Military Comedy Films

ALSO BY HAL ERICKSON AND
FROM MCFARLAND

*The Baseball Filmography,
1915 through 2001,* 2d ed. (2002; paperback 2010)

"From Beautiful Downtown Burbank": A Critical History of Rowan and
Martin's Laugh-In, *1968–1973* (2000; paperback 2009)

*Encyclopedia of Television Law Shows: Factual and Fictional Series
About Judges, Lawyers and the Courtroom, 1948–2008* (2009)

*Sid and Marty Krofft: A Critical Study of Saturday Morning Children's
Television, 1969–1993* (1998; paperback 2007)

*Television Cartoon Shows:
An Illustrated Encyclopedia, 1949 through 2003,* 2d ed. (2005)

*Syndicated Television:
The First Forty Years, 1947–1987* (1989; paperback 2001)

*Religious Radio and Television in the United States, 1921–1991:
The Programs and Personalities* (1992; paperback 2001)

Military Comedy Films

A Critical Survey and Filmography of Hollywood Releases Since 1918

Hal Erickson

McFarland & Company, Inc., Publishers
Jefferson, North Carolina, and London

Unless otherwise indicated, all photographs and illustrations
are from the author's personal collection.

LIBRARY OF CONGRESS CATALOGUING-IN-PUBLICATION DATA

Erickson, Hal, 1950–
Military comedy films : a critical survey and filmography
of Hollywood releases since 1918 / Hal Erickson.
    p.   cm.
Includes bibliographical references and index.

ISBN 978-0-7864-6290-2
softcover : acid free paper ∞

1. War films— United States— History and criticism.   2. Comedy
films— United States— History and criticism.   I. Title.
PN1995.9.W3E75   2012   791.43'658 — dc23   2012025244

BRITISH LIBRARY CATALOGUING DATA ARE AVAILABLE

©2012 Hal Erickson. All rights reserved

*No part of this book may be reproduced or transmitted in any form
or by any means, electronic or mechanical, including photocopying
or recording, or by any information storage and retrieval system,
without permission in writing from the publisher.*

Front cover: Robin Williams as Adrian Cronauer in
Good Morning Vietnam, 1987 (Photofest)

Manufactured in the United States of America

*McFarland & Company, Inc., Publishers
Box 611, Jefferson, North Carolina 28640
www.mcfarlandpub.com*

To my son, the doctor,
Peter Erickson.
"Hey, Doc. It hurts every time I go like *that*."

Table of Contents

Preface 1
Introduction 3

1. "I surrounded them!" Charlie Chaplin and *Shoulder Arms* 17
2. Run Silent, Run Shallow: The Silent Service Comedies 22
3. First Line of Offense: "Professional" Comedians in Talkie Service Comedies 48
4. Abbott and Costello Meet the Ripoffs 90
5. Repeated Rounds: The "Series" Films 106
6. You Know What Sailors Are: Comedies About Seafaring Men 133
7. The Few, the Proud, the Funny: Comedies About the Marines 145
8. You Read the Book! You Loved the Play! Now See the Movie! 159
9. It's Still the Same Old Story ... Sort Of: *See Here, Private Hargrove* and *Biloxi Blues* 189
10. Stranger Than Fiction 199
11. The Wheeler Dealers 213
12. It Ain't Stupid If It Works: The "Misfit-Makes-Good" Comedy 240
13. The Children's Crusade: Military-Academy Comedies 253
14. "Holy Smokes! A Dame!": Women in the Military 265
15. Special Ops 276
16. PR/CYA 285
17. The Home Front 298
18. No Laughing Matter? Comedies About the Civil War and Vietnam 314
19. "One, Two Three, What Are We Fighting For?" Anti-War and Anti-Military Comedies 337
20. "The Mother of All Movies": Satires and Parodies 358
21. Extra Added Attractions: The Cartoons 369

Filmography 377
Bibliography 395
Index 401

Preface

Why a book about Hollywood military comedies? Because I *like* Hollywood military comedies. That is, I like the best of them. Reason enough.

Please forgive the flippancy. It's just that I am anticipating objections to a lifelong civilian having the audacity to write about service comedies. While I was not required to have extensive baseball experience to write about baseball movies, nor was I obliged to possess a gift for drawing funny pictures to write about television cartoon shows, it might be different in the realm of comedy films about the Army, Navy and Marines. Though no one in my circle of friends and relatives who *has* served this country in uniform would suggest that I should have avoided writing a book dealing with a profession and lifestyle for which I have no firsthand knowledge, there may be those among my readers who do harbor such objections.

So let's clear up some things here and now. I am neither a slacker nor a draft-dodger. At the time I was eligible for military duty — the Vietnam era, for those who *really* need to know my age — I was given a college deferment. Once I was out of college, I grimly and nervously awaited what I thought would be the inevitable "Greetings" from Uncle Sam, but the number I had been assigned in the 1969 draft lottery (#129) had still not been called up. Within a few years the war was over and the draft abolished, and I was a free man again. Unlike Christopher Buckley and other writers who have expressed guilt over having avoided their military obligations, feeling perhaps that because of their absence thousands of other young men were forced to bleed and die in their place, it is my firm belief that the American military was better off without me. Judging from my record of ineptitute in other jobs for which I was totally unsuited (such as the miserable summer I spent as a plumber's assistant), I cannot help but feel that I may have actually *saved* lives by not serving in uniform.

And may I also state unequivocally that I have nothing but the highest respect and esteem for those courageous and selfless men and women who have chosen to make the military their life. As these words are being written a few days after the 70th anniversary of Pearl Harbor, I can only say, "God bless you and Godspeed."

And also, "Thanks for instilling in me an appreciation for military comedies." While I was growing up, I was intrigued by my war-veteran father and his contemporaries laughing immoderately while they watched films like *Mister Roberts* and *No Time for Sergeants*. I found these films funny as well, but certainly not in the same way. There was a special "in the know" attitude shared by veterans that prompted them to laugh at little bits of dialogue and stage business that didn't seem amusing to me at all. Why, for example, did my Dad chuckle every time he saw a "Kilroy Was Here" sign in an old war movie? Why was he amused when the camp cook in a military comedy was named "Shingles"? And why did he smile knowingly when such deceptively harmless acronyms as "Snafu" and innocently misquoted catchphrases as "Grab your socks and grab your hats" were bandied about?

For reasons I can't entirely explain, I have always been fascinated by comedy films that entertain on two levels: on one level for the average audience member, and on another for those who have intimate knowledge of the characters and circumstances depicted on screen. So it is with military comedies. And now that we're nearing the end of this preface, I shall say no more.

Except to acknowledge those individuals and organizations who have, in one way or another, provided help, material, illustrations and inspiration during this book's gestation. In alphabetical order, I thank the Bobke family (Carl, Cari and David), Denis Clark, Dale Craven, Jim Feeley, Wayne and Rita Hawk, Greg Hilbrich, Jane and Mark Martell, Lee Matthias, Movie Market, Movie Poster Shop, Movie Star News, the Movie Store, Moviegoods.com, James L. Neibaur, Peggy Peterson Ryan, David Seebach, Roger Sorenson and Bill Sprague.

For my wonderful wife Joanne and sons Brian and Peter, there are not enough thanks.

And now, let's grab our socks, etc., and begin our full frontal assault on military comedy films.

Introduction

Director Billy Wilder's *Stalag 17* (Paramount, 1953) takes place in a German POW camp in 1944. Among the incarcerated American soldiers are a couple of inveterate cut-ups named Animal and Harry. While drunk, Animal imagines that Harry is his favorite movie star Betty Grable. He also imagines that he's gone blind from bootleg booze when his hat falls over his eyes. At one point, Animal and Harry get themselves assigned to painting detail so they can catch a glimpse of some pretty female Russian POWs in the shower stalls. Elsewhere, the prisoners place bets on which rat can run the fastest around a tiny makeshift "racetrack"; a pompous German guard is ridiculed by the POWs, who don fake Hitler mustaches and shout "Seig Heil!" in unison; another German guard gets so excited over a volleyball game that he unwittingly hands his weapon to one of the prisoners; and a newly arrived POW regales his fellow inmates with celebrity impersonations of Clark Gable, Jimmy Cagney and Cary Grant. At the end of the picture, Stalag 17's least likable prisoner Sgt. Sefton stages a daring escape, whereupon Animal grumbles that Sefton's ulterior motive was to steal a pair of barbed-wire cutters. The distinguished film critic Pauline Kael has described *Stalag 17* as a "rowdy prisoner-of-war comedy," while the film's original advertising campaign included such tag lines as "Hilarious!" and "The Star-Spangled Laugh-Loaded Salute to Our PW Heroes!"

So why isn't it included in this book on military comedy films?

Try this alternate synopsis on for size. Billy Wilder's *Stalag 17* takes place in a miserable, freezing, lice-infested POW camp where the prisoners' desperate escape efforts are constantly thwarted by a Nazi spy within their own ranks. Already two of their number, Manfredi and Johnson, have been shot in cold blood, and a later getaway attempt threatens to yield similarly tragic results because the hidden spy has been placed in charge of "security" by the unwitting POWs. Wrongly suspected of being the traitor, the cynical Sefton is beaten to a bloody pulp by the other prisoners, and when the real spy is exposed, he is bound, gagged and ghoulishly taunted with graphic descriptions of his imminent demise. Among the POWs is a downed fighter pilot from whom the sadistic camp commandant tries to extract military secrets by using such refined torture methods as starvation and sleep deprivation. Then there's a tragic young prisoner named Joey, who after witnessing the bloody slaughter of his comrades has retreated into a catatonic state from which he will likely never recover.

Well, *that's* sure rowdy, hilarious, and loaded with laughs, isn't it?

Anyone who has seen *Stalag 17* will recognize that both of the above descriptions are accurate — as far as they go. And therein lies the quandary in which I presently find myself: How, precisely, does one define the term "military comedy"? War films like *The Big Parade, Wings, Guadalcanal Diary, The Story of G.I. Joe, The Great Escape* and *Three Kings* undeniably contain some hilarious moments within the traditional boundaries of "comedy relief," but none can be labelled comedies, not even by those whose sense of humor borders on the warped. The confusion arising from *Stalag 17* can be blamed (if that's the proper word) on producer-director-cowriter Billy Wilder, who throughout his career loved to keep audiences on their toes by constantly switching moods within the same film. For example, though Wilder's *The Apartment* (1960) was adver-

Though many people regard Billy Wilder's *Stalag 17* (Paramount, 1953) as a military comedy, much of the film is as grim as the expression on star William Holden's face (*courtesy Jim Feeley*).

tised and accepted as a comedy, it could just as easily have been described as a bittersweet drama about a callous young man who exploits the sexual peccadilloes of his fellow workers to get ahead in the business world, and a pathetic young woman who carries on an affair with a married executive while kidding herself that her paramour is genuinely in love with her. And while we're on the subject of *The Apartment*, few filmmakers besides Billy Wilder would be so brazen as to interrupt the flow of a "funny" scenario with an attempted suicide — a stunt he'd already successfully staged in 1954's *Sabrina*.

Though Wilder was the master of this brand of mood-mixing, a number of other filmmakers have tried pulling off the same trick, with variable results. As will be seen in the synopses of such military comedies as *Mister Roberts, Imitation General, The Wackiest Ship in the Army?, Soldier in the Rain, Catch-22* and *Buffalo Soldiers*, a few ambitious writers and directors have endeavored to stimulate the audience by tossing in unexpectedly dramatic and unpredictably tragic curves in the middle of what is supposed to be a laugh riot. Still and all, the above-mentioned films *are* comedies, and were planned and designed as comedies. Thus, unlike *Stalag 17*, they are duly covered in this book.

For this book, "military comedy," and the alternate designation "service comedy," is defined as any film in which the main purpose is to arouse laughter with leading characters who are members of one or another branch of the armed services, and/or any film which is dominated by a humorous slant on military life. While there are a few borderline cases in this book — as witness the films in Chapter 17, "The Home Front"—for the most part our definition will suffice.

At the same time, a few exclusions had to be made to avoid ending up with multiple volumes.

On the other hand, don't be misled by Buster Keaton's dour countenance: This scene *is* from a military comedy, the 1930 MGM release *Doughboys (courtesy James L. Neibaur).*

First to go were approximately 90 percent of all wartime and military musicals. Films like *You'll Never Get Rich, This Is the Army, Rookies on Parade, The Sky's the Limit, Hey Rookie, Rosie the Riveter, Reveille with Beverly, Priorities on Parade, Tars and Spars, Here Come the Waves, The West Point Story, Starlift, G.I. Jane, Three Sailors and a Girl, Mardi Gras* and others certainly have their mirthsome moments, but in the final analysis they are more musical than comedy (the producers of *Reveille with Beverly* were evidently so intent upon emphasizing its musical content that *not one* of the film's impressive lineup of character comedians— Franklin Pangborn, Tim and Irene Ryan, Wally Vernon, Andrew Tombes, Doodles Weaver — receives an on-screen credit!) Also, most of the comedies concerning the "space race" of the 1950s and 1960s won't be found here, even though all astronauts of the period were required to be military officers with test-pilot experience. The humor in these films is by and large predicated on situations that have little to do with military matters; thus, don't look for titles like *Moon Pilot, Way Way Out* or *The Reluctant Astronaut* within these pages—though for reasons hopefully made clear in the text, a handful of films involving guided missiles (*Rally 'Round the Flag, Boys!, Everything's Ducky, Sergeant DeadHead*) *did* make the cut.

Other films that aren't analyzed here include a few that have sometimes been classified as service comedies because of the preponderance of military characters, American and otherwise. Both *The Russians Are Coming, the Russians Are Coming* (1966) and *1941* (1978) involve the screwball behavior of civilian and military personnel alike when it appears that a foreign invasion has taken place on American soil. But because these two films are so scattershot in their satire of home-grown paranoia, poking fun at a wide variety of personalities and professions, it would be insufficient to classify them simply as service farces. (One of the characters in *1941* is a guy in a Santa Claus costume: does that make *1941* a Christmas picture?) As for 2008's *Tropic Thunder*, it's perfectly understandable that some people have described the film as a lampoon of serious war pictures, inasmuch as the protagonists are a bunch of self-centred movie actors who end up smashing a Southest Asian drug operation while under the mistaken impression that they're filming a *Rambo*-like action flick. Overall, however, *Tropic Thunder* is a broad, sweeping satire of the entire Hollywood motion picture industry, with the "war" angle merely one of many ingredients spicing up the proceedings.

Finally, I have limited coverage to American films that have been released theatrically. To include, say, the military comedies produced in England for domestic English audiences (*Bell-Bottom George, The Midshipmaid, Carry On Sergeant, Private's Progress*, among others) would have probably burst the binding of this book: the British naval comedies alone would have required an extra volume. This, however, *doesn't* mean that we've excluded Hollywood films made abroad (*Catch-22*, the 1997 version of *McHale's Navy*), or partially financed by non–American concerns (e.g. *All the Queen's Men*). As for the "theatrical" qualification, all made-for-TV service comedies (*Wake Me When the War Is Over, She's in the Army Now,* and so on) have been excluded, as well as films like 1994's *Ernest in the Army*, which though intended for a theatrical release ended up going straight to home video— a fate narrowly averted by the likes of *Going Under, Major Movie Star* and *Military Intelligence and You!*, all of which have been included and documented here.

So much for what *isn't* in this book. What I *have* included are well over two hundred feature-length military comedies produced between 1918 and 2009, and a sizeable selection of short subjects and cartoons produced during roughly the same time frame ("roughly" because a handful of pre–1918 releases have managed to sneak in). Some films are discussed in depth (especially in **Chapters 8, 9** and **19**), others in passing, depending on the circumstances. Occasionally the more "famous" service comedies will receive less space than the second-echelon pictures, but again the circumstances will dictate this. The titles have *not* been arranged alphabetically or chronologically, but rather are discussed within narrowly defined categories: Silent films, Navy comedies, Marine pictures, movies about females in the military, pictures about military schools, anti-war films ... well, you get the drift. This approach may sometimes appear as helter-skelter as the plotline of *Catch-22*, with its constant backward and forward time-leaps, but don't despair: Taking a cue from the military-manual style sheet, any entry in this book that requires a cross-reference to an earlier or later chapter will be noted in the text, with the referenced chapter in **bold**. My fervent hope is that this procedure will prove to be less confusing and more pleasurable to read than your average military manual.

A chronological list of the feature films cited in this book, with basic cast and production credits, can be found in the **Filmography**. To make things a bit easier from the outset, the following pages provide an historical and contextual overview of the entire military-comedy genre.

Since my focus is on American films, our time spent within the realm of non–American historical precedents will be brief. It goes without saying that the military comedy did not emerge overnight upon the formation of the United States in the late 18th century. Like any other subject ripe for ridicule, the more odious examples of miltary groupthink — war for political gain and personal glory, the subjugation of people without weapons or resources, corruption within the ranks — have been prime targets for comedy writers since the world began. Greek playwright Aristophanes was taking satirical potshots at wars and warriors as far back as the 5th century BCE with such stage comedies as *The Babylonians* and *Lysistrata*. Aristophanes' principal villains were the thick-eared military leaders appointed from the ranks of royalty and aristocracy, rather than the common foot soldiers, most of whom were either slaves or prisoners from conquered lands. Those paid mercenaries who fought only when money crossed their palms — and who as a rule were more interested in rape and plunder than defending their host nation — were given a thorough drubbing by another Greek playwright named Menander, and an even worse one by Roman playwright Plautus, who flourished in the 3rd century BCE. The storyline of Plautus' *Miles Gloriosus* is built entirely around a popular stock comic character of the day: the "braggart warrior," invariably depicted as a swell-headed mercenary who roamed the countryside weaving tall tales of his battlefield victories, often accompanied by a toadying yes-man (accurately described by Plautus as a "parasite") who kept himself fed and clothed by constantly massaging the warrior's ego.

Leave it to old Bill Shakespeare (if I may be permitted a 1800-year quantum leap) to go the Romans and Greeks one better by combining Plautus' braggart soldier and Aristophanes' warmongering nobleman into one corpulent body. Arguably the single most memorable character in Shakespeare's two-part historical drama *King Henry IV* (circa 1598) is Sir John Falstaff, a fat and fatheaded knight who spends most of his waking hours drinking, wenching, and boasting about his largely imaginary exploits. Providing a comic contrast to King Henry's honorable and valiant war against the rebellious Henry "Hotspur" Percy, Falstaff is shown organizing a ragtag miniarmy of his own, comprised of doddering oldsters, borderline imbeciles and other choice specimens from the dregs of the rural English bourgeoisie. Shakespeare is careful to establish that Falstaff has gotten his officer's commission only by virtue of his knighthood and his friendship with the King's wayward son Prince Hal — and also that whenever the going gets tough on the battlefield, Falstaff is usually nowhere to be found.

Funny though these early examples of service humor may be, they are essentially products of men on the outside looking in (Aristophanes *may* have had some military experience, but the records are hazy; as best as can be determined, Shakespeare was a lifelong civilian). Even with the "democratization" of the armed services during the American Revolution, in which the Yankee army was mostly comprised of men who actually *wanted* to fight rather than those forced or paid to do so, the business of chronicling the war for posterity was largely in the hands of non-combatants and the officer class, with the voice of the lowly "grunt" generally remaining unheard. The accelerated literacy rate in the post–Revolutionary years has left us with reams of correspondence sent by soldiers, sailors and Marines to their friends and loved ones, but surprisingly little of a humorous nature was written down — not even when there was something to laugh about, such as the United States Cavalry's experimental use of camels as pack animals in the Southwestern territories. Occuring in the decade just prior to the Civil War, this experiment was taken quite seriously at the time, though in the ensuing years the more ludicrous aspects of the idea have provided comic material for a number of articles and books, as well as a brace of lighthearted Hollywood westerns, *One Little Indian* (1973) and *Hawmps* (1976).

Not until the American Civil War was there a significant body of written humor arising from the day-to-day experiences of enlisted men. Befitting this long, devastating and appallingly bloody conflict, many of the jokes circulating throughout the war can best be described as "gallows humor," the desperate, defense-mechanism comedy common to men facing death and deprivation on a 24-hour basis. Typical is an 1864 anecdote from Patrick O'Flaherty's *A History of the 69th*: "One slightly wounded man complained that he had to walk to the rear. A more seriously wounded comrade replied, 'Ah Duffy, hold your tongue. There's a lad over there with his head shot off and he's not making a complaint at all.'" An even richer vein of gallows humor can be mined from the experiences of Northern POWs confined to such infamously brutal Confederate prison camps as Andersonville. To keep up their morale in circumstances for which the word "adverse" is pitifully inadequate, many of these prisoners passed jokes to one another via secretly published in-house periodicals. A favorite topic of conversation was the food that the POWs were forced to consume. In his book *Civil War Humor*, Cameron C. Nickels has preserved a letter written by a Union prisoner to his family, in which he claims that his food is so rife with maggots that "we have to have an extra gard [sic] to keep them from packing it clear off."

The homegrown humorists of the Civil War also emulated such earlier wits as Aristophanes by referring to the North-South conflict as "rich man's war, poor man's fight." Southern soldiers were especially virulent in their derision of the "gold-braided gentry," blue-blooded Confederate officers who were long on arrogance and short on competence. Few of these rebel soldiers were aware that the men in charge of the Confederacy were capable of even more egregious behavior than they'd exhibited on the battlefield. Historian John Pimpernell has done a great deal of research on a long-range strategy devised by Confederacy president Jefferson Davis and General Robert E. Lee to infiltrate the North with inherent Southern sympathizers. The plan was to recruit prostitutes from brothels below the Mason-Dixon line to become sex partners of unwitting Union troops, passing along their "Southern genes" so that the bastard children resulting from these assignations would grow up to carry on the Confederate cause for generations to come! (If you think that's insane, wait til we get to the synopsis of 2009's *The Men Who Stare at Goats* in **Chapter 10.**) While the Davis-Lee "soiled dove" strategy might seem to be a natural premise for a service comedy, once Hollywood actually focused on the Civil War the films that resulted were mostly sympathetic to the fallen South. As Buster Keaton, creator-star of the 1927 Civil War comedy *The General*, explained on several occasions, the Confederacy had suffered such a total and humiliating defeat that they were automatically relegated to "underdog" status—and audiences, even Northern ones, generally tend to root for the underdog.

After the Civil War the ranks of America's standing army diminished, wherupon military comedy largely became the province of the United States Navy, which like the navies throughout the world remained on call whether a war was raging or not. Without specifically citing the works of such authors as Homer, Herman Melville and Eugene O'Neill, it is safe to say that the lure of the sea and its promise of limitless adventure has been a constant throughout history, hence the predominance of the mariner-warrior class in the late 19th century. Much of the humor favored by sailors—both in and out of the "official" Navy—has traditionally focused on the colorful sexual escapades purportedly enjoyed while in various exotic ports; thus, many of the ripest (and best) comic anecdotes arising from naval service have not always made it to the printed page. When the movies finally got around to sailors, the heavy hand of censorship continued to prevail, though certain inventive filmmakers were able to circumvent the bluenoses through inference and innuendo, as in such films as Howard Hawks' *A Girl in Every Port* (1928) and Raoul Walsh's *Sailor's Luck* (1933). When the censorial battlements finally toppled in the 1960s and 1970s and Hollywood filmmakers were permitted to be more explicit in their language, among the first films to fully reap the benefits of this new-found freedom was a Navy comedy, *The Last Detail* (1973).

Outside of the occasional foreign entanglements involving the globetrotting Navy and Marine Corps, the next time that a large body of servicemen was involved in a serious skirmish was the Spanish American War of 1898, which didn't last long enough to leave behind a significant reservoir of military jokes. Less than two decades later, the United States was swept up in its first major overseas conflict: the First World War. At the outbreak of hostilities in 1914, Americans—and

American filmmakers—tended to be ambivalent. There was as much pro–German sentiment in the United States as there was pro–British and pro–French, a situation inadvertently helped along by the British government, which at first refused to allow movie cameramen any closer than 30 miles from the battlefield for fear that the resulting films could be used for espionage purposes. The Germans on the other hand permitted cameramen wider access to their military maneuvers and personnel; consequently, most American moviegoers of 1914 could *only* witness the conflict from the German point of view. (This would have made excellent material for a comedy about wartime bureaucracy had anyone dared to exploit it!) But with the sinking of the British ocean liner *Lusitania* on May 6, 1915, in which many American lives were lost, President Woodrow Wilson's insistence upon maintaining a neutral stance in World War I was met with open hostility by former president Theodore Roosevelt and other prominent "warhawks," all of whom promoted intense hatred against Germany and its ruler Kaiser Wilhelm.

Though the *Lusitania* incident went a long way toward stirring up anti–German fervor with the American public, Hollywood's response to the sinking was for the most part slow in coming, with such propagandistic fictionalizations of the tragedy as Cecil B. DeMille's *The Little American* not seeing the light of day until after America had entered the war on the side of Britain and France in April of 1917. An interesting contrast to this foot-dragging was *A Submarine Pirate*, a 4-reel comedy released by Mack Sennett's Keystone studio some six months after the *Lusitania* sank beneath the waves. In typical Sennett fashion, there is no propaganda of any kind in *A Submarine Pirate*: the climactic sinking is merely the outcome of a farcical set of circumstances involving a greedy waiter (Syd Chaplin) who assumes command of a midget submarine for the purpose of robbing a ship laden with gold bullion.

In the words of historian Kevin Brownlow, America's entry into World War I has been portrayed on film "with a feverish montage of flags and bands, marching troops and ecstatic civilians." The actual immediate reaction was less euphoric: Most American were unclear regarding the political intrigues that had brought about the war, and there were still many ethnic communities where pro–German (or at least anti–British) sentiments ran high. It became necessary for the government to stir up enthusiasm for the war, and the motion picture industry joined the campaign by sending its biggest stars (Mary Pickford, Douglas Fairbanks and others) out on enlistment drives and "Liberty Loan" rallies. At first, the films resulting from the join-the-fight movement were rather low-key appeals to patriotism and pointed attacks against men who avoided the draft (the first Selective Service Act had been put into effect on May 18, 1917). Most films like these avoided a comedic approach, with such exceptions as *Bud's Recruit* (1918), one of the earliest surviving films of director King Vidor. In this 2-reel epic, teenager Bud (Wallis Brennan) organizes his friends into an unofficial military unit, and for the first six minutes or so the film derives laughter from the kids' sincere but risible efforts to emulate their elders. Then things take a serious turn, more or less, when Bud disguises himself as a grown-up (looking for all the world like Groucho Marx!) and fills out an enlistment application on behalf of his "slacker" older brother Reggie (Robert Gordon), who is so moved by his sibling's red-blooded patriotism — and so shamed by his own lack of intestinal fortitude — that he immediately joins up for real.

Later films were less subtle in their propaganda, as Hollywood endeavored to stir up anti-Germanism with a plethora of vicious "Hate-the-Hun" melodramas like *My Four Years in Germany, The Kaiser — Beast of Berlin, To Hell with the Kaiser* and *The Prussian Cur*. Very few laughs there: In fact, if one had a hankering for military comedy, one was best advised to avoid movies and focus on the literature of the period, as well as the anecdotes of the boys in uniform who'd been discharged or had come home on furlough (technically, the Selective Service act did not require soldiers to remain in service for the duration of the war, though most of them did). Typical of what passed for service humor during this era was Edward Streeter's weekly newspaper column "Dere Mable," ostensibly written by an illiterate "doughboy" (contemporary slang for an American infantryman) to his girl back home. Laden with deliberate misspellings and malapropisms, Streeter's columns don't hold up very well today, but they pleased the audiences of their era.

In the gallows-humor tradition of the Civil War, a lot of the humor favored by World War I's front-line soldiers had to do with the crummy food, the muddy accommodations and the "cootie" attacks endured by American soldiers in France, as well as the universal contempt held for obnoxious and inept second lieutenants, too many of whom were merely political appointees who had no business anywhere near an armed conflict (this generalization has been verified by war historians and veterans). Another favorite target of ridicule was the bullying top sergeant, frequently an Army "lifer" who'd signed up because he'd been unable to find work in the civilian sector, though this particular character was seldom held in as low esteem as those officers who had earned their stripes only because of family influence and social connections. On a lighter note, and one reflective of the *joie de vivre* of those Yankee soldiers who spent less time on the battlefield than they did behind the lines (of the 4,272,000 mobilized Americans, only a fraction actually ever saw combat), there was plenty of Navy-style ribaldry involving the promiscuity, actual and alleged, of the French female population. Anyone who's ever heard *all* the lyrics of the popular marching song "Mademoiselle from Armentières" will know what I'm talking about, especially in regards to the verse that begins "The French they are a funny race, parlez-vous...."

It wasn't until the war was practically over and won that Hollywood's first major service comedy, Charlie Chaplin's *Shoulder Arms* (1918), even went into production. For Chaplin, the notion of using the war as a comedy backdrop would seem to have been a natural: As the world's most popular entertainer, he'd previously been given *carte blanche* to exercise his creative freedom by extracting laughter from such otherwise doleful subjects as slum-dwelling (*Easy Street*) and alcoholism (*The Cure*). But for reasons noted in **Chapter 1**, Chaplin was extremely trepidatious about making light of the war and spent several months agonizing over the prospect that the public's reaction to *Shoulder Arms* would be violently negative. As it happened, Americans had grown so dog-weary of the war and the resultant propaganda pictures that they were very much in the mood to laugh off their woes. While many of Hollywood's expensive military dramas were playing to empty houses (forcing theater owners to post such assurances as "*NOT A WAR PICTURE!*" on their marquees), *Shoulder Arms* ended up as Chaplin's biggest success to date, not only in the United States but throughout the world. For several years thereafter, virtually the only war-related films to enjoy any sort of popularity were such comedies as *Yankee Doodle in Berlin* and *23½ Hours' Leave*.

The 1920s came, and, with them, the Great Disillusionment. Many Americans who'd fought in the war, especially those who'd suffered serious injuries, had lost arms and legs on the battlefields of France, or returned home beset with profound emotional difficulties, began questioning the necessity of entering into a foreign conflict in which the United States apparently had no real stake. The literature of the "Lost Generation" was abundant with trenchant commentary on the dismal spectacle of young men shedding blood to settle the differences of old men safely ensconced in their lavish homes and palaces, with precious few positive results. As a result, the marketability of military films fell off sharply in the early years of the Roaring Twenties. Virtually the only service comedies that enjoyed any sort of acceptance were peacetime frolics involving sailors (*A Sailor-Made Man*, *Shore Leave*), who were always good for a laugh or two.

The revival of interest in war dramas occurred only after the 1924 Broadway premiere of *What Price Glory?*, a play cowritten by World War I veteran and confirmed pacifist Laurence Stallings. While graphically elucidating General Sherman's famous declaration "War is Hell," *What Price Glory?* also scored points with its equally graphic comedy content involving a pair of perpetually cursing, brawling, drinking and womanizing American Marines named Capt. Flagg and. Sgt. Quirt. Laurence Stallings was also on the ground floor of the first truly successful war film of the Jazz Age, MGM's *The Big Parade* (1925). Like *What Price Glory?*, *The Big Parade* had more than its share of raucous comedy, mostly concentrated in the early reels as three diverse "citizen soldiers" played by John Gilbert, Karl Dane and Tom O'Brien dallied with the mademoiselles, drank cognac with abandon, and pulled all manner of jokes on each other. But unlike *What Price Glory?*, which packed most of its "War is Hell" message into the second act and then reverted to comedy in the third, *The Big Parade* forsook its laugh potential the moment the three protagonists arrived at the front, whereupon the film became a chilling cavalcade of combat horror climaxed by the nerve-shattering "death march" through Belleau Wood. Ironically, *The Big Parade* was directed by King Vidor, with nary a trace of the fervent flag-waving sentiments which distinguished his earlier *Bud's Recruit*.

The Big Parade single-handedly made World War I movies bankable again, a fact that considerably boosted the box-office value of the inevitable 1926 film version of *What Price Glory*—which, though it had its share of harrowing moments, not only retained the comedy content of its theatrical predecessor, but actually increased that content with a prewar prologue involving Flagg and Quirt's carnal pursuits in the Orient. In between *Big Parade* and *What Price Glory* came the first major World War I comedy feature of the 1920s, Paramount's *Behind the Front*. The success of this film resulted in a profusion of comedies which poked fun at the war and the men who fought it. Nineteen twenty-six yielded not only *Behind the Front* but also five other World War I–related laughfests including *Private Izzy Murphy*, *The Better 'Ole* and *Tin Hats*. The following year, audiences were regaled by eight similar comedies, many of them emulating *Behind the Front*'s teaming of Wallace Beery and Raymond Hatton by featuring such daffy duos as Karl Dane and George K. Arthur, Sammy Cohen and Ted McNamara, and Charlie Murray and George Sidney. The genre flourished into 1928 with nine additional service comedies, six of them featuring storylines set during the war years.

Following the talkie revolution of 1928–29, the public's demand for war films diminished in favor of musicals and dialogue-laden stage adaptations. The 1930 release of the relentlessly grim war drama *All Quiet on the Western Front* revitalized interest in the genre, just as *The Big Parade* had done in 1925. The Army comedies that resulted from this resurgence generally took place during World War I, pitting such popular comedians as Wheeler & Woolsey, Laurel & Hardy and Joe E. Brown against the stern and humorless military establishment, arousing laughter with the contrast between the goofy stars and their somber surroundings. Comedies featuring "straight" actors (such as James Ellison in the 1937 remake of *23½ Hours Leave*) were likewise often as not set during the war years—not so much out of nostalgia for a non–Depression era gone by as a reflection of the fact that the ranks of the United States Army had thinned considerably in the years following the war, an outgrowth of public demand that America encourage pacifism by maintaining only a bare minimum of defensive military strength (the wartime draft had ended in 1920). Contemporary comedies about the Army were few and far between in the 1930s for the simple reason that there weren't all that many soldiers to poke fun at.

Meanwhile, Navy comedies set in "modern" times continued to prosper, the glamorous aspects of a life at sea remaining relatively untarnished even after the Great War, and the comic potential of carefree gobs on shore leave in pursuit of willing ladies continuing to be exploited by filmmakers. During this period, actor Jack Oakie virtually carved a second career out of portraying simpleminded gobs in such films as *Hit the Deck*, *Sea Legs* and *Sailor Be Good*. Similarly, the peripatetic United States Marines were amply represented comedically in the first decade of the talkies, not only by the two *What Price Glory* sequels *The Cock-Eyed World* and *Women of All Nations*, but also by such lightweight efforts as *Leathernecking*, *Come On, Marines* and the Gary Cooper-Jack Oakie-Roscoe Karns segment in the all-star *If I Had a Million* (1932).

As threats of a second World War intensified in Europe and Asia during the late 1930s, the United States Army enjoyed an upsurge in enlistments, though it still lagged behind the Navy. Once America's entry into World War II seemed to be just a matter of time, the government took decisive action to increase the nation's military might. On September 14, 1940, the Selective Training and Service Act, America's first peacetime draft, was signed into law, requiring all able-bodied

Hollywood's fanciful spin on the typical American fighting man, vintage 1929: Victor McLaglen dallies with Lili Damita in Fox's *The Cock-Eyed World*.

men between the ages of 21 and 36 to register for conscription; the age range was later amended to 18–45. Originally, the term of service was to be 12 months, inspiring any number of movie scenes in which a young draftee assures his girlfriend that he'll only be gone a year — a remark usually followed by a sarcastic "That's what *you* think" from a pal or passerby. As America's entry into the war went from possibility to probability, the length of service was extended to 18 months — and after the Pearl Harbor attack on December 7, 1941, all military personnel found themselves facing a tour of duty lasting "the Duration plus six months."

The compulsory nature of the Draft meant that, unlike the situation that prevailed during World War I, it was not necessary for Hollywood to shame or frighten young men into signing up for military service. As a result, the first volley of films resulting from the Selective Training and Service Act endeavored to blunt the trauma of being uprooted from home and shipped off to basic training, thence to combat duty abroad, by prettying up the process with bouncy musical numbers and uproarious comedy routines. Beating all other studios in rushing a conscription comedy into theaters was Universal, whose Abbott & Costello and Andrews Sisters extravanganza *Buck Privates* (1941) was a smash hit beyond the studio's wildest dreams. *Buck Privates* was followed in quick succession by a pair of "draft" comedies that had been in preparation at the same time as the Universal picture, Bob Hope's *Caught in the Draft* (1941) and Jimmy Durante's *You're in the Army Now* (1941), as well as two additional Abbott & Costello service farces, *In the Navy* and *Keep 'Em Flying* (both also 1941). Then came the inevitable *Buck Privates* ripoffs, wherein various other comedy duos were placed in a military-training milieu: Laurel & Hardy in *Great Guns* (1941),

Frank Faylen & Charlie Hall in *Top Sergeant Mulligan* (1941), Jackie Gleason & Jack Durant in *Tramp Tramp Tramp* (1942) and Wally Brown & Alan Carney in *Adventures of a Rookie* and *Rookies in Burma* (both 1943). Not since the post–*Behind the Front* comedy boom of the 1920s were so many military comedies unleashed upon the public—some two dozen films within a two-year period, ten in 1941 alone!

While most of these films enjoyed the services of genuine military personnel as technical directors, and a few (notably *Caught in the Draft*) used bonafide Army trainees as extras, none were told from the first-person viewpoint of an actual draftee. That honor was reserved for *See Here, Private Hargrove*, a 1944 MGM comedy based on the best-selling memoirs of Sgt. Marion Hargrove, who'd been in uniform since just before Pearl Harbor. With *See Here, Private Hargrove*, World War II became the first major war in which the regular "boots on the ground" actually had significant input in the literary and cinematic efforts of the period; no longer would the flow of information from the front be the exclusive domain of newspaper reporters, officers and diplomats. Among the non-commissioned military correspondents contributing to wartime humor was Sgt. Bill Mauldin, cartoonist for the Army periodical *Stars and Stripes*, whose comic panels about the hardscrabble existence of "typical" infantrymen Willie and Joe were much prized by Mauldin's fellow soldiers, and were ultimately translated to the Big Screen in the postwar years—as were the comic-strip misadventures of Sgt. George Baker's hapless PFC "The Sad Sack," who starred in the pages of *Yank* magazine.

Though Mauldin's Willie & Joe frequently spoke "truth to power" by ragging on the more pretentious members of the officer class, by and large the cartoonists of World War II, together with the manufacturers of movie comedy, sidestepped harsh reality in favor of harmless escapism. Not only did civilian audiences respond more favorably to having their minds taken off the problems of a war-torn world, but so too did movie fans in the military prefer such escapist fare as musicals, comedies and Westerns. Indeed, many soldiers, sailors and Marines were known to boo and jeer at "serious" war pictures, especially when forced to endure the synthetic larger-than-life heroics performed by such draft-proof movie stars as John Wayne and Errol Flynn.

The fact that servicemen derived great pleasure from lighthearted and non-issue-driven entertainment was not the only reason that Hollywood tread very carefully when dealing with war-related matters during the early 1940s. Two short-lived regulatory agencies, the Office of War Information (OWI) and the Office of Censorship, combed through every inch of film to make certain that everything shipped out to the public adhered to a strict set of requirements and restrictions. Of the two agencies, the Office of Censorship was less concerned with entertainment films than with newsreels and documentaries, checking to see that "reality" shots of war production plants did not reveal any secret military projects, and that civilian complaints about rationing restrictions and "labor, class or other disturbances" be minimized to prevent the enemy from propagandizing such elements. To be sure, the mainstream Hollywood product—especially animated cartoons—contained a lot of jokes about the inconvenience of food, gas and rubber rationing, but the practice *itself* was not criticized.

More aggressive in monitoring Tinseltown comedies was the OWI, who judged all submitted scripts by such criteria as: "Will this picture help win the war?"; "If it is an 'escape' picture, will it harm the war effort by creating a false picture of America, her allies and the world we live in?"; and "Does it merely use the war as a basis for a profitable picture, contributing nothing of real significance to the war effort and possibly lessening the effort of other pictures of more importance?" Since comedies were as rule dismissed as being of "less importance" than dramatic films, they received closer scrutiny for perceived departures from the OWI's exacting standards. Thus, any joke or gag that could remotely prove detrimental to the war effort was strongly discouraged. As one of many examples of the agency's taboos, filmgoers could no longer enjoy the *What Price Glory?*-style spectacle of overseas troopers drinking themselves into oblivion and indulging in hands-on fraternization with the local womenfolk. Nelson Poynter, the notoriously presumptive head of the OWI's Bureau of Motion Pictures, went so far as to pressure RKO Radio into totally withdrawing from circulation the 1942 comedy *Call Out the Marines* because he regarded the film as a gross insult to the integrity of the Marine Corps—and never mind that if RKO complied, it would cost the studio $450,000.

In theory, none of the major studios was required to follow the "advice" of the OWI to the letter. However, since the agency had the power to withhold the use of technical advisors, uniforms, military weaponry, transport vehicles and Signal Corps stock footage from the producers of fictional war pictures, the studios were reluctant to put up resistance to the OWI's demands. But even if Hollywood had totally ignored the agency, they were still at the mercy of their own in-house regulators. Among the "requests" made by the Hays Office (which had overseen movie censorship since the 1920s) was that the makers of slapstick comedies refrain from such "wasteful" practices as pie-throwing and furniture-smashing, so as not to offend civilians who were forced to ration such items. Even the members of the Screen Writers' Guild, normally the staunchest of First Amendment advocates, got into the act. Joining forces with the morale-boosting Hollywood Writers Mobilization, the Guild warned comedy writers that "a very funny line may make black-market dealings seem innocent and attractive," and insisted that "respect for officers must be maintained at all times, in any scene, in any situation." (So much for all those second lieutenant gags from World War I.)

After World War II ended in 1945, service comedies were allowed more leeway in ribbing authority figures and commenting caustically on the downside of military life — even during the subsequent Korean War (1950–1953)—though filmmakers still watched their step in order to secure military cooperation when needed. The "voice" of military humor was now primarily the collective domain of ex-servicemen who knew whereof they spoke and whose jokes and gag situations had an aura of verisimilitude frequently lacking in prewar comedies. A whole new generation of comedy writers had honed their talents while in uniform — with the not-inconsiderable financial assistance of the postwar GI Bill — and were more than willing to share their wartime experiences for the purpose of mass-market entertainment. This bright young talent pool included Thomas Heggen (*Mister Roberts*), Vern Sneider (*The Teahouse of the August Moon*), Mac Hyman (*No Time for Sergeants*), Neil Simon (*Biloxi Blues*, TV's *You'll Never Get Rich*), William Bowers (*Imitation General, The Last Time I Saw Archie*), David Stern (*Francis the Talking Mule*), Sy Gomberg, William J. Lederer, William Brinkley, Donald R. Morris and many others.

It helped immeasurably that the new crop of miltary humorists were speaking to a well-informed civilian audience that understood exactly what they were talking about, who needed no explanation of wartime conditions and required no translations of such war-related nomenclature as "Seabee," "Howitzer," "bazooka," "Molotov cocktail," "reconnaissance," "camouflage," "commando," "guerrilla," "pincer movement," "flak-happy" and "halftrack." Nor did the non-combatant public suffer much confusion over the myriad of military acronyms which circulated freely throughout the war: AAA, APO885, CCS, DUKW, LCM, LST, MI, MP, MTB, OCS, OSS, PT, SHAEF, and, of course, SNAFU. As Edward R. Murrow once observed, World War II was "the greatest mass adventure Man has yet undertaken," and virtually every man, woman and child in the United States felt as though he or she were a part of the Big Picture, civilian or no. As such, the average American homebody in the World War II years was just as savvy about "inside" military terminology and slang as any soldier in the field. Listen to a few Bob Hope radio shows of the era, and you'll receive a crash course in Army, Navy and Marine jargon.

Not only did movie comedies about World War II proliferate in the two decades following the conflict, but there was also a wealth of comedies revolving around the modern peacetime military. In contrast with the post–World War I era, the Selective Service process that was put into effect in 1940 had not been dismantled after VE Day. The renovated Selective Service Act of 1948 declared that every male 18 or over had to register for service, and that those between the ages of 19 and 26 were eligible for the draft and a 21-month tour of duty. Budgetary limitations kept the number of processed men to a minimum until the Korean War, at which time the Universal Military Training and Service Act went into effect, lowering the draft age to 18½ and increasing the compulsory service period to 24 months (subject to change depending on the branch of service: for example, if you volunteered for the Navy, you were in for four years). Though married men with children, college students, business trainees and conscientious objectors could request exemptions, most young men of draft age in the years 1950 through 1965 resigned themselves to the inevitability of service time. It was this audience that most readily identified with the protagonists of such postwar military comedies as *Let's Go Navy, Sound Off, Jumping Jacks, Off Limits, The Perfect Furlough, A Private's Affair, All Hands on Deck* and *The Honeymoon Machine*.

The Cold War of the 1950s suddenly heated up in the early 1960s thanks to the increasing animosity between the United States and the Soviet Union—and especially the ever-escalating conflict in Vietnam, with thousands of young Americans shipped off to fight and die in a war that wasn't even supposed to be a war. It was during this period that the voices of burgeoning anti-war movement began making themselves heard, not only in the real-life media but also in such penetrating "black" military comedies as *Dr. Strangelove* and *The Americanization of Emily* (both 1964). America's active involvement in Vietnam was entering its second decade when on November 26, 1969, the Military Service Act of 1967—which had expanded the draft age from 18 to 35 and decreed that all college deferments were null and void upon the deferee's 24th birthday—was radically amended. The draft was now based on a lottery system, each number corresponding to a calendar day. No longer could eligible males rely on a high draft-registration number or a deferment to avoid conscription: If your birthday happened to fall upon a low lottery number, your chances of remaining a civilian were considerably curtailed. Not surprisingly, the end-the-war movement *really* caught fire after this amendment went into effect on December 1, 1969. Hollywood wasted no time exploiting these sentiments with a whole slew of anti-war and anti-establishment films, including two hard-hitting service comedies that had been in preparation *before* the lottery: *MASH* and *Catch-22*, both 1970 releases.

After the United States pulled out of Vietnam in 1975, the military-comedy genre went into a total eclipse, at least on the big screen (the TV series *M*A*S*H* was by now virtually alone in representing the serviceman's POV in humorous terms). The genre was briefly reactivated in 1980 with the release of *Private Benjamin*, an up-to-date comedy about women in the military starring Goldie Hawn. The success of *Private Benjamin* was too big to ignore, and within a year another cinematic goldmine debuted: the Bill Murray vehicle *Stripes*, likewise a comic slant on the modern military. Unlike their predecessors of the 1950s, these two Army farces could not rely upon a built-in audience of genuine military personnel to bolster their success. Since 1973, the Army had been an all-volunteer operation; the draft was permanently halted, and the registration requirement came to an end in 1976. Four years later, Proclamation 4771 reinstated compulsory registration for men between the ages of 18 and 26, but once registered they weren't required to join up. Thus, both *Private Benjamin* and *Stripes* played to a largely civilian audience and a comparative handful of military volunteers.

Unfortunately, both films also reflected an inconvenient truth about the state of things in the early 1980s. The combination of an unpopular and wasteful war in Vietnam and a series of deep defense-budget cuts between 1975 and 1980 had left the American military—the Army in particular—in a severely demoralized and debilitated condition. The salary was so low on many bases that the families of enlistees had to subsist on food stamps, while much of the available training equipment was outdated and in deplorable shape. Like the protagonists of *Private Benjamin* and *Stripes*, a lot of the young men and women in uniform had signed up only because they had run out of options in civilian life—and since the military could not afford to be as choosy as in the past, some of the new enlistees weren't entirely "all that they could be." Now burdened with a last-resort onus, the military establishment was in danger of becoming a festering ground for desperation, defeatism and substance abuse. (The highly skilled and highly motivated officer graduates of such venerable military academies as West Point, Annapolis and The Citadel were spectacular exceptions to this generalization.)

Things took an upward swing before the end of the 1980s with increased defense spending, a strengthened and improved training process for enlistees and non-commissioned officers, and especially the morale-boosting internal collapse of the East European Communist bloc. The subsequent upsurge in enthusiastic and well-prepared American troops did not, however, result in an increased number of Hollywood service comedies. From 1984 to 2009, an average of only one such film per year was produced, with only the retrospective *Good Morning, Vietnam* and the genre spoof *Hot Shots!* enjoying the same blockbuster status as *Private Benjamin* and *Stripes*— though *serious* military films like *Platoon, Top Gun, A Few Good Men* and *Saving Private Ryan* flourished mightily during these years.

Beyond the absence of the sort of universally shared experience that fostered the popularity of funny films about World War II, it isn't easy to explain from the vantage point of 2011 why service comedies have fallen from favor in the past three decades. Certainly the demand for entertainment during this period has increased dramatically among military personnel, especially those brave men and women who enlisted in the War on Terror in response to the horrific events of September 11, 2001. These valiant volunteer warriors have as a rule been too modest and unassuming to demand a steady supply of comedy films to provide relief from their perilous mission, but if anyone has ever *deserved* to be entertained, it is they. And yet, since 9/11 a mere half dozen military comedies have seen the light of day, with only two such efforts—*Delta Farce* and *The Men Who Stare at Goats*—exhibiting the sort of relevance and timeliness that had helped make Chaplin's *Shoulder Arms* and Abbott & Costello's *Buck Privates* so popular and profitable in years (and wars) past. Unfortunately, neither film was a box-office hit, so the impulse to cash in on them, as Hollywood had previously done with *Shoulder Arms* and *Buck Privates*, has been nonexistent.

Still, it may be too early to write off the service comedy as a dead issue. Previous obituaries for such specialized movie genres as the Western, the musical and the religious epic have proven premature, as seen in the phenomenal success of *Dances with Wolves, Chicago* and *The Passion of the Christ*. Perhaps generations yet unborn will be regaled by the future equivalents of such military-related laughspinners as *The General, Buck Privates, Mister Roberts, No Time for Sergeants, Operation Petticoat, MASH, Private Benjamin* and *Hot Shots!* We can only hope and and pray that any such resurgence of popularity will not require a brand-new war to set it in motion.

1

"I surrounded them!"
Charlie Chaplin and Shoulder Arms

Released by First National Exchange on October 20, 1918, Charles Chaplin's *Shoulder Arms* has been described as the first truly great American war comedy — or at the very least, the first truly great military comedy. Well and good, but a few "experts" have gone further by classifying the film as the first military comedy *period*, which it most certainly wasn't. Chaplin's former boss Mack Sennett had delved into the genre even before World War I with the 1913 Civil War farces *The Battle of Who Run* and *Cohen Saves the Flag*, both discussed in **Chapter 18**. Once the war was under way, the film industry responded with comedies referencing the conflict, just as virtually every other aspect of society was considered fair game for fun-poking. Many of the war-related comedies were less concerned with the military than with the impact of the war on the civilian population. Sennett's *Her Torpedoed Love* (1916) used a sea skirmish merely as a plot device to complicate a standard romantic triangle, while films like *Swat the Spy* (1917) and Larry Semon's *Huns and Hyphens* (1918) capitalized on widespread rumors of German espionage activities in the United States.

A handful of pre–*Shoulder Arms* releases did experiment with Army humor. Released by Vim Comedies in September 1916, *Love and Duty* was part of the "Plump and Runt" series of one-reelers headlining 24-year-old Oliver Hardy as Plump and Billy Ruge as Runt. In this one, the boys are both in love with the Colonel's daughter, with Plump the girl's favorite until Runt proves that his rival is also wooing "The Pet of the Regiment." Arrested on trumped-up charges, Plump clears himself when he rescues the Colonel from drowning — then decides that the old man's daughter isn't worth all the bother. Jester Comedies' *The Recruit* (February 1918) was also part of a series, this one starring Marcel Perez (aka Marcel Fabre) as a character variously known as Tweedle-Dum, Tweedle-Dan and Tweedy. Cast as a raw rookie, the star tilted with his sergeant and spooned with his sweetie, played by Perez' wife Dorothy Earle. Filmed in Florida, *The Recruit* was an early directorial effort by William A. Seiter, who later piloted such comedy classics as *Skinner's Dress Suit* and *Sons of the Desert*.

Then there was Universal's *The Geezer of Berlin* (August 1918), a takeoff of the serious propaganda picture *The Kaiser — Beast of Berlin*, in which doughboy Monty Banks crossed swords with the Kaiser (here billed as "Willie A'Mighty") and his stooges "The Clown Quince," "Von Hindenboig," "Von Turpentine" and "Cancellor Von Bethmann-Bowlegs." An argument could be made that *The Geezer of Berlin* was a direct precursor to *Shoulder Arms*, which also featured Kaiser and Crown Prince caricatures. However, it is more likely that Universal was taking advantage of Chaplin's notoriously slow working methods (he'd started *Shoulder Arms* in May and wouldn't wrap things up until mid–September), allowing the studio to rush its own war comedy through production and into theaters two months ahead of Chaplin, thereby cashing in on the publicity attending Charlie's picture-in-progress.

There was no shortage of buzz surrounding *Shoulder Arms*. The single most popular entertainer on earth, Chaplin was under round-the-clock scrutiny from the press — especially in his home country England, where certain self-appointed arbiters of patriotism were busy browbeating young men of military age to enlist in the Great War. Never mind that Charlie Chaplin is a Hollywood movie star, admonished these ageing armchair generals. He's an Englishman, and all red-blooded Englishmen must respond to their nation's call immediately. As Kevin Brownlow has written, "Chaplin not only received white feathers, but also threatening letters and public attacks in the papers." In contrast, British and American government authorities shared the opinion that Chaplin could do more good by continuing to make films that kept the troops laughing than he could in the trenches. "Mr. Chaplin has a perfect right right to resent being termed, in any sense, a 'slacker,'" noted *Motion Picture News* in July of 1917, adding: "People fail to realize that at this depressing time the man who can make them smile and forget the terrible, world-wide gloom is doing a real good for humanity." Still, the perception lingered that Charlie had managed to evade military service because of fame and wealth, while middle-class British families who had lost fathers, husbands and sons were not granted this reprieve. The nastiest response to Charlie's supposed lack of fortitude was a scatological soldier's song, "The Moon Shines Bright on Charlie Chaplin." Decades after the fact, Charlie recalled to both Alistair Cooke and Garson Kanin that he spent the war years terrified that this song might inspire some deranged veteran to attack him in the street.

Chaplin wore his patriotism on his sleeve by leading and contributing to a variety of war-fund drives, and by headlining an amusing propaganda short, *The Bond*, which concluded as Charlie's "Little Tramp" pummelled the Kaiser into insensibility with a huge mallet labelled LIBERTY BONDS. He also issued statements solidifying his commitment to the Allied cause: "I only wish that I could join the English Army and fight for my mother country," he told *Pictures and Picturegoer* magazine in February of 1918, "but I have received so many letters from soldiers at the front, as well as civilians, asking me to continue making pictures that I have come to the conclusion that my work lies right here in Los Angeles." In the end, Charlie decided that the most effective assault he could muster against the Central Powers would have to be conveyed in the language he knew best — the language of laughter.

Shoulder Arms was advertised as "The Million Dollar Picture" in reference to Chaplin's new contract with First National, which guaranteed him a salary of $1,000,000 (sixteen million in 2011 dollars) and a bonus of $75,000 for delivery of twelve films. Chaplin disappointed neither his distributor nor his fans with his initial First National effort *A Dog's Life* (April 1918), at three reels his longest starring film to date, and one that represented a maturity in Chaplin's approach and technique: the settings were realistically grimy, unlike the near-fantasy world of his Mutual comedies; the camerawork (by Rollie Totheroh) was smoother and more sophisticated; and the gags were better paced and motivated. When critics praised *Dog's Life* as Chaplin's pinnacle, the comedian vowed to top himself with *Shoulder Arms*, going so far as to plan his next picture as his first feature-length comedy (discounting 1914's *Tillie's Punctured Romance*, which was not a vehicle for him nor filmed under his control).

Press releases were issued to the effect that *Shoulder Arms* would open with a prologue showing henpecked husband Charlie escaping his termagent wife and howling children (one of whom was played by future screenwriter True Boardman) by joining the Army. Two weeks were spent filming this opener, in which a near-naked Charlie dazedly wanders through a maze of lookalike cubicles and indifferent female stenographers at the induction center. No sooner was this sequence in the can that Chaplin decided to drop the whole business and open "cold" with Charlie already in boot camp. Rescued from deterioration in the mid-1970s, this abandoned prologue has been restored and reassembled by Kevin Brownlow and David Gill, revealing that one of the stenographers is played by Chaplin's perennial leading lady Edna Purviance, who also appears in the later war sequences as a woebegone French peasant. Some have suggested that this double casting was carelessness on Chaplin's part, while others have opined that Purviance's presence was meant to tip off the audience that the subsequent battlefield scenes were all part of an elaborate dream, imagined by Charlie before he'd even set foot in France.

With the prologue removed, *Shoulder Arms* was redesigned as a three-reeler, running approximately 45 minutes when projected theatrically. For the benefit of those who've never seen it (imagine any writer saying *that* 40 or 50 years ago!), Charlie is introduced as a member of the "awkward squad," comprised of rookies so inept that they have to be segregated from the other recruits and trained on their own. After reducing the drill to a shambles, Charlie collapses on his cot, whereupon we immediately switch to the trenches "Over There." The plotline abandons the strictures of the dugout halfway through and moves to open country, where while carrying out a high-risk assignment Charlie rescues heroine Edna (characterized as "Poor France") from various and sundry predatory Germans. From the moment the enemy troops are paid a surprise visit by Kaiser Wilhelm and the Crown Prince, the audience begins to sense that things aren't quite what they seem — a sense heightened when Charlie takes both men prisoner and turns them over to the Allies (the original cut included a sequence in which Charlie is fêted for his heroism by all the important Allied dignitaries). Our suspicions are confirmed when the whole story turns out to have been dreamed by Charlie while supine on his Army cot back in training camp.

Even as production on *Shoulder Arms* drew to a close in early September 1918, and despite an increase in reports from the Front regarding the morale-boosting value of Chaplin's earlier 2-reelers, the comedian began to have second thoughts about releasing the completed film, worried that even remotely kidding the war would be regarded as offensive and insulting. A few industryites, notably Cecil B. DeMille, advised Chaplin to either delay the release or permanently shelve the picture, while a few hostile journalists made clear that they were prepared to hate the film on sight whether it was funny or not. According to Chaplin, only the enthusiastic support of his good friend Douglas Fairbanks Sr. ("my greatest audience") persuaded him to release *Shoulder Arms* as scheduled, less than three weeks before the Armistice. It turned out be just the right film at the right time, as observed by critic Walter Kerr: "With their worries ended, audiences could openly enjoy what had appalled them so long."

In Joe Franklin's 1959 coffee-table book *Classics of the Silent Screen*, it is noted that *Shoulder Arms* "somehow still managed to convey the tragedy of war without holding up any of the fun." Those unfamiliar with Chaplin might well be turned off by the critics' rhapsodizing over the pathos in his films, imagining that the comedian was more interested in wheedling pity than summoning laughter. Nothing could be further from the truth. Chaplin's "Little Tramp" was popular not because audiences felt sorry for him, but because they admired the character's resilience and resourcefulness: His genius for making the absolute best of bad situations, his versatility in adapting the props around him for utmost comfort and utility (a cheese grater in *Shoulder Arms* proves to be an excellent backscratcher during a "cootie" attack), and the manner in which his jaunty gentleman-hobo demeanor made the most shabby of surroundings seem as luxurious as the finest metropolitan hotel. When in *Shoulder Arms* Charlie settles down to sleep in a flooded dugout, his pantomime does not convey the attitude "What a miserable state of affairs!" but rather "Oh, well, one works with what one gets"— illustrating this philosophy by delicately arranging his soaking pillow to fit his weary head. When Charlie can find no other food to eat than the cheese in a mousetrap, he treats this repast as if it was a gourmet smorgasbord. And when during mail call he receives no letters of his own, Charlie peeks over the shoulder of another soldier as the man reads a message from home, vicariously experiencing the same joys and sorrows as the reader. (In this, Chaplin is behaving like a typical movie fan: If I can't have my own happiness, I can always tune in on someone else's.)

Chaplin is at his very best as both actor and director during the scenes in Edna Purviance's bombed-out cottage. A lengthy establishing shot of the girl sitting morosely on her crumbling doorstep, then wandering disconsolately amidst the rubble of what once had been her home, seems at first glance a heavy-handed reminder that War is Hell even in a comedy. What the audience doesn't realize is that Chaplin is setting up every square inch of that ruined cottage — the open ceiling, the rickety floor, the tiny windows, the narrow doorways, the gaping shell-holes, the distressingly easy access between the first and second stories—for future comic use. Only when Charlie leads a platoon of pursuing German soldiers on a merry chase all over, around and through the cottage does it become obvious what the comedian is up to. Chaplin is not wallowing in the horrors

Prepared for any and all emergencies, Charlie Chaplin goes to war in 1918's *Shoulder Arms*.

of war; instead, he is using the tragedy of the situation as groundwork for the comedy, making the gags even funnier by providing context and substance.

Shoulder Arms turned out to be Chaplin's biggest financial and critical success to date. The *New York Times* commented that even those who'd shown up at the premiere for the express purpose of finding fault with the film laughed hysterically and went home happy. One Chaplin detractor in the audience was heard to exclaim, "The fool's funny!"—a sound-bite which would soon be incorporated in First National's ad campaign along with such blurbs as "Putting the Silver Lining to the Clouds of the World." Other reviews were just as enthusiastic, and some a lot more analytical like *Motion Picture* magazine in January 1919: "Underneath all the farce of it, we are in close sympathy with the little man and conscious of a touch of true pathos which makes us realize that this Chaplin who calls himself a comedian is perhaps the greatest (a word I dislike to use but which seems necessary in this case) actor of the screen today. Truly, with each release does he prove the value of his making only a few pictures a year. Not only is the perfection of three months' work apparent as compared to the three weeks expended upon other feature films [sic], but the public does not have an opportunity to become satiated with the star."

Only in retrospect can we recognize that such effusions of praise would have a detrimental effect on Chaplin. Now that he was an acknowledged "genius," he felt obligated to behave like one, and as a result his post–*Shoulder Arms* comedies tended to be more labored and ponderous than his previous work (though he would eventually return to the old form with his 1925 masterpiece *The Gold Rush*). Also, now that critics were willing to "forgive" the lengthy gaps between his films, the comedian would work at an even more decelerated pace throughout the next decade, with years rather than months going by before a "new" Chaplin comedy hit the screens. To fill this void, various exhibitors kept the comedian's earlier comedies in constant distribution — including *Shoulder Arms*, which was given two major reissues by Pathé in 1923 and 1927 (the same year that Chaplin settled a lawsuit with one Leo Loeb, who claimed that the film was plagiarized from his own stage play *The Rookie*).

Naturally, any film this popular would have a lasting effect on the movie industry. Not only was *Shoulder Arms* the yardstick by which all future Chaplins would be measured, but the film's best gags—Charlie masquerading as a tree behind German lines, using limburger cheese as a weapon, opening a bottle of wine by having the cork blown off by enemy gunfire, fretting over various bad-luck omens before going "Over the Top"—would be lifted and repeated *ad nauseam* by practically every second-tier comedian in Hollywood. Other filmmakers acknowledged Chaplin's influence without resorting to outright imitation: Most war comedies of the 1920s and beyond would follow *Shoulder Arms*' example by focusing on the day-to-day activities of the "regular" soldiers and noncoms, rather than the gallantry and sacrifice of the officer class. It is even possible to trace certain camera setups during the harrowing "Belleau Wood" sequence in King Vidor's landmark 1925 World War I drama *The Big Parade*, with its hundreds of doughboys nervously marching through row upon row of sniper-infested trees, all the way back to Chaplin's more lighthearted forest perambulations in *Shoulder Arms*.

Does the film hold up for modern audiences? Most of the gags still induce laughter, but the timeliness and immediacy of a World War I comedy released at the tail end of that conflict is now understandably lost. Also, the film's reputation as a penetrating anti-war doctrine — a reputation largely fabricated by film pundits of the Vietnam era — tends to wither in the cold light of day. "*Shoulder Arms* will disappoint those expecting a biting satire of war," wrote Andrew Sarris in a February 6, 1964, critique for *The Village Voice*, adding: "The most pacifistic films are usually made long before or long after there is any serious need for them." Those seeking out a more explicit screed on pacifism from Charles Chaplin are advised to watch his 1940s films *The Great Dictator* and *Monsieur Verdoux*, both of which fulfill Chaplin biographer John McCabe's description of the comedian's later efforts as "medicine-coating the sugar." Those who prefer their sugar without medicine can relax with *Shoulder Arms*.

2

Run Silent, Run Shallow
The Silent Service Comedies

Feature Films

With the release of *Shoulder Arms* and the cessation of hostilities in the fall of 1918, it suddenly became safe for movies to kid wartime military activities. Leading the assault on the audience's funnybone was "King of Comedy" Mack Sennett, who on March 2, 1919, arranged a press preview of his 5-reel feature *Yankee Doodle in Berlin* (working title: *The Kaiser's Last Squeal*). Mostly filmed in November and December of 1918, *Yankee Doodle in Berlin* has sometimes been characterized as a lampoon of the serious "Hate the Hun" propaganda films of the World War I years. Sennett himself described the film as a satire of German militarism, or so his publicity people told *Variety*: "Sennett believes with Alexander Pope that ridicule and satire are the most effective weapons in the world to employ when the over-estimated and over-praised are to be given their true and just treatment.... The Kaiser ... is shown up in *Yankee Doodle in Berlin* for what he is, a pitiable spectacle of an inflated egotist, vicious in mind and depraved in habits." Beyond the likelihood that Sennett never heard of Alexander Pope (nor for that matter knew the meaning of the word "depraved"), an examination of the film suggests that the producer regarded the wartime framework as merely an excuse to show people kicking each other, clobbering one another with croquet mallets, throwing furniture, taking pratfalls, bursting bathroom pipes and frantically running in and out of bedrooms—in other words, a typical Mack Sennett farce on a higher budget than usual.

In keeping with Sennett's policy of showcasing such Broadway luminaries as Marie Dressler and Raymond Hitchcock in his "special" productions, *Yankee Doodle in Berlin* is a vehicle for Danish-born entertainer Bothwell Browne (1877–1947), a female impersonator second only to the legendary Julian Eltinge in popularity. Browne was cast as American aviator Bob Adams, sent behind enemy lines to steal the Kaiser's war plans. Crash-landing in "Hun-land," Adams eludes capture by harking back to his "college plays" and dressing up as a *femme fatale*. Using faux feminine wiles to wrap the Kaiser, the Crown Prince and Von Hindenburg around his little finger, he caps his masquerade with a Mata Hari-like exotic dance. While Bothwell Browne's cross-dressing mimicry is impressive, one can't help observing that he is far more attractive as a man than as a woman. (Throughout the film, director F. Richard Jones stresses the red-blooded masculinity beneath Browne's frilly finery by showing the actor beating the bejeepers out of every German soldier he meets, sometimes taking on two or three at a time. Even so, Browne's delicate features and lamby-pie eyes are at odds with this forced machismo.)

Other than the star and the bit actors playing the Allied troops, the cast is recruited entirely from Sennett's world-famous gallery of grotesques. Ford Sterling plays the Kaiser exactly as he played Chief Teeheezel in the Keystone Kops 1-reelers, grimacing and gesticulating outrageously. As Von Hindenberg, bulbous Bert Roach relies on sheer *avoirdupois* (with a bit of extra padding from the prop department) to get laughs, while future director Mal St. Clair plays the Crown Prince as a milksop mama's boy. Chester Conklin administers as many kicks to the posterior as traffic will allow in the role of a military commander; cross-eyed Ben Turpin staggers about as an amorous sentry; and shifty-eyed Heinie Conklin and gargantuan Kalla Pasha patiently stand in wait until the other comics stop making funny so they can throw in their own routines. The most memorable performance comes from the literally immense Eva Thatcher as Kaiser Wilhelm's wife, variously referred to as "The Kaiserine" and "The Mrs." After an introductory scene in which she is shown swilling a huge stein of beer and devouring what appears to be an ulcerated sausage, Thatcher proves beyond doubt that *Yankee Doodle in Berlin,* for all its "topicality," is at base an old-style domestic farce. Pelting her husband with crockery, breaking a bass fiddle over the Imperial noggin, and pursuing "Bill" around their boudoir after catching him in a compromising position, Eva Thatcher works long and hard to earn her belly-laughs.

That *Yankee Doodle in Berlin* was initally planned as a 2-reeler and expanded to feature length during production is made painfully obvious by the chaotic plotting, the abrupt jumps in scene and mood, and especially the cavalier treatment of two leading characters: an Irish POW played by Charlie Murray, and a captured Belgian lass enacted by Marie Prevost. After going to great lengths to establish these characters—Charlie picks lice from Chester Conklin's walrus moustache and defiantly blows his nose on the German flag, while Marie heaves rocks at the *Boche* before escaping her captors in male drag—the film abruptly drops them and moves on to other things. Though Prevost briefly reappears during the climax, Murray totally vanishes after Reel Two. The film's ending likewise suffers from paste-and-paper construction. In the midst of an epic battle scene highlighted by convincingly choreographed troop movements and stunning aerial photography, Sennett falls back on standard 2-reel gaggery with a patently artificial shot of the Kaiser and his minions being chased around the studio treadmill by a prop bombshell emblazoned with the letters "U.S."

For the film's national release in June 1919, distributor Sol Lesser marketed *Yankee Doodle in Berlin* on a reserved-seat "road show" basis. In the larger cities, the film was preceded by a live stage presentation headlined by Bothwell Browne in person, featuring a lavish musical tableau spotlighting the Sennett bathing beauties in such roles as "The Victory Girl," "The Sand Witch" and "The Ocean Tramp"; among the young hopefuls performing in this extravaganza was Virginia Fox, future wife of 20th Century–Fox head man Darryl F. Zanuck. *Yankee Doodle* broke box-office records throughout the nation ("In no time at all, I was an impresario," noted Sol Lesser years later) and was equally well received in Great Britain, where it was diplomatically retitled *Tommy Atkins in Berlin.* In the 1920s, the film was theatrically reissued in 2-reel form, doing no damage whatsoever to its continuity. The current archival print, restored from several battered and slightly deteriorated sources, runs approximately 59 minutes. As one of the few propaganda features from the World War I period still in existence, its historical value is immeasurable, though its entertainment value has tarnished considerably over the decades.

Ford Sterling masticates the scenery while lampooning "Kaiser Bill" in this frame capture from Mack Sennett's *Yankee Doodle in Berlin* (1919). Mal St. Clair, as the Crown Prince, looks on.

Other feature-length military comedies tended

to steer clear of Sennett-style slapstick in the immediate post–World War I years, relying on characterization and situation for laughs. Produced by Thomas H. Ince for Paramount release, 1919's *Hay Foot, Straw Foot* was a vehicle for the incredibly popular Charles Ray. Generally cast as either a passive juvenile who allowed others to walk all over him or a small-town braggart who needed to be taken down a peg or two, Ray promised his fans an "entirely new characterization" in this film. The star played Ulysses S. Grant Briggs, grandson of a self-proclaimed Civil War hero (Spottiswoode Aitken). When America enters World War I, Ulysses' grandpa joins forces with his lifelong rival (William Conklin), a former Confederate soldier, to train Ulysses for Army service — warning him to steer clear of "play-actresses" like Betty Martin (Doris Lee) if he wants to stay in prime fettle. But the boy is so smitten by Betty that he goes AWOL to rescue her from a would-be seducer. Refusing to explain his actions lest he compromise Betty, Ulysses languishes in the guardhouse until the girl comes forth and tells all to his commanding officer. Though Ulysses has yet to go anywhere near a battlefield, his grandfather and grandpa's rival agree that, through his noble silence, the boy exhibited just as much courage as the original Ulysses S. Grant. While audiences may have been disappointed that Charlie Ray was never seen in a combat situation, the actor compensated to a degree by performing genuine magic tricks during an onscreen camp show, earning praise from several professional magicians.

Tired of his constant contractual battles with the egotistical Charles Ray, producer Thomas Ince called the actor's bluff by developing a "new" Ray in the form of light comedian Douglas MacLean, whom Ince teamed with ingenue Doris May (previously billed as Doris Lee in *Hay Foot, Straw Foot*). The producer boosted MacLean and May to full stardom in the army comedy *23½ Hours' Leave*, directed by Henry King and released approximately one year after the Armistice. The film was based on a 1918 magazine serial-*cum*-novel by Mary Roberts Rinehart, whose research on barracks life was gathered while she was a wartime news correspondent. One of a half-dozen popular novels purchased by Ince for a lump sum of $67,000, *23½ Hours' Leave*, despite its comic nature, is paced and plotted like one of Rinehart's later mystery stories, the author providing fragmentary plot information on a "need-to-know" basis until everything is explained at the end. The film version wasted no time with this literary coyness, allowing the audience to figure out where the plot is going long before the slightly dense hero catches on. Otherwise, the film was a reasonably faithful rendition of its source, moving *Photoplay* to comment that the Rinehart original had been perfectly transferred to the screen.

Douglas MacLean was cast as Sgt. William Gray, a rule-bending wiseacre ("Laws are for slaves!") who bets his barracks buddies that within the titular 23½ hours he will be sitting down for breakfast with the General. But it doesn't look like he'll have much time to ingratiate himself with the General, nor even go on leave: In trouble for wearing a tailor-made uniform rather than his government-issued duds, Gray has been confined to barracks. Through a stratagem too complicated to explain here, Gray escapes from camp wearing only his BVDs, and it is his buddies who end up confined to quarters. Covering his embarrassment with a raincoat, Gray hitches a ride to town with pretty Peggy Dodge (Doris May), who unbeknownst to him is the General's daughter (she's his niece in the novel). Though he wants to treat her to dinner and a show, she insists upon making a quick stop at the local photo studio. The foolhardy Gray begins to gossip about military secrets (of which he knows absolutely nothing) to the shop's owner, little suspecting that the man is a German spy. Spotted by his angry Army pals, who intend to get even for being punished because of his insubordination, Gray takes refuge in the photo shop, where after figuring out that skullduggery is afoot he single-handedly subdues a brace of enemy agents. As a reward for his bravery, Sgt. Gray does indeed have breakfast with the General — and wins Peggy as a bonus.

Motion Picture News' Tom Hamlin gave the film an unqualified rave as "the best all-around comedy of the season." An even greater honor bestowed upon *23½ Hours' Leave* was the wholehearted endorsement of the American Legion, who invited star Douglas MacLean to be guest of honor at several Legion posts throughout the nation. Present-day audiences won't have much of a chance to form their own opinions of the film: Like most of MacLean's starring pictures, *23½ Hours' Leave* is currently unavailable for reappraisal, the one reportedly extant print incomplete and in bad shape. One can, however, get a pretty good idea of the silent film's quality by watching the 1937 talkie remake produced by Douglas MacLean for Grand National Pictures, a small but ambitious "indie." The remake retains the World War I setting, the main characters, the major plot points, a number of comic setpieces (including a mammoth pillow fight!) and a great deal of the novel's original dialogue. It also carries over several of the alterations made between novel and screen for the 1919 version, including the addition of a handsome young officer who vies with the hero for the heroine's attentions. For publicity purposes, producer MacLean sought out the sons of several American Legionnaires who'd played bit parts in the original film to fill the same roles in the remake.

James Ellison is seen in the talkie version as Sgt. Gray, with Terry Walker as Peggy and Paul Harvey (*not* the radio commentator) as the General. Featured in the cast are two actors whose names would carry more box-office weight in the years to come, Arthur Lake and Ward Bond. For reasons that he would take to his grave, Douglas MacLean opted to gin up the remake by adding musical numbers, many of these popping up without warning in the unlikeliest places.

A Sailor Made Man (Hal Roach, 1921): It's obvious that Navy life agrees with Harold Lloyd.

During an otherwise mundane mess hall scene, Sgt. Gray abruptly breaks out in the Nelson Eddy-style anthem "We Happen to Be in the Army," segueing into a mini-production number using pots, pans and eating utensils as musical instruments: even Ward Bond joins in a chorus. The silliest of these songfests occurs during a nightclub scene in which Gray is invited by the orchestra leader to sing "Goodnight My Lucky Day"— and when his fellow soldiers show up with the intention of knocking him senseless for getting them confined to barracks, they are instantly pressed into service as Gray's backup singers.

But we digress: Let's get back to the silent era, and beyond Thomas H. Ince, to see how the slapstick rivals of Charlie Chaplin handled the military-comedy format. By 1920, Chaplin's supremacy was being challenged by three comedians: Roscoe "Fatty" Arbuckle, Harold Lloyd and Buster Keaton. Of the three, only Arbuckle had already moved into feature films, and only Arbuckle abstained from service comedies. Harold Lloyd's producer Hal Roach tentatively dipped his toes into producing comedies longer than two or three reels with the 4-reel Lloyd vehicle *A Sailor-Made Man* (released by Pathé in December 1921), described by historians as either a "long short" or a "semi-feature." In addition to being Lloyd's most ambitious comedy to date, the film was the bespectacled comedian's only extended foray into military humor.

In the manner of Charles Ray, Lloyd alternated between playing nice young men who were put upon by society and impudent sprouts who succeeded through sheer audacity. It is in the latter guise that Harold is seen in *A Sailor-Made Man*, cast as a wealthy idler smitten by equally wealthy Mildred Davis. Brashly informing Mildred's father, "I've decided to marry your daughter," Harold is told that he hasn't a chance until he proves he "can do something besides loaf." In the next scene Harold shows up at a recruiting office, declaring with customary cheekiness, "I've decided to join your navy." Imagining that he'll immediately be promoted to Admiral, the boy instead finds himself a common sailor on board the U.S.S. *Frederick* (the actual ship is used for these scenes, with real sailors as extras). Surprising everyone with his willingness to work both humbly and hard, Harold climaxes this early stage of his Naval career by forging a strong alliance with the *Frederick*'s toughest tar, played by Noah Young. Once this is established, *A Sailor-Made Man* forsakes its nautical ambience and shifts sights to the mythical Eastern kingdom of Khaipura-Bandanna, where Harold and Noah rescue the heroine from the clutches of lecherous maharajah Dick Sutherland. Though structurally *A Sailor-Made Man* looks like three or four short subjects strung together, its success emboldened Hal Roach to move Lloyd out of 2-reelers and exclusively into features, beginning with 1922's *Grandma's Boy*.

Highlighted by a flashback to the Civil War, *Grandma's Boy* might marginally be classified as a service comedy, though it would fall to two other major comedians of the 1920s, Raymond Griffith and Buster Keaton, to fully exploit the struggle between North and South as a comedy backdrop in their respective 1926 vehicles *Hands Up* and *The General*, both discussed in detail in **Chapter 18**. By the time these films were in circulation, Keaton had joined Chaplin and Lloyd as the great comedy triumvirate of the silent era (Fatty Arbuckle's career having been destroyed by scandal several years earlier), though all three of these laugh makers were being given a run for

Though in the film itself his weapon of preference is a slingshot, this still from *The Strong Man* (First National, 1926) finds Harry Langdon manning a World War I-vintage machine gun.

their money by a newcomer to the Pantheon, baby-faced Harry Langdon. Perhaps because the comic contrast between Langdon's infantile behavior and the raw maturity of the World War I fighting forces was too good to resist, Harry ended up making more service-related comedies than any other major comedian of his time.

The first of these were short subjects, filmed while Langdon was working for Mack Sennett. The 2-reel *All Night Long* (1924) is an extended flashback to Harry's wartime experiences in France, introduced with a characteristic shot of the dopey doughboy wistfully peeling the puniest potato in a veritable Everest of spuds. In love with local mademoiselle Natalie Kingston, Harry suffers in silence as burly sergeant Vernon Dent tries to horn in on the girl. When it becomes obvious that Natalie prefers Harry, Vernon vengefully transfers the timorous soldier to No Man's Land, giving Langdon the opportunity to perform a brilliant piece of physical business as he sits atop a wooden post and nimbly "compartmentalizes" his body to avoid the many shells whizzing past him. Illustrating director Frank Capra's theory that Langdon's character was so helpless that "only God" could help him triumph, Harry rescues a colonel by sheer chance and earns a promotion to lieutenant. With its flashback framework (clumsily) intact, *All Night Long* was remade in a South American setting as *The Leathernecker* (1935), one of Langdon's talkie 2-reelers for Columbia Pictures.

In 1926, Langdon returned to battle-scarred Europe in another Sennett comedy, the 3-reel *Soldier Man*. Taken prisoner by the Germans on the day he arrives at the front, Harry makes his escape while his captors are "celebrating something or other," that something-or-other being the Armistice. The scenes of Langdon wandering aimlessly around the deserted countryside of "Bomania," vaguely curious as to why there aren't any other soldiers around, are among the comedian's funniest screen moments. The military aspect of the story ends somewhere around Reel Two, giving way to a *Prisoner of Zenda* spoof as Harry is dragooned into impersonating his look-alike, a dissolute monarch. The World War I segment in Langdon's classic feature-length comedy *The Strong Man* (First National, 1926) is briefer still, confined to a prologue in which Belgian soldier Harry ineptly practices his marksmanship on a tin can just before he is captured by German trooper Zandow (Arthur Thalasso), in civilian life a circus strongman who retains Harry's services as a general factotum after the war.

Langdon backtracked to World War I territory in his final silent starring feature, the 1928 First National release *Heart Trouble* (working title: *Here Comes the Band*). Playing the son of German immigrants, Harry patriotically rushes to the Big City to enlist when the war begins, but has trouble finding a recruiting station that will overlook his slight stature and muscular deficiencies. To save face with his hometown sweetheart (Doris Dawson), Harry inaugurates a body-building regimen by taking on several manual labor jobs, with a noteworthy lack of success. Again and again he tries to enlist, but his persistence only makes matters worse. Once again, however, Providence comes to Harry's rescue when he stumbles upon the headquarters of some German spies (a gag Langdon would echo in another of his Columbia 2-reelers, 1943's *Blitz on the Fritz*). More dumb luck ensues, enabling Harry to turn the spies over to the authorities and simultaneously rescue an American army captain — who happens to be the same recruiting officer who has repeatedly turned Harry down for military service in the preceding reels.

Heart Trouble has not been seen since its final overseas play dates in 1931, and is now considered a lost film. Some of the available information indicates that the picture was a total failure, the latest in a series of fiascoes arising from the arrogant Langdon's decision to direct as well as star in his own productions. With the comedian's critical and fan following seriously eroded by the disastrous *Three's a Crowd* (1927) and *The Chaser* (1928), First National decided to sever their relationship with the Harry Langdon Corporation and to release *Heart Trouble* as a low-echelon programmer (it was seen as the bottom half of a double bill for its only New York showing). Besides, with the talking-picture revolution well under way, the studio had no compelling reason to get behind a silent comedy with a rapidly fading star.

Thanks to such latter-day Langdonphiles as Walter Kerr and Kevin Brownlow, a modest legend has grown up around *Heart Trouble*, suggesting that it was far better than its reputation would indicate. While the most frequently quoted review of the film is *Photoplay*'s terse "Just a lot of silly gags, no story and enough inane situations to spell the exit of Harry Langdon," Langdon historian William Schelly has taken the trouble to reprint a more laudatory critique from *Variety*, which counted the film among the "best of the few" of Harry's features, adding, "The gags are not numerous but the ones used are good." British film historian Harold Truscott, who claimed to have seen *Heart Trouble* as a youngster, retained fond memories of the experience, adding that the film actually did good business overseas. Whether *Heart Trouble* was a mess or a masterpiece, it certainly would be lovely to see the picture for oneself—but it isn't likely that this will ever happen.

Of course, we *could* be wrong. For decades, Warner Bros.' 1926 war comedy *The Better 'Ole* was regarded as a lost film, an ignominious fate for the second-ever silent feature to be released with a Vitaphone musical score and sound-effects track (the first, of course, was John Barrymore's *Don Juan*). In 1975, Walter Kerr reported that a print of *The Better 'Ole* had been located and archived, but in an incomplete state. In the mid-1990s, the film's five-minute musical prologue, featuring the Warner Bros. orchestra, premiered on the Turner Classic Movies cable service. Several more years passed before TCM screened *The Better 'Ole* itself, albeit a severely truncated version running a little over an hour. Finally in 2010, UCLA's fully restored 95-minute print of *The Better 'Ole* was unveiled on TCM, accompanied by the original Vitaphone music track (including one spoken word: "Coffee"). Beyond its historical significance, the film takes on added value as one of the few surviving features starring Charlie Chaplin's half-brother Syd Chaplin, who though more widely known as Charlie's longtime business manager was also an excellent comedian in his own right. Generally cast in parts that emphasized his handsome features and his gifts as a light *farceur*, Syd Chaplin headlines this World War I comedy in the wholly uncharacteristic role of a plump, phlegmatic, pipe-smoking, paintbrush-mustached Cockney "career private" known to one and all as Old Bill.

The character was invented by British artist Bruce Bairnsfather (1887–1959), an officer in the Royal Warwickshire Regiment. Serving in Flanders during World War I, Bairnsfather drew from his own experiences to launch a series of comic magazine illustrations revolving around the exploits of three "typical" British Tommies, Old Bill and his scraggly mates Bert and Alf. The most famous of these cartoons shows Bill and another soldier squatting uncomfortably in a foxhole as dozens of mortar shells explode directly overhead. Obviously responding to a complaint about their muddy accommodations, Bill grumbles sarcastically, "If you know a better 'ole—go to it." The "Old Bill" cartoons were so popular with real-life soldiers that the British government, recognizing the character's propaganda value, removed Bruce Bairnsfather from the battlefield and reassigned him as an Allied artist-correspondent. Bairnsfather has since been credited with keeping up the morale of the British troops to the extent that one observer has proclaimed, "He won the World War," in much the same way that Bill Mauldin's "Willie & Joe" cartoons (see **Chapter 5**) lifted and sustained the spirits of American GIs during World War II. Old Bill himself became a mass-entertainment superstar, the character "starring" in a musical comedy cowritten by Bairnsfather and Arthur Elliot which had its London premiere in 1917 under the title *The Better 'Ole: The Romance of Old Bill* (a later Broadway production starred Mr. and Mrs. Charles Coburn). The following year, the play was adapted as the first of several "Old Bill" motion pictures produced in England during the silent era. Thus, Syd Chaplin's *The Better 'Ole* is actually a remake.

Stationed in France for the duration (the backlot exterior sets, created by French expatriate Ben Carré, are unusually convincing), Old Bill has been a Tommy so long that he has managed to befriend several officers, notably young lieutenant Bert Chester (Harold Goodwin). But the veteran campaigner has failed to win over antagonistic Corporal Austin (Edgar Kennedy), who considers the day wasted that he doesn't consign Bill and his diminutive buddy Alf (Jack Ackroyd) to yard duty. Bill downs tools long enough to steal a chicken from a nearby barn, which action leads him to discover that a wine barrel in the cellar of the local inn is being used as a coop for carrier pigeons. It turns out that innkeeper Gaspard (Theodore Lorch) is sending messages about British troop movements to the Germans—and further, that Gaspard is in league with a German spy (Charles K. Gerrard) who is posing as a British major. Though Bill rounds up the pigeons and turns them over to his superiors, he is unable to convince anyone of the Major's treachery. It isn't until the village in which the British are billeted is captured by the Enemy that Bill is able to obtain photographic proof that the Major is a secret German operative. After a neck-risking motor chase through the countryside, Bill makes it back to his own lines, only to be accused of treason and sentenced to a firing squad. The last-minute intervention of Bert Chester (actually a British secret service agent) prevents Bill's military career from coming to a sad end. As a reward for his patriotism, Bill is granted his lifelong wish to become a sergeant. Turning to Alf and exclaiming "Blimey, this ain't a bad war after all," Old Bill brings this chapter of his life to a close by settling accounts with Cpl. Austin in the most fundamental manner possible.

An artist's rendering of Syd Chaplin as Old Bill in *The Better 'Ole* (Warners, 1926), enlarged from a vintage cigarette card.

Though in cold print *The Better 'Ole* comes off as excessively melodramatic, and despite the ghoulishness of certain isolated sequences—the German spy shooting Gaspard down in cold blood, Cpl. Austin gloating over Bill's imminent execution—the film is played for laughs from start to finish under the direction of former Charlie Chaplin associate Charles F. Reisner, who cowrote the script with future movie mogul Darryl F. Zanuck. Syd Chaplin fleshes out his droll interpretation of Old Bill with a million-and-one comic nuances and subtle bits of business, reaping the harvest of his training in British music-hall pantomime. According the *Photoplay* review: "There is one gag that places Syd right up with the immortals. Bill and Alf, playing front and hind legs of a horse, respectively, are left in a French town that is captured by the Germans. The gorgeous adventures of that horse will always be stored in our mind as one of our Beautiful Memories of the Eighth Art." Seen today, this particular gag (later revived in the Harry Langdon talkie feature *A Soldier's Plaything*) seems to be protracted far beyond its worth, just as *The Better 'Ole* itself is a shade too long to sustain its overall level of humor (apparently planned as a 7- or 8-reel programmer, the film was expanded to 10 reels during production to make it "worthy" of an expensive Vitaphone score). Funnier by far is the brief sequence in which Old Bill, seated on the chest of an unconscious German soldier, distracts his captors by manipulating the other man's extremities so that the German's legs and Bill's torso appear to be attached to the same body.

While some of the gags and plot devices in *The Better 'Ole* may seem overfamiliar due to being repeated *ad infinitum* in later service comedies, this film has one distinction that its latter-day derivations cannot boast. Rather than try the audience's patience with a tacked-on romantic subplot, the film runs its happy course with virtually no "feminine interest" whatsoever. Doris Hill, the only actress with any sort of substantial role, isn't even credited onscreen. "There is neither love nor heroine in *The Better 'Ole*," remarked the *Picture Play* reviewer with admiration. "Instead we have humanness and wholesome laughter. Don't pass this up; it's great."

The week after *The Better 'Ole* went into release in October 1926, Warner Bros. served up another service comedy with another prominent comedian, this one better known for his stage work. *Private Izzy Murphy* was tailored to the talents of George Jessel, whose association with the brothers Warner went all the way back to his debut film *The Other Man's Wife* (1917). The comedian deigned to star in *Private Izzy Murphy* on condition that Warners purchase the screen rights to Jessel's great stage success *The Jazz Singer*. The studio agreed, but when they subsequently refused to increase Jessel's salary upon deciding to add Vitaphone-recorded singing and dialogue sequences to *The Jazz Singer*, Jessel refused to appear in the film — then had to simmer in silence as *Jazz Singer* not only made movie history but also a megastar out of rival entertainer Al Jolson.

Ballyhooed by the studio as a "serio-comic heart drama," and "a comedy drama that will make your sides shake and your heart ache" (a painful prospect indeed), *Private Izzy Murphy* cast Jessel as a Jewish delicatessen owner who changes his last name to Murphy when he moves into an Irish neighborhood. Upon America's entry into World War I, Izzy joins an all–Irish Army regiment (presumably Wild Bill Donovan's predominantly Hibernian "Fighting 69th"), leaving his Irish sweetheart Eileen (Patsy Ruth Miller) anxiously waiting at home until it's over Over There. Suffering mightily when Izzy is reported killed in battle, Eileen rapidly recovers when her boy returns home to a hero's welcome — but there's still trouble in store for the couple thanks to certain anti–Semitic elements lurking about. The studio press book assured us that the ensuing complications "are so mirth-provoking, so human, that everyone in the audience forgets that such things as rancor and prejudice can exist in the world! It is one of those rare plays which have universal appeal. It is as American as baseball. As all-inclusive as the circus!" For once, the Warners publicity machine didn't oversell its product. Despite studio concerns that the racial prejudice angle would lessen its box office appeal, *Private Izzy Murphy* was a smash hit.

Jessel followed this triumph one year later with a markedly less popular sequel, *Sailor Izzy Murphy*, which eschewed the pathos of the first film in favor of what the trade ads described as a "Grouch Cure." Replacing *Private Izzy Murphy*'s director Lloyd Bacon was venerable slapstick merchant Henry "Pathe" Lehrman, whose lack of subtlety and taste was surpassed only by his utter disregard for the safety and sensibilities of his actors (When Lehrman carped that Jessel's performance wasn't "sparkling enough," Georgie shot back, "I did not know I had been engaged to be a bottle of Canada Dry.") This time, Izzy is a perfume peddler who decorates his bottles with pictures of the heroine (Audrey Ferris), then tries to sell his "Dream of Love" formula to the girl's perfume-manufacturer father (Warner Oland). But Father kicks Izzy out on his *tuchus*, prompting our hero to chase after the old man's yacht to serve him with damage papers. The yacht is hijacked by a group of lunatics (I didn't know lunatics traveled in groups) led by "Orchid Joe" (John Miljan), a *meshuggenner* who hates the girl's poppa because he kills flowers to make perfume. Posing as one of the crazies, Izzy is elected "lord high executioner" and ordered to knock off the heroine and her dad, but he turns the tables on the looney-tunes at the end. *Sailor Izzy Murphy* is not technically a service comedy — Izzy is neither a real sailor nor a real Murphy (his last name is Goldberg) — but who could resist recounting that pixilated plotline?

In between the two Jessel films, pasty-faced comedian Larry Semon honored the world with the 5-reel war farce *Spuds* (Pathé, 1927). Best remembered for such 2-reel slapstick festivals as *The Show* and *The Sawmill*, in which the comedian and his supporting players were forever falling out of buildings, hurling wooden crates and other such missiles at each other and wallowing in enormous mud puddles, Semon enjoyed immense popularity in the 1920s; Buster Keaton once claimed that he'd never heard an audience laugh louder than when watching Larry in action. The comedian's feature films were just as messy and chaotic as his shorts, notably a whacked-out 1925 adaptation of *The Wizard of Oz* with Semon as the Scarecrow, his wife Dorothy Dwan as Dorothy, and Oliver Hardy as the Tin Man. But by 1927 Larry was having trouble finding backers for his increasingly ambitious productions. The problem was not a drop in popularity, but the fact that he invariably spent more money on his films than they could possibly earn. *Spuds* represented both a comeback and a last stand for Larry Semon; it was his final starring feature, released one year before his premature death from a combination of pneumonia and a nervous breakdown.

An introductory title places the film in the French village of "Mayonnaise," giving us a pretty good idea of what we're in for. Semon plays Spuds, a doughboy so named because of the hours he spends manicuring potatoes. Like Old Bill in *The Better 'Ole*, Spuds has a good buddy in the form of Captain Arthur McLaughlin (Edward Hearn) but a sworn enemy in the person of his overweight sergeant (Kewpie Morgan, latest in a long line of fat comedians whom Semon used as foils). The plot gets rolling when Captain McLaughlin is suspected of hijacking an Army payroll car carrying $250,000. Recovering the stolen vehicle, Spuds drives it back to American lines through a No Man's Land festooned with the comedian's beloved mud puddles, winning the eternal devotion of the lovely Madelon (Dorothy Dwan). Critical response to Larry Semon's valedictory feature provides an interesting contrast to the praise lavished on *The Better 'Ole*, with one reviewer noting, "*Spuds* has no human interest, and the gags, though well dovetailed at times, never mean much."

Two later silent war comedies bore the same titles as a pair of talkie-era Army farces, but otherwise there was no connection between the earlier and later films. Released by poverty-row Anchor Films in early 1928, *Top Sergeant Mulligan* featured Wade Boteler (whose association with military comedies can be traced back to 1919's *23½ Hours' Leave*) in the title role, with onetime child star Wesley "Freckles" Barry as buck private Mickey Neilan (an inside joke referencing the prominent movie director of the same name). While helping his vaudeville partner Lila (Lila Lee) exhort a group of civilians to join the Army, song-and-dance man Mickey ends up enlisting himself. Once in uniform, Mickey is harrassed by Sgt. Spike Mulligan, who has designs on Lila — as does a handsome YMCA employee. Shipped off to France, Mulligan and Mickey bury the hatchet long enough to costar in a camp minstrel show, and while still in blackface the boys are captured by the Germans, one of whom is identified as "Fritz Von Lang" (probably the handiwork of the same gag writer who came up with "Mickey Neilan"). The balance of power shifts when the two soldiers capture a notorious spy (Sheldon Lewis); but even though the Sergeant and the Private now have enough medals to start their own pawnshop, Lila spurns them both and strolls into the sunset with the guy from the "Y." *Top Sergeant Mulligan* might well have been "the funniest comedy of the year" as advertised, but today it is even more obscure than the same-named 1941 comedy from Monogram Pictures.

As noted in **Chapter 4,** the 1941 edition of *Top Sergeant Mulligan* was a low-budget knockoff of Abbott & Costello's smasheroo *Buck Privates.* Universal had previously used *that* title for another 1928 service comedy, a 7-reeler starring sleek Malcolm McGregor as Private Smith and jowly Eddie Gribbon as Sergeant Butts. Stationed in an occupied German village just after the Armistice, Smith and Butts battle for the affections of Annie (top-billed Lya de Putti), daughter of the town's leading citizen (James Marcus). When the Army issues orders against fraternization, Smith chances a court-martial by secretly meeting Annie in her father's garden. Both lovers are punished for their indiscretion: Smith is arrested by Butts, and Annie's outraged father cuts off her long flowing hair. Butts agrees to drop all charges against Smith if Annie promises to marry the sergeant, but frumpish fraulein Hulda (ZaSu Pitts) takes Annie's place during the ceremony, allowing the heroine to escape on a motorcycle with her true love. Contemporary reviewers of the silent *Buck Privates* enjoyed such buffoonery as Private Smith being booted onto the sidewalk by Annie's father and Sgt. Butts getting clunked on the casaba by a falling flowerpot. But most of the critical attention was reserved for leading lady Lya de Putti, celebrated worldwide for her performance as the sloe-eyed seductress who drives Emil Jannings to murder in E.A. DuPont's German masterpiece *Variety* (1925), and here cast radically against type as a demure and dainty damsel.

Having launched the post–*Shoulder Arms* cycle of Army comedies with 1919's *Yankee Doodle in Berlin*, Mack Sennett brought things full circle with one of the last silent films in that cycle, *The Good-Bye Kiss* (released by First National in 1928). Much was made at the time of Sennett's willingness to risk a million-dollar production on a cast comprised largely of unknowns and newcomers. The leading lady was Mack's latest discovery Sally Eilers, described by the producer as "one girl in a million," with Alma Bennett as the soubrette. The male players included Matty Kemp as the hero and Johnny Burke as the comedy lead; Andy Clyde, cast as Eilers' grandfather, was the only prominent holdover from Sennett's familiar stock company. *The Good-Bye Kiss* was the first feature film to be personally directed by Mack Sennett since 1921's *Molly-O*, as well the first feature edited by William Hornbeck, who later won an Academy Award for his work on George Stevens' *A Place in the Sun* (1951).

Advertised as "nine reels of love and laughs" but copyrighted as an 8-reeler, *The Good-Bye Kiss* revolved around the romance between Sally (Eilers) and Matty (Kemp). When Matty is drafted into World War I, he bestows a good-bye kiss upon Sally, inspiring her to stow away on her sweetheart's troop ship and join the Salvation Army upon arrival in France. Matty proves to be a coward in battle, but Sally shames him into bravery during an air raid and he redeems himself by capturing a German spy. In a syndicated newspaper article allegedly written by himself, Mack Sennett claimed that the film's plot was based on incidents in his own life, specifically the "thrill" of a first kiss. Sennett added that "we all know a woman will stick by her man when he is on top, but our drama is of a girl who is with her man through thick and thin, for ever and ever"—which may have been a subtle dig at Sennett's former leading lady and erstwhile sweetheart Mabel Normand, who famously walked out on Mack when she found him *in flagrante delecto* with another actress. The producer closed with a prediction: "I think *The Good-Bye Kiss* is a picture that all movie fans will like. First, because it is human. Second, because it has romance. Third, because it has a well-balanced blending of comedy and drama. Fourth, because it is clean!" Given Sennett's track record of throwing off the balance of his "dramatic" efforts with steaming heaps of gratuitous slapstick, to say nothing of his not-so-clean "Tired Businessman" 2-reelers starring Billy Bevan, one is skeptical of Mack's assurances that *The Good-Bye Kiss* was a deviation from his norm. But as in the case of Harry Langdon's *Heart Trouble*, we'll probably never know for sure: All nine (or is it eight?) reels of *The Good-Bye Kiss* have apparently vanished from the face of the earth.

You may have noticed that the above-mentioned silent comedies tended to favor the Army over the other service branches. Those silent and sound comedies involving the Marines are referenced in **Chapter 7**, while Navy comedies of the talkie era are analyzed in **Chapter 6**. Of the latter group, several were variations on the storyline of the first important seafaring comedy of the silent period, the 1925 adaptation of the stage hit *Shore Leave*, which dealt with the off-and-on romance between a restless sailor and a newly rich woman. A lively spin on the *Shore Leave* formula was deployed in the silent 7-reeler *A Sailor's Sweetheart* (Warner Bros., 1927) starring seasoned funsters Louise Fazenda and Clyde Cook. Upon inheriting a fortune, spinster Cynthia Botts (Fazenda) weds Mark Krissel (John Miljan), a con artist posing as a banker. Discovering that Krissel is a bigamist (his wife is played by a young Myrna Loy), the outraged heiress skirmishes with the scoundrel and falls into the ocean, where she is rescued by shrimpy sailor Sandy MacTavish (Cook), who is unaware of Cynthia's millions and has always worshipped her from afar. Pursued by the predatory Krissel, Cynthia and Sandy are kidnapped by bootleggers, then mistakenly arrested as crooks by a detective (William Demarest) and his minions. The two lost souls wriggle out of their multitude of dilemmas by invoking *Yankee Doodle in Berlin*, with Sandy disguising himself as a woman.

At least one late silent—which included a sound-on-disc music score and a handful of "live" songs—was something of a precursor to the *other* most-often imitated theatrical Navy farce, 1933's

Sailor Beware (discussed more thoroughly in **Chapter 6**). Paramount's *The Fleet's In* (1928) starred Clara Bow as Roseland dance-hall hostess Peachy Deane, torn between two sailor boyfriends named Eddie Briggs (James Hall) and Searchlight Doyle (Jack Oakie in the first of several such roles). A few of the film's significant plot devices were later wedged into Paramount's first two talkie versions of *Sailor Beware*, 1936's *Lady Be Careful* and a 1942 musical also titled *The Fleet's In*, wherein Clara Bow's role was more or less taken over by Dorothy Lamour.

A couple of silent Navy comedies produced by Fox Studios were likewise retreaded as talkies. *Sharp Shooters* (1928) stars George O'Brien as an amorous sailor named George, who promises eternal devotion to every girl he meets, secure in the knowledge that he'll never see her again once he sets sail. But one of his casual sweethearts, a cute French blonde named Lorette (Lois Moran), takes George at his word thanks to a prank letter delivered by George's fellow swabs Tom (Noah Young) and Jerry (Tom Dugan). Lorette trails George to the U.S. for matrimonial purposes, and after several reels of humorous convolutions finally drags him to the altar. The reviewer for *Time* magazine described *Sharp Shooters* as "one more reversal of that familiar proverb, the gobs will get you if you don't watch out," expressing pleasant surprise at the spectacle of Lois Moran, who normally played the "embodiment of all that a good girl should be," performing a provocative bump-and-grind in a Moroccan dive. In Fox's 1934 talkie remake *She Learned About Sailors*, Moran's role is assumed by Alice Faye, who sings but doesn't shimmy in a Shanghai cabaret patronized by skirt-chasing sailor Lew Ayres. The two capricious gobs who mislead Alice into believing that Ayres wants to marry her are here played by the knockabout comedy team of Frank Mitchell and Jack Durant, whose roughhouse antics are a bit hard to endure when seen today.

The other 1928 Fox release, *A Girl in Every Port*, is a service film in the sense that the two protagonists are professional sailors, though not official members of any navy. It is also a comedy in the sense that (a) it's very funny, and (b) there isn't a believable moment in the film, not even during its "serious" passages. But lack of credibility does not signify a lack of hilarity, certainly

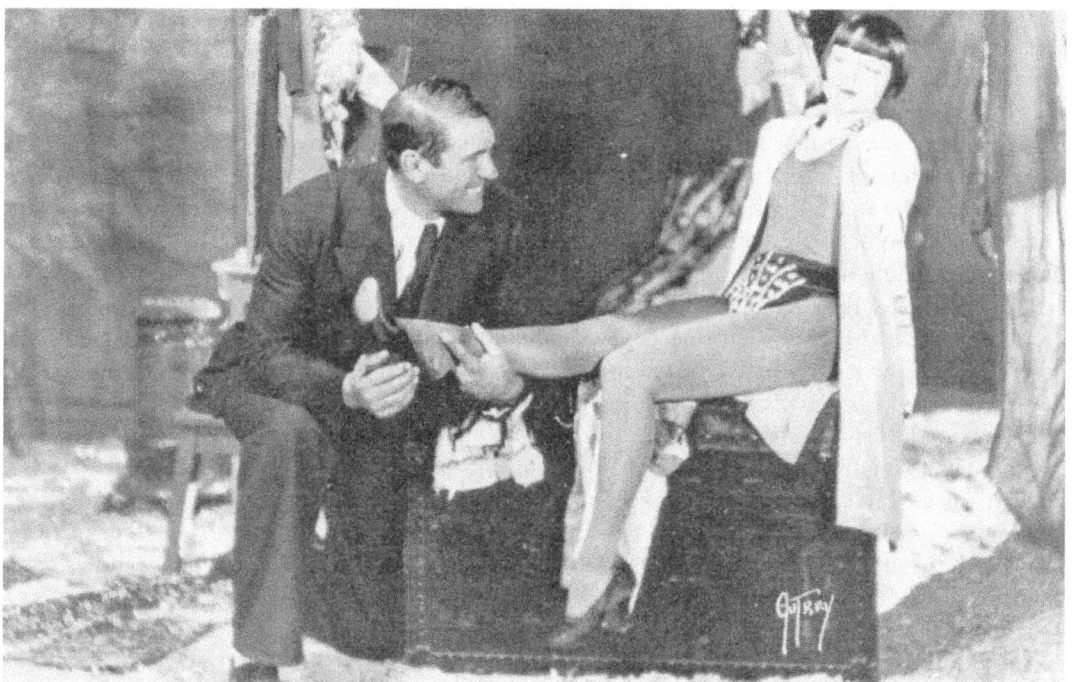

Sailor Victor McLaglen may be out of uniform, but entertainer Louise Brooks is definitely wearing *her* working clothes in *A Girl in Every Port* (Fox, 1928).

not with Howard Hawks in the director's chair (Hawks also wrote the original nine-page story treatment).

The introductory scenes of this silent film (with Movietone musical score) belong to Victor McLaglen as Spike, whom we first meet as he disembarks from a tramp schooner and sets foot in an ersatz Amsterdam (we know it's Holland because of the windmills and wooden shoes). Choosing one of the local Little Dutch Gals as his favorite, Spike is about to move in for the moment of truth when he notices that the *mejuffrow* is wearing a bracelet with an anchor design. It's the same bracelet and anchor he's seen on girls in five previous ports, and the same bracelet and anchor he's *going* to see during an upcoming visit to Rio. Obviously some "snoopin' sea-snipe" has beaten Spike to the finish line in all these ports — and when another anchored bracelet appears on another female wrist in Panama, Spike vows to catch up with his rival and whale the tar out of him. On cue, merchant seaman Salami (Robert Armstrong) swaggers into view, forming a fast alliance with Spike as the two men beat up a battalion of local cops. Glancing in a mirror and spotting the familiar anchor mark on his chin, Spike figures out that Salami is his peripatetic nemesis. He posts Salami's bail for the express purpose of knocking the man's brains out, but after the two tars rescue each other from drowning, they decide that their new friendship is stronger than any animosity over dames.

By the time they reach Marseilles, Spike and Salami are "shipmates for life"— or so they think. While Salami is confined to bed with a toothache, Spike takes in a local carnival, where the star attraction is high-dive artist Mam'selle Godiva (the hauntingly beautiful Louise Brooks). Falling hard for Godiva, Spike is primed to give up his wandering ways and settle down with the girl, but not before introducing her to Salami. Giving Godiva the once-over, Salami makes an insulting comment, whereupon Spike exclaims that their friendship is over. Though Salami instantly apologizes ("I didn't mean that your skirt was a tramp"), he's just trying to spare his pal's feelings. It seems that Salami had previously known Godiva when she was "Tessie of Coney Island"— and he knows from experience than she plans to soak Spike for every cent he's got. It looks like Spike will be taken to the cleaners until he discovers that Godiva is wearing a tattoo ... in the shape of an anchor. With the fury of an enraged bull, Spike vows to punch Salami into the next world, but all ends happily when he finds himself saving Salami from yet another saloon brawl.

In accordance with the film's title, Fox had announced plans to feature well-known actresses in each of Spike and Salami's ports of call. In addition to Louise Brooks in Marseilles, the boys were to meet Natalie Joyce in Panama, Natalie Kingston in the South Seas, and fabled fan dancer Sally Rand in the South Pacific; but not all of the supporting actresses listed in the film's publicity packet appear in the longest available print, which at 78 minutes seems to be complete (unmentioned by the publicists was a slinky starlet named Myrna Loy, virtually unrecognizable as a Chinese lass). At any rate, these girls would have wound up playing second fiddle to the impenetrable bond between male leads Victor McLaglen and Robert Armstrong, which Howard Hawks has described as "a love story between two men." Though little of an explicitly gay nature is hinted at — surprising for a Hawks film, in which the subtext is always half the fun — it's worth noting that the most overt gesture of affection between Spike and Salami consists of a running gag in which one of the guys' fingers goes out of joint and the other guy pulls the finger back into place. Howard Hawks later told historian Joseph McBride that this mildly suggestive bit of business was inspired by a brief skirmish between the director and Ernest Hemingway (a story that must be taken with the proverbial grain of salt, since virtually all of Hawks' most colorful anecdotes seem to involve world-famous people).

Fox's talkie remake of *A Girl in Every Port*, 1931's *Goldie*, was every bit as raucous and misogynistic as the original, though Benjamin Stoloff's static direction can't match the cheerful vulgarity of Howard Hawks. Taking over from McLaglen and Armstrong as Spike and Salami (renamed "Bill" in the 1931 film) are Warren Hymer and Spencer Tracy, who'd previously costarred in John Ford's *Up the River*. The titular Goldie, the remake's equivalent of Louise Brooks' Godiva, is enacted by an almost unbearably sexy Jean Harlow, billed in the ads as "the heroine of *Hell's Angels*."

During production of *Goldie*, Harlow and Spencer Tracy became lifelong friends when he advised Jean to drop her affected "Stage British" and speak in her normal voice on-screen. Though both actors went on to successful careers at MGM, the ensuing years were less kind to Warren Hymer, who literally pissed away his career when he urinated on the desk of Columbia Pictures chief executive Harry Cohn. But in 1931, Hymer was considered as big a star as Spencer Tracy by his home studio Fox, who tried to build up the two actors as a "new comedy team." While this was a misreading of Hymer and Tracy's relationship in *Goldie*, the military-comedy genre was inarguably a breeding ground for comedy teams in the 1920s, and we have Paramount's 1926 effort *Behind the Front* to thank for this phenomenon.

Filmed under the working title *Two Soldiers*, *Behind the Front* was based on the 1925 *Saturday Evening Post* short story "Spoils of War" by Hugh Wiley, better known as the creator of the erudite Chinese detective Mr. Wong. Taking a break from the serious and villainous roles that had been his stock in trade during the 1920s, Wallace Beery returned to his slapstick-comedy roots as beefy detective Riff Swanson, who while patrolling the streets of New York on the day the city is celebrating America's entry into World War I has his watch stolen by pickpocket Shorty McGee, played by Raymond Hatton. Though he doesn't get a good look at the thief, Riff chases him into the mansion of society belle Betty Bartlett-Cooper (Mary Brian), the sister of an Army captain (Hadley Stevenson), who is presently holding a recruiting party. Upon meeting face to face, Riff and Shorty become fast friends, though Riff has a gnawing feeling that he's seen Shorty somewhere before. Both men are smitten by Betty, who persuades them to enlist in the Army by giving each man a locket with her picture, inscribed "To My Hero." Unaware that Betty has presented a similar locket to several other men in the room, Riff and Shorty mistake this token of esteem as a promise of marriage, so they march off to war with a smile on their lips and a song in their hearts. The smile is dimmed and the song stilled when they meet their merciless drill sergeant (Tom Kennedy), who nips at their heels all the way to France. Accidentally poking a general in the *derrière* with a bayonet, Riff and Shorty are marched to the guardhouse, where they cultivate an intense hatred for an unappetizing brand of hardtack biscuit, manufactured by some guy named Brown.

After dallying with the local female talent, the two doughboys inadvertently volunteer for a dangerous mission in No Man's Land. When their clothes are rent asunder by enemy fire, the boys don German uniforms and are "rescued" by the very soldiers who'd been trying to kill them a few minutes earlier. Escaping to their own lines in a stolen tank—and nearly preventing the Armistice from taking place—Riff and Shorty return home as heroes, only to find that their mutual heart-throb Betty is about to wed another man (Richard Arlen). The wedding degenerates into a donnybrook when the two veterans discover that Betty's intended is Percy Brown, son of the "hardtack king." This might well have been the fadeout gag were it not for Riff's inevitable realization that his bosom companion Shorty is the same jasper who swiped his watch way back in April of '17.

When *Behind the Front* was first announced in the trades, Victor Fleming was listed as director and Mildred Harris, a once major star on the downgrade, was slated for a comeback in the role of Betty. But Fleming was replaced by Edward Sutherland in his first important screen assignment, while the part of Betty went to Paramount contractee Mary Brian, who was less expensive and more reliable than the substance-abusing Ms. Harris. It was Eddie Sutherland who sought out the services of Ralph Spence, the highest-paid writer of subtitles in the movie business. Much prized for his ability to come up with hilarious dialogue and turns of phrase without relying on cheap wisecracks, bad puns, or excess verbiage, Ralph Spence's contributions to the overall frivolity of *Behind the Front* were invaluable. In one example of Spence's comic prowess, Shorty storms up to the bullying sergeant and says via subtitle "You big stiff, you hit me," whereupon Sarge grabs Shorty and hangs him halfway up a wooden wall, leaving Riff to survey the scene and laconically remark: "You showed him up." A couple of reels later, Spence encapsulates the two privates' nerv-

Doughboys Wallace Beery (left) and Raymond Hatton share a gripe in the World War I farce *Behind the Front* (Paramount, 1926).

ousness during their first night in the trenches with ten pithy words: "Listening post — where men are men, but wish they weren't." Ralph Spence would continue providing one-liners and swift rejoinders for a variety of military comedies well into the 1940s.

The visuals in *Behind the Front* were every bit as amusing as the titles. Among the highlights is a sequence in which, after spending several backbreaking hours cleaning every speck of mud from a village street, Riff and Shorty can only look on in mute frustration as a huge mounted Cavalry regiment marches past them. But the one gag that seems to stick in the mind of everyone who's ever seen the picture (which happily still exists, albeit in the slightly abridged version prepared for nonprofessional and home screenings) is a magnificently timed and staged "black" joke. While crawling through the grime and debris of No Man's Land, Riff encounters a German soldier who turns out to be Mr. Schultz, his former New York butcher. Almost immediately, Schultz demands payment of the eight dollars Riff owes him. Seconds after the cash is exchanged, a bomb explodes. When the smoke clears, Schultz has vanished — and Riff is seen casually stuffing the eight bills back into his own pocket.

Released in February 1926, *Behind the Front* was Paramount's top-grossing film of the year, encouraging the studio to churn out five subsequent films teaming Wallace Beery and Raymond Hatton. Of these, two were service farces, *We're in the Navy Now* (1926) and *Now We're in the Air* (1927), the latter featuring Louise Brooks in a dual role. By the time Beery and Hatton got around to *Now We're in the Air*, the two actors were having a field day mouthing whatever dirty words came into their minds while the cameras were grinding, knowing full well that their profanities would be purified by the insertion of non-profane subtitles — forcing Ralph Spence to spend many a sleepless, whiskey-sodden night trying to come up with "safe" comic dialogue that would fit the lip movements. The Beery-Hatton series came to an end in 1928; while Wallace Beery remained at the top of his profession until his death in 1949, Raymond Hatton's career suffered an eclipse near the end of the silent era, though he rallied in the 1940s as a cowboy sidekick in a variety of westerns produced by Republic, Monogram, and other second-echelon studios.

The astounding success of *Behind the Front* had exactly the same effect on other studios that the phenominal popularity of the Abbott & Costello starrer *Buck Privates* would have on Universal's rivals in 1941. Paramount's competitors fell over one another in a rush to create their own comedy teams, hoping to match the box-office pull of Beery and Hatton. MGM was the first to tap into this lode when studio producer Harry Rapf summoned contract players Karl Dane and George K. Arthur to his office and calmly informed them that henceforth they would be costarred in a series of feature-length comedies. Dane, a gargantuan, horse-faced Scandinavian, had developed a following after providing comic relief in the studio's otherwise serious World War I epic *The Big Parade*, while Arthur, a diminutive, oval-faced Englishman, had played the title character in the 1926 MGM giggler *The Boob*. Most comedy duos of the silent era (notably the prolific "Ham and Bud" combination of the pre–1920 era) were cast from the same mold as comic-strip favorites Mutt and Jeff: one small, the other tall; one chubby, the other skinny. Sometimes the tall one was chubby and the small one skinny, as in the case of Beery & Hatton; sometimes it was the other way around, as in the case of Dane & Arthur. Whatever the combination, the studios were counting on the "comedy of opposites" to carry the day.

Walter Kerr has characterized MGM's Dane & Arthur series as merely the Beery & Hatton series all over again. This was also noted by contemporary reviewers, who readily recognized the patterned followed by both teams' vehicles, beginning with the fact that each duo's inaugural effort was an Army comedy. Dane & Arthur's *Rookies* was released in April 1927; this 7-reel feature represented the first MGM assignment for Sam Wood, an all-purpose director best known to comedy buffs for his two Marx Brothers films of the 1930s, *A Night at the Opera* and *A Day at the Races*.

George K. Arthur played sissified cabaret dancer Greg Lee, while Karl Dane was cast as bellicose army sergeant Diggs. When Diggs tries to move in on Greg's dancing partner Zella Fay (Louise Lorraine), Greg gets even by publicly humiliating the sergeant. Arrested for this impertinence, Greg is sentenced to serve six weeks in one of the many Citizen's Military Training Camps that proliferated in the 1920s. There needs no ghost come from the grave to tell us that Sgt. Diggs is stationed at this very same camp. The fire-eating topkick goes out of his way to persecute the wimpy rookie during his enforced enlistment, while Greg reciprocates by bombarding Diggs with an arsenal of practical jokes. The animosity between the pair is heightened when both Diggs and Greg fall in love with Betty Wayne (Marceline Day), daughter of the judge who sentenced Greg to the camp. Greg not only wins Betty's hand but also Diggs' unswerving friendship when, using acrobatic skills acquired during his show-business career, he rescues the girl and the sergeant from a runaway balloon. Costing considerably less than the average MGM feature, and a *lot* less than the star comedies turned out by such autonomous laugh makers as Chaplin, Lloyd, and Keaton, *Rookies* benefited from extensive location filming at actual civilian training camps in and around Los Angeles. The balloon sequence, which took a week to produce, was filmed just as the audience saw it, with virtually no special-effects fakery; contemporary reviewers were impressed by the fact that one could clearly see the Hollywood Hills on the horizon.

This authenticity wouldn't have amounted to a hill of beans if the film hadn't clicked with the public. *Rookies* tapped into an audience demographic hitherto overlooked by the mighty MGM, whose prestige pictures with such prestige stars as Greta Garbo and Lon Chaney could be counted on to perform well in big cities, but generally met with a mild reception in midwestern and rural communities. For the first time since its formation in 1924, the studio had found a formula guaranteed to rake in big bucks in the hinterlands. This was reflected in the rave reviews from small-town exhibitors in the pages of *Motion Picture Herald* and other trade publications. A representative of the Schanberg theater circuit in Kansas gushed: "Screened *Rookies* tonight.

Absolutely the greatest comedy ever produced bar none. Unquestionably will prove a natural at box office. I would be ungrateful if I failed to express appreciation for this one." And a theater manager in Atkinson, Nebraska, stated succinctly: "This one's a scream."

In response, MGM got behind *Rookies* in a big way, promoting the comedy as the studio's third-anniversary "special" and engendering exhibitor goodwill by charging a lot less for rentals than their standard fee (another break from the tradition established by such top comedians as Chaplin and especially Lloyd, both of whom were regularly chastised in the "trades" for their exorbitant rental and profits-percentage rates). Critical response to the film's general release was, if anything, even more enthusiastic than the preliminary reports from theater owners. Here's what *Screenland* magazine had to say on July 27, 1927: "My, my—the regulars and the recruits won't know themselves when they see this picture. Probably they never suspected that a soldier's life is such a merry one.... After the French-pastry farce they have been feeding us lately, *Rookies* is like hamburger smothered in onions; and if the accent is on the ham, who cares? Go ahead and laugh."

Of the seven Karl Dane & George K. Arthur comedies produced by MGM from 1927 to 1929, at least five films are presently known to exist, either in complete or partial form. Surveying the material that has survived, it is difficult to pinpoint any one of the team's efforts as a "typical" or "representative" vehicle, mainly because the two comedians' characterizations were so wildly inconsistent. Adversaries in their inaugural feature *Rookies*, they would in subsequent vehicles run the gamut from boon companions to bitter enemies depending on the dictates of the script. Also, whereas most comedy duos have sharply defined "smart-dumb" or "dominant-passive" characters, Dane & Arthur switched these designations as often as they changed costumes. In *Rookies*, Dane is the aggressive one and Arthur the patsy; but in their penultimate silent comedy *All at Sea* (1929), it is Arthur who dominates and Dane who plays the fall guy.

Directed by former Harold Lloyd associate Alf Goulding, *All at Sea* found George K. Arthur portraying cocky stage magician Rollo the Great, who during one performance is heckled by Karl Dane, playing a sailor named Stupid McDuff. As in *Rookies*, Rollo gets even by making a public spectacle of McDuff, hypnotizing the goofy gob into performing ridiculous stunts. A reel or so later, circumstances force Rollo to shed his tuxedo and don a Navy uniform. Again running afoul of McDuff, Rollo puts the big lug into another hypnotic trance, resulting in chaos and slapstick galore at a fancy-dress officer's ball. A later highlight is a gunnery-practice sequence in which the boys end up suspended from two giant cranes, a "high and dizzy" gag obviously inspired by the balloon antics in *Rookies*. Once again, the production values of this economically-produced film were enhanced by using actual locations, including a Navy training depot, a Marine barracks, and an arsenal that was set ablaze for the Wow Finish.

In addition to being their next-to-last MGM starring feature, *All at Sea* represented Dane & Arthur's final venture into military humor. The coming of talkies prompted a nervous MGM to drop Dane's contract for fear that the actor's thick Scandinavian accent would not register well on the soundtrack, even though he proved that this would not be the case with a supporting appearance in the seriocomic 1929 William Haines vehicle *Navy Blues*. Dane remained partnered with George K. Arthur in short subjects and vaudeville until he was overwhelmed by profound financial and emotional problems in 1932; two years later, Karl Dane was dead by his own hand.

Soon after MGM unveiled the Dane-Arthur team in 1927, Fox Studios followed suit with their own fabricated duo, though unlike Karl Dane and George K. Arthur, Fox's combination had previously worked together as supporting players. 33-year-old Ted McNamara had signed with Fox not long after his screen debut as a two-fisted sailor named Smith in Paramount's *Shore Leave* (1925), while 26-year-old Sammy Cohen had made his first appearance under the Fox banner as "Morris Pincus" in the 1926 Gladys Brockwell vehicle *The Skyrocket*. McNamara and Cohen were then respectively cast as Marine privates Kiper and Lipinsky in the World War I comedy-drama *What Price Glory* (see **Chapter 7**). Lightly trading on ethnic stereotypes, the two "boots" indulged in pantomimic references to Kiper's Scots-Irish heritage (though McNamara was actually Australian) and Lipinsky's Jewish upbringing. Several reviewers singled out the scenes between McNamara and Cohen as high points of hilarity in *What Price Glory*, encouraging Fox to thrust stardom upon the two actors as a challenge to Dane & Arthur. The studio also elected to keep the two comic actors in uniform for their first official vehicle, 1927's *The Gay Retreat*.

Cowritten by William Conselman (creator of comic-strip heroine Ella Cinders) and directed by Ben Stoloff, this 6-reeler bestowed top screen billing upon romantic leads Gene Cameron and Betty Francisco, with Cohen and McNamara listed fourth and seventh; but as far as the trade ads and the filmgoers were concerned, there was no question as to who the real stars were. Gene Cameron played wealthy young Dick Wright, rejected from active military service during World War I because of his chronic sleepwalking. Undaunted, Dick joins an ambulance unit, by accident ending up in the regular army. Worried that Dick's somnambulism may have fatal consequences, the boy's faithful valet Sammy Nosenbloom (Cohen) and chauffeur Ted McHiggins (McNamara) enlist so that they can protect Dick in the trenches. All three men become heroes, but not before a few mix-ups with a Red Cross nurse (Francisco), a French girl (Judy King) and a troublesome refugee kid (played by Jerry Madden, a juvenile star billed as "Jerry the Giant" in Fox's 2-reel Sunshine Comedies). If the plot sounds familiar, it's because Fox partially remade *The Gay Retreat* as the 1941 Laurel & Hardy service comedy *Great Guns* (see **Chapter 4**).

Gay Retreat is apparently lost, but the next Cohen-McNamara opus *Why Sailors Go Wrong* (1928) is still very much with us—and to a few cynics, it offers a persuasive argument *against* the restoration of silent films on the basis of historical rather than entertainment value. This time "Mac" (playing Angus McAxle) is the owner of a rundown hansom cab, and Sammy (saddled with

Disguised as Germans, Yankee soldiers Sammy Cohen (left) and Ted McNamara (right) pretend to put their sleepwalking buddy Gene Cameron under arrest in ***The Gay Retreat*** (Fox, 1927).

yet another execrable surname, "Beezeroff") is a taxi driver. Both men climb aboard a yacht to collect the $1000 promised them by their latest fare, wealthy Jimmy Collyer (Nick Stuart). The vessel sets sail and the two hackies are pressed into service as sailors; a shipwreck follows. "Waves of Laughter, Oceans of Fun," promised the newspaper ads for *Why Sailors Go Wrong*. The waves of laughter include Mac being awakened by a slapping chimp on the shores of "Pongo Pongo," while the oceans of fun involve cannibals and crocodiles.

Director Henry "Pathe" Lehrman appeared to be operating on the theory that if you don't have good material to work with, then throw as many gags as possible on the screen and hope that at least a few of them stick. Reviewers of the period indicate that audiences howled at even the hokiest comic bits, so who are we to say that Lehrman was wrong? In notes written for the Theodore Huff Society on June 4, 1968, noted film scholar William K. Everson has this to say: "*Why Sailors Go Wrong* must be one of the most monumentally foolish films ever made ... McNamara and Cohen belong as supporting, and cutaway comedians, not as leads (they did of course fill that supporting niche very effectively in *What Price Glory?*) Still, there are some good gags—the best being of a black and somewhat outrageous quality, revolving around seasickness, implied nudity and the like—and the film is fast and unpredictable even when it isn't being terribly funny." Whether *Why Sailors Go Wrong* was sufficiently amusing to warrant further Cohen-McNamara efforts will never be known. Ted McNamara died suddenly on February 3, 1928, leaving Sammy Cohen to briefly team with plug-ugly Jack Pennick (a supporting player in *Sailors*, and a stalwart of the John Ford stock company), then go it alone as a character comedian and bit player until his retirement in 1946.

Which brings us back to Paramount, where all this "team" business began. While Beery and Hatton were headlining films from Paramount's West Coast facilities, the company's East Coast operation in Astoria, Long Island was busily cranking out a group of feature comedies starring Broadway luminary W. C. Fields. The Great Man's surviving silent efforts—including *So's Your Old Man*, *It's the Old Army Game* and *Running Wild*—indicate that while Fields was more than capable of getting big laughs through pantomime alone, the loss of his inimitable wheezy voice and muttered asides was a decided handicap. Operating on only half strength, Fields was unable to build up a following amongst movie fans, leading Paramount to assume that he couldn't carry a feature by himself. The studio's solution was to team Fields with a proven favorite, walrus-mustached Chester Conklin, hoping that enough sparks of hilarity would fly between this very odd couple to buoy up the box office.

The three resultant Fields-Conklin features are no longer in existence, a fact that Fields scholar Simon Louvish finds "irksome." But even Louvish hasn't much good to say about the second of the three films, *Tillie's Punctured Romance*, produced by the Los Angeles-based Christie comedy studio and released by Paramount in 1928. Though directed by *Behind the Front*'s Eddie Sutherland, who worked copacetically with Fields on other occasions, *Tillie's Punctured Romance* doesn't seem to have been worth the effort made by Christie to purchase the title and literary rights from Mack Sennett, who had produced the original film version of the property in 1914 with Marie Dressler, Charlie Chaplin and Mabel Normand as stars. Throwing out everything from the original except the heroine's name, the 1928 *Tillie* starred Louise Fazenda as a farm girl who runs off to join a circus, where Chester Conklin is the owner and W.C. Fields the ringmaster. The two men have nothing in common but a mutual hatred, each man conspiring to have the other devoured by the circus' only lion. Okay, so why is this in a book about military comedies? Simply because scriptwriters Monte Brice and Keene Thompson, with visions of *Behind the Front* dancing in their heads, contrived to send Conklin's circus overseas to entertain the Allies during World War I. Hopelessly lost behind enemy lines, the little troupe accidentally joins the German army, where their combined ineptitude contributes mightily to the Allied victory. Stills from *Tillie's Punctured Romance* show W.C. Fields, Chester Conklin and Louise Fazenda in a goose-step march, kicking each other in the behind. The film's producer might have made a better target.

While the Fields-Conklin pairing was (perhaps mercifully) brief, the team of Charlie Murray and George Sidney managed to survive well into the talkie era. Laboring in the same Irish-Jewish "culture clash" field that was also tilled by Ted McNamara and Sammy Cohen, the wizened Charlie Murray and the rotund George Sidney scored an instant hit in the *The Cohens and the Kellys*, Universal's 1926 adaptation of the ethnocentric stage comedy *Two Blocks Away*. This picture led to a lengthy series of "Cohens and Kellys" follow-ups, as well as several other non-series comedies costarring Murray and Sidney, filmed between 1927 and 1935. Among these efforts was First National's *Lost at the Front* (1927), which cast Murray as Irish cop Pat Muldoon and Sidney as German barkeeper August Krause, both rivals for the affections of svelte sculptress Olga (Natalie Kingston). Comes the War and Pat joins up with the Russian (!) Army, while August loyally aligns with the Germans. Reunited on the battlefield, the two men first attempt to take each other prisoner, then don female drag in order to take refuge within the "Battalion of Death," the famed Soviet women's army unit. Managing to survive unscathed—and after fending off the amorous advances of the male Russian soldiers—our heroes return home to find that Olga has wed another fellow in their absence. *Lost at the Front* and *Tillie's Punctured Romance* are anomalies among the feature-length silents discussed in this chapter, in that each film starred a comedy duo that was formed *outside* the military-comedy genre.

During this period there were a handful of "instant" teams that never made it past their first in-tandem film appearance. Released in November 1926, MGM's *Tin Hats* avoided imitating the comedy-duo setup in *Behind the Front*. Instead, the picture emulated the pre-battlefield sequences

Tin Hats (MGM, 1926): Americans George Cooper, Conrad Nagel and Bert Roach (left to right) are welcomed as conquerors in a post–Armistice German village.

in MGM's own *The Big Parade* by offering a trio of doughboys performing hijinks reminiscent of those indulged in by John Gilbert, Karl Dane and Tom O'Brien in the earlier picture. O'Brien in fact appeared in *Tin Hats*, not as a member of the comic threesome but as their beetle-browed topkick.

Set in the immediate post–Armistice period, *Tin Hats* starred Conrad Nagel as rich man's son Jack Benson, George Cooper as ex-gangster Lefty Mooney and Bert Roach as German-American brewery heir Dutch Krausemeyer. Wandering into a German village ahead of the other Allied troops on Armistice Day, the boys "liberate" the village and place themselves in charge of everything except an ancient castle occupied by Princess Elsa (Claire Windsor) and her hyperprotective servants. Jack falls in love with Elsa, Lefty pitches woo at giggling fraulein Freida (Eileen Sedgwick), and Dutch uses his ability to speak fluent German to his own advantage. Though advertised as "The Funny Little Brother to *The Big Parade*," the MGM publicists took great pains to emphasize that *Tin Hats* was not a war picture and there were no battle scenes. The jocular nature of the proceedings was further underlined with the ad-poster art by famed "Roaring Twenties" illustrator John Held, Jr., and by such chucklesome subtitles (again by Ralph Spence) as "The Cocktail's Red Glare, Corks Bursting in Air — Gave Proof Though the Night That Our Jag Was Still There" (an irreverent riff that was censored in several states!). Just how funny this "laugh-riot of three rollicking rhinestones" truly was is hard to determine today, since the only known print is incomplete and in tatters. (An amusing rewrite of the film's opening "liberation" sequence was seen in the World War II-vintage MGM comedy *What Next, Corporal Hargrove?*)

The existing reference copy of another one-time-only "team" comedy, the 1927 United Artists release *Two Arabian Knights*, isn't in much better shape than *Tin Hats*, with several scenes so deteriorated and mottled that they appear to have been filmed during an attack by flying jellyfish. Yet unlike *Tin Hats*, which isn't currently a high priority on anyone's preservation list, *Two Arabian Knights* was rescued from the brink of disintegration when a print of the long-missing film showed up at the University of Nevada-Las Vegas, part of a huge donation made by the estate of the picture's producer Howard Hughes. Painstakingly restored on a frame-by-frame basis, this offbeat military comedy more than justifies the Academy Award bestowed on director Lewis Milestone for "best comedy direction," the only time that an Oscar was ever presented in that category.

Though Howard Hughes and Lewis Milestone undoubtedly had the success of *Behind the Front* in the back of their minds when they collaborated on *Two Arabian Knights*, the film actually has more in common with *What Price Glory?* (see **Chapter 7**) — a commonality that Milestone downplayed in a late–1960s interview with Charles Higham and Joel Greenberg: "*What Price Glory?*, which happened to be one of my favorite plays, had much more of a story than *Two Arabian Knights*. The only resemblance between the two pieces was the animosity of the protagonists: but it was not really animosity, just their idea of humor — to put the other fellow into trouble." Maybe so, but it's worth noting that one of Milestone's stars, Louis Wolheim, had played Captain Flagg in the original Broadway version of *What Price Glory?*

Gorilla-visaged Wolheim appears in *Two Arabian Knights* as Sgt. Peter O'Gaffney, with chiseled-profile leading man William Boyd (borrowed by Hughes from Cecil B. DeMille) as Private W. Dangerfield Phelps III. Having carried on a feud throughout World War I, O'Gaffney and Phelps continue their personal battle when they find themselves sharing the same foxhole. Punching each other senseless, the two soldiers end up in the custody of the Enemy. Confined to a POW camp in the frozen tundra of northern Germany, O'Gaffney and Phelps agree to call a truce long enough to engineer an escape. They make their getaway wrapped in burnooses stolen from a couple of Arab prisoners, then hop a steamer headed for the Arabian province of Jaffa. Here the boys both fall in love with Princess Mirza (Mary Astor), who is en route to an arranged marriage. Phelps makes so much headway with Mirza that he persuades her to lift her veil, which immediately results in a sentence of death for himself and O'Gaffney. The Princess' father orders his minions

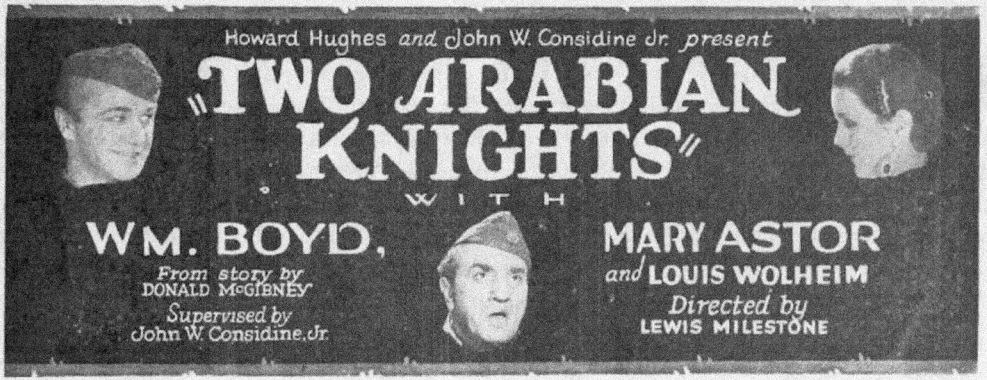

A glowing trade advertisement for *Two Arabian Knights* (United Artists, 1927), originally published in *Film Daily*.

to assassinate the infidels on sight, while Mirza's fiancee Shevket Ben Ali (Ian Keith) salivates at the prospect of challenging Phelps to a duel. The two Americans manage to squeeze out of their predicament through sheer yankee pluck, allowing them to escape with Mirza in tow. Unfortunately, the surviving print of this film does not include the scene in which William Boyd, who later portrayed that bastion of virility Hopalong Cassidy, plants a kiss on the cheek of a harem eunuch. (No doubt about it: Lewis Milestone really deserved that Oscar!)

Two Arabian Knights—"A barrage of fun with the war left out—the laughs left in!"—was such a money-spinner that Howard Hughes spent the better part of the next two decades planning a remake: In 1944, this project was announced to the press, with William Bendix, John Payne and Linda Darnell proposed as the stars. Though *Two Arabian Knights* would never be officially remade, an all-talkie Hughes production released by United Artists in 1932 was very much in the spirit of the earlier film. *Sky Devils* (working title: *Ground Hogs*) stars Spencer Tracy and George Cooper as Wilkie and Mitchell, a pair of monumentally stupid soldiers who'd been drafted in Army after flunking out as lifeguards (no one told them that they'd have to learn to swim). Since World War I doesn't agree with them, the two chowderheads attempt to desert by stowing away on a transport—which takes them directly to the war zone, leaving them at the mercy of volcanic Sgt. Hogan (played by William "Stage" Boyd, so billed to avoid confusion with the William Boyd who'd appeared in *Two Arabian Knights*). Going AWOL, Wilkie and Mitchell scrap over the affections of heroine Mary (Ann Dvorak), then become heroes by accidentally strafing and destroying a German ammo dump (courtesy of leftover aerial footage from the 1930 Hughes production *Hell's Angels*).

If this seems to make even less sense than the scenario for *Two Arabian Knights*, just imagine what *Sky Devils* looked like in its original version (featuring yet another harem sequence!) directed by Edward Sedgwick, which was rejected *in toto* by Howard Hughes and refilmed from top to bottom under the direction of Eddie Sutherland, with Ann Dvorak replacing Lola Lane and William "Stage" Boyd taking over from Sidney Toler. Alas, all this retinkering was for naught: *Sky Devils* flopped so resoundingly that Howard Hughes completely withdrew from the motion picture business for nearly ten years.

For better or worse, *Sky Devils* still exists, worth a look if for no other reason than seeing the brilliant Spencer Tracy play a total imbecile. And as mentioned, we still have the film's prototype *Two Arabian Knights*, albeit in an imperfect state. Conversely, the final silent "team" comedy in this chapter is not only a missing film, but there are many social historians who fervently hope that it will stay missing. Directed by Rol Del Ruth and released as Warner Bros.' 1927 Christmas attraction, *Ham and Eggs at the Front* was a 6-reel regression into the sort of racial insensitivity that had typified the American entertainment world of the mid–19th century. Ham and Eggs are two black vaudevillians who join an "all-colored" regiment in order to serve in World War I. Our heroes go AWOL in France and take refuge at an inn run by German spy Friml, who instructs his Sengalese waitress Fifi to flirt with Ham in order to extract vital military information. The climax borrowed liberally from Dane & Arthur's *Rookies*, with Ham and Eggs trapped in a runaway balloon.

The ads for *Ham and Eggs at the Front* touted the picture as "more fun than a dozen minstrel shows." Contributing factors to the "fun" included stolen chickens, watermelon, dice, razors and ghosts, while the subtitles were overstocked with exaggerated dialect jokes and malapropisms. These demeaning witticisms were largely the handiwork of Warners scenarist Darryl F. Zanuck, the same man who later produced such distinguished anti-prejudice films as *Gentleman's Agreement* and *Pinky*—possibly as an act of absolution.

The film would have been offensive enough had the cast been comprised of genuine African Americans, but the offense was compounded by exclusively casting white actors wearing blackface. Tom Wilson, a Caucasian specialist in Negro characterizations, played Ham, with comedy "regulars" Heinie Conklin as Eggs, Tom Kennedy as Pvt. Lazarus, Noah Young as the Sergeant and Louise Fazenda as Ham's hometown gal Callie. The worst we've saved for last: Seen as the alluring Sengalese spy Fifi was none other than Myrna Loy, who ever afterward expressed mortification over having had anything to do with the picture. "How could I have ever put on blackface?" she asked in her autobiography. "When I think of it now, it horrifies me. Well, our awareness broadens, thank God."

Selected Shorts, Part One: The Silents

The silent era was the golden age of 2-reel comedies, a time when filmmakers unfettered by Political Correctness were free to poke fun at everything and everybody — including the military and the recent World War. We've already referenced the two Harry Langdon army-comedy shorts of the 1920s, *All Night Long* and *Soldier Man*. To say there was "more where that came from" is hardly sufficient.

Langdon's onetime boss Mack Sennett was responsible for the 1925 two-reeler *Over Thereabouts*, starring Billy Bevan as a pampered playboy who upon being drafted into World War I must humble himself as the orderly for his former personal secretary (Ernest Wood), now a high-ranking officer. Madeleine Hurlock costars as a socialite whose gorgon-like mother had been trying to force her into a marriage with Billy, even though Madeleine loves the secretary. After a bumpy airplane ride (featuring some of the least convincing double-exposure work ever to emerge from the Sennett factory), Billy helps his superior officer outwit the Germans and steal an enemy munitions truck, allowing Madeleine to wed her true love and Billy to win the girl's mother as *his* bride. Like many Sennett shorts of the era, *Over Thereabouts* was constructed as a two-part story, Part One involving wealthy Billy and his long-suffering servants, and Part Two comprised of the war scenes, in which those same servants pop up among the German ranks. The continuity is so disjointed that some prints of the film show the reels in reverse order, suggesting that Billy has hired his former enemies *after* the war in the spirit of "no hard feelings."

Other Sennett military farces included the 1928 double-reeler *Smith's Army Life,* one of the long-running "Smith Family" series starring Raymond McKee, Ruth Hiatt and 4-year-old Mary Ann Jackson. Touching upon a contemporary fad previously exploited in the feature-length *Rookies*, suburbanite Smith (McKee) signs up for a hitch at a Civilian Military Training Camp, with his busybody wife (Hiatt) and precocious daughter (Jackson) tagging along. The expected complications ensue, resulting in Mr. Smith seeing the inside of an Army kitchen with alarming regularity. All-around comedy man Alf Goulding directed this assemblage of familiar awkward-squad gags, described by *Film Daily* as "laughable stuff."

Mack Sennett didn't hold a monopoly on this sort of nonsense; there were several of the comedy producer's former employees laboring in the same cornfield. Sennett alumnus Chester Conklin was starred in the 1920 Fox Sunshine comedy *Her Private Husband*, the story of a doughboy's futile efforts to spend quality time with his wife. This plot would later be turned inside out for Hal Roach's *One Hour Married* (1927), the last in a group of 3-reelers starring former Sennett headliner Mabel Normand, trying to stage a comeback after several professional and personal setbacks. In order to be near her new husband Creighton Hale, Mabel disguises herself as a male soldier and sneaks into Hale's barracks. Discovering that hubby has already been shipped out, Mabel ends up trailing after him all the way to France. Without access to a copy of this film, one can't say for certain if it was funnier than it sounded: It is, however, a matter of record that *One Hour Married* represented Mabel Normand's final screen appearance before her death in 1930.

Just as Mack Sennett had defectors, so too did Hal Roach sever ties with a few of his more prominent stars during the 1920s. Breaking with Roach over money matters in 1925, Snub Pollard, he of the upside-down Kaiser Bill mustache, joined forces with Weiss-Artclass films as both star and producer. Among Pollard's earliest Weiss-Artclass efforts was *The Doughboy* (1926), filmed on a large and elaborately detailed foreign-village exterior set that had obviously been constructed for another film. Opening with an awkward-squad routine as Snub and his fellow rookies train with broomsticks substituting as rifles, the film quickly moves to "Anybody's Land" in France, where the little comedian is ordered to guard the rear flank while the rest of the regiment moves forward. This plot tangent is abandoned for a scene in which Snub flirts with a French miss and promises to look after her kid brother. Man and boy are captured by the Germans, but Snub effects a rescue by posing as an enemy officer (it's never explained how he managed to slip out of his jail cell and into a German uniform). Pausing long enough to save the girl from a lustful Hun, Snub throws the enemy into confusion by wearing his boots on his hands. (If it had been *that* easy, the Allies would have been home by the summer of 1917.) Typical of Snub Pollard's Weiss-Artclass vehicles, *The Doughboy* has some excellent isolated gags but absolutely no sense of story or structure; the gags never "build," while the action comes to a halt only because the alotted two reels are used up.

Another Hal Roach star, Clyde Cook, appeared in 2-reelers for several other studios prior to his Roach contract. One of these was 1924's *The Misfit* (filmed in 1923 with the working title *Under Orders*), in which Army rookie Clyde is assigned the unenviable task of guarding the stockade. Filmed at the former Buster Keaton Studio with Keaton costar Joe Roberts in the cast and several of Buster's gag writers contributing to the script, *The Misfit* was released by Educational Studios, which in addition to distributing the output of several independent producers also had a healthy manifest of home-grown product. *Jolly Tars* in 1926 was a showcase for one of Educational's top stars, Lloyd Hamilton, cast as a flabby, pussy-footing sailor who spends his first night at sea wrestling with a troublesome hammock (a gag reprised by Lou Costello in 1941's *In the Navy*); the following year, Hamilton played an improbable doughboy at odds with his remonstrative sergeant (Stanley Blystone) in the 2-reel *At Ease*. Another Educational favorite, the great British music-hall entertainer Lupino Lane, headlined the 1929 military fantasy *Battling Sisters*. The film is set in 1980, when traditional sex roles are reversed and women wage war while the men stay home and knit. In a near-surrealistic parody of World War I-era propaganda pictures, helpless husband Lane must fight off the rapacious advances of an invading female officer while his soldier wife rushes home to save him from a Fate Worse Than Death.

Many of Lupino Lane's comedies cast him as a comic sailor, with his brother Wallace Lupino playing a shipmate. Over at Christie Studios, rubber-limbed Billy Dooley fashioned a whole career out of playing a silly swabbie in such 2-reelers as *A Goofy Gob*, *A Salty Sap*, *A Briny Boob* and *The Dizzy Diver*. Many of Dooley's comedies still survive, albeit cut down from two reels to one: On the whole they're quite funny, though Dooley himself was an undistinguished performer whose single memorable trait was a V-shaped smile.

Christie Studios was also the home base for *Shell Socked* (1923), featuring pencil-moustached Jimmie Adams as a private who vies with fellow soldiers Eddie Baker and George Burton for the attentions of Red Cross nurse Vera Stedman. To cut down competition, Eddie and George arrange to send Adams on a dangerous mission — which consists of escorting Vera to her father (William Irving), a general who is so impressed by Jimmie's fortitude that he promotes him on the spot. And in Christie's *Yes Yes Babette* (1925), saucer-eyed Army private Bobby Vernon cuts loose in Gay Paree (or a reasonable facsimile thereof).

It is hard to find a comedian of the 1920s who *didn't* show up in uniform at one time or another. Jimmy Aubrey, a British comic whose screen image would mature from the baggy pants and crepe mustaches of an earlier era to the natty man-about-town preferred by audiences of the Jazz Age, starred in Vitagraph's 1923 military comedy *Forward March*. A couple of years later, Aubrey was signed by independent producer Joe Rock, who at the same time was shipping out a series of 2-reelers featuring the "Ton of Fun"—a.k.a. Frank Alexander, Hillard Karr and Kewpie Ross, a trio of fat comedians made even fatter with obvious padding. Renting studio space at Universal, Rock had access to a number of impressive exterior sets, one of which served as the backdrop for the Ton of Fun's 1926 offering *The Heavy Parade*. Per its title, this elaborate 20-minute comedy (set in 1917 B.P.—"Before Prohibition") is a takeoff of the World War I feature *The Big Parade*, including a lengthy lampoon of the earlier film's classic scene in which lovesick heroine Renee Adoree desperately clings to John Gilbert as he marches off to the front. In *Heavy Parade*, frowzy mademoiselle "Clora Form" similarly attaches herself to the obese Frank Alexander, going so far as to grab hold of his transport wagon — which promptly reveals itself to be a pickup truck, dumping its corpulent contents on the ground. A later sequence in the trenches finds the "Three Fatties" (as they were known in the trades) using a single rifle to bring down a pesky German attack plane, at last enabling the boys to "enjoy this war."

Also under contract to Joe Rock during this period was Stan Laurel, whose twelve 2-reelers for the producer included 1925's *Navy Blue Days*. Playing a sailor stationed in South America (courtesy of another Universal standing set), Stan wangles an invitation to a dinner attended by his Chief Petty Officer, where he falls for the attractive hostess. Not only must Stan do battle with the CPO to win over the girl, but both men are forced to contend with a local swain named Peter Vermicelli. *Navy Blue Days* was written by Tay Garnett, who later directed several major features with seafaring themes (*One Way Passage, China Seas, Slave Ship*, etc.).

After leaving Joe Rock, Stan Laurel settled at Hal Roach Studios, where he began appearing opposite Oliver Hardy, first in supporting roles and then as a full-fledged team. Despite their titles, the early Laurel and Hardy efforts *Why Girls Love Sailors* and *Sailors Beware* (both released by Pathé in 1927) are not service comedies, though the duo would dutifully explore that genre in several other films discussed in **Chapter 3**.

Taking a novel approach to the military-comedy *ouevre* were several 2-reelers featuring children. One of the best of these was the Our Gang comedy *Dogs of War* (Hal Roach/Pathé 1923), which opens with the "Great Battle of Kelly's Tomato Patch." Characteristically treating their "pretend" world with utmost seriousness, the kids have set up quite a Theater of Operations, with five little commanding officers (including "Gang" favorites Mickey Daniels and Jack Davis) and a single private (black child Allen "Farina" Hoskins, effectively integrating the Armed Forces a quarter of a century before it actually happened!). Six-year-old Mary Kornman pitches in as a Red Cross nurse, complete with field hospital and improvised bandages, while the boys put up a valiant defense of their lines with an endless supply of rotten vegetables. Though Farina nearly brings about a premature Armistice by coaxing a skunk onto the battlefield, peace is not declared until Mary is called away by the nearby "West Coast Studios" (actually the thinly disguised Hal Roach lot) to play a small movie role. The rest of the film is devoted to the gang's antics while being chased around by the irate studio guards, climaxing with another "gas attack" from one of Farina's beloved skunks.

Less elaborate but no less lively was *The Big Pie-Raid* (Bray Studios, 1927) featuring an Our Gang knockoff called the McDougall Alley Kids. Though inferior to *Dogs of War*, this comedy at least does not repeat the earlier film's mistake of dropping its war-spoof gags before the first reel is over, instead reserving the sham-battle highlight for the final sequence. After a kiddie football game, heroine Mary (Annabel Magnus) invites the winners to a party at her house. Early skirmishes with such missiles as ice cream and cake are but prologue to the "Big Push" at the climax, when the losing team entrenches itself in the backyard next door. With the battle lines defined by a large hedge, the youngsters stage an impressive contretemps using mud and bean shooters as weapons; and when a pie wagon breaks down on a nearby street, guess what happens next. Yet another "skunk" gag wraps up this derivative but energetic 2-reeler, released the same year that Al Jolson's *The Jazz Singer* sounded the death knell for the Silent Cinema — but hardly for the world of the military comedy.

3

First Line of Offense

"Professional" Comedians in Talkie Service Comedies

The majority of service comedies produced during the talking-picture era are categorized and dealt with with elsewhere in this book. The following chapter, covering a period of eight decades, concentrates on the many Army and Navy comedies featuring professional comedians, rather than merely "straight" actors who only occasionally raised laughs on screen. Such individual efforts as Tiffany-Stahl's *Troopers Three* (1930), Universal's *Private Jones* (1933), Grand National's *We're in the Legion Now* (1937) or Warners' *Three Sons O' Guns* (1941) may be considered hilarious by some, but they won't be discussed in this chapter because their stars were not exclusively comedians. Besides, until a print of *Private Jones* turns up, it is hard to determine if it *was* hilarious, having been described as a rollicking comedy by some contemporary reviewers and a stark drama by others (conversely, I've seen *We're in the Legion Now* three times and I *still* don't know if it's supposed to be funny or not). Also absent from this section are the wartime farces of Abbott & Costello and their imitators — but be patient, we'll get to those guys in their proper place.

Buster Keaton

With the spectacular exception of *The General* (see **Chapter 18**), Buster Keaton shied away from making war or army comedies during the silent era. The comedian's biographers have suggested that Keaton found his own military experience during World War I so unpleasant that he just couldn't see the humor in it. Be that as it may, when talkies came in Buster had less to say about the content of his feature comedies than before. No longer in charge of his own studio, he was now just a salaried employee at MGM, obliged to accept whatever the writers handed him. One such assignment was a war comedy, initially titled *The Big Shot* and ultimately released in late 1930 as *Doughboys*.

Reviving the upper-class-twit character he'd essayed so well in his silent *The Navigator* (1924), Buster is cast as wealthy Elmer J. Stuyvesant, who when America enters the Great War loses his chauffeur to the Army. Elmer heads down to an employment agency for a replacement, little realizing that the agency has been converted into a recruiting office. A bit slow on the uptake, Elmer can't understand why the two uniformed men in the office are so eager to take off his clothes and submit him to a physical exam. By the time he's figured out what's what — and has issued a harsh reprimand to the Army for failing to respect his social standing — Pvt. Elmer J. Stuyvesant is packed off to training camp, where he and the rest of his "awkward squad" display their resilience by fainting dead away during bayonet practice. He also makes a powerful enemy in the form of vitriolic Sergeant Brophy (Ed Brophy) and finds a close friend in the form of ukelele-strumming Nescopeck (Cliff Edwards).

3. First Line of Offense

En route to France via troop ship, Elmer renews his acquaintance with Red Cross nurse Mary (Sally Eilers), whom he's been trying to woo and win since Reel One. The romantic angle is temporarily forgotten when, while on the front lines, Elmer comes face to face with his former butler Gustave (Arnold Korff), now a member of the German army. Generously offering to find food for the starving *Boche*, Elmer somehow gets hold of a strategic map and is hailed as a hero by the Allies. Granted a furlough, he again tries to link up with Mary, but by now bombs are falling and the two erstwhile sweethearts are forced to make an escape in a truck loaded with explosives. Managing to avoid being blown to bits, Elmer and Mary end up in a foxhole, surrounded by the Enemy. It looks pretty hopeless until Gustave pops up again and announces that peace has been declared—and that he is now *Elmer*'s prisoner.

Of the seven MGM starring features he made during the early-talkie era, Keaton always cited *Doughboys* as his personal favorite. With special dispensation from studio production head Irving Thalberg, Buster was allowed to develop his own screen story (though official credit went to Al Boasberg and Sidney Lazarus) and to devise all the main gag sequences, luxuries normally denied him at MGM. Buster also enjoyed working with director Edward Sedgwick, though eyewitnesses recall a few tense moments when Sedgwick had to bawl the comedian out for blowing his lines. When seen today, *Doughboys* is hardly a cause for enthusiasm; in fact, many Keaton devotees regard it as one of his worst pictures. Part of the blame can be leveled at the film's protacted 8-reel length, forcing the comedian into repetition and predictability, but the primary cause of *Doughboy*'s poor reputation is the fingernails-on-the-blackboard performance by Ed Brophy as Buster's obnoxious sergeant. Formerly the production manager for Keaton's MGM unit, Brophy was promoted to character roles by virtue of his memorable dressing-room scene with Buster in *The Cameraman* (1928). Judging from his work in *Doughboys*, Ed Brophy should have kept his day job.

If one can get past its shortcomings (which the comedian's fans were certainly able to do in 1930), *Doughboys* contains several entertaining moments, with the early recruiting-office scene a standout—so much so that Keaton reprised the sequence in his 1941 Columbia 2-reeler *General Nuisance*. Unfortunately, not *all* of Buster's proposed gags were included: One routine, in which an entire platoon marches right over our hero when he forgets to about-face, was excised from *Doughboys*, though it would ultimately be performed by Keaton in 1965's *Sergeant DeadHead* (see **Chapter 12**).

Conversely, the war scenes feature some marvelous touches. An American officer's glowing description of "Sunny France" is instantly followed by a shot of the new recruits slogging around in the wettest, sloppiest downpour imaginable. Another characteristic Keaton moment occurs when Elmer and Mary prepare themselves for certain doom as German troops bear down on their foxhole. Handing Mary an artillery belt, Elmer grimly tells the girl to save the last bullet for herself should she fall into the clutches of the hideous Huns. But when his ex-butler Gustave humbly announces that the Armistice has been declared, Elmer resumes his former aristocratic hauteur without batting an eyelash, magnanimously giving Gustave his old job back and bidding a courteous farewell to the rest of the Germans: "I'll run into you in some other war sometime."

Best of all are the film's musical numbers, showcasing the versatility of the vaudeville-bred Keaton. The first such number is a seemingly impromptu ukelele duet between Buster and Cliff Edwards, which might have been even more enjoyable had it not been interrupted by the egregious Ed Brophy. The second, taking place during a camp variety show, features Buster in drag performing a violent Apache dance that degenerates into a wrestling match—a routine that may well have inspired the similar Apache spoofs in Joe E. Brown's *Sons O' Guns* (1936) and Jimmy Durante and Phil Silvers' *You're in the Army Now* (1941).

After his fall from grace at MGM—let's skip the all-too-well-known details—Keaton staged a comeback at Educational Studios, where he starred in sixteen cheap but lively 2-reelers between 1934 and 1937. Buster had made his share of "seafaring" pictures in his glory days (*The Boat, The*

Preoccupied with fending off the German army, Sally Eilers and Buster Keaton seem unaware that the enemy is literally breathing down their necks. From *Doughboys* (MGM, 1930) (*courtesy James L. Neibaur*).

Love Nest, The Navigator), but the 1935 Educational short *Tars and Stripes* was the only time he actually wore a regulation Navy uniform. Filmed at the Naval Training Station in San Diego, *Tars and Stripes* casts Buster as another "Elmer," who spends the first reel giving apoplexy to the exasperated chief gunner's mate, played by perennial Three Stooges foil Vernon Dent. Reel Two is an extended chase, as Dent pursues Elmer on land and sea to prevent our hero from winning over the officer's girlfriend (Dorothea Kent), a plot device lifted from *Doughboys*. There's a cute bit in which Elmer, assigned to punishment drill, pivots a huge hole in the parade grounds, and another in which he vainly tries to jockey for first-in-line position at the mess hall. Otherwise, *Tars and Stripes* has little to recommend it.

Six years later, Keaton was making short comedies at Columbia; ten such films were churned out in quick succession, with *General Nuisance* (1941) in the Number Nine slot. Directed with the fury of a mad dog by the redoubtable Jules White, this one features Buster *not* as a guy named Elmer, but as millionaire Peter Hedley Lamarr Jr. (33 years before Mel Brooks modified this punny name for the Harvey Korman character in *Blazing Saddles*). Hoping to make an impression on pretty nurse Dorothy Appleby, Lamarr enlists in the Army, where he is assigned a job eminently suited to his qualifications: cleaning out the officers' spittoons. The one outstanding scene in this negligible 2-reeler is another musical interlude, this time with raucous comedienne Elsie Ames, whom Columbia was grooming to be the next Martha Raye. The scene ends with a quote from Keaton's best Educational short *Grand Slam Opera* (1936), as Buster and Elsie perform a mixed-culture dance consisting of a jitterbug, a Viennese waltz, a Russian mazurka, a ballet *pas de deux*—and several Jules White-style pratfalls.

Buster Keaton spent the last decade of his life (1956–1966) playing supporting and cameo roles in a multitude of films both good and bad. His penultimate film, released nearly a year after

Eleven years after *Doughboys*, Buster repeats one of the film's key gag sequences in the Columbia 2-reeler *General Nuisance*, with the assistance of Monty Collins (right). The actor at left is unidentified (*courtesy James L. Neibaur*).

his death, was a military comedy variously titled *Two Marines and a General* and *War Italian Style*. Despite the preponderance of American actors in the cast (including Martha Hyer and Fred Clark), the film is a European production geared for the fans of Italian comedians Franco and Ciccio, and as such outside the realm of this book. Suffice to say that Buster portrays the sweetest and most lovable Nazi general in movie history.

Harry Langdon

Though not as many Hollywood careers were ruined by talkies as legend would have it, there were quite a few silent stars whose fame and popularity waned when the movies began to speak. The case of baby-faced comedian Harry Langdon is a bit unusual in that he was considered washed up *before* the advent of talkies. As noted in **Chapter 2**, his last silent starring feature *Heart Trouble* was deemed such a disaster that First National Pictures passed on renewing their contract with the Harry Langdon Corporation. Ironically, it was the same First National, now folded into Warner Bros., who offered Langdon a comeback opportunity in early 1930.

His descent from his late-'20s superstardom notwithstanding, Langdon was still treated as a valuable commodity by Warner Bros.-First National, who paid him $2500 per week for his work in the feature-length Army comedy *A Soldier's Plaything* (working title: *Easy Go*). From the looks of things, this was a quite an expensive production, as well as one of a handful of Warner-First National films photographed in an early widescreen process called Vitascope (a "flat" version was simultaneously lensed to accommodate theaters not equipped with anamorphic lenses; it is the latter version that survives today). While Langdon is given top billing in most of the newspaper and trade ads, *A Soldier's Plaything* was actually designed to showcase a new studio contractee, Budapest-born actress Lotti Loder — who, oddly enough, doesn't even make an appearance until the second half of the film. Also heavily promoted by the studio publicity machine was the film's romantic lead Ben Lyon, who had recently negotiated a lucrative new contract with Warner-First National on the strength of his excellent showing in Howard Hughes' 1930 aviation epic *Hell's Angels*. The attention lavished on Loder and Lyon in the trade papers might lead one to conclude that Langdon's screen time in *Soldier's Plaything* was severely limited despite his prominent billing. While this is inaccurate, it cannot be denied that Harry's personality does not dominate the proceedings as it did in his silent work. Also, there is a concerted effort throughout the film to create a team out of Langdon and Ben Lyon in the equal-time manner of *What Price Glory?*'s Victor McLaglen and Edmund Lowe (see **Chapter 7**).

Based on a story by Viña Delmar, whose reputation was founded on such "scandalous" novels as *Bad Girl*, *A Soldier's Plaything* gets under way shortly before the Armstice, with gambler Georgie Wilson (Lyon) on the lam from the cops because he thinks he's killed a guy. As a means of escape, Georgie and his goofy pal Tim (Langdon) enlist in the Army of the Occupation. The gregarious Georgie has an easier time getting along with his fellow soldiers (if not his superiors) than the bumbling Tim, who can't help committing such accidental infractions as dropping a large weight on an officer's head. Both Georgie and Tim spend a lot of time with shovels in hand as "stable police," a circumstance that indirectly leads to a comic setpiece in which the boys try to cross the French-German border dressed in a horse costume (someone at the studio obviously remembered how funny this bit was in Syd Chaplin's *The Better 'Ole*). Stationed in the German town of Koblentz, Georgie falls for innkeeper's daughter Gretchen (Lotti Loder), but holds off proposing to her so long as he has a murder charge hanging over his head. Tim tries to make time with the local frauleins as well, but his courtship technique leaves a lot to be desired. All ends happily when Georgie's "victim" shows up very much alive.

Langdon's best moment in the picture is evocative of his scenes with the blind heroine in the silent feature *The Strong Man*. Smitten by a pretty girl, Harry noisily tries to attract her attention, only to discover that she is deaf. The potential for sticky pathos is hilariously cut short when Harry, evidently not as innocent or childlike as in his silent films, declares his intentions by flashing a dirty French postcard! Film historian William K. Everson praised this sequence in his program notes for a 1974 screening of *A Soldier's Plaything* at the New School for Social Research: "it revives that odd combination of subtle pantomime and black humor that was Langdon's forte."

This said, Everson felt compelled to issue a disclaimer: "I am well aware that *A Soldier's Plaything* may be considered *the* programming mistake deluxe in our entire twenty-series history." Warners-First National knew they had a dog on their hands long before that. Originally running 71 minutes, the film previewed so poorly that it was hacked down to 57 minutes, rendering several scenes incomprehensible and reducing supporting actor Jean Hersholt to a mere walk-on. The sole remarkable aspect of *A Soldier's Plaything* is that it represents the only collaboration between Harry Langdon and director Michael (*Casablanca*) Curtiz. It was also Curtiz's biggest money-loser until the 1950s.

His comeback feature a failure, Harry Langdon would have to make do with whatever film roles he could scrounge up for the rest of his career — though contrary to the distorted recollections of his coworkers Mack Sennett and Frank Capra, the comedian seldom lacked for work, appearing steadily in both features and shorts until his death (*not* in poverty) in 1944. Langdon made one additional service comedy in the talkie era, the 1935 Columbia 2-reeler *The Leathernecker*, mentioned in **Chapter 2**.

Laurel and Hardy

The only bonafide service comedy made jointly by Stan Laurel and Oliver Hardy during the silent era (see **Chapters 1** and **2** for references to their solo work) was filmed before they were officially a team. At this point in time, Laurel & Hardy were members of the Hal Roach Studio's "All-Stars," a collection of talented comedians appearing in a variety of characterizations. Considering the frequency with which studios like Paramount and MGM conspired to mold synthetic comedy teams out of the likes of Wallace Beery, Raymond Hatton, Karl Dane and George K. Arthur, Hal Roach was surprisingly oblivious to the fact that he had a "natural" team right under his nose. Curiously, when Roach finally did recognize the chemistry between Laurel & Hardy (with the encouragement of his ace director Leo McCarey), he didn't envision them as a duo but as two-thirds of a trio, with double-take expert James ("Doh!") Finlayson as the third member. From mid-1927 to early 1928, audiences were treated to the Laurel/Hardy/Finlayson triumvirate in such 2-reelers as *Love 'Em and Weep* (in which Hardy barely appears), *Do Detectives Think?*, *Flying Elephants* and *Sugar Daddies*— as well as the threesome's second joint appearance in *With Love and Hisses* (1927).

Little more than a loosely threaded string of gags, *With Love and Hisses* casts Laurel as a delicate Army private, Hardy as a blustery topkick, and Finlayson as a gimlet-eyed general. Hardy is held in reserve during the first half of the picture while Laurel crosses swords with Finlayson, first on a troop train and then during a practice drill — the latter sequence featuring an uninhibited slice of gay humor as the epicene Laurel misinterprets one of Finlayson's orders as a come-on! The second reel is devoted to Laurel & Hardy, climaxing with a brilliant sight gag involving a huge billboard for the Cecil B. DeMille production *The Volga Boatmen*, used as a convenient hiding place when Stan, Ollie and the other soldiers are forced to skulk around the countryside buck-naked after their uniforms have been set afire. Subtlety is not the strong suit of *With Love and Hisses*, which also features a risibly repulsive repertoire of body-odor jokes.

In retrospect, Laurel & Hardy were wise to avoid service comedies once they'd achieved star billing as a team. The concept of a misfit duo in uniform was by 1928 already a shopworn cliché thanks to the Beery-Hatton comedies and their imitators (see **Chapter 2**). Stan and Ollie play sailors in the silent classic *Two Tars* (1928) and the early talkie *Men O' War* (1929), but there are no training or combat scenes; instead, both films are hilarious essays in "reciprocal destruction" (tit-for-tat battles between the two gobs and various civilian opponents) while the boys are trying to enjoy shore leave with their empty-headed girlfriends. The closest Laurel & Hardy ever get to the bounding waves in *Men O' War* is when they hire a rowboat in a lakeside park — then proceed to go in circles as each man rows in the opposite direction. And though the boys play merchant seamen in the 1936 feature *Our Relations*, they spend most of their time on dry land, snuggling with another pair of dockside doxies.

Of the team's 1930s feature films, three could be regarded as military comedies (1938's *Block-Heads* opens with a brief World War I sequence, but the bulk of the comedy takes place when ex-doughboys Stan and Ollie are reunited twenty years later). The first, *Pack Up Your Troubles* (Hal Roach/MGM, 1932), boasts a consistent level of hilarity but suffers from the same structural problem as their previous feature *Pardon Us* (1931); the comedians had been 2-reel stars for so long that they were having trouble putting together a cohesively plotted 7-reeler.

All of the Army comedy in *Pack Up Your Troubles* is concentrated in the first half hour or so, beginning with Stan & Ollie reluctantly conscripted into the Great War, a sequence containing the sort of "black humor" gag that only Laurel & Hardy could pull off tastefully: Hoping to avoid military service, the boys briefly pretend to be amputees! Then we're off to the obligatory awkward-squad sequence as the two rookies infuriate a bulldog-faced drill sergeant ("*Halt* means to *stop*!"). Comparing this scene to the faster-paced, gag-packed boot camp routines performed by

Raw (but polite) recruits Stan Laurel and Oliver Hardy try to ingratiate themselves with their superiors in this posed shot from *Pack Up Your Troubles* (Roach, 1932) (*MOVIE STAR NEWS*).

Abbott &Costello and the 3 Stooges, one is impressed by the casual expertise with which Laurel & Hardy can milk the maximum comic value from a minimum of gag material.

We next find the boys hauling garbage cans from the camp kitchen. "What are we supposed to do with this stuff?" Ollie asks the cook (played by George Marshall, the film's director). "Are you guys tryin' to kid somebody?" the cook sneers contemptuously. "Take it to the General!" Failing to recognize sarcasm when they hear it, and determined to "follow the Army curriculum with discipline" so they won't get in any more trouble, our heroes follow the cook's "orders" to the letter, depositing the smelly, fly-infested trash receptacles in the General's living room — and since we're still in Hal Roach Land, the General is once again James Finlayson. This memorable scene was huffily condemned as "disgusting" by the reviewer for *New England Film News*, who was already steamed over the fact that Hal Roach and MGM were charging higher rental fees for the Laurel & Hardy comedies than the other Roach films.

The next major sequence is set on the battlefields of France: "Somewhere in nowhere, where the cannons boomed all day and the cooties boomed all night." Some of the team's funniest and most characteristic material occurs in a lengthy dugout scene, beginning with the boys contentedly snoozing the night away in nonregulation nightshirts with a hot water bottle at their feet, then proceeding as Stan washes his hands and face in stale coffee and combs his hair with a mess-kit fork. The scene's climax takes place in No Man's Land, with Laurel & Hardy accidentally becoming heroes by getting stuck in a runaway tank and wrapping up a whole brigade of German soldiers in yards of barbed wire. Unfortunately, this also wraps up the "war" portion of *Pack Up Your Troubles*. The remaining four reels are a variable blend of comedy and sentiment, as Laurel & Hardy search for the grandparents of a little war orphan (Jacquie Lyn).

The *Pack Up Your Troubles* formula was reversed in *Bonnie Scotland* (Roach/MGM 1935), shifting the military portion of the storyline to the final two-thirds of the film. The initial three reels focus on Stan & Ollie's escapades in Scotland, where the boys have journeyed so that Stan can claim his share of a family fortune. Somewhere around the 30-minute mark, the twosome inadvertently join His Majesty's Services, mistaking a recruiting office for a tailor's shop in a scene slightly reminiscent of Buster Keaton's *Doughboys*. Assigned to the "Third Battalion, Caledonia Highlanders" in the Northwest Province of India, Laurel & Hardy once again match half-wits with James Finlayson, cast as a Sergeant Major. And, once again, they become heroes by chance when with the help of a swarm of animated-cartoon bees (a gag lifted from *With Love and Hisses*) they put down a Hindu uprising. Though *Bonnie Scotland* was the team's biggest international moneymaker to date, the film tends to disappoint when seen today. Plunking Laurel & Hardy into a *Lives of a Bengal Lancer* setting never lives up to its full satiric potential (the result of radical re-editing after several previews), and far too much footage is wasted on an asinine romantic subplot. Even so, two of the "Army" routines rank among the team's best work: Stan & Ollie's impromptu Highland fling while cleaning up the parade grounds, and the legendary scene in which Stan, resolutely out of step during a forced march, somehow manages to communicate his incompetence to the rest of the regiment — and before long *everyone* is out of step.

Their third service feature was 1939's *The Flying Deuces*, produced by Boris Morros, released by RKO, and now available from every cheapjack DVD company in the known universe thanks to its public domain status. The film is a partial remake of Laurel & Hardy's 4-reel short *Beau Hunks* (Roach/MGM 1931), in which the boys join the Foreign Legion to forget Ollie's unfortunate love affair with "Jeanie-Weenie." Its title a play on the classic adventure yarn *Beau Geste*, *Beau Hunks* ends with Stan & Ollie defending a desert fort from a Riff rebellion, using tacks to incapacitate the barefoot insurgents. *Flying Deuces* likewise finds a heartbroken Ollie joining the Foreign Legion to get over his one-sided romance with cute French waitress Georgette (Jean Parker), dragging Stan along with him. This time out, "forgetting" becomes problematic indeed, inasmuch as their commanding officer (Reginald Gardiner), the man who suggested that the boys sign up with the Legion, turns out to be Georgette's husband. In emulation of both *Pack Up Your*

Troubles and *Bonnie Scotland*, *Flying Deuces* is highlighted by a scene in which rookies Stan and Ollie make a shambles of a marching drill. And while there is no native uprising on this occasion, *Deuces* comes to a rousing finale when Laurel & Hardy, condemned to the firing squad for setting the camp's laundry ablaze (another quote from *With Love and Hisses*), make their escape in an out-of-control airplane. Oh, and did we mention that James Finlayson is also in the film?

Laurel & Hardy's final expedition into the world of military humor, 1941's *Great Guns*, is covered along with all the other Abbott & Costello/*Buck Privates* rip-offs in **Chapter 4**.

Joe E. Brown

Most of the comedians who came to prominence in the early talkies were vaudeville veterans who relied upon jokes and wisecracks. Cavern-mouthed funster Joe E. Brown had an added advantage: Trained as a circus acrobat, he was one of the few major comedians of the 1930s who was equally as accomplished with visual humor as with dialogue—perhaps even more so. Brown's starring features for Warner Bros.-First National took full advantage of all his comic gifts, establishing a formula whereby Joe E. would talk himself into a ridiculous situation, then be forced to rely upon physical comedy—slapstick preferred—to worm his way out of trouble.

The first of Brown's two service comedies for Warners-First National, 1933's *Son of a Sailor*, was based on "The Gob," a comedy sketch written by Paul Girard Smith that the comedian had performed on Broadway in *The Greenwich Village Follies of 1923*. The sketch involved a brash young sailor who uses a pair of baby shoes to make time with several young ladies, weaving a different heartrending story about the origin of the shoes (a gift from his poor grey-haired grandma, a token of affection from a long-lost sweetheart, etc.) with each successive damsel. Brown wanted to add "The Gob" to his permanent repertoire, but when the play's producers wouldn't pay for the rights he quit *The Greenwich Village Follies* and purchased the sketch with his own money. In 1930, *The Gob* was filmed by Warner Bros. as a 2-reel "Vitaphone Variety," starring Hal Skelly as the title character; Joe E. Brown himself waited three more years to use the sketch as the foundation for the feature-length *Son of a Sailor* (originally filmed as *Son of a Gob*, which sounds more like a horror picture).

In a refreshing break from standard studio procedure, the film's first two reels were entirely location-shot on the U.S.S. *Saratoga*, with real sailors appearing as background players amongst such familiar character actors as George Chandler, Joe Sawyer, Jack Pennick and Gary Owen. Brown plays titular sailor's son "Handsome" Callahan (tantamount to calling a bald-headed man "Curly"), who when he isn't bragging about his expertise in all things nautical is boasting about his prowess with the ladies. His shipmates try to show Handsome up by arranging for him to fight the fleet's boxing champ, but by a fluke he manages to win the bout and a huge reserve of cash. Now more determined than ever to make Handsome look silly, the other sailors slip a pair of baby booties in his pocket just before he goes on shore leave. Upon discovering the booties, Handsome uses them as a means of breaking the ice with a procession of impressionable ingenues played by Noel Francis, Sheila Terry and Merna Kennedy, winning each of their hearts with three different pick-up lines explaining how the tiny shoes came into his possession. He then tries the same technique on the demurely delectable Helen (Jean Muir), who knows darn well that the booties don't belong to him, mainly because she'd given them as a present to her sailor boyfriend Duke (Johnny Mack Brown). Amused by our hero's guileless prevarications, Helen doesn't let on that she knows he's a fraud, smiling graciously when Handsome claims to be a personal friend of Admiral Farnsworth (Samuel S. Hinds)—who happens to be Helen's grandfather. While juggling a multitude of deceptions during a dinner party at Helen's home, Handsome catches the eye of a slinky baroness (Thelma Todd), who has reason to believe that he knows something about a remote-control aerial bombing device invented by Duke. The Baroness, you see, is a foreign spy in league with another party guest named Williams (Kenneth Harlan) who is dead set on stealing the invention for his own country. Slapstick and suspense collide head-on when Handsome, chasing after Williams, takes flight in a pilotless airplane controlled by Duke's device, then parachutes onto the deserted deck of the U.S.S. *Covington*, an obsolete Navy vessel slated to be bombed out of the ocean by the robot plane.

As can be gathered, the "money scene" in *Son of a Sailor* is the climactic demolition of the *Covington*, with Handsome not only escaping death by the hair of his chinny-chin-chin but also earning a promotion for ferreting out the spies—after serving some heavy brig time for going AWOL. For all that, the scene in the film which gets the biggest laughs today occurs early in the proceedings, when Handsome teaches a few lovemaking techniques to his girl-shy shipmate Gaga (wonderfully enacted by Frank McHugh, who drops out of the story *way* too soon). As Handsome plays the "boy" to Gaga's "girl," the other sailors laugh and hoot derisively, topping off their ridicule by handing Handsome a freshly-plucked pansy! Let's leave *Son of a Sailor* on this high note and ignore the post-production headaches wherein Joe E. Brown and his studio were sued for plagiarism by writer Edward A. Lynch, who claimed that the portions of the film that couldn't be traced back to "The Gob" were actually stolen from a screenplay of his own.

Brown's other military farce of the 1930s was also Broadway-derived. Opening November 26, 1929, at the Imperial Theater, *Sons O' Guns* was a musical comedy with songs by J. Fred Coots (best known for "Santa Claus Is Coming to Town"), lyrics by Arthur Swanstrom and Benny Davis, and libretto cowritten by the play's star Jack Donohue. A rose-colored backward glance at World War I, *Sons O' Guns* concerned a coddled playboy named Jimmy Canfield (Donohue) who reluctantly joins the Army, only to find that his former valet Hobson (William Frawley) is now his top

Recently arrived in France, soldier-by-accident Joe E. Brown is unexpectedly reunited with old flame Wini Shaw, while his new *amour* Joan Blondell looks askance. From *Sons O' Guns* (Warners, 1936).

sergeant. Suffering under a heap of "payback" from his onetime employee, Jimmy finds comfort in the arms of luscious French pastry Yvonne (Lily Damita). Falsely accused of being a German spy, Jimmy clears himself one beat ahead of the firing squad, winning Yvonne's admiration and love. Despite the ravages of the Depression, *Sons O' Guns* ran for 295 performances, the third most successful musical of the 1929–30 Broadway season and another feather in the cap of stage favorite Jack Donohue—who unfortunately died before Warner Bros. was able to commit the property to film in 1936. Luckily, Joe E. Brown was still under contract, hotter than ever thanks to the success of his 1935 baseball comedy *Alibi Ike*. Though dismissed by Brown biographer Wes D. Gehring as "minor but serviceable," and admittedly not as consistently amusing as *Son of a Sailor*, the film version of *Sons O' Guns* is one of the comedian's most lavishly mounted movie vehicles, and his last major release under the Warners banner.

As a means of showcasing the star's singing and dancing expertise, *Sons O' Guns* was rewritten so that hero Jimmy Canfield is a Broadway headliner, playing a soldier in a splashy patriotic stage revue titled "Men in Uniform." When America enters World War I, Jimmy does everything he can avoid conscription, cheerfully admitting he has neither the nerve nor the inclination to fight: "I'm just not mad at anybody." This is not to the liking of Jimmy's frosty fiancée Mary Harper (Beverly Roberts), whose Army-general father (Joseph King) refuses to consent to the marriage unless Jimmy signs up immediately. No sooner has this occurred than cabaret dancer Bernice (Wini Shaw) comes a-knocking at Jimmy's door with a breach of promise suit. In an effort to escape Bernice, Jimmy pretends to have joined the Army by marching in a military parade, still dressed in his stage uniform. Like Bob Hope in *Caught in the Draft* (see **Chapter 4**), Jimmy's phony enlistment turns out to be the real thing, and before long he is sweating and straining under the baleful eye of his top sergeant—and ex-valet—Hobson, played by British actor Eric Blore. Funny though William Frawley must have been as Hobson in the stage version of *Sons O' Guns*, Blore's casting works even better in the movie, the actor's droll line delivery enhancing every scene in which he alternately barks orders at his former boss and humbly apologizes for his effrontery.

Once Jimmy arrives in France, a third girl enters his life: Vivacious French barmaid Yvonne, played with an enchantingly awful Gallic accent by Joan Blondell. Unbeknownst to Yvonne, her stepfather Pierre (Robert Barrat) is an enemy spy who uses carrier pigeons to relay information to the Germans (shades of Syd Chaplin's *The Better 'Ole*, likewise a Warners release). Arrested by General Harper on a charge of being Pierre's accomplice, Jimmy breaks out of the stockade by pretending to be a British captain, complete with monocle and upper-crust accent. In this masquerade he is ordered behind enemy lines to wipe out a machine gun nest. Managing to lose his clothes during heavy bombardment, Jimmy quickly assumes another disguise, adopting a "diz muzz be der place" dialect and improvising a German uniform. This last deception evolves into an elongated parody of the Sergeant York legend (later filmed on the square by Warner Bros. with Gary Cooper in the lead), as Jimmy manages to persuade a trio of battle-weary German soldiers that the war is pointless. Before long, this pacifistic message has spread throughout an entire enemy regiment, with each and every soldier happily throwing down his weapons and following Jimmy back to the American lines! Convinced that Jimmy has single-handedly captured hundreds of Germans without firing a shot, crusty old General Harper graciously puts aside his original plan to execute our hero, plastering the boy's chest with medals instead of bullets. The trademarked Joe E. Brown "yell" closes the picture as Jimmy embraces Yvonne.

None of the original Broadway score is used in the film version of *Sons O' Guns*—not even the stage version's two biggest hits, "Why" and "Cross Your Fingers." Of the new songs written for the film by resident Warner Bros. tunesmiths Harry Warren and Al Dubin, the best is "On a Buck and a Quarter a Day," wonderfully performed as an eccentric song-and-dance routine by Joe E. Brown and Joan Blondell. Also well worth having is a mock Apache dance reminiscent of a similar highlight in Buster Keaton's *Doughboys*, with a mustachioed Brown tossing around his female partner (actually Frank Mitchell in drag) like a second-hand mop.

Though Joe E. Brown never again starred in a service comedy, he remained an active and enthusiastic contributor to military entertainment throughout World War II with his innumerable USO tours. The loud and loving laughter greeting his appearances undoubtedly provided great comfort to the aging comedian, whose son Don, an Army Air Force officer, had been killed in a 1942 training accident. Brown's indefatigable trouping throughout the war would earn him the Bronze Star, an honor given to only one other civilian, correspondent Ernie Pyle.

Bob Hope

An entertainer whose name has become inextricably linked with the American Armed Services by virtue of his tireless entertaining on behalf of military audiences throughout several wars, Bob Hope also made his fair share of service comedies during his four-decade film career. I haven't seen so much olive drab since Bing Crosby's face after he lost his putter, but I wanna tell ya....

Hope's earliest foray into service comedy occurred before he'd struck it big in feature films. While appearing on Broadway, Bob headlined five 2-reel comedies filmed at the Vitaphone studios in Brooklyn. The second of these, released in March 1935, was *Calling All Tars*. The fragmentary storyline has Bob and his pal Johnny Berkes (a cut-rate Jimmy Durante–type) donning sailor costumes in order to pick up girls, only to be nabbed by the Shore Patrol and forced to sail with the Fleet. After blowing up a ship's galley, the boys are stranded on a tropical island, bombarded by falling cocoanuts. Hope's dialogue in *Calling All Tars* consists mainly of asking Berkes to repeat everything he says, or repeating it for him; as historian Leonard Maltin has written, the film shows "a brash young comic ... who had a good sense of delivery, but no material to deliver." And though he gets top billing, Bob is barely in the climactic scene, as Johnny Berkes launches into a pantomime of ineptitude preparing an explosive meal.

Following his first feature *The Big Broadcast of 1938*, Hope served an apprenticeship as nominal leading man in a string of medium-budget Paramount comedies. In 1938's *Give Me a Sailor* he is billed below comedienne Martha Raye, who is cast as Letty Larkin, ugly-duckling sister of self-centered Nancy Larkin (Betty Grable). Nancy is the heartthrob of sailor Walter Brewster, played by British-born Jack Whiting, a gifted singer-composer who curiously made no impression at all in films. Hope plays Walter's brother Jim, also a sailor and also in love with Nancy. Jim persuades Letty to help him break up the romance between their respective siblings; Letty agrees, but only if Jim helps her land Walter. Once the story gets under way, Jim and Walter forsake Navy garb in favor of mufti (except for a climactic wedding scene), so it isn't necessary to dilate the rest of the plotline. We note in passing that the film's oddest moment occurs when Martha Raye and not Betty Grable wins a "beautiful legs" contest — but then, this *is* a Cinderella story, at least according to the Paramount publicity department. Though *Give Me a Sailor* is amiable enough, both Raye and Hope would be better served in the Preston Sturges-scripted *Never Say Die* (1939).

Finally moving into the top rank of motion picture stars with 1939's *The Cat and the Canary*— and simultaneously cementing the joke-a-second "courageous coward" character that became his stock in trade — Hope was immediately elevated to productions that would show him off to best advantage. When Paramount entered the army-comedy sweepstakes sparked by the peacetime conscription act of 1940, the studio selected Hope to star in 1941's *Caught in the Draft*, which because it was beaten to the theaters by Abbott & Costello's *Buck Privates* several months earlier is discussed in full in **Chapter 4.**

Were it not for the sake of topicality, Hope's 1943 effort *Let's Face It* wouldn't have been a military comedy at all. The property began life as *The Cradle Snatchers*, a play by Russell Medcraft and Norman Mitchell. In this popular domestic farce, a trio of middle-aged wives try to teach a lesson to their roving husbands by hiring three college boys as gigolos. *The Cradle Snatchers* opened on Broadway in 1926 with Edna May Oliver, Mary Boland, Gene Raymond, and a callow juvenile named Humphrey Bogart in the cast. In 1928 the play was adapted as a silent film by Fox Studios, directed by Howard Hawks and featuring Louise Fazenda, Arthur Lake, Franklin Pangborn and J. Farrell MacDonald. It was remade as the 1929 talkie *Why Leave Home?*, de-emphasizing the older cast members in favor of Fox's rising young romantic team of Nick Stuart and Sue Carol.

Flash-forward to October 29, 1941, at which time the peacetime draft had been in effect for some thirteen months. On this particular evening, the new Cole Porter musical *Let's Face It* opened at New York's Imperial Theater, settling in for a healthy run of 547 performances. Scripted by Dorothy and Herbert Fields, with lyrics by Porter, Sylvia Fine and Max Liebman, the musical was inspired by a newspaper article about civilian women doing their bit for Uncle Sam by entertaining soldiers in their homes—innocently and with no exchange of sexual favors, of course. In *Let's Face It*, three wives in their early 30s discover that their husbands have been somewhat less than faithful; to get even, the wives throw a party for Army recruits Jerry, Frankie and Eddie, paying them handsomely to pose as their lovers. Little of a prurient nature actually occurs, but there's hell to pay when the three husbands, their current paramours, and the soldiers' girlfriends all converge on the house at the same time. It didn't take a intelligence-gathering mission to determine that for all its up-to-date trappings, *Let's Face It* was simply the newest edition of *The Cradle Snatchers*. Among the stars of the Porter musical were Eve Arden, Nanette Fabray, Vivian Vance, and a brash young bundle of talent named Danny Kaye, who stopped the show each night with the tongue-twisting specialty number "Melody in 4F." (Also on the premises was Eve Arden's understudy, Carol Channing.)

Purchased by Paramount Pictures at a cost of $225,000 ($100,000 going to 20th Century–Fox to secure the picture rights of the original *Cradle Snatchers*), *Let's Face It* went before the cam-

G.I. Bob Hope wages a fierce battle to prevent Betty Hutton from stealing the scene in *Let's Face It* (Paramount, 1943).

eras after the musical closed on Broadway. Only two songs were retained from the original show, the others replaced with new compositions by Jule Styne and Sammy Cahn. Bob Hope was tapped for the Danny Kaye role, Army private Jerry Walker, though Kaye was seriously considered for a while. Another Paramount favorite, Betty Hutton, was cast in the expanded part of Jerry's fiancee Winnie Potter, played on stage by Mary Jane Walsh. Eve Arden repeated her Broadway role as neglected housewife Maggie Watson; the other two wives were played by ZaSu Pitts and Phyllis Povah, while Cully Richards and Dave Willock were seen as Jerry's Army buddies Frankie and Barney (originally Eddie), who at one point join Jerry for an intricate dance routine, advertised by the studio as Bob Hope's first-ever movie dancing scene.

The role of Jerry was extensively retailored to fit the established Hope personality. The comedian stamps the character as his own property in his very first appearance: Spotting a group of overweight women at a health farm, he quips, "How come they have so much when the butcher shop has so little?" Likewise introduced in this scene is Betty Hutton as Winnie, owner of the farm, who is leading the dieting damsels in a harsh reducing regimen. Having smuggled an assortment of candies and cakes from the Camp Arthur mess hall, draftee Jerry sneaks into the farm to sell his black-market goodies to the ravenous females — much to the annoyance of Winnie, who has placed her chubby charges on a strict calcium diet. Before long, we've established that hardworking Winnie is anxious to wed, but Jerry has always managed to avoid matrimony by pleading poverty.

As Jerry returns to camp, he makes the acquaintance of the three wives, who happen to be clients of Winnie. The ladies want to purchase the services of three young soldiers to make their wayward husbands jealous, but Jerry turns down their entreaties. Soon afterward, he crashes his jeep through the camp canteen wall, whereupon Sgt. Wiggins (Joe Sawyer) tells him he'd better pay for the damages OR ELSE. Not wishing to be "OR ELSE'd," Jerry accepts the wives' $300 offer and invites his pals Frankie and Barney to accompany him to Mrs. Watson's weekend party in Southhampton. He fakes a head injury so he can slip out of camp, then fabricates a tall tale for Winnie's benefit about a top-secret mission: "Men have been shot doing this kind of work," he mutters ominously. Therafter, the complications pile up like cordwood, at one point requiring Jerry to feign insanity as a result of his "injury" and to submit to Winnie's bizarre notions of first-aid treatment (including a tourniquet around the neck). As often happens in wartime farces, the plot is resolved by the abrupt arrival of German spies, whom Jerry manages to lure into captivity by holding a mirror in front of a submarine periscope.

For many years withheld from exhibition because the story rights had expired, *Let's Face It* is today available only in washed-out TV prints. Even in pristine form the film had a rather sparse look for an "A" production due to wartime budget cutbacks at Paramount. Planned for the film but abandoned before shooting was a sumptuous meal sequence at the Southhampton home of Mrs. Watson. The decision to modify this scene arose less from expense concerns than in the interest of public morale: audiences coping with food rationing might have resented the spectacle of rich movie stars enjoying steaks, sugar, champagne and other such luxuries.

Though Bob Hope is ideally suited to his role as a trouble-prone GI, his funniest scene has nothing to do with the Army. In a wicked lampoon of the 1942 Bette Davis picture *Now, Voyager*, Bob emulates the urbane romanticism of Paul Henreid by sharing a cigarette with a lady — only to be stuck with a mouthful of smoldering cancer sticks as more and more ladies stream into view. When all is said and done, however, *Let's Face It* is stolen hands down by the boisterous Betty Hutton, belting forth such rat-a-tat musical numbers as "Who Did? I Did! Yes I Did!" and "Let's Not Talk About Love" (which includes a lyric about "Paramount minus Bob Hope"!) While he was willing to share the spotlight with Martha Raye in his formative movie years, and though he was personally fond of Betty Hutton, by 1943 Hope had enough clout to make damn sure that never again would a leading lady get more laughs than he did.

Bob's next service comedy didn't come along until after the War. Originally titled *Military*

Policemen, Paramount's *Off Limits* (1953) stars Hope as Wally Hogan, manager and trainer of promising young boxer Bullet Bradley (Stanley Clements). After Bullet is drafted, Hogan's disreputable business partners Vic and Babe Breck (Marvin Miller, Richard Weil) strong-arm Wally into enlisting in the Army so he can keep an eye on "their boy." But when Bradley is declared unfit for service, Wally catches on that the Breck brothers have forced him into uniform so they can ace him out of his share of Bullet's championship purse. Meanwhile, pint-sized private Herbert Tuttle (Mickey Rooney, in a role originally intended for Alan Young) attaches himself to Hogan, hoping that Wally will train him to be a prizefighter. Wally isn't interested until he meets Herbert's shapely young aunt, nightclub singer Connie Curtis (Marilyn Maxwell)—who hates boxing and is dead set against her nephew pursuing a pugilistic career. Enamored of Connie, Wally promises to discourage Herbert, all the while secretly grooming the boy for an important interservice bout with Navy boxer Art Aragon (as himself), and a later bid for the lightweight championship against Bullet Bradley. As the main plot plays itself out, Wally and Herbert are dragooned into becoming military policemen by pompous training officer Karl Danzig (Eddie Mayehoff), a rules-are-rules fanatic who frowns upon such civilian pursuits as prizefighting. To make a long story short, Wally's former partners get their comeuppance when Herbert defeats Bullet in the ring with the help of instructions relayed by walkie-talkie. Wally wins Connie's hand in marriage, and the overbearing Danzig finds out there's more to life than the Army rulebook.

Off Limits was made during that awkward period in Hope's film career when the middle-aged comedian was straining to recapture the youthful zest of his 1940s vehicles. Only one of Hope's solo scenes truly evokes fond memories of his earlier efforts: Prodded by Connie to stand up to his crooked ex-partner Vic Breck, Wally (Bob) gleefully inflicts all manner of damage on what he assumes to be Breck's fancy new automobile—little imagining that he is actually demolishing a general's staff car.

In her second costarring assignment with Hope (the first was *The Lemon Drop Kid*), Marilyn Maxwell was savvy enough not to overstep her bounds and upstage Bob as Betty Hutton had done. As for the ebullient Mickey Rooney, his scenes with Hope are smoothly handled, neither comedian overtly trying to outshine the other. Though they were never offscreen buddies—and despite a potentially alienating incident when Mickey showed up late and hungover for an expensive location shoot in a crowded boxing arena—Hope and Rooney respected each other's talents and worked harmoniously together, most memorably in the breezy musical duet "Military Policemen," written by Jay Livingston and Ray Evans. It's possible that Bob and Mickey refrained from hogging one another's spotlight to form a united front against the film's premier scene-stealer Eddie Mayehoff, whose overripe portrayal of Karl Danzig exhibits all the restraint of Genghis Khan.

Off Limits did not exactly break any box-office records, nor were the critics supportive of Paramount's decision to team Bob Hope with Mickey Rooney. One jaundiced reviewer tipped his readers off to the surprise appearance of Bing Crosby, who shows up on a TV screen near the end of the picture. The reviewer noted that Crosby's unbilled cameos in Hope's films were well on their way to becoming as much a trademark as Alfred Hitchcock's celebrated walk-ons. Perhaps in response, *Off Limits* represented the last time this gimmick would be trotted out until Hope's final film, 1972's *Cancel My Reservation*.

We next find Bob in uniform in the Anglo-American coproduction *The Iron Petticoat* (MGM, 1956). At last playing a character closer to his own age (though not *that* much closer), Hope is seen as Captain Chuck Lockwood, an Air Force pilot stationed in England. Just before going on leave for a prestigious but passionless marriage to a wealthy heiress (Noelle Middleton), Chuck is handed a delicate assignment by superior officer Col. Tarbell (Alan Gifford). It seems that Captain Vinka Kovelenko (Katharine Hepburn—you heard that right, *Katharine Hepburn*), a world-famous Russian jet pilot, has fled her homeland after being passed over for promotion. Sensing a major propaganda coup for the American government, Tarbell orders Chuck to win the dogmatically Communistic Vinka over to capitalism by any means necessary. The military aspect of *Iron*

Petticoat is for the most part subordinate to screenwriter Ben Hecht's futile effort to recapture the charm and sophistication of the earlier West-meets-East romantic comedy *Ninotchka*. Towards the end of the film, Hope belatedly brings his character's Air Force background to the fore as he hijacks the plane that is transporting Vinka back to the USSR. Since Bob's character is more mature than earlier Hope incarnations, there is not a hint of incompetence; his flight skills are as sure-handed as if James Stewart or John Wayne were at the controls.

Like *Let's Face It, The Iron Petticoat* is rarely shown today because of entanglements involving distribution rights. Take our word for it, you're not missing anything, unless you're unable to die happy until you've witnessed Katharine Hepburn's worst-ever performance, bellowing her lines in a ridiculous Slavic accent. The film's most noteworthy aspect is the surprising rapport between Hope and Hepburn — all the more surprising considering the two stars detested each other. Nor did Hope see eye to eye with screenwriter Ben Hecht, who not only demanded that his name be taken off the credits but also savagely attacked the comedian in the trade papers.

Bad though *The Iron Petticoat* may be at times, it is a Palme D'Or candidate compared with Bob Hope's final service comedy. By the 1960s, Hope was involved in so many business interests that filmmaking was no longer a priority. As long as he could grind out a picture on a modest budget and be assured a decent box-office return, he was satisfied. Whether filmgoers who could remember the comedian's best work were satisfied by such dreck as *Boy, Did I Get a Wrong Number* and *Eight on the Lam* barely seemed to matter to him. In a 1968 interview, AP correspondent Hal Boyle asked the 65-year-old comedian, whose personal worth was estimated at $200 million, why he continued making movies when he certainly didn't need to. Hope responded by assuring Boyle that the work was fun and not at all difficult: "The only real labor is in having to get out of bed so early. After that, somebody just has to point you to the studio." Released by United Artists in 1968, *The Private Navy of Sergeant O'Farrell* suggests that Bob should either have stayed in bed or found somebody with a poorer sense of direction.

The film was partially financed by the NBC TV network through a subsidary called Naho, as part of a deal whereby NBC would get first-telecast rights, as if that was some sort of prize or something. Filmed in Puerto Rico but set on the fictional South Pacific atoll of Funapee, *The Private Navy of Sergeant O'Farrell* takes place in the final months of World War II. The title character (played by Hope, who may not be acting his age but certainly looks it) has been having a morale problem with his men ever since the sinking of a cargo boat carrying a huge shipment of beer — "Milwaukee's holy water," as O'Farrell describes the lost treasure in the first of the film's slightly distasteful laugh lines. (Later on he makes a quip about a Japanese sailor "leaking soy sauce." You get the idea.) In lieu of the brewskies, the Sergeant prevails upon Army Captain Prohaska (John Myhers) to ship a group of gorgeous American nurses to Funapee so the guys will know what they're fighting for. But the only nurse who shows up is frazzle-haired Nellie Krause, played by Hope's protegee Phyllis Diller in their third film together. Clearly Nellie isn't going to satisfy anyone's cravings, so O'Farrell begins an unauthorized search for the MIA beer with the help of Calvin Coolidge Ishimura, a Japanese-American who is AWOL from Tojo's Army (this demeaning role was played by Mako, who always chose his words very carefully when discussing the film in later years). Along the way O'Farrell commandeers an abandoned Japanese torpedo boat and rescues two damsels in distress: The sergeant's former fiancee Maria (Gina Lollobrigida, who like Hope was a bit long in tooth for her character) and her niece Gaby (Mylène Demongeot, in a role turned down by Jean Seberg of *Breathless* fame).

Several boring reels later, a Kamikaze plane crashes into the ocean near Funapee, causing thousands of beer cans, all prominently labeled Pabst Blue Ribbon, to float to the surface. (The cans rise when they're full and sink when they're empty. Don't ask.) After the beer is loaded onto the torpedo boat, O'Farrell goes off and captures a Japanese submarine. In the process he is lost at sea and presumed dead, leading to a ripoff of *No Time for Sergeants* (see **Chapter 8**) as our hero suddenly reappears in the middle of his own memorial service. O'Farrell marries Maria, Helen

Krause cracks one joke too many about her homeliness, and supporting players Jeffrey Hunter, Dick Sargent and Henry Wilcoxon begin pondering the wisdom of entering the acting profession.

Sadly, *The Private Navy of Sgt. O'Farrell* was the last film directed by Frank Tashlin, who had previously brought out the best of Bob Hope in the brilliant western spoof *Son of Paleface* (1952). His days as a darling of the *auteur* theorists long behind him, Tashlin only sporadically returns to his old form with such cartoonish gags as having an enemy sailor speak English with Japanese subtitles, and with a genial takeoff of the beach scene in *From Here to Eternity*, substituting Hope and Gina Lollobrigida for Burt Lancaster and Deborah Kerr. There's also a nightmare sequence in which costar Jeffrey Hunter envisions Phyllis Diller as Eve and Cleopatra, which is funny if you find Phyllis Diller funny. Some people don't.

Enough diehard Bob Hope fans still existed in 1968 to ensure a $2.5 million North American gross for *The Private Navy of Private O'Farrell*. The newspaper ads for the film declared, "War is Heck! Hic Hic Hooray!" Even *that* was funnier.

Danny Kaye

Though denied the opportunity to recreate his Broadway stage role in the film version of *Let's Face It*, multifaceted entertainer Danny Kaye could take heart in the fact that his first starring feature *Up in Arms* (1944) was like his Broadway show a musical comedy with a military theme. As a bonus, Danny was allowed to repeat his showstopper from *Let's Face It*, "Melody in 4-F," cowritten by his wife Sylvia Fine.

Promoted by producer Sam Goldwyn as Kaye's film debut — neatly sweeping under the rug Danny's previous work in such Educational Studios 2-reelers of the 1930s as *Dime a Dance* (in which he played a sailor) and *Getting an Eyeful*—*Up in Arms* is a reworking of Goldwyn's 1930 Eddie Cantor vehicle *Whoopee!*, which in turn was inspired by Owen Davis Sr. and E. J. Rath's 1923 play *The Nervous Wreck* (itself filmed in 1926, with the "other" Harrison Ford). Neither of the earlier versions was a service comedy, but *Up in Arms* (working title: *With Flying Colors*) was made at the height of World War II, so the original storyline about a sickly young man who goes West for his health would have to be revised and updated.

Kaye plays pill-popping hypochondriac Danny Weems, whose nurse Virginia Merrill (Dinah Shore) is secretly in love with him. But Danny has eyes only for another nurse, Mary Morgan (Constance Dowling) who in turn loves Danny's roommate Joe Nelson (Dana Andrews). When he receives his draft notice, Danny is terrified by the allergy risks of a trip overseas, but ends up donning khaki all the same. Joe is also conscripted and Virginia enlists as a WAC nurse, while Mary stows away on the troop ship in male drag to be near Joe. The rest of the film is a virtually plotless, catch-as-catch-can affair, with an overstocked barrel of comic and romantic complications. Finally Danny overcomes his imaginary illnesses long enough to single-handedly capture a group of Japanese soldiers.

Writing about Goldwyn's Eddie Cantor musicals of the 1930s, critic Howard Thompson encapsulated the whole batch in a single word: "Elephantine." The same is true of Goldwyn's Danny Kaye vehicles of the 1940s, which smothered the comedian with garish Technicolor photography, bloated production values and overarranged musical numbers spotlighting the thinly garbed "Goldwyn Girls." Poor Danny is seldom given a chance to act, or even develop a believable character in these films. To Goldwyn, all that mattered were Kaye's trademarked tongue-twisting wordplay, double-talk dialect routines and "git-gat-gittle" musical specialties; story and characterization be damned. All of which is a shame, because *Up in Arms* had real potential. Director Elliott Nugent, choreographer Danny Dare and art director Stewart Chaney clearly envisioned the film as a deliberately exaggerated send-up of the brassy, flag-waving wartime musicals that proliferated during this period. The sets and photography are impressionistic, almost Caligariesque in their forced-

3. First Line of Offense

perspective surrealism; even the "exteriors" on the Japanese-held island resemble an artificially foliated theme park. That this "only a movie, folks" ambience was not decided upon casually is evidenced in the dialogue. Watching a bunch of swimsuit-clad nurses sunbathing on the deck of a troop ship, sergeant Lyle Talbot comments to corporal Elisha Cook, Jr., "We never had anything like this in the last war." To which Cook replies, "Sergeant, we don't have anything like it in *this* war either!"

Elliott Nugent had intended to carry this aura of fantasy right up to the very last scene. In a 1969 interview with Leonard Maltin, the director recalled his planned finale for *Up in Arms*: "It had an ending which Don Hartman wrote, kind of an oddball thing which was going to be done by Disney, where the screen falls apart and roaches, or bugs of some kind eat up the film, and you see this happening ... Disney wanted I think $10,000 for this little bit of film, and I think they paid it and then it wasn't satisfactory. But I felt that the film should end with a number, and I had arranged toward the end a place where you could dissolve into a musical number. Finally it turned out I was right, but somebody was smarter than I was; they didn't make a new musical number — they reprised the dream sequence." As a result, the ending seems terribly abrupt, just as the rest of the film shows signs of being extensively re-edited before its release, forcing offscreen narrator Knox Manning to "explain" a few missing plot points. Despite all this, *Up in Arms* made a fortune at the box office, and also provided Danny Kaye with one of his all-time best patter routines, "The Lobby Number," a brilliant five-minute takeoff of the movie going experience in the 1940s.

Bypassing the early wartime scenes in 1954's *White Christmas*, the next time we find Kaye in uniform is in the 1961 Paramount release *On the Double.* No longer answerable to Sam Goldwyn,

Danny Kaye assumes a dual role in *On the Double* (Paramount, 1961). That's the fearless General Mackenzie-Smith on the left (with Gregory Walcott standing behind him), and the gormless Private Ernie Williams on the right (with Wilfred Hyde-White over Ernie's left shoulder).

Danny and Mrs. Kaye (who coproduced the film) exercised considerable control over this film, jettisoning anything (like gratuitous musical numbers or chorus lines) that might divert attention from the star. Also, Danny had proven himself an able actor and convincing romantic lead in the years since *Up in Arms*, in which he'd been obliged to make funny faces and noises rather than portray a genuine human being, and to relinquish nominal leading lady Constance Dowling to supporting player Dana Andrews. Finally, whereas *Up in Arms* was a haphazard hodgepodge in which the specialty numbers stuck out like sore thumbs, *On the Double* is sustained by a solid and credible plotline, building logically to a climactic fifteen-minute *tour de force* in which Kaye's character must assume a variety of disguises to stay alive.

Filmed in both Hollywood and London, *On the Double* was inspired by the true-life story of British actor M.E. Clifton-James, who during World War II was recruited to impersonate General Bernard Law Montgomery, to whom he bore a startling likeness. The strategy was to use Clifton-James to divert the Nazis and mislead them regarding the General's plans in the North African campaign. The story had already been filmed as *I Was Monty's Double* (1957), a surprisingly light-hearted take on a serious subject with M.E. Clifton-James playing both himself and "Monty." *On the Double* took an even more irreverent approach to the premise, with Danny Kaye stepping into the dual role of timid American Army private Ernie Williams (again a hypochondriac!) and his dashing, dauntless look-alike, British General Sir Lawrence Mackenzie-Smith, utilizing a new matte process enabling both Kayes to share the same screen without the slightest hint of trick photography.

While doing an imitation of the General for the amusement of his fellow GIs, Ernie is collared by British Intelligence operative Colonel Somerset (Wilfred Hyde-White, who also narrates the film) and "requested" to keep up the masquerade, the better to prevent a covey of Nazi spies from learning about the upcoming Normandy Invasion. When the real Mackenzie-Smith is reported killed, Ernie is forced to carry on the charade indefinitely. He must also contend with the various women within Mackenzie-Smith's orbit: The General's neglected wife Lady Margaret (Dana Wynter, who in one scene sheds her ladylike screen image by clobbering her costar with a cold salmon), his pulchritudinous mistress Bridget (Diana Dors, whose then-husband Richard Dawson plays a bit role as a sentry), and his dotty aunt Lady Vivian (Margaret Rutherford, in her first American film). Captured by the Nazis and bundled off to Berlin, Ernie makes his escape during an air raid by rapidly changing costumes and personalities, at one point posing as a Dietrich-like cabaret singer who regales "her" audience with a rendition of "Cocktails for *Zwei*." Ernie even disguises himself as Adolf Hitler, successfully pulling off the ruse until he comes face to face with the genuine Fuhrer — played as ever by Bobby Watson, moviedom's foremost Hitler imitator.

Directed and co-written by Danny Kaye's frequent collaborator Mel Shavelson, who always enjoyed working with the capricious entertainer (not everyone did), *On the Double* is today regarded as Kaye's last truly good film. Critics of the early 1960s, however, had become a bit blasé regarding the comedian's fondness for dual roles, vis-à-vis his earlier *Wonder Man* (1945) and *On the Riviera* (1951). *The New York Times* dourly described *On the Double* as "a melancholy dive into self-plagiarism"; *Life* magazine was more positive but equally dismissive, noting, "Connoisseurs of Kaye comedy will not rate this as his best, but it is satisfying all the same."

Dean Martin and Jerry Lewis

Discounting his later films *Way Way Out* (1966), in which he briefly dons a Naval uniform as an astronaut, and *Which Way to the Front?* (1969), which casts him as a millionaire 4F who organizes a civilian commando group during World War II, Jerry Lewis has starred in five military farces—all released within the same decade, three of them while Jerry was still teamed with Dean Martin.

3. First Line of Offense

Following their movie debut as supporting players in *My Friend Irma* (1949), Martin & Lewis—then the hottest act in show business—struck a deal with their Paramount producer Hal Wallis, allowing them to appear in at least one "outside" project per year. As a result, the team's second feature (albeit the third to be released) was *At War with the Army*, distributed by Paramount and independently produced by Dean and Jerry's own York Productions in association with former playwright and studio executive Fred Finklehoffe. In keeping with the Abbott & Costello tradition, it was decided to "officially" launch the team's movie career with a service comedy. Beyond the fact that he had co-authored the popular military comedy *Brother Rat* (see **Chapter 13**), it's easy to see what attracted Fred Finklehoffe to *At War with the Army*: A Yale Law School graduate, he was undoubtedly impressed that the property was based on a Broadway play written by a Yale drama student, and featuring several stalwart Yalies in the original cast.

Opening March 8, 1949, at the Booth Theater and running a respectable 151 performances, the original *At War with the Army* was a three-act farce by James B. Allardice, better known for his long association with Alfred Hitchcock (it was Allardice who scripted the wickedly amusing introductory comments for Hitch's TV anthology). All the action takes place in the company orderly room of an Army training camp, somewhere in the Kentucky boonies. Despite the play's title and its late–1944 setting, the only war onstage is the battle of nerves between a bunch of khaki-clad "desk jockeys" and their stuffed-shirt superiors. The plot is a plethora of complications, convolutions and misunderstandings, all solved by a few words of explanation in the final scene. Doors swing open and slam shut with machine-gun precision. Characters suddenly pop in to declare themselves in hilarious fashion, then just as suddenly pop out. People fall on their backsides and props malfunction spectacularly on cue. Comic catchphrases abound, notably a prickly drill sergeant's petulant "That don't make no difference!" And running gags are rampant, ranging from the lazy non-coms' frantic efforts to look busy whenever the Colonel strides past the office, to the periodic drop-ins by an officer's wife, the only person in camp who really knows what the upper-echelon Brass is planning—simply because she's been trading gossip with the *other* officer's wives.

There are a few satirical swipes at military bureaucracy and doublespeak, the boredom of being stuck in the sticks while other boys are out fighting World War II, the blatant black-marketeering of enterprising supply sergeants, and the promiscuous mating habits of Our Men in Uniform. But for the most part the play aspires to nothing more than, in the words of *Time* magazine, "wooing the funnybone via Memory Lane, using every last boys-will-be-boisterous trick of farce." Directed with razor-sharp timing by Ezra Stone, *At War With the Army* was just the sort of light entertainment demanded by postwar audiences: Fast, funny, and forgettable.

But how could Martin & Lewis fit into all this? For one thing, *Army* is not a star vehicle but an ensemble piece, "all of whose parts are of nearly equal importance," to quote the New York *Herald Tribune*. For another, none of the characters could be described as suitable for Dean Martin and Jerry Lewis. Well, practically none. James Allardice's original stage notes provide descriptions for three of the principals:

1st Sergeant Robert Johnson, portrayed on Broadway by Gary Merrill. Age approximately 25, "better than average intelligence and ... a sense of humor. In dealing with his men he is frequently like the typical old army 1st sergeant, probably acting in unconscious imitation of one under whom he has served. Johnson resents the army's lack of respect for his wishes to the extent that he believes 'they' are always out to frustrate him." Johnson is ticked off over his superiors' refusal to ship him overseas; he is also a world-class womanizer who spends most of the play trying to arrange a tryst with his current sweetie Helen, all the while avoiding his pregnant ex-girlfriend Millie.

PFC Alvin Hawkins, a "gangling" lad of about 19, originally played by William Lanteau. "He is a simple Kentucky hillbilly with little formal education ... Hawkins is mystified by the complexity of the army and never quite understands it." PFC Hawkins is forever pleading for a three-day pass to visit his expectant wife, but his entreaties earn him nothing more than a round of painful tetanus shots.

The Lost Private, a role created on stage by future Pulitzer-winning playwright Tad Mosel (*All the Way Home*). A brand-new draftee, the Lost Private has stumbled into the wrong army camp. No longer a civilian and not yet a soldier, he is doomed to wander aimlessly through "the maze of organizations and red tape." Though he never speaks a word, the Lost Private is provided with plenty of eloquent pantomime routines.

With a bit of rewriting and a change of ethnicity, 1st Sgt. Robert Johnson was transformed into 1st Sgt. Vic Puccinelli, a serviceable role for the smooth, seductive Dean Martin. Likewise, PFC Alvin Hawkins was stripped of his hayseed veneer, retooled as a displaced New Jerseyite, and redubbed PFC Alvin Corwin, a better fit for the nerdish personality of Jerry Lewis. Since in the original play Alvin Hawkins is a much smaller role than Sgt. Johnson, Alvin was combined with the character of the Lost Private, allowing Jerry to indulge in the gawky physical *shtick* he did so well.

In the play, the Sergeant and the Private are in no way, shape or form a "team." Outside of sharing a couple of brief dialogue exchanges, the two characters appear together only in a climactic scene in which their Captain is misled to believe that the Private, and not the Sergeant, is the father of Millie's baby. To establish a bond between the characters, screenwriters James Allardice and Fred Finklehoffe created a backstory establishing that Vic and Alvin had grown up together and were a songwriting team in civilian life. This device permits the downtrodden Alvin to bemoan the fact that his former best buddy Vic now bullies and humiliates him at every opportunity. (Dean Martin is here far nastier to his partner than in any subsequent film, perilously close to the comic villainy of Bud Abbott.) Also, the songwriting angle logically accommodates the tunes written for the film by Mack David and Jay Livingston.

The screen version of *At War With Army* all too obviously betrays its stage origins. At least 85 percent of the film take place in a dingy, cluttered orderly room, with an inordinate amount of time spent on characters other than Martin & Lewis. The only scenes taking place outside the main set are those that were added to showcase the stars: The opening musical number "Beans," with K.P. Jerry rhythmically dishing out a most unappetizing repast in the mess hall; a romantic duet in a recording booth between Dino and Polly Bergen (making her second screen appearance in the role of Helen); a short burst of slapstick with Jerry on the obstacle course; and an extended barroom routine in which an AWOL Jerry, in grotesque Marlene Dietrich drag, attempts to distract his drunken drill sergeant (Mike Kellin, repeating his Broadway role) with a sultry torch song. The screenwriters also developed a subplot involving the rehearsals for a camp variety show, with Martin & Lewis' longtime nightclub bandleader Dick Stabile wielding his baton in the role of Private Pokey. The rehearsal scenes allow Dean and Jerry to perform a tantalizingly brief sampling of their stage act, including an affectionate musical spoof of the 1944 film *Going My Way* with the boys impersonating Bing Crosby and Barry Fitzgerald.

At War with the Army's comic high point is the payoff to a running gag. Throughout the film, several of the characters feed nickels into a temperamental Coca Cola machine, which greedily gobbles up the money but stubbornly refuses to surrender any bottles. Somewhere around Reel Seven, an exhausted Alvin Corwin staggers into the orderly room after a grueling training session. Accidentally bumping into the Coke machine, Alvin unexpectedly hits the jackpot, as dozens of pop bottles—and one milk bottle—tumble into his lap and onto the floor. This delightful vignette is so "typical" a Jerry Lewis routine that one might conclude it was specifically written for the comedian. Not so: the Coke-machine gag, replete with renegade milk bottle, appears in the original Broadway play, and in fact was singled out as the hit of the show by such publications as *Billboard* and *Life* magazine. The stage version also includes a punchline that isn't in the film: as the wide-eyed Lost Private gathers up his bounty of bottles, the machine suddenly belches forth all the nickels that had previously been "donated" by the rest of the troops.

Though a financial success upon its national release in January 1951—and thanks to its Public Domain status, Martin & Lewis' most easily accessible film today—*At War With the Army* is a somewhat unsatisfying effort, less a vehicle for Dean and Jerry than a film in which Dean and Jerry happen to appear. This cannot be said of the team's next service comedy, 1952's *Sailor Beware* (originally titled *At Sea With the Navy*), which is so dominated by Martin & Lewis' personalities that the plot proper doesn't get under way until half an hour into the picture.

Sailor Beware is based on the 1933 Broadway comedy of the same name, discussed in detail in **Chapter 6**. The play was initially considered so raunchy that the Hays Office forbade the use of the original title for the first film version, which was shipped out as *Lady Be Careful* in 1936. By the time Martin & Lewis got their hands on *Sailor Beware*, the censors had relaxed their ban on the title, providing that the third filmization of the Kenyon Nicholson-Charles Robinson stage piece was nothing more than good, wholesome fun. This version was scripted by James Allardice (who'd been hired when the film was originally slated as an immediate sequel to *At War with the Army*) and seasoned comedy writer Martin Rackin, from an adaptation by veteran 2-reeler gagman Ellwood Ullman and with additional dialogue by longtime Abbott & Costello jokemeister John Grant. The presence of the two last-named gentlemen may explain why the plot takes a back seat to the comedy throughout — especially the visual comedy.

The dual-hero dichotomy established for *Lady Be Careful,* wherein the part of the protagonist was divided between costars Lew Ayres and Buster Crabbe, is retained for this version. Martin plays nightclub singer/chick magnet Al Crowthers, while Lewis plays Melvin Jones, who is allergic to girls—or rather, the cosmetics worn by girls. We meet both characters at a Naval induction center, where Al is bidding a passionate farewell to his latest conquest (played *sans* screen credit by Betty Hutton as an inside reference to her leading role in *The Fleet's In*, the 1942 musical version of *Sailor Beware*), mournfully telling her that marriage is out of the question because he's going off to sea for four years— secure in the knowledge that the Navy has rejected him on medical grounds several times before. Of course, *this* time he's accepted, but not before making an enemy of irascible CPO Lardoski (Robert Strauss). Meanwhile, Melvin is so anxious to sign up that he manages to get on the wrong side of a surly Chief Bosun's Mate (Donald MacBride), who to exact revenge on Melvin sees to it that the poor jerk is immediately processed no matter what his physical shortcomings—leading to an overlong but hilarious string of "induction" and "examination" jokes, and also Melvin's meeting with pretty Navy nurse Hilda Jones (Marion Marshall), who wears no cosmetics and thus doesn't impel the poor boy to break out in sneezes.

While attending a TV broadcast where Al is singing, Melvin is by a fluke selected as "Mr. Temptation" in a contest sponsored by a lipstick company, which offers a passel of big prizes to the lucky girl who kisses our hero. As a result, Melvin is mobbed by scores of squealing young ladies, earning him a reputation as the Don Juan of the Pacific Fleet. Al and his shipmates place a wager with CPO Lardoski that Melvin will be able to melt the "Miss Deep Freeze" of Pearl Harbor, nightclub thrush Corinne Calvet — played, in a master stroke of casting, by Corinne Calvet. Once in Hawaii, Lardoski pulls out every dirty trick in the book to keep Melvin and Corinne apart, but in the end the wager is won, Melvin is reunited with Hilda, and lucky Al winds up with Corinne.

Though Paramount's publicity made no mention of *Sailor Beware*'s source material, reviewers with long memories readily recognized it as the latest — and cleanest —version of the notorious 1933 play. In a reversal of the *At War with the Army* situation, the plot of *Sailor Beware* is virtually an afterthought; what little remains of the original play is merely a backdrop for an endless parade of sight gags, one-liners, comedy setpieces and musical numbers. And thanks to the input of Paramount producer Hal Wallis, *Sailor Beware* is a far more lavish production than the somewhat seedy-looking *At War with the Army*, with extensive location filming at San Diego harbor, the Long Beach Naval Station, and the submarine U.S.S. *Bashaw*.

Many aficionados regard *Sailor Beware* as the best of the early Martin & Lewis vehicles, and certainly the duo's routines are well above average, capped by a superb boxing sequence (in which — all together now!— James Dean appears in a bit part). Though Dean and Jerry were fairly evenly matched in *At War with the Army*, Jerry is the dominant force in *Sailor Beware* as he remains hopelessly out of synch with hundreds of genuine sailors during close-order calisthenics, scuttles a rowboat in a training operation, impersonates an oriental rickshaw driver and a Samoan knife dancer, and in the film's funniest scene, goes into full panic mode when he's stranded on the deck of a submerging submarine.

Perhaps significantly, this was the first Jerry Lewis film to grab the attention of the French new-wave critics, who apparently regarded Jerry as the apotheosis of a "typical" postwar American. Here are some musings from a 1952 review by François Truffaut: "Jerry Lewis, the new comedian, puts on the face of an American *avant-gardiste*, very effeminate, with a short hairdo and bangs. It goes without saying that he is also overpowered by all the known signs of degeneracy: a fat chin, thick lips, and the hint of a goiter. …At the end, in accordance with the axiom 'heal bad with bad,' he becomes normal, like everyone else, like you and me! … The film may give back some confidence to American—and other—spectators who are deprived of physical attractiveness by nature. Therein lies the objective of this new comic strategy.…"

Despite the emphasis on Jerry, Dean Martin is permitted a few pleasant musical interludes, notably a well-edited production number titled "The Sailor's Polka." And during the Hawaiian nightclub finale, Dino is given ample opportunity to shine as he joins Jerry for a song-and-dance duet, backed up by the ineluctable Dick Stabile and his orchestra.

Carefully adhering to the tried-and-true Abbott & Costello formula (see **Chapter 4**), Martin & Lewis moved from land and sea to the air in their third service comedy *Jumping Jacks* (Paramount, 1952). Dean and Jerry adhered to their own formula as well, with Jerry as focal character and plot motivator, and Dean along for the ride to romance the leading lady and warble the latest batch of Mack David–Jay Livingston tunes. Following the precedent of *Sailor Beware*, a goodly portion of *Jumping Jacks* was lensed on location at the Airborne Department of the Infantry School at Fort Benning, Georgia, where the 249-foot parachute drop towers seen in the film (modeled after a similar structure at the 1939 World's Fair) remain standing to this day. Finally, Robert Strauss reprises his *Sailor Beware* role as a tough topkick, here named Sgt. McCluskey. The major differences between *Jumping Jacks* and its two predecessors are the choice of director, with Norman Taurog replacing Hal Walker, and the fact that the film is not based on a stage play.

Which is *not* to say that the screenplay was originally conceived with Martin & Lewis in mind. Written in 1943 by Fred Rinaldo and Robert Lees (whose previous credits included several Abbott & Costello vehicles) from a story by Brian Marlow, the script, initially titled *Ready, Willing, and Four F*, was intended as a vehicle for either Bob Hope or Danny Kaye, both of whom turned it down. Producer Hal Wallis purchased the still-unfilmed script in 1952, updated the story from World War II to the postwar era, and divided the leading role between Martin and Lewis.

Jerry plays nightclub comic Hap Smith, who'd been teamed with singer Chick Allen (Dean) until Chick joined the Infantry. Hap is now performing a double act with vocalist Betsy Carter (Mona Freeman), highlighted by a specialty number requiring him to wear an Army uniform. On the verge of landing a spot in a Broadway musical, Hap receives a telegram from Chick, instructing him to go to Fort Belding for what is described as a secret mission. Upon arrival, he discovers that Chick, a corporal in the paratrooper-training program, needs Hap's help in staging a camp variety show, one that will hopefully convince a humorless general (Ray Teal) that "soldier shows" are good for morale. Thus, it's necessary for Hap to retain his prop uniform and pretend to be a real soldier for the duration of the show. You guessed it: Hap is mistaken for a genuine private and whisked off to paratrooper school along with Chick. To avoid arrest for impersonating a soldier, Hap must assume the guise of Pvt. "Dogface" Dolan (Richard Erdman), who in turn must remain in hiding so that eagle-eyed Sgt. McCluskey won't catch on. No matter how often Hap tries to escape the training school, Chick and his buddies conspire to keep him there, at least until their show, which is now touring the bases on orders from the General, has played its final performance. The situation forces Chick to cover for Hap during basic training by taking the blame for the

3. First Line of Offense 71

Dean Martin and Jerry Lewis in the third of their military comedies, *Jumping Jacks* (Paramount, 1952).

phony private's blunders and passing off his own accomplishments as Hap's—so naturally, McCluskey is convinced that Hap is a model soldier and Chick is a hopeless foul-up.

An examination of *Jumping Jacks* indicates how the film could easily have been a wartime comedy as originally intended, rather than a peacetime farce. The elaborate wargames sequence in which the terrified Hap becomes a hero in spite of himself might just as well have taken place during a genuine combat situation. Similarly, when the real Dogface Dolan is assumed to be an impostor and accused of being a Communist spy, the situation would have been equally ridiculous had the interrogators mistaken poor Dogface for a Nazi agent. Too, one can envision first-choice stars Bob Hope or Danny Kaye going through the same paces as Martin & Lewis, especially in the screamingly funny dining-car scene where Hap and Chick hide Dogface under a table and attempt to sneak him a sandwich without arousing the suspicions of Sgt. McCluskey. And thanks to the input of original scripters Fred Rinaldo and Robert Lees, there's a lot of Abbott & Costello in the climax, wherein Hap finds himself entangled in Chick's parachute as the two troopers rapidly descend to Earth. Unlike *Sailor Beware*, which is carefully geared to the unique talents of Martin & Lewis, *Jumping Jacks* would have been just as effective with any other comedians in the lead. Though inspired by an old play and boasting some *very* old jokes (including the "human sieve" gag as Jerry springs several leaks after a barrage of hypodermic needles), *Sailor Beware* comes off as a dish served piping hot; *Jumping Jacks* is for the most part a plate of stale leftovers.

It was also the last of the Martin & Lewis military comedies, though the team would continue turning out top-grossing films for Paramount until their highly publicized breakup in late 1956. At that time, Hal Wallis optimistically announced that Dean and Jerry would somehow reconcile long enough to complete two scheduled Paramount films, *The Delicate Delinquent* and *The Sad Sack*. But the split was irrevocable, forcing Wallis to revise both films as solo Jerry Lewis vehicles, with Darren McGavin taking Dean's part in *Delinquent*, and David Wayne handling the straightman duties in *Sad Sack*.

Contrary to popular belief, the designation "Sad Sack" (as in "sad sack of shit") did not originate with the comic strip created in May of 1942 by Sgt. George Baker for the weekly army magazine *Yank*. The phrase had been in popular usage as far back as World War I, describing any doughboy who was born with two strikes against him and thus unable to conform to Army life. Prior to Baker, *The Sad Sack* was used as the American title of the 1928 French film *Tire au Flanc*, directed by Jean Renoir, in which a physically awkward poet and his resourceful valet find their social positions reversed upon joining the Army. Highlights of *Tire au Flanc* include a chaotic drill scene, with the poet and his fellow rookies—Sad Sacks all—unable to see where they're going with their gas masks on.

As envisioned by ex–Disney artist George Baker, the Sad Sack (no other name given him) was a disheveled, basset-faced, tuber-nosed American Army private who just plain couldn't win for losing. In such pantomimic misadventures as "The Physical" and "Orders," the Sack was forever at the mercy of bullying superiors, soulless military bureaucracy, and his own naïvete. "The underlying story of the Sad Sack," explained Baker, "was his struggle with the army in which I tried to symbolize the sum total of the difficulties and frustrations of all enlisted men." A few of Baker's *Yank* pages also appealed to the average enlistee's love of ribald humor. Youngsters who grew up reading Harvey Publications' sanitized *Sad Sack* comic books of the 1950s, 60s and 70s might get quite a jolt from the character's wartime exploits, such as the episode in which, after being scared witless by an anti–VD training film, the Sack refuses to shake hands with a girl until he slips on a rubber glove.

Like *Jumping Jacks*, the film version of *The Sad Sack* was at first slated to star anybody *but* Jerry Lewis. In 1951, Lippert Studios entered into negotiations with George Baker for a series of *Sad Sack* B–pictures starring Mickey Rooney, not unlike Hal Roach's "Sgt. Doubleday" films of the 1940s (see **Chapter 5**). Lippert was outbid by Paramount, who purchased the film rights as a vehicle for Alan Young. The property then passed to producer Hal Wallis, who hoped to use the Baker material for a Martin & Lewis picture. Newly shorn of his partner and not keen on starring in a film in which the romantic subplot would be handled by a supporting player, Lewis agreed to make *Sad Sack* and one additional film merely to finish off his contract with Wallis, whom the comedian had grown to dislike. This initial reluctance may explain why Jerry's performance in *Sad Sack* is downright lackluster at times.

Released in November 1957, the film, scripted by Edmund Beloin and Nate Monaster, uses the title of the George Baker comic strip and the "misfit" aspect of the character—and nothing else. Lewis plays Pvt. Meredith Bixby, who has spent a record seventeen months in basic training. Bixby isn't really stupid; far from it. He is blessed with a photographic memory enabling him to recite obscure rules and regulations down to the page, paragraph and sentence; he is an expert in all manner of self-defense, especially judo; he is a master of several languages, including French and Arabic; and he is one of the few men in the Army capable of assembling the new, top-secret R2 rapid fire rocket. Problem is, Bixby is catastrophically clumsy and careless; even before the film begins, he has "distinguished" himself by losing a tank and blowing up a civilian truck. Small wonder that Bixby becomes a test case for Army psychiatrist Major Shelton, who happens to be an attractive WAC (played by Phyllis Kirk). Convinced that even a "Sad Sack" like Bixby would make a good soldier if given proper guidance, Shelton asks Cpl. Larry Dolan (David Wayne) to take Bixby under his wing and help him complete training. A shameless schemer and habitual goof-off, Dolan agrees to mentor Bixby for two reasons: He and his cohort Pvt. Stan Wensalawsky (Joe Mantell) can theoretically use Bixby as a pigeon to take the blame for their own insubordinations; and frankly, Dolan has gone ga-ga over the shapely Shelton.

The disjointed storyline moves along fitfully until, for no other reason than there is extra footage to go, Bixby, Dolan and Wensalawsky are transferred to Morocco, where their unit is assigned to investigate the theft of some valuable Army munitions. Stumbling into the thieves' hideout, Bixby is spared a horrible death when the villains find out that he is capable of piecing together the R2 rocket (remember?). Duped into believing he's been sworn into the Foreign Legion secret service, Bixby is spirited away to the desert, while Dolan and Wensalawsky race to the rescue. Wackiness ensues, as wackiness is wont to do, and by film's end Pvt. Meredith Bixby has become a decorated hero through a combination of courage, fortitude and dumb luck.

Whenever he granted an interview, *Sad Sack* director George Marshall would proudly proclaim that his career stretched all the way back to 1912. Some of the comedy material in the film stretches back even farther. En route to camp by train, Bixby accidentally pulls the emergency brake. Ordered to move a dump truck, Bixby grabs the wrong lever and deposits a ton of gravel on a grouchy sergeant. Unwittingly sparking a barroom brawl, Bixby is the only participant to emerge unscathed. Returning to the base in the dead of night, Bixby inadvertently sneaks into the WAC's quarters. And when assigned to the rifle range, Bixby completely misses the target and—you're way ahead of us—shoots down a duck. It's not that this material is never funny, simply that, as in the case of *Jumping Jacks*, it would have been just as funny in the hands of a Mickey Rooney or an Alan Young. Not only does *The Sad Sack* forsake the special qualities that endeared the George Baker comic strip to millions of servicemen; the film also robs Jerry Lewis of the very uniqueness that made him a star.

Nor is Lewis the only actor ill served in *Sad Sack* (and let's not dwell on Jerry's rendition of the title song, co-written by no less than Burt Bacharach in the vain hope of duplicating Lewis' previous success with his hit single "Rock-a-Bye Your Baby"). David Wayne and Phyllis Kirk seem far too intelligent to be mouthing the banalities in the romantic scenes originally intended for Dean Martin and whichever starlet Hal Wallis was promoting at the time. In a stock performance as a tough sergeant, Gene Evans exhibits none of the brilliance of his even tougher sergeant in Samuel Fuller's *The Steel Helmet* (1951). And the magnificent Liliane Montevecchi, who later starred in such Broadway musicals as *Grand Hotel* and *Nine*, is totally wasted as a slinky cabaret chanteuse. Only Peter Lorre, who doesn't show up until the film is practically over, transcends the mediocrity with his subversively self-mocking portrayal of a knife-wielding Arab ("Pleeeease, can I kill him *now*?").

For all its faults, *The Sad Sack* posted a tidy profit for Paramount, a fact taken into consideration when Hal Wallis made his peace with Jerry Lewis and signed the actor to a better contract. Determined to exploit the potential of "Jerry in Uniform" to the utmost, Wallis came up with one of the comedian's best-ever vehicles, 1959's *Don't Give Up the Ship*.

Amazingly, this fanciful farce is based on a true story. While serving as a supply officer in the Army film division at Fort Roach in Culver City, California, during World War II, Hollywood screenwriter Edward Anhalt signed a requisition for a captured German Messerschmitt, to be used as a prop in a training film. Over a decade later, Anhalt was approached by a Military Intelligence agent and informed that he owed the government $175,000 for the now-missing Messerschmitt. The writer spared himself a lot of grief when he located the "lost" fighter plane, which was serving as a mock-up on the MGM backlot. This anecdote quickly grew into a Hollywood legend, getting better and more outlandish with each retelling.

TV writer Ellis Kadison built upon the story for a half-hour episode of NBC's *Alcoa Theater*. Telecast December 2, 1957, "Souvenir" starred Jack Lemmon as Ed King, an ex–Navy officer turned college professor who is forced to account for a missing destroyer escort that he'd commanded at the end of the War. Joan Marshall—who as "Jean Arless" went on to play the androgynous murderer in William Castle's *Homicidal* (1961)—costarred as Navy investigator Ensign Rita Benson, and Dick Wessel was seen as Ed King's former Bosun's Mate Cedric Wychinski. Ellis Kadison is given story credit for the subsequent film version of "Souvenir," retitled *Don't Give Up the Ship*, while scriptwriters Herbert Baker, Henry Garson and Edmund Beloin (a carryover from *The Sad Sack*) were responsible for fine-tuning the material to fit the talents of Jerry Lewis. The protagonist "Ed King" becomes "John Paul Steckler VII," no longer a professor but a Navy lieutenant, the last in a long and not-so-illustrious line of seafaring men. It need hardly be added that Lewis is assigned this role.

Congressman Mandeville (Gale Gordon), an anti-military blowhard, holds up a $4 billion appropriation until the Navy can explain the disappearance of the U.S.S. *Kornblatt*, a 306-foot destroyer escort that was last commanded by Lt. Steckler just after V-J day. The fittingly yclept Admiral Bludd (Robert Middleton) snatches the nonplussed Steckler away from his honeymoon with new bride Prudence (Diana Spencer) and gives the poor schnook ten days to locate the *Kornblatt* or face a court martial. Assigned to keep tabs on Steckler is curvaceous Ensign Rita Benson (Dina Merrill), whose presence Steckler has a heap of trouble explaining to the increasingly impatient Prudence. A flashback to 1945 reveals that junior officer Steckler had been placed in charge of the *Kornblatt* when all the other officers were mustered out and sent home. With the help of Bosun's Mate Stan Wychinski (Mickey Shaughnessy), the greenhorn Steckler managed to keep the *Kornblatt* from smashing into another destroyer, but not from beaching on a reef surrounding an uncharted island. While exploring the island, Steckler dropped out of sight and was assumed to be dead, but in fact had been captured by a group of Japanese sailors who refused to believe that the War was over. Barely escaping a firing squad, Steckler made his way to the spot where the Kornblatt had docked, only to find that the ship had completely vanished. Back in the present, Steckler and Ensign Benson track down Wychinski, the one man who might know the ultimate fate of the *Kornblatt*. Unfortunately Wychinski is now a professional wrestler, whose memory evaporates whenever he gets struck on the head. The former Bosun's Mate recovers long enough to guide Steckler to the location where the *Kornblatt* had been sunk during Naval target practice. Steckler not only finds the missing destroyer, saves his career and returns to the loving arms of Prudence, but in a supremely satisfying plot twist he deflates Congressman Mandeville and wangles an extra billion bucks out of the old windbag.

Under the direction of Norman Taurog, Jerry Lewis delivers what is arguably his finest and most mature performance to date. The central situation permits the comedian to temporarily park his "crazy kid" characterization and act his real age (33), while the innumerable plot convolutions provide both motive and opportunity for his periodic lapses into the "Niiiice lady DON'T hit!" looniness that his fans adore. Also, while the fact-based story retains its basic realism — enhanced by extensive location shooting on an actual destroyer escort, the U.S.S. *Vanmen*— the scripters are able to insert a bit of Lewis' patented surrealism into the proceedings, notably an underwater sequence in which the scuba-diving Steckler envisions mermaids while experiencing "rapture," without doing any harm to the overall credibility. And unlike the hit-or-miss *Sad Sack,* each and every scene in *Don't Give Up the Ship* propels the plot forward while simultaneously delivering a generous serving of laughs. This formula wouldn't have been appropriate for *every* Jerry Lewis film (think *The Bellboy* or *The Disorderly Orderly*), but here it works magnificently, a thoroughly successful and fulfilling climax to the "military" phase of the comedian's career.

In the Wake of Dean and Jerry: The Bernard Brothers, Noonan & Marshall

The phenomenal postwar popularity of Martin & Lewis encouraged Hollywood studios to repeat their response to the similar ascendency of Abbott & Costello just before World War II: Specifically, to find their *own* Martin & Lewis and sup full of the gravy train. The most blatant of the M & L wannabes was the team of Duke Mitchell and Sammy Petrillo, whose imitation of Dean and Jerry was so close to the real thing that legal action was taken by the more famous comedy duo. Fortunately, Mitchell & Petrillo's only starring film, the imperishable *Bela Lugosi Meets a Brooklyn Gorilla* (1952), is not a service comedy, so we won't have to inflict an analysis on you.

A couple of other teams did however show up in uniform on screen, in obvious emulation of Martin & Lewis. It is unfair to describe the Bernard Brothers as a ripoff, since they had been active in show business long before Dean and Jerry had ever met. Truth to tell, the Bernard Brothers weren't brothers at all. Prior to 1932, George Bernard and Herbert James "Bert" Maxwell had been working as singles in American vaudeville, each performing an eccentric song-and-dance routine. Upon teaming with George Bernard, Bert Maxwell euphoniously assumed his partner's last name. As the Bernard Brothers, the twosome did a burlesque ballet act which achieved great success in Paris and London. By 1938 they were performing their most famous routine, "Off the Record," in which they pantomimed to popular recordings. Though such "record acts" were a novelty at the time, they soon became commonplace thanks to the success of the Bernards. One fledgling comic who got his professional start doing a similar act was 17-year-old Jerry Lewis.

Playing top-of-the-bill bookings in Great Britain throughout the war years, George and Bert Bernard reached their pinnacle when they appeared with Danny Kaye, the Nicholas Brothers and

3. First Line of Offense

With two luscious leading ladies like Dina Merrill (left) and Diana Spencer, no wonder Jerry Lewis is grinning in this publicity shot from *Don't Give Up the Ship* (Paramount, 1959).

13-year-old Julie Andrews in a Royal Command Variety Performance on November 1, 1948. Three years later the Bernards made their feature-film bow in a French production, *Nuits de Paris*. Around this time their act was seen by Hollywood mogul Herbert Yates, head of Republic Pictures. Sensing that the Bernards could be Republic's "answer" to Martin & Lewis (we didn't hear the question), Yates signed them to a one-picture deal, resulting in a slick but uneven melange of comedy, music, and satirical spy melodrama: *Gobs and Gals* (1952), scripted by Arthur T. Horman of *Buck Privates* fame.

Advertised by Republic as "international favorites," the Bernards are cast as sailors Sparks Johnson and Salty Connors, assigned to a lonely Naval weather observation station in the South Pacific. To earn extra money, Sparks and Salty begin releasing weather balloons with notes asking for pen pals, attaching pictures of their handsome superior officer Lt. Steve Smith (Robert Hutton) so that the women retrieving the balloons will send back gifts, homemade desserts and other items exchangeable for cash. During shore leave in San Francisco, Steve can't understand why he is besieged by so many unattached females—nor can his suspicious and unforgiving fiancee Betty Lou Prentice (Cathy Downs), the daughter of a senator (Emory Parnell) whose committee is dead set on vetoing Navy appropriations. Steve's C.O. orders him to reconcile with Betty for the sake of the Service, while Sparks and Salty scramble to hide the trunk containing the money they've accumulated from their scheme before the authorities catch up with them. At the same time, the trunk is assumed to contain secret government documents by a group of Soviet spies, who demonstrate their acuity for assimilation by openly reading the latest issues of *Pravda* (with Stalin's picture splashed over every page) and speaking in accents so thick that they make Boris and Natasha sound like Julius and Ethel Rosenberg. Once in a while, the hectic plotting calms down long enough for the Bernards to do a pantomime sketch, or to show up in drag as "Mabel and Myrtle Mansfield." The film ends with a slapstick chase that is funnier and better staged than anything else in the picture (Republic never faltered when delivering an action sequence), and a final Bernard Brothers turn as they mime to a recording of "East Indian Polka."

Gobs and Gals did some business in the hinterlands and none in the big cities; it was released to television in 1958, made the syndication rounds until the early 1970s, then retreated into obscurity. George and Bert Bernard appeared in one other film, playing comic villains in the international production *Decameron Nights* (1953), and cohosted a syndicated TV anthology, *Tales of Hans Christian Andersen* (1954). They continued to prosper as stage performers, reviving their old parody-ballet routine after prohibitive royalty payments forced them to abandon their record act, until George Bernard's death in 1967.

Unlike the Bernard Brothers, Tommy Noonan and Peter Marshall were not a permanent comedy team; working together only when both were available at the same time, they otherwise pursued separate careers. Tommy Noonan had made his stage debut in the company of his actor brother John Ireland in 1934. Before the War, Noonan headed his own repertory company, and after Navy service he made his first film appearance in *George White's Scandals* (1945). When his brother John married actress Joanne Dru, Noonan befriended Dru's brother Peter Marshall, an aspiring singer. Impressed with the popularity of Martin & Lewis, Noonan and Marshall decided to form a team of their own, with Noonan as the manic Lewis-type comic and Marshall as the smooth Martinesque vocalist — though in fairness, Tommy and Peter took great pains to avoid outright imitation. The team made its film debut in 1950 as a specialty act in the Lippert Studios musical revue *Holiday Rhythm*, then moved to Warner Bros. to enact a brief sketch in 1951's *Starlift,* returning to Lippert to perform an old burlesque chestnut in the 1952 cheapie *FBI Girl*. Noonan & Marshall periodically broke up throughout the 1950s, allowing Noonan to accept choice supporting roles in such films as *Gentlemen Prefer Blondes* (as Marilyn Monroe's rich boyfriend), *A Star Is Born* (as Judy Garland's musician confidante) and *Bundle of Joy* (as the pompous floorwalker who loses Debbie Reynolds to Eddie Fisher). During this period Peter Marshall also made strides as a solo entertainer, notably in a 1956 TV dramatization of composer Gordon Jenkins' celebrated tone poem *Manhattan Tower*. On those occasions when the two performers reteamed, they concentrated on nightclub work, and at one point headlined the CBS TV special *Café Mardi Gras*, produced by Jackie Gleason.

In 1958 Noonan & Marshall again linked up as part of a master plan concocted by Tommy Noonan to produce and star in a series of low-budget film comedies. Their first project, filmed independently on a rock-bottom budget and released by 20th Century–Fox in 1959, was *The Rookie,* a service farce with occasional songs. Comedian George O'Hanlon, best known for his "Joe McDoakes" short subjects and his cartoon voicework as George Jetson, cowrote and directed the film, later expressing pride and satisfaction over the results. Well, far be it from us to burst O'Hanlon's bubble, except to observe that the writing of *The Rookie* was just as good as the direction — that is to say, not good at all.

Tommy Noonan plays a radio-station page named "Tommy Noonan," who receives his draft notice on the last day of World War II. Stubbornly determined to serve his country despite the cessation of hostilities, Tommy takes his demands all the way to the Pentagon, where thanks to the antics of two drunken janitors (Vince Barnett, Rodney Bell), he is assigned to an all-but-deserted training camp overseen by sergeant Peter Marshall (likewise playing "himself"). Poised to close down the camp and return to his movie-starlet girlfriend Lili Marlene (Julie Newmar), Marshall changes his mind when the girl's sleazy agent (Jerry Lester) convinces him that keeping the camp open for "the last rookie" would be an excellent publicity stunt to advance Lili's career.

There follows a stupefyingly unfunny series of basic-training gags before Noonan and Marshall are shipped off to Japan, where they capture an enemy submarine manned by a pair of goofs who haven't yet heard about V-J day. Public Relations being what they are, Tommy and Peter are brought back to America and fêted with a ticker-tape parade as the heroes who ended the war!

So many things go wrong with this film that one hardly knows where to begin. Starting with a wretched "Italian chef" routine that hadn't been any more amusing when Noonan performed it in *Starlift,* and ending with the lamebrained concept of having Noonan & Marshall also portray the two Japanese sailors—caricatures so offensive that they make Jerry Lewis look like Toshiro Mifune—*The Rookie* lives down to Leonard Maltin's description as "one of the most abominable movies ever made." In an effort to put lipstick on this pig, 20th Century–Fox advertised *The Rookie* as an "all star comedy," citing the many veteran comic actors in the supporting cast, including Jerry Lester, Joe Besser, Doodles Weaver, Vince Barnett, Frank Mitchell and Paul "Mousie" Garner. But Nick St. Marie of the *Third Banana* website was closer to the mark when he described the cast of *The Rookie* as "the 'desperate comedians' ... those poor souls who'd outlasted the days of real comedy films and waited around for people like Tommy Noonan, or Jerry Lewis, to throw them a bone."

Noonan & Marshall made one more film together, *Swingin' Along* (1961), then broke up for good. Tommy Noonan would gain a measure of notoriety as star and director of the pioneering soft-core nudie films *Promises Promises* (with Jayne Mansfield) and *Three Nuts in Search of a Bolt* (with Mamie Van Doren) before his death in 1968. Peter Marshall achieved his greatest fame as host of the long-running TV quiz show *The Hollywood Squares.*

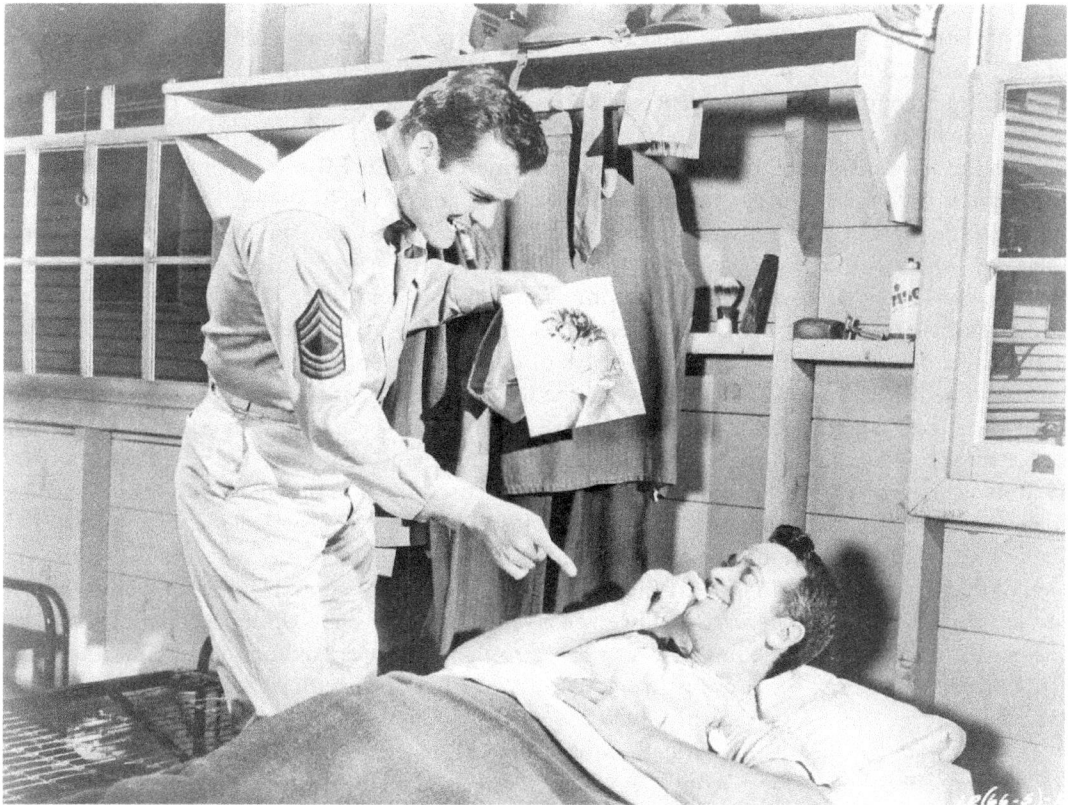

Peter Marshall (standing) and Tommy Noonan eagerly anticipate a visit from Julie Newmar (in photograph) in this buoyant scene from the otherwise dreary *The Rookie* (20th Century–Fox, 1959).

Other Talkie Comedians: From the Two Black Crows to Larry the Cable Guy

Chronologically speaking, the first all-talking feature film that can be designated an "Army Comedy" was *Anybody's War*, released by Paramount in 1930. It was the second starring feature for the blackface team of Moran & Mack, billed in those less enlightened times as "The Two Black Crows." Having joined up in the early 20th century, George Moran and Charles E. Mack became vaudeville and Broadway stars with a fast-paced patter routine featuring Moran as the silver-tongued straight man and Mack as the whining, worrying comic. Speaking in an exaggerated "darkie" dialect, the team achieved phenomenal popularity in the late 1920s with a series of 78-rpm comedy discs for Columbia Records, selling nearly seven million copies of such titles as "In the Jailhouse" and "Foolishments." Inevitably, the team was invited to Hollywood for their feature film debut in the musical comedy-drama *Why Bring That Up?*, which despite its sluggishness was one of Paramount's biggest moneymakers of 1929.

Just as their popularity was at its peak, George Moran dropped out of the act. Depending on the source one believes, Moran was either miffed about the amount of money he was getting, or upset over his onscreen billing. Charlie Mack promptly called upon Bert Swor, the brother of his former stage partner John Swor, to don blackface as Moran's replacement. This "new" team was still billed as "Moran and Mack" in the World War I comedy *Anybody's War* (1930)—and apparently their fans couldn't tell the difference (though they *could* have if they'd bothered to read about the substitution in *Time* magazine's review of the film).

Based on Charlie Mack's novel *The Two Black Crows in the A.E.F*, the film followed the adventures of Amos and Willie Crow, a couple of Tennessee boys who march off to battle in the company of their trained dog "Deep Stuff." As in *Why Bring That Up?*, a romantic subplot was handled by the "white" second leads, in this case Neil Hamilton and Joan Peers. But unlike the earlier film, which concluded with a lachrymose hospital scene wherein Mack brought his comatose partner back to life by launching into one of their old routines, *Anybody's War* was comedy through and through: As the breezily insensitive newspaper ads declared, "You'll laugh till you're black in the face!" In the most celebrated scene, a crap game between Amos and Willie is interrupted when their dog swallows the dice, whereupon the boys borrow an X-ray machine so they can continue their game—a gag later appropriated (minus the racial subtext) by Abbott & Costello in *Here Come the Co-eds* (1945). This scene excepted, contemporary viewers could not help but notice that Charlie Mack was getting the lion's share of the footage, notably a solo routine in a potato bin. As noted in Harold W. Cohen's review for the Pittsburgh *Post-Gazette*, Mack's partner was little more than "an atmospheric shadow." It was almost as if George Moran wasn't there at all.

Although Moran & Mack would eventually reconcile and reunite, their vogue was over by 1930, as the new blackface duo of Amos 'N' Andy surpassed them in popularity. At the same time, the whiteface musical-comedy team of Bert Wheeler and Robert Woolsey were riding high as RKO Radio's most consistent moneymakers. Launching their Hollywood career with the 1929 film version of their Broadway hit *Rio Rita*, Wheeler & Woolsey served as comedy relief for a brace of follow-up songfests before they were finally given a vehicle all their own. Undoubtedly impressed by the earlier success of such teams as Beery & Hatton and Dane & Arthur in military comedies, RKO placed Wheeler & Woolsey against a World War I background for the team's first "official" starring feature, *Half Shot at Sunrise* (1930).

As indicated by the opening title, the story is set in 1918 Paris. Tommy Tanner (Bert Wheeler) and Gilbert Simpkins (Robert Woolsey), a jaunty pair of AWOL privates who like to impress the mademoiselles by posing as officers, are the bane of the existence of Col. Marshall (George MacFarlane). In the course of events, Tommy romances Marshall's hoydenish daughter Annette (W&W's perennial leading lady Dorothy Lee), while Gilbert pitches woo at the Colonel's "special" lady friend Olga (Leni Stengel). Annette and Olga decide that the only way to keep Tommy and Gilbert out of the stockade is to get the boys to perform an act of bravery on the battlefield. This plan goes awry, and it looks as if the daffy duo is headed toward a firing squad. Thanks to a last-minute reversal of fortune, our heroes are placed in the position of blackmailing the very married Col. Marshall with some love letters written by Olga. Coinciding with Armistice Day, Tommy and Gilbert are released to their respective sweethearts, while the Colonel must make do with his not-entirely-forgiving wife (Edna May Oliver).

Superficially, *Half Shot at Sunrise* is everything a starring vehicle should be. Both Bert Wheeler and Robert Woolsey are given ample opportunity to trot out their individual comic specialties: Wheeler shares a charming duet with Dorothy Lee and solos with an impressive roller-skating routine, while Woolsey rattles off such wisecracks as "I became an aviator because they told me I was no good on earth!" and performs an energetic song and dance (in which he loses most of his clothes) with Leni Stengel. Both comedians join forces with Dorothy Lee for a sprightly mock ballet, which like all of the film's best scenes is performed outdoors—quite a novelty at a time when most movie musicals were still stagebound. The film's laugh content is given a booster shot by the uncredited (but well-compensated) gag contributions of former comedy star Roscoe "Fatty" Arbuckle.

Unfortunately, *Half Shot at Sunrise*, which since lapsing into public domain has become one of the most frequently shown Wheeler & Woolsey vehicles, is not among their best. The directorial pacing (by Paul Sloane) is habitually a few beats off, the two comedians laugh at their own jokes to save the audience the trouble, and nominal "heavy" George MacFarlane is too much the buffoon

Half Shot at Sunrise (RKO, 1930): Diligent doughboys Robert Woolsey (left) and Bert Wheeler manage to locate an actual Frenchwoman in the streets of Paris.

to provide any sort of credible comic menace. In addition, the film is hampered by a climactic sequence which, in the words of Wheeler & Woolsey biographer Ed Watz, "leaves an unpleasant aftertaste with most viewers, after the lighthearted frolics that had preceded it."

Throughout the first three-quarters of *Half Shot at Sunrise*, the morbid realities of World War I are blissfully ignored. In fact, with the exception of the starring duo's Army uniforms, no effort is made to authentically recreate the pre–1920 era: The ladies are costumed in the latest 1930 fashions, while the comedians make quips about such anachronisms as Eskimo Pie, an ice-cream confection not invented until 1921. All this is perfectly attuned to the joyously artificial musical comedy *ouevre* of Wheeler & Woolsey. Then, suddenly and without warning, the team is motorcycled off to a starkly realistic World War I battlefield, replete with foxholes, barbed wire and whizzing shells. When volunteers are requested for a suicide mission, Gilbert (Woolsey) glibly offers the services of Tommy (Wheeler), then instantly regrets it. The two men share a deadly serious farewell scene, followed by a horrifying shot in which Tommy, apparently hit by a mortar blast, is buried up to his neck in mud and debris. Gilbert rushes to help his friend, who croaks painfully that he "can't feel a thing" in his legs. Though ending on a comic note (it turns out that Tommy is completely uninjured, and has landed on top of an equally hale-and-hearty soldier), this episode is both jarring and disturbing, and it takes a while for the film to recover. Blending comedy with tragedy is a delicate procedure, best left to specialists like Chaplin and not interns like Wheeler & Woolsey.

Although every conceivable movie genre from murder mystery to Western was represented in the team's 22 starring films, *Half Shot at Sunrise* was Wheeler & Woolsey's only service comedy. A case *might* be made for their 1933 political farce *Diplomaniacs*, which concludes as the comedians are conscripted into the Army after their knuckleheaded efforts to secure universal peace at the Geneva Convention result in the launching of the Second World War. The Marx Brothers' *Duck Soup* (1933), a similar but far superior political satire, likewise contains elements of the service-humor genre. This is especially true in the film's cartoonlike battlefield finale, during which the brothers play various members of the mythical Freedonian army, with Groucho wearing a different uniform — running the gamut from the Confederacy to the Boy Scouts— in every scene.

Away from his brothers, Groucho Marx managed to squeeze one Navy comedy into his schedule. Released by RKO in 1952, *A Girl in Every Port* (no relation to the 1928 film of the same name) offers the curious spectacle of 61-year-old Groucho and 46-year-old William Bendix as a pair of screw-up sailors named Benny Lynn and Tim Donovan. Adhering to the *Sailor Beware* pattern, the plot is the old saw about a bunch of gullible gobs investing all their money in a "sure thing": In this case, Benny and Tim inveigle their shipmates into betting on a broken-down racehorse that Tim has purchased — or rather, the horse's twin brother, a genuine champion. The outcome of the story hinges on dimwitted carhop Jane (Marie Wilson), the only person who can tell the two nags apart. At one point, Benny poses as a wealthy Southern colonel, allowing Groucho to trot out the cornpone accent he'd previously "auditioned" in *A Day at the Races* (1937). With sailors, gangsters and saboteurs mixed up in the storyline, you'd think that something funny would have to happen every so often. It does, but not every so often enough.

The quality of *A Girl in Every Port* can be summed up by observing that its best joke was spoken by Groucho Marx in real life rather than on film: When a reporter asked why he wore his Navy uniform while driving to and from the studio, Groucho explained, "I might be drafted while I'm on my way to work." Over two decades later, the comedian claimed that he agreed to star in the film when the producer promised to give him a trip around the world — for which he was still waiting. Beyond its script and production deficiencies, *A Girl in Every Port* suffers from a lack of even surface credibility. By 1952 Groucho Marx was too firmly entrenched as the wittily caustic host of TV's *You Bet Your Life* to be convincing as a luckless, self-defeating sailor: Leo Miller of the Bridgeport (Connecticut) *Sunday Herald* commented that Groucho was "looking every minute as if he would be happier in back of a microphone giving money away to contestants." Meanwhile, costars William Bendix and Marie Wilson work so hard at playing "stupid" that they come off as brain-damaged. Much better represented are the film's supporting players, among them Don Defore, Gene Lockhart, Teddy Hart (brother of lyricist Lorenz Hart) and Dee Hartford (soon to be Groucho's sister-in-law). Otherwise, we can be grateful that RKO Radio did not carry out their announced plans for a sequel to *A Girl in Every Port*. Once was quite enough, thank you.

We've covered the military comedies starring Moran & Mack, Wheeler & Woolsey and (peripherally) the Marx Brothers, so can the The Ritz Brothers be far behind? Before you non–Ritz fans answer, "Yes, *far* behind!" it must be noted that the Ritzes were one of the biggest and best-paid nightclub acts of the past Century. It wouldn't be fair to completely ignore them, even though their film work was extremely variable, scaling the heights with *The Three Musketeers* (1939) and plumbing the depths with *Hi'ya, Chum!* (1943). After a couple of happy years performing specialty routines in 20th Century–Fox musicals, the Ritzes were promoted to top-billed stardom in *Life Begins in College* (1937), which showed their precision dancing and incessant mugging to good advantage. But there was just so much Fox could do to sustain the Brothers' stardom; they were not actors in the accepted sense, and outside of the much-admired Harry Ritz (hailed as a genius by such savants as Pauline Kael and Mel Brooks) they had no distinctive screen personalities. This, together with some well-publicized battles with the Fox hierarchy over matters of money and story material, had seriously eroded the Ritzes' appeal by 1939. Irrefutable evidence of how far they had slipped can be found in their last Fox feature, *Pack Up Your Troubles* (working title: *Tin Hats*), in which they were billed below child star Jane Withers.

Pack Up Your Troubles bears no relation to the same-named 1932 Laurel & Hardy film beyond its World War I setting. Billed as "The Silly Schultzes," the Ritzes are a trio of vaudevillians specializing in a German-dialect routine, hardly a ticket to success in those anti–German times. Following a disastrous audition at a theatrical booking agency (the best scene in the picture), the boys decide to join the cavalry — the mule division, of course — where they are at the mercy of tough sergeant "Angel Face" Walker (Stanley Fields). Once in France, the threesome befriends American waif Collette (Jane Withers), whose French father Capt. Paul Didiot (Joseph Schildkraut) has been reported killed in battle. Donning phony German uniforms to perform their vaudeville act for the French troops, our heroes are set adrift in a balloon which crash-lands behind enemy lines. After much byplay and horseplay — some of which involves a seductive German spy played by third-billed Lynn Bari — the Brothers locate the still-alive Capt. Didiot and rescue him from a firing squad.

Clearly intended as the film's main attraction, little Jane Withers handily upstages the Ritz Brothers with her singing, dancing, and uncanny imitations of George M. Cohan and Eva Tanguay. If the Ritzes felt slighted playing second fiddle to a 13-year-old kid, imagine what was going through the mind of Oscar-winning actor Joseph Schildkraut, who was consigned to fourth billing — or if you want to get technical, sixth billing. In a scathing review of *Pack Up Your Troubles* ("dry, dull and diffident"), Harold W. Cohen of the Pittsburgh *Post-Gazette* touched upon the shabby treatment afforded both Schildkraut and another prominent Broadway veteran in the film: "The casting at least reaches a new high — in incongruity. Imagine finding two such distinguished actors as Mr. Joseph Schildkraut and Mr. Fritz Leiber in such impoverished circumstances. Even now old Rudolph Schildkraut, Joseph's father, and the ghost of Mr. Leiber's 'Hamlet,' must be turning fitfully in their graves."

Modern-day viewers who stumble upon the Ritz Brothers or Wheeler & Woolsey on late-night cable might either react favorably or with head-scratching incredulity: "How could any audience in their right minds *laugh* at these idiots?" The same question could well be posed by film fans of the distant future when they review the output of certain comedians who have held appeal for members of our generation. What, for example, will the reaction be when a casual TV viewer of 2060 AD witnesses the comic capers of Pauly Shore or Larry the Cable Guy? We haven't chosen these examples randomly: At their peak popularity, both of these comedians were starred in military comedies. Undoubtedly their fans were thrilled; non-fans are rumored to have tolled bells in the streets while shouting, "Unclean! Unclean!"

When 21-year-old standup comedian Pauly Shore was promoted to stardom as an MTV host in 1989, there were those who smugly assumed that he'd attained this lofty goal through the showbiz connections of his mother Mitzi Shore, owner of the fabled Comedy Store in Los Angeles. Though in truth Pauly was as hard a worker as anyone in his profession, it was smart business to promote the idea that he'd gotten where he was through no real effort of his own: Who else could appeal more to the "slacker generation" than a fellow slacker? Fracturing his fans with his disorganized comic rantings and his world-owes-me-a-living attitude, Pauly rode high, wide and homely throughout the early 1990s with such films as *Encino Man* (1992) and *Son in Law* (1994).

Released by Hollywood Pictures/Buena Vista in 1994, Shore's third starring feature *In the Army Now* casts him as Bones Conway, an indolent electronics-store employee who is fired when caught sneaking away from his duties for a quickie with his girlfriend. Does this mean that Bones and his nerdy buddy Jack (Andy Dick) will have to give up their dreams of owning their own video-game store? Not if they both join the National Guard, where Bones is certain they can earn a lot of money for doing practically nothing: "It's like a health spa, only they pay us." We're off to the requisite boot camp routines, filmed at Fort Sill, Oklahoma, and involving a sexy-but-stern female drill sergeant, well played by Lynn Whitfield. Eight agonizing weeks later, Bones, Jack and their new friends Fred (David Alan Grier), a dental student who is afraid of everything *including* his own shadow, and Christine (Lori Petty), a gonzo gal who bristles over the fact that women aren't allowed in combat, have made the cut for the Army's Water Purification Division (a branch of service chosen by Bones because his brother is a pool boy). Just when it looks as if Bones has glommed onto a sweet deal as a "weekend warrior," Libya declares war on Chad. In a twinkling, the Water Purification Division is mobilized and shipped overseas, where Bones is once again at the mercy of a tyrannical sergeant (Esai Morales), this one a member of Special Ops. Before the film is half over, Bones, Jack, Fred and Christine have been stranded in the desert (California's Imperial Valley doubling for Chad and Libya) with no vehicle or backup troops. Assuming command by virtue of his rank — he's the only Private First Class in the bunch — Bones stumbles onto a Libyan outpost, stocked with confiscated American tanks and artillery and geared for an all-out missile strike on Chad. It might have been refreshing if the four protagonists had been reduced to cinders by the bad guys, but this a comedy, so Bones spearheads an assault on the Libyans, blowing up everything in sight and assuring plenty of medals and glory for himself and his friends.

Unlike its obvious inspiration *Stripes* (see **Chapter 12**),

Reservist Pauly Shore makes America safe for democracy — or, at the very least, for idiotic comedies like *In the Army Now* (Hollywood/Buena Vista, 1994).

which starts slowly and builds to a hilarious climax, *In the Army Now* shoots its wad at the very beginning with a spectacular slapstick sequence, then works its way down to deadening dullness as Pauly Shore and his costars spend more time wandering in the desert than Moses. Though five writers are given screenplay credit, they seem merely to have gotten in each other's way. Far too often, gags are carefully set up, only to remain unresolved by payoffs or punchlines; a "funny" camel is even less amusing here than in the benighted Dustin Hoffman-Warren Beatty vehicle *Ishtar*; and most damaging of all, virtually no comic advantage is taken of the fact that the four principals are attached to Water Purification. One would think we'd be treated to at least *one* sight gag showing Bones et al. subduing the Libyans with a high-powered hose; instead, all we get are a few outsized explosions. These pyrotechnics don't even seem logical in context: How can blowing up a single solitary tent set off a chain reaction that destroys all of the enemy's scud missiles?

And while we're on *that* topic, what sort of "logic" was behind robbing Pauly Shore of his slacker appeal (such as it is) by shearing off his trademarked unruly hair and trading his familiar scrawny torso for abs of steel? This is almost as misguided as the decision to surround Shore with costars like Andy Dick, David Alan Grier and Lori Petty, all of whom are heaps funnier than he is. It's like watching a Marx Brothers picture in which Zeppo gets all the best lines.

Because the film is scrupulously respectful in its treatment of the "real" Armed Forces (if only by default), *In the Army Now* was produced with full military cooperation. As observed by P.J. Budahn, author of *What to Expect in the Military: A Practical Guide for Young People, Parents and Counselors*, the film is "surprisingly accurate in catching the tone of life among troops, and by Hollywood standards a not too bad depiction of boot camp and Army life." And though it fell short of the profits accrued by Pauly Shore's previous film *Son-in-Law*, *In the Army Now* managed to rake in $29 million. While this was no assurance that the star would remain a box-office draw (last time we looked, he was nowhere to be found) it was impetus enough for a virtual remake of *In the Army Now* thirteen years later by a comedian who was even more of an acquired taste than Pauly Shore.

Larry the Cable Guy wasn't his real name, of course. Using his given name Dan Whitney, the portly, bearded humorist eked out a modest living as a traditional standup comic in the 1990s, doing mother-in-law jokes and other such stuff—until, like Pauly Shore before him, he stuck his shovel in the ground and tapped into a rich vein of anti-intellectualism. By that time, the self-styled slackers of the '90s had been supplanted by the self-styled rednecks of the early 21st century. Both groups were immoderately fond of jokes about scattershot sex and body functions, and both had a low opinion of college-educated people in top-level jobs. The main difference was that rednecks perceived themselves as having a stronger work ethic than their shiftless predecessors. Note that when he changed his professional name, Dan Whitney was Larry the Cable Guy, not Larry the Lazy Pig Who Lives in His Parents' Basement. And note that in contrast with Pauly Shore's whiny catchphrases "Buuud-dy" and "Weasels!" Larry the Cable Guy's mantra was "Git-'r'-done!" Whether or not this makes Larry funnier than Pauly, or whether either man is funny at all, is open to debate. If earning power is any indication of quality (which it isn't), *Forbes* magazine has reported that as of 2007, Larry the Cable Guy was pulling in $20 million annually.

During the era of the second Gulf War, Larry and his fellow redneck comics Jeff Foxworthy, Bill Engvall and Ron White comprised a unit show called the Blue Collar Comedy Tour, performing extensively for civilian and military audiences alike. Larry was gratified that the men and women in uniform were as enthusiastically supportive of his brand of humor as he was of their courageous efforts in Iraq, Afghanistan and other international hot spots. This was the audience to whom Larry geared his second starring feature, *Delta Farce* (Lionsgate, 2007). The comedian even previewed the film for the troops at Andrews Air Force Base. "The USO set it up ... and we had all the guys from Walter Reed come down with their families and I knew they were going to like it," Larry recalled to Fox News' Greta Van Susteren. "But when we showed it, it got even a better reaction than I thought it would. I mean, the troops really liked it and I am glad they did, because, you know, it was for them and it was to make them laugh a little bit and something they could relate to, as well. So, we were real happy with that."

The similarities between *Delta Farce* and *In the Army Now* are blatant: A wacky gross-out comedian in the lead; a group of foul-ups who have joined the Reserves as an easy and painless way to earn extra cash; the rude awakening when our heroes are marched off to a real shooting war; the *Full Metal Jacket*-style sergeant (Esai Morales in the first film, Keith David in the second) who in a weak moment admits he'd be happier in a less stressful career (Morales had wanted to go into ballet, David had dreamed of being an aerobics instructor); the villain who keeps tabs on the outside world by watching an American cable-news channel; a series of near-catastrophes ending in victory and adulation for the protagonist and his hangers-on; and withal, a reverent attitude towards actual combat troops—even though the U.S. military yanked its cooperation at the last minute in the case of the second film. Beyond all that, *Delta Farce* is less a clone of *In the Army Now* than a rehash of the 1985 comedy *¡Three Amigos!*, which starred Larry's idol Steve Martin.

Recently fired-and-jilted restaurant manager Larry, unhappily married "professional sue-er" Bill (Bill Engvoll) and gun nut-*cum*-sex deviate Everett (DJ Qualls) are looking forward to their monthly weekend with the Reserves, if only to escape their dismal civilian lives. This weekend, however, they are mobilized for battle in Iraq at the insistence of their iron-jawed topkick Sgt. Kilgore (Keith David). En route to Falujah via transport plane, Larry, Bill and Everett try to grab some shuteye by sneaking into a Humvee—which is promptly jettisoned and parachuted to earth when the plane runs into turbulence over the California-Mexico border. Emerging unharmed from the vehicle, the Three Stoopids are convinced that they've landed in Iraq, but the audience knows that they're really only 500 miles from Mexico City. Mistaking the residents of a tiny Mexican village for Iraqis, Larry and his buddies discover that the town is being besieged by bandits, who of course are assumed to be enemy insurgents. Once they've realized their error, our heroes nonetheless dig in their heels, fulfilling their oath to fight terrorism no matter where it occurs: In other words, to "Stay the course." While protecting the villagers from the bandit hordes, Larry et al. find time to rescue Sgt. Kilgore, who has somehow also ended up in Mexico.

At one point Kilgore is kidnapped by the bandit gang and subjected to the inhuman torture of singing "I Got You Babe" with the gang leader's gay nephew. Lest you think that this is the *only* joke at the expense of homosexuals in *Delta Farce*, you just don't know Larry the Cable Guy. If you like hearing Kurds and Shi'ites referred to as Turds and Shit'ites; if you enjoy watching a man drink a canteen full of urine and eat a chunk of someone else's spit; if you laugh out loud at references to "Camel's Ass Tacos"; and if you revel in witnessing a young man's spiritual growth from sleeping with blow-up dolls to becoming the world's skinniest *Lucha Libre* wrestler; then, Mister, this is the picture for you. To describe *Delta Farce* as being in poor taste would be assuming the producers actually *have* any taste.

There were a few cautious yea-sayers like John Anderson of *Variety*, who described the film as "rife with fat, fart and Falujah jokes, but with a subcutaneous wit that has a lot to do with Iraq war fatigue." But most critics concurred with *The Onion*'s Steven Hyden: "Like *Paths of Glory*, *Apocalypse Now*, and *Platoon*, *Delta Farce* is a difficult, harrowing work offering little relief or humor. Unlike those movies, though, *Delta Farce* is supposed to be funny." And yet ... the film is, in its own tacky way, a lot more amusing and better constructed than *In the Army Now*. At least *Delta Farce* manages to extract humor from its characters rather in spite of them; better still, whenever a verbal or visual gag is set up in this film, you *know* there's going to be a strong payoff. And when all else fails, *Delta Farce* can always fall back on the uproarious comic performance of veteran movie hardcase Danny Trejo as a scarred and scowling bandit chieftan named Carlos Santana!

"Here's a sobering thought," shuddered Scott Brown of *Entertainment Weekly*. "If every war gets the comedy it deserves, could *Delta Farce*, a strenuously unfunny *Three Amigos* knockoff, be our *M*A*S*H*?" Not likely, any more than Wheeler & Woolsey's *Half Shot at Sunrise* ended up as the Depression generation's *Shoulder Arms*. However, it's a certainty that comedians yet unborn will continue rising up to star in military comedies for all future wars — assuming that anyone will still be alive to watch.

Selected Shorts, Part Two: The Talkies

Hollywood continued grinding out one- and two-reel comedies into the late 1950s, but the status of live-action comedy shorts had diminished by the mid–1930s thanks to the rising popularity of animated cartoons and the double-feature policy. Unlike the golden days of Lloyd Hamilton, Lupino Lane and Billy Bevan, far fewer comedians specialized in shorts in the talkie era than in the silent period — meaning of course that there were also fewer 10- and 20-minute service comedies.

A few names of importance managed to flourish and prosper despite being limited to the short-subject form. Specializing in situation comedies and domestic farces, Charley Chase was one of Hal Roach's most important stars of the 1920s, and happily he was able to sustain his popularity well into the 1930s, no small thanks to his expertise as a singer, dancer and musician. During the 1930–1931 season, Chase starred in a brace of 3-reel Army comedies that could easily have been run in tandem as a 6-reel "feature."

In *High-Cs* (1930), directed by James W. Horne, Charley is cast as a World War I sergeant who'd rather sing than fight (in fact, he performs six songs in the course of the film's 29 minutes). His irreverence towards military protocol and his frequent musical interludes with his pals The Ranch Boys — Jimmie Adams, Frank Gage and Marvin Hatley — hardly endear Charley to his nononsense C.O. (Carleton Griffin), but prove quite charming to demure French barmaid Antoinette (played by Chase's frequent costar Thelma Todd). Once in No Man's Land, Charley is forced to confront the grim realities of warfare when his buddy Jimmie Adams is shot — not fatally, but in the adam's-apple, ruining his beautiful tenor voice. Determined to capture a German soldier who can also sing tenor, Charley convinces a group of enemy POWs that Germany has won the war, so that they will lure their melodious comrade over to the American trenches. Once in custody, the *Deutsch Sänger* reveals that he can't speak English, so Charley and the Ranch Boys accommodate their prisoner with a chorus of "Du, Du Liegst Mir im Herzen," complete with yodels (*All Quiet on the Western Front* this isn't). The film ends on Armistice Day, with everyone in a celebratory mood but Charley: it seems that the Ranch Boys have been thrown in the guardhouse. What else is there for Charley to do but get himself arrested as well?

Picking up where *High-Cs* left off, the 27-minute sequel *Rough Seas* (1931) was directed by Chase's brother James Parrott. According to the introductory titles, the film takes place during "A great month in the lives of the American Dough Boys — The war was over! — They were going home! — And several Second Lieutenants had fallen overboard!" Most of the action transpires on a New York–bound troop ship carrying Charley, his prickly CO (Carleton Griffin again) and the Ranch Boys, now four in number (the German tenor having apparently switched sides). Charley sneaks his lady love Antoinette (Thelma Todd again) aboard ship by hiding her in his duffel bag, a strategy sabotaged when the girl's shapely leg pokes through the canvas (a sight gag lifted from Chase's silent comedy *What Price Goofy*?). Later on, Charley instructs his pet monkey Napoleon to steal an Army uniform for Antoinette, which she dutifully dons, albeit retaining her high heels. "You can't wear those shoes, dear heart," remonstrates Charley. "This isn't a musical comedy." Ultimately Antoinette and Charley are married by ship's captain Frank Brownlee; in the meantime, the film goes off on several other tangents, including a musical number in which Charley performs a *basso profundo* rendition of "Asleep in the Deep." And in the resolution of a situation established in *High-Cs*, nutty ship's doctor Jerry Mandy performs an operation to restore Jimmie Adams' tenor voice, with surprising results. Not as well paced as its predecessor, *Rough Seas* nonetheless benefits from the boundless energy of the leading players, and the delightful background music by LeRoy Shield. (A Spanish-language version of *Rough Seas* was released under the title *Monerias*, featuring Angelica Benitez in Thelma Todd's role.)

Charley was reunited with the Ranch Boys (minus their German *kamerad*) in a pair of military-themed 2-reelers released back to back in 1933. *Arabian Tights* finds the old war buddies attending an American Legion convention in postwar Paris, where they accidentally sign up with the Foreign Legion. Captured by a genial, Oxford-educated sultan (Philip Sleeman), Charley saves the lives of himself, the Ranch Boys and girl friend Muriel Evans by teaching the potentate's harem girls how to square-dance! And in *Sherman Said It*, Charley and the Boys backtrack to World War I, encountering all manner of difficulty trying to get out of France and return home. Though no director is credited for *Arabian Tights*, *Sherman Said It* was helmed by Chase himself, billed as Charles Parrott.

Fired by Hal Roach in 1936, Charley Chase spent the remainder of his career as an actor and director at Columbia Pictures, where the Three Stooges had been headlining their own 2-reel comedy series since 1934. Over the next 25 years, and through several changes of personnel (Moe Howard and Larry Fine appeared in all the films, while the role of the third stooge was assumed first by Curly Howard, then Shemp Howard and finally Joe Besser), the team showed up in a vast array of movie genres, from western parodies to science-fiction spoofs. Moe Howard once theorized that the Stooges' knockabout humor was most effective when the trio was dropped into surroundings where they were most out of place — including the various branches of the Armed services.

Discounting *Uncivil Warriors*, discussed in **Chapter 18**, the team's first military comedy was 1936's *Half Shot Shooters*, in which hoboes Moe, Larry and Curly are hoodwinked into signing up

The Three Stooges — Moe, Curly and Larry — stare down the barrel of their own Army's artillery in the 1940 Columbia two-reeler ***Boobs in Arms***.

for the Army, where they immediately run afoul of Sgt. McGillicuddy (Stanley Blystone), the same topkick who'd made their lives miserable during World War I. The 18-minute short comes to a literally explosive climax wherein the Stooges, assigned to gunnery practice, commandeer a cannon and manage to lay waste to a bridge, a smokestack, a private bungalow and the Admiral's flagship! In *Three Little Sew-and-Sews* (1939), the Stooges are Navy tailors who steal some officer's uniforms in order to attend a fancy party. Facing a firing squad for their insubordination, the boys redeem themselves by subduing a pair of foreign spies (Harry Semels, Phyllis Barry) who have hijacked a submarine. And in *Boobs in Arms* (1940), the Stooges are greeting-card salesmen who join the Army to escape the vengeance of an angry customer (Richard Fiske) — only to find that the selfsame customer is now their drill sergeant. One of the Stooges' funniest outings, *Boobs* features an extended Army-drill routine which ranks among the team's best work (it later showed up as stock footage in their 1943 short *Dizzy Pilots*).

Curiously, all three of these pre–World War II service comedies end with images of death. In *Half-Shot Shooters*, the exasperated sergeant takes charge of the cannon and blows the Stooges clear out of their boots. In *Three Little Sew-and-Sews*, Curly accidentally detonates a bomb which sends everyone winging toward the Pearly Gates. And in *Boobs in Arms*, the Stooges, incapacitated by laughing gas, are last seen astride a flying mortar shell, guffawing hysterically as they disappear into the clouds. Evidently it was reasoned that the three comedians were *so* inept that the only way to keep America safe for Democracy was to kill them off! (The boys were allowed to survive past the "End" title in their 1938 Foreign Legion comedy *Wee Wee Monsieur*, but that one didn't take place in America.)

Once World War II was under way, it would have been bad for national morale to show the uniformed Stooges meeting an untimely demise; thus, in *Back From the Front* and *Higher Than a Kite* (both 1943), they manage to remain unscathed all the way to the end. *Back From the Front* casts the boys as members of the Merchant Marine, set adrift on a makeshift raft after their ship is torpedoed by a Nazi sub. Clambering aboard another vessel, our heroes discover that they are now on the deck of the "S.S. Schickelgruber," forcing them to pose as German sailors until they can make good their escape. When they learn that their former commanding officer Lt. Dungen (Vernon Dent) is actually a German spy, the boys determine to get even with him while simultaneously striking a blow for the Allies. After subduing the entire crew, the Stooges disguise themselves as Nazi dignitaries (with Moe launching into his familiar Adolf Hitler imitation) to dispose of Dungen and his conspirators. A peppy if uninspired effort, *Back from the Front* is distinguished by the excellent fog-shrouded camerawork of cinematographer John Stumar.

In *Higher Than a Kite*, the three comics are garage mechanics for the R.A.F., somewhere in England. After systematically destroying a colonel's staff car, the boys are forced to go into hiding lest they be torn asunder by their infuriated sergeant (Duke York). They take refuge in what appears to be a drainpipe, but is actually the empty shell of a blockbuster bomb. Dropped out of a plane over Germany, the Stooges crash-land at the headquarters of "General Bommel" (Dick Curtis) and "Marshal Boring" (Vernon Dent). Moe and Curly elude capture by donning German uniforms, while Larry puts on female drag as a temptress named Moronica (replete with Veronica Lake-style "peekaboo bangs"). Stealing the Nazis' war plans, the Stooges make their getaway, but not before a United States Marine bulldog takes a bite out of Curly's posterior. The brightest moment in *Higher Than a Kite* is the sort of gag that drew howls from 1943 audiences, but is totally lost on today's younger viewers: Unable to obtain the proper gas-rationing card, Marshal Boring must travel around on a kiddie scooter!

After Shemp Howard took over from his brother Curly as the third Stooge in 1947, the team made only a smattering of service comedies, if indeed they could be categorized as such. *Punchy Cowpunchers* (1950) casts the trio as U.S. Cavalrymen, circa 1868, who aid the handsome but clumsy cowboy hero (Jock Mahoney in a side-splitting performance) as he rids the west of the dreaded "Killer Dillons." *Love at First Bite* (1950) features a flashback sequence as each Stooge recalls how he met his foreign-born fiancee while serving overseas. And in the 1955 "Dragnet" parody *Blunder Boys*, Moe tells the audience how he and his partners became heroes during the War ("We were fighting a rear-guard action — the only action we knew how to fight"). Following Shemp's death in 1955, he was replaced by Joe Besser, who participates in a reworking of the *Love at First Bite* wartime flashback (with the help of stock footage) in the 1958 2-reeler *Fifi Blows Her Top*.

As a utility comedian with the Warner Bros./Vitaphone short-subject unit in the early 1930s, past-and-future Stooge Shemp Howard appeared in support of a number of prominent comic actors. Teamed with Jack Haley in 1933's *Salt Water Daffy*, Shemp plays a pickpocket who ducks into a Navy recruiting station to avoid arrest. Both Shemp and Jack try to avoid enlistment by pretending to be unfit for duty, with Jack feigning deafness and Shemp launching into an uproarious "blind" routine. But it's all for naught: Soon the boys are in uniform, spending most of their time eluding their commanding officer, from whom Shemp had stolen a watch just before signing up, and escaping the wrath of their gravel-voiced CPO, played by a decidedly pre–*Hart to Hart* Lionel Stander. The 2-reeler ambles to a moderately amusing climax as Shemp and Jack flush out a foreign spy (Chales Judels). On his own, Shemp headlined another Vitaphone short, *The Officer's Mess* (1935), playing an obnoxious National Guardsman who unwittingly humiliates his new commanding officer (Charles Kemper) at a posh French restaurant.

Similarly, Joe Besser soloed in a group of 2-reelers prior to his association with the Stooges, produced by Columbia between 1949 and 1956. Taking their cue from Besser's superb performance as a dimwitted private in the 1943 Ann Miller musical *Hey, Rookie*, five of his ten Columbia shorts had him portraying a soldier. *Dizzy Yardbird* (1950) finds Besser on permanent KP duty due to the failed efforts of his apoplectic sergeant (Dick Wessel) to turn Joe into a lean, mean fighting machine. In *Aim, Fire, Scoot* (1952), Joe and his buddy Jim Hawthorne (a popular California-based radio humorist) are at the mercy of pitbull-visaged drill sergeant Henry Kulky; this film recreates the drill sequence from the Three Stooges' *Boobs in Arms* almost word-for-word, and closes with a fadeout gag lifted from the Stooges' *Half Shot Shooters*. And in *Spies and Guys* (1953), Joe foils a band of enemy agents with the aid of swimsuit-clad WAC Angela Stevens (the film also features Besser's distinctive take on a familiar Columbia-comedy gag: jabbed in the butt by a bayonet, Joe squeals, "Owwww! I'm losing my *miiiind!*"). *Dizzy Yardbird* and *Aim, Fire, Scoot* were respectively remade as *GI Dood It* (1955) and *Army Daze* (1956) — though "remade" is perhaps too lofty a term, since both of the later shorts are largely comprised of stock footage from the earlier films, with new "framing" devices (a dog's narration in *GI Dood It*, a dash of espionage in *Army Daze*) hastily assembled so that Columbia could pass off these patchworks as "new" productions.

A handful of other military comedy shorts appeared in the years between 1931 and 1945. Over at Hal Roach Studios, ZaSu Pitts and Thelma Todd were seen in the World War I comedy *War Mamas* (1931), which appears to have been filmed on the same locations as Charley Chase's *High C's*. Cast as Red Cross nurses, ZaSu and Thelma take a wrong turn in an Army truck and end up at a French chateau where a group of German soldiers are billetted. Aided by a sympathetic French countess (Claire Daumery), our heroines demoralize a pair of besotted enemy officers (Charles Judels, Stuart Holmes) with a game of strip poker (the girls win and the men lose, worse luck). Co-directed by Marshall Neilan, a prominent filmmaker of the silent era who had fallen from favor by the time the talkies rolled around, *War Mamas* is not one of the better Pitts-Todd comedies, but does have its moments, especially whenever ZaSu salutes her superiors with her trademarked fluttery hand gestures.

A former Hal Roach attraction, the kiddie contingent Our Gang, appeared in 1941's *Fightin' Fools*, the 27th of 52 one-reelers that the Gang made for MGM Studios between 1938 and 1944. A very loose remake of the kids' 1923 silent effort *Dogs of War* (see **Chapter 2**), *Fightin' Fools* pits the youngsters—"Spanky" McFarland, "Froggy" Laughlin, "Buckwheat" Thomas, Mickey Gubitosi (aka Robert Blake) and the rest — against a rival gang in a mock military battle, using such ammunition as tomatoes, watermelons, and the inevitable limburger cheese. Unfortunately there isn't enough variety of gags to make this 10-minute epic truly memorable, and after a while one's attention is diverted from the kids in the foreground to the field of oil wells sprouting from the Los Angeles hills in the distant background.

Too bad there wasn't anything to distract the viewer from the goings-on in another "kid" comedy of the talkie era. Released in 1933 by Educational Pictures, *War Babies* was the last and least of the studio's single-reel "Baby Burlesks," in which children wearing oversized diapers appeared in broad and tasteless parodies of adult feature films. The leading performer in these pathetically unfunny efforts was a pre-stardom Shirley Temple, who on this occasion portrays the "Charmaine" counterpart in a wretched lampoon of *What Price Glory?* (see **Chapter 7**). A French-accented shimmy dancer at Buttermilk Pete's Café, five-year-old Shirley coquettishly toys with the affections of a pair of pugnacious pre-school Marines named "Sergeant Flirt" and "Captain Gagg." ("Oui, mon cap-ee-tan!" she coos, almost as if she actually understands her lines.) Principal gags include a pair of dice stenciled on the diaper of a black child, a toddler getting "drunk" on sour milk, and the grand finale in which Captain Gagg triumphs over Sgt. Flirt by claiming possession of Shirley's diaper pin. The less said about this the better.

Finally, dialect comedian El Brendel, onetime darling of Fox Studios who found himself relegated to Columbia 2-reelers in the 1940s, showed up as an overage conscriptee in two separate shorts. *The Blitzkiss* (1941) casts Brendel as a Swedish gardener who carries on a feud with fellow groundskeeper Tom Kennedy when both men join the Army. A wearisome routine with a baby pig, a few extremely painful gags involving a gopher trap, and an airborne finale with El trapped in a target balloon, all add up to a generally mediocre effort, yet somehow *The Blitzkiss* managed to cop an Academy Award nomination. Slightly better is *I Spied for You* (1943), filmed on the same huge shipboard set seen in the Three Stooges' *Back from the Front*. This lively little opus finds bumbling sailor Brendel inadvertently thwarting a gang of Nazi spies, accidentally sinking an enemy sub with a depth charge, and incredibly capturing the heart of the captain's daughter (Katherine Keys).

4

Abbott and Costello Meet the Ripoffs

When President Roosevelt signed the first peacetime conscription act into law on September 14, 1940, requiring all men aged 21 through 35 to register for the draft, the major Hollywood studios jockeyed to be the first to capitalize on this historic event. The three studios most aggressively vying for this honor were Paramount, Warner Bros. and Universal. Given its second-class industry status, it was assumed that the Universal effort would be dwarfed by the films turned out by its two rivals—especially Paramount, who had already sent out publicity that their top comedy star Bob Hope would be headlining a timely blend of music and laughs titled *Caught in the Draft*. No one could have predicted that Universal would steal Paramount's thunder by serving up their own Army comedy a scant four months after the draft went into effect, while *Caught in the Draft* was still in its preproduction stage. And absolutely no one could have predicted the phenomenal popularity of a pair of former burlesque comedians named Bud Abbott and Lou Costello.

It is fashionable for those who don't like the thin, sardonic Abbott or the rotund, whiny Costello to dismiss them as minor-league comics who lucked into the Big Time with an up-to-date service comedy that happened to strike a responsive chord with 1941 filmgoers. This theory fails to acknowledge the fact that Bud and Lou were established headliners well before *Buck Privates*: radio stars since 1938, and Broadway favorites thanks to their successful run in the hit 1939 revue *The Streets of Paris*. Also, the team's feature-film debut as supporting players in the 1940 Universal musical *One Night at the Tropics* had garnered the best reviews for that otherwise negligible effort. Anxious to cast Abbott & Costello in a film more worthy of their talents and one that would tap into their youthful fan following, Universal drew up plans to costar the team with another up-and-coming specialty act, the singing Andrews Sisters. Like A&C, Patty, Maxine and Laverne Andrews had earned critical plaudits for their supporting work in *their* first film, the otherwise unsuccessful 1940 Ritz Bros. vehicle *Argentine Nights*. Universal reasoned that both Abbott & Costello and the Andrews Sisters would have better movie-star potential if they were rescued from the ranks of "extra added attractions" and allowed to headline their own films.

Reams of Hollywood mythology have been written about the gestation of *Buck Privates*, mostly based on the reminiscences of Universal producer Alex Gottlieb, the man who first recommended Bud and Lou to the studio. According to Gottlieb, no fewer than 17 Universal scriptwriters turned down the assignment of fashioning Abbott & Costello's first starring feature, a story which presupposes that the famously parsimonious studio actually *had* 17 writers on its payroll. The first scrivener to take a whack at a film combining Abbott & Costello with the Andrews Sisters was Harold Shumate, who in November 1940 submitted a story idea that also incorporated the highly exploitable "draft" angle. In Shumate's proposal, the comedians and the singers were members of a theatrical troupe touring Army camps around the country. Adhering to musical-comedy tradition, neither A&C nor the Andrews girls were expected to carry a "straight" romantic plotline. While the comics and the vocalists went through their traditional paces the plot proper would be handled by another member of the traveling show, a young millionaire who aspired to be a songwriter against his family's wishes.

4. Abbott and Costello Meet the Ripoffs

Universal liked the Army-camp setting and the wealthy-hero angle, but rejected practically everything else in this first treatment (elements of Shumate's scenario would later resurface in the movie adaptation of Olsen & Johnson's Broadway extravaganza *Hellzapoppin'*). Arthur T. Horman was assigned to rewrite the property in such a way that Abbott & Costello would not merely entertain soldiers but actually be soldiers themselves, thereby establishing audience identification with the team and allowing for richer comic possibilities. In Horman's version, Bud and Lou portray sidewalk peddlers Slicker Smith and Herbie Brown, who inadvertently join the Army while escaping the wrath of an angry cop, only to find that the same cop is now their drill sergeant. The rich hero is refashioned as a worthless wastrel who, after first trying to use his father's influence to secure a draft deferment, eventually "mans up" as an Army draftee, making him a more desirable sweetheart for the poor-but-proud heroine, a USO hostess who is also being wooed by the wastrel's former chauffeur. The USO angle also neatly accommodated the Andrews Sisters, who weave in and out of the story to perform a succession of Army-related songs. Assigned to direct the picture was Arthur Lubin, who worked so well with Abbott & Costello that Universal retained his services for five of the team's pictures.

The title *Buck Privates* had already been registered by the studio for a 1928 war comedy starring Malcolm McGregor (see **Chapter 2**). To beat Paramount's *Caught in the Draft* to the punch, the Abbott & Costello film was assembled in a swift 24 days, using several of Universal's standing sets to keep costs under control. Location shooting was minimal, except for a few sequences staged at California's Providence Ranch and some atmosphere shots lensed at Fort Ord near Monterey Bay. Over the years there have been several estimates of the film's budget: The Universal publicists,

Buck Privates (Universal, 1941). Maxine Andrews sidles up to Lou Costello, while her sisters Patty (center) and Laverne snuggle with Bud Abbott. If any studio portrait ever screamed "1941!," this is it (*courtesy Jim Feeley*).

sensing that moviegoers adored Cinderella stories about minor pictures that turned out to be major hits, claimed that *Buck Privates* was brought in for less than $100,000; other contemporary reports estimated the tab in the $150,000–$180,000 range. Tireless Abbott & Costello historians Bob Furmanek and Ron Palumbo have recently confirmed that the final budget was $245,000 — not precisely the "lowly B picture" that *Buck Privates* is often described as being, but still a very modest programmer. Released January 31, 1941, the film proved to be a cash cow from the word go. In several major cities, where the average run for a new picture was two weeks at most, *Buck Privates* was held over for several times that length; in New Orleans, the film was screened at a single theater for a record-breaking eight weeks. The movie ended up raking in four million dollars, proportionately Universal's biggest domestic hit until 1975's *Jaws*.

In a 1941 article about Army comedies, *Life* magazine noted that the handful of "preparedness" pictures made just before the Draft had not done too well, citing such barely profitable examples as 1940's *Flight Command*. While the subject matter of *Buck Privates* was unquestionably a major contributor to its popularity, there had to be other reasons for its spectacular success. Abbott & Costello themselves theorized that the film was a hit because there were thousands upon thousands of filmgoers who'd never seen the team in burlesque and never heard their classic routines and timeworn jokes. To these deprived souls, everything old was suddenly new. Interviewed by Hubbar Keavy of the Special News Service, Bud Abbott commented: "Perhaps the boys who used to go to burlesque shows will not think our material funny. They'll recognize it. But there are millions who never saw us. And there's a new generation."

For argument's sake, let's say that the average *Buck Privates* fan was interested in neither the timely storyline nor the ancient wheezes of Abbott & Costello. Perhaps these folks were drawn to the picture by the Andrews Sisters, here performing some of the finest musical material they ever had. Or was it remotely possible that movie fans were lured into theaters by the three-way romance between "straight" leads Lee Bowman (the rich draftee), Jane Frazee (the USO sweetheart) and Alan Curtis (the ex-chauffeur rival)?

Buck Privates was a success not only because it was a good service comedy but because it was a good film by any standard, blending all the elements for success with near-perfect symmetry. Abbott & Costello's routines may have been older than the audiences watching them, but the team had the advantage of a brilliant writer named John Grant, a fellow graduate of burlesque with an uncanny gift for freshening up the stalest material — and better still, for adapting venerable routines so that they would logically fit into the film's storyline. An early scene in which the comedians are being transported to boot camp by train turned out to be an ideal spot for the old "dice game" bit. Once the boys arrive at camp, where better to insert the classic "drill" routine, with acting corporal Abbott barking orders at left-footed private Costello? The night our heroes receive their first Army paychecks was the perfect setting for a bit of verbal chicanery in which Abbott flim-flams Costello to the point that Lou not only loans him all his cash, but actually finds himself in debt to Bud. And when everybody in the barracks was supposed to go to sleep after "Taps," the time was ripe to haul out the noisy burlesque chestnut "Go Ahead and Sing," with choleric sergeant Nat Pendleton added to the mixture. Unlike *One Night in the Tropics*, in which Abbott & Costello seemed to be an afterthought with little relevance to the storyline, the boys are an integral part of the action in *Buck Privates*— simply because the action has been made an integral part of the comedy.

The same is true of the Andrews Sisters, whose songs follow a logical plot progression, beginning with their introductory welcome-to-the-Army number "You're a Lucky Fellow, Mr. Smith," continuing through the first-leave interlude "Apple Blossom Time," and climaxing with the Sisters commenting on a specific aspect of daily military life with the film's best number, "Boogie Woogie Bugle Boy" (which unexpectedly gained a new lease on life three decades later, courtesy of Bette Midler). Like the felicitous combination of Abbott & Costello and John Grant, the Andrews Sisters were provided with the perfect collaborators: choreographer Nick Castle to map out the girls' synchronized movements, and songwriters Don Raye and Hughie Prince to provide their pitch-perfect harmonies.

Even the least compelling aspect of the film, the secondary love triangle, sustains audience interest thanks to the sincerity of the three "straight" leads—not to mention the fact that Abbott & Costello and the Andrews Sisters are never absent from the screen long enough to let boredom set in. Only in the final reel does the film falter. Inexplicably, Universal chose to remove Abbott & Costello from the climactic "war games" sequence early in the proceedings, in order to resolve the animosity between the characters played by Alan Curtis and Lee Bowman. Audiences conditioned to expect a slam-bang slapstick finale involving the star comedians could not help but feel cheated, thereby assuring that the studio's scriptwriters would never make this narrative mistake again. And after the box-office returns came rolling in on *Buck Privates*, Universal would never again make the economic mistake of booking an Abbott & Costello film at the lower B-picture rate; henceforth, the studio would demand and receive a hefty A-picture rental.

While *Buck Private*s was being readied for release, Universal kept their new comedy team busy with the modest 65-minute haunted house farce *Oh, Charlie*. Once the team's first starring feature scored a hit, the studio decided to temporarily shelve their second vehicle and rush Bud and Lou into another service comedy, reuniting the comedians with the Andrews Sisters and providing them with a bigger budget and a more stellar supporting cast (Universal simultaneously retooled *Oh, Charlie*, adding brassy musical numbers with the Andrewses and shipping the picture out as an 85-minute "A," retitled *Hold That Ghost*). Abbott & Costello's third starring feature was thus the second to be released: Originally titled *Hello, Sailor*, it eventually hit the screens as *In the Navy* on May 28, 1941—while Paramount's competing *Caught in the Draft* was still in post-production!

Approximately ten percent of *In the Navy*'s $379,000 budget went to costar Dick Powell, here genially ribbing the service musicals (*The Singing Marine, Shipmates Forever*) he'd filmed at Warner Bros. in the 1930s. As with *Buck Privates*, the "straight" lead carried the main plot, with Powell cast as Tommy Halstead, a popular radio crooner who escapes his screaming fans by enlisting in the Navy under an alias. Plucky photojournalist Dot Roberts (Claire Dodd) dogs Tommy's trail in hopes of getting a picture of him in uniform, a mission requiring her to sneak on board ship in male drag with the unwilling help of sailors Abbott & Costello, cast respectively as electrician's mate Smokey Adams and ship's baker Pomeroy Watson. That's just about the extent of the connection between A&C and the principal plotline: Otherwise, the boys have their own subplot to deal with, as Costello aspires to win the heart of Patty Andrews (playing "herself") by pretending to be an experienced seaman, when in fact he has spent six years in the Navy without ever going near the ocean.

Once again, the team's pet writer John Grant reconfigured several time-honored burlesque routines to fit perfectly into the film's nautical setting, including the "Lemon Bit" (Abbott tries to gull Costello out of his money with a variation of the old shell game), "Buzzin' the Bee" (the boys take turns spitting water at each other during a shipboard club initiation), and a routine that probably dates back to the Babylonians, as Costello successfully proves to Abbott that $7 \times 13 = 28$. More so than in *Buck Privates*, the scriptwriters take advantage of Costello's potential as a pantomimist in several key sequences, notably a lengthy bit involving a recalcitrant hammock that was deemed worthy of a two-page *Life* magazine photo spread.

So as not to repeat their *Buck Privates* error, Universal made certain that Abbott & Costello dominated the final reel of *In the Navy* with an extended slapstick sequence in which Costello pretends to be the captain of a battleship in order to impress the Andrews Sisters. Abbott is supposed to help Costello with an elaborate charade suggesting that Lou is issuing orders to the crew, but things go awry and the tubby comedian actually takes charge of the ship, with the confused crewmen dutifully following his half-witted instructions during a genuine naval-maneuver exercise. As the ship perilously dashes and darts around the rest of the Pearl Harbor fleet, narrowly

Lou Costello and Bud Abbott inspect a fleet of doughnuts while serving *In the Navy* (Universal, 1941) (*MOVIE STAR NEWS*).

averting disaster at every turn, a visiting dignitary (Thurston Hall) marvels at how "brilliantly" the cardboard captain is handling his vessel. As a result, the bewildered Costello is fêted as a hero and master navigator. At least, that's the way the scene was *supposed* to have played. In its capacity as the film's technical advisor, the U.S. Naval Department objected to the entire climax, complaining that it made the Navy look ridiculous. Not wishing to reshoot what was already the film's most expensive segment, Universal saved the day by adding a handful of scenes explaining away Costello's chaotic maritime maneuvers as a dream, with Lou merely imagining that he's in charge of the battleship. The Navy's objection and Universal's mollification were hardly unique to *In the Navy*. One recalls that after an AWOL Joe E. Brown successfully thwarts an espionage plot in 1933's *Son of a Sailor* (see **Chapter 3**), he *still* has to spend a few hours in the brig for insubordination so that Warner Bros. could secure full Naval Department cooperation.

In the Navy raked in even more money than *Buck Privates,* ending up the sixth biggest-grossing picture of 1941. The film's success proved beyond question that Abbott & Costello's popularity vis-à-vis *Buck Privates* was not a fluke, nor could it be totally attributed to the topicality of the earlier picture. Whereas *Buck Privates* was locked into a specific time period, *In the Navy* could just as easily have been made in the 1920s or 1930s for all its relevance to America's prewar preparedness. Whether critics of the comedians liked it or not, *In the Navy* was a hit solely because of Abbott & Costello.

Universal placed the team in a non-military setting for their next picture, *Ride 'Em Cowboy*. But theater owners and exhibitors, still convinced that the comedians' success was pegged to a military milieu, insisted that Universal ship out more of the same as quickly as possible. Thus, *Ride 'Em Cowboy* was withheld from view until February 1942, while A&C's fifth starring vehicle *Keep 'Em Flying* (working title: *Up in the Air*) was rushed into release as their *fourth* starrer on November 28, 1941. Though Universal regarded this commitment to service comedy as simply a smart business move, producer Alex Gottlieb insisted that he was guided by loftier motives, noting that if America should enter World War II as everyone was predicting, there were "going to be plenty of sick people in the audience — people who have lost a husband, son, brother or boyfriend — who will want and very much need the healing unguent of laughter."

While Abbott & Costello still enjoyed the services of writer John Grant and director Arthur Lubin, the Andrews Sisters were absent from *Keep 'Em Flying*, having been awarded their own series of starring musicals for Universal. (One of these, a brazen *Buck Privates* retread titled *Private Buckaroo*, featured another frequent Abbott & Costello costar, Shemp Howard.) Both music and plot motivation were supplied by male romantic lead Dick Foran, previously an *In the Navy* supporting player, accompanied by female romantic lead Carol Bruce. Recalling the positive audience feedback from the pairing of Lou Costello with raucous comedienne Joan Davis in *Hold That Ghost*, Universal cast zany comic actress Martha Raye opposite Costello in *Keep 'Em Flying*, with Martha giving a terrific performance in a dual role as twin sisters, one demure, one rambunctious. (It's likely that this film inspired Paramount to go the twin-sister route with their own house *farceusse* Betty Hutton in the 1944 musical *Here Come the Waves*.)

By this time, every branch of the Armed Services was keenly aware of Abbott & Costello's huge following among servicemen. None of the top brass in the Army or Navy was presumptuous enough to claim that the comedians' service films were responsible for the recent upsurge in enlistments: the Draft had taken care of that. Conversely, the Army Air Corps was not comprised of ordinary draftees, but was instead a select group of highly trained specialists. One was not drafted into the Air Corps, nor did one simply enlist: A rigorous qualification process had to be passed before a candidate was even considered for the grueling 20-week training program. The Air Corps had no shortage of men willing to undergo this ordeal: The problem lay in persuading those candidates who had "washed out" as aviators (usually because of eyesight or equilibrium problems) to remain with the Corps in other capacities rather than transferring elsewhere. It was vital to assure the candidates that each and every job in the Corps was important — and to do that, the organization elected to use Abbott & Costello's *Keep 'Em Flying* as a recruiting tool.

This game plan is fully articulated in *Life with the Flying Cadets* (1941), a 1-reel short produced by the Army Air Corps and featuring selected highlights from *Keep 'Em Flying*. The entertainment is periodically interrupted by an upbeat narrator who assures potential Air Cadet School graduates that they would all be matched with commissions best suited to their specific skills. Those who didn't make the grade as "sergeant pilots" could otherwise function as navigators, aerial photographers, mechanics and ground-crew personnel. Once it is established that you have to be awfully damn good to make it into the Air Corps in any capacity, the narrator exults over the euphoria of being a solo pilot — "There can be no greater feeling for a man than to be at the controls of one of these super powered ships" — while simultaneously emphasizing the importance of *every* member of the team. "Behind every pilot, behind every ship that takes to the air, is the skill, industry and devotion of the heroes of the ground, without whose aid it would be impossible to 'keep 'em flying.'"

In *Keep 'Em Flying* itself, Lou Costello, playing a character named Heathcliff, delivers a brief non-comic speech which feeds into the Corps' propaganda campaign. Heathcliff and his pal Blackie (Bud Abbott) have tagged along with their stunt-pilot chum Jinx Roberts (Dick Foran) to Cal-Aero Air Academy, where Jinx intends to sign up as a cadet. The commanding officer solemnly informs Heathcliff and Blackie that there's no place for men without qualifications in the Academy. Pleading his case, Heathcliff recalls that as a child he was too fat to play on the baseball team, so he was made a batboy; and he was too slow to join the football team, so they made him the water boy. "And now, Major, when you're training the biggest team we ever had, there surely must be a place for Blackie and I ... maybe as a water boy ... or a bat boy?" Touched by this eloquence, the C.O. assigns the boys to the ground crew. Contrary to appearances, the Air Corps did not insist on having Lou Costello temporarily drop character to deliver this stirring monologue. The decision was made by director Arthur Lubin, to prove to the Universal higher-ups that Costello was capable of handling pathos as well as humor.

Costello's speech is a lot easier to take than the heavy dollops of propaganda and jingoism throughout the rest of *Keep 'Em Flying,* in which reckless "lone eagle" Jinx Roberts must learn the value of teamwork the hard way. Washed out of the academy for pulling off a stunt that nearly costs the life of the heroine's brother, Jinx redeems himself by rescuing Craig Morrison (William Gargan), his rival for the girl's affections, in a thrilling airborne finale (made rather less thrilling than intended by the overuse of a process screen). This situation is a direct steal from the final reel of *Buck Privates,* and it isn't the only moment in *Keep 'Em Flying* where the Abbott & Costello formula is showing signs of wearing thin. Elsewhere in the film, the comedians make a totally gratuitous visit to a carnival funhouse, where Costello registers gibbering terror when confronted by a man in a gorilla suit — an attempt by Universal to replicate the hilarity of the classic moving-candle routine in *Hold That Ghost.* Though the funhouse scene works well enough, neither this bit nor the bulk of the other comedy highlights (except for A&C's inevitable ascents into the Wild Blue Yonder) are as expertly integrated into the "military" motif as the A&C routines in *Buck Privates* and *In the Navy.* Though *Keep 'Em Flying* posted a healthy profit, it fell short of the money accrued by the team's two earlier service comedies, prompting Universal to keep the boys out of uniform for the immediate future.

In between *In the Navy* and *Keep 'Em Flying,* Paramount's long-awaited *Caught in the Draft* was finally unveiled on July 4, 1941. Though *Buck Privates* blocked this Bob Hope vehicle from being the first major-studio comedy to deal with the Selective Service Act, *Caught in the Draft* held its own with fans and critics alike, and was never disparagingly compared to the Abbott & Costello effort by contemporary reviewers. In fact, not a few commentators preferred the Hope film to *Buck Privates,* if only because Bob was a better-known commodity with a proven movie track record.

Superficially, *Buck Privates* and *Caught in the Draft* have a lot in common. The protagonist is a wealthy, pampered, self-centered young man who after striving to avoid the draft is nonetheless conscripted and subjected to all the indignities and heavy duties heaped upon the other draftees. His efforts to impress the leading lady come acropper until, at the very end, he proves himself a topnotch soldier during a sham-battle exercise. The added spark in *Caught in the Draft* is the fact that the romantic lead is not the colorless Lee Bowman but the charismatic Bob Hope, here cast as vainglorious movie star Don Bolton, whose on-screen heroics are considerably at odds with his real-life cowardice. Terrified of loud noises, Don is relieved that he won't be exposed to the sound of artillery fire because he's over the age of 35, the original cut-off point for the Draft. But when Uncle Sam raises the eligibility age to 42, there is no escape. After arranging a phony induction procedure that somehow turns out to be the genuine article, Don is marched off to training camp along with two members of his Hollywood entourage, Steve Riggs (Lynne Overman) and Bert Sparks (Eddie Bracken). At first, Don intends to merely go through the motions of soldiering for the benefit of his studio's publicity department, but changes his mind for the sake of his sweetheart Antoinette "Tony" Fairbanks (Dorothy Lamour), daughter of commanding officer Colonel Fairbanks (Clarence Kolb). The Colonel, however, refuses to consent to a marriage between Don and Tony until Don is able to earn the rank of corporal. After several disastrous false starts on the rifle range, in a runaway tank and during parachute training, Don finally proves his mettle in the climactic war-games sequence.

Caught in the Draft is a slicker and costlier effort than *Buck Privates;* at times it's even funnier, particularly when making satiric swipes at Hollywood in the early scenes. Yet it lacks the charm

A lyrical magazine ad for Bob Hope's *Caught in the Draft* (Paramount, 1941), sung to the tune of (what else?) "Thanks for the Memory."

and durability of the Abbott & Costello film. Cinema historian William K. Everson analyzed the major difference between the two properties in a 1990 review of *Caught in the Draft* for the New School of Social Research: "What it *really* lacks...is a sense of the period. Abbott & Costello's *Buck Privates* really did capture the fervor and energy of the period, almost in the same way that King

Vidor's *The Big Parade* did for World War 1. *Caught in the Draft* seems to see the period merely as a convenient background for Hope's antics, and to aim at nothing more."

Another of the film's shortcomings can be attributed to Paramount, who ever since Bob Hope graduated to full stardom had endeavored to make him part of a comedy team. This worked magnificently when Hope was paired with Bing Crosby in the wonderful "Road" pictures, and reasonably well when Bob traded quips with black comedian Willie Best in *The Ghost Breakers* and *Nothing But the Truth*. But in *Caught in the Draft*, Hope seems ill at ease sharing the spotlight with those inveterate scene-stealers Eddie Bracken and Lynne Overman. While the decision to cast Hope as a team member may have been to emphasize the necessity of the new draftees putting aside selfish considerations and "pulling together" for the common good, this message is not adequately conveyed in the film itself. It is this aspect of *Caught in the Draft* that relegates the film to a lower echelon in the Bob Hope canon. It may also lead those unfamiliar with movie history to wrongly conclude that teaming Bob with two other comics was a desperate attempt to ape the success of Abbott & Costello in *Buck Privates*, when in fact the Hope film was on the drawing board well before Bud and Lou were even being considered for a service comedy.

That said, it cannot be denied that several other post-*Buck Privates* military films *were* conceived in the hope of matching Abbott & Costello's popularity by featuring a team of misfit soldiers who were Bud and Lou in everything but name. This was painfully obvious in the Laurel & Hardy comedy *Great Guns* (working title: *Forward March*), released by 20th Century–Fox on October 10, 1941. Not only did the shooting script contain a heavy-handed dialogue exchange that made specific references to *Buck Privates* (an exchange that was mercifully excised before the film's release), but the Fox people did everything in their power to reformat the unique talents of Stan Laurel and Oliver Hardy into a rank imitation of Bud Abbott and Lou Costello, complete with misfire wisecracks and abysmal puns ("Sanka?" "You're welcome").

Possibly to avoid accusations of out-and-out plagiarism, Fox tweaked the *Buck Privates* formula just enough so that *Great Guns* wasn't an *exact* replica of its prototype. Wealthy hero Daniel Forrester (Dick Nelson) does not try to buy his way out of the draft; on the contrary, he eagerly welcomes Uncle Sam's call to arms, if only to prove to his overprotective aunts that he isn't the sickly hothouse flower that they've raised him to be. Heroine Ginger Hammond (Sheila Ryan) works at the hero's Army camp just as in *Buck Privates*, but in the photo shop rather than the USO canteen. Tough sergeant Hippo (Edmund MacDonald), and not the hero's ex-employee, is Daniel's romantic rival. And instead of accidentally joining the Army, Laurel & Hardy enlist on purpose: As Daniel's loyal valet and chauffeur, they are determined to accompany him to camp and make certain that his allegedly fragile health is not compromised by the rigors of army life. Ironically, Fox's attempts to give the material an "original" slant weren't all that original themselves. At closer examination, *Great Guns* turns out to be a reworking of the 1927 Fox silent *The Gay Retreat* (see **Chapter 2**), in which the comedy team of Sammy Cohen and Ted McNamara played a valet and chauffeur who joined the Army to safeguard *their* wealthy young master, an incurable sleepwalker.

Laurel & Hardy chroniclers Randy Skretvedt and Scott MacGillivray have already done such an excellent job itemizing the strengths and weaknesses of *Great Guns* that there's little to be gained by going over the same territory here. It's worth mentioning that the L&H film has one distinct advantage over *Buck Privates* in that the two star comics are allowed to dominate the climactic war-games sequence, and even partially determine its outcome. It must also be noted that for all its faults, *Great Guns* is excellent audience material. This author has seen three separate public showings of the film, and in each case the antics of Laurel & Hardy have brought down the house. Certainly *Great Guns* met with exactly the same response in 1941, encouraging 20th Century–Fox to amend its one-picture deal with Stan and Ollie and sign the team for a series of profitable comedies, the last of which was released in 1945.

With no Abbott & Costello or Laurel & Hardy on their payroll, other studios who hoped to feed from the *Buck Privates* trough were obliged to create their own comedy teams out of whole cloth. There's a likelihood that Warner Bros.' conscription comedy *You're in the Army Now* was originally planned for a solo star, a la *Caught in the Draft*. But by the time the Warners film was released on Christmas Day of 1941, there were two powerhouse comedians in the leading roles. The studio claimed to have tested 22 different comic combinations before deciding upon Jimmy Durante, whose flagging screen career had recently received a booster shot with Warners' *The Man Who Came to Dinner*, and Phil Silvers, borrowed from 20th Century–Fox. In his autobiography, Silvers stated that he and Durante were longtime pals who respected each other's talents and didn't squander energy trying to upstage each other. Frankly, they didn't have to. Though Warners insisted in its ad copy that Durante and Silvers were a team in every sense of the word, *You're In the Army Now* is scripted and staged as a Jimmy Durante vehicle pure and simple, with Phil Silvers merely an added attraction (Jimmy also received ten times Phil's salary).

Silvers has written that both he and Durante were amused rather than disheartened by the understanding that their film was a deliberate *Buck Privates* ripoff. The two stars also found it risible that Warners was so intimidated at the prospect of turning an "A" picture over to a pair of homely laugh makers that the studio submitted Jimmy and Phil to the traditional Hollywood glamour treatment, including a pair of lavish toupees for the two famously follicle-challenged funsters. Durante in particular seemed determined to have as much fun as possible on and off the set, endlessly ribbing Warners' top producer Hal Wallis by referring to Wallis' actress wife Louise Fazenda as "Trixie Friganza." These extracurricular hijinks undoubtedly contributed to providing *You're in the Army Now* with a carefree buoyancy that many of the other *Buck Privates* wannabes sorely lacked.

Durante and Silvers are cast as Homer Smith and Beezy Jones, door-to-door salesmen for the Whirlaway vacuum cleaner company. Ever on the prowl for customers, the boys try to hawk their wares at an Army recruiting station, only to accidentally sign up for a one-year hitch. There are some mirthsome moments as Homer and Beezy try to adjust to their ill-fitting uniforms and Homer is forced to go barefoot during a marching drill before the plot proper rears its head. The film's "straight" lead Captain Joe Radcliffe (Regis Toomey) is trying to convince stubborn Colonel Dobson (Donald MacBride), an old-school Cavalry officer, to replace the outmoded horses in his unit with up-to-date tanks. Radcliffe also happens to be in love with Dobson's perky daughter Bliss, played by Jane Wyman at her pre–*Johnny Belinda* cutest. Homer and Beezy try to help Radcliffe win the Colonel over by using tank power to move the Dobsons' house to a new location. Unfortunately the house ends up teetering on the ledge of a high cliff, but the boys save the day by deploying a tank to pull the structure and its occupants to safety.

Working on the theory that the secret to Abbott & Costello's success was the team's reliance upon old jokes, the scriptwriters crammed *You're in the Army Now* with some of the most cobwebbed material they could dredge up, including that venerable 2-reel comedy cliché involving alum and pursed lips (though this routine is brightened by an unanticipated twist). A camp-show sequence borrows from both Buster Keaton's *Doughboys* and Joe E. Brown's *Sons o' Guns*, with Durante donning drag as an involuntary participant in a violent Apache dance. And the house-on-the-precipice climax was lifted bodily from Charlie Chaplin's *The Gold Rush*—a fact that did not go unnoticed by Mr. Chaplin, who threatened to sue Warners for plagiarism. Apparently, however, nobody in 1941 took notice of *You're in the Army Now*'s curious homage to Jean Renoir's *Le Grande Illusion*: Repeatedly sentenced to the stockade, Durante begins to cultivate a potted plant in the window of his cell, a plant that grows larger and larger the more time Jimmy spends in stir.

Fans of Jimmy Durante will probably enjoy *You're in the Army Now* more than anyone else, since the star is given several opportunities to strut his stuff musically, beginning with a characteristic "poundin' the ivories" number titled "If You Own a Whirlaway." Though eclipsed by Durante's shadow for the most part, Phil Silvers does get a couple of shining moments, repeating his classic "elocution lesson" routine and joining Jimmy and Jane Wyman for the ensemble number

"I'm Glad My Number Was Called." Durante and Silvers aside, *You're in the Army Now* is best remembered for a well-circulated bit of Hollywood trivia. According to several "authoritative" sources, a love scene between Jane Wyman and Regis Toomey set a record for the longest sustained kiss in film history, lasting three minutes and five seconds. Alas, at this point we must assume the mantle of mythbuster: A recent viewing of *You're in the Army Now* reveals that the legend of the long kiss is just that—a legend. At most, Wyman and Toomey lock lips for a few seconds shy of one minute, in a scene broken up by several cutaways to supporting player Donald MacBride. (In any event, this "record" was shattered by the six-minute smooch in 2005's *Kids in America*, which is not an Army comedy and won't be mentioned again if we can help it.)

Another fabricated comedy duo came to us by way of Monogram Pictures. Borrowing its title and nothing else from a 1928 Wesley Barry vehicle (see **Chapter 2**), Monogram's *Top Sergeant Mulligan* (1941) stars Nat Pendleton, the topkick who'd bullied and browbeaten Abbott & Costello in *Buck Privates*, as the title character. The comedy team in this one ("Look What the Draft Blew In!" trumpeted the film's newspaper ads) consists of prolific supporting players Frank Faylen and Charlie Hall, the latter beloved of Laurel & Hardy fans for his superlative fall-guy work in such comedies as *Them Thar Hills* and *Tit for Tat*. The roughhewn Faylen and the diminutive Hall (who'd previously worked together in Monogram's *Father Steps Out*, albeit not as a preplanned team) receive sixth and seventh billing as cash-strapped pharmacy owners Pat Dolan and Budd Doolittle. Upon learning that the government has declared a "debt moratorium" on servicemen, the two pill-pushers devise a scheme whereby they will pretend to enlist as a means of dodging their creditors. Sure as shootin,' the two goofs sign up for real and are assigned to the platoon of Sergeant Herman Mulligan—who, wouldn't ya know it, is also the relentless bill collector who'd nipped at their behinds in civilian life. Once in uniform, Dolan and Doolittle get mixed up in the star-crossed romance of wealthy private Don Lewis (Tom Neal) and nightclub singer Gail Nash (Marjorie Reynolds), forcing the boys to commandeer an experimental Army jeep to keep the AWOL Don from getting into trouble. The wild motor chase that follows results in triumph rather than tragedy when the Army congratulates the two rookies for proving the resiliency of their new jeeps. (Not content with merely stealing from *Buck Privates*, Monogram cribs notes from *In the Navy* as well!)

Featured in the cast are Sterling Holloway in the atypical role of a fast-talking con artist, Frank Faylen's real-life wife Carol Hughes as a wily gold-digger, and black comedian Wonderful Smith, best known for his stooge work opposite Red Skelton on radio, as a fellow draftee. (The fact that the services weren't integrated in 1941 didn't faze Monogram; the studio had a sizable fan following in African American communities thanks to their many films showcasing the immortal Mantan Moreland.) Uncharacteristically, Monogram shelled out good coin for the right to use a then-popular song in *Top Sergeant Mulligan*: the Felix Bernard-Raymond Klages composition "21 Dollars a Day—Once a Month," a jocular reference to the pay scale for the average buck private.

Beyond this distinction, *Top Sergeant Mulligan* was typical of the bargain-basement Monogram releases of 1941. Columbia's entry in the *Buck Privates* sweepstakes, *Tramp Tramp Tramp* (1942), was likewise par for this studio's B-picture division. In a brash move, Columbia not only patterned *Tramp Tramp Tramp* after *Buck Privates*, but actually invited comparison to the Abbott & Costello vehicle in the ad campaign, which promised that their two leading characters "get into more amusing situations than any other two movie 'raw recruits' in pictures which have appeared hitherto."

With the Three Stooges already on their payroll, it's puzzling that Columbia would choose to reach beyond its contract list to create an ersatz Abbott & Costello, but that's exactly what happened. The Torch Lady's "Abbott" was tall and relatively good-looking Jack Durant, a Broadway and nightclub entertainer who'd already been one-half of a comedy duo with Frank Mitchell in the 1930s (see notes on *She Learned About Sailors* in **Chapter 2**). The "Costello" equivalent was a

Not quite as chubby but every bit as self-confident as in his network-TV heyday, Jackie Gleason takes center stage in Columbia's 1942 military comedy *Tramp Tramp Tramp*. He is shown here with his one-time-only comedy partner Jack Durant and leading lady Florence Rice.

porcine Manhattan-based funster who while under contract to Warner Bros. had billed himself as Jackie C. Gleason. His coronation as "The Great One" several years in the future, 26-year-old Jackie Gleason had previously appeared in one service comedy, Warners' *Navy Blues* (see **Chapter 6**), where the thunder had been stolen by his better-known costars Jack Oakie and Jack Haley (Years later, Gleason ruefully ripped his own performance: "I acted as if I was watching the picture being made.") *Tramp Tramp Tramp* was Jackie's first real opportunity to score as a film personality, and he made the most of it, even though his material was hardly conducive to developing a fan base.

Tramp Tramp Tramp (working title: *Camp Nuts*) gets off the ground with a rehash of the medical-examination scenes in *Buck Privates*. With all their regular customers being drafted left and right, small-town barbers Jed Hart (Durant) and Hank Tomlin (Gleason) decide to follow those customers to the local Army camp and enlist themselves. The highlight of this sequence occurs when Hank tells the Army doctor that he can't read the eye chart. "You mean you can't see that chart?" asks the doc. "No," Hank replies sheepishly. "I can't read."

All opportunities for training-camp humor would seem to be squelched when Jed and Hank are classified 4-F. But wait! At this point, the film becomes a forerunner to the popular British TV series *Dad's Army*, with the two comedians organizing all the other 4-Fs in town into a home-defense unit. So we're treated to all those familiar "drill" scenes after all, the essential difference being that the trainees aren't technically soldiers—and one of them is a midget. Jed and Hank's home guard earns its chops at film's end when the Army rejects subdue a gang of fugitive criminals (among them future leading man Forrest Tucker) who've been using the civilian training camp as a hideout.

In *Buck Privates* tradition, the lead comedians spend most of their time making funny while the "serious" plot is propelled forward by the romantic leads, soldier Tommy Lydel (Bruce Bennett) and girl reporter Pam Martin (Florence Rice). In a refreshing break from that tradition, comic

Jackie Gleason is awarded his *own* love interest, played by brassy singer-comedienne Mabel Todd, who like Jackie had previously been a Warner Bros. contractee. And let's not forget the picture's big-time musical act, Borrah Minnevitch and his Harmonica Rascals (not quite as pretty as the Andrews Sisters but every bit as melodious—and very funny besides). While *Tramp Tramp Tramp* would probably never have been made had not Columbia wanted to capitalize on the success of *Buck Privates*, in one respect the film returned the favor to Abbott & Costello: The director of *Tramp Tramp Tramp* was Charles Barton, who went on to helm some of Bud and Lou's best postwar films, including *Abbott and Costello Meet Frankenstein*.

The most transparent of all the Abbott & Costello/*Buck Privates* imitations was perpetrated by RKO Radio Pictures in 1943. Committed to yearly blocks of inexpensive "series" films—*The Saint, The Falcon, Mexican Spitfire*, et al.—RKO used the *Buck Privates* format as a springboard for a new series of military comedies. The creative team for this project was already under contract to the studio: Both producer Bert Gilroy and director Leslie Goodwins were longtime members of RKO's short subject unit. As for their Abbott & Costello clones, all RKO had to do was find a pair of seasoned vaudevillians who bore an approximate likeness to Bud and Lou. The men needed were the men found: Wally Brown and Alan Carney.

An angular, pomade-haired standup comedian, 38-year-old Wally Brown specialized in a breathless routine in which he'd begin talking on one subject, then continually change that subject in mid-sentence and sometimes even mid-word, never quite finishing *any* of the thoughts he'd started. The routine bore a close resemblance to the "interrupted-talk" exchanges made famous by the comedy team of Mantan Moreland and F.E. Miller, except that Wally Brown did it without a partner. Existing transcriptions of Brown's radio appearances in the 1940s indicate that his act was a real crowd-pleaser, with audiences breaking out in applause even before he'd wrapped up.

While performing at Loew's State Theater on Broadway, Brown was signed by RKO to play supporting roles in the studio's comedy features and 2-reelers. At the same time that Wally was fracturing audiences at Loew's, chubby, rubber-faced comedian Alan Carney was playing across the street to enthusiastic crowds at the Paramount Theater. Though the 33-year-old Carney hadn't developed a distinct comic image, he did quite well for himself as a dialectician and celebrity impressionist. RKO caught Carney's act and signed him to a contract around the same time they hired Brown. Making an excellent impression as a comic hoodlum in the 1943 Cary Grant vehicle *Mr. Lucky*, Carney started being groomed for stardom.

Though Wally Brown and Alan Carney had known each other for years, they'd never worked together until RKO decided to promote the duo as the studio's "answer" to Abbott & Costello. RKO announced plans to cast the comedians in a whole series of Army comedies, having them play the same characters—Brown as Jerry Miles and Carney as Mike Strager, "a pair of slaphappy, slapsticky and not too bright soldiers"—in each picture. To keep things topical, Jerry and Mike were slated to show up in uniform wherever the American forces happened to be serving at the time of production. But the first film on the docket, 1943's *The Adventures of a Rookie*, did not take place in Sicily or the South Pacific: Instead, the film returned to *Buck Privates* country by focusing on the boys' training-camp period.

Strictly speaking, Brown and Carney were part of a trio in their inaugural starring effort. The third member of the "team" was juvenile lead Richard Martin, who would achieve his greatest fame under the RKO banner as cowboy star Tim Holt's semicomic sidekick Chito Rafferty. *Adventures of a Rookie* begins as the three leads—vaudeville entertainer Jerry Miles, truck driver Mike Strager and aspiring musician Bob Prescott (Richard Martin)—receive their draft notices. The son of an Army colonel, Bob stands a good chance of becoming an officer, but his dreams of a commission are dashed by the clumsy boot-camp antics of fellow rookies Jerry and Mike. Nonetheless, the three pals stick together for a 48-hour leave, hitching a ride from the lissome Peggy Linden (Margaret Landry), who invites the boys to an all-girl dinner party. Upon arrival, Bob gravitates to Peggy, Jerry links up with soubrette Patsy (Patti Brill), and Mike is left holding the bag (actually he's holding an egg, the payoff to an earlier comic setup). A doctor who misdiagnoses a case of strawberry rash as scarlet fever quarantines Peggy's house, forcing the three rookies to spend two weeks billeted with a bevy of gorgeous damsels (RKO used this arrangement to audition its latest crop of starlets, foremost among them the alluring Rita Corday). For Jerry and Mike, the situation is Heaven on Earth, but there's Hell to pay when their surly top sergeant Burke (Erford Gage) is quarantined along with them.

Somewhere around the fifth reel the scarlet-fever business is dropped and we move to San Francisco, where Jerry, Mike and Bob accidentally go AWOL (the episodic storyline suggests that producer Bert Gilroy's heart was still in 2-reelers). After a few misadventures at the Frisco docks and an Army hospital, our heroes manage to link up with their unit just before they're shipped overseas. All this transpires in a brisk 64 minutes, with time to spare for Wally Brown to go into a few of his interrupted-sentence harangues and Alan Carney to imitate Edward G. Robinson and Charles Laughton.

In a 1943 interview with syndicated columnist Robbin Coons, Brown and Carney both claimed that they'd developed much of their own comedy material for the film, often adlibbing new business while the cameras were rolling just to see if they could throw each other off; they even encouraged "straight" lead Richard Martin to ad-lib as well. With all this improvisation, one wonders how much the film's official co-scripter William Bowers (whose later military comedies included *Imitation General* and *The Last Time I Saw Archie*) actually contributed to the festivities. It can be presumed that future Oscar-winner Bowers would hesitate to take credit for the following exchange:

> CARNEY: My stomach's getting too fat.
> BROWN: You oughta diet.
> CARNEY: What?
> BROWN: Diet.
> CARNEY: Naw, I *like* it this color.

With material of this caliber, the RKO publicity flacks were valiant souls indeed to bill Brown and Carney as "the funniest pair to hit the screen in years!" In all fairness, the two comedians do

Adventures of a Rookie (RKO, 1943): Alan Carney, Richard Martin and Wally Brown (left to right) cool their heels in the stockade.

earn a fair share of laughs, but mostly in the scenes where they perform their individual specialties. Unlike Abbott & Costello, Brown & Carney aren't really a team, just two guys who happen to talk to each other a lot. And while it's no trick to tell Bud and Lou apart, I defy you to close your eyes, listen to the soundtrack of *Adventures of a Rookie*, and figure out which is Brown and which is Carney.

Though something of an endurance test today, *Adventures of a Rookie* went over big with entertainment-hungry wartime audiences, clearing a profit of $198,000. During production, Wally Brown made a self-deprecating remark to Robbin Coons in response to Alan Carney's warning that they'd have to rush production of their next picture because he was about to be drafted. "Heh," Wally snickered, "here we are talking about our next picture, and we haven't finished this one." Neither comedian had anything to worry about: Not only was Carney not drafted, but RKO wasn't about to let two of their biggest moneymakers go idle.

Four months after the release of *Adventures of a Rookie*, Brown and Carney were back as Jerry Miles and Mike Strager in the sequel to their earlier hit, *Rookies in Burma* (1943). Though Richard Martin is absent from this tour of duty, the dorky duo is reunited with Erford Gage as the combustible Sergeant Burke (Ironically, Gage would soon leave show business to enlist in the Army as a staff sergeant; he was killed in the Philippines in March 1945). The fun-and-games begin when Jerry and Mike march into the Burmese jungle with their company, where in no time flat the two knuckleheads are captured by the Japanese. The enemy captain (Ted Hecht) orders the boys to translate some coded messages given them by the likewise imprisoned Sgt. Burke, but they manage to outwit their captor with a barrage of Brooklynese slang (apparently the captain missed "vernacular night" in English class). Mike, Jerry and Burke eventually escape by disguising themselves as Japanese soldiers, replete with those hideous buck teeth so often worn by comedians during the War years. Making their way to a friendly village, the two privates and the sergeant come across a pair of stranded American entertainers, Connie (Claire Carleton) and Janie (Joan Barclay). Determined to aid the girls in their flight from the Japanese, Mike and Jerry trade one offensive racial stereotype for another, blacking up as Burmese natives. During the climactic getaway, Mike and Jerry commandeer an elephant — with Mike getting seasick as the pachyderm bounces through the underbrush — and, like so many comedians before them, end up in a runaway tank.

Rookies in Burma performed almost as well at the box office as its predecessor, and it appeared as though RKO could settle back, relax and wait for the money to roll in as Brown & Carney continued to caper about in uniform. But after viewing a work print of *Rookies in Burma*, the Office of War Information declared that the film had reached "a new low" and pressured RKO to pull the plug on the "Rookie" series. With the exception of the 1944 Navy musical *Seven Days Ashore*, in which Brown & Carney aren't really the focal point despite being top-billed, RKO rerouted the comedians into a variety of non-military stories, including the deathless "scare" farce *Zombies on Broadway* (1945). Curiously, Wally and Alan continued to play "Jerry Miles" and "Mike Strager" in their subsequent starring vehicles, suggesting that the two hapless rookies had been dishonorably discharged while no one was looking. After *Genius At Work* in 1946, RKO dissolved the team of Brown & Carney; the two comedians went their separate ways, appearing onscreen together one last time in Disney's *The Absent Minded Professor*, released shortly before Wally Brown's death in 1961. Alan Carney remained active until he passed away in 1973; he is perhaps best known to modern viewers for his performance as police chief Spencer Tracy's deputy in *It's A Mad Mad Mad Mad World*.

By the end of World War II, it would seem that Hollywood's casting agencies had run dry of Abbott & Costello imitators. This left only Abbott & Costello to imitate themselves, which they did in the 1947 Universal picture *Buck Privates Come Home*, a sequel to their 1941 breakthrough film. The boys play the same characters, Slicker Smith and Herbie Brown, and are reunited with the same irascible top sergeant played by Nat Pendleton, now an equally irascible police officer. Except for a few excerpts from the *Buck Privates* drill routine in the opening sequence and a couple of lengthy scenes in a homebound troop ship and the Fort Dix separation center (where Herbie almost re-enlists by accident), *Buck Privates Come Home* ceases being a Army comedy early on, morphing into an unaccredited remake of Laurel & Hardy's *Pack Up Your Troubles* (see **Chapter 3**) as Slicker and Herbie try to find a proper home for a precocious war orphan (Beverly Simmons).

The team's final service farce was 1950's *Abbott and Costello in the Foreign Legion*, a strictly-from-hunger affair with the aging funsters plodding through a dreary parade of dog-eared routines. *Foreign Legion* is enlivened only by an early scene lampooning the artificiality of professional wrestling, and a lengthy episode in the desert in which the biggest laugh is delivered by neither Abbott nor Costello, but by uncredited "Bowery Boys" regular David Gorcey. On this occasion, Universal's rival studios did not fall over themselves trying to create a new Bud Abbott and Lou Costello. After all, they were too busy trying to create a new Dean Martin and Jerry Lewis (see **Chapter 3** again).

5

Repeated Rounds
The "Series" Films

Nothing pleases Hollywood more than a guaranteed profit. And from the earliest nickelodeon days on, there were few commodities more guaranteed to turn a profit than what we now call the "Franchise," but for many years was simply known as the "Series." Until the advent of weekly TV shows, inexpensive series films proliferated from studios both big and small, bearing such blanket titles as "The Cohens and the Kellys," "The Jones Family" "Andy Hardy," "Dr. Kildare," "Charlie Chan," "The Whistler," "Boston Blackie" and "Inner Sanctum." And of course the tradition continues to thrive into the 21st century; take, for instance, the economical, profitable and seemingly interminable "Saw" and "Twilight" franchises.

This chapter concentrates on individual movie-series entries that have dealt with military themes in a lighthearted manner. To qualify for entry, the series must have at least two titles in this category; excluded, for example, is the one-and-only Army comedy in the entire 28-film "Blondie" series, the 1950 Columbia release *Blondie's Hero*. (This also saves me the trouble of having to sit through *Blondie's Hero* again. It's a dog — and it ain't Daisy.)

Sgt. Doubleday (1941–1943, 1951–1952)

The only significant series of the talkie era to focus exclusively on military comedies was produced by Hal Roach Studios between 1941 and 1943. Never given an official umbrella title, the films were known variously as the "Sgt. Doubleday" comedies and the "Dodo" pictures, the latter referring to the lead character's nickname.

In 1938, independent producer Hal Roach severed his association with MGM, who had been distributing his films since 1927, and entered into an arrangement with United Artists, who promised Roach a larger percentage of his film's profits. But there was a downside: While MGM had always co-financed his features, Roach now had to arrange his own financing. Consequently, though Roach reaped the box-office benefits of such successes as *Topper Takes a Trip* (1939) and *One Million BC* (1940), he also had to absorb the losses incurred by such misfires as *Zenobia* (1939). By the early 1940s, both Roach and United Artists had fallen upon hard times, forcing the producer to totally realign his production policy. He wanted to continue offering quality product, while simultaneously cutting down production time and the physical print cost. His solution was the outgrowth of an idea Roach had been nursing since the mid-1930s; the assembly-line production of "streamliners," each running between 40 and 50 minutes and designed as co-features for double bills.

Roach first experimented with the streamliner format by releasing his 1940 Laurel & Hardy comedy *A Chump at Oxford* at a length of 42 minutes, but exhibitor demand required him to stretch the running time to feature length by shooting several additional scenes. One year later, the producer revitalized the streamliner policy by proposing a series of 4½-reel military comedies starring Laurel & Hardy, but the team had left the studio with no intention of returning. Fortunately, Roach was still able to sell the Army-comedy concept to United Artists, who like everyone else in Hollywood was anxious to emulate the success of Universal's *Buck Privates*. The first entry in the new series, *Tanks a Million*, went before the cameras in the summer of 1941.

With an average budget of $100,000 per picture, Roach was unable to attract big names to the project, so he settled for a cast of inexpensive but well-known character actors. Top billing went to 23-year-old William Tracy, a chubby juvenile who after garnering excellent notices as beleaguered military-academy "plebe" Misto in *Brother Rat* (1938) had gone on to such prestige items as Ernst Lubitsch's *The Shop Around the Corner* and John Ford's *Tobacco Road*. Second-billed James Gleason, a Hollywood fixture since 1926, was well known for his acidulously comic characterizations in such films as *Here Comes Mr. Jordan* and *Meet John Doe*; the wizened, nasal-voiced Gleason has been described by film maven Leslie Halliwell as "one character actor who never let us down."

Also appearing in *Tanks a Million* are Roach contractee Noah Beery Jr. (son of venerable screen heavy Noah Beery and nephew of MGM star Wallace Beery), who had drawn attention to himself with supporting roles in *Only Angels Have Wings* (1939), *Of Mice and Men* (1939) and *Sergeant York* (1941); and fourth-billed Joe Sawyer, previously Joseph Sauers, whose movie career had been on the ascent ever since his performance as Humphrey Bogart's hero-worshipping henchman in *The Petrified Forest* (1936). Fashion model Elyse Knox, famous for her magazine-ad appearances as "The Chesterfield Girl," was selected to play the love interest; later the wife of football star-turned-sportscaster Tom Harmon, Knox is best known today as the the mother of *NCI*'s star Mark Harmon.

Scripted by Edward E. Seabrook, Paul Girard Smith and Warren Wilson, the 50-minute *Tanks a Million* casts William Tracy as Dorian "Dodo" Doubleday, an owlish young man blessed with a photographic memory. We first see Doubleday demonstrating his phenomenal mental backlog of trivia and minutiae on a radio program hosted by announcer Knox Manning, who has invited our hero to appear before the microphone as a *rara avis*: A railroad-station information clerk who can actually provide information. In the studio audience is Charlie Cobb (Noah Beery Jr.), Doubleday's rival for the affections of the toothsome Jeannie (Elyse Knox). Called up by the Draft, Doubleday and Charlie report for duty at Camp Carver, where Dodo immediately runs afoul of Sergeant William Ames (Joe Sawyer), a thick-eared career soldier with an intense hatred for know-it-all draftees. The situation hardly improves when Dodo so impresses Lt. Caldwell (Harold Goodwin) with his encyclopedic knowledge of the Army manual that he is sent to non-com training, where in a single day he earns the same sergeant's chevrons that it took Ames twenty years to attain. Outraged that Sgt. Doubleday is now Caldwell's pet soldier, Sgt. Ames and Capt. Rossmead (Douglas Fowley) assign the "24-hour wonder" to Company F, the worst platoon in camp — where the lazy Charlie Cobb has also been shunted off. Ames' and Rossmead's hopes of getting Doubleday busted to private are dashed when, through a combination of good fortune, book-smarts and purity of heart, the youthful sergeant whips Company F into tip-top shape.

Enter Colonel "Spitfire" Barkeley (James Gleason), a crusty old campaigner who happens to suffer from a severe case of "mike fright," shivering at the mere prospect of delivering a speech. Appointed Barkeley's adjutant, Doubleday impulsively tries the Colonel's uniform on for size, just as his girlfriend Jeannie shows up at camp. Jeannie's assumption that Dodo has been promoted to Colonel leads to a comedy of errors as the stammering Sergeant, mistaken for Barkeley, is forced to make a coast-to-coast radio speech. Ames and Rossmead take fiendish delight in this turn of events: They're certain that once Doubleday's true identity is revealed, he will be sent to Leavenworth for impersonating an officer. But the Pentagon officials are so moved by Doubleday's extemporaneous speech about democracy and duty that he is forgiven his deception — even by the bombastic Barkeley, who orders Dodo to write *all* of his speeches from now on.

Tanks a Million represented a comeback for director Fred Guiol (pronounced "Gill"), who had first signed with Hal Roach as a prop man in 1918, quickly moving up the studio ladder as photographer and director. Guiol's best 2-reelers for Roach include Laurel & Hardy's *The Second 100 Years* (1927), Max Davidson's *Pass the Gravy* (1927) and Charley Chase's *Limousine Love* (1928). When fellow cinematographer George Stevens graduated to directing, he invited his old friend Guiol to join him at RKO, where Stevens had just finished two successful Wheeler & Woolsey vehicles. Unable to helm the team's next film *The Rainmakers* (1935), Stevens recommended Guiol for the job—which proved a grievous error in judgment. Though extensively experienced in 2-reelers, Guiol seemed incapable of assembling a feature-length film; worse still, his lack of organizational skills caused him to go way over budget. Guiol's three Wheeler & Woolsey features were disasters, transforming one of RKO's most saleable commodities into a box-office liability. Apparently washed up as a director by 1936, Guiol signed on as an associate director and screenwriter for his pal George Stevens, earning plaudits for his work on such pictures as *Gunga Din* (1939) and *Vigil in the Night* (1940). At Stevens' urging, Hal Roach rehired Guiol in 1941 to direct *Tanks a Million*—and miracle of miracles, the 4½-reel streamliner length turned out to be ideally suited to Guiol's limited talents. Though the derivative director brought nothing new to the table, his 1940s efforts for Roach were brisk, breezy little entertainments, benefiting rather than suffering from the director's habit of recycling old gags. In *Tanks a Million*, for example, the physical consequences of a forced march are represented by a closeup of the rookies' bare toes, which bulge and pulsate before our eyes—a gag that can be traced back to Guiol's 1927 Roach comedy *With Love and Hisses*. Fred Guiol went on to direct four more of the "Doubleday" comedies, and served as producer for the remaining entries of the 1940s.

All industry eyes were on *Tanks a Million* when it hit America's movie screens on September 12, 1941: Could Hal Roach truly strike box-office gold with a second feature running slightly less than five reels? He could and did; *The Hollywood Reporter* gave it an enthusiastic review: "The show is a solid howl and a sure hit attraction on any bill. If Roach can hold to the quality of this 50 minutes of screamingly funny farce, his idea of shorter features is certain to prove a winner." *Tanks a Million* received top-of-the-bill bookings in several cities, and also earned an Oscar nomination for Edward Ward's musical score. Though Roach would develop several other streamliner series, the "Doubleday" films would be his biggest moneymakers of the 1940s.

This success cannot be attributed to timeliness alone. The surehanded comic performance of William Tracy, who manages to make Dodo Doubleday both irritating and adorable all at once, is the show's main attraction. In this first entry, Tracy is essentially a solo player; beginning with the second "Dodo" picture *Hay Foot* (released January 2, 1942), Roach began exploring the potential of a creating a new comedy trio out of Tracy and supporting players Joe Sawyer and Noah Beery, Jr., respectively repeating their roles as Sgt. Ames and Charlie Cobb. Sawyer is co-billed with Tracy over the title in *Hay Foot*, with Beery, James Gleason, and Elyse Knox in the featured cast. Now also a sergeant, Cobb has become Sgt. Ames' co-conspirator in the ongoing campaign to discredit Doubleday and get him reduced in rank—and just as in the first film, the harder Ames tries to make Dodo look bad, the more stupid and incompetent he himself appears. Previously cast as Doubleday's girlfriend Jeannie, Elyse Knox here plays Betty Barkeley, daughter of General Barkeley (Gleason again).

In the 48-minute *Hay Foot*, Dodo's photographic memory is of no help to him on the firing range; though he may know all there is to know about ballistics and trajectory, he is unable to shoot straight or even handle a gun properly. Ordered to practice alone in the woods, Dodo accidentally shoots a hawk and a fish (!) dead-center. Impressed by the boy's "marksmanship," Gen. Barkeley invites Dodo to his house for dinner, with Betty addressing the invitation to "the best shot in the regiment." Having both won medals for their own shooting skills, Ames and Cobb read the invitation and show up at Barkley's house, each assuming that the letter was addressed to him. When Dodo arrives, the other two sergeants throw him out of a window—twice. In contrast with his passivity in *Tanks a Million*, Doubleday decides to exact vengeance on Ames and

5. Repeated Rounds 109

Frame capture of a typically jaunty opening title from Hal Roach's popular "Sergeant Doubleday" series of the 1940s.

Cobb in this picture. Knowing that the pair are scheduled to participate in a national shooting contest, he swipes their pistols and places the weapons on a plank precariously balanced on the edge of a deep well, with his dog Jeep on the other end of the plank. If Dodo should whistle, Jeep will jump up and the pistols will be "drowned." With this threat hanging over their heads, Ames and Cobb have no choice but to follow Dodo's orders in full view of Gen. Barkeley, forced to exhibit such ridiculous behavior as playing patty-cake and singing falsetto. But Dodo overplays his hand and whistles by mistake — and "plunk" go the pistols, prompting the two surly sergeants to hatch their own revenge scheme. Sneaking into the barracks late at night, Ames and Cobb toss Dodo's bed out a second-floor window — little realizing that the bed is occupied by General Barkeley, who is spending a night in the non-coms' quarters as part of his program to "democratize" the military. This sort of material has less to do with Army life than with producer Hal Roach's career-long commitment to the Comedy of Embarrassment, and on this level it succeeds admirably.

With Noah Beery Jr. spun off into a separate series of streamliners teaming him with Will Rogers' son Jimmy, William Tracy and Joe Sawyer are all that remain of the *Hay Foot* comic trio in the third "Doubleday" comedy *About Face* (April 16, 1942). It was by now obvious that Roach was endeavoring to mold Tracy and Sawyer into a new Laurel & Hardy; indeed, the final reel of the 43-minute *About Face* is basically a remake of Stan & Ollie's classic silent short *Two Tars* (1928).

Dodo's photographic memory figures into the plot only as a device enabling him to win a contest sponsored by Rice Puffies Cereal. This time, Ames is not preoccupied with ruining Dodo's career; on the contrary, he goes out of his way to ingratiate himself with his fellow sergeant. That's because Ames is flat broke, and is hoping to use Dodo's contest money for a night on the town (echoing another Laurel & Hardy silent, *Their Purple Moment*). The comedy arising from this premise has little relation with things military until the film's midsection, when Dodo is invited by socialite Betty Marlowe (Marjorie Lord) to attend a debutante tea party. Under the misapprehension that some wild reverie is in the offing, Ames tags along with Dodo. Presiding over the party is the magnificent Margaret Dumont as Mrs. Culpepper, head of the Home Defense League. Mrs. Culpepper delivers a lecture about vocational training, using Doubleday to represent the new "brains" army and Ames to illustrate the old-fashioned "brawn" army. Metaphorically, explains Mrs. C., Dodo is a "modern mechanized tank," while Ames is an "outmoded Army mule." Soon the plot takes another direction as Ames and Dodo rent a car (from veteran screen sourpuss Charles Lane) and drive their dates to an Army-Navy dance at the Lakeside Country Club. Here the boys become involved in a minor accident with another motorist, which quickly escalates into a *Two Tars*-style exercise in reciprocal destruction wherein several servicemen (including such familiar toughies as Mike Mazurki and Matt Willis) tear each other's cars apart, smashing fenders, ripping off grills and breaking windshields with orgiastic abandon. The film concludes in the same manner as its predecessors, with Ames trying to heap the blame for all the damage on Doubleday, only to have his strategy backfire spectacularly.

In addition to future *Danny Thomas Show* regular Marjorie Lord, *About Face* boasts a dynamic female supporting cast, including brassy Veda Ann Borg as a high-maintenance blonde and irresistibly cute Jean Porter (later the wife of director Edward Dmytrk) as a flirtatious jitterbugger who repeatedly embarrasses Dodo in the eyes of his girlfriend Betty, a running gag reminiscent of Roach's earlier comedies with Charley Chase. Best of all is perennial Marx Brothers foil Margaret Dumont, delivering a polished and superbly nuanced performance which firmly puts the lie to Groucho Marx's assertion that she never understood any of her dialogue. Dumont's disparaging comment that a squad car full of good-time girls looks more like a "squab car" is comic timing at its best.

Fall In (March 5, 1943) was the fourth in what was now being regularly promoted as the "Dodo" series. From being erstwhile pals in *About Face*, Doubleday and Ames resume their adversarial relationship in *Fall In*, though Dodo tries his best to make friends with the irascible Ames; also, the two actors are not technically teamed in this one, except at the very end of the picture. Considered the best of the series, the 48-minute *Fall In* is certainly the best constructed entry since *Tanks a Million*, and the one that takes the fullest comic advantage of the photographic-memory angle.

When Dodo is selected for Officer Training School, Ames' jealousy soars to new heights. Knowing that Dodo's promotion hinges on his ability to take charge of a group of new recruits, Ames arranges for his nemesis to be place in command of a cantankerous collection of Kentucky hillbillies. Dodo can't get these scraggly-haired, rifle-totin' backwoodsmen to pay any attention to him until one of the rustic rookies (played by Arthur Hunnicutt, later a favorite of director Howard Hawks) lets slip that they'll only take orders from a fellow Kentuckian. Summoning his vast knowledge of the Blue Grass state — gleaned from memorizing the *Encyclopedia Americana* at age eight — Dodo adopts a thick Southern drawl and claims to hail from the hillbillies' home turf, whereupon the bucolic recruits agree to do anything he tells them. Impressed by the shooting-range expertise of Dodo's platoon, the boys' captain assigns them to MP duty, ordering them to make sure the other GIs behave themselves in town on payday. Meanwhile, Ames is enjoying himself at a military rec hall set up in the mansion of wealthy Mr. Benedict (Clyde Fillmore, who'd played a colonel in *Tanks a Million*) and his niece Lydia (Rebel Randall, previously one of the debutantes in *About Face*). Working as a volunteer hostess at Benedict's house is Dodo's girlfriend Joan (Jean Porter, another carryover from *About Face*, also playing a different character). When she discovers that the house is bugged with microphones, the better to pick up any and all secret information from the garrulous GIs, Joan deduces that Benedict is actually a Nazi spy (his full

5. Repeated Rounds

"Dodo" Doubleday (William Tracy, left) in the iron grip of scowling fellow sergeant Ames (Joe Sawyer). A frame capture from *Fall In* (Hal Roach, 1942), Number Four in the "Doubleday" series.

name in the original shooting script was Arnold Benedict!), and manages to summon help from Dodo and his mountain-grown MPs before she's kidnapped. The final slapstick free-for-all between the MPs and the spies reprises all sorts of sight gags from Hal Roach's silent Harold Lloyd and "Our Gang" comedies. Once the villains are routed, Dodo tunes in on the Nazis' short-wave radio and memorizes the orders being issued to the local fifth columnists. Unfortunately he's conked on the head and loses his memory, but Ames saves the day by re-conking Dodo with a handy mallet.

By now, Tracy and Sawyer had their characterizations and familiar bits of business (such as Ames grabbing Dodo by the scruff of the neck) down to a science. Sensing it was time to freshen up the formula, screenwriters Eugene Conrad and Edward E. Seabrook placed the two stars in a brand-new setting for the fifth entry, *Yanks Ahoy* (June 29, 1943)—which may not have been "The Funniest Army Comedy Yet!" as advertised, but at 58 minutes was certainly the longest "Dodo" comedy to date. It's possible that after two years of turning out streamliners, Roach was hoping to ease his way back into feature-length comedies with *Yanks Ahoy*.

When Doubleday is finally assigned to overseas duty, Ames has one more reason to detest his fellow non-com: After all, of what value would a wonky weakling like Dodo be in a combat situation, especially since the Army already has such a fine physical specimen as Ames? While on board the same Navy transport ship with Doubleday, Ames works overtime to discredit the little guy in the eyes of their superior officer (Walter Woolf King), as usual succeeding only in making himself look like a moron. Adopting a new strategy, Ames tries to convince his CO that he himself has war-hero potential, but it is Doubleday who is covered with glory when, in the absence of the ship's quartermaster, he draws upon his vast knowledge of ocean charts to safely navigate the vessel through a treacherous strait. Finally Ames manages to get Doubleday busted to private by arranging for his nemesis to be caught sneaking around the nurse's quarters, which also puts Dodo in bad with heroine Phyllis (played by Marjorie Woodworth, who had once been promoted by Hal Roach as the "new Jean Harlow"). But even this setback is turned to Doubleday's advantage when, while taking a break from KP duty, he agrees to help the ship's cook reel in a fish — and hooks a Japanese submarine instead.

The 6-reel length of *Yanks Ahoy* only serves to prove that the series was at its best when it was at its briefest. The film suffers from repetition and padding, with two sequences in particular — a prolonged and somewhat nauseating "seasick" gag and an exhumation of the ancient "crying while peeling onions" routine — slowing the pace to a crawl. The submarine-capture finale, which should have been a highlight, is lethargically staged in the same cramped studio tank that had diminished the closing scenes of Laurel & Hardy's *Saps at Sea* (1940), using miniatures that wouldn't pass muster in a bathtub. Only the expertise of the two stars rescues the film from total worthlessness — that, and the unexpected appearance of onetime Hal Roach Studio fixture James Finlayson in the tiny role of ship's cook Flynn.

After delivering one more streamliner to United Artists, the Hitler spoof *Nazty Nuisance* (1943), Hal Roach turned his facilities over to the American armed services for the production of wartime propaganda shorts. Three years after the end of World War II, Roach attempted to jump-start his movie career with a new gimmick: the ready-made double feature, consisting of two short feature films in a single package. The second — and last — of these dual-picture offerings went out in 1948 under the blanket title *Hal Roach Laff-Time*. This package contained *Who Killed Doc Robbin?*, a 51-minute failed attempt to bring back the "Our Gang" series with a new kiddie cast; and *Here Comes Trouble*, a 58-minute continuation of the "Dodo" franchise with William Tracy and Joe Sawyer reprising their roles. Our heroes have returned to civilian life in this one, with Doubleday a cub reporter and Ames a beat cop. No sooner have they renewed their contentious relationship than the boys are mixed up in the murder of a blackmailing striptease artist, culminating in a frantic backstage chase at a burlesque theater. Cheap and shoddy every inch of the way, *Here Comes Trouble* did nothing to advance the careers of either the producer or the stars. The film's sole virtue was its Cinecolor photography, a virtue lost in the surviving black & white TV prints.

With the Roach lot now in the hands of the producer's son Hal Roach, Jr., the studio forsook the manufacture of theatrical films to concentrate on television production. In 1951, the younger Roach took another fling at big-screen moviemaking, with bargain-basement Lippert Studios rather than United Artists handling distribution. Despite the dismal box office of *Here Comes Trouble*, it was decided to once more revivify the "Dodo" series, again starring Tracy and Sawyer and with Fred Guiol back in the director's chair. The first of these follow-ups to Roach's most successful franchise of the 1940s was released on October 5, 1951, under the title *As You Were*.

Contrary to previously published reports, the 57-minute *As You Were* was not merely a cobbled-together reissue of two earlier "Doubleday" comedies, though generous footage from *Tanks a Million* is used in a flashback sequence. The action takes place during the Korean War, with plenty of references to that then-current conflict. Back in uniform, Sgt. Ames is having trouble recruiting new soldiers in a train depot. In desperation, Ames persuases Doubleday, who has gone back to his prewar career as an information clerk, to re-up. It's *déjà vu* all over again when, after impressing Col. Lockwood (Russell Hicks) with his photographic memory, Dodo is instantly promoted to master sergeant — outranking the fuming Ames. The presence of Joan Vohs as an attractive WAC sergeant tips the audience off well in advance to the inevitable "Oops, we're in the women's barracks!" routine. Still, no one could be entirely prepared for the spectacle of William Tracy and Joe Sawyer in drag.

With the same stars and director, the "new" Doubleday series trundled forward with the 65-

minute Lippert release *Mr. Walkie-Talkie* (November 28, 1952), the only series entry set in a combat zone (South Korea, which bears a marked resemblance to LA's Griffith Park). Sgt. Ames has had himself transferred to the front lines in hopes of escaping the pesky Doubleday, but you and I know that ain't gonna happen. A notch or two better than its predecessor, *Mr. Walkie Talkie* includes some amusing byplay between Dodo and his pet duck Clarence, and a truly hilarious army-games sequence involving Dodo's ability to imitate the sound of a quail. New to the franchise are comic singer Margia Dean, who performs the novelty number "I Love the Men," and Alan Hale Jr. as the inappropriately nicknamed "Tiny."

After *Mr. Walkie Talkie*, the "Dodo" series called it a day. Though not particularly well known except among comedy buffs and Hal Roach scholars, the seven military comedies in the series have never entirely been out of circulation. They were frequently revived theatrically well into the 1950s, and were all early arrivals on television courtesy of such distributors as Favorite Films and Comet Productions. In the mid-1980s, the newly reformed Hal Roach Studios prepared two of the films for TV and theatrical reissue, editing *Fall In* and *Yanks Ahoy* together as a 97-minute feature. Apparently no one took time to notice that supporting player Frank Faylen is cast as an Army lieutenant in *Fall In* and a Navy quartermaster in *Yanks Ahoy*. And here's one for all you classic-TV fans out there: Faylen's character name in *Fall In* is Lieutenant Gillis. Mayhaps this is the same fellow who later resurfaced as "Herbert T. Gillis," father of sitcom hero Dobie Gillis—*you* know, that small-town grocer who was always bragging about serving "in Dubya Dubya Two! The Big One! *With* the Good Conduct medal!"

The Bowery Boys (1946–1958)

Outside of the "Doubleday" films, no other movie series offered as many military comedies as "The Bowery Boys." Of the 48 feature-length comedies in this series produced by Monogram Pictures and its successor Allied Artists between 1946 and 1958, five of them found the "Boys" in one branch or other of the armed services.

The Bowery Boys have been described by author James Robert Parrish as a "mongrelization" of several other movie franchises. It all began in 1937 with Sam Goldwyn's film version of Sidney Kingsley's 1935 Broadway drama *Dead End*, featuring six of the teenage actors who had played street-gang members in the original stage version: Billy Halop, Bobby Jordan, Leo Gorcey, Huntz Hall, Gabriel Dell and Bernard Punsly. The "Dead End Kids" scored such a hit in the Goldwyn picture that their contracts were purchased by Warner Bros., who cast the boys as essentially the same wisecracking punks in six films, ranging from the classic James Cagney vehicle *Angels with Dirty Faces* (1938) to the 60-minute quickie *On Dress Parade* (1940). In 1938, Halop, Hall, Jordan, Dell and Punsly splintered off into a similar aggregation at Universal, "The Dead End Kids and Little Tough Guys," with youthful character actor Billy Benedict joining the gang. Two years later at Monogram, producer Sam Katzman launched "The East Side Kids," which would eventually include all the aforementioned Dead End Kids and Little Tough Guys except Halop and Punsly, plus Leo Gorcey's younger brother David (for many years billed as David Condon), who'd been in a handful of the Universal entries. During the World War II years, a few of the East Side Kids pictures contained elements of the military-comedy genre—the boys show up in uniform at the end of 1943's *Kid Dynamite*, and are home on furlough in 1944's *Follow the Leader*—but none of the 22 series entries was a full-fledged service farce.

The popularity of the East Side Kids enabled Leo Gorcey and his agent Jan Grippo to break away from Katzman and reorganize the group into still another franchise, "The Bowery Boys," beginning with the 1946 Monogram release *Live Wires*. Having gone through a variety of character names, Gorcey was now firmly established as group leader Terrence Aloysius "Slip" Mahoney, with Huntz Hall as goofy second banana Horace Debussy "Sach" Jones, Billy Benedict as the affable

Whitey and David Gorcey (or Condon) as the nondescript Chuck (Bobby Jordan remained with the series until 1947, while Gabe Dell dropped out in 1950). The first six years' worth of Bowery Boys pictures were produced by Grippo, with Gorcey exercising most of the creative control—including the decision to downpedal the dramatic elements of the earlier films and focus on comedy. By the early 1950s, the Boys were no longer pugnacious slum kids but a bunch of amiable, underemployed thirty-somethings who hatched various comic schemes while hanging around the Bowery sweet shop owned by the easily swindled Louie Dumbrowsky (Bernard Gorcey, Leo's real-life father). Leo and David Gorcey were still with the team, along with Hall, Benedict, and a revolving retinue of newcomers like Bennie Bartlett and Buddy Gorman.

Non-fans of the Bowery Boys often complain that it's impossible to tell their pictures apart. To be sure, certain comic bits are repeated *ad infinitum:* Slip Mahoney's endless malapropisms and habitual hat-slapping of subordinate Sach Jones, Sach's "motor lips" and occasional magic powers, the mountain of IOUs piling up at Louie's Sweet Shop, and the numerical cataloging of fight signals ("Okay, fellas, Routine Six!"). Still, the series' producers did their best to inject some variety in the formula. One of their most effective methods was to lampoon every movie genre in existence. Gangster Melodrama, Western, Mystery, Ghost Story, Newspaper Yarn, Film Noir, Jungle Epic, Sci Fi/Fantasy—you name it, the Bowery Boys trashed it.

The series finally got around to service comedies with 1951's *Bowery Batallion*, which begins with Sach, Whitey, Chuck and Butch (Buddy Gorman) signing up for the Army after being scared witless by a mock air raid. Slip races to the recruiting office to stop them, only to be tricked into enlisting himself. Arriving at Fort Stockton, the boys waste less time than usual getting into trouble, and before the second reel has ended they've been sent to the guardhouse, thereby establishing the film's running gag of repeated incarceration. Meanwhile, their old pal Louie Dumbrowsky, a World War I hero known as "the fighting corporal," has been summoned to the Pentagon for a top-secret espionage mission. His former commanding officer Col. Masters (Selmer Jackson) gives Louie a Major's commission and leaks the slightly misleading information that the new officer is the inventor of a revolutionary "hydrogen ray," the better to bait and hook a gang of enemy agents. Also assigned to Fort Stockton, Major Dumbrowsky appoints Slip, Sach and the rest as his orderlies, despite their inability to follow the simplest order correctly (since *Bowery Batallion* required Army cooperation to film several scenes at an actual base, the script is careful to point out that the Bowery Boys are the *only* foul-ups amongst the new recruits). Unbeknownst to anyone, Army secretary Marsha (Virginia Hewitt) is one of the enemy spies, and it is she who arranges for her two confederates (John Bleifer, Al Eben) to abduct Louie right from under the Boys' noses. Fortunately Louie manages to tip Sach off by whispering, "Routine Eleven!" which prompts the Boys to dash to the rescue. Unfortunately, they have to go AWOL to accomplish this, and in the last scene our heroes are marched off to the stockade for the fourth time in the same picture.

Overall, *Bowery Batallion* is the weakest of the series' military comedies, hampered by an inconsistent script with too many loose plot strands. The direction by William Beaudine (who helmed more Bowery Boys entries than anyone else) is perfunctory at best, bringing little to the film that hasn't already been written down. Still, *Bowery Batallion* has its good points, notably some prime Leo Gorcey malaprops ("Let's sympathize our watches," "A whole spittoon of soldiers is on their way") and a priceless training scene in which Huntz Hall gets a free mud treatment. The film's funniest moments belong to saber-toothed Donald MacBride, who in the role of exasperated topkick Sgt. Frisbie is able to generate more laughs with a raised eyebrow than most actors with fifteen pages of jokes. MacBride is even allowed to deliver the picture's Pirandellian punchline: Slamming the door of the stockade cell that will be the Boys' home for the next few days, the actor turns to the camera and chortles, "As far as I'm concerned, this is the greatest finish to any picture I've seen!"

The Bowery Boys' next service comedy *Let's Go Navy* (1951) is one of the series' finest entries, its most memorable gags and routines emerging from a logical progression of events and the unique characterizations of the stars. After collecting $1600 for charity, Slip and Sach are mugged and robbed by two men dressed as sailors (one of the assailants is played by Tom Neal, the luckless protagonist of the quintessential low-budget film noir *Detour*). Suspected of stealing the cash themselves, the Boys vow to track the crooks to the ends of the earth, even if they have to join the Navy to do it. In order to avoid a full four years' service, Slip takes advantage of a mix-up at the recruiting station and pilfers the enlistment papers of five other guys, reasoning that once their mission is completed he and the Boys can inform the Navy of their "mistake" and receive instant discharges. Thus, Slip spends the rest of the picture posing as "Seaman Dobson," Sach is identified as "Seaman Hobenlocker," and Whitey, Butch and Chuck pretend to be "Schwartz," "Stevenson" and "Merriwether," respectively. Slip's brilliant scheme demonstrates anew his bad habit of leaping without looking: While the Boys spend the next twelve months at sea, the two thieves—who aren't sailors at all, merely civilians posing as gobs—remain safely sequestered in the apartment directly above Louie's Sweet Shop.

"Man the Laff-Boats!" was the main advertising tag for *Let's Go Navy*, which like the previous *Bowery Battalion* was filmed with full military cooperation (including the input of technical advisor Lt. Robert M. Garick, USNR) and thus avoided casting aspersions upon the Navy by again depicting the Bowery Boys as the only maladroits in the picture. While Gorcey's marvelous malaprops are at a minimum ("Chief Petting Officer" is the best of a meager lot), the film's key running gag—Sach accidentally causing CPO Longnecker (Allen Jenkins) to be thoroughly drenched with water—is infinitely better than *Battalion*'s tiresome repeat visits to the stockade, with each new variation on the gag genuinely taking the audience by surprise (director William Beaudine is in top form here). Also praiseworthy is the scene in which the Boys make good their $1600 debt with

The Bowery Boys invade the South Seas in *Let's Go Navy* (Monogram, 1951). From left: David Gorcey, Leo Gorcey, Buddy Gorman, Charlita, Huntz Hall and Billy Benedict.

a lucky gambling streak, as Sach outwits a thimble-rigging sailor (Frank Jenks, who'd earlier played the recruiting sergeant in *Battalion*) with the help of Davy Jones, a garrulous parrot he'd picked up during a stopover in a tropical port. In its review of *Let's Go Navy*, the traditionally hard-bitten *Motion Picture Herald* enthused: "Any resemblance between this and any other Bowery Boys picture is purely geneological. It is far funnier, faster and more fruitful as to audience reaction than anything the Leo Gorcey-Huntz Hall duo has furnished their following."

Though it doesn't quite live up to the standard set by *Let's Go Navy*, the 1952 Bowery Boys epic *Here Come the Marines* (working title: *Bowery Leathernecks*) is an enjoyable outing, one of the better entries produced by Jan Grippo's successor Jerry Thomas. With Billy Benedict and Buddy Gorman out of the series, their slots in the five-man Bowery Boy lineup were filled by Gil Stratton Jr. as Junior and Bennie Bartlett as Butch. It is clear that unlike its predecessors, *Here Come the Marines* was filmed without the cooperation of the U.S. Marine Corps. Beyond the fact that the picture's officers and non-coms sometimes behave as foolishly as the Boys, it's doubtful that the organization would have countenanced such a gaffe as having Slip Mahoney receive a draft notice from the Marines. Fiercely proud of its "elite" status, the Corps did not regularly draft recruits until the Vietnam era — and then only on a *very* selective basis, while the men were standing in line at the induction center.

The series' love affair with running gags reaches its pinnacle (or pinochle, as Slip might put it) in *Here Comes the Marines*; one could even say that the entire plot is a running gag. Through a series of lucky accidents, Sach Jones is promoted from buck private to sergeant his very first day in the Corps — and the more Sach messes up throughout the picture, the higher he is promoted! This premise would be better developed in 1965's *McHale's Navy Joins the Air Force* (see **Chapter 12**), but it's still fun to see the feckless Sach barking orders at the scowling Slip instead of the other way around. Even more galling to Slip is the knowledge that Sach enjoys a warm friendship with Col. Brown (Hanley Stafford), who during World War I had been best buds with Sach's father, Sgt. "Hardhead" Jones.

As Sergeant Sach toots his ear-shattering whistle and imperiously marches his pals down a country road, Slip comes upon a beaten and half-dying marine sprawled in a ditch. A curiously designed playing card found on the marine's body leads Slip and his pals to a crooked gambling joint run by Jolly Joe Johnson (Paul Maxey), which specializes in shaking down servicemen. In their efforts to avenge the murdered marine, Slip and Sach apprise Col. Brown of what's transpiring at Jolly Joe's. Agreeing to act as decoys to expose the baddies, the Boys nearly get court-martialed when Jolly Joe orders his personal "Mata Hari" Lulu Mae (Myrna Dell) to sneak into the Marine barracks as a means of discrediting our heroes. This sets up one of the film's myriad of service-comedy cliches — hiding a girl from the CO during inspection — but the payoff is quite ingenious, if a bit unbelievable. Anyway, the Boys manage to bust up Jolly Joe's racket, and as a bonus Slip turns the tables on the power-mad Sach for the finale.

Here Come the Marines is out of favor with many Bowery Boys purists because of Sach's overbearingly obnoxious behavior while pulling rank on his buddies — and admittedly, he blows his damn whistle so often that we'd like to ram it down his throat. But screenwriters Tim Ryan (who also appears in the film as a corrupt sheriff), Charles R. Marion and Tim Crutcher manage to keep Sach lovable by having him perform such generous gestures as securing 12-hour passes for his pals, and arranging for Louie Dumbrowsky to take over the PX so that the Boys will continue receiving their daily allotment of free banana splits. Also, Sach admits that he's "just havin' fun" lording it over Slip and the others, so we can't stay mad at him very long. But for all its scripted humor and sight gags, the single most amusing aspect of *Here Come the Marines* is unintentional. Though director William Beaudine and cinematographer Marcel le Picard do their best to camouflage the fact, it is obvious that all the film's exterior marching scenes were shot on the same day — and during the same rain shower.

Having lain waste to the Army, Navy and Marines, the Bowery Boys invade the Air Force in

1953's *Clipped Wings*, the funniest of the series' military farces. By this time, Ben Schwalb had taken over as the franchise's producer, adjusting the format so that the Boys are no longer semi-believable overgrown urchins, but instead come off as total buffoons. The films themselves have taken on the appearance of extended 2-reel comedies, with many of them directed by Edward Bernds and scripted by Ellwood Ullman, alumni both of Columbia Pictures' short-subject unit. The best director the series ever had, Ed Bernds moved his nine Bowery Boys efforts along at a breakneck pace, with Ullman expertly melding the verbal and visual gags with solid story values provided by Bernds and other collaborators (he shares screen credit in *Clipped Wings* with series regular Charles R. Marion). The Boys themselves are now four in number, Gil Stratton Jr. having dropped out after *Here Come the Marines*; but though David Gorcey and Bennie Bartlett are prominently billed in *Clipped Wings*, they disappear for reels at a time. Like most of the remaining series entries, this is Gorcey and Hall's show all the way.

We begin the picture as the Boys share a brief reunion with their old neighborhood chum Dave Moreno (played by Todd Karns, aka "Harry Bailey" in *It's a Wonderful Life*), now an Air Force lieutenant. Not long afterward, word arrives that Dave has been arrested and confined to quarters on suspicion of treason. The minute we see a furtive-looking Moreno conspiring to steal military secrets with a trio of criminals (Phil Van Zandt, Frank Richards, Michael Ross), we can rest assured that Dave is *not* a traitor, and that he is working undercover with the FBI to trap the crooks. Of course, Slip and Sach are ignorant of such tried-and-true movie plot devices, and thus make a beeline to Allen Air Force Base to get the whole story from Dave, only to accidentally sign up for a hitch themselves. Though their flight-school test results indicate that Slip and Sach "have a combined IQ of minus eighteen," the boys are assigned to ground-crew detail and ordered to pick up their barracks assignments. Sach having signed his name as "H. Jones," his enlistment papers are confused with those of another H. Jones, and as a result he is assigned to Barracks C— home of the base's all-girl WAF unit. Flustered female sergeant Anderson (a terrific performance by Renie Riano) tries to rectify this error, but the officer who signed Sach's papers has been called overseas and the assignment stands. (Though the studio had to get Air Force cooperation for permission to film on a genuine air base, the powers-that-be evidently weren't offended by this sly satire of military bureaucracy.) Given separate quarters in the WAF laundry room, Sach nonetheless basks in the attention of all the pretty young aviatrixes, while Slip must sweat it out with the rest of the guys scrubbing down wings and propellors.

After a few well-timed gag sequences enhanced by Martin Skiles' Mickey Mouse musical score (not to mention the ridiculous nightcap and floor-length gown that Sach *always* wears to bed in his military comedies), the plot resumes as Slip and Sach put a tail on Dave to find out if he's really betrayed his country. During a public air show being held on the base, the boys inadvertently knock out Moreno's two FBI contacts, leaving Dave helpless and vulnerable when the villains— aided by treacherous PX waitress Dorene (June Vincent)— kidnap him. Racing to the rescue, Slip and Sach board a single-seat airplane, Sach confidently assuring his buddy that he knows all about flying because he's taken a correspondence course. What he doesn't know (but we do) is that they've climbed into a remote-controlled target plane, bound for an aerial gunnery demonstration. The usual dumb luck guides Sach's hand as he avoids getting shot down and takes control of the plane, conveniently landing a scant quarter-mile away from the farmhouse where Dave is held prisoner. There follows the traditional bang-slam-pow climax and nonsensical fadeout punchline, this one informed by the strategic application of a syringe filled with truth serum.

Though all the Bowery Boys films could rely upon a built-in audience, the studio never missed a chance to promote the pictures to filmgoers outside the usual fan base. This included the occasional advertising tie-in, such as the Atomic Jet kiddie ride seen in the beginning of *Clipped Wings*. The ride was a genuine coin-operated device manufactured by Conat Sales and prominently featured in the film as part of a joint promotional campaign devised by Conat president Nat Cohen and Allied Artists' publicity head Murray Goldstein. According to *Billboard* magazine, Conat agreed to install an Atomic Jet ride in front of every theater showing *Clipped Wings*. Now *there's* a choice collectible to watch for on eBay.

The last of the Bowery Boys' military comedies returns them to the tender mercies of the Army. *Looking for Danger* was released by Allied Artists in 1957, two years after Leo Gorcey had left the series, insisting that he could no longer go on playing Slip Mahoney following the death of his father Bernard Gorcey in a car accident. Leo's replacement was Stanley Clements as Duke Covaleski, an agreeable performer in an agreeable role who was never quite able to replicate Leo's roughneck charm. Now elevated to top billing, Huntz Hall was indisputably center of attention in the final seven Bowery Boys entries, with producer Ben Schwalb remaining with the franchise until he ceded power to Richard Heermance (hitherto Allied Artists' chief film editor, and the brother of actress June Collyer). Likewise still in attendance was David Gorcey as Chuck, with Jimmy Murphy and Eddie LeRoy joining the club as Myron and Blinky, respectively. The group's center of operations had moved from Louie's Sweet Shop to Mike Clancy's Café (actually the same shabby set with rearranged furniture), with Percy Helton playing Clancy in *Spook Chasers* (1957) before he was replaced by Dick Elliott in the last three films; this change occurred a few days before shooting began on *Looking for Danger*, probably because Helton had prior commitments (one cannot imagine the ineluctable Percy Helton ever turning down a picture). On the whole, the seven Gorcey-less Bowery Boys pictures are abysmal, though *Looking for Danger* is a welcome exception. Scripted by old reliables Edward Bernds and Ellwood Ullman and directed by Austin Jewell (Bernds no longer functioned as director because he'd developed an intense dislike for Huntz Hall, a feeling that was apparently mutual), this 46th series entry represents a near-total formula overhaul, using a period setting (World War II) and exotic foreign milieu (North Africa), featuring a sexy leading lady who can actually be trusted, and showcasing the traditionally timorous Sach as a man of fearless fortitude ("They don't call me the Fighting Coward for nothin'").

The story is told in flashback, as Duke explains to War Department auditor Bradfield (John Harmon) how he managed to lose a aluminum cooking pot worth $4.85 during World War II. Dispatched on a secret spy mission by the Allies, Duke and Sach disguise themselves as Nazi officers Schultz and Von Schnaubel in order to locate "The Hawk," the leader of the anti-German underground in the city of Raz-Mamuth. Before long they discover that the "The Hawk" is actually the gorgeous Shareen (Lili Kardell), Number One harem girl in the palace of Sultan Sidi-Omar (Michael Granger). Unaware that the Sultan is in cahoots with the Nazis, Sach spills all he knows about his mission and ends up locked in a dungeon with Duke. The other Bowery Boys sneak into the palace and rescue everyone we care about, enabling the Allies to avoid a trap set by Sidi-Omar and to vanquish the Afrika Korps in a crucial battle. It all sounds quite fantastic—and no wonder, since not a word of it is true. Not only has Duke woven this incredible tale out of whole cloth, but he never gets around to explaining what happened to the missing pot ... which, now serving as a plant holder in Mike Clancy's Café, ends up rendering poor Mr. Bradfield unconscious.

Despite its impoverished production values—the dimly-illuminated native tavern where the conspirators regularly gather looks more like a hastily redecorated Santa Monica barbecue pit—*Looking for Danger* is fast-paced and consistently amusing. Scripters Bernds and Ullman effectively trot out some of their best 2-reeler material (including a routine first performed by Gus Schilling and Richard Lane in the 1946 Columbia short *Hot Water*, wherein Duke and Sach are ordered to give each other the "third degree") while throwing in a healthy supply of fresh and inventive gags (Sach plugging a portable fan into a cactus tree). The film might have served as a triumphant finale to the 12-year Bowery Boys saga were it not for the fact that there were two more pictures to go, one of them (*Up in Smoke*) as bad as any comedy ever made by anyone, anywhere, any time.

As a postscript to the Bowery Boys service comedies, we note that a solo Huntz Hall was showcased as an addlebrained air cadet in the 1943 United States Navy training film *Don't Kill Your Friends*. Though his character name is Ensign Dilbert, Hall remains in full "Sach" mode as he provides a series of examples of what not to do during aerial gunnery practice. "Don't be a Dilbert," admonishes the narrator at the end of this 14-minute object lesson. "*Don't* kill your friends!"

Francis the Talking Mule (1949–1956)

While it is safe to assume that the escapades of the Bowery Boys were not inspired by any sort of real-life experiences, another popular film series from the same era, based on a novel by David Stern III, did have a foundation in reality (sort of). The son of the publisher of the *New York Post*, Stern had already worked in an executive capacity on several newspapers when, in 1943, he joined the Army as an ordinary private. Submitting to the usual classification interviews, the 34-year-old Stern was confident that the officer in charge would fit him to the job best suited to his talents. Instead, he ended up as assistant driver on a garbage truck.

Though he went on to attend OCS, rise to the rank of captain and write for such prominent military publications as *Stars and Stripes*, Stern never forgot his initial humiliation, nor did he overcome his disdain for superior officers. To stimulate his imagination while working on an obscure Army newspaper in Hawaii, he sketched out a series of fanciful discourses between a lowly second lieutenant and a talking Army mule named Francis—who was not only brighter than his human friend, but also possessed a higher IQ than most other officers of his acquaintance. The notion of a loquacious and somewhat condescending mule proved so fascinating to Stern that he simply couldn't stop writing about the animal. "With memories of OCS fresh in my mind I thought I might rid myself of the creature by shipping him off to become a second lieutenant," explained Stern years later. "Francis outwitted me. He refused to go."

After the war, Stern organized his "Francis" stories into a novel, which in 1946 was among the first books published by the upstart firm of Farrar & Strauss (Giroux hadn't joined the company yet). *Francis* tells the story of young "second looie" Peter Stirling, who while trapped in the Burmese jungle is rescued from the Japanese by the titular Francis. Not only has the veteran Army mule (serial number M52519) memorized every existing field manual down to the last comma, but he is also a brilliant military strategist—and when the need arises, he is even able to fly a plane. The Top Brass naturally assumes that Francis' wartime heroics are actually being performed by Peter Stirling. Every time our young protagonist (who narrates the novel) tries to convince his superiors that his "military adviser" is a talking mule, he is bundled off to the psychiatric ward; it seems that Francis refuses to speak to anyone but Peter. When Stirling's flabbergasted C.O. finally acknowledges Francis' military expertise, the American press corps tries to write the whole thing off as a publicity stunt, hurling personal insults at the hapless mule during a press conference. This is too much for Francis to bear, and he abruptly breaks his silence: "I have heard more than my share of fool remarks! I have tuned in on radio commercials where men try to be funny about laxatives! I have heard the ravings of delirious men on the battlefield! There was a time when I endured the stupidity of half-baked recruits. But, by the tail of my great-aunt Regret, who won the Derby, I have never suffered through such disgusting hogwash as you so-called newspapermen are spouting!" The reporters are dumbfounded: so you really *can* talk, they exclaim. "I hope to kiss a duck I can talk!" Francis shoots back, proceeding to demonstrate the scope of his knowledge by itemizing the various ethical lapses perpetrated by each reporter's home newspaper. (*Francis* not only attacks the narrow-minded military establishment, but also aims a few broadsides at the author's journalistic rivals.) In the end, both Francis and Peter bid farewell to the Army and hit the road for new adventures.

Francis sold briskly enough to spawn a sequel, also by David Stern. Published in 1948, *Francis Goes to Washington* is a political satire in which Francis manages Peter Stirling's mayoral campaign against a crooked incumbent. Thereafter, Stern abandoned fiction to devote his energies to the

New Orleans *Item*, a daily newspaper he purchased in 1949. That same year, Universal-International came knocking at Stern's door, offering a princely $300 for the film rights to *Francis*.

Immediately following the studio's merger with International Pictures in 1946, Universal's executive staff issued lofty statements to the effect that the lowly Abbott & Costello comedies, garish Maria Montez-Jon Hall Technicolor extravaganzas, cheap B westerns and threadbare serials that had been the studio's bread and butter were to be eliminated. Henceforth, Universal-International would offer only "prestige" pictures along the lines of *All My Sons, Another Part of the Forest* and *Letter from an Unknown Women*. But as noted in *Life* magazine, by 1949 the studio's ledgers "were deeply dyed in red. Out the window went prestige, and the Universal program was aimed at a more universal appeal." Typical was U-I's response to the critical and financial success of two 1948 comedies, *Abbott and Costello Meet Frankenstein* and *The Egg and I*. The Abbott & Costello effort yielded a string of spinoffs in which the team "met" everyone from Dr. Jekyll and Mr. Hyde to the Keystone Kops; *The Egg and I* spawned a series centering around two of the film's supporting characters, the backwoods duo Ma and Pa Kettle (Marjorie Main, Percy Kilbride). Made for less than $500,000, the initial entry in the Kettle series is said to have single-handedly saved U-I from bankruptcy, encouraging the studio to cast about for other properties with series potential.

Back in 1941, Universal had averted another financial crisis with Abbott & Costello's *Buck Privates*, directed by Arthur Lubin (see **Chapter** 4). In a later interview with Ronald L. Davis, Lubin claimed it was he who brought *Francis* to the studio's attention. "Universal was very skeptical of the idea of a talking mule, and the higher-ups at the studio didn't want to make the original movie. At first I couldn't sell the idea to anyone. I had an agent, Mike Levy, who was a very important man. I still have a letter of his where he said, 'Dear Arthur, if anyone buys this script I'll eat it.' Universal only made the picture because they had Donald O'Connor under contract, and if they didn't have a picture for him within a certain date, they were going to lose $30,000. The studio needed the money in those days."

Donald O'Connor turned out to be the ideal choice to play the flustered Peter Stirling. At 24, he was just the right age for the part; and having been a professional entertainer since childhood, his comic timing was flawless. Moreover, he was totally believable in those scenes requiring him to carry on a lucid conversation with a talking mule, never hoking up his reactions or playing for easy laughs. Though O'Connor was unenthusiastic about appearing in the *Francis* series from the outset, he enjoyed working with Molly, the female mule purchased by Universal (for the staggering sum of $350) to play Francis. The actor not only developed a rapport with the "lead" mule, but also with her two understudies (also female, to avoid the potential censorship hassles of showing a full-frontal naked male mule on screen). Molly, aka Francis, responded in kind with a magnificent performance, one that earned her the very first PATSY award, an acronym for "Picture Animal Top Star of the Year."

To sustain the level of credibility established by Donald O'Connor, Arthur Lubin avoided hiring comedy "regulars" for the supporting parts, relying instead on such solid dramatic performers as Ray Collins and John McIntire to play Stirling's superiors. Even comedienne ZaSu Pitts, as the Army nurse supervising Peter during his frequent stopovers at the psych ward, keeps her standard fluttery gestures and "Oh, dear, oh my" asides to the barest minimum. The only performer who overplays is Patricia Medina as a deceptively friendly French damsel who turns out to be a German spy, but her role requires this sort of acting to keep the story's espionage angle from lapsing into melodrama.

Though both Donald O'Connor and Arthur Lubin would repeatedly insist that they'd been sworn to secrecy regarding the method used to make it appear that Francis was talking, it was well known within Hollywood circles that Molly's trainer Les Hilton utilized a thin pair of strings to manipulate the mule's "lips," gently pulling the strings through Molly's mouth and causing her to twitch her jaw as if forming words. As for the voice of Francis, character actor Chill Wills (who

The title character of *Francis* (Universal-International, 1949) passes along some military wisdom to his human confidante Peter Stirling (Donald O'Connor).

received no screen credit) was hired because Lubin felt that "a mule, being a big animal, should have a rough voice. I thought the best kind of voice might be somebody like a cowboy, and it worked out that way." That's why Francis, a snide Runyonesque type in the novel, sounds like a B-western sidekick on film (Andy Devine was considered for the role, but rejected because audiences familiar with his voice would be thinking of Andy instead of Francis). The Universal sound crew enhanced Chill Wills' natural "mulishness" by electronically lowering his vocal timbre in post-production.

According to Lubin, Universal didn't know they had a hit on their hands until *Francis* was screened before a preview audience. Once convinced, the studio pulled out all stops to promote the picture. The coming-attractions trailer is a masterpiece of showmanship, beginning with an animated-cartoon tour of the "Comedy Hall of Fame," with statues dedicated to past Universal successes like *My Man Godfrey*, *Buck Privates* and *The Egg and I*. At the conclusion of the tour, a new monument is unveiled to honor *Francis*, revealing just enough to hint at the film's content without giving away the plot. Cut to a live-action sequence with *Jack Benny Show* announcer Don Wilson standing outside a preview theater and interviewing the departing patrons (actually Hollywood bit players), who are laughing too hard to give any sort of coherent critique of the new film. To further arouse the audience's curiosity, though Francis is identified over and over as "The Talking Mule," his voice is never heard.

Filmed on a budget of approximately $350,000, *Francis* grossed nearly ten times that amount upon its initial release during the 1949–50 movie season. There was no question that the film would be the vanguard for a series: But how would it be possible to maintain the freshness of the initial entry? Universal's answer was to treat each subsequent *Francis* film as if it was the first in the series, with Peter Stirling finding himself trapped in a devastating dilemma that can only be straightened out by his four-legged pal Francis—who still speaks only to Peter, with no one else in the cast believing the human hero's outlandish stories about a talking mule until the final reels. Since Universal could rely upon each of the *Francis* films to earn between two and three million dollars, no one was about to rock the boat by tampering with a proven formula. Thus, of the five *Francis* programmers produced between 1951 and 1955, three were military comedies.

The third entry in the series, *Francis Goes to West Point* (1952), was designed to mollify an increasingly dissatisfied Donald O'Connor by fashioning the script to focus more on Peter Stirling than Francis, especially during the climactic intrigues surrounding the annual Army-Navy football game. O'Connor has no trouble extracting laughs and sympathy from his character's trials and tribulations in the early campus scenes (of the 687 cadets in his West Point class, he ranks 687th). But from the moment the Point's football-team mascot Francis begins tutoring Peter so he'll qualify for graduation, even Robert de Niro would have had trouble grabbing attention away from the multiloquent mule. Making the situation even more galling for O'Connor was that he'd been forced to absent himself from the "Broadway Melody" number in the concurrently produced *Singin' in the Rain* because of his commitment to *Francis Goes to West Point*.

The fifth series entry, *Francis Joins the WACs* (1954), finds Peter Stirling the victim of a clerical error assigning him to the Women's Army Corps, with Francis getting himself transferred to a WAC medical unit in order to lend Peter a helping hoof. The film could, in a pinch, be considered an early endorsement of Women's Liberation, as Peter (aided by Francis) helps a group of smartly uniformed female warriors emerge victorious over a chauvinistic regiment of male combat veterans during a large-scale camouflage exercise. Lynn Bari, usually cast in conniving "other woman" roles, seems to be relishing the opportunity to play a sympathetic part as WAC Major Louise Simpson, while Julie Adams is seen as the no-nonsense Captain Jane Parker, who is determined to prove herself the equal, if not the superior, of any man—especially Peter. ZaSu Pitts returns to the fold as the same character she played in the original *Francis*, while the mule's "ghost voice" Chill Wills appears on-screen as a misogynistic general.

Francis Joins the WACs serves a purpose established at the very beginning of the series: to provide exposure for Universal's latest crop of young contract players. Tony Curtis had shown up in a minor role in *Francis*, Piper Laurie appeared in *Francis Goes to the Races* (1951) and David Janssen, Leonard Nimoy and Paul Burke were seen in *Francis Goes to West Point*. Fulfilling their contractual duties in *Francis Joins the WACs* are such budding actresses as Mara Corday, Allison Hayes (later the star of *Attack of the Fifty-Foot Woman*), and, as "Corporal Bunky Hilstrom," the pneumatic Mamie Van Doren. In 1961, Universal recycled the script of this *Francis* installment as the storyline for a cost-conscious second feature titled *The Sergeant Was a Lady,* in which the locale was changed to a WAC outpost in the South Pacific, with Martin West in the Donald O'Connor role as the misplaced male. Though there was no mule on this occasion, the studio followed the lead of the earlier film by trotting out a fresh batch of fetching starlets, among them Venetia Stevenson and Francine York.

By 1955, Donald O'Connor was making no secret of his displeasure over how Universal was wasting his talents on a string of cookie-cutter programmers. Early in the proceedings O'Connor was able to joke about playing second fiddle to a mule; Tony Curtis has recalled that during filming of *Francis*, the star frequently broke the tension on the set by making self-deprecating comments about "that fucking idiot Donald O'Connor." But it was no laughing matter when during shooting of *Francis Joins the WACs*, O'Connor contacted a disease known as "Q Fever" from the mule, which knocked him out of the cast of Paramount's *White Christmas*. That, as they say, tore it: Arthur Lubin could not help but notice that the normally cooperative and convivial O'Connor was now drinking heavily, showing up late, and swearing a blue streak at anything that provoked him. Nonetheless, Universal had lined up another episode in the talking-mule saga, *Francis in the*

Navy, and fully expected O'Connor to do his box-office duty. The actor agreed to headline this film on two conditions: That his role be expanded, and that the studio would release him from his contract after the picture wrapped.

Filmed partially on location at the Navy's Amphibious Training Base in Coronado, California, *Francis in the Navy* is a cut above its predecessors if only because of O'Connor's dual role as the perenially luckless Peter Stirling and his exact look-alike, a cocky, two-fisted, skirt-chasing sailor named Slicker Donovan. While trying to save Francis from being auctioned off as "war surplus," Peter is held responsible for Slicker's various insubordinations, a hassle that hounds our hero right up to the closing credits. *Francis in the Navy* is noteworthy today as the second film appearance of Clint Eastwood, playing a gob named Jonesy (Eastwood had been discovered by director Lubin, who hoped that by building up the boy's role in this film, Universal would take notice. Universal didn't). The film was just as profitable as the previous series entries, but this meant nothing to Donald O'Connor. The actor's famous explanation as to why he quit the series at this juncture has been reprinted innumerable times: "When you've made six pictures, and the mule still gets more fan mail than you do..." Nor was O'Connor the only one to take a walk: both director Arthur Lubin and Francis' voice actor Chill Wills likewise bade *adios* to the series. The final entry, *Francis in the Haunted House* (1956), stars Mickey Rooney as the human hero, with Charles Lamont directing and Paul Frees voicing the mule.

In the wake of the first *Francis* movie, the other Hollywood studios, displaying the originality and innovation that made the motion picture industry great, tripped over themselves looking for similar "clever animal" properties with movie-series possibilities. It wasn't long before filmgoers were besieged with larcenous squirrels (*The Great Rupert*), cats who inherited baseball teams (*Rhubarb*), Great Danes who were reincarnated as Dick Powell (*You Never Can Tell*) and chimpanzees who shared breakfast with Ronald Reagan (*Bedtime for Bonzo*). There was even one picture of this nature that was based on an honest-to-goodness true story: MGM's *Fearless Fagan* (1952), also the only one of the aforementioned films with a military background.

As reported in the February 12, 1951, issue of *Life* magazine, Army private Floyd C. Humeston, a circus clown in civilian life, had recently stirred up a tsunami of sensational wire-service stories when he asked the warrant officer at Fort Ord, California for a 14-day emergency furlough so he could return home and take care of his pet cat. Nothing out of the ordinary here, unless one takes into consideration that the "cat" was a 400-pound male lion named Fagan. Weaned on chocolate milk and trained for a show business career by Floyd's brother Earl, Fagan had spent most of his life with his master's menagerie of exotic pets, including an alligator, a boa constrictor and six *other* lions. Inseparable as Damon and Pythias, Floyd and Fagan shared the same house, performed their daily ablutions at the same time, ate at the same table, and on cold nights slept under the same blanket. Upon being drafted, Floyd had problems finding a suitable temporary home for Fagan and asked permission to bring the lion with him to training camp. When the Army objected (what was up with *them*?), Fagan was briefly placed with the Monterey Humane Society, seven miles from Fort Ord. The lion was later hired by the Mills Brothers and Clyde Beatty circuses, with occasional furloughs to tour with Earl Humeston in a nightclub wrestling act. Given a full-page photo spread in *Life*, Fagan became a worldwide celebrity, and within six months his life story was purchased by MGM assistant producer Sidney Franklin, Jr., who earned a promotion as a result. Reading these accounts some 60 years later, one feels a bit manipulated by the story's calculated whimsy, the whole yarn coming off more like a carefully preplanned publicity stunt than the warmhearted saga of a boy and his lion. But the general reading public of 1952 was enchanted by Fagan, making MGM's movie adaptation a foregone conclusion — and in same tradition as Audie Murphy and Jackie Robinson, Fagan himself was chosen to star in his own biopic (with MGM's "house lion" Jackie as occasional stand-in).

Originally titled *Homer and the Lion, Fearless Fagan* was planned as an economical programmer along the lines of *Francis*, though MGM's idea of "economical" cost over twice as much as the Universal picture. Whereas outside of Donald O'Connor most of the participants in *Francis* were enthusiastic over the project, several of the people involved with *Fagan* had to be forced to do the film. Having just come off the landmark musical *Singin' in the Rain*, director Stanley Donen at first resisted the opportunity to give stage directions to a lion, but finally acquiesced because (a) he was impressed that the film was based on a true story and (b) MGM threatened to put him on suspension. Leading lady Janet Leigh (replacing Sidney Franklin Jr.'s first choice Deborah Kerr) also initially balked at appearing in the film, as did song-and-dance man Carleton Carpenter, even though the role of Private Floyd Hillstrom (a fictional composite of Floyd and Earl Humeston) was to be Carpenter's first starring assignment. Beyond regarding the property as beneath them artistically, the director and the stars were also trepidatious over sharing scenes with a full-grown lion — and let's face it, given a choice between a lion and a mule, most actors would prefer working with a critter who isn't apt to "do lunch" with you as the lunch. On brief furlough from the Army, Floyd Humeston was slated to double for Carleton Carpenter in several scenes, a sensible decision in that Fagan's behavior could be unpredictable (to say the least) if Floyd wasn't there to mollify him. But when Humeston was obliged to return to Fort Ord, MGM had to make do with its own stable of stunt doubles and animal wranglers, resorting to split screen and double exposure in certain difficult scenes pairing the lion with his human costars. The studio also made sure that there was always a lady lion within roaring distance of the set, since Stanley Donen had been informed that male lions were at their most manageable when their libidos were aroused (exactly the opposite of most MGM stars, but we won't go into that).

His recalcitrance aside, Stanley Donen handled the material in the same believable, low-key fashion exhibited by *Francis*' Arthur Lubin. The mood is established immediately after the opening credits, with Keenan Wynn, cast as the film's narrator Sgt. Kellwin, matter-of-factly informing us that what we're about to see is "the true story you've all read about." As often happened in service comedies, Wynn all but steals the show with his expertly shaded and textured performance, most memorably in the lengthy scene wherein Kellwin, with ever-mounting frustration, phones one organization after another in search of a proper home for the troublesome lion.

Since there really isn't much more to Fagan's story than what was printed in that *Life* article, the screenwriters had to fabricate a few dramatic complications, such as a villainous lion trainer (Parley Baer with a Sig Ruman accent) who victimizes the beast in Floyd's absence, and a third-act crisis in which Fagan is threatened with euthanization because of his mercurial behavior. Also pulled from thin air are such high-larious highlights as poor Sgt. Kellwin hanging upside down from a tree after triggering a lion trap, and Fagan "invading" the WACs' quarters to listen to a recording of Mario Lanza singing "The Loveliest Night of the Year" (a right-between-the-eyes plug for MGM's recent Lanza vehicle *The Great Caruso*). And in an effort to remove the "cheap publicity stunt" onus from the proceedings, the writers tack on a scene in which a stern Army officer accuses movie star Abby Ames (Janet Leigh) of feigning concern over Fagan's plight merely to advance her own career.

Though according to *Variety* the film was expected to do only "okay box office," the MGM publicists made certain that the entire nation was *Fearless Fagan*-conscious, first sending Fagan out on a tour of Army camps, then distributing photos of the lion undergoing a screen test (the A.D. holding up a slate marked "Mr. Fagan") and making a chauffeured stopover at the MGM administration building, with a very nervous-looking Esther Williams strolling alongside the limousine. *The Hollywood Reporter* came right out and stated what the studio merely hinted at, that *Fagan* was intended as the opening salvo in a new *Francis*-like film series. While this project would be abandoned once the MGM executives weighed the advisability of keeping a hungry and temperamental lion on the payroll for only one picture per year, it's a bit odd that the studio didn't pick up on a minor story element of *Fearless Fagan* and develop a "Ma and Pa Kettle" style series based on the rustic lion-farm owners played in the picture by Ellen Corby and John Call. The final word from *Fearless Fagan* was heard in March of 1953 when the titular star won that year's PATSY award, beating out such stiff competition as Bonzo and Trigger.

Eight more years passed before Hollywood again tried to emulate *Francis* by combining an intelligent animal with the service-farce format. The 1961 Columbia release *Everything's Ducky* was largely driven by its star Mickey Rooney, who owned 50 percent of the picture and was determined to crack the lucrative kiddie-matinee market that had recently been reactivated with Columbia's Three Stooges vehicle *Have Rocket, Will Travel*. Rooney's project was highly derivative of the *Francis* series, though Mickey was able to justify this by claiming that the first *Francis* picture had been offered to him before the studio settled on Donald O'Connor. This doesn't quite jibe with Arthur Lubin's recollection of the events surrounding *Francis*, but Mickey Rooney has always had a habit of remembering things a bit differently than others. From time to time, Rooney has indicated that he'd plucked Buddy Hackett from the obscurity of the New York nightclub circuit to give him his first big movie break in *Everything's Ducky*—and never mind that Buddy had been prominently featured on screen since 1953.

Rooney and Hackett play a pair of Navy electricians' mates, with Mickey cast as Beetle and Buddy as a gob whose full moniker is Admiral John Paul Jones. Considered unfit for active duty because Beetle lacks a sense of direction and Jonesy gets seasick, the boys are consigned to a dummy training submarine in the middle of the desert bordering a Navy missile site. Because they happen to be available, their CO assigns Beetle and Jonesy to find a new home for Scuttlebutt, the pet duck of recently deceased rocket scientist Dr. Serkin. What no one knows—but the gobs will soon find out—is that Serkin had taught Scuttlebutt how to talk (his voice is provided by Walker Edmiston, doing a Hans Conried imitation), and that the mallard is the only living being who knows all of the late scientist's guided-missile secrets. Our heroes are convinced that Scuttlebutt is worth a fortune to them, but in fine *Francis* tradition they can't convince anyone that the duck has the power of speech—and more vexing still, Scuttlebutt has a fondness for martinis that tends to get his human pals into trouble. Feeling protective of their new feathered friend, Beetle and Jonesy attempt to rescue Scuttlebutt from being launched into outer space as part of "Operation Birdbrain," only to end up sealed in the missile's nose cone themselves. En route to the stratosphere, the boys and the duck enjoy the sensation of weightlessness, and the film stops. Not ends, just stops.

To their credit, scripters Benedict Freeman and John Fenton Murray go to heroic lengths to avoid making *Everything's Ducky* an all-out *Francis* ripoff. For starters, Scuttlebutt does not display Francis' reluctance to speak to anyone other than his human master: On the contrary, the duck is willing to shoot the breeze with anyone who'll listen. The gag here is that practically no one *wants* to listen—and those that do listen either assume that Beetle and Jonesy are practicing ventriloquism, or that Scuttlebutt has a computer chip planted in his brain. And in a reversal of the *Francis* running gag in which Donald O'Connor is constantly being shipped off to the psych ward for insisting that he chums around with a talking mule, no sooner have Beetle and Jonesy told their story to the base psychiatrist (played by Jackie Cooper, evidently as a favor to fellow ex-child star Rooney) than the shrink accuses them of bucking for a Section Eight and boots both sailors out of his office. Beyond the film's central gimmick, the writers manage to get off a few satiric jabs that transcend the juvenile nature of the project. In one scene, Scuttlebutt refuses to divulge his missile secrets because he's a pacifist—and an attempt to appeal to his patriotism fails because he happens to be a Canadian duck.

The casting of the supporting players is also praiseworthy, though more in line with a TV comedy show than a theatrical feature, with such sitcom standbys as Roland Winters, Gordon Jones, James Milhollin, Richard Deacon, Alvy Moore and Elizabeth MacRae (*Gomer Pyle USMC*'s Lou Ann Poovie) in attendance. The one performer who isn't seen to good advantage is leading lady Joanie Sommers, a popular singer of the day. Despite the fact that three songs are listed in the credits, Joanie never sings a note—and apparently doesn't speak a word either, since her voice seems to have been dubbed by another actress.

Though billed as Scuttlebutt, the central character was played by a duck named Herbie, trained by Ralph Helfer (who also supplied three webfooted stand-ins). In his autobiography, Helfer wrote that while Herbie was fairly compliant, he was extremely problematic in one respect: Put delicately, a duck cannot be housebroken. Herbie not only left droppings all over the set but also deposited an abundance of calling cards on his human costars. When Herbie relieved himself in Buddy Hackett's hand during one scene, Buddy nonchalantly placed that hand on Mickey Rooney's shoulder, his angelic expression never tipping off the "gift" he had bestowed on his fellow thespian until the cameras stopped rolling. The film's director Don Taylor has indicated that this practical jokery was S.O.P. on the set, telling interviewer Tom Weaver that despite a tight 11-day shooting schedule Rooney and Hackett insisted upon eating up valuable time with their schoolboy shenanigans. Further, Taylor complained that Herbie was totally uncooperative from start to finish, never more so than when Mickey and Buddy "helped" the duck play his martini-drinking scenes by plying him with vodka.

Only a fraction of this offscreen merriment comes across on screen. Though family-oriented periodicals like *Boys' Life* and *PTA Magazine* were kind to *Everything's Ducky*, most mainstream publications regarded the picture as beneath critical comment. While not deserving of its place of dishonor in the Medved brothers' egregious *Golden Turkey Awards*, the film lacks the overall hilarity needed to sustain its fanciful premise. It's possible that if *Everything's Ducky* had clicked, Mickey Rooney would have tried to parlay the property into a series of low-budget comedies. As it happened, the only benefit arising from the project was the fact that producer Stanley Kramer was so impressed by the rapport between Mickey Rooney and Buddy Hackett that he reteamed the actors in his all-star comedy epic *It's a Mad Mad Mad Mad World*. Now *that* was funny—and with nary a talking duck in sight.

Snuffy Smith (1942)

The smashing success of Columbia's *Blondie* series in the late 1930s inspired other film studios to thumb through the funny pages in search of comic-strip properties with movie potential. Taking into account its sizeable box-office receipts from rural communities, Monogram Pictures elected to bestow film stardom upon Snuffy Smith, a pint-sized hillbilly character introduced in 1934 by artist Billy DeBeck in his long-running *Barney Google* strip. With rustic humor all the rage thanks to the Broadway hit *Tobacco Road*, DeBeck transported his leading player Barney Google, a small-time sports promoter, to the hills of North Carolina, where Barney had inherited an estate (which turned out to be a squalid shack). Shortly thereafter, city-slicker Google made the acquaintance of rifle-totin' Snuffy Smith and his gargantuan wife Loweezie, both of whom harbored an inbred mistrust of "furriners" who didn't hail from the mountains—especially "Revenooers" (government revenue agents) who were bent upon closing down Snuffy's illegal moonshine still. By the early 1940s, Snuffy had eclipsed Barney in popularity, and the strip was accordingly retitled *Barney Google and Snuffy Smith* (which it remains to this day, even though Barney is long gone). And just as DeBeck had popularized such slang expressions as "Osky-wow-wow" and "Heebie-Jeebies" during Barney's heyday, the introduction of Snuffy brought forth a whole new supply of colloquialisms like "great balls o' fire!"; "shif'less skonk"; "time's a-wastin'"; "bodacious"; and "tetched in the haid." When Barney and Snuffy joined the Army in 1941, a new phrase was added to the American lexicon: "yard bird," referring to incompetent or incorrigible military recruits who were relegated to such menial tasks as sweeping the camp grounds and shoveling manure.

Once Monogram had secured the picture rights to DeBeck's strip, they were faced with the formidable task of casting an actual human being as the grotesquely caricatured Snuffy Smith. The studio hired diminutive Bud Duncan, who as one-half of the "Ham and Bud" team (Lloyd Hamilton was "Ham") had been a silent comedy star of the World War I era, and who later teamed with Thelma Hill in another comic-strip derivation, the *Toots and Casper* 2-reelers of the 1920s. When Monogram engaged Duncan's services in 1942, the little actor had been away from films for eleven years, prompting the studio's publicity department to hail the triumphant comeback of this old "favorite." Costarring as Snuffy's spouse Loweezy was Sarah Padden, an actress literally twice Duncan's size (height-wise, that is). Both actors were outfitted with cartoonlike costumes and makeup approximating the DeBeck originals: Duncan now sported a bulbous nose, paintbrush mustache and prosthetic bald wig (in which the folds and creases were all too visible), while Padden was provided with a lycanthropic set of false teeth.

Released in January 1942, the 67-minute *Private Snuffy Smith* (working title: *Snuffy Smith the Yardbird*) opens with a cast-credit sequence in which DeBeck's cartoon renditions of the main characters dissolve into close-ups of the actors playing these roles (a device lifted from the first *Blondie* feature). Fade in to the Great Smoky Mountains, where in the tiny community of Hootin' Holler bullets are a-flyin' between Snuffy's fellow moonshiners and a band of "Revenooers" led by Ed Cooper (Edgar Kennedy). To stay out of the hoosegow, Snuffy decides to join the Army, an especially appealing prospect in that he stands to earn "thutty dulars a month." Though too short to qualify for military service, Snuffy manages to earn a uniform when he saves the life of General Rosewater (J. Farrell MacDonald), albeit only under "Special Classification Z"—a polite way of labeling Snuffy a permanent yard bird. This is hardly to the liking of Snuffy's new top sergeant, none other than his old nemesis Ed Cooper (the gimmick of a uniformed antagonist following the comic hero into the Army was lifted from Abbott & Costello's *Buck Privates*). Meanwhile, handsome mountaineer-turned-private Don Elbie (played by future *Mickey Mouse Club* emcee Jimmie Dodd) has perfected an automatic range finder, which he hopes to sell to the Army and thus earn enough money to wed his hometown sweetheart Cindy (Doris Linden)—and also end the feud between the sweethearts' families. A gang of Fifth Columnists conspires to steal the range finder, just before Gen. Rosewater is able to deploy the device to beat the Blue Army in the war-game maneuvers held near Snuffy's home turf. With the help of Snuffy and Loweezie, the spies are routed, the invention is recovered, the lovers are reunited, and the war games are won by Rosewater.

Sprinkled throughout are the familiar catchphrases ("balls o' fire!" et al.) from the *Barney Google* comic strip, which must have proven confusing if not totally incomprehensible when *Private Snuffy Smith* was released in Great Britain by Pathé Pictures. The film also boasts a number of running gags, one involving a dog rendered invisible (a not-bad special effect) by Loweezie's homemade soap mixture. Another recurring gag concerns the bags of flour used in lieu of ammunition during the war games: whenever a soldier is hit by flour he is declared "dead" and out of the game—prompting one frustrated officer to smash himself with a flour bag, thereby "committing suicide."

With slightly higher production values than the average Monogram product and benefiting from the extensive comic knowhow of director Eddie Cline (whose previous films included W.C. Fields' masterpiece *The Bank Dick*), *Private Snuffy Smith* was a promising debut for the intended "Snuffy Smith" series—with one glaring exception. Watching Bud Duncan slog through his paces as Snuffy, it "ain't hard to figger" why the actor had been out of films for so long; he is hopelessly bad, his artless performance grinding the picture to a dead halt on several occasions. Infinitely better are the always reliable Edgar Kennedy as Sgt. Cooper, and young Jimmie Dodd as Pvt. Elbie. Whenever the pace begins to flag, Dodd grabs a guitar and bursts into song, performing such forgettable but hummable compositions as "Time's a-Wastin,'" cowritten by comedians Olsen & Johnson and the youthful songwriting team of Jay Livingston (here billed under his given name Levenson) and Ray Evans.

Private Snuffy Smith performed well enough for Monogram to slap together a sequel, the sublimely titled *Hillbilly Blitzkrieg* (1942). This one was directed by Roy Mack, formerly associated with Vitaphone's 2-reel comedy product of the 1930s, so it's not surprising that the film plays like an elongated short subject, replete with Three Stooges-style sound effects and Sennettesque sight gags. Bud Duncan is back as Snuffy, less a tribute to his talents than an admission that Monogram couldn't find anyone else to fit the uniform. Several other actors are carried over from *Private Snuffy Smith*, albeit with different character names. Though still playing Snuffy's topkick, Edgar Kennedy now goes by the name of Sgt. Gatling. Doris Linden's heroine has been rechristened Julie, no longer a hillbilly gal but the citified daughter of eccentric Professor James (Lucien Littlefield). And the previous film's romantic lead Jimmie Dodd has been demoted to a minor role, with Alan Baldwin taking over as Julie's sweetie Corporal Bruce. New to the franchise is comedian Cliff Nazarro as the living embodiment of Snuffy's comic-page cohort Barney Google. Though camouflaged to resemble Billy DeBeck's visualization of Barney (derby hat, cigar, prop mustache), Nazarro is essentially his same old obnoxious self, hauling out his irritating double-talk routines whether we like it or not.

Evidently Snuffy has broken up with Loweezie, who doesn't appear in this film. In her stead, Snuf has been carrying on a pen-pal correspondence with one Eliza Murdock, who sends him various gifts and eatables which he shrewdly sells to his fellow soldiers. In exchange, Eliza asks for a photograph of Snuffy — and rather than risk scaring her away, he sends her a snapshot of handsome Corporal Bruce. Once these preliminaries are dispensed with, Sgt. Gatling takes a six-man detail (including Snuffy) to the Big Smokies, where they are to stand guard during the test flight of a radio-controlled rocket invented by Professor James. The soldiers set up headquarters at a ramshackle lodge owned by Snuffy's cousin, that "Shif'less Skonk" Barney Google. Having sunk all his money into the Professor's invention, Barney is left with only one asset, his broken-down racehorse Sparkplug (covered with the same personalized blanket he'd worn in his comic-strip appearances of the 1920s and 1930s). To raise the $500 required to purchase a new stabilizer for the rocket, Snuffy enters Sparkplug in a race against Sgt. Gatling's entry, a liquor-swilling Army mule named P-40. It is emblematic of *Hillbilly Blitzkrieg*'s shoddy construction that the race sequence, which should have been a last-reel highlight, is over and done with before the picture is half over.

A new story tangent is introduced when Snuffy's pen-pal Eliza is revealed to be an enemy agent named Lisa (Nicolle Andre), part of a spy ring determined to sabotage the rocket. Dispatched to woo Snuffy and distract him from his guard duties, Lisa at first mistakes Cpl. Bruce for the hillbilly, then assumes that Sgt. Gatling is the genuine article. Despite Edgar Kennedy's priceless facial expressions when Eliza turns on the charm, this segment spirals downward very quickly. The slapstick climax, in which Snuffy takes flight in Professor James' moonshine-fueled rocketship, falls totally flat thanks to some truly horrendous special effects, with the prop missile somehow managing to cast a shadow on the sky.

The funniest thing about *Hillbilly Blitzkrieg* is its title; the film brought the "Snuffy Smith" series to a swift and merciful end. More than likely, it wasn't a loss of box-office revenue that prompted Monogram to terminate the series (since the films cost practically nothing to make, they couldn't help turning a profit), but simply that the rights to the comic strip had gotten too expensive to warrant further sequels. The studio would fare better with its later funny-paper spin-offs, the "Joe Palooka" and "Jiggs and Maggie" films of the postwar era.

Willie & Joe (1951–1952)

Another brief series borne of the comic pages was inaugurated by Universal-International in 1951. Whereas *Barney Google and Snuffy Smith* was aimed at a mass civilian audience, cartoonist Bill Mauldin's bearded, bedraggled, battle-weary infantry troopers "Willie and Joe" were featured in the Army periodicals *45th Division News* and *Stars and Stripes* for a select audience of American combat soldiers. An infantry sergeant himself, Mauldin formally introduced Willie and Joe in

5. Repeated Rounds

1943, turning out as many as six single-panel cartoons per week. The polar opposite of the clean-shaven, eager-beaver soldiers idealized in Hollywood films and by the military's public-relations department, Mauldin's dogface duo gained instant popularity by totally rejecting artifice and speaking the language of the average GI, mirroring his fears, frustrations, desires, and most of all his gripes about everything from lousy K-rations to the inequities of rank.

Mauldin's fondness for parodying the peremptory attitude of officers who cared less about the hearts and souls of the men under them than they did about demanding blind obeisance to rules and regulations, and who somehow believed that a couple of extra stripes on the sleeve made one an inherently superior being, earned the cartoonist the adoration of the uniformed men on the ground — and the wrath of such high-rankers as General George Patton. Called on the carpet by Old Blood 'N' Guts to justify his "disrespectful" and "dissension-spreading" cartoons, Mauldin nervously explained the fundamental appeal of Willie and Joe: "The soldier is back in his foxhole stewing about officers and thinking he's got the short end of the stick in everything.... Whether it makes sense or not, the fact is he feels there's been an injustice, and if he stews long enough about this, or about any of the other hundreds of things soldiers stew about, he's not going to be thinking about his job. All right, sir, he picks up his paper and he reads a letter or sees a cartoon by some other soldier who feels the same way, and he says, 'Hell, somebody else said it for me,' and he goes back to his job.'" Just as Bruce Bairnsfather's pen-and-ink creation Old Bill was a gigantic morale booster for British "Tommies" in World War I (see notes on *The Better 'Ole* in **Chapter 2**), so too were Willie and Joe for American troops in World War II. (Not surprisingly, General Patton despised Bairnsfather as much as he did Mauldin!)

Published stateside by United Features Syndicate under the blanket title *Up Front*, Mauldin's cartoons gained him a following far beyond his fellow infantrymen. Many of the illustrations and captions chronicling the saga of Willie and Joe became classics of the comic form, and would pop up time and again in other media. A Mauldin cartoon showing an MP explaining the various ribbons on his chest ("an' the real purdy one wid all th' colors is fer being in this theater of operations") found its way into William Wellman's 1945 war film *The Story of GI Joe*, while the artist's personal favorite of all his panels, in which a cavalry sergeant stoically prepares to shoot his crippled jeep, would be recreated three decades later in the TV series *M*A*S*H*.

In 1946, Mauldin was approached by William Goetz, CEO of the independent movie firm International Pictures, to develop a live-action comedy feature revolving around the characters of Willie and Joe — albeit minus most of the anti-authoritarianism of the cartoons, lest the Army raise a stink. Goetz sweetened the pot by promising that the 24-year-old cartoonist would be given full creative control over the project. Bill's first suggestion was to hire his three *Stars and Stripes* colleagues Herbert Mitgang, Dave Golding and Bill Hogan to do the story treatment and to incorporate many of the best-loved *Up Front* captions in the dialogue. After International Pictures merged with Universal, Mauldin's film was temporarily put on hold on the theory that the immediate-postwar public was growing tired of service pictures. Approximately two years later, Universal-International pulled *Up Front* out of mothballs, assigning Ring Lardner Jr. and his brother John to write the screenplay. When Ring Lardner Jr. was rendered undesirable as one of the HUAC's "Unfriendly Ten," Mauldin himself toiled away on the script for four weeks. At this juncture, producer Leonard Goldstein took over the project and hired his own writer, Stanley Roberts. Goetz' original assurances notwithstanding, neither Goldstein nor Roberts accepted any of Mauldin's suggestions, so Bill washed his hands of the matter, going so far as to return the $10,000 he'd been paid as technical advisor. This experience, coupled with Mauldin's disatisfaction over his acting debut as "The Loud Soldier" in John Huston's 1951 filmization of *The Red Badge of Courage* (though he received excellent reviews, he was unhappy with MGM's slash-and-hash editing job on the completed picture) pretty much soured Bill on Hollywood. He didn't even bother to see the finished version of *Up Front* when it premiered in early 1951, telling *Newsweek*, "I've just heard that it had a lot of jokes and everybody laughed."

Several established Hollywood names were considered for the film's leading roles—William Bendix, Donald O'Connor, Van Heflin, Jack Carson—before Leonard Goldstein decided to go with a couple of recent Broadway recruits. Tom Ewell and David Wayne had both been officially "introduced" to movies in MGM's 1949 comedy *Adam's Rib*, with Ewell as a boorish philandering husband and Wayne as an effete Cole Porter-esque songwriter. Neither actor was handsome in the accepted Hollywood sense; Tom Ewell in particular wasn't handsome in *any* accepted sense, possessing a face like a battered baseball glove. While no one could be quite as homely and haggard as Mauldin's concept of Willie and Joe, Ewell and Wayne came awfully darn close. (Incidentally, though the characters were always billed as "Willie and Joe" in the advertising, David Wayne as Joe received top billing on screen.)

The story is set in 1943, just after the American invasion of Italy. Given the last names of Wingfield and Cooper in the picture, Willie and Joe are a pair of mud-caked infantrymen stationed a few miles from Naples. Like their comic-page counterparts, the boys are efficient but reluctant soldiers; unlike those counterparts, they are also expert goldbricks, prodigious drinkers, indefatigable womanizers and petty-larceny thieves. Lest the reader bemoan these questionable "improvements" on the source material, it should be observed that Bill Mauldin himself had come up with the two protagonists' less admirable character traits as a means of fleshing out the characters for dramatic purposes. This element was one of the few holdovers from the original late-1940s screen treatment for *Up Front*, along with the decision to weave nearly two dozen of Mauldin's celebrated cartoon captions into the dialogue. Within the first three reels, the viewer is treated to such choice Mauldinisms as "I can't get no lower, Willie. Me buttons is in th' way"; "He's right, Joe. When we ain't fightin' we should act more like sojers"; and, as the boys wander dazedly through a

If you're looking for Robert Taylor and Tyrone Power, you're in the wrong theater: David Wayne as Joe (and) and Tom Ewell as Willie in the Bill Mauldin-inspired comedy *Up Front* (Universal-International, 1951).

bombed-out saloon littered with smashed wine bottles, "Them rats! Them dirty, cold-blooded, soreheaded, stinkin' Huns! Them atrocity committin' skunks!"

While these quotations are today much prized by Mauldin aficionados, in 1951 some observers complained that the filmmakers were none too subtle in their application. The *New York Times*' Bosley Crowther commented: "It is not hard to spot the derived lines ... Alexander Hall, who directed, does everything but set up finger-posts." Reviewers also groused about the film's over-reliance upon slapstick at the expense of logic, especially in the climactic battlefield sequence wherein Willie and Joe's craven efforts to escape punishment for their latest infraction somehow result in a German retreat and an Allied victory. Likewise given short shrift by critics were the circuitous subplots involving a gung-ho captain (Jeffrey Lynn) determined to shake our heroes out of their chronic slothfulness, and a bombastic Italian patriarch (Silvio Minciotti) who sidelines in bootleg cognac. Few, however, found fault with the film's leading lady, Italian actress Marina Berti, whose physical attributes made up for her thespic shortcomings. Filmed economically on Universal's backlot, with many of the familiar studio landmarks camouflaged with dust and rubble, *Up Front* was what the industry called a "Nervous A": Neither expensive enough to qualify as an "A" picture nor inexpensive enough to be relegated to "B" status, and as such eminently suitable for either top- or bottom-billed bookings in double feature situations.

As part of its ongoing committment to the manufacture and promotion of series films (see previous notes on *Francis*), Universal-International already had a sequel to *Up Front* in the oven before the first film went into distribution. Still tied to a short-term Universal contract, Tom Ewell returned as Willie for the second entry *Back at the Front*, this time billed first in accordance with the film's alternate title *Willie and Joe Back at the Front*. With David Wayne under contract to 20th Century–Fox, the part of Joe was recast with service-comedy *habitue* Harvey Lembeck. Though a gifted comic actor, Lembeck did not mesh with Ewell as well as Wayne did, partially because of the discrepancy in ages between the two actors; while Ewell and Wayne were born only five years apart, Ewell was sixteen years older than Lembeck, and looked it. As for Bill Mauldin, his contribution to the sequel extended only as far as selling the character rights to the studio.

In a break from Hollywood tradition (especially at budget-conscious Universal), *Back at the Front* was a more costly undertaking than its predecessor, with the studio shipping cast and crew to Japan for location shooting, setting up temporary production headquarters at Tokyo's Imperial Hotel. According to *Billboard* magazine, Tom Ewell and Harvey Lembeck's costuming was so convincing that while taking an afternoon stroll in the streets of Tokyo, the two actors were nabbed by the local American MPs for wearing sloppy uniforms. *Billboard* also reported that director George Sherman was impressed by the fact that Japanese film technicians tended to complete each scene in a single take — not because of absolute perfection on the first try, but because their equipment was substandard and prone to unpredictable breakdowns.

And just how did Willie and Joe end up in Tokyo? No, they hadn't been transferred to the Pacific theater immediately after V-E Day: *Back at the Front* takes place in the year of its release, 1952, with the two GIs volunteering for reserve duty in Japan to avoid being sent to Korea. Any resemblance to the *Stars and Stripes* version of *Up Front* is purely accidental, as Willie and Joe indulge in broad physical humor and vaudevillian verbal exchanges while helping Military Intelligence track down a renegade American (Russell Johnson) who is using cans of crab meat to smuggle dynamite to the North Koreans. Further severing all ties with the Mauldin original is a drawn-out sequence in which the boys try to escape arrest by dressing up as geisha girls. The leading lady this time out is that porcelain princess Mari Blanchard, playing a Eurasian seductress in league with the villain. Near the end of the picture, an uncredited David Janssen arrives just in time to provide the stars with a set-up for the fadeout punchline.

Though both of the "Willie & Joe" movies remained in active distribution well into the late 1950s, neither was a conspicious success, and no further series entries were produced. Tom Ewell elected to return to Broadway after completing *Back at the Front*, almost immediately scoring a personal triumph in the stage version of *The Seven Year Itch*. Bill Mauldin continued to avoid Hollywood like the plague, even though other job offers were scarce in the years that followed, and a 1956 bid for a political career came to naught. He finally got back on his feet in 1958 when he succeeded the legendary Daniel Fitzpatrick as editorial cartoonist for the *St. Louis Post-Dispatch*. The winner of two Pulitzer Prizes for his illustrated commentaries, Mauldin died at age 82 in 2003 — and as far as we can determine, he never *did* see the movie version of *Up Front*.

6

You Know What Sailors Are
Comedies About Seafaring Men

As noted elsewhere in this book, practically every major movie comedian has at one time or another donned a Navy uniform; in particular, Billy Dooley made playing a comic sailor his life's work in a series of silent 2-reelers for the Christie studio. This chapter deals with *some* of the post-silent-era films starring actors not exclusively limited to comedy who have occasionally dipped into the waters of maritime humor. (For a book dealing with every seafaring comedy ever made, you'll have to look for someone made of stronger stuff than your humble correspondent.)

The essential ingredients of the Hollywood Navy Comedy remain virtually unaltered from picture to picture. When they aren't on board ship swabbing decks, cleaning guns and pulling galley duty, sailors have but two things on their mind: Money and Sex. Seldom do sailors venture into port alone, preferring to travel in packs of two or three. If there are two sailors, there's bound to be a fistfight over money or girls early in the proceedings, frequently at an off-limits saloon in an exotic foreign port. Otherwise, the two protagonists spend their time trying to outfox each other, forming a united front only when a third party (usually a soldier, marine or civilian) threatens physical harm to themselves or the heroine. If there are three sailors, often as not the handsomest of the three is the "brain," forever angling to enlarge his bankroll or add some fresh female talent to his little black book; the largest one is the "brawn," slow on the uptake but mighty useful in a brawl; and the third gob, generally the smallest in stature, is the nerdish patsy who invariably gets the worst of every situation. Whether acting solo or as part of a team, the comic sailor's principal enemies include the shore patrolman, the chief petty officer, and the oily civilian lounge lizard with whom the heroine is wrongheadedly enamored. Depending on the year in which a Navy comedy was made, the sailor protagonists may also find themselves trading blows with enemy spies.

The women in these sailors' lives fall into the either-or categories of virgins and whores, with a handful of redeemable "soiled doves" showing up in the pre–Production Code efforts. Our heroes may dally with a few tramps and trollops (who always seem to be a lot smarter than their male companions, especially in financial matters), but they'll more than likely settle down with the virtuous lass who refuses to give them anything but her time. Frequently, the "good" girl is the daughter of a captain or an admiral, or at the very least the offspring of an old salt who knows first-hand what's on the typical sailor's mind and refuses to let his darling daughter have anything to do with the hero — until said hero proves to be 100 percent true-blue in the final reel. Women are also useful for such farcical situations as smuggling a girl on board ship, usually in an oversized uniform to camouflage the proportional discrepancies, or the fact that the lady has somehow lost her own clothes along the way.

A number of maritime comedies have derived from two main theatrical sources. The first of these protypical plays is *Shore Leave*, written in 1920 by Canadian author Hubert Osborne and initially staged by the Edwin H. Robins Players in Toronto, under the direction of Broadway impresario David Belasco. The show finally made it to New York on August 8, 1922, after Belasco protegee Frances Starr signed on to play the heroine. Though dismissed by influential critic George Jean Nathan as "a mild and pleasant little thing," *Shore Leave* ran a solid 151 performances at the Lyceum Theater.

Ms. Starr portrayed Connie Martin, progeny of a marriage between a ship's captain and a circus acrobat, who has forsaken the restless lifestyle of her parents to settle down as a dressmaker in a New England port town. Resigned to spinsterhood, Connie changes her mind when sailor Bilge Smith (originally played by James Rennie) saunters into her life. Upon discovering that Connie is a skipper's daughter, Bilge grins and says, "Put it there, sister. I knew there was something different about you — that's it — the sea — you've got it in you." (The dialogue was praised for its naturalism back in 1922.) Bilge lets slip that his one compelling ambition in life is to command his own freighter. After he leaves on a tour of duty, Connie sells a valuable necklace left to her by her mother to buy and salvage a freighter as a gift for Bilge. Two years later, while throwing a party for a group of sailors on the deck of the freighter (which she has redesigned as a floating café), Connie is reunited with a drunken Bilge, who once he sobers up admits he is still in love with her — but when he finds out that she's purchased the freighter for his sake Bilge is outraged, insisting he "ain't the sorta guy that'd live off'n a *woman!*" Concluding that the money earned from the freighter is an obstacle to romance, Connie sells the vessel and disposes of the cash. Two more years pass: Having gotten word that Connie is penniless, Bilge works his way back to port as a stoker in hopes of a reconciliation. Alas, he becomes convinced that her so-called poverty is actually a frame-up devised to trap him under false pretenses. But Connie informs him that her money is being held in a trust fund, not for herself, but for her son should she ever have one — and *only* on the condition that her son is named "Smith." Tossing off his cap and shouting an exultant "Hell!," Bilge plants a kiss on Connie as the curtain falls.

The first film version of *Shore Leave* was a silent production, directed by John S. Robertson and released by First National in 1925, with Dorothy Mackaill as Connie and Richard Barthelmess as Bilge. Portions of the film were shot on the decks of the battleship *Arkansas* during a cruise from New York to Newport News, a location jaunt advertised as a "first" in motion picture history; fifty actual seamen and two petty officers served as extras. For a film produced at the height of the Jazz Age, *Shore Leave* is a surprisingly relaxed effort, relying totally upon the charisma of the two stars to sustain audience interest. The film's only significant action sequences involve Bilge Smith and his shipboard rival, played by Ted McNamara: A knock-down, drag-out fight on board the reconverted freighter, and an interlude set in Egypt (but actually filmed in Central Park) wherein the two tars go for a camel ride.

Shore Leave was remade thrice during the talkie era, each time as a musical. Two of these films were derived from *Hit the Deck*, the 1927 Broadway musical-comedy adaptation of *Shore Leave* with book by Herbert Fields, music by Vincent Youmans, and lyrics by Leo Robin and Clifford Grey. The heroine of *Hit the Deck*, now named Loulou, starts off managing a coffee shop in Newport, Rhode Island, then becomes an heiress. The hero, still named Bilge Smith, falls for Loulou but is reluctant to marry a woman of wealth. As Bilge travels all over the world Loulou traipses after him, hoping that he'll overcome his class prejudice and pop the question. Finally he does so, but only after Loulou follows the example of her *Shore Leave* predecessor Connie Martin by signing away her money to the couple's first-born child. Charles King, two years away from his movie debut in the Oscar-winning *Broadway Melody*, played Bilge, while Louise Groody was Loulou. The main attraction of *Hit the Deck* (which ran 201 performances longer than *Shore Leave*) was neither stars nor story, but the show's cavalcade of catchy songs, including "Sometimes I'm Happy" and "Hallelujah."

Hit the Deck first went before the cameras in 1930 as an RKO Radio Pictures super production, partially lensed in Technicolor. In one of his many appearances as a likeable but lunkheaded sailor, Jack Oakie played Bilge, with Polly Walker as Loulou and Marguerita Padila handling several musical numbers in the secondary role of Lavinia (a character created for the 1927 stage musical). The

Archetypal movie sailor Jack Oakie shares an intimate moment with Polly Walker in the first film adaptation of the Broadway musical *Hit the Deck* (RKO, 1930).

fact that Jack Oakie frequently listed *Hit the Deck* among his favorite films makes it all the more frustrating that only the soundtrack of the 1930 version is known to exist. Conversely, the 1955 MGM remake of *Hit the Deck* has been safely preserved for all you fans out there of Vic Damone, Jane Powell, Tony Martin, Ann Miller and Debbie Reynolds. The original storyline is totally jettisoned in this Cinemascope-and-Metrocolor remake: according to the new script, Jane Powell aspires to star in a stage revival of *Hit the Deck*, but is frustrated by a trio of well-intentioned sailors who hope to protect her from a womanizing producer. Three of the songs and none of the jokes were salvaged from the 1927 Broadway production. (An interim 1941 version of *Hit the Deck*, intended as a Ray Bolger vehicle, was announced by RKO but never produced.)

The best of the extant *Shore Leave* remakes—musically if not comedically—is the 1936 RKO production *Follow the Fleet*. What's left of the 1922 plotline is in the hands of Randolph Scott as Bilge Smith and Harriet Hilliard (aka Harriet Nelson) as Connie Martin. But who's paying any attention to Randy and Harriet as long as the film's *real* stars Fred Astaire and Ginger Rogers (cast as Bilge and Connie's best friends) are center stage to sing and dance such Irving Berlin hits as "Let Yourself Go" and "Let's Face the Music and Dance"?

The second theatrical "horn of plenty" for lighthearted Navy films is *Sailor Beware*, written by Kenyon Nicholson and Charles Robinson and initially housed at the Lyceum Theater (previously the home of *Shore Leave*) for 500 performances beginning September 28, 1933. Described by its authors as "Variations on a Familiar Theme in Eight Acts," this is the salty saga of swaggering sailor Chester Jones, nicknamed "Dynamite" for his sexual combustibility. While on leave in Panama, Dynamite's shipmates literally bank on his reputation, betting the ranch that he can successfully seduce sexy resort hostess Billie Jackson—better known as "Stonewall" Jackson because of her uncanny ability to resist the advances of any man. As sexually explicit as a legitimate play could be in 1933 without bringing down the vice squad, *Sailor Beware* was condemned by critics but adored by the public. After its Broadway run, the play flourished on the road and in stock, and was successfully revived by the all-black Harlem Players in a 1935 production featuring Juano Hernandez, Canada Lee and Juanita Hall (who later created the role of Bloody Mary in *South Pacific*).

Optioned by Paramount Pictures in 1935, *Sailor Beware* was deemed so "filthy" a property that the Hays Office refused to allow it to be filmed without extensive laundering—and even then, Paramount was forbidden to use the original title. The management of New York's Rialto Theater cheekily thumbed their noses at the censors (and risked an injunction in the process) by emblazoning the words "SAILOR BEWARE" on the theater's marquee to herald the premiere of the 1936 film version *Lady Be Careful*. Painstakingly purged of its most questionable elements by screenwriters Dorothy Parker and Alan Campbell—whom the press dubbed "the spot removers" for their cleansing efforts—*Lady Be Careful* sidesteps censorship by splitting the main character in two. The self-proclaimed lothario is now named Jake, played by Buster Crabbe; Jake's fellow sailor, played by Lew Ayres, is known as "Dud" because of his shyness around women. While docked in Panama, Dud falls overboard and is rescued by a group of leggy ladies on board a sailboat. When he is returned to his ship, the other sailors assume that Dud has been having a roaring good time with the damsels, whereupon he is rechristened "Dynamite"—though both Dud and the audience know that he remains pure and chaste. Only then does the wager involving the virginal Billie "Stonewall" Jackson (Mary Carlisle) enter the plot, with Dud/Dynamite endeavoring to plant a kiss on Stonewall's lips to win the bet, and Jake doing his best to beat our hero's time with the heroine. The plot devices of a timid tar with an undeserved reputation and an ice-princess heroine ripe for thawing were retained for Paramount's second adaptation of *Sailor Beware*, the 1942 musical *The Fleet's In*, starring William Holden, Dorothy Lamour and, in her feature-film debut, the irrepressible Betty Hutton. (This version also lifted elements from two other Paramount features, the otherwise unrelated *The Fleet's In* [1928] and *True to the Navy* [1930], both starring Clara Bow.) In 1951, the property was remade under its original title as a vehicle for Dean Martin and Jerry Lewis—an adaptation examined in detail in **Chapter 3**.

It is sometimes more difficult to tell Navy comedies apart than to determine the difference between a male and female caterpillar, but we'll give it a try. Discounting popular comic actor William Haines' first talkie vehicle *Navy Blues* (MGM 1929), which starts as a comedy but grows more serious with each passing reel, among the earliest seagoing chucklefests of the sound era was *Sailor's Holiday* (1929), a six-reeler released by Pathé in both sound and silent versions. Alan Hale Sr. and George Cooper topped the cast as a pair of swabbies who embark upon a search for the missing brother of heroine Sally Eilers. A quest of a different sort was the substance of Universal's *Dames Ahoy* (1930), featuring Glenn Tryon, Otis Harlan and Eddie Gribbon as three tars who spend the majority of the picture tracking down the larcenous lady who has swindled one of them. Alas, only the 51-minute silent version of *Dames Ahoy* survives, depriving us of the scene in which Glenn Tryon performed a sanitized rendition of the bawdy old sea chanty "Barnacle Bill." Helen Wright and Gertrude Astor supply the feminine interest, while Walter Brennan and Andy Devine pop up in bit roles.

Nineteen-thirty also brought forth archetypal "dumb gob" Jack Oakie in Paramount's *Sea Legs*, a semi-sequel to the 1928 silent *The Fleet's In* (see **Chapter 2**) and the first talking picture built around one of the mainstays of service comedies, the dimwitted Navy boxing champion. As in the earlier film, Oakie is cast as Searchlight Doyle, the fleet's top lightweight contender. Shanghaied and carried off to the mythical land of St. Cassette, Doyle is ordered to serve as a substitute for another sailor, the AWOL son of a prominent financier. As the plot charts its course, Doyle is accused of murdering the guy he's impersonating, putting a crimp in his romance with the Captain's daughter (Lillian Roth). Planned as a musical, *Sea Legs* was released with only one song intact.

6. You Know What Sailors Are

Jack Oakie was back three years later in *Sailor Be Good* (working title *Tars and Feathers*), a Jefferson/RKO Production directed by James Cruze, a major figure of the silent era then on the downslide. Yet again, Oakie plays a Navy pugilist, one Kelsey Dugan. During a drunken shore leave, Dugan falls in love with jaded dance-hall hostess Red (Vivienne Osborne). After an interim marriage to a pretentious socialite (Gertrude Michael), Dugan returns to Red, reversing the *Shore Leave* premise by reforming the harlot and convincing *her* to settle down. Elsewhere in 1933, director William Wyler, still serving his apprenticeship in Universal programmers, dashed off the modestly enjoyable *Her First Mate*, one of several comedies teaming gangly Slim Summerville with gawky ZaSu Pitts. Another *Shore Leave* derivation (and also based on a stage play), *Her First Mate* casts off when the heroine purchases an old car ferry so that her boyfriend, a candy butcher on the Albany night boat, can realize his dream of being a captain.

Unlike William Wyler, Raoul Walsh was firmly established as an A-list director in 1933, meaning that even such shabby material as *Sailor's Luck* had a more prestigious veneer than it deserved. The last of Walsh's assignments for Fox Pictures, *Sailor's Luck* was originally titled *Bad Boy* in hopes of cashing in on the success of *Bad Girl* (1931), Fox's previous pairing of the studio's popular new stars James Dunn and Sally Eilers. The original ad campaign made no secret of this strategy: "BAD GIRL and her BOY FRIEND in the story of a nautical-minded miss who made a broad-minded sailor walk the straight and narrow!"

Promising to settle down and marry the experienced but essentially decent Sally Brent (Eilers) when he returns from his next voyage, randy sailor Jimmy Harrigan (Dunn) jealously breaks off the engagement when Sally enters a marathon dance contest promoted by her lecherous landlord Baron Portola (played by a deliciously slimy Victor Jory in his first major screen role). A typically Walsh-ian ballroom brawl follows, as do a plethora of *Shore Leave*-ish misunderstandings and missed opportunities before Jimmy and Sally finally fasten the half-hitch. Though it takes a bit too long getting started, *Sailor's Luck* is chock full of marvelous bits of business: Round-heeled Esther Muir's musical invitation to her male admirers; ex-boxer Frank Moran's portrayal of a roughneck with intellectual pretentions (a characterization Moran would hone to perfection in his later work for director Preston Sturges); and a wild swimming-pool sequence featuring one of the most outrageous homosexual stereotypes you're ever likely to see, even in a Pre-Code picture ("Gay-zee ansy-pay!")

Less ribald but no less entertaining are Joan Blondell and Glenda Farrell in Warner Bros.' Post-Code effort *Miss Pacific Fleet* (1935). Joan and Glenda play Gloria and May, a pair of gold diggers working San Diego Harbor, fleecing various sailors and marines. A beauty contest promoted by henpecked husband Freytag (Hugh Herbert) somehow makes an honest woman out of Gloria, who ends up marrying nice-guy Marine sergeant Tom Foster (Warren Hull). Allen Jenkins steps into the traditional Jack Oakie role of punchdrunk Navy boxer Kewpie Morgan.

Oakie himself would weigh anchor at Warners in the 1941 musical comedy *Navy Blues* (not a remake of the 1929 William Haines picture), which emulates *Sailor Beware* by having the star and his shipmates Jack Haley (a last-minute replacement for Eddie Albert) and Jackie Gleason ("of nightclub fame," trumpeted the studio publicists) going heavily into debt to wager on the outcome of a gunnery-practice contest between the battleships *Montana* and *Wisconsin*. A surprisingly bucolic Ann Sheridan, showing off a hitherto untapped talent as a hog-caller, is the heroine; Martha Raye plays Jack Haley's alimony-chasing ex-wife; and Herbert Anderson, Dennis the Menace's future TV dad, is cast as the singing juvenile. Just before shooting began on *Navy Blues*, Warners conducted a poll amongst the sailors at San Diego Naval Base to choose six gorgeous women from hundreds of applicants to appear as singers and dancers in the film. The girls selected were all ex-models, at least three of whom went on to enjoy a modicum of stardom: Georgia Carroll, Marguerite Chapman, Kay Aldridge, Peggy Diggins, Leslie Brooks and Claire James (Alexis Smith, one of the original finalists, was pulled out to appear in another Warner production, *Dive Bomber*). Christened "The Navy Blues Sextette," this attractive aggregation was prominently fea-

"Now I know I have a heart; it's tattooed on my chest." Jack Haley as a wistful gob in *Navy Blues* (Warners, 1941).

tured in both *Navy Blues* and the Jimmy Durante-Phil Silvers vehicle *You're in the Army Now* (see **Chapter 4**), with Alix Talton replacing Claire James in the second picture. Like several other Navy films of the immediate pre-war period, *Navy Blues* was extensively location-filmed at Pearl Harbor, which is the main reason that Warners discreetly withdrew the picture from distribution after December 7.

Naval themes have also drifted in and out of the many B films produced by the minor studios. Grand National Pictures' 1937 quasi-musical *Sweetheart of the Navy* is a vehicle for the popular juvenile team of Eric Linden and Cecilia Parker, both playing worldlier characters than usual. When hard-bitten Joan (Cecilia) is in danger of losing ownership of the Snug Harbor Café, a pair of sympathetic tars arrange a fundraising boxing match (what else?), with egotistical sailor Eddie (Linden) fighting on the girl's behalf. Commander Lodge (Roger Imhof), who doesn't want Eddie to ruin his chances of entering Annapolis, urges him not to fight, but the desperate Joan vamps him into it, pretending to be a sweet churchgoing girl from his home town. Another Grand National quickie, *Swing It Sailor* (1938), is not a musical despite its title. On this occasion, Ray Mayer channels Jack Oakie as Navy boxer Husky Stone, who aspires to wed the deceptively genteel Myrtle Montrose (Isabel Jewell in a rare starring role). This threatens the well-ordered existence of Stone's buddy Pete Kelly (Wallace Ford), who is accustomed to using Husky as a stooge to fight his battles and perform his shipboard duties. Sensing that Myrtle is a phony, Pete determines to woo her away from Husky in order to teach his buddy a lesson. All is forgiven when Pete saves Husky from being blown to bits during aerial bombing practice. The most novel aspect of this obscure potboiler is that the scripted stupidity is not the exclusive domain of pea-brained Husky Stone: *All* the main characters are blockheads, including the heroine.

Over at budget-conscious Republic Pictures, scripters Gordon Kahn and Eric Taylor cooked up a Navy comedy which not only incorporated many of the usual plot devices, but also refreshingly offered several unexpected story developments. Released in 1937, Republic's *Navy Blues* (no relation to either the 1929 MGM film or the 1941 Warners effort of the same name) features the requisite team of sailor protagonists, this time four in number: Habitual liar and self-proclaimed chick magnet Rusty Gibbs (Dick Purcell), aspiring boxer Biff Jones (Warren Hymer), and eternally frustrated Chips (Joe Sawyer) and Gateleg (Horace MacMahon). Hoping to get even with Rusty for past misdeeds, his three shipmates set him up on a blind date with Doris Kimbell (Mary Brian), who though described by the trio as a ravishing beauty is actually a dull, bespectacled librarian (a faint echo of *Shore Leave*). If Rusty is able to win Doris' heart during a 48-hour leave, he'll also win 25 bucks; if he fails, he'll have to do his pals' laundry for a month (a less faint echo of *Sailor*

Beware). Obstacles in Rusty's path include Doris' sailor-hating Aunt Beulah (Lucille Gleason) and the girl's erstwhile beau, wimpy head librarian Julian Everett (Edward Woods, a long way from playing Jimmy Cagney's mobster buddy in 1931's *Public Enemy*). Conversely, Doris' milquetoast uncle Andrew (Chester Clute) is fond of Chester and helps him promote the romance. In the first of the film's many plot twists, Uncle Andrew turns out to have been a champion college athlete, and in this capacity he gives boxing lessons to the hulking Biff.

While it's hardly surprising that smooth-talking Rusty inspires ugly-duckling Doris to evolve into a beautiful swan (especially since, in the opening cast credits, we see Mary Brian both before and after her makeover), the rest of the film goes off on a variety of unpredictable tangents. Early on, Rusty tries to make time with Doris by feigning interest in an algebra textbook, which sparks the interest of her boss Julian. We soon learn that Julian is a member of an enemy spy ring, using algebraic equations to decipher coded messages as part of a plot to assassinate a foreign politician. Meanwhile, Rusty spins his customary web of prevarications in order to impress Doris, claiming at one point to be a secret government agent. From the evidence at hand, the enemy spies conclude that that Rusty is telling the truth — and so do the *real* Naval Intelligence operatives assigned to protect the targeted politician. Misunderstandings and misapprehensions mushroom to the extent that Rusty, Doris and Uncle Andrew are captured and held prisoner by the bad guys. With the help of his sailor buddies, Rusty manages to vanquish the villains, prevent the assassination, land the heroine and win his bet.

Navy Blues is no masterpiece, but credit Republic Pictures for putting a fresh coat of paint on an old bucket of cliches. That's more than can be said for another Republic opus, 1941's *Sailors on Leave*, which not only cannibalizes *Sailor Beware* but also Buster Keaton's *Seven Chances* (1925) and the hoary old stage farce *Charley's Aunt*. Lest they lose a bet, comic tars Swift (Chick Chandler) and Mike (Cliff Nazarro, he of the tiresome doubletalk routines) try to prevent misogynistic shipmate Chuck (William Lundigan) from getting married before his 27th birthday in order to inherit a fortune. Thinking their money is safe when they pair Chuck off with man-hating nightclub thrush Linda (Shirley Ross), the two funnymen are foiled when Chuck and Linda fall in love. To bust up the romance, Swift and Mike disguise themselves as Chuck's ex-wife and maiden aunt. All that's worth mentioning about this mechanical melange is the original song "I'm Proud I'm a Navy Man," written by Frank Loesser and Jule Styne.

Navy comedies proceeded full speed ahead throughout the 1940s, their titles, plots and characters interchangeable. *Sailor's Lady* (20th Century–Fox, 1940) deserves a nod for the direction by the prolific Allan Dwan, the script by real-life Navy pilot Spig Wead (himself the subject of the 1957 biopic *Wings of the Eagles*), the presence in the cast of a pre-stardom Dana Andrews, and the fact that the studio had to hire five on-set attendants to look after the adorable little baby who motivates the storyline. *Sailor's Holiday* (Columbia, 1944), not a remake of the same-named 1929 Pathé release, is worth a footnote as one of a handful of features starring Arthur Lake during the brief period in the mid-'40s when the *Blondie* series was on hiatus; and as the first significant movie appearance of Shelley Winters (billed as Winter), playing a Hollywood extra who weds nominal leading man Lewis Wilson. And Universal's *Hi'ya Sailor* (1943) involves a $200 investment ponied up by two sailors on behalf of a third, a swindle perpetrated by a civilian, and a climactic floor show. Donald Woods, Phyllis Brooks, Eddie Quillan and Elyse Knox are among the cast members, but it hardly mattered. Wartime audiences were so hungry for entertainment that a team of trained poodles could have appeared in *Hi'ya Sailor* and still posted a profit for the studio.

The stock characters of Depression-era navy comedies tended to fade away during the World War II years, as the Office of War Information encouraged (a nicer word than "strong-armed") Hollywood to sanitize the image of American sailors and the ladies in their lives for the sake of civilian morale. The clean-cut navigators played by Gene Kelly and Frank Sinatra in the 1945 musicomedy *Anchors Aweigh* are a far cry from the tattooed libertines depicted in the films of the pre-war era, just as wholesome Kathryn Grayson and healthily hoydenish Pamela Britton are the diametric opposites of the painted chippies, buttoned-up spinsters and frosty misandrists who populated the Navy films of the 1930s.

Gene Kelly and Frank Sinatra were still pure of heart and intention when they were reteamed in the 1949's *On the Town*, the exuberant story of three sailors (Jules Munshin completed the trio) who find fun and romance during a 24-hour leave in New York City. *On the Town* is today regarded as among the best of the Arthur Freed-produced MGM musicals, largely on the strength of its unforgettable opening number, composed by Leonard Bernstein with lyrics by Adolph Green and Betty Comden, and staged on location in the streets of Manhattan with as many innovational camera angles, jump-cuts and terpsichorean turns as codirectors Gene Kelly and Stanley Donen could jam into five minutes' footage. Indeed, so overpowering is this opener that the rest of the film is unable to live up to its promise. This is particularly true in the film's comedy setpieces, which — except for an extended cross-purposes musical number staged in a cramped taxi between Frank Sinatra and lady cabbie Betty Garrett — are never quite as funny as the actors seem to think they are. (Am I the only person on earth who's never been trapped into laughter when the main characters cause the collapse of a dinosaur skeleton?) Nonetheless, *On the Town* is invariably described as both a musical *and* a comedy; accordingly, the cookie-cutter Navy pictures that tried to emulate its success in the early 1950s—*Three Sailors and a Girl, Skirts Ahoy* and others—did their best to provide generous helpings of songs and laughs.

The most shameless of the *On the Town* imitations was Columbia's *All Ashore* (1953), a Technicolor follow-up to the studio's earlier Army comedy *Sound Off* (see **Chapter 12**) with the same combination of talents: Star Mickey Rooney, producer Jonie Tapps, director Richard Quine,

On the Town (MGM, 1949): Taking a quickie musical tour of New York City, sailors Frank Sinatra, Jules Munshin and Gene Kelly (left to right) burst out in song in front of Rockefeller Center (*courtesy Jim Feeley*).

scriptwriters Quine and Blake Edwards and composer George Duning. Whereas *Sound Off* was a solo vehicle for Rooney, *All Ashore* goes the Kelly-Sinatra-Munshin route by teaming The Mick with singer Dick Haymes and dancer Ray McDonald. Just as *On the Town* was largely location-filmed in New York City, the majority of *All Ashore* was lensed on Catalina Island, with emphasis on the fabled Avalon ballroom. And in lieu of *On the Town*'s dancing damsels Ann Miller and Vera-Ellen and female comic Betty Garrett, *All Ashore* combines all three characters into the single form of Peggy Ryan, who for the first three reels or so provides both laughs and fancy footwork, usually in combination with her frequent movie partner (and later real-life husband) Ray McDonald.

With eight musical numbers crammed into the film's 80 minutes, there isn't much time for the plot, which finds sailors Haymes and McDonald formulating various moneymaking schemes to bankroll Rooney's "dream" vacation to Catalina. Cast as the perennial fall guy, forever sacrificing his cash and his girlfriends (notably costar Jody Lawrance) to his two sharpie shipmates, Rooney might have been more appealing had his character (named Moby Dickerson!) not wallowed in self-pity, at one point singing the plaintive ballad "I'm So Unlucky" to an audience consisting of one tropical bird. In the final scenes, Mickey's luck changes spectacularly when he rescues millionaire's daughter Barbara Bates from drowning. Though most of the comedy is as threadbare as the storyline, a few highlights emerge. An early scene in which the three sailors are rolled in a cheap dive by a bevy of B-girls includes such cute gags as a spiked drink that causes instant immobility, and such offbeat touches as a twelve-fingered piano player. Later on, Rooney is chased

The dream sequence from Columbia's 1953 musical *All Ashore*: Sailor Mickey Rooney, imagining himself "Sir Francis the Bold," clashes steel with shipmates Ray McDonald (in back, center) and Dick Haymes, while damsel-in-distress Barbara Bates placidly awaits rescue.

through a motel courtyard by veteran Hollywood stuntman Dick Crockett, eluding his pursuer (and impressively doing his *own* stunts) by ducking and dodging up, down, around and through the playground equipment. And in a fantasy sequence which simultaneously lampoons movie swashbucklers and Nelson Eddy-Jeanette MacDonald operettas, Rooney and Barbara Bates sing an impassioned love duet (with patently obvious dubbed voices) while jockeying to upstage each other.

As late as 1984, the *On the Town* formula was reactivated minus the music (and most of the humor) in Marimark Productions' *Weekend Pass*. In the 35 years since *On the Town,* the sublime postwar innocence of movie sailors had reverted to the seen-it-all rowdiness of the 1930s, while most of the sailors' girlfriends underwent the same moral retrogression. Aimed straight at the drive-in trade, *Weekend Pass* revolves around four young sailors from different cultural backgrounds — played by four young actors you've never heard of, so why embarrass them by mentioning names? — who arrive in L.A. on a 72-hour leave. The black sailor returns to the old 'hood and immediately gets caught up in a gang war. The Jewish-nerd sailor performs an amateur stand-up gig at a comedy club (Phil Hartman, the only recognizable cast member, plays the club owner. He must have lost a bet.) The self-proclaimed "cool" sailor, looking forward to an ecstatic weekend with a "wild" girl, recoils in horror when she turns out to be a bit *too* wild. And the requisite virginal sailor, after failing to score with a Chinese masseuse named Chop Suzi, settles for the only female virgin left standing in Southern California. This being a 1984 film, everybody ends up at a disco party — where, in the tradition of *Porky's* (another teen-raunch comedy of the era) — the manly-man sailors learn to be tolerant of a gay character. There's also a beach scene with acres of bikinied babes, and a strip-club scene with plenty of babes but no bikinis. *Weekend Pass* was written by a fellow straight out of college (it shows) and distributed by Crown International, the same folks who brought you such cinematic triumphs as *Galaxina* and *The Pom Pom Girls*.

Other individual films about sailors are covered elsewhere in this book (see **Chapters 2** and **3** in particular). We'll knot up the loose ends with two comedies that deal with the Shore Patrol, a branch of Navy service often maligned in films but seldom given "hero" status.

At the time of its release in late 1973, Columbia's *The Last Detail* generated a great deal of industry buzz because of the uninhibited use of profanities by the film's star Jack Nicholson, cast to perfection as a muscle-flexing, cigar-chewing Navy lifer named Buddusky. The film's language was regarded as so obscene in Robert Towne's original script (based on a novel by Darryl Ponicsan) that the studio refused to make the picture until Towne agreed to tone things down. As the writer recalled years later, one executive sat him down and inquired in a paternal tone, "Bob, wouldn't *twenty* motherfuckers be more effective than *forty* motherfuckers?" Towne refused to alter a word, and the script remained in limbo for nearly three years before Hollywood's rating system relaxed sufficiently for Columbia to produce the film exactly as written — and reap a box-office fortune as a result. (The studio's ad campaign was more cautious than the film itself in flaunting this new-found freedom, beginning its first sentence with the comic-book expletive "No *#@!!*")

The plot harks back to the three-sailors-on-the-prowl formula of earlier Navy comedies, but with a few noteworthy nuances. Career petty officers "Bad-Ass" Buddusky and "Mule" Mulhall (Otis Young) are ordered to escort a pimply young gob named Meadows (Randy Quaid), sentenced to an eight-year jail term for a relatively minor theft, from a Virginia naval base to a New Hampshire brig. At first, the two hardened salts regard this detail as a paid vacation and their prisoner as a loser. By and by, Buddusky sizes up Meadows as a boy who's never truly "lived," and now won't have much of a chance to do so. With a reluctant Mule in tow, Bad-Ass vows to treat Meadows to the best time of his life during the kid's last few hours of freedom, and to teach him how to survive in a man's world along the way. Essential ingredients to Meadows' rite of passage are liquor bottles, card games, and a loss of virginity to a young whore (billed only as "Young Whore" — you could get away with that in 1973 — and portrayed by Carol Kane). Amazingly, even the bowdlerized version of *The Last Detail* currently making the commercial-TV rounds manages to retain the

6. You Know What Sailors Are

Otis Young (left) looks on with trepidation as fellow shore patrolman Jack Nicholson cooks up some R-rated deviltry in *The Last Detail* (Columbia, 1973).

Rabelaisian exuberance of the original version, thanks to the free-swinging direction by Hal Ashby and the towering performance of Jack Nicholson in his first flush of superstardom. Roger Ebert has commented that Nicholson "creates a character so complete and so complex that we stop thinking about the movie and just watch to see what he'll do next."

If anyone cares what the characters will do next in the 1994 Morgan Creek/Warner Bros. production *Chasers*, I've yet to meet them. Like *Last Detail*, *Chasers* is an R-rated "shore patrol" comedy about an unusually eventful prisoner transfer. And in the tradition of *Last Detail*'s Jack Nicholson, *Chasers* utilizes the talents of a former participant of the 1969 counterculture classic *Easy Rider*, in this case director Dennis Hopper. But that's where all resemblances come to a screeching halt.

Chasers does, however, bear traces of previous Navy comedies by offering a money-hungry sailor protagonist and a larcenous-hearted "sailor's girl." Having coasted through his Navy hitch on sheer *chutzpah*, Eddie Devane (William McNamara) has formulated a system to become filthy rich and purchase a Porsche at the government's expense just before his discharge. But Eddie's plans are derailed when is assigned to Shore Patrol duty with granite-jowled veteran Rock Reilly (Tom Berenger). Their detail is to escort a brash young Marine named Toni Johnson, described as a "dangerous criminal," to a maximum-security prison. Well, guess what: Toni Johnson turns out to be a well-proportioned blonde female, played by Erika Eleniak. And this Toni Johnson is one sharp cookie, who can figure out more methods of evasion and on-the-spot scams than any busty blonde in movie history, even Joan Blondell. Having met his match, Eddie naturally falls in love — and into bed — with tawny Toni.

Chasers is highly recommended for those who think that the mere mention of the word "tampon" is a cause for jubilation, and for those who are aroused at the sight of a thinly clad Erika Eleniak in handcuffs (shucks, she had *my* attention). With the exception of *New York Times* critic Janet Maslin, whose fondness for Dennis Hopper outweighed her indifference toward the film, *Chasers* was as roundly booed by reviewers as *The Last Detail* was heartily cheered. Some observers have suggested that the famously iconoclastic Dennis Hopper agreed to make a formula product like *Chasers* as a means of ingratiating himself with the studio bigwigs, so that he'd be allowed back in the directorial mainstream and make the films he really wanted to make. Given the fact that Hopper surrounded himself with several old acting cronies (Dean Stockwell, Seymour Cassel, etc.), and reserved for himself a flashy cameo role as a slavering underwear salesman, one must face the disillusioning prospect that this *was* the film he really wanted to make.

If nothing else, *Chasers* confirms what Navy comedies have been telling us since movies began: The two principal motivating factors in the life of a typical sailor are money and sex. And lots of both.

7

The Few, the Proud, the Funny

Comedies About the Marines

"Tell it to the Marines! Those lovable lugs with wonderful mugs who we now love more than ever! Tell 'em they're still the greatest guys in the world."

This advertising blurb for the 1950 war drama *The Halls of Montezuma* (immortalized 20 years later as one of the anonymous P.A. announcements in Robert Altman's *MASH*) neatly sums up Hollywood's attitude toward the United States Marine Corps: Tough but Lovable — or if you prefer, Tough *and* Lovable. But it was not always thus: until Fox Pictures' *What Price Glory* hit the screen in late 1926, the movie image of the Marine Corps was merely "Tough," period.

Introduced during the Revolutionary War but not official formed until 1798, the U.S. Marines have always taken great pride in their perpetual state of preparedness. Combining the best elements of the Army and Navy, this elite corps ("the few, the proud") was created as a rapid-response team, stationed on sailing vessels as infantry units and trained to provide power protection for American ground troops. The Corps had cemented its reputation during the Battle of Derne in 1805 by utterly decimating the Barbary pirates on the "Shores of Tripoli." Unlike the general run of Army and Navy enlistees, most of whom had no practical combat experience, the Marines seldom entered any armed conflict without already having put boots on the ground elsewhere. This was especially true when America entered World War I in 1917. By the time the Marines arrived in France, most of them had seen combat duty during the American occupation of Nicaragua ("The Halls of Montezuma"), which had begun in 1912 when the Corps landed to provide cover for rebel leader Juan José Estrada in his power struggle against the country's president (and perceived Yankee-hater) José Santos Zelaya.

It was the 20-year Nicaraguan occupation that did the most to solidify the Marines' heroic image in the eyes of the movie going public. By the mid-1920s, there was hardly a film fan living who wasn't well versed in the various nicknames used to describe Marines: The most popular of these included "Leathernecks," referring to the neckband that was once a part of the official uniform, and "Devil Dogs," derived from the Germans' begrudging admiration of the *Teuful Hunden*'s courage and tenacity during the battle of Belleau Wood. And never mind that the oft-repeated admonition "Tell it to the Marines" originated as a derisive comment (usually made by a soldier or sailor) upon the mental inferiority of the average Marine recruit. By the time this catchphrase was used for the title of a 1926 William Haines vehicle, it was generally accepted as a compliment, as well as the perfect squelch for any enlistee who had the gall to whine that military life was too rough ("You think *you've* got it bad, soldier? Tell it to the Marines!").

The notion of treating the Marine Corps in a comic fashion did not occur to moviemakers until after the first week of September in 1924, when three new plays about World War I premiered on Broadway: *Nerves*, *Havoc* and *What Price Glory?*. Although the last-named play opened with the least amount of advance publicity, it was the only one of the trio to score a hit, lasting 433 performances at New York's Plymouth Theater. Cowritten by poet-playwright Maxwell Anderson and journalist Laurence Stallings, *What Price Glory?* shocked the opening-night audience with its unvarnished depiction of warfare as a hellish slaughterhouse — a startling contrast to the many previous films and plays that had treated the War to End All Wars as a glorious adventure. No one could accuse co-author Laurence Stallings of being a dilettante: A decorated hero of World War I, he had lost a leg as a result of injuries sustained at Château-Thierry. Stallings' front-line experiences had transformed him into as outspoken a pacifist as his collaborator Maxwell Anderson, and this epiphany was reflected in *What Price Glory?*'s bitter observations about the futility of warfare, the rottenness of "a world that's gotta be wet down every thirty years" with the blood of innocent boys, and the hypocrisy of superior officers who blithely send their minions on suicide missions while weeping crocodile tears over not being permitted to participate in combat themselves.

But the play's tragic elements were not *What Price Glory?*'s main selling card. Except for a grim second act set in a besieged "cellar in a disputed town," most of the action took place far removed from the front lines. Act One was set at Marine headquarters in a small French village, where several leathernecks passed the time by bragging about their sexual conquests and bitching about their superior officers. The final act occurred in a saloon owned by one Cognac Pete, where the play's two rough-and-ready protagonists, well fortified with cheap liquor, battled over the affections of a saucy little baggage known as Charmaine.

The play's original subtitle — "A Comedy with a Few Deaths" — said it all. Despite such horrific second-act highlights as a delirious officer raving hysterically over the carnage and a fatally wounded private begging the medics to "Stop the blood!" playgoers were principally attracted to the raucuous comedy content of *What Price Glory?* The boisterous barracks-room humor was spiced up with some of the most explicit expletives ever spoken on the legitimate stage. Though the play was not, as has often been alleged, the first to use excessive profanity (earlier works like Clyde Fitch's *The City* and Somerset Maugham's *Rain* had already blazed that trail), the plethora of "Goddamns," "Hells," "Jesus Christs" and "Sons-of-Bitches" tripping from the tongues of the *What Price Glory?* cast members, to say nothing of the relentless sexual innuendoes and casual references to "broads," "sluts" and "tarts," did not normally constitute an evening of theatrical entertainment in 1924. The impact of this crude candor on the first-night audience has given rise to an apocryphal story involving one of the theater patrons, a sweet-natured old dowager who after the final curtain allegedly whispered to her companion, "Now where in hell did I put my goddamn galoshes?"

Prior to its Broadway debut, *What Price Glory?* was subjected to intense scrutiny from both the public-morals watchdogs and the federal government. The play's "problem" was not so much its unbridled Anglo-Saxonisms as its emphasis on the Marines' sexual hijinks and nonstop drinking — which, it was feared, would lead audiences to conclude that a hitch in the Corps was little more than a round-the-clock debauch. A more vexing issue was the play's robust disrespect for authority figures, as manifested in the sarcastic and mutually recriminating dialogue exchanges between the two main characters, Captain Flagg and Sergeant Quirt. The playwrights agreed to tone down some of the riper dialogue, and to add a few lines indicating that the lack of discipline and disregard for protocol exhibited by the Marine characters occurred *only* when they were off duty, and never during critical moments on the battlefield. Chances are, however, that the civilian and military bluenoses who disapproved of *What Price Glory?* would not have been able to stop the production, since technically the playwrights had broken no federal or municipal laws. Citing the fact that most of the play's characters performed heroically and unswervingly when the necessity arose, Laurence Stallings and Maxwell Anderson were able to successfully argue that they did not "bring disrespect or reproach upon the United States Army, Navy or Marine Corps."

The success of MGM's *The Big Parade* in early 1925 had the other Hollywood studios scrambling for war-related properties that could be adapted as films. It has been claimed that William

Fox purchased the movie rights to *What Price Glory?* as an immediate response to *The Big Parade*, but in fact Fox's first major entry in the World War I–flick sweepstakes was the 1925 adaptation of another theatrical piece, *Havoc*. Directed by Rowland V. Lee (another front-line war veteran), *Havoc* was largely filmed at Westwood, California, where the studio dug several hundred yards of trenches for the battle scenes. Never one to let anything go to waste, William Fox would leave these trenches intact for use in several future films— including *What Price Glory?*, which Fox had purchased for $100,000 in the fall of 1925 as one of a group of theatrical favorites the studio intended to commit to celluloid, including *The Music Master, The Auctioneer, The Return of Peter Grimm* and *The Cradle Snatchers*.

Any fears that Fox would allow the anti-war message of *What Price Glory?* (the titular question mark was removed for the film version) to undermine the public's respect for the Military and its leaders were allayed by the studio's choice of director: Raoul Walsh, a man who by no stretch of the imagination could be described as pacifistic or anti-military, as proven by such subsequent gung-ho epics as *Objective Burma, Battle Cry* and *Marines, Let's Go*. In many a later interview, Walsh would proudly boast that his adaptation of *What Price Glory?* "promoted more enlistments in the Marine Corps than any picture ever made"— though he readily admitted that this was due to his rosy depiction of the Corps as "happy-go-lucky guys with gals and this and that." (Walsh also claimed that while filming *Battle Cry*— or maybe it was *Marines, Let's Go*, he wasn't sure— an irate Marine general approached him with clenched fists and grumbled, "You bastard. You got

The infernal triangle: Sgt. Quirt (Edmund Lowe, left) and Captain Flagg (Victor McLaglen) prepare to duke it out for the love of the gorgeous Charmaine (Dolores Del Rio) in Fox's 1926 silent version of **What Price Glory** (*MOVIE STAR NEWS*).

me into this." We'd love to believe this anecdote, but this is the same Raoul Walsh who for years dined out on his story about stealing the corpse of John Barrymore from a funeral parlor to play a practical joke on Errol Flynn.)

Louis Wolheim, self-proclaimed "ugliest man in the movies," was originally slated to repeat his stage role as Capt. Flagg, but Victor McLaglen won the part with a self-financed screen test (Wolheim would later play a Flagg-like character in Howard Hughes' 1927 service comedy *Two Arabian Nights*, as noted in **Chapter 2**). Edmund Lowe, then being built up as a matinee idol by Fox, was assigned the role of Sgt. Quirt, created on stage by William Boyd—not the *Hopalong Cassidy* star, but another actor with the same name. Mexican actress Dolores Del Rio, whose accent would of course pass undetected in a silent film, was cast as Charmaine, sharing some extremely torrid love scenes with both her male costars.

Though it could hardly be described as a 100 percent comedy—certainly not with such harrowing highlights as a long trench caving in on a helpless group of soldiers, leaving them to suffocate while their bayonets still poked above ground—*What Price Glory* emerged onscreen with all the best comic moments from the stage version intact, along with some freshly minted material by director Walsh, scenarist James T. O'Donohue and title writer Malcolm Stuart Boylan. Particularly delightful is the film's pre-war prologue set in the Orient, which finds Quirt and Flagg vying for the attentions of swivel-hipped adventuress Shanghai Mabel (Phyllis Haver)—who, it is explained via subtitle, "has just divorced the Army and is announcing her engagement to the Marines." When Quirt bursts upon a cozy tête-à-tête between Flagg and Mabel, the audience is quickly made aware that the imprecations and blasphemies spoken in the stage version of *What Price Glory?* will not be expunged from the screen version. To be sure, the censors have been mollified by the insertion of the occasional "harmless" subtitle, but the steady stream of obscenities mouthed by both Victor McLaglen and Edmund Lowe can be easily lip-read, with "Son of a Bitch" and "Prick" seemingly the expletives of preference.

Legend has it that this "cuss-word puzzle" (as it was described in the trade papers) triggered thousands of protests from outraged filmgoers. These complaints certainly didn't discourage the producers of such subsequent service comedies as *Rookies* and *Now We're in the Air* from allowing *their* stars to mouth every oath that happened to pop into their heads while the cameras turned. Reviewers of the period seemed to delight in warning spectators of the bawdy badinage in these films, while simultaneously assuring their readers that these verbal improprieties actually made the films all the funnier. The critic for the *Reading* [Pennsylvania] *Eagle* went so far as to congratulate the makers of *What Price Glory* for not relying upon multiple subtitles to convey what the characters were talking about, as many other silent films were forced to do: "Capt. Flagg and Sgt. Quirt, 'dressing each other down' with strong language on the screen, not only fails to shock their audiences, but sets a new style for conveying their remarks to their 'hearers.' One must see *What Price Glory* to appreciate this particular angle."

Also established in the film's early scenes is the paradox of Raoul Walsh. Though capable of such subtleties as establishing the intimate relationship between Quirt and Charmaine by the discreet exchange of a hairpin, Walsh was the perpetrator of some of the basest and most infantile attempts at humor ever seen in a major adult-oriented motion picture. The closeup of Mabel's pet monkey ducking into a chamber pot while Quirt and Flagg pummel each other is admittedly a surefire laugh-getter, but one can't help concurring with the opinion of Walsh's fellow director John Ford: "When I have to resort to monkeys jumping into pisspots to get a laugh, I'm getting out of this business."

For its initial run in late November of 1926 at New York's Roxy Theater (where the film set a weekend box-office record), *What Price Glory* was accompanied by a live orchestral score composed and conducted by Ernö Rapée, featuring the hit theme tune "Charmaine." Roxy patrons were also treated to a spectacular stage prologue, magnificently recounted in Joe Franklin's *Classics of the Silent Screen*: "Bombs burst, scenery tumbled, red glares lit up the theatre, and just as all hell was breaking loose and patrons were thinking of heading for cover, the main titles of the film flashed on the screen!" The enthusiasm of filmgoers over *What Price Glory*— which earned $2.4 million during its first domestic run, the fourteenth biggest moneymaker of the entire silent era — was almost surpassed by the showers of praise from reviewers and exhibitors. As one forages through the mountains of positive press coverage, it is almost a relief to come across a mildly negative comment from the manager of the Princess Theater in Vermont, Illinois: "A great war picture, but for our patrons not so great entertainment."

The enduring legacy of *What Price Glory* included the establishment of the U.S. Marine Corps as a future source for film comedy, and the formation not one but *two* new screen teams. In addition to stars McLaglen and Lowe, character comedians Ted McNamara (Scots-Irish) and Sammy Cohen (Jewish) were featured in the film as Privates Kiper and Lipinsky. These characters were singled out by the *Reading Eagle* as "two inseparable war buddies who add so much warmth and humor to scenes behind the lines. They are living prototypes of thousands of our boys who even under fire never lost their sense of comedy and good fellowship." In answer to public demand, Fox spun McNamara and Cohen off into their own starring series of service comedies, eschewing the aforementioned "warmth" in favor of stereotypical ethnic humor as McNamara's Gaelic viewpoint clashed with Cohen's Hebraic perspective and vice versa. (Universal was simultaneously covering the same ground in their "Cohens and Kellys" film series). Only two films, *The Gay Retreat* and *Why Sailors Go Wrong* (both covered in **Chapter 2**), managed to make it to the screen before Ted McNamara's death in early 1928 dissolved his partnership with Sammy Cohen.

With both Victor McLaglen and Edmund Lowe still in fine fettle after completing *What Price Glory*, there was no chance that Fox would blow the opportunity to revive the characters of Flagg and Quirt in at least one movie sequel. As it happened, there were three sequels, beginning with the 1929 talkie *The Cock-Eyed World*, which reunited McLaglen and Lowe with director Raoul Walsh and writers Laurence Stallings and Maxwell Anderson (the virtually plotless film was based on their unproduced play *Tropical Twins*). While opinions differ over whether to classify *What Price Glory* as a comedy, *Cock-Eyed World* definitely falls into that category, even in those scenes where it isn't supposed to be funny.

The World War in Europe is over, but the personal war between Flagg and Quirt rages on, with the boys, still in uniform, duking it out over an assortment of tootsies in Vladivostock, Coney Island and (inevitably for a 1920s Marine film) Nicaragua. While the fickle Charmaine is gone — but definitely not forgotten — our heroes console themselves with such distaff companionship as randy Russian lass Olga (Leila Karnelly), gum-chewing New Yawker Fanny (Jean Bary) and hot Nicaraguan number Elenita (Lily Damita, aka the first Mrs. Errol Flynn). The "war is hell" message of the theatrical *What Price Glory*, already tamped down in the 1926 screen version, barely

The Cock-eyed World (Fox, 1929): In the first sequel to *What Price Glory*, Flagg (Victor McLaglen, left) and Quirt (Edmund Lowe) go cheek-to-cheek with hot tamale Elenita (Lily Damita).

exists at all in the 1929 sequel, save for a few acid comments about civilian war profiteers. Some of the most cherished bits of business from *Glory* are repeated in *The Cock-Eyed World*, notably Flagg and Quirt's endless "Sez you-sez me" exchanges. And while there are no pantomimed profanities this time, the euphemisms uttered by the protagonists (many of them penned by showman Billy K. Wells, celebrated for some of the filthiest stage reviews ever to hit the Big Apple) are quite an earful in themselves—plus there's a risqué sight gag during the "End" title that's a beaut! A running joke introduced in *What Price Glory* likewise spills over into *Cock-Eyed World*, as Quirt "proves" eternal devotion to his girl of the moment by presenting her with his most cherished possession, a sharpshooting medal (of which he has dozens of replicas in reserve).

Also echoed are a few key sequences from the earlier film, including Quirt's abrupt recovery and return to active duty after a bout with illness, and a blush-inducing episode illustrating the consequences of unprotected sex (a "shotgun wedding" in *What Price Glory*, an inconvenient pregnancy in *Cock-Eyed World*). And while Ted McNamara and Sammy Cohen are M.I.A., the sequel's consignment of ethnic humor is delivered by Swedish-dialect comedian El Brendel, here marginally more tolerable than in his other Fox Film appearances of the period. As Private "Yump" Olsen, Brendel is given the film's funniest scene, yet another example of Raoul Walsh's adolescent brand of humor: Ordered by Captain Flagg to get "the lay of the land," the obliging Olsen returns with a map in one hand and a sexy brunette in the other.

The Cock-Eyed World affects different film historians different ways. Leonard Maltin has scorned the picture as "absolutely deadly," further remarking that it is "slow as molasses" when seen today. Conversely, the late William K. Everson, while admitting that the picture is overlong (at 113 minutes, it is only slightly shorter than *Glory*), has qualified this by remarking that "it is nevertheless for 1929 — and especially in comparison with Walsh's very slow, measured and lethargic *In Old Arizona*—a very slick and fast-paced production." In notes written for the Theodore Huff Society in 1970, Everson also touched upon the one aspect of the film that at times makes it virtually unwatchable today: "Conscious of the fact that it is a talkie, it delivered the goods of this new toy with a vengeance!" Indeed, the film's soundtrack is so shrill and cacophonous (including "live" musical performances by a balalaika troupe and a marimba band) that even those 21st-century filmgoers inundated with such ear-shattering digital sound extravaganzas as *The Dark Knight* and *Transformers* are likely to emerge from a screening of *The Cock-Eyed World* with a splitting headache.

Audiences in 1929 evidently weren't bothered by the assault on their aural cavities, nor by the film's flimsy plot structure. *The Cock-Eyed World* earned even more money than *What Price Glory*, grossing a whopping $500,000 in its first three weeks at the Roxy and ending up as the ninth most profitable film of the 1920s. Fox's response to this was as inevitable as night follows day: Another sequel. And so it came to pass that the third installment in the ongoing saga of Captain Flagg and Sergeant Quirt, *Women of All Nations*, was unveiled in the late spring of 1931.

This one is "narrated" by director Raoul Walsh via a series of introductory and transitional subtitles. According to Walsh (if indeed he did write the text), Laurence Stallings had "introduced" him to Flagg and Quirt during World War I, compelling the director to continue chronicling the boys' postwar peregrinations. The picture begins with an outsized battlefield sequence, played completely straight. After a stopover in Panama, we pick up the action in New York, where while trying to scare up new Marine recruits Captain Flagg is reunited with ex–Sergeant Quirt, now passing himself off as a French health-spa owner (a clever ploy to meet beautiful girls and get paid for it). On the lam from the law, Quirt hurriedly re-ups for another hitch in the Marines, whereupon the boys are sent on a goodwill mission to Sweden. Here Quirt adopts another disguise, dressing as Santa Claus (would we lie to you?) to beat Flagg's time with spunky Swedish heartbreaker Elsa (Greta Nissen). Beaten to a pulp by Elsa's behemoth boyfriend Olaf, Quirt and Flagg make a quick getaway, briefly helping out earthquake victims in South America (the film's other "dramatic" sequence) before accompanying their regiment for a tour of duty in a country that looks a lot like Turkey. Who should also turn up in this exotic locale but our gal Elsa, now the favorite wife in the harem of the fearsome Prince Hassan, played with great relish and a bit of pickle by an uncredited Bela Lugosi. No, Elsa does not yearn to be rescued from the evil Hassan: She is quite comfortably settled in the harem, bribing the eunuchs to smuggle various lovers into her chambers. Picking up Elsa's cue, both Quirt and Flagg sneak into Hassan's palace, whereupon the film devolves into a bedroom farce with turbans. Barely escaping death (or worse!) at the hands of the Prince's minions, the two Marines rejoin their regiment and march off God-knows-where to new adventures.

If one cannot imagine an even more episodic and less coherent film than *The Cock-Eyed World*, one hasn't seen *Women of All Nations*, which appears to be held together with spit and baling wire. There's a possibility that its original form the film might have actually had a semblance of a storyline: Running a bare 72 minutes, *Women of All Nations* shows signs of wholesale cutting just before its release, with certain elaborately-mounted sequences—notably the South American earthquake—appearing only fleetingly onscreen. Also, though both Humphrey Bogart and Nat Pendleton are prominently listed in Fox's publicity packet, neither actor appears in the picture, nor is there the slightest hint of what their function in the "story" might have been. (On the other hand, vivacious comedienne Marjorie White—who like Bela Lugosi receives no screen credit—appears to have been inserted in the proceedings at the last minute to goose an otherwise dull expositional scene.) And if you're looking for any vestiges of the original play's "war is hell" theme, forget it. Only during the earthquake scene (a tragedy which can hardly be blamed on politics) does one of the characters die, a demise that might have been more shocking had it not been tipped off well in advance, at the very moment when this foredoomed fellow bids a tearful farewell to his father before shipping overseas.

Now that we have an idea what *isn't* in the picture, what does *Women of All Nations* have to offer? Well, the film persists in repeating treasured bits from the first two Flagg-Quirt endeavors, with Quirt still handing out sharpshooter medals to any skirt who gives him a second glance, and the two antagonists going through their patented "Sez You-Sez Me" banter, which by now sounds as silly as Bugs and Daffy's "Rabbit Season-Duck Season" routine. Held over from *Cock-Eyed World* is supporting buffoon El Brendel as Olsen, here saddled with horrible puns (when someone mentions Brigham Young, he replies, "Bring 'em young and bring 'em often") and a repulsive running gag involving a "Bronx cheer." Apparently operating on the theory that if one dialect comedian is funny, three will be even funnier, El Brendel's castmates include French-fried Fifi D'Orsay and Jewish jokester Jesse Devorska (D'Orsay's foreign accent is as bogus as Brendel's; Devorska's is evidently the real deal). Though this comic triumvirate does their very best, they aren't even half as funny as Bela Lugosi—and he's the only actor taking things seriously ("Ba-a-ar the gates and sharpen the kn-i-i-ives!").

The level of wit in *Women of All Nations* makes one nostalgic for the sophisticated repartee of *The Cock-Eyed World*. Early in the film, screenwriter Barry Conners gets off an amusing jab at *What Price Glory*'s "cuss-word puzzle": As Flagg is about to let loose with a profanity, Quirt reminds him that the government doesn't allow Marines to swear any more, thereafter limiting the boys to such pejoratives as "You big custard!" and "You big quince!" Unfortunately (or fortunately, depending on one's viewpoint) the rest of the picture represents Raoul Walsh at his gutter-minded lowest. The incongrous appearance of a tiny monkey during the Swedish sequence is merely an excuse for the pesky primate to crawl into El Brendel's trousers, allowing the comedian to shock his dancing partner by exclaiming, "I yoost sat on my monkey!" And if you happen not to care for *that* little double-entendre, consider the scene in which Quirt and Flagg, waxing nostalgic over their lost love Charmaine, leeringly remind one another that the old girl made a terrific "plum pudding." Regarded as pretty spicy stuff in its time, *Women of All Nations* nowadays comes across like a 1931 episode of *Beavis and Butt-head*.

Most critics were kinder to the picture than it deserved. "This new contribution is reminiscent of *The Cock-Eyed World*," wrote Mordaunt Hall of the *New York Times*. "It has the same repre-

Film Daily advertisement for *Women of All Nations* (1931), the second of Fox's three followups to *What Price Glory.*

hensible sort of fun, which succeeded in provoking the much-desired gusts of laughter from an audience at the first showing yesterday afternoon." *Exhibitor's Forum* was also complimentary: "Plenty of names that mean money at the box-office and good direction and photography put it over well." Unfortunately, those gusts of laughter soon trickled down to a faint breeze; and for all its "name" value, the film's box-office was disappointing. Raoul Walsh later chalked up the failure of *Women of All Nations* to the fact that the public had grown tired of Flagg and Quirt. Even so, Fox churned out one more comedy featuring these characters, this time with John G. Blystone handling the direction. *Hot Pepper* (1933) isn't a service comedy and thus will not be analyzed, except to mention that Victor McLaglen and Edmund Lowe appear in mufti as nightclub owner "Jim" Flagg and prohibition agent "Harry" Quirt, fighting over fiery songstress Lupe Vélez. (*Variety* complained that the two stars had by now "degenerated into a couple of slapstick clowns.") El Brendel is also back as Olsen, as good a reason as any to skip *Hot Pepper*.

McLaglen and Lowe costarred in several other films throughout the 1930s in such guises as sandhogs, deep-sea divers, detectives and reporters (they were still in harness as late as 1956, popping up among the celebrity cameos in the Oscar-winning *Around the World in Eighty Days*). Only in the early 1940s would the boys again show up as Marines, both still cutting quite a figure in their dress uniforms despite being collectively 106 years old. Released in 1942 but obviously completed before Pearl Harbor, the RKO 7-reeler *Call Out the Marines* stars the two venerable actors as Flagg and Quirt in everything but name. Not having seen each other for 15 years, ex–Marine sergeants Jimmy McGinniss (McLaglen) and Harry Curtis (Lowe) are reunited at a race track, where Jimmy is working as a sanitation engineer and Harry as manservant to a gouty old grouch. Less than two minutes after their reunion, the boys are once again scrapping over a doll, in this case snazzy blonde Vi (Binnie Barnes), a hostess at the Shore Leave Club. The establishment is owned by the boys' former captain Jim Blake (Paul Kelly), who shamefacedly tells them that he's been cashiered from the Corps on suspicion of stealing government documents. Called back to active duty, Jimmy and Harry end up stationed at a Marine base where another document theft occurs. Having seen Blake conspiring with suspicious-looking recruit Billy Harrison (Robert Smith), the two sergeants jump to the obvious conclusion and literally smash into Blake's office to retrieve the valuable papers. Little do they realize that Blake and Harrison are both working undercover for the Marine Corps, and that big-hearted Vi is actually an enemy agent.

With the Production Code holding Hollywood by the short hairs in 1942, McLaglen and Lowe could no longer exchange their old double-meaning insults, reduced instead to such defanged epithets as "Old Scuttlebutt" and "Super Stupid." Another sign of changing times is the fact that no longer does every available female prostrate herself at the two Marines' feet. Except for Vi, who has a hidden agenda, most of the film's damsels give the boys a shoulder so cold that they almost get frostbite. With the laissez-faire lewdness of their earlier movie escapades carefully sifted out of the script, McLaglen and Lowe have no other choice but to indulge in Sez You-Sez Me wisecrackery, outrageous slapstick (including *two* extremely well-staged car chases) and the sort of improbable gags that were usually confined to 2-reel comedies. They even break down the "fourth wall" *à la* Groucho Marx and Bob Hope, with both Vic and Edmund directly addressing the camera at several junctures. Also, the shadow of Abbott & Costello's *Buck Privates* looms large over *Call Out the Marines*, which features four entirely dispensable musical numbers performed by The King's Men, Six Hits and a Miss, Corinna Mura and Dorothy Lovett. It would appear that the film boasted two directors (Frank Hamilton and William Ryan) so that one could handle the "plot" scenes and the other could take care of the musical interludes.

Though Victor McLaglen and Edmund Lowe strain so hard to be funny that they're actually kind of cute, some of the film's biggest laughs are delivered by the supporting players: Franklin Pangborn as a snippy waiter, George Cleveland as a scowling bartender (his disgusted close-up reaction to McLaglen's "Brazilian Alpaca Coat" is beautifully timed and staged), and George Lloyd as a mousy enemy spy with a cleft palate, who figures into the film's longest, most tasteless and arguably funniest comedy setpiece. Of course, not everyone was amused by the proceedings: the wartime Bureau of Motion Pictures put pressure on RKO to withdraw the film, citing its "negative" portrayal of the USMC. Whether or not the studio agreed to shelve the film, *Call Out the Marines* was still included in the RKO television package syndicated by C&C Films in 1955.

Despite compelling evidence that McLaglen and Lowe held the monopoly on Marine comedies, a few other actors were allowed to take a crack at the genre. Douglas MacLean, star of the 1919 Army comedy *23½ Hours' Leave* (see **Chapter 2**), was cast as a devil-may-care Marine sergeant in the 1927 Universal silent feature *Let It Rain*, directed by Keystone alumnus Eddie Cline. The plot found "Let-It-Rain" Riley (MacLean) taking time out from the ongoing war of words and fists between the Marines and the Navy to pitch woo at a pretty telephone operator (Shirley Mason). Tossed in the brig for something or other, Riley breaks out to visit his sweetheart, ending up a hero when he foils a mail robbery. This "rollicking farce" (to quote *Motion Picture World*) was distinguished by a handful of Technicolor scenes.

The early Technicolor process was given an even healthier workout in another of Eddie Cline's directorial assignments: The 1930 RKO musical *Leathernecking*, adapted from the 1928 Rodgers & Hart Broadway hit *Present Arms*. Eddie Foy Jr. starred as Marine private Chick Evans, a bumptious Brooklynite stationed at Pearl Harbor. To impress the aristocratic Delphine Witherspoon (Irene Dunne), Chick passes himself off as a captain, "borrowing" an officer's uniform and a Distinguished Service Medal. No sooner has Chick begun hobnobbing with Delphine's ritzy friends at a society soirée than his Marine buddies crash the joint and expose him as a fraud. To win Delphine back, Chick conspires with his pal Frank (Ken Murray) to fake a shipwreck, emerging heroically when the phony disaster turns out to be real thing. "If a marine's life is anything like *Leathernecking*," mused the *New York Times* critic, "then it must be one continual round of parties, yachting trips and pillow fights among the boys in the barracks.... The film's chief virtue is its failure to

A moment of truth (more or less) from RKO's *Leathernecking* (1930). From left, Lilyan Tashman, Wilhelm von Brincken, Werther Neidler, unknown Marine, Irene Dunne (in her film debut), Ken Murray, Eddie Foy Jr. and Benny Rubin.

take itself seriously, and in so doing frolics along to a slapstick beat...." Initially planned as a faithful adaptation of *Present Arms*, *Leathernecking* was ultimately stripped of all but two of the original Rodgers-Hart songs ("You Took Advantage of Me" and "A Kiss for Cinderella"), with new tunes by other composers in their place. Long considered a lost film — only the soundtrack is presently available, though recent reports indicate that a complete picture print has been found — *Leathernecking* would be worth exhuming if only to see Irene Dunne in her first movie role as the haughty Delphine.

Later in 1930, Fox Films elected to make a Quirt-and-Flagg comedy with different character names and minus one-half of the starring team. *A Devil with Women* (working title: *On the Make*) top-bills Victor McLaglen as Marine troubleshooter Jerry Maxton, with 31-year-old Humphrey Bogart making his second film appearance as Jerry's soldier-of-fortune buddy Tom Standish. The boys have landed in Central America, there to capture rebel leader Morloff (Michael Vavitch). Complications ensue when both Jerry and Tom fall for sloe-eyed Rosita (Mona Maris), who is smuggling guns to the insurgents. Recognizing the similarities between this film and the Quirt-Flagg "series," Mordaunt Hall of the *New York Times* observed that Victor McLaglen seemed happy to be "reappearing in the familiar khaki and Sam Browne belt of his earlier successes." As for newcomer Humphrey Bogart, Hall found him "both good looking and intelligent." Though he hadn't yet matured into our beloved "Bogie," the youthful actor delivers such a smooth and self-assured performance that McLaglen has quite a time asserting the fact that *he* is supposed to be the star. Bogart's scene-stealing prowess might well have been the reason that his entire role in the subsequent Quirt-Flagg comedy *Women of All Nations* ended up on the cutting room floor.

Jumping ahead to the immediate post–Production Code era, 1934 brought forth a couple of similarly-titled Marine movies, both of which start out as comedies before crossing over to the adventure category in the terminal footage. Mascot's *The Marines are Coming* represented the screen swan song of popular silent leading man William Haines, cast as ever in the role of an audacious young rule-bender who gets his act together just in time to save his superior officer (Conrad Nagel) from a band of South American *insurectos*. And in Paramount's *Come On, Marines*, directed by Henry Hathaway, top sergeant Richard Arlen leads his fellow leathernecks on a mission to rescue a flock of swimsuit-clad debutantes (among them Ida Lupino and Ann Sheridan!) who've been stranded on a tropical island.

After several years' liberty from Comedy Detail, the Marines established a brand-new beachhead with the coming of World War II. In 1943, producer Hal Roach announced plans to curtail his long-running series of 45-minute "streamliners" (see **Chapter 5** for notes on Roach's "Sgt. Doubleday" featurettes) and film a pair of feature-length comedies starring contractee William Bendix: a Marine yarn titled *Yanks Down Under* and a fight picture called *The Tennessee Tornado*. Production of the first film began on the Roach lot with studio mainstay Fred Guiol functioning as producer-writer and frequent Laurel & Hardy collaborator Charles Rogers among the scripters. After receiving an officer's commission in the Army, Hal Roach found himself too preoccupied with military matters for any personal or financial involvement in *Yanks Down Under*. Thus, Roach forged a deal with independent producer Edward Small, who agreed to bankroll the film in exchange for the screenplay rights and William Bendix's services. Not long afterward, United Artists freed Roach from his remaining contractual obligations; as a result, *Yanks Down Under* was released in 1944 as an "Edward Small Production" under the title *Abroad with Two Yanks*. (*Tennessee Tornado* was never filmed.)

Filmed at the Roach and RKO-Pathé facilities under the skilled hand of director Allan Dwan, *Abroad with Two Yanks* displays the same breezy, irresponsible spirit — and slapdash plot construction — of the old Quirt-Flagg pictures, though out of deference to the toughened Production Code the comedy content is as clean as a hound's tooth. The film's Marines are the quietest and politest bunch of leathernecks you're ever likely to meet, with even the tough sergeant (James Flavin) giving out with "Please" and "Thank You." The Two Yanks in question are Biff Koraski

(William Bendix) and Jeff Reardon (Dennis O'Keefe), American Marines on furlough in Australia. Having saved the life of Aussie pilot Cyril North (John Loder), Biff promises to look up North's lifelong friend Joyce Stuart (Helen Walker) and give her Cyril's best regards. Setting his own sights on Joyce, Jeff gains entrance to the girl's house by passing himself off as Biff — and thus begins a riotous round robin of deception and doublecross, with Biff and Jeff constantly trying to outsmart each other but succeeding only in outsmarting themselves.

Though no longer a Hal Roach production, *Abroad with Two Yanks* bears earmarks of the vintage Roach two-reelers of the 1920s and 1930s with such familiar plot pegs as mistaken identity, feigned insanity and female impersonation. The best sequence could easily have been lifted from one of Roach's classic Laurel & Hardy comedies: Squaring off for a fight, Biff and Jeff take great pains to avoid making any noise lest they attract the attention of the MPs. After 80 hectic minutes, things wrap up with our heroes raising a ruckus at a charity bazaar while dressed in female drag (and not bad lookers at that!) For all the film's farcicality, director Allan Dwan manages to invest his characters with a soupçon of sincerity, notably in the poignant scene where the oafish Biff proposes to a startled Joyce.

The next Marine comedy in this chapter was released during the Korean conflict by low-budget Lippert Pictures, starring the studio's resident utility comedian, jug-eared Sid Melton. In *Leave It to the Marines* (1951), Gerald Meek (Melton) shows up at the county courthouse with his fiancee Myrna McAllister (Mara Lynn) to get a marriage license, but the little jerk is so dumb that he wanders into the wrong office and signs up for a three-year hitch in the Marines. Though he'd like to weasel out of this commitment, Gerald is dissuaded by his grandmother (Ida Moore), who tells him about the heroic exploits of his grandpa, likewise a Marine (shades of Preston Sturges' *Hail the Conquering Hero*). Stuck with traditionally obnoxious drill sergeant "Foghorn" McTaggert (George Martell), Gerald is crestfallen when he's led to believe that McTaggert has stolen his girl (not true, but we've got 66 minutes to fill). And so it goes until the slapstick finale, wherein Gerald mistakes a powerful new bomb for a hot-water heater. Lippert followed this little gem with another Sid Melton service comedy, *Sky High* (1951), in which he plays an Air Force tailgunner posing as his look-alike, a notorious saboteur. The fact that both films boasted the same cast, same director (Sam Newfield) and same production team suggests that *Leave It to the Marines* and *Sky High* were filmed simultaneously — a typical cost-cutting ploy of Lippert Pictures, who in 1950 had lensed a series of six westerns starring Russ Hayden and Jimmy Ellison within a space of four weeks!

Though billed as "Hollywood's New Comedy Team," costars Sid Melton and Mara Lynn hardly constituted a threat to Burns and Allen. A few years after *Leave It to the Marines* was released theatrically (and almost immediately syndicated to television), Melton found his true calling as one of TV-dom's favorite second bananas, racking up such roles as Ichabod "Icky" Mudd on *Captain Midnight*, nightclub owner Charlie Halper on *The Danny Thomas Show* and plumber Alf Monroe on *Green Acres*.

Like most post–1933 Marine comedies, the two Sid Melton films were scrupulously decent, family-friendly entertainments, scrubbed clean of the old Quirt-Flagg bawdiness in order to satisfy the grand poobahs of the Production Code. However, one 1953 Paramount comedy seemed to hold out promise of something a bit racier. *The Girls of Pleasure Island* was written and co-directed by F. Hugh Herbert, then at the center of a storm of controversy regarding his stage play *The Moon Is Blue*, which producer-director Otto Preminger planned to film with such mildly risque dialogue bites as "professional virgin" intact — not only fully aware that he would be denied a Production Code seal of approval, but actually priding himself on the fact. Pre-release publicity for the enticingly titled *Girls of Pleasure Island* was chock-full of titilating prose arising from the film's storyline, to wit: On a remote island in the South Pacific, bookish Britisher Roger Halyard (played by Leo Genn) has raised his three daughters Hester, Violet and Gloria (played by "New Paramount Personalities" Audrey Dalton, Joan Elan and Dorothy Bromiley) in a virtual vacuum, never allowing them to meet any males their own age. Now in the early stages of womanhood, the three budding maidens are about to experience an awakening with the arrival of 1500 girl-starved American Marines (among them future TV star Gene Barry).

Sounds rife with possibilities, doesn't it? But this was still 1953, and not every filmmaker was a taboo-smasher like Otto Preminger. Despite the occasional compromising situation and a few scenes in which the three ingenues appear in skimpy costumes, *The Girls of Pleasure Island* is no more sexy or provocative than that same year's *Peter Pan*. Getting down to basics, the picture is a crashing bore, redeemed only by the delightful Elsa Lanchester as the girls' wiser-than-she-looks nanny. As for the films' antiseptic depiction of the Marine Corps, we refer you to the scene in which one of the heroines congratulates her new leatherneck boyfriend for his chivalrous behavior when his jeep runs out of gas. If Victor McLaglen and Edmund Lowe hadn't been alive at the time, they would have turned over in their graves.

The Girls of Pleasure Island should have been the final entry in this chapter, but we must at least touch upon John Ford's lackluster 1952 remake of the picture that started the whole Marine-comedy cycle, *What Price Glory*. Actually, 20th Century–Fox's predecessor Fox Studios had had a remake on the drawing board as early as 1932, not starring the original's Victor McLaglen and Edmund Lowe but instead teaming Spencer Tracy and Ralph Bellamy, with William K. Howard replacing Raoul Walsh as director. This project was eventually rejected as too expensive (Fox was going through one of its retrenching periods), and Tracy and Bellamy were rerouted to a medium-budget crime drama, *Young America*. With the advent of World War II a decade later, *What Price Glory* was rendered anachronistic and by and large forgotten by Hollywood, though it was occa-

Thoroughly laundered — in every sense of the word — are Corinne Calvert as Charmaine and Dan Dailey as Sgt. Quirt in John Ford's flaccid talkie remake of ***What Price Glory*** (20th Century–Fox, 1952).

sionally revived on stage, most memorably in a 1949 touring production mounted for charity purposes by the Masquers Club, an actor's fraternity. Among the stellar participants in this brief revival were John Wayne, George O'Brien, Maureen O'Hara, and Oliver Hardy. The director was John Ford, who two years later contracted with 20th Century–Fox for a Technicolor remake of the property, part of a general wave of early-1950s nostalgia for the "Roaring Twenties" (during this period there were also movie remakes of such 1920s theatrical favorites as *No No Nanette*, *Show Boat*, *The Jazz Singer* and *Rain*).

According to a 1951 *Hollywood Reporter* article, the new *What Price Glory* had been planned as a musical comedy, rechristened *Charmaine* and with French actress Micheline Presle in the title role. For that purpose, a boy-girl subplot was added by screenwriters Phoebe and Henry Ephron, with secondary character Pvt. Lewisohn ("Stop the blood!") built up as the juvenile lead and a new character, convent girl Nicole Bouchard, as the ingenue. In his autobiography, James Cagney stated that he'd agreed to star as Captain Flagg when John Ford assured him that the film would be a musical, but that once shooting started Cagney got the impression that Ford had misrepresented the project. Indeed, though Fox had announced that several World War I–vintage songs were to be performed by the leading actors, the only tunes heard beyond a few familiar background pieces and the evergreen romantic leitmotiv "Charmaine" were the old Fred Fisher composition "Oui Oui Marie," performed by Corinne Calvet (who had replaced Micheline Presle as Charmaine), and a new number, "My Love, My Life," written by Jay Livingston and Ray Evans and sung by Marisa Pavan (Nicole). That John Ford probably never had the slightest intention of making a musical would seem to be confirmed by the fact that his first choice for Flagg had been John Wayne, a carryover from the 1949 stage revival. Alas, neither James Cagney nor his costar Dan Dailey (cast as Sgt. Quirt) were permitted to show off their remarkable dancing skills—and if that wasn't enough of an affront, Dailey was forced to take third billing below Corinne Calvet, who'd been billed below *him* only two years earlier in Ford's *When Willie Comes Marching Home* (see **Chapter 17**).

With the Hollywood censors still holding sway in 1952, the Ephrons were prohibited from using the raw language and sexual banter from the 1924 stage play, even though certain setpieces from the original—notably the third-act drinking scene in which Flagg and Quirt alternately exchange dire threats and toast each other's health — were retained. The end result was a toothless, eviscerated *What Price Glory* that might have been specially prepared for high school drama clubs and church groups, not unlike the laundered *Les Misérables* which made the amateur-theatrical rounds in the 1990s. A random sampling of contemporary reviews includes such pointed adjectives as "soft-boiled," "ineffectual" and "deplorable," with several snarky references to James Cagney's un–Marine like corpulence. No one denied that the film was occasionally funny, but no one took the stand that it was anywhere close to being *as* funny as the original.

In retrospect, the most amusing aspect of the 1952 *What Price Glory* is a typical example of John Ford's sadistic sense of humor. Buried among the minor players in the nonspeaking role of a priest is Barry Norton, who in the years since playing Pvt. Lewisohn in the original 1926 *Glory* had been reduced to the ranks of bit players and extras—and who, reportedly, had been hired by Ford as a cautionary lesson on the fickleness of fame for the benefit of the new version's Pvt. Lewisohn, a green-gilled youngster named Robert Wagner.

8

You Read the Book! You Loved the Play! Now See the Movie!

The postwar surge in comic novels with military themes resulted in three international bestsellers: *Mister Roberts* (1946), *The Teahouse of the August Moon* (1951) and *No Time for Sergeants* (1954). In turn, each of these three novels yielded a long-running stage play and a successful motion picture — and in two cases, a short-lived TV series.

All three books were penned by ex-servicemen, all three were loosely based on the authors' own wartime experiences, and all three were first novels (in two instances, the *only* novel published by the author in his lifetime). None of the three novels contained any combat sequences, instead focusing on men far removed from the hostilities. All three dealt extensively with the comedy of frustration, a common theme in military humor. And when these three novels were adapted for the stage, each was highlighted by a riotous drinking scene.

Narrowing things a bit, two of the three novels engaged the services of a whimsical narrator when transferred to the stage. Two of the three theatrical versions were heavily male-centric, with only one female cast member in each. Two of the play versions were produced by the same man, just as two of the film versions shared the same director. Also, two of the film versions featured the same star who'd appeared in the original Broadway production. And last but not least, two of the dramatic adaptations featured a funny goat.

Mister Roberts (and Sequel)

In July 1944, 25-year-old Navy Lieutenant Thomas Heggen was piped aboard the U.S.S. *Virgo*, an attack transport stationed in the Marshall Islands. Having previously served on the transport *Rotanin*, Heggen hoped that his transfer would bring him closer to the real shooting war. But though the threat of danger loomed large as the *Virgo* moved cargo and troops from one West Pacific port to another, the crew saw little enemy action — and except for a few air raid drills, the *Virgo* would ultimately survive World War II with nary a scratch.

As communications officer, Lt. Heggen performed his duties without complaint, though inwardly he yearned to be more actively involved in the war, and on several occasions he applied unsuccessfully for another transfer. Heggen found himself with so much slack time during his fourteen months on the *Virgo* that he began writing short stories focusing on the experiences of himself, his fellow officers and the men serving under him. After the war, Heggen's summary of life on a wartime cargo vessel would achieve worldwide fame: "For the most part it stays on its regular run, from Tedium to Apathy and back; about five days each way. It makes an occasional trip to Monotony, and once it made a run all the way to Ennui, a distance of two thousand nautical miles from Tedium." One of Heggen's strategies to battle boredom was using the sighting telescope of a five-inch gun to spy into the bathroom window of a dockside hospital, where a bevy of unclad nurses were blissfully unaware that their daily ablutions could be viewed unobstructed from the *Virgo*'s deck.

In August 1944, the ship took on a new skipper: Lt. Cmdr. Herbert Randall of the Naval Reserve, described by maritime historian Hugh M. Heckman as "an unpolished merchant marine officer who didn't take kindly to Navy ways." A humorless martinet who earned the enmity of the crew by refusing permission for a long-overdue liberty in San Francisco, Randall also had more than his share of eccentricities. In particular, he was enamored of a pair of palm trees that had caught his eye during a layover in the Leyte Gulf. Ordering the trees replanted in two paint cans, Marshall reserved a place of honor for his leafy trophies on the *Virgo* bridge. This was too good to resist for Tom Heggen, who one fine evening impulsively tossed the palm trees overboard—and repeated this insubordination when the truculent Randall replaced the trees.

Resuming his job as a *Reader's Digest* editor after the War, Heggen set about submitting short stories to various other magazines. His first published work, "Night Watch," appeared in *The Atlantic Monthly* in April 1946. This virtually plotless story is an unsentimental journey through the private thoughts of Lieutenant Doug Roberts, cargo officer of the U.S.S. *Reluctant*. While pulling night-watch duty somewhere in the Pacific, Lt. Roberts—addressed as Mister Roberts, in keeping with Navy protocol—exchanges a few pleasantries with Quartermaster Dolan. As Dolan drones on about various sexual conquests, Roberts reminisces about his own past. The reader learns that Doug Roberts is 26 years old; that he tossed away an airtight deferment by dropping out of medical school to join the Navy; and that he is aching to be an active participant in the War, which is rapidly winding down. There isn't much humor in "Night Watch"; the meat of the story is Roberts' desperation over being trapped for two years on a rusty old transport, under the thumb of a captain identified only as "Stupid."

The publishing firm Houghton Mifflin suggested that Heggen expand "Night Watch" into a novel. Digging into his old sea bag, Heggen came up with several other, more comedic tales of the mythical *Reluctant* that he'd penned during the war. He had wanted to title his novel *The Iron-Bound Bucket* (the crew's affectionate nickname for the *Virgo*), but Houghton Mifflin chose *Mister Roberts* instead.

Heggen's physical description of Lt. Doug Roberts is hazy: we know he is tall and blonde, and that's about all. Though his thought processes are meticulously detailed, only occasionally does Roberts actually say anything: the two most prominent examples are his heated debate with the *Reluctant*'s doctor over the horrible necessity of World War II, and a briefly triumphant moment when he challenges the wildly contradictory orders issued by the cranky Captain. Otherwise, what we know about Roberts during the first portions of the novel is revealed piecemeal. One perceives a decent, idealistic young man who recognizes that authority must be tempered with courtesy and common sense: Roberts never pushes his men, allowing them to sleep late, indulge such leisure activities as reading and gambling, and take their time going about their duties so long as the job is done well. His laissez-faire attitude is defined not only by his own actions but also in comparison with other characters, notably the mercurial Captain. Then there's young Ensign Keith, an Academy shavetail who drives the crew crazy by insisting that all buttons be buttoned and hats worn properly, and who commits the unspeakable atrocity of tossing a precious cache of contraband beer overboard. Roberts' involvement in *l'affaire* Keith is marginal; he calmly tries to talk sense to the "boot Ensign," but Keith cannot be budged. Nevertheless, Roberts' casual approach to maintaining authority and delegating responsibility is manifested in the actions of Bosun's Mate Dowdy, who figures that the best way to "humanize" Keith is to get the kid stinking drunk on a potent concoction known as Jungle Juice.

Many readers have opined that Doug Roberts is nothing more than the alter ego of Thomas Heggen, and there is sufficent evidence to support this. In *Mister Roberts,* Heggen lovingly recreates the *Virgo* "palm tree" incident, and hilariously expands his clandestine surveillance of the nurses' quarters. In the novel, this voyeurism becomes a spectator sport for the entire crew—until one of the nurses, the "blonde with the birthmark," finds out what our lustful lads have been up to, whereupon shades are immediately installed in all bathroom windows.

Other aspects of Roberts' personality were gleaned from a man named Don House, assistant gunnery officer of the U.S.S. *Rotanin*, where Heggen had served before the *Virgo*. In a postwar interview, former Chief Pharmacist's Mate Dale Allen Bullock vividly recalled how House, who was also the *Rotanin*'s legal officer, diplomatically smoothed the ruffled feathers of local authorities after an embarrassing incident during a stopover in the Fiji Islands. It seems that several *Rotanin* crew members, upset over being hoodwinked into mistaking the home of the French Ambassador for a house of ill repute, proceeded to totally trash the place. This incident served as the basis for one of *Mister Roberts*' funniest chapters: the bawdy, boisterous liberty in the fictional port of Elysium.

Also on the *Rotanin* was an officer named Richard Pulver, whose last name Tom Heggen borrowed for the character of the *Reluctant*'s lazy, lecherous, hero-worshipping Ensign Frank Pulver. Intensely devoted to his friend and mentor Doug Roberts, the novel's Pulver is forever hatching insanely impractical schemes to drive the despicable Captain out of his mind. Finally working up the nerve to plant a firecracker beneath the Captain's bunk, Pulver is foiled when his scheme literally blows up in his face, and it isn't until the end of the story that the hapless Ensign is able to reassemble his shattered ego with an act of unexpected bravado. Next to Roberts, Pulver is the most memorable of Heggen's characters—and never mind that the real Richard Pulver, who retired with the rank of Lieutenant Commander, was nothing at all like his fictional counterpart.

As writing on *Mister Roberts* progressed, Houghton Mifflin admonished Heggen for his lack of a unifying plotline and a strong climax—and admittedly, even in final form the novel is little more than a random collection of anecdotes until the author finds a way to bring closure in the final chapters. Early in the proceedings, the reader is told that Roberts' monthly transfer requests have been turned down because the Captain begrudgingly acknowledges that the Lieutenant is his best officer and doesn't want to lose him. Several chapters later, Roberts humiliates the Captain in full view of the crew; as the men congratulate him for his courage, the Lieutenant shakes his head and mutters, "The Captain always wins," all too aware that he has squelched his last chance for transfer. Soon afterward, news arrives that the Germans have surrendered, and it looks as if the War will soon be over in the Pacific as well. Enraged over the likelihood that he will never see combat, Roberts marches up to the bridge and throws the Captain's beloved palm tree overboard. Though he regards this as a small and futile gesture, the crew sees things differently, awarding Roberts with a tiny, tree-shaped medal which they dub The Order of the Palm—"for action against the enemy, above and beyond the call of duty." This moment not only brings unification to all that has gone before, but also solidifies the special place that an officer like Mister Roberts holds in the hearts of his beleaguered shipmates. It also establishes that even in wartime, a man can be a hero without ever firing a shot.

While Heggen was polishing his manuscript, Houghton Mifflin let it be known that they expected a steady stream of *Mister Roberts* sequels. Already worried over coming up with enough material for even a second novel, Heggen had no desire to milk the character of Mister Roberts beyond its value. This may explain why he "violated" the comic form by killing off his protagonist in the final chapter. Ironically, Roberts' death occurs just after he has finally gotten his long-awaited transfer—and it occurs in as ignominious a manner as possible. But Heggen trumps this tragedy with a solid laugh as the timorous Ensign Pulver, galvanized by Roberts' demise, suddenly develops a backbone and becomes the new champion of the *Reluctant* crew by tossing the Captain's latest batch of palm trees—all *four* of them—into the briny deep.

When Broadway producer Leland Hayward optioned *Mister Roberts* for a stage version, playright-director Joshua Logan invited Tom Heggen to collaborate on the script. Heggen had already started work on a dramatization of *Roberts* with comic novelist Max Shulman, but according to theater historian David Sheward there "was no dramatic conflict or suspense" in this first draft, save for a plot device that combined two of the novel's otherwise unconnected plot strands. In the original novel, the *Reluctant* crew is granted liberty in Elysium, with no interference from the

Captain. In the play version, the Captain threatens to cancel liberty unless Roberts agrees not to write any more transfer requests; bucking for a promotion, the Captain doesn't want Roberts' complaints to sully the *Reluctant*'s spotless record. Thus is Mister Roberts forced to sacrifice his own desires for the sake of the crew, which not only underscores the character's integrity but also provides an excellent first-act curtain. Josh Logan rewote Act One so it would build to this critical scene, using several of the novel's isolated anecdotes as subplots and recurring gags. Logan then restructured Act Two to resolve the main conflict, and a number of lesser ones, in a way that would lead inexorably to the heady combination of gut-wrenching drama and gut-busting comedy at the end. Max Shulman ankled the project, leaving Logan and Heggen to complete the play.

Recognizing the necessity of developing a colorful cast of supporting characters to give Mister Roberts a breather once in a while, the playwrights fleshed out the already plum role of Ensign Pulver. The character's new designation as the *Reluctant*'s "Officer of Laundry and Morale" provides Pulver with a terrific second-act entrance, covered in soapsuds after the firecracker intended for the Captain explodes prematurely in the laundry room. Roberts was also provided with the traditional sounding board/father figure/severest critic in the form of the *Reluctant*'s middle-aged doctor. The "Doc" of the novel is a snide, saturnine figure with a low opinion of what he regards as a crew of bellyachers and malingerers. In the play, Doc is warmer and more avuncular, still sarcastic but without the cruel edge of his literary model. To supply this character with a reserve of rich dialogue, Logan lifted whole passages from the *non*-dialogue sections of the novel. Many of Doc's cleverest turns of phrase—the young lady described as "rendered pregnant," Pulver's worshipful assessment of Mister Roberts as "approximately God," the tally of Hollywood-style heroics that Pulver might actually accomplish should he ever invest as much energy in his duties as in his goldbricking, skirt-chasing and plot-hatching—can be found in Heggen's original third-person narrative.

The character of the Captain is likewise built up. The Captain of the novel is not so much a villain as a menace, motivated less by inherent evil than by monumental stupidity and mortal terror of anyone smarter than he is. The Captain of the play is vicious, vitriolic and vengeful. In a pathological rampage, he tells the college-educated Roberts that he has despised "you superior bastards" ever since he'd been a lowly restaurant busboy—but now that he's a captain in the U.S. Navy and there's a war on, he's by God going to get even with the world no matter whose heart he has to stomp on in the process.

This beefing-up process also extended to Mister Roberts, who speaks up a lot more often in the play than he ever did in the original text. Roberts' confrontation with the Captain in front of the crew, which originally took place when the novel was practically over, becomes an early highlight of Act One. The novel's drunk scene with Ensign Keith (a character written out of the play) is adroitly refashioned as a showcase sequence for Roberts and Doc, who join forces to brew up an ersatz bottle of scotch using grain alcohol, Coca-Cola and iodine—all so that Ensign Pulver can score with a pretty nurse. And during the indispensible "liberty" scene, it is Roberts who stands watch at dockside, making pungent and poignant comments while the crewmen drunkenly stumble back to the *Reluctant* after wreaking havoc upon Elysium. The comic value of this sequence is heightened when, taking a cue from a single sentence in the novel, one of the bibulous sailors tries to sneak a stolen goat on board—and of course, Roberts has a deadpan response to this as well. No matter how much time Mister Roberts spends offstage, and despite his total absence in the play's final scene, the character is never overshadowed by the supporting players.

To attract backers for the Broadway version of *Mister Roberts*, it was vital to cast a major name in the title role. Both Heggen and Logan had envisioned Logan's old friend Henry Fonda in the part, but were worried that the actor, recently returned from Naval duty and bound to several movie commitments, would be neither interested in reviving his stage career nor inclined to accept a lower salary than what he could command in Hollywood. So the authors approached rising young actor David Wayne, who since January of 1947 had been knocking 'em dead as Og the Leprechaun in the Broadway musical *Finian's Rainbow*. Both Wayne and Fonda were present at the first reading of the manuscript in Logan's apartment. Initially, Fonda wasn't keen on doing a play, feeling that *Roberts* had better potential as a movie; but by the time Logan read the last line of the script, Fonda was won over. Graciously, Wayne accepted the secondary role of Ensign Pulver.

Even before the star had been signed, the producers began filling the rest of the play's thirty speaking parts, giving preference to ex-sevicemen who would best appreciate the mood of the story. The first actor cast was Harvey Lembeck, late of the USN Submarine Service, who landed the role of Seaman Insigna. Other Broadway newcomers in *Mister Roberts* were Steven Hill, Murray Hamilton, Ralph Meeker and Tige Andrews. The larger roles of the Captain and Doc were respectively taken by Joshua Logan's brother-in-law William Harrigan (memorable as Claude Rains' treacherous assistant in the 1933 film version of *The Invisible Man*) and by Robert Keith (who arranged for his son Robert Jr. to fill a small role in the play, long before the youngster achieved film and TV fame as Brian Keith).

Casting the male roles was a breeze compared to finding an actress for *Mister Roberts*' sole female character: Lt. Anne Girard, the young nurse whom the libidinous Pulver invites on board the *Reluctant*—and who spoils Pulver's seduction plans by leaving in a huff upon discovering that she and the other nurses have been providing a free "nudie show" for the binocular-equipped crewmen. Originally cast as Anne Girard was Peggy Maley, who unfortunately came off as too brittle. She was replaced by 24-year-old Eva Marie Saint, who perfectly matched the novel's description of Lt. Girard; but Saint was also dismissed when the producers determined that she was so cute and cuddly that the audience would want her to keep coming back after her one-and-only scene. Finally, Henry Fonda suggested an old friend from his stock-company days in Omaha, neither too jaded nor too pretty—whereupon Jocelyn Brando, sister of you-know-who, joined the cast.

Despite the presence of such high-strung artists as Logan, Fonda, and Hayward, rehearsals for *Mister Roberts* proceeded smoothly, a strong cameraderie forming among the actors, crew members and production personnel. The New York opening at the Alvin Theater on January 18, 1948, met with such rapturous applause that during the curtain call, Fonda grinned at the audience and said, "That's all Tom and Josh wrote.... If you want us to do it again, we will"—and was met with even a louder ovation. In his review for the New York *Daily News*, John Chapman confessed, "I hung around for a while, hoping they *would* do it again." Other reviewers were equally rhapsodic, placing *Mister Roberts* firmly in the S.R.O class for 1,157 performances; the play went on to win the Tony Award and was nominated for a Pulitzer Prize, barely losing the latter to *A Streetcar Named Desire*. Henry Fonda, who ever after cited Doug Roberts as his all-time favorite role, stayed with the Broadway production almost to the end, then took the play on the road. John Forsythe headed the first national touring company, and in 1956 Forsythe directed a new staging at the New York Civic Center, starring Charlton Heston as Roberts, Orson Bean as Pulver and Fred Clark as Doc. Other actors who have portrayed Mister Roberts on stage range from Tyrone Power in the London production to Martin Sheen in a 1980 revival directed by Josh Logan for the Burt Reynolds Theater in Florida.

Tragically, the one person who did not reap the full benefits of *Mister Roberts*' success was the man who first brought the property to life. Having found it impossible to cope with overnight fame and fortune, unable to gather his thoughts together for a second novel, and heavily reliant upon liquor and barbituates to counteract his depression and despair, 30-year-old Tom Heggen drowned in the bathtub of his Manhattan apartment on May 19, 1949.

The play's extended stage life delayed the movie adaptation of *Mister Roberts* for nearly seven years. It was first assumed that Henry Fonda would reprise his role on film, but by the time Warner Bros. was ready to start production, Fonda's participation seemed to be a moot point. Having been away from Hollywood since 1948, Fonda was no longer considered bankable by Warners, who offered the role of Roberts first to William Holden and then Marlon Brando. Too, time was not on Fonda's side; at age 49, he was now deemed too old to convincingly portray the 26-year-old Roberts. Fonda likewise felt that his age was an obstacle, and had resigned himself to missing out on the movie.

William Holden turned down the offer, declaring that the part of Doug Roberts was Fonda's and Fonda's alone. Brando was more receptive, and his casting would likely have met with the approval of Josh Logan, who'd long been on the inside track to direct the film. As it turned out, Warners had no interest in securing the services of Logan; the studio insisted upon a "name" movie director who'd draw crowds above and beyond the *Mister Roberts* fan base. And fewer names were bigger in 1954 Hollywood than John Ford, who'd just put the finishing touches on Columbia's prestigious 30th Anniversary "special" *The Long Gray Line*. Warners' selection of Ford proved to be more than simply a smart box-office move. The Navy's Office of Information was at first disinclined to extend cooperation to the production, citing the scurrilous portrayal of the Captain and the crew's rapacious behavior during the liberty scene. Fortunately, Ford had served with distinction as a Navy officer during World War II, putting his life on the line to film the award-winning documentaries *The Battle of Midway* and *The Fighting Lady*. Having left the service with the rank of Rear Admiral, John Ford had no difficulty assuring the Office of Information that the Navy would be treated with the utmost respect throughout *Mister Roberts*.

Though some sources suggest that Ford initially balked at the opportunity to helm *Roberts*, allegedly dismissing it as "that homosexual play," he accepted Warners' offer—but not their proposed star Marlon Brando. After all, Ford and Henry Fonda had previously made cinema magic with such classics as *Young Mr. Lincoln, The Grapes of Wrath,* and *My Darling Clementine*. Either Warner Bros. hired Fonda to play the movie Roberts, demanded Ford, or they could get another director. Warners acceded to this demand, covering their bets by casting two top-rank film personalities in support of Fonda. The studio sent out press releases intimating that Spencer Tracy had been selected to play Doc; and when James Cagney was told that Tracy was a "lock," he agreed to sign on as the Captain of the *Reluctant*. But by the time Cagney reported for work, Tracy was out of the picture, and William Powell was on board as Doc. (It remains unclear whether Tracy had actually been approached, or if his name had merely been floated to secure Cagney's services.)

For the last of the four major roles, the studio decided upon a comparative newcomer. After energetically lobbying for the assignment, Jack Lemmon landed the role of Ensign Pulver, which would ultimately earn him an Oscar for best supporting actor. The story goes that Ford chose Lemmon on the basis of the actor's screen test for the Tyrone Power role in *The Long Gray Line*; in later years, Lemmon claimed he'd been cast as Pulver *despite* his test, in which he'd been weighed down with old-age makeup and a motley wig. Another relatively new face was chosen for the slightly expanded role of Lt. Ann Girard; Betsy Palmer, who unlike Lemmon *had* been in *The Long Gray Line*.

John Ford reserved several supporting roles for members of his unofficial stock company, among them Ward Bond, Ken Curtis, Patrick Wayne (son of John), Danny Borzage, Jack Pennick, and Harry Carey Jr. In his autobiography, Carey recalls that many of the Ford "regulars" arrived on location in Hawaii not knowing which parts they'd end up playing; only after a few days did the director match each man with the appropriate role. Others in the ensemble included Olympic swimming champion and stunt diver Stubby Kruger, who in the climax of the "Elysium liberty" scene drove a motorcycle straight off a pier and into the ocean; and two future TV favorites in their first screen appearances, Nick Adams and Frank Aletter. Featured in the role of Wiley is Tige Andrews, who along with Henry Fonda was carried over from the Broadway production.

While the Ford unit was on location, initially at Midway Island (the first civilians permitted there since the War) and then in Hawaii, Warner Bros. cheerfully assured the public that the bulk of the raunchy and rowdy elements of the stage version would be left intact, though concessions were made to the Production Code. Beyond changing "goddam" to "stinkin,'" "virgin" to "maiden," and eliminating the vivid descriptions of Pulver's sexual shenanigans, it was announced that play's most censorable moments would be supplanted with slapstick and comic exaggeration, not only to mollify the censors but also to appeal to a general audience. Warners had first approached John Patrick, who'd successfully pepped up the stage version of Vern Sneider's novel *The Teahouse of the August Moon* (discussed later in this chapter) with a broad comedy approach, to adapt *Mister Roberts* for the screen. But John Ford selected his longtime collaborator Frank Nugent, who in addition to increasing the slapstick content also contributed such typically Fordian touches as having Doc portrayed as a borderline alcoholic.

Few of these changes met with the approval of Josh Logan or Henry Fonda, who regarded the play as the Holy Writ. A quarter century after the fact, Logan was giving interviews in which he lamented, "The movie is an absolute disgrace to the play," describing John Ford as "a sinner to do what he did." In his autobiography, Fonda groused, "I didn't like it. Josh and Tom Heggen had written an excellent play, and very subtly, the dialogue had been changed around. Not a helluva lot, but enough to lose the laughs and the nuances of frustration and pain." The actor was especially perturbed by Ford and Nugent's excesses, citing the decision to "enhance" the scene with nurse Ann Girard by having no fewer than half a dozen well-endowed nurses clamber aboard the *Reluctant*, presumably on the theory that six girls would be six times funnier. John Ford himself felt hamstrung by Fonda's intractable insistence upon playing the comedy scenes with the same pacing and timing he'd developed on stage. Though *Mister Roberts* was largely lensed outdoors on the deck of the Navy cargo ship *Hewell*, Ford worried that the finished film would come across as a photographed stage play. The director's unhappiness trickled down to his "regulars"; as Harry Carey Jr. remembered, "There was never the 'Ford mood' on that set." If we are to believe Josh Logan, Ford broke his long-standing personal vow of abstention while making a film, and began drinking heavily on the eighth day of shooting.

According to Henry Fonda, the tension between himself and Ford reached the crisis stage when, during an argument over Ford's unwillingness to shoot retakes—which was particularly hard on the aging William Powell, who was having difficulty remembering his lines—the director took a swing at Fonda and knocked the actor down. Though Jack Lemmon later insisted this never happened, and James Cagney liked to pretend he knew nothing about the confrontation, it was obvious that the animosity had gone past the point of no return. Less than two months into production, John Ford was flown back to Hollywood; the official story was that he needed an emergency gall bladder operation.

With barely enough time to read

Not exactly in his mid-twenties anymore, but he doesn't look like he's approaching fifty either (though he was). Henry Fonda repeating his stage role as the title character in ***Mister Roberts*** (Warner Bros., 1955).

the script, veteran all-purpose director Mervyn LeRoy flew to Hawaii to pick up where Ford had left off. LeRoy vowed to complete the film exactly the way it was started, screening the rushes over and over so he could copy Ford's style to the letter; the only significant change made by LeRoy was to downplay Doc's liquor intake (both Ford and LeRoy would be credited on-screen). The hostile atmosphere subsided, though Fonda griped that there was still too much low comedy and slapstick; indeed, Warners felt that Ford hadn't been slapsticky *enough*, and wanted LeRoy to lay it on even thicker. Meanwhile, James Cagney, who had openly disliked LeRoy since the 1930s, kept to himself as much as possible on the set, spending his free time relaxing on the beaches of Hawaii with his friend William Powell. Next to Jack Lemmon, Powell was regarded as the most convivial of the four main players, though privately he grew so anxious over his failing memory that he vowed to quit show business cold the moment *Mister Roberts* wrapped — which he did.

After principal shooting ended, the studio dictated a few additional changes. With Mervyn LeRoy occupied elsewhere, Josh Logan directed a handful of scenes without screen credit, including the deathless finale in which Pulver, outraged over Mister Roberts' sudden demise, bursts into the Captain's cabin and exclaims, "It is *I*, Ensign Pulver, and I just threw your stinkin' palm tree overboard! Now, what's all this crud about no movies tonight?" Harry Carey, Jr., normally a John Ford loyalist, was among those who felt that Logan should have directed the film from the start. Logan himself has characterized the final product as "a spit-and-toothpick version of *Mister Roberts*.... It hasn't been one of the great, huge pictures it should have been."

Maybe not, but *Mister Roberts* turned out to be a great, huge box-office success, the second top-grossing film of 1955. Audiences responded enthusiastically to all of the surefire comic setpieces carried over from both the novel and the play: The long-distance ogling of the nurses' quarters, the Elysium bacchanale, the explosion in the laundry room, Roberts' defiant "execution" of the Captain's palm tree, and Pulver's sudden conversion from mouse to man at fadeout time. Equally well received were the highlights that had not appeared in the novel but had originated in the play: The scotch-brewing scene, the Captain meeting Pulver for the first time after the cowardly Ensign has been avoiding such a meeting for fourteen months (a scene that proved so hilarious to the actors that James Cagney demanded numerous rehearsals so he wouldn't break up laughing), and Doc's loving recollection of the crew's well-lubricated "contest" to forge the Captain's signature on Roberts' transfer orders.

To give Henry Fonda and Josh Logan their due, some of the attempts to goose the laugh content fall flat, notably composer Franz Waxman's musical "wolf whistle" accompanying the scene in which the crew spies upon the nurses. Likewise irksome is Mervyn LeRoy's tendency to duplicate John Ford's fondness for outrageous overacting from the supporting players, with the usually reliable Martin Milner one of the worst offenders as a Southern-accented MP. On the other hand, a lot of the much-despised slapstick works beautifully, especially the marvelous shot of Ensign Pulver happily floating in a sea of detergent bubbles after his firecracker has lain waste to the laundry.

One addition to the film version scores on a purely sentimental level. Reaching back to the original Tom Heggen novel, adaptor Frank Nugent provides a touching coda to the Rabelaisian liberty scene, as virginal Seaman Bookser (Patrick Wayne) returns to the *Reluctant* hand in hand with a sweet young lady whom he met while attending a church service.

Overall, *Mister Roberts* remains as entertaining to modern film fans as it was to audiences of 1955, though most of today's viewers may have some trouble relating to the frustrations of the crew, and might not understand why anyone in his right mind would want to be involved in combat when he can sit out the war in safety, even on a "bucket" like the *Reluctant*. Also, the more PC-sensitive viewers will likely be turned off by the film's vigorously unabashed sexism, and thus disinclined to appreciate the humor in a bunch of horny sailors invading a formal dinner dance in Elysium and manhandling a group of proper young ladies (an outrage not shown on screen, but tersely described by shore patrolman James Flavin). But for all the backstage bickering, the participation of three different directors, and the potential imbalance of flanking Henry Fonda with two dynamic old pros like Cagney and Powell, *Mister Roberts* flows smoothly and assuredly from beginning to end, the actors working copacetically as a team throughout. Never once does the film betray the sort of artistic indecision or raggedness found in such other troubled productions as *The Magnificent Ambersons* (1942) and *Cleopatra* (1963); if one were not apprised of the difficulties during filming, one would assume that the participants had as much fun making *Mister Roberts* as the audience has seeing it.

Mister Roberts went on to be adapted as an NBC television series, which ran from September 17, 1965, through September 2, 1966. This half-hour sitcom version starred Roger Smith as Roberts, Steve Harmon as Pulver, Richard X. Slattery as the Captain and George Ives as Doc. The only noteworthy aspect of this tired, cliché-ridden effort was the decision by the producers to withhold the otherwise ubiquitous "canned laughter" during the confrontations between Roberts and the Captain—predating a similar decision by the producers of the TV version of *M*A*S*H*. Far more interesting, and more faithful to its source, is a later television production of the original Logan-Heggen play. Telecast live by ABC on March 19, 1984, and presently available on home video, this *Mister Roberts* stars Robert Hays in the title role, Charles Durning as the Captain, Howard Hesseman as Doc, Marilu Henner as Anne Girard, Joseph Pantoliano as Insigna, and some green kid by the name of Kevin Bacon as Pulver.

Oh, lest we forget: In 1964, Joshua Logan directed and co-wrote a movie sequel to *Mister Roberts*, released by Warner Bros. under the title *Ensign Pulver*. Picking up its story a few weeks after the death of Doug Roberts, the sequel again largely takes place aboard the *Reluctant*, still making its dreary cargo runs to obscure military installations in the Western Pacific—though this time out, location shooting took place in Mexico and Puerto Rico. Having lost the momentum of his character conversion at the end of *Mister Roberts*, Ensign Pulver is just as timid and wishy-washy as ever. An effort is made to "man up" the character by having him aspire to become a doctor in order to live up to the accomplishments of his older brothers, war heroes all. Pulver has also abandoned his love-'em-and-leave-'em attitude as he pursues a serious romance with a comely Navy nurse named Scotty, who in turn loves the Ensign in spite of his imperfections—and in a way, *because* of them.

Without a strong antagonist like Mister Roberts to keep him in check, the *Reluctant*'s Captain has become even more dictatorial, sadistically refusing to grant his crew any sort of privileges as he strives to break a cargo-shipping record so he can be promoted to Commander. Within this setup, the obligatory climax in which Pulver finally triumphs over the Captain grows less from Pulver's inner strength than from an incredibly contrived chain of circumstances.

With no one else available, the nervous Pulver is forced to go to the Captain's rescue when the old reprobate falls overboard during a heavy storm. Drifting in a leaky rubber raft for several days, Pulver tries to allay his own fears by keeping a diary of his ordeal. Meanwhile, the Captain, angered at having to rely on Pulver for his survival and insisting that he has never needed anyone's help in his life and isn't about to ask for it now, slowly succumbs to delirium, babbling about his miserable childhood, his many failures in life, and his innermost fears. The two castaways finally wash up on the shore of a lush tropical island, not far from where a plane carrying a group of nurses has been forced down by the storm. When the Captain is stricken with appendicitis, Pulver again has "greatness thrust upon him." With the assistance of Scotty and the other nurses, he performs an emergency operation, following instructions via radio from an increasingly besotted Doc. Anesthetized with an intoxicating native beverage, the Captain drops all his defenses and begins behaving like a real human being, singing happily and even flirting with the head nurse. But upon returning to the *Reluctant* after an eight-week convalescence, and despite his new promotion to Commander, the Captain is as mean and spiteful as ever, threatening dire consequences to the crew for their frolicsome behavior in his absence. In a last-ditch confrontation, Pulver threatens to make public the contents of his diary and reveal to the world that the Captain is just as prone to weakness, vulnerability and sentimentality as anyone. Practically in tears, the Captain shouts back that he is incapable of changing his ways—but he *can* agree to drop all threats of punishment, request a transfer, and leave the *Reluctant* in the hands of second-in-command Lt. LaSeuer (Gerald S. O'Loughlin). The shaken Pulver realizes that this is the only way that the Captain is capable of saying "thank you" for saving his life. Thus, the big epiphany in *Ensign Pulver* is not undergone by the hero, but by the villain!

Outside of the character names, the setting, and the cumbersome necessity of reiterating incidents from the earlier film, only twice in *Ensign Pulver* are there any vestiges of the original *Mister Roberts*. In both cases the screenwriters harked back to incidents in the Thomas Heggen novel that had not previously been dramatized. In the first instance, Pulver accepts a challenge from Doc to strike out at the Captain, using a slingshot to fire a ball of leadfoil and nails at the skipper's hindquarters while the old fart is watching a horror movie on deck. In the second, the ship's radio operator John X. Bruno goes berserk when he is refused liberty after finding out that his infant daughter has died, whereupon he grabs a Luger and threatens to kill the Captain. (In the novel, the grieving sailor overcomes his anger and gets on with his life without meting out retribution.)

Chosen to play Ensign Pulver was 23-year-old Robert Walker, Jr., son of the late film star Robert Walker and actress Jennifer Jones. Hollywood columnists magnanimously avoided unfairly comparing Robert Walker Jr. to Jack Lemmon by unfairly comparing Robert Walker Jr. to Robert Walker Sr. (it didn't help that the actor dropped the "Jr." in his on-screen billing). Young Walker took it all in stride, cheerfully declaring that he was a lucky fellow to have such a distinguished pedigree, and that he hoped *Ensign Pulver* would do for his career what *See Here, Private Hargrove* (see **Chapter 9**) had done for his father's. But though he gave it the old college try, Walker was

Forever hatching schemes to confound the Captain of the *Reluctant*, Frank Pulver (Robert Walker Jr., replacing Jack Lemmon) shows off his new arsenal to the quizzical Doc (Walter Matthau taking over from William Powell) in the *Mister Roberts* sequel *Ensign Pulver* (Warner Bros., 1964).

not quite ready to carry a major motion picture, nor did the uneven script of *Ensign Pulver* give him much to work with. Better served within the framework are Walter Matthau as the philosophical Doc, played along broader and boozier lines than William Powell, and Burl Ives in the much-expanded role of the Captain, though at times Ives' performance comes nervously close to "Big Daddy at Sea." Pulver's girlfriend is wittily portrayed by former *Diary of Anne Frank* star Millie Perkins (Sandy Dennis had auditioned for the role, but her screen test was sabotaged by an ill-fitting push-up bra), while Kay Medford, a last-minute replacement for Dody Goodman, is seen as the no-nonsense nurse who assists Pulver during the appendectomy. As the unfortunate Bruno, Tommy Sands was the latest in a long line of singing idols making the transition to heavy dramatics—a point emphasized in the film's theatrical trailer, which gives Sands almost as much attention as Robert Walker Jr.

The huge cast also features a stunning roster of stars in the making. African American actors Al Freeman Jr. and Diana Sands struggle to transcend stereotype as a pair of missionary-educated natives; and among the officers and sailors are Larry Hagman, Peter Marshall, James Farentino, George Lindsey and James Coco—not to mention Jack Nicholson, who despite recent claims that his sizeable supporting role was whittled down to a bit part, actually has quite a few good moments. In later years, both Nicholson and Larry Hagman recalled that *Ensign Pulver* was a tough shoot, fraught with such costly technical snafus as the flock of expensive white doves that refused to fly on cue, spoiling take after take—and when the doves finally took wing, they all descended straight into the ocean, where they were eagerly devoured by sharks.

Though Josh Logan could with some justification attribute the shortcomings of *Mister Roberts* to John Ford and Frank Nugent, he had only himself to blame for the pedestrian quality of *Ensign Pulver*. Participants in the production remember that Logan was uncommunicative with the younger actors, refusing to be bothered with questions about character interpretation while he was "thinking" between scenes. Also, Logan, who suffered from a variety of physical and mental ailments, was so over-medicated that at times he seemed totally oblivious to what was going on.

For contemporary viewers, the star-studded cast of minor players, and the clever redeployment of excerpts from the 1936 Boris Karloff vehicle *The Walking Dead* as the "horror film" the Captain is enjoying when he receives the leadfoil fusillade, are the principal attractions of the serviceable but unremarkable *Ensign Pulver*.

The Teahouse of the August Moon (and Derivations)

Though many sources state that Vern J. Sneider was born in Ontario, the city of Monroe, Michigan, has always claimed him as a native son; despite international fame as an author, Sneider lived in Monroe virtually all his life, and passed away there at age 64 in 1981. Whatever his country of origin, he served in both Army and the Navy of the United States in World War II. Just before the end of the war, Sneider was transferred to the military government and sent along with the invasion forces to Okinawa, where he was placed in charge of a native refugee camp (population 5000) in the village of Tobaru.

During this difficult transitional period in which, according to Sneider, "the United States began to find itself in the Military government business," he and his fellow officers "were at a complete loss" as to how to go about it. The only official guide to the job at hand was a xenophobic tome written in 1917 for the Occupation forces in the Rhineland. Sneider found it far more helpful to refer to John Hersey's novel *A Bell for Adano*, the warmhearted story of an American army major who cuts through a jungle of red tape to bring order and democracy to a small Italian town—and in the process invests in the war-weary villagers a renewed sense of self-respect and self-determination. The lesson Sneider took away from *Adano* was that the United States could not force democracy or the American way of life down the throats of a conquered people. He concluded that the best way a military government officer could handle his assignment is "if he looks to the wants of the people under him, then tries to satisfy those wants."

Sneider did his best to follow this creed in Tobaru, and after VE Day in the Kyong Province of Korea, where he reopened 500 of the area's schools. In both cases, he was often compelled to undo the damage wrought by well-meaning but clueless American officials whose idea of democratization was to ignore the natives' basic needs, empirically setting up "model" governments and businesses based more on theory than practicality. He also despaired over the inability of certain higher-ups to gain even a rudimentary knowledge of local customs, traditions and taboos. Most of all, he was appalled by the openly racist attitudes of many American officers and politicians towards the very natives to whom they were supposed to be spreading the philosophy of All Men Created Equal. In his later novels and short stories, Sneider would angrily bear down on these "Ugly American" aspects of the Occupation; but when time came to write his first novel, he elected to set forth his philosophy of tolerance, cooperation and understanding with light humor and gentle satire.

The Teahouse of the August Moon (Putnam, 1951) is the story of Jeff Fisby, a balding, porky, slightly slovenly Army captain. Assigned the job of administrator in the Okinawan village of Tobeki, Fisby is ordered to carry out "Plan B," fomulated by the vainglorious Colonel Wainwright Purdy III for the purpose of educating the natives in all things American — and if the Colonel can get himself a promotion in the process, so much the better. Purdy himself is the servant of two masters: The Pentagon, and his own formidable wife Mrs. Purdy, president of the Tuesday Club of Pottawattamie, Indiana. To curry favor with Washington, Purdy has made the casual suggestion that Tobeki's new schoolhouse be built in the shape of the Pentagon. To mollify his wife, Purdy has instructed Fisby to establish a Tobeki Womens' League for Democratic Action, and to set up a daily menu for the natives including such Tuesday Club delicacies as chicken aspic and fruit compote.

But nothing in Plan B prepares Tobeki for the sudden arrival of two geisha girls, First Flower and Lotus Blossom, whom a friendly Okinawan has given Fisby as "souvenirs." The village's male population now insists that the building of a schoolhouse take second priority to the construction of a *cha ya*, or teahouse. Here the men will be able to forget the pressures of their lives, relax, and be treated with kindness and respect by the geishas, who will provide a friendly cup of tea, a pleasant song, and a sympathetic ear as the men unburden their problems and concerns. Fed up with bending over backward to keep the locals from "losing face" by behaving contrary to their traditions, Fisby at first resents this new complication in his life. Gradually, however, he learns to respect the strong-willed First Flower, who not only supervises construction of the teahouse but also conceives a whole new town around the structure, including such Okinawa-centric business concerns as a sandal-manufacturing shop and a distillery for sweet potato brandy. The male residents, who'd previously dragged their heels implementing Plan B, suddenly spring into action to fulfill First Flower's expansive visions. As for the new Women's League for Democratic Action, the forceful president Mrs. Higa Jiga is not so much interested in politics as in persuading the menfolk to treat herself and the other ladies as nicely and deferentially as the geishas. For this purpose, she insists that First Flower and Lotus Blossom set up classes to teach the women how to dance, sing, and dress geisha-style.

In carrying this out, Fisby must beg, borrow and virtually steal the supplies necessary for the construction and maintenance of the teahouse and its environs. All this proves confusing to Col. Purdy, who is peeved that none of his Plan B has been carried out. What Purdy doesn't grasp until the end of the novel is that, with the combined input of Fisby and the locals, Tobeki has become a flourishing textbook example of the U.S. Free Enterprise System — and all on the Okinawans' terms.

Throughout the narrative, born-and-bred midwesterner Fisby has progressively gone native, lounging in a kimono and sipping tea as he contemplates his existence. The pervasiveness of the

Okinawan lifestyle has also spread to an Army psychiatrist named McLean, initially dispatched by Purdy to spy on the "eccentric" Fisby. An organic gardener in civilian life, Fisby is so blown away by the growth potential of Tobeki that he establishes a thriving agricultural system that will allow the locals to sustain themselves forever — and allow *him* to cast off military protocol and, like Purdy, enjoy life for a change. Reviewing *Teahouse of the August Moon*, *Time* magazine stated: "How Fisby got around the Purdy plan and built himself a miniature Utopia full of happy Okinawans is the story of Vern Sneider's nimble novel ... Sneider has written a shrewd fantasy about the American in the uncomfortable role of conqueror."

Time also described *Teahouse* as a "short story puffed up to novel length," which might have led potential readers to conclude that the book was as short and spare as *Mister Roberts,* when in fact it is over twice as long. John Patrick, a popular American playwright with such Broadway successes as *The Hasty Heart* and *The Curious Savage* in his portfolio — and himself a war veteran, who had served in the medical division of the American Field Service and with the British Army in the Far East — would most likely not have concurred with *Time*'s assessment of the novel. Josh Logan's task in *Mister Roberts* had been to expand the plotline, flesh out the characters, and elaborate upon the dialogue to bring the novel up to a workable two-act length. John Patrick's challenge was to take the overabundance of plot, incident, characters and talk in the original *Teahouse of the August Moon* and slim them down to a manageable *three* acts. If any man could pull this off, it was Patrick, whose past credits included the 45-minute radio series *Streamlined Shakespeare*.

Whereas the action in the novel sprawls all over Okinawa, the play is confined to four small acting areas representing Purdy's office, Fisby's headquarters, the teahouse and the village of Tobeki. The timeframe of the story is telescoped from several months to a few weeks. The huge cast of characters is narrowed to five principals, four supporting roles and nineteen bit parts. The number of geisha girls presented to Fisby is reduced from two to one, with the important character of First Flower eliminated entirely. Finally, the many successful business enterprises established by the villagers are pared down to the one with the most comic potential: The manufacture of brandy from sweet potatoes.

Responding to those who felt that his novel was as serious as it was amusing, Vern Sneider replied that *Teahouse* was meant to be whatever the reader wished it to be. What John Patrick clearly wished it to be was the sort of "well-made" Broadway comedy that pushed all the right buttons and left 'em laughing. The languid pace of the novel was abandoned in favor of dynamic, expertly timed entrances and exits, sharply defined character "types," and dialogue chock full of setups, punchlines and catchphrases like "What in the name of the Occupation *is* this?" And in the tradition of *Mister Roberts*, Patrick concocted a number of comic setpieces involving a crowded jeep, an Okinawa-style wrestling match, a giggling geisha who undresses a blushing Army captain while he is trying to carry on a phone conversation with his C.O., and a drinking scene with a brandy-swilling goat (who actually guzzled Coca-Cola on stage). All this builds up to a cliffhanger crisis — the threat of a court-martial for Fisby and the demolition of the village's beloved geisha house — invented by Patrick for the end of Act Two, which is hilariously resolved by a *deus-ex-machina* — the U.S. government's endorsement of Tobeki's unique spin on American capitalism — at the end of Act Three.

Acknowledging that the "blue-haired ladies" who controlled Broadway ticket sales preferred to see good-looking young leading players, Patrick transformed Captain Fisby from chubby, unattractive and hair-challenged to slim, handsome and full-follicled. Also recognizing that an audience instinctively empathizes with an underdog, Patrick ignored the passages in the novel establishing Fisby as a fairly prosperous civilian pharmacist, reinventing him as a well-meaning bumbler who has failed miserably in all his other assignments — and for whom Tobeki is his make-or-break Last Chance. In addition, Patrick performed a bit of creative surgery on Fisby's antagonist Colonel Purdy, who in the Sneider original not only bends to the wishes of his social-climbing wife but is also easily swayed by his sycophantic, self-serving fellow officers. In the play, the impracticality of Purdy's "Plan B" is shown to be a one-man folly rather than idiocy planned by committee. This deflected potential criticism that the play was biased against the entire Occupation Army, and also eliminated several superfluous characters.

The novel's backstory indicates that Fisby has been in Tobeki for several weeks before the actual plot gets under way. Patrick gives the action more immediacy by having Fisby confront the villagers for the very first time in Act One, just as the audience members have *their* first brush with the culture-clash issues which motivate the story. In a similar vein, once we meet Army psychiatrist McLean in the novel, it is several chapters before we discover that he has been sent to Tobeki to evaluate Fisby's mental state. Patrick gives McLean a far more effective entrance by letting the audience in on his mission from the outset, setting up a superb duel of cross-purposes as McLean misinterprets every innocent word spoken by Fisby as a sign of incipient insanity.

John Patrick's biggest creative challenge was to represent the Okinawan point of view in such a way that a non–Asian audience would both comprehend and sympathize. What was needed was a persuasive Okinawan "voice" to elucidate the philosophical differences between Americans and Asians, and to demonstrate that the local population was willing to adopt certain American standards while remaining true to their own traditions. The device Patrick hit upon, in his own words, was "a dash of kabuki": The inclusion of an onstage narrator, who could not only accomplish the above-mentioned tasks but also set the mood and rhythm of the play, swiftly and economically conveying time and scene transitions without excess verbiage or an overreliance on stage machinery.

Throughout the first half of Vern Sneider's novel, Captain Fisby's 22-year-old native interpreter Sakini is a character without a character. His job is to translate the words of the other Okinawans into English, and to explain and clarify the local customs and social rules for Fisby's benefit. He does this job calmly and efficiently, never betraying his own emotions or opinions—except once. After the arrival of the geisha girls, it is Sakini who emphatically insists that Fisby, Colonel Purdy, the United States Government and (up to this point) the reader have all been laboring under a misapprehension: Geishas are not, repeat *not,* prostitutes. This was all John Patrick needed. He had found his narrator — and the American Theater was blessed with one of its most memorable characters.

In the play's opening scene, Sakini politely introduces himself to the "Lovely Ladies, Kind Gentlemen" in the audience, and with pithy geniality describes his countrymen as having enjoyed the "distinguished" history of being constantly invaded and conquered by others: "Okinawans very fortunate. Culture brought to us. Not have to leave home for it." Through this process, Sakini's people have discovered over the centuries that "world full of delightful variations." Withal, Sakini assures us that "Okinawans most eager to be educated by conquerors. Not easy to learn. Sometimes very painful. But pain make man think. Thought make man wise. And wisdom make life endurable." In less than three minutes, Sakini has set forth all we need to know about what has happened before the opening curtain rises, and what *will* happen before the final curtain falls.

As a narrative device, Sakini is indispensable. As a plot motivator, he is delightfully sly and manipulative. Unlike his counterpart in the novel, who takes no active or personal part in the Americanization of the orientals and the orientalization of the Americans, the Sakini of the play is obviously "interpreting" to the advantage of himself and his people, not overtly twisting the words spoken in Okinawans but slightly bending them to his needs. But as a character pure and simple, Sakini poses a major problem for contemporary audiences. Though he speaks with poetic eloquence, he uses Pidgin English throughout (as opposed to his near-perfect English is the novel), and is doggedly deferential to the American characters. Thus it is not surprising that Sakini is now dismissed as a racial stereotype, a perception fueled by the fact that the character has almost exclusively been portrayed by non–Asian actors.

The theatrical adaptation of *Teahouse of the August Moon* was optioned by British actor-producer Maurice Evans, fresh from his Broadway success in the suspense play *Dial M for Murder.*

Evans had hoped to play Sakini himself (no longer pigeonholed at 22, the character was described as being of indeterminate age), but director Robert Lewis persuaded him to seek out an Asian actor for the role. This proved all but impossible; in 1953, there were no Asians in New York who could carry an entire Broadway show. "There were so few opportunities for them that none had the experience to do it," Lewis later explained. "The crowd in the play were a whole mixture of Asians. We had Japanese, Chinese, even blacks. But Sakini was a starring part where he had to not only act in all the scenes but also step out of the play and talk to the audience all evening and be an emcee. To do that, you have to have a certain charm and ability to make the audience laugh." After a tortuous audition process, Evans and Lewis chose Sho Onera, a prominent Japanese journalist who spoke English beautifully and possessed a marvelous sense of humor. But as Lewis recalled, "We brought him to the theater and started to work with him ... and he just couldn't do it." Onera was retained as technical advisor, translating the Japanese dialogue spoken by the minor characters (written phonetically in the script). Ultimately, a Caucasian was selected to play Sakini: David Wayne, *Mister Roberts'* original Ensign Pulver and a man described by onetime costar Una Merkel as "one of the finest actors we have. He's so good they don't know what to do with him."

The rest of the casting proceeded painlessly, with John Forsythe (another *Mister Roberts* alumnus) chosen as Fisby, Paul Ford assigned to Col. Purdy, Larry Gates cast as McLean and Harry Jackson tagged for Purdy's deadpan assistant Sgt. Gregovich (a throwaway character in the novel). And although non–Asians were given the larger Okinawan speaking roles, Japanese actress Mariko Nikki, who never appeared on Broadway before or after, landed the major (and virtually non-speaking) role of geisha girl Lotus Blossom. Despite some flareups between playwright Patrick and director Lewis (*de rigueur* for major stage productions of the 1950s), *The Teahouse of the August Moon* opened as scheduled at the Martin Beck Theatre on October 15, 1953, scoring an immediate hit.

Comparing the play with the novel, critic Brooks Atkinson wrote: "By eliminating details, sweetening the humor and sharpening the conflict between the wily natives and the naive captain, Mr. Patrick has made a pungent comedy with a tangible theme that delights everyone who distrusts military authority in civilian affairs. Mr. Sneider's novel provides the basic material. Mr. Patrick, working on it with fresh relish, has made a fresh piece of writing out of it." Four years later, theater historian John Gassner had this to say: "Many American plays dealt forcefully with man's inhumanity to man; this work had the opposite effect of showing man's humanity to man.... It was a genial play, composed as a theatrical experience even if its political implications were evident.... An allowable criticism that the second act was weak or that the American officers were cartoons, and they were, was of minor consequence on Broadway. It was a droll play of theater and a lightly satirical one, and it took a pleasantly romantic view of the Orient and its people. All this could endear a play about the problems of an Army Occupation to a public that did not exact and was not being promised profound revelations." The ultimate accolade arrived when *Teahouse* won the Pulitzer Prize, the Critics' Circle Award and the Tony Award — the first Broadway comedy to earn all three statuettes.

Five touring companies were sent to major cities in the United States and Great Britain. Eli Wallach played Sakini in the London production, where the live goat in the drinking scene, originally identified on stage as "Lady Astor," was rechristened "Elsa Maxwell" by order of the local censors. There were several subsequent stagings throughout the world; the German production, translated by Oskar Karlweiss, ran even longer than the Broadway version's stunning 1,077 performances. And though modern viewers may be offended by the ethnic stereotypes, Asian audiences of the 1950s loved the show. In Japan the play boasted an interracial cast, with Americans playing the American roles and the Japanese the Okinawan roles, each speaking their own language.

Teahouse of the August Moon had few more fervent fans than Marlon Brando, who saw the original Broadway production three times. Brando later confessed that during one evening at the

Martin Beck, "I laughed so hard I almost ended up beating the hat of the lady in front of me." The play's message inspired the actor to donate a generous portion of his movie earnings to establish an Asian film program for the United Nations; it also prompted him to lobby for the role of Sakini in MGM's upcoming film version of the play. Though John Patrick could only express faint enthusiasm over the prospect of Brando playing an amiable Oriental, MGM was eager to snap up the services of Hollywood's hottest young actor. "If he had wanted to play Little Eva," remarked studio head Dore Schary, "I would have let him." There was an added incentive to MGM's acquiescence: By the time *Teahouse* went into production in early 1956, Marlon Brando was the most popular non–Asian actor in Japan.

Marlon Brando goes native as the cheerful, crafty Okinawan interpreter Sakina in MGM's 1956 filmization of the Broadway hit ***The Teahouse of the August Moon.***

Since the role of Captain Fisby was as a large and as important as Sakini, an actor of stature equal to Brando's was required. The studio's choice of Glenn Ford was in its own way as radical as the casting of Brando: Prior to *Teahouse*, Ford had built his reputation on a series of *noir*-ish tough guy roles in films like *Gilda* and *The Big Heat*, with very little time spent in light comedy. The part of Lotus Blossom went to Japanese actress Machiko Kyô, who had gained international renown for her searing performances in such landmark Japanese films as *Ugetsu*, *Rashomon* and *Gate of Hell*. To state that *Teahouse* was her first English-language role would be stretching things; except for the phrases "hot water" and "happy birthday," she speaks Japanese exclusively throughout the film. Other casting choices adhered strictly to formula: Longtime MGM contractee Louis Calhern as the pompous Col. Fisby, Eddie Albert as the enthusiastic Capt. McLean, and Harry Morgan as the laconic Sgt. Gregovich. It cannot, however, be said that the director was typecast: Delbert Mann was hardly a comedy specialist, having previously helmed such dramas as *Come Back, Little Sheba* and *I'll Cry Tomorrow*.

In keeping with the prevailing industry trend of bypassing Hollywood facilities in favor of location filming, the *Teahouse* company set up shop in Kyoto, Japan, with the eleven-acre Tobeki set constructed in the temple city of Nara. The crew arrived in April 1956, hoping to take full photographic advantage of the blooming cherry blossoms. To prepare for his role, Brando brought along his Japanese vocal coach Bob Okazaki, worked out every day to lose the weight he'd gained in Hollywood (he would eventually drop 30 pounds), and wore patches on his eyes to achieve the proper Oriental slant. In the light of latter-day criticism aimed at Brando for allegedly caricaturing the part of Sakini, it should be noted that costar Machiko Kyô was favorably impressed by the actor's transformation, as well as his on-set deportment. "Brando is like a small boy," she explained through an interpreter to a *Life* magazine correspondent. "But once he gets on the set he is all they say he is. He radiates, always joking.... He tried so hard to look like an Okinawan. When I saw him I didn't know it was Brando."

Of Glenn Ford, Kyô commented, "Ford and Brando are most different. Ford is quiet, very *yawarukai* [tender]." Nor was this the only difference between the two actors. Clashes between the stage-trained Brando and Hollywood-bred Ford commenced almost from the outset, with Brando accusing Ford of scene-stealing and Ford griping about Brando's method techniques. Director Daniel Mann grew so weary of the two actors' bickering that he finally halted them in mid-take and exclaimed, "You're not really doing a scene—you're doing a show about two actors trying to fuck each other." The other performers did their best to remain aloof from this diva behavior, and to keep the company's spirits high. Louis Calhern was in an especially festive mood, surprising in that his fourth marriage had recently broken up and he'd resumed the heavy drinking that had nearly wrecked his career. Nonetheless, everyone involved in the production was appreciative of Calhern's buoyant efforts to maintain a happy set. *Someone* had to play the role of morale-booster: In addition to the warfare between Brando and Ford, *Teahouse* was plagued by unseasonably rainy weather, which ruined many a day's location shooting.

On May 12, 1956, just days before the unit was to move to Daiei Studios in Tokyo, Louis Calhern succumbed to a fatal heart attack. This, coupled with the fact that expenses had been mounting steadily throughout the many delays on location, forced MGM to move production to their California studios, where, with the exception of an elaborate geisha dance staged at the Yamashiro Restaurant on Sycamore Avenue in Los Angeles, filming would be completed. Paul Ford, from the original Broadway cast, was hastily recruited to replace Calhern as Col. Purdy, spurring the MGM publicity department to make much of the fact that Ford was a proven audience favorite by virtue of his continuing role as Colonel Hall on the popular Phil Silvers TV series *You'll Never Get Rich*—a role he'd landed largely on the strength of his work in the stage version of *Teahouse*. Fortunately both Marlon Brando and Glenn Ford got along famously with Paul Ford, and filming resumed with a minimum of friction (beyond the ongoing feud between the two stars). The five-minute MGM short subject *Operation Teahouse* (1956), swiftly assembled to promote the upcoming feature, mentions neither Louis Calhern nor Paul Ford, focusing instead on the "scenic beauty of Japan," Brando's exhaustive preparation for his role, the construction of the Tobeki village set, and the "introduction" of Machiko Kyô (in her 29th film!) as narrator George Fenneman helpfully provides a definition of the word "geisha."

With John Patrick adapting his own play, the differences between the stage and screen versions of *Teahouse* are minimal, save for the usual bones thrown to the censors. In the crucial scene where Sakini clarifies the function of the geisha girl, the word "prostitute" is inferred but never spoken; on the other hand, Sakini is still permitted to contrast the Oriental and Occidental attitudes toward female nudity by observing, "Conclusion: Pornography is a question of geography."

Because he was still just an actor and not yet an Institution in 1956, Marlon Brando was reviewed on the merits of his performance as Sakini rather than in relation to his entire career. The tone of the criticism was mostly positive, along the lines of *Variety*'s assessment that "Brando is excellent as the interpreter, limning the roguish character perfectly." Even when chastizing the actor for being "too elaborate, too consciously cute" and playing Sakini as "less a charming rascal than a calculated clown," *The New York Times*' Bosley Crowther gave Brando points: "However, he fits the farcical pattern that Mr. [Daniel] Mann pursues." Interestingly, except for an occasional comparison to Fu Manchu or Jerry Lewis, few observers of the period felt that Brando's portrayal of an Okinawan was offensive or demeaning—and this includes reviewers in Asian countries. Only since the late 1970s have the pundits of Political Correctness weighed in, allowing such questionable social arbiters as the Medved brothers, in their infamous tome *The Golden Turkey Awards*, to label Marlon Brando's Sakini as "The Most Offensive Portrayal of an Oriental" in movie history. Brando himself would join the choir in his 1996 autobiography: "a well-written play is nearly actor-proof, but in *Teahouse* Glenn Ford and I proved how easily actors can ruin a good play or movie when they're so self-absorbed with themselves and their performances that they don't act in concert. It was a horrible picture and I was miscast."

Viewed objectively, Brando *is* a trifle precious, but he comes off a lot better than Glenn Ford, whose dithery portrayal of Captain Fisby was accurately summed up by Bosley Crowther: "Mr. Ford ... throws himself into this enjoyment with such grinning and grotesque gusto that one gets the uneasy feeling that his captain is mildly mad. He flings his arms wildly and vainly. He stammers and yelps what he has to say. And he works up such sheer intoxication that you wait for him to swoon." In fact, Ford received some of the most negative reviews of his career for this film. Audiences, however, responded enthusiastically to the "new" Glenn Ford, who continued scampering around like a summer-stock juvenile in such comedies as *The Gazebo* and *Pocketful of Miracles* for the rest of his career. Indeed, Ford's ascension to number-one male box office attraction in 1958 was at the time largely attributed to the upsurge of comedy films in his manifest.

The supporting actors may be playing clichés, but they're undeniably funny clichés; Paul Ford in particular is so good as the windbag Colonel Purdy that it is hard to imagine the more florid Louis Calhern being any better. The most charming aspect of *Teahouse* is the throughly natural, utterly captivating performance by Machiko Kyô as Lotus Blossom. During the classic scene in which she merrily chatters away in Japanese while nimbly disrobing the mortified Captain Fisby, it is well nigh impossible to reconcile *this* Machiko Kyô with the actress who so chillingly portrayed the wraithlike Lady Wakara in Kenji Mizoguchi's *Ugetsu*.

The success of *Teahouse of the August Moon* ($5,712,000 in domestic rentals on a $2 million investment) bred the inevitable imitations. Less than six months after *Teahouse*'s December 1956 national release, Universal-International had *Joe Butterfly* ready for shipping. Like *Teahouse*, *Joe Butterfly* was based on a stage play (albeit unproduced), this one written by Jack Ruge and Evan Wylie. Like *Teahouse*, *Butterfly* was filmed on location in Japan, totally rather than partially on this occasion. And like *Teahouse*, *Butterfly* was the story of a cunning Oriental chap (Japanese, not Okinawan, though *Teahouse* never truly differentiated between the two) who wraps a group of American soldiers around his little finger.

A ripoff it may have been, but *Joe Butterfly*'s cast and production credits were top-drawer. The title role, a lovably conniving black marketeer, was first offered to David Wayne, a logical choice inasmuch as the character was essentially Sakini with a better wardrobe. When Wayne proved unavailable, the role went to Burgess Meredith, who had briefly replaced Wayne as Sakini on Broadway and had headlined one of the *Teahouse* road companies. The "Captain Fisby" counterpart, a trouble-prone Army photographer named Pvt. John Woodley, was assigned to war hero-turned-Western star Audie Murphy. Jesse Hibbs, Murphy's favorite director, was assigned to the film at the same time. The script was cowritten by Marion Hargrove, of *See Here, Private Hargrove* fame (see **Chapter 9**), and Sy Gomberg, whose previous war-comedy assignment was John Ford's *When Willie Comes Marching Home* (see **Chapter 17**).

Taking place shortly after VJ Day, *Joe Butterfly* concerns five staff members of *Yank* magazine, who are among the first U.S. troops in Tokyo. Their mission is to turn out a special post-victory issue of *Yank*—and they have exactly three days to do it. Among the staffers is Pvt. Woodley, already in the doghouse for having stolen gin and olives from Colonel E.E. Fuller (Fred Clark) to make martinis, and for insulting snooty civilian magazine editor Harold Hathaway (Keenan Wynn). Unable to meet their deadline while billeted with the rest of the troops, the five GI jounalists turn to the resourceful Joe Butterfly, who arranges for the staff to set up headquarters in a palatial mansion owned by wealthy Mr. Sakiama (Tatsuo Saiko)—which of course is strictly against regulations. While straight-arrow Sgt. Ed Kennedy (George Nader) struggles to maintain discipline and decorum, Pvt. Woodley thoroughly enjoys his lavish surroundings, and especially the presence of Mr. Sakiama's lovely niece Chieko (Kieko Shima). Through the machinations of Joe Butterfly, Woodley and his buddies end up helping the devastated Japanese civilians outside the mansion find food, rebuild their homes and get back on their feet. As a bonus, Woodley, who has gone AWOL, redeems himself in the eyes of the Brass when he snaps a photo revealing the whereabouts of notorious wartime propagandist Tokyo Rose.

Joe Butterfly's heart is in the right place, but the film's unsteady blend of comedy and pathos never jells. Critics compared the film unfavorably to *Teahouse of the August Moon*, though they were kindly disposed towards Audie Murphy is his first comedy role, and particularly impressed by the actor's persuasive handling of dialogue expressing the sentiment that it was no longer possible for him to hate the former enemies of America (it will be remembered that Murphy had become the nation's most highly decorated soldier by killing some 240 German troops during World War II). Oddly, very little mention was made of Burgess Meredith's superb portrayal of the title character; evidently critics took it for granted that he'd be terrific. When Leonard Maltin brought up the subject of *Joe Butterfly* to Meredith in a 1968 interview, the actor replied that he "had great hopes for it but it didn't turn out very well; but it was a very funny character."

As it happened, neither Burgess Meredith nor the film received much exposure. Universal-International was in the late 1950s controlled by executives with a cavalier attitude toward any film that didn't have "box-office smash" written all over it, tending to withhold such properties from first-run theaters in the big cities, and dumping them on lesser regional houses and the drive-in circuit. Such was the fate not only of *Joe Butterfly*, but also such perceived "losers" as Orson Welles' *Touch of Evil* (1958).

Stretching a point, the second of the cinematic *Teahouse of the August Moon* derivations can be said to have a female counterpart to Sakini (not as much of an innovation as one might think; from time to time, Sakini *has* been played on stage by a woman). Adapted by Richard Breen from a novel by Howard Singer, *Wake Me When It's Over* (20th Century–Fox, 1960) top-bills Ernie Kovacs as Captain Charlie Stark, commanding officer of a lonely Air Force radar station on the microscopic island of Shima, just off the coast of Japan. With the war long over, Stark and his men have virtually nothing to occupy their spare time — and practically nothing *but* spare time. To keep up morale, the captain organizes bird-watching expeditions and sports events (his athletic director is somewhat incongruously played by Don Knotts), but to little avail. So bored is Stark that he's beginning to display eccentric behavior that borders on madness, prompting station physician Doc Farrington (Jack Warden) to assign nurse Nora McKay (Margo Moore) to keep close watch over the increasingly addled C.O. A rocky romance blossoms between nurse and captain, with Ernie Kovacs uncharacteristically going through his Romeo paces in a gentle, low-key manner.

The "Captain Fisby" equivalent is Gus Brubaker (Dick Shawn), a World War II veteran and civilian restauranteur. Goaded by his wife Marge (Noreen Nash) to file for his GI insurance, Brubaker is enmeshed in a bureaucratic blunder: Because he'd been inaccurately declared dead during the War, Gus has been issued two serial numbers — and when his first number is reactivated, he is recalled to duty and assigned to Shima. Begging for a transfer, Brubaker is stopped cold by Captain Stark, who laughingly informs him that he'll have to wait in line until all the other transfer requests — hundreds of 'em — are processed. Moping around the island, Gus meets a distaff Sakini in the form of the lovely Ume (Nobu McCarthy), daughter of the local mayor. Ume informs Gus that Shima rests atop a natural spring that gurgles forth health-giving waters. She subtly suggests that this spring could be of mutual benefit to both the impoverished islanders and the Air Force. Summoning his entrepreneurial knowhow, and with the enthusiastic aid of Captain Stark, Gus begins construction of a combination health spa and resort hotel using the piles of surplus materials that Stark has accumulated over the years, as well as spare parts from various planes that have crashed in the vicinity. At first hostile over the intrusion of the Americans, the natives change their minds when they consider what a financial boon a health spa would be, and soon every one of them has signed on to work for the hotel-in-progress as a bellhop, maid or construction laborer. Occasionally stopping to ask himself if all this activity is strictly according to regulations, Stark rationalizes that the Air Force has long forgotten that Shima even exists. As for Brubaker, he is provided with several opportunities to leave the service and return to his wife, but is so swept up in the project that he elects to stay.

Before long, the jerry-built resort has become the garden spot of the Sea of Japan, with servicemen traveling from miles around to enjoy its hospitality. Captain Stark no longer has a morale problem on his hands: His only problem is where to stash all the money pouring in. But things go sour after a national magazine article is published about the resort. Suspecting that Brubaker and Stark's "hotel" is nothing more than a glorified brothel and clip joint (yet another echo of *Teahouse*), a fatuous senator (Ralph Dumke) demands an investigation. The ensuing court-martial of Gus Brubaker degenerates into a media circus, with Gus managing to escape prosecution through the same bureaucratic snafu that had forced him back in uniform. The final scenes belong to Stark and Nora, patching up their often fractious relationship with promises of eternal devotion (though Kovacs can't quite suppress his "Oh, yeah?" grimace).

Going off on too many tangents at once, and hampered by the unimaginative direction of Mervyn LeRoy, *Wake Me When It's Over* is nowhere near as memorable as *Teahouse of the August Moon*. Still, it's nice to find Ernie Kovacs, so frequently cast as unsympathetic authority figures (see notes on *Operation Madball* in **Chapter 11**), playing a lovable character for a change. Besides, it's hard *not* to like a film featuring a Japanese character (played by Tommy Nishimura) who speaks fluent Yiddish.

The third and final *Teahouse of the August Moon* wannabe does not include a "Sakini" character, though several other elements are firmly in place: Glenn Ford in the lead, on-location filming in Japan (except for a few interiors and a shot of Long Beach Pier doubling for Yokohama Harbor), and a passel of pretty geisha girls. Adapted by Irving Brecher from a novel by George Campbell, the 1961 Columbia release *Cry for Happy* (its title inspired by the Japanese predilection for reversing "normal" emotions) is set in 1952, the second year of the Korean war. Glenn Ford plays Navy photographer Andy Cyphers, who with his colleagues Prince (Donald O'Connor), Suzuki (James Shigeta) and Lank (Chet Douglas) are flown to Japan for R-and-R after covering a combat mission. Lifting a page from *Joe Butterfly*, the boys buck regulations by billeting in a geisha house which they believe to be deserted. This turns out not to be the case, as four lovely geishas named Chiyoko (Miiko Taka), Haru (Miyoshi Umeki), Harakichi (Michi Kobi) and Koyuki (Tsuruko Kobayashi) suddenly flutter into view. Apparently having forgotten the lessons learned in *Teahouse*, the four Americans jump to the conclusion that the girls are merely "comfort women," only to be sorely disappointed when they realize that geishas are nothing of the sort. Meanwhile, a jocular newspaper story filed by Cyphers suggesting that the Allies are fighting in Korea for the express purpose of helping orphaned children receives widespread circulation in the States. When the Navy Department sends representatives to investigate, Cypher prevails upon the geishas to "borrow" a few neighborhood kids to pass off as orphans. You can fill in the rest by yourself: Our heroes become *real* heroes when the geisha house is transformed into a thriving orphanage—and they win the love of the four geishas in the bargain.

The most original aspect of the story finds the freewheeling photographers picking up a few extra bucks by helping a Japanese movie producer complete a home-grown western titled *The Rice Rustlers of Yokohama Gulch*. This was intended as a spoof of the cheaply produced imitation-Hollywood action films being churned out by Japan during the early 1960s, and it earns laughs on its own unsubtle level. In all fairness, however, at least *one* contemporary critic might have pointed out that Hollywood itself had recently produced a western called *The Magnificent Seven*, which happened to be a remake of the Japanese epic *The Seven Samurai*.

8. You Read the Book! You Loved the Play! Now See the Movie!

Glenn Ford (far right) returns to *Teahouse of the August Moon* territory for the derivative comedy *Cry for Happy* (Columbia, 1961). Here we see Ford surreptitiously coaching Donald O'Connor (far left) to give just the right answers to visiting civilians Harriet MacGibbon and Joe Flynn.

Trading the blushes of *Teahouse* for the leers of *Cry for Happy*, Glenn Ford delivers a capable comic performance under the direction of his frequent collaborator George Marshall. Donald O'Connor is even more effective as Ford's buddy, though the script never permits him to do anything of a musical nature (singer Bobby Darin was considered for O'Connor's role, but chose not to break his nightclub contract with his mentor George Burns). The Asian actors are uniformly fine, especially Oscar-winning Japanese actress Miyoshi Umeki and her future *Flower Drum Song* costar, the Hawaii-born James Shigeta. *Cry for Happy* is an amusing time-filler, though it still falls short of its template film *Teahouse of the August Moon*.

Getting back to the source, while *Teahouse* did not inspire a weekly TV series a la *Mister Roberts*, the John Patrick play was amply represented on the small screen via an exquisitely mounted production directed by George Schaefer for the monthly anthology *The Hallmark Hall of Fame*. Originally telecast by NBC on October 26, 1962, this color-videotaped, two-hour staging reunited the three stars from the Broadway version: David Wayne, John Forsythe and Paul Ford. Miyoshi Umeki costarred as Lotus Blossom, William LeMassena was seen as Captain McLean, and filling the supporting part of Mr. Sumata was Khigh Deigh, best known today as master criminal Wo Fat on *Hawaii Five-O*.

Finally, a musical version of *Teahouse*, adapted by John Patrick with music and lyrics by Stan Freeman and Franklin Underwood, opened December 28, 1970, at New York's Majestic Theater under the title *Lovely Ladies, Kind Gentlemen*. Starring Kenneth Nelson as Sakini, Ron Husmann as Fisby, Eleanor Calbes as Lotus Blossom and David Burns as Purdy (who won a Tony Award for his performance), this overproduced and underdeveloped effort ran a grand total of nineteen performances.

No Time for Sergeants

No Time for Sergeants is a classic example of the old adage that begins "Success has many fathers." Credit for its worldwide popularity as a novel, play and film must be evenly distributed amongst Mac Hyman, William Blackburn, John Selby, Bennett Cerf, Ira Levin, Maurice Evans, Emmett Rogers, Morton da Costa, Peter Larkin, Mervyn LeRoy ... and last but far from least, Andy Griffith.

First, Mac Hyman. Born in 1923 in the tiny Georgia village of Cordele, Hyman developed his talent for putting words together in a funny fashion while writing articles for his high school newspaper. Though reluctant to leave Cordele, he managed to pry himself away to attend both North Georgia College and Duke University in North Carolina. Called to the colors in 1943, he spent World War II as an Army Air Corps photo navigator. Returning to Duke after the war, he signed up for a creative writing course taught by William Blackburn, who became his lifelong friend and mentor. It was Blackburn who encouraged Hyman to organize his humorous recollections as a self-proclaimed "country bumpkin" in the Armed Services into a short story or two. The author began work on this project in 1947, supporting himself and his family with a progression of "Joe Jobs" and taking time off for another three-year hitch with the Air Corps. In 1952 Hyman signed up for a writing workshop at New York's Columbia University, where as a class project he put the finishing touches on his short-story collection, which by now had evolved into a novel. Earning an "A" from workshop instructor John Selby, Hyman was emboldened to submit his novel to several publishers under a variety of prospective titles.

He received nothing but turndowns until he sent the manuscript to Random House, then under the aegis of celebrated editor and humorist Bennett Cerf. Renowned as a man who enjoyed a good laugh (as proven whenever he went into a paroxysm of giggles over his own remarks as a panelist on TV's *What's My Line?*), Cerf saw potential in Hyman's novel, but felt it was more a "string of pearls" than a coherent story. Assigning his staff editors to assist Hyman in formulating a workable plotline with a "wow finish," Cerf also came up with the final title *No Time for Sergeants*, a takeoff on the S.N. Behrman stage play *No Time for Comedy*.

Written in a colloquial dialect and told in first-person singular, *Sergeants* is the story of young Will Stockdale, a hulking, beefy, incredibly naïve Georgia backwoodsman loosely patterned after Mac Hyman himself. When Will receives his draft notice, the letter is destroyed by his iron-willed father, who uses barbed wire and buckshot to scare off the local draft board. Figuring that it would be best for all concerned if he obeyed the law, Will walks the full 27 miles to the town of Callville, where he is placed in custody as a draft dodger and shipped off to basic training. Here he is mercilessly bullied by an obnoxious draftee named Irvin, but sweet-natured Will refuses to be provoked because he's been told that Irvin has had ROTC, which our hero assumes to be some sort of exotic disease. He also befriends pint-sized Ben Whitledge, who as the last in a long line of infantrymen feels grossly insulted over the prospect of joining the Air Corps. Another principal character is sarcasm-spouting Sergeant King, who at first regards Will as just another of the "bums and idiots" they always send to his barracks. Soon, however, King is taking full advantage of Will's guilelessness by keeping the boy from being classified so that he will remain the barracks' "Permanent Latrine Orderly"—a position in which Will takes chest-swelling pride.

Eventually King's C.O. finds out what the sergeant has been up to and orders him to classify Will immediately or risk losing his stripes. King conspires to have Will booted out of the service by getting the boy drunk; true mountaineer that he is, Will ends up drinking the sergeant under the table with absolutely no ill effect on himself. Inevitably, King is demoted, and Will and Ben are transferred to a faraway Air Corps base along with all the other misfits and losers. This would have been a logical final chapter, but Bennett Cerf insisted upon a funnier ending. Inspired by an episode in Mark Twain's *The Adventures of Tom Sawyer,* Hyman came up with a riotous finale in which Will and Ben, presumed to have been killed in a training flight, wander back to their base just as a memorial service is being held in their honor. To avoid a public-relations nightmare, the officers on the base go into full "CYA" mode by secretly pinning undeserved medals on both of the not-quite-dead soldiers—all of which is taken in stride by good ol' Will, who has no firmer grasp of the situation now than when we first met him.

It isn't hard to understand why *No Time for Sergeants* spent 66 weeks on the best-seller list. The humor works on two levels, both of which proved irresistible to the Postwar reading public. First, there was the satirical slant on the frustrations and foibles of the entire military system, most memorably during the lengthy sequence in which Will must undergo a series of by-rote examinations in order to be classified. Second, there was the character of Will himself: delightfully ingenuous, unassailably cheerful, eternally eager to please, and utterly incapable of seeing anything but the best qualities of his fellow human beings. Like the Good Soldier Schweik before him and Forrest Gump afterwards, Will Stockdale is a protagonist that even the most cynical ex–GI could instantly take to his heart—and surreptitiously identify with. In the words of one of the novel's biggest fans, Will Stockdale is "at least one of the most, if not *the* most Christlike character I ever met."

Those words were spoken by Andy Griffith, who at the time of the novel's first appearance in 1954 was rapidly gaining professional ground as a comic monologist, regaling sophisticated nightclub audiences with his "rube's-eye-view" commentaries on topics ranging from football to Shakespeare. Upon reading *No Time for Sergeants*, Griffith felt that the novel was prime material for a monologue about Army life, so he contacted Mac Hyman in hopes of securing permission to perform such a routine. Hyman was flattered, but informed Griffith that *Sergeants* had already been optioned as a television play by the Theater Guild's weekly anthology *The U.S. Steel Hour*. The writer chosen for the TV adaptation was 24-year-old Ira Levin, then enjoying his first brush with fame as author of the suspense novel *A Kiss Before Dying*. Like Hyman, Levin was able to bring a serviceman's perspective to the material: Though too young for World War II, he was in the process of completing a two-year hitch with the Army Signal Corps. Fortunately he was stationed in Queens, New York, enabling him to secure work as a TV writer while fulfilling his military obligations.

Though a mere comedy monologue was now out of the question, Andy Griffith still felt that the character of Will Stockdale was ideally suited to his own comic persona. On either side of his graduation from the University of North Carolina, Griffith had had some practical acting experience as Sir Walter Raleigh in Paul Green's perennial outdoor drama *The Lost Colony*. But he had never played a dramatic role on Broadway or television, so it was with no little trepidation that he auditioned for the TV version of *Sergeants*. Ira Levin was so impressed by Griffith's cold reading that he began refashioning the dialogue to conform to the young comedian's unique speech cadence. Sensing that Griffith was still more at ease as a nightclub monologist than as an actor, the producers of *The U.S. Steel Hour* broke precedent by agreeing to stage *No Time for Sergeants* before a live studio audience.

In adapting Hyman's novel as a 60-minute TV play (52 minutes minus commercials), Levin was neither forced to expand the dialogue and incidents, as Josh Logan had done with *Mister Roberts*, nor invent comic highlights, as John Patrick had done with *Teahouse of the August Moon*. The dialogue and action was already fully and firmly in place in the novel; so were all the comedy setpieces, each one a self-contained gem. And with Will Stockdale already established as the "voice" of the novel, Levin had the added advantage of a built-in narrator who could deliver the expositional information that the playright had been forced to telescope or remove to accommodate the hour-long format. The use of a narrator in this capacity was an accepted television technique, carried over from radio. Audiences of the era felt no more disorientation when Andy Griffith broke the "fourth wall" to directly address the camera than when Paul Newman did likewise in *The U.S. Steel Hour*'s 1956 TV adaptation of Mark Harris' novel *Bang the Drum Slowly*. In both cases, the deployment of a narrator also eliminated the necessity of building complete standing sets that would have been cumbersome to move or disassemble for scene changes. Audiences willing to suspend disbelief and accept a character who periodically interrupted the action to speak to them directly were equally willing to accept unrealistic, fragmentary stage settings.

Levin placed special emphasis on the sequences in the novel that were proven audience favorites: The first meetings with the overzealous Ben Whitledge and the long-suffering Sergeant King; a fistfight in the barracks, which Will regards as nothing more than good clean fun with a bunch of likeable guys; Will's encounter with an Army psychiatrist, whose efforts to goad the boy into revealing his hidden neuroses succeed only in driving the shrink himself to the edge of insanity; and King's foredoomed efforts to get Will kicked out of the service by plying him with liquor. The TV version ends with King's demotion and Will and Ben's transfer, several chapters short of the novel's denouement. Ira Levin evidently agreed with the critical consensus that the original ending, involving Will's supposed demise and the attendant embarrassment when he shows up very much alive, was the weakest and most contrived part of the story. And besides, Levin had had so much fun adapting the earlier chapters that he'd plumb run out of time to tackle the rest of the book.

A few adjustments had to be made with the source material to pacify the ABC Standards and Practices Division. In the novel, Will does such a fabulous job cleaning the barracks latrine (which he doesn't realize is actually punishment duty) that Sgt. King decides to keep him in this position, with the admonition that Will is never, ever to tell anyone — particularly an officer — that he has been appointed Permanent Latrine Orderly. Unfortunately for King, Will chooses to stage a spectacular demonstration of his efficiency when the C.O. shows up for inspection, wiring all the toilet seats to pop up simultaneously. Inasmuch as American Network Television had not yet acknowledged the existence of toilets in 1955 (except in Ajax cleanser commercials), this marvelous sight gag would have to be modified for *The U.S. Steel Hour*. Accordingly, Will arranges a reception for the Captain consisting of loud music, unfurling flags and a ton of confetti. It still gets a huge laugh from the studio audience, but imagine the reaction had the original punch line been retained.

To discuss another example of Levin's pre-emptive censorship, we must tread carefully. It is established early in the novel that Will, a white man, is quite fond of the African Americans he has met in the course of his life — though as a mid-20th-century Georgian, he has some peculiar notions as to how black people should talk and behave. Will also has no qualms about using the "N" word on occasion. He uses it without malice or hostility; it is simply the way he has been raised to talk, just as Huckleberry Finn uses the offending word as a common noun rather than a pejorative.

Halfway through the novel, Will meets a black Army officer, who speaks to him curtly and authoritatively. Will is both astonished and impressed: Not only has no black man ever spoken to him this way, but he has never heard a black man use such "white" words. When he tells Ben that he'd like to get to know this black officer better, Will innocently drops the "N" bomb. Outraged, Ben ripostes that an officer is an officer. He is neither a black man nor a white man. He's an officer, and Will should take notice of nothing other than the rank and the uniform. All this is prologue to the moment in which Sgt. King and a few other non-coms make a reference to the same black officer, whereupon Will insists that all he sees is the officer, not his color. Nervously, King digests the "evidence." Will is obviously color-blind, meaning he will fail his physical and not be classified — and if he isn't classified, King will lose his stripes.

Well, try to get *that* scene past a TV censor in 1955. Even if the "N" word was removed — which of course it would have to be — surely some bigoted yahoo would write an angry letter to U.S. Steel (assuming he could write), complaining that the company had profaned the network by allowing a white man to emerge from a "confrontation" with a black man looking like an idiot. Ira Levin's solution was disarmingly simple: he changed the officer from a black male to a white *female*. In the TV play, Will's dumbfounded reaction arises not from racial but from sexual stereotyping: No mere woman has ever spoken to him so harshly and mannishly. The ensuing lines were altered so that Ben could admonish Will for taking notice of the officer's gender: An officer is an officer, not a man, not a woman, etc. Thus, the new payoff to the scene finds Sgt. King in mortal fear that Will Stockdale is not merely color-blind, but *totally* blind. In retrospect, this isn't half as funny as Mac Hyman's punch line, but it still works well in performance.

Though Levin uses the combined "voice" of Mac Hyman and Andy Griffith in his adaptation, in one respect he adds a personal touch. Reflecting Hyman's experiences, the novel is implicitly set during World War II; accordingly, Sgt. King is a typically venomous World War II non-com. Will misinterprets King's sarcasm as kindness and courtesy, but the reader understands that there is nothing remotely likable about the sharp-tongued sergeant. Outside of his obsessive affection for his shiny new car (an element removed entirely from Levin's dramatization), King can barely be regarded as a human being, and as such he gets exactly what he deserves when he loses his stripes—which, in the novel, happens twice.

Unlike Mac Hyman, Ira Levin was a product of the peacetime military, so his attitude toward sergeants was slightly different. Levin's version of Sgt. King is grouchy and combustible, but not unsympathetic. A career soldier, King regards his barracks as own private little world. Serene and secure, he bothers no one and no one bothers him. As long as his superior officers are happy, he is happy, and he's not about to risk rocking the boat—to say nothing of losing his pension—by allowing Will Stockdale to louse things up. Though this new dimension of Sgt. King's personality is underdeveloped in the TV play, the audience is "with" the character all the way, feeling his pain when, at the end of the story, he is demoted to private—and worse, is shipped off to the same training camp with his numbskull nemesis Will.

Directed by Alex Segal, who won an Emmy Award for his labors, *No Time for Sergeants* originally aired live on March 15, 1955. Happily, a kinescope exists of this production, allowing future generations to bear witness to the birth of a major star in the role of Will Stockale: As noted by *Time* magazine, "Andy Griffith was convincing as the Georgia rookie with two left feet and an unconquerable spirit." The ease and confidence with which Griffith periodically interrupts the flow of the plotline to make a reflective observation to the audience—almost as if he exists in both the "Now" and "Then" simultaneously—belies the fact that the actor was admittedly terrified at the prospect of carrying an hour-long TV play by himself.

Comic foil Eddie LeRoy, best known for his appearances as the bespectacled Blinky in the final four *Bowery Boys* pictures, plays the role of Ben Whitledge to the hilt, and then some. Harry Clark, a Broadway regular who as a musical-comedy gangster in Cole Porter's *Kiss Me Kate* introduced the spicy specialty number "Brush Up Your Shakespeare," is blunt but effective as Sgt. King. Among the supporting players are TV favorites Bob Hastings as a non-com named Lucky, and Robert Emhardt as the harried Army psychiatrist.

Among the millions of viewers impressed by the TV play in general and Andy Griffith in particular was Maurice Evans, who with his producing partner Emmett Rogers had purchased the theatrical rights to *No Time for Sergeants*. Evans was so bowled over by Ira Levin's adaptation that he engaged the writer's services for the theatrical version, dropping his announced plan to hire *Stalag 17* co-authors Edmund Trzcinski and Donald Bevan. Though Levin jumped at the opportunity, Evans had to use all the persuasive powers at his command to persuade the reticent Griffith to sign a long-term contract.

In the tradition of both the Mac Hyman novel and his own previous staging of *Teahouse of the August Moon*, Evans opted to use an onstage narrator to bind the episodic storyline together. Ira Levin developed the framing device of a Georgia town-hall meeting, where Will Stockdale endeavors to explain to his friends and neighbors how he earned a medal of valor. The rest of the play unfolds in flashback, retaining the TV version's Brechtian device of having Will occasionally come "out" of the story to comment on the action (Levin's skill at capturing Andy Griffith's distinctive speech patterns, right down to the performer's emphasizing a point by exclaiming "It *did*!," is nothing short of brilliant).

All of the comic vignettes that had scored in the TV production were transferred to the stage play, with the psychiatrist scene a singular highlight (it was given a two-page spread, with photos and quotes, in *Life* magazine). Taking advantage of Broadway's looser censorial strictures, Levin restored the scene in which Will rigs all the toilet seats to "salute" his C.O., and also Will's nonplussed reaction to being ordered around by a black officer (whom he now characterizes as "colored"). In expanding the play to two acts, Levin packed all the action from his TV script into Act One, then used the climactic chapters from the Hyman novel for the incidents in Act Two. As in the novel, the climax is the least effective portion of the play, though Levin enlivens things with a surfeit of slapstick and the introduction of several new characters, including a pair of monumentally incompetent Air Force pilots and a flock of flustered lieutenants, captains, colonels and generals.

Likewise expanded was the role of Sgt. King, with Levin masterfully fleshing out the character's "don't make waves" philosophy and his smoldering desperation when waves are made. In an early scene, the scabrous Irvin (he's the one suffering from ROTC, remember?) insists upon bringing Will's "draft dodger" status to the attention of the C.O. The complacent King halts Irvin in his tracks by comparing Army life to "a big lake, nice and calm; I'm in one canoe, you're in another ... but for your information, you got the smallest canoe in the whole damn lake." King's ultimate downfall thanks to the well-meaning ineptitude of Will Stockdale has all the ironic inevitably of a Laurel & Hardy comedy — and is just as hilarious.

To properly coordinate the many scene changes and multitude of characters, Maurice Evans hired 31-year-old director Morton Da Costa, direct from the Broadway musical *Plain and Fancy*. Having made his New York acting debut in Thornton Wilder's similarly rambling *The Skin of Our Teeth* (1942), Da Costa was well schooled in the art of bringing control and comprehensibility to what otherwise might have been a chaotic theatrical experience. He would go on to helm such equally extravagant Broadway productions as *Auntie Mame* and *The Music Man,* both of which he later transferred to film. Working hand in glove with Da Costa in moving *Sergeants* along with speed and dexterity was scenic designer Peter Larkin, who did his job so well that many observers never realized that the play had only two "complete" sets; all the rest were miracles of illusion, conveyance, and forced perspective. In his *Billboard* magazine review of *Sergeants*, Bob Francis enthused over "some of the most extraordinary scenic effects by Peter Larkin to be seen on a Stern platform in a long, long time." Larkin's crowning glory was the Second Act sequence in which Will and Ben parachute from a disabled airplane — an episode that appears nowhere in the novel (in which the two recruits never even leave the ground), but was purely the invention of Ira Levin.

Other than Andy Griffith, none of the actors from the TV version was carried over for the stage production. In the interests of cast insurance, the producers called upon two supporting players who in 1955 enjoyed far wider name recognition than the play's leading man. British-born Roddy McDowall, a film star since childhood and a theatrical favorite since his Broadway bow in the 1953 revival of Shaw's *Misalliance*, was signed to play Ben Whitledge. Myron McCormick, who, along with Henry Fonda and Joshua Logan, was one of the mainstays of the Princeton University Players in the early 1930s, and who in 1949 had scored a personal triumph as Luther Billis in the Josh Logan-directed musical *South Pacific*, was tapped to play Sgt. King. Other familiar faces in the cast included the versatile Robert Webber as Irvin, longtime Hollywood character player Howard Freeman as General Bush, and 78-year-old Floyd Buckley, at that time Broadway's oldest working actor, as Pa Stockdale. Several other players used *Sergeants* as a springboard for their own lengthy TV and Hollywood careers, most notably James Milhollin, a latter-day Franklin Pangborn type, as the officious Army psychiatrist. Young Earle Hyman, best known to sitcom addicts of the 1980s as Cliff Huxtable's father on *The Cosby Show*, was also seen in the small but key role of the African American officer. (When Roddy McDowall and Earle Hyman left the play, they were replaced respectively by Arte Johnson and Ossie Davis.)

Another up-and-coming actor was cast in two roles, first as the Georgia preacher who introduces Will Stockdale in the opening town-hall scene, then more conspicuously as a squeaky-voiced classification corporal who is driven to hysteria while testing Will's hand-eye coordination. These roles were filled by 31-year-old West Virginia native Don Knotts, who like Andy Griffith was just starting to make inroads as a nightclub comedian. Knotts' brief but unforgettable turn in *Sergeants* not only landed him a four-year stint as a regular on Steve Allen's NBC TV variety show, but also gained him a lifelong friend in Andy Griffith, who in 1960 recommended Knotts for his signature role as deputy Barney Fife on *The Andy Griffith Show*.

Opening October 20, 1955, at the Alvin Theatre, *No Time for Sergeants* was an instant hit with playgoers but a qualified one with critics. The gentlemen of the press could not deny that they were amused, but even their most positive words were tinged with condescension. *Sergeants*, you see, was not a "significant" play like *Mister Roberts*, which blended high comedy with heavy drama, or *Teahouse of the August Moon*, an acknowledged mandate for racial tolerance. *Sergeants* was designed purely to tickle the funnybone for two-and-a-half hours and send the audience home happy and satiated: No message, no moral, just a plain old-fashioned "laff riot." Jack Gaver of United Press International set the tone for most of the critics: "A strong case could be made that *Sergeants* isn't a very good play by the usual standards—or that it isn't a play at all. But is certainly is a funny, funny show." In somewhat the same vein, though more indulgent, were the words of *Billboard*'s Bob Francis: "So who cares whether or not it's a play, when [Andy] Griffith can wind up an uproarious evening with practically everybody on stage riddled with harpoons, except himself." Samuel French, publishers of the acting edition of *Sergeants*, wisely chose to bypass the more patronizing critiques by quoting the New York *Post*: "Take a simple and lovable innocent, guileless, gullible and without malice, and place him in juxtaposition to the pompous earnestness of military discipline and bureaucracy, and you have the springboard for mockery that can be both devastating and heartwarming ... its gift for uproarious lampooning is matched only by its genial good nature." Perhaps the most objective and insightful observer was theatrical archivist John Gassner. Writing in 1957, just as *Sergeants* was wrapping up its 796-performance Broadway run, Gassner praised the play for its "almost fairy tale quality of unreality," comparing the piece to a classic "tall tale" in the tradition of Paul Bunyan.

Andy Griffith emerged from *Sergeants* an even bigger star than before, though curiously the play failed to perform the same magic for the competent but obscure actors who replaced him after his contract had run out (Barry Nelson, already an established name, headed the 1956 London production). Once the Hollywood bidding wars were over, Warner Bros. emerged with the film rights to *Sergeants*—and given that Warners regularly offered their filmed stage plays to major motion picture stars (remember how Cary Grant, and not Robert Preston, was first choice for the 1962 adaptation of *The Music Man?*), the studio broke its own tradition by going directly to Andy Griffith, who had never before appeared in a movie. But Griffith was forced to demur, at least temporarily. Director Elia Kazan had already secured the actor's services to play the beguilingly sinister country singer Lonesome Rhodes in his upcoming Budd Schulberg-scripted drama *A Face in the Crowd*, also slated for a Warner Bros. release. Though *Face in the Crowd* is today acknowledged as a masterpiece, the film tanked at the box office in 1957, and Griffith worried that its poor reception would hurt his chances to star in Warners' filmization of *Sergeants*. Happily, both studio head Jack L. Warner and director Mervyn LeRoy were still firmly in Andy's corner.

In addition to Griffith, Myron McCormick repeated his stage role as the choleric Sgt. King, as did James Milhollin as the prissy psychiatrist and—blessedly—Don Knotts as the hypertense classification corporal. The rest of the casting was along standard Hollywood lines, though each actor was ideally suited to his role: A very young Nick Adams as Ben Whitledge; all-purpose screen menace Murray Hamilton as Irvin; Raymond Bailey, future Mr. Drysdale on *The Beverly Hillbillies*, as the Base Colonel; jowly Howard Smith as Maj. Gen. Bush; Sydney Smith (no relation) as Maj. Gen. Pollard, who unexpectedly provides the film's terrific closing gag; and William Fawcett, a grizzled character actor who seemed to have been born at the age of 65, as Pa Stockdale. Uncredited as a bumbling Air Force pilot is an angular young character player named Jameel Farah, who in later years did rather better for himself under his professional name Jamie Farr. Another unbilled performer was the film's technical advisor, Air Force Master Sergeant Albert Williams, who with great reluctance accepted a small role as a corporal (maybe it was the loss in rank that bugged him).

Of the three stage adaptations referenced in this chapter, the film version of *No Time for Sergeants* bears the closest resemblance to its theatrical original. This can be attributed to film director Mervyn LeRoy's decision to emulate stage director Morton Da Costa's original approach to the material, in the same manner that LeRoy slavishly copied John Ford's established style in *Mister Roberts*. In general, LeRoy's derivative technique is effective, though at times the actors seem to be leaning heavily upon their "stage voices," shouting and overenunciating for the benefit of the folks in the cheap seats. (Years later, Andy Griffith expressed the feeling that the film was a bit too overacted.) In contrast with the ego clashes and backstage bickering which plagued *Roberts* and *Teahouse of the August Moon*, LeRoy maintained a happy set on *Sergeants*, so much so that Jack L. Warner frequently dropped in while shooting was in progress, spoiling several takes by dissolving into loud laughter (though knowing J.L. as we do, it is just as likely that the studio boss was chortling over one of his own abysmal puns).

The screenplay was by John Lee Mahin, who'd just finished collaborating with Mervyn LeRoy on the movie version of another Broadway hit, *The Bad Seed*. Mahin sagaciously left the best of both Mac Hyman and Ira Levin intact, with a few emendations and alterations. The town-hall

As Ben Whitledge (Nick Adams, right) looks on, Will Stockdale (Andy Griffith) demonstrates the intricate wiring necessary for the infamous "toilet salute" in *No Time for Sergeants* (Warners, 1958).

framing device was no longer necessary and thus jettisoned, though Will Stockdale's narration is still occasionally heard on the soundtrack, and on two occasions Will addresses the audience directly as he had on stage (a device that doesn't entirely work on film). The final sequence involving the crippled airplane is effectively expanded and made more "cinematic," including one priceless sight gag in which the pilots, thinking they're approaching an illuminated landing strip, accidentally buzz a drive-in movie. And since the Production Code was still in effect, all "damns," "hells" and "bastards" are dutifully excised. Finally, Mahin was obliged to make one important concession to prevailing racial sensitivities, just as Ira Levin had on television: Will's encounter with the black male officer was once more rewritten to accommodate a white female. This diluted episode actually plays better in the movie, thanks to the casting of a sexy, shapely young woman (Jean Willes) as the WAF Captain rather than the starchy matron (Adnia Rice) of the TV version.

Filmed in black & white to keep the budget under control, *No Time for Sergeants* accumulated $7,500,000 in domestic rentals upon its release in 1958. Warner Bros. responded to this windfall by rushing Andy Griffith into another service film, also based on a recent novel. Written by Weldon Hill (a pseudonym for William R. Scott), *Onionhead* is a semi-autobiographical paean to the U.S. Coast Guard. Protagonist Al Woods is an aimless, antagonistic young Oklahoman who a few months before Pearl Harbor joins the Coast Guard, thinking it will be an easy hitch. He quickly learns otherwise when he's assigned to the galley of the U.S.S. *Periwinkle*, under the baleful eye of hard-drinking ship's cook "Red" Wildoe. Though he remains basically unsympathetic from first page to last, Al eventually comes to appreciate the value of self-discipline and devotion to duty, especially after America enters the war.

Straining to recapture the appeal of *No Time for Sergeants*, Warner Bros. promoted the 1958 film version of *Onionhead* (directed by Norman Taurog) as if it was a rollicking farce, emphasizing Al Woods' disastrous attempt to prepare a breakfast of cinnamon rolls for his shipmates, the attenuated drunk scene between Andy Griffith as Al and Walter Matthau as Red Wildoe, and an episode in which Al, worried that he's going bald, submits to an experimental scalp treatment requiring him to shave every hair from his head (hence the film's title). Also heavily publicized was the presence in the cast of comedian Joey Bishop, playing a gob whose reputation as a womanizer is so tarnished that girls slap him in the face before he even says "Hello." But *Onionhead* is anything but humorous for most of its running time, wallowing in such unsavory elements as a sleazy ensign (Ray Danton) who skimps on the *Periwinkle*'s food budget in order to fatten his own wallet, and the extamarital canoodling between Al Woods and Red Wildoe's sluttish wife Stella (Felicia Farr). Anticipating a continuation of the hilarity in *No Time for Sergeants*, audience were sorely disappointed by the paucity of laughs in *Onionhead*. So miserably did the film perform at the box office that Andy Griffith was forced to abandon any aspirations of movie stardom; not until the debut of *The Andy Griffith Show* two years later did the performer truly regain the ground lost with *Onionhead*.

Minus Andy Griffith, *No Time for Sergeants* spawned a half-hour TV situation comedy, produced by George Burns for Warner Bros. and unveiled by ABC on September 14, 1964. For his Will Stockdale, Burns selected another North Carolina boy named Sammy Jackson, who coincidentally had played a bit role in the film version of *Sergeants*. (Former *Sugarfoot* star Will Hutchins, who had essayed a larger role in the 1958 film, was briefly considered for the TV series.) Harry Hickox, best known to moviegoers as anvil salesman Charlie Cowell in the 1962 filmization of *The Music Man*, was cast as Sgt. King. Virtually all of the charm and wit of the original novel, play and film were syphoned out of the TV series in favor of stale sitcomery: Will was saddled with a funny bloodhound named Blue, a buoyant girlfriend named Millie Anderson (Laurie Sibbald), and Millie's cantankerous grandfather, so obviously conceived as a clone of the Walter Brennan character in the popular series *The Real McCoys* that he was played by former *McCoys* costar Andy Clyde. Though a few of the episode plotlines had merit, notably one in which Will and an Air Force buddy are hypnotized and conditioned to respond to "trigger words" à la *The Manchurian*

Candidate, in sum total the TV *No Time for Sergeants* was as disposable as George Burns' other series for the 1964–65 season, *Wendy and Me*. Even if it had been better, the series was laboring under two additional disadvantages: The debut that same year of the thematically similar, and infinitely funnier, CBS comedy weekly *Gomer Pyle USMC*; and the decision by ABC to schedule *Sergeants* on Monday evening at 8:30 P.M.—smack dab opposite *The Andy Griffith Show*.

Mac Hyman, the man who started at all, had nothing to say on the occasion of ABC's *No Time for Sergeants*, for the simple reason that he was no longer among the living. Though financially well off thanks to royalties and residuals from *Sergeants*, Hyman wrote very little thereafter, and never published another novel in his lifetime. He died of a heart attack in 1963, one month before his 40th birthday. After his death, his friend and mentor William Blackburn oversaw the publication of Hyman's second novel *Take Now Thy Son*, as well as a collection of the author's letters titled *Love, Boy*.

I would love to have given this chapter a funnier ending, but the Fates were against me. The reader is strongly recommended to expunge the melancholy by renting DVD copies of *Mister Roberts*, *The Teahouse of the August Moon* and *No Time for Sergeants* for a weekend military-comedy marathon.

9

It's Still the Same Old Story ... Sort Of
See Here, Private Hargrove *and* Biloxi Blues

Marching off to World War II as either a draftee or an enlistee was for many American males the most overwhelming shared experience of the 20th Century. While there were quite a few men who returned from the war disinclined to discuss the experience with their friends and loved ones, there was a far larger number of ex-warriors who'd expound upon their participation in "The Big One" at the drop of a hat, frequently supplying their own hats. So many novels and memoirs were published by servicemen during and after World War II that cartoonist Mischa Richter knew he could raise a hearty laugh with his 1945 *Collier*'s magazine panel in which a bookstore clerk proudly proffers a hot-off-the-press volume and says to a customer: "Now here's something new and startling. It's a book written by a professional writer."

For the purposes of this chapter, we'll ignore the myriad of publications from novice or one-time-only writers and focus on two World War II-based pieces that were penned by professionals. Both of these works were humorous in nature; both were intensely autobiographical; both dealt with the author's Army experiences, focusing on induction-and-training process prior to being shipped overseas; and both were ultimately made into popular films. The essential difference between Marion Hargrove's *See Here, Private Hargrove* and Neil Simon's *Biloxi Blues* is one of perspective: The first title was written while World War II was still in progress; the second was written four decades after the fact.

Born in Mount Olive, North Carolina, in 1919, Edward Thomas Marion Lawton Hargrove Jr. was a professional journalist by the age of 21, working in various editorial capacities—from the "women's page" to the obituary column—at the *Charlotte News*. Though supremely confident of his writing skills, Marion Hargrove was by all accounts (including his own) less comfortable with what we now term "people skills." As a teenager, he'd lost out on getting a high-school diploma because of his uncompromising refusal to take a geometry exam; and around the newspaper office he was the butt of his colleague's jokes because of his flippant attitude and terminal clumsiness. Drafted into the Army in July of 1941, Hargrove didn't fare much better as a soldier than as a civilian. Within a few weeks of his arrival at Fort Bragg, he was voted "worst selectee" by his fellow soldiers, an honor in which he took perverse pride.

During those rare moments when he wasn't pulling KP duty, Hargrove (who somehow made it to the rank of sergeant before war's end) translated his training-camp travails into a series of humorous articles for the *Charlotte News* and for the military publication *Yank*, where his editor was Hartzell Spence, author of the popular autobiographical novel *One Foot in Heaven*. Soon afterward, the young selectee became a protegé of author/poet Maxwell Anderson, whose own works included the World War I play *What Price Glory?* (see **Chapter 7**). While visiting Fort Bragg,

Anderson read a collection of Hargrove's articles and sent them to editor Bill Sloane of Henry Holt & Company, suggesting that they might be organized into a book. "You know," Sloane replied, "this stuff is almost a book as it is." Published in 1942 under the title *See Here, Private Hargrove*, the baby-faced author's reminiscences became a runaway best-seller to the tune of over 400,000 hardcover editions and 2.2 million paperback copies. There were many explanations as to why Hargrove's novel struck such a responsive chord while other wartime memoirs from more experienced authors gathered dust on the shelves. Lewis Gannett of the *New York Times* opined: "Civilian America, tired of reading what other people's sons were doing on other continents, took to its heart Private Hargrove's unassuming stories of what American boys were doing in American training camps." *Life* magazine further stated that Hargrove's novel "owed its special charm to the fact that it treated Army life in a way that civilians could comprehend. The story ... was successful largely because it scrupulously avoided 'inside' GI humor and lingo. Hargrove, after all, was a stranger there himself."

Hargrove set the tone of his novel — and simultaneously made certain that the Office of War Information would approve its publication — at the end of Chapter One: "Watch your attitude, do your work, respect your superiors, try to get along with your fellow soldiers, keep yourself and your equipment clean at all times, and behave yourself. Do these and you won't have any trouble with the Army.

"For what happens when you don't do them, let us now look into the case of Private Hargrove, U.S.A."

Much of the novel's comedy is grounded in frustration, a subject on which Hargrove could rise to great metaphoric heights, as when he describes the task of cleaning dirt from an Army oven: "Like the magic pitcher in the old Greek legend, the more you take out the more there is inside." Hargrove also possesses a remarkable gift for conveying the loneliness of barracks life, and the uncertainty of what lay ahead of the average GI once he was shipped overseas, without losing his sense of humor or resorting to bathos. There is even a note of optimism in the final pages, when Hargrove and his fellow draftees, apprised of the attack on Pearl Harbor, come to the sobering realization that all their grunt work has been absolutely necessary.

Establishing himself as an incurable wiseguy, given to clicking his heels European-style when saluting his superiors, Hargrove invests his novel with a gently mocking tone. His characters converse in a Damon Runyon cadence, couching their anger with strained *politesse* (upset that Hargrove has been placed on KP thrice in a single week, a sergeant moans "Oh, I get so discouraged sometimes") and faux intellectualism. (Fagged out after a long drilling session, Hargrove mutters, "It has been, withal, a very busy day.") Though a few curse words make their way into the text, Hargrove prefers such colorful euphemisms as "Great gods and little paychecks!" And whenever he veers too close to preciousness, Hargrove pulls back by admitting that he *can* be precious: Preparing to relate an oft-told barracks anecdote, he warns us with the three-word preface "Have a chestnut." Readers came away from *See Here, Private Hargrove* feeling confident about the war's outcome, certain that if every GI was possessed of the same wry sense of humor as Marion Hargrove, the dark and humorless forces of the Axis didn't stand a chance. The book also reassured new selectees that while training camp may at times seem all "brutality and sadism," in the long run it was worth the pain and degradation — and that even a congenital foul-up like Marion Hargrove could be molded into a semblance of a good soldier.

He could also become a rich soldier overnight. In 1944 MGM paid Hargrove $100,000 for the movie rights to his novel, and also for permission to use his characters in a possible sequel. Comedy-construction specialist Harry Kurnitz was assigned the task of bringing coherence to the novel's loose gathering of anecdotes. In an interview with Douglas Heil, Hargrove had nothing but praise for Kurnitz's craftsmanship: "I thought the movie was brilliant. Harry Kurnitz did a wonderful job with the adaptation, spinning a series of disparate episodes into dramatic form." Wesley Ruggles, brother of comic actor Charlie Ruggles and past collaborator with such laughgetters as Mae West, Carole Lombard and Burns & Allen, was tapped as director; it would be Ruggles' last American film, with only the British musical *London Town* ahead of him before retirement.

A comparative newcomer was chosen to play the title role: 25-year-old Robert Walker, who'd recently made a vivid impression as a doomed soldier in MGM's *Bataan*. Walker's All-American-Boy vulnerability was a perfect fit for the apple-cheeked Marion Hargrove, the actor's ingenuous line delivery removing the sting and retaining the charm of Hargrove's youthful arrogance. Ironically, Walker had originally balked at playing Hargrove, worried that he'd become typecast as a typical American GI. Forced to exude cheerfulness before the cameras day after day, Walker grew increasingly sullen off-screen, eventually (and ominously) taking solace in liquor.

The movie version of *See Here, Private Hargrove* begins with a few minutes' worth of establishing material showing the civilian Hargrove wreaking havoc in a small-town newspaper office; when he receives his draft notice, no one is happier than Hargrove's flustered editor (Ray Collins). En route to Fort Bragg for training, Hargrove befriends small-time sharpster Tom Mulvehill (Keenan Wynn), gravel-voiced Brooklynite Bill Burk (William "Bill" Phillips) and countrified Orrin Esty (George Offerman Jr.), with Mulvehill becoming his closest pal. In the book there *is* a Pvt. Mulvehill, whom Hargrove's sergeant lovingly describes as "Your dear friend, the bum," but he is a minor character compared with the author's actual best friend, symphony-loving Sgt. Maury Sher — who didn't make the cut in the screenplay. The many irascible sergeants who express frustration over Hargrove's incompetence in the book are amalgamated onscreen into the fictional

See Here, Private Hargrove (MGM, 1944): Definitely not as dumb or naïve as he looks, Marion Hargrove (Robert Walker Sr.) spends a little quality time with sweetie Carol Holliday (Donna Reed).

Sgt. Cramp, superbly enacted by Chill Wills. It is Cramp who is given one of the book's most famous and most profane vignettes, albeit cleaned up for mass consumption. While administering the Oath of Allegiance to a rowdy bunch of selectees, an unflappable officer (Louis-Jean Heydt) politely endeavors to calm the group down with the soft-spoken admonition "Gentlemen, please." Once the Oath is taken, the officer quietly concludes with "You are now members of the Army of the United States"—at which point Sgt. Cramp bellows, "Now SHUT UP!"

Hargrove's near-perpetual KP duty becomes a running gag in the film, with Marion forced to clean and polish garbage cans after each and every infraction—and not even getting *this* duty right. In a fit of poetic license, screenwriter Kurnitz gives Hargrove a girlfriend named Carol Holliday, played by Donna Reed. The romance is deftly dovetailed into the main plotline involving Hargrove's efforts to sell his novel of Army life, when while making the rounds of publishers in New York he pays Carol a visit. This allows supporting player Robert Benchley to feast upon his tiny role as Carol's father, a World War I veteran who while feigning interest in Hargrove's military experiences insists upon boring the youngster with windy reminiscences of his own adventures in uniform.

The I-Want-To-Be-An-Author throughline provides third-billed Keenan Wynn an opportunity to shine (to the extent of nearly taking over the picture!), as the enterprising Mulvehill forms himself, Hargrove, Burk and Esty into a corporation, dedicated to promoting Marion's literary efforts and sharing the royalties. Kurnitz also adroitly uses this conceit to help him tie all the loose plot ends into a pretty bow. Having arranged for himself and Hargrove to avoid combat duty by joining the Army's public relations unit, Mulvehill alienates both Burk and Esty, who disgustedly drop out of the corporation. Their consciences gnawing at them as they sit safely behind stateside typewriters, Hargrove and Mulvehill finally decide to lobby for an overseas assignment, but are told it's too late for such a move. At this juncture, we are reintroduced to General Dillon (Edward Fielding), with whom Hargrove had had a comic run-in during that earlier trip to New York (the private had accidentally gotten hold of Dillon's coat and was nearly pinched for impersonating an officer). The boys plead their case to the general, who arranges for their transfer overseas and sets the stage for what was considered a happy ending in 1944. This frantically funny closing sequence was an eleventh-hour replacement for the film's original serious ending, which emulated the closing chapter of the book wherein all fun-and-games suddenly cease when Hargrove hears of the Pearl Harbor attack. After the first ending tested badly with preview audiences, MGM instructed Kurnitz to concoct a more upbeat coda. With Wesley Ruggles already in England hard at work on *London Town*, Tay Garnett took over direction of the new finale.

Though it moves at a far more rapid pace than most MGM films of its vintage, and despite a topnotch cast and a consistently hilarious screenplay, *See Here, Private Hargrove* has not aged too well, and not only because of the utterly pointless 40s-style musical number "In My Arms," written by Frank Loesser and sung by Bob Crosby. With the welcome exception of the vitriolic Sgt. Cramp, the military characters seem too courteous, well-spoken and vice-free to be entirely believable, while the barracks and training grounds are so scrupulously spic-and-span that the film might as well be set in a hospital. Critic James Agee was among the few in 1944 who were put off by the film's MGM-ized artifice: "It is callow, puppyish, whimsically amusing—to those who can easily swallow that contradiction—and uninteresting in telling the truth even about training.... There is something unpleasantly cuddly about it—a sort of cross between *Stalky* [a Victorian novel about boarding-school life] and the pansy-truck-driver sort of *New Yorker* humor." But Agee was in the minority: Most reviewers and audiences loved *See Here, Private Hargrove*— and like the book before it, the film was warmly embraced even by genuine GIs who "knew the score."

Released by MGM in November 1945, *What Next, Corporal Hargrove?* suffered the fate of most sequels in being neither as good nor as fresh as the original. Beyond the use of his name,

Marion Hargrove had nothing to do with the sequel; it was entirely the work of Harry Kurnitz, who received an Oscar nomination for "best story." Which beggars the question, "*What* story?" since there are several plotlines in play, none of them as well developed or unified as in *See Here, Private Hargrove*. Too, the direction by Richard Thorpe has little of the enthusiasm and gusto exhibited by the earlier film's Wesley Ruggles and Tay Garnett; though *What, Next Corporal Hargrove?* is five minutes shorter than its predecessor, it seems ten minutes longer.

Robert Walker and Keenan Wynn respectively return as Marion Hargrove and Tom Mulvehill, who by now have evolved into a comedy team, with Wynn upstaging his costar to an even greater degree than in the first picture. Also back for more are Chill Wills as ill-tempered Sgt. Cramp and William "Bill" Phillips as roughhewn Pvt. Burk, the latter making up for his reduced screen time with a fitfully funny running gag involving his efforts to speak French. Echoes from the original *Hargrove* film are sparse, but they're there if you dig for them. The hero makes repeated references to his girlfriend Carol (who never appears, Donna Reed being otherwise occupied in bigger-budgeted films like *The Picture of Dorian Gray* and *They Were Expendable*) and a fleeting reference to the royalties accrued from his writing career. Hargrove continues to be assigned punishment duty on a regular basis, with the added humiliation of repeatedly being promoted to corporal only to be demoted a few days (and sometimes a few hours) later. And the sequel opens and closes with vestiges of one of *See Here, Private Hargrove*'s most memorable episodes, in which the protagonist, in charge of a transport truck, leads his buddies to several wrong locations during a sham battle. In *What Next*, Hargrove manages to get a truckful of troops stuck in a muddy ditch — twice.

The 1945 film takes place in France just after D-Day. Separated from their field-artillery unit, Cpl. Hargrove and his charges carry out previously issued orders to liberate the village of Mardenne (with one of MGM's all-purpose "foreign" exterior sets standing in for the community). Trouble is, Mardenne has already been liberated by its own residents, but Hargrove hasn't gotten the new orders to bypass the town. Decked out in ludicrous camouflage outfits, Marion, Mulvehill and the others arrive to a hero's welcome in Mardenne, with Marion, still faithful to his gal back home, attracting the unwanted attentions of the amorous Jeanne Quidoc (Jean Porter), daughter of the town mayor (Hugo Haas). Because he has "invaded" Mardenne without permission, Hargrove is busted to private, but he and Mulvehill have made such a positive impression on the villagers in general and Jeanne in particular that the Army decides to send the boys back into town as goodwill ambassadors during the establishment of a provisional military government. Much of the material in these opening scenes appears to be based upon the 1926 MGM Army comedy *Tin Hats* (see **Chapter 2**), in which a wandering trio of doughboys similarly "liberate" a German village well ahead of the Allied troops.

Despite Hargrove's protestations, the Army orders him not to tell Jeanne that he has no interest in her lest Army-Civilian relationships be compromised. Meanwhile, in his efforts to flimflam the locals, Mulvehill is himself suckered by a larcenous watch merchant who sells him a phony treasure map. Jeanne is temporarily disposed of when Mulevehill talks her into joining the French WACs, the better to be "reunited" with Hargrove when the Americans roll into Paris. Several desultory escapades later, Hargrove and Mulvehill accidentally go AWOL and end up in Gay Paree, where while following his treasure map Mulvehill lands them both behind bars. To get out of jail, Mulvehill collars a chaplain (Richard Bailey) and fabricates a sob story of how Hargrove deserted his unit only to be near his sweetheart. Once freed, the boys run into Jeanne again and the lie is thrown back in their faces. Fed up with Mulhevill's chicanery (just as the audience has already been for several reels), Hargrove tells his ex-buddy that he never wants to see him again. Still and all, when Mulvehill disappears just before the Army is about to go on an important mission, Hargrove makes an unauthorized return trip to Paris to search for his erstwhile friend — accompanied by Sgt. Cramp, making one of the most abrupt and unbelievable character about-faces in movie history.

If the sterile sanitary conditions of the barracks and parade grounds in *See Here, Private Hargrove* were hard to swallow, the squeaky-cleanliness of the exterior scenes in *What Next, Corporal Hargrove?* could make one choke to death. In the film's sole battlefield scene, all the soldiers—American and German alike—are clean-shaven and well-groomed, with barely a speck of mud on their uniforms; even the debris looks like it was freshly scrubbed and carefully arranged by the art director. And though we hear the sounds of guns and cannon fire, no one is even slightly wounded; when Hargrove is captured by Germans, then rescued when the Germans themselves are captured, nary a shot is fired. How many lives could have been spared had Louis B. Mayer and not Dwight Eisenhower been supreme commander of the Allied Expeditionary Force.

Let's be fair: This is, after all, a comedy. We know it's a comedy because of the preponderance of thick foreign accents, double takes, pratfalls, drunk scenes and breakaway props. The warmth and humanity of *See Here, Private Hargrove* are smothered and buried by the slaphappy excesses and the unremitting stupidity of the principal characters in *What Next, Corporal Hargrove?*, which pleased the crowd in 1945 but is far less satisfying when seen today. The film is redeemed only by the performances of Robert Walker, Keenan Wynn, Chill Wills and especially Jean Porter as the irrepressible Jeanne Quidoc, whose character deserves a lot better than the casually cruel treatment she receives here.

Marion Hargrove was able to rise above this ill-conceived project to stake out a long and fruitful career as a novelist and screenwriter. His only return to barracks comedy was the peacetime-army novel *The Girl He Left Behind*, filmed in 1956 as a non-comic vehicle for Tab Hunter. Otherwise, mention of the name Marion Hargrove is less likely to invoke memories of the book that put him on the map than to conjure up pleasant recollections of his extensive contributions to such TV series as *Maverick* and *The Waltons*, and his many movie assignments, including his Oscar-nominated 1962 adaptation of the Broadway hit *The Music Man*. Marion Hargrove died in 2003: the "family business" has been ably carried on by his son Dean Hargrove, who in partnership with Fred Silverman developed and nurtured such popular TV properties as *Matlock* and *Diagnosis: Murder*.

To itemize *all* the differences between *See Here, Private Hargrove* and its postwar stepchild *Biloxi Blues* (Rastar-Universal, 1988) would be a tedious exercise. But before delving any deeper into the second film, it might be worthwhile to at least touch upon the main contrasts between the two properties. For starters, while *Hargrove* is a Story of the Moment, chronicling a major military mobilization that was occurring even while the film was in production, *Biloxi* is a Remembrance of Things Past, the distance of time allowing the author the luxuries of objectivity and insight. Whereas all the soldiers in *Hargrove* are White Anglo-Saxon Protestant, there is a broader ethnic spectrum in *Biloxi,* beginning with Jewish protagonist Eugene Morris Jerome and his best bud and *lantzman* Arnold B. Epstein. *Hargrove* was an assembly-line studio product with an assembly-line studio look; *Biloxi* was Rastar Productions' one and only 1988 release, and as such boasts a veneer of individuality that its 1944 predecessor lacks. While *Hargrove* was answerable to the prohibitive commandments of the Production Code, *Biloxi* is permitted to discourse freely on such onetime taboo topics as homosexuality, masturbation, prostitution and flatulence. Finally, *Biloxi Blues* represents a growth process and radical change of lifestyle, which *See Here, Private Hargrove* does not. Already a published author in his early 20s, Marion Hargrove had no doubts whatsoever about his talent; and as a North Carolinian born and bred, his being billeted in a Southern boot camp hardly constituted a culture shock. *Biloxi's* teenage hero Eugene Jerome is merely an aspiring author, still none too certain that he has anything truly worthwhile to contribute to the world of journalism — to say nothing of the world itself. And as a child of Brooklyn, Eugene's relocation to Biloxi, Tennessee, is roughly the equivalent of being abandoned on the dark side of the Moon.

Making its Broadway premiere on March 28, 1985, *Biloxi Blues* was the second in a trilogy of autobiographical coming-of-age plays written by Neil Simon, a man who needs no introduction and won't get one here. Prior to marching off to World War II, Simon's alter ego Eugene Jerome and his family struggled with the privations of the Depression in *Brighton Beach Memoirs*, which opened on Broadway in 1983. After *Biloxi*, the author's *Broadway Bound* (1986) detailed Eugene's postwar trials and tribulations as a fledgling radio comedy writer. Throughout most of his career, Neil Simon had resisted the temptation to capitalize on past successes by writing sequels. Quoted by David Sheward, the playwright explained: "When I wrote *Brighton Beach Memoirs*, I never intended it to be a trilogy. When it turned out to be so successful [1580 performances!], I was encouraged to write a sequel.... When I thought of what would be the next obvious step in my life, some momentous occasion, it was when I went into the Army.... *Biloxi Blues* is Eugene stepping out of New York and the comfort and safety of home into a whole new world."

As written by Simon and staged by Gene Saks, the original *Biloxi Blues* was stylistically similar to the 1955 Broadway hit *No Time for Sergeants* (see **Chapter 8**), with the protagonist narrating the story in the "Now" while periodically stepping into and out of the "Then" of basic training in 1943. The sets by scenic designer David Mitchell were fragmentary and impressionistic, allowing for a smooth and even narrative flow. Not as tightly structured as Simon's other works, *Biloxi* is like *Private Hargrove* a series of anecdotes linked together by a common wartime theme. In the course of his two-and-a-half hours' traffic on stage, Eugene struggles to cope with the anti-semitism and negative behavior of certain fellow rookies; endures the near-psychotic tirades of his drill instructor Sgt. Toomey, who hates all New Yorkers on general principle; develops a taste (sort of) for the non–Kosher chow ladled out at the camp commissary; learns the hard way the importance of teamwork and accepting responsibility for one's actions; loses his virginity to a pragmatic prostitute named Rowena; and falls chastely in love with a sweet high school *shiksa* named Daisy Hannigan. Most importantly, Eugene develops his talent and confidence as a writer by jotting down his daily observations and accepting the constructive criticism of his pal Arnold: "You're always standing around watching what's happening, scribbling in your book what other people do. You have to get in the middle of it. You have to take sides. Make a contribution to the fight." Eschewing the joke-a-second clockwork of such earlier successes as *The Odd Couple* and *The Sunshine Boys*, Neil Simon set out in *Biloxi Blues* to "write drama and tell it as a comedy." Critic John Simon (no relation) was among those who were both surprised and gratified that Simon did not pen a pure farce this time out but instead produced a play of depth and emotion, with the laughs arising naturally from the situation and characters: "By George, he's done it!" was John Simon's Henry Higgins-esque accolade.

Matthew Broderick as the gefilte-fish-out-of-water Pvt. Eugene Jerome in Neil Simon's *Biloxi Blues* (Rastar/Universal, 1988).

Repeating his role from *Brighton Beach Memoirs*, Matthew Broderick was the first actor to portray Eugene in the original Broadway version of *Biloxi Blues*, which though not as a big a hit as *Brighton* still enjoyed a comfortable 524-performance run; the play also earned the Theatre World Award and four Tonys. Broderick was again seen as Eugene in the 1988 movie version, adapted for the screen by Neil Simon and directed by Mike Nichols, whose previous collaborations with Simon included the Broadway stagings of *Barefoot in the Park*, *The Odd Couple*, *Plaza Suite* and several other plays. This, however, was the first time that Nichols helmed a Simon-scripted movie.

In opening up the play for the screen while simultaneously shortening the running time to 106 minutes, Simon dispensed with a lot of exposition, verbal character descriptions and other elements. Among the passages missing from the film is the delightful scene in which Eugene and his Catholic girlfriend Daisy (played in both the stage and screen versions by Penelope Ann Miller) compare their respective religious holidays, and the disillusioning moment wherein the prostitute who'd deflowered Eugene barely recognizes him during a second meeting. Also gone are most of the songs performed by Sinatra wannabe Pvt. Carney (Alan Ruck in the play, Casey Siemaszko in the movie) which on stage served as transitions from one scene to the next. While such vignettes were effective on a theatrical level, they didn't really advance the story and were thus regarded as dispensable. Additionally, Simon moved the action up from 1943 to 1945, thereby providing the film with an ironic coda: For all their grueling boot-camp training, neither Eugene nor any of the other rookies will ever see combat duty.

Some critics were unenthused over other alterations made for the film version, notably the beefing up of Matthew Broderick's role at the other actors' expense. In the play, Eugene is more observer than catalyst, suggesting that Neil Simon created the supporting role of Arnold Epstein (Barry Miller on stage, Corey Parker in the film) so he could personalize the two warring sides of the teenaged Simon's real-life psyche: the agreeable, conciliatory Eugene vs. the rebellious, pugnacious Arnold. This, according to *New York Magazine* critic David Denby, provided the play with the potentially intriguing yin-and-yang of "the impractical but principled Jew and the sane but compromising one." We say "potentially" because this dichotomy is rather underdeveloped in the play, but at least it's *there*. Not so in the film, where most of Arnold's major scenes are either cut out entirely, or rewritten so that they happen to Eugene instead. The most glaring example of this is the play's highly anticipated showdown between the combative but physically frail Arnold and the terrifying Sgt. Toomey. In the film, however, Arnold is literally shoved into the background so that Eugene can have the climactic confrontation with Toomey—which, in context, makes no sense whatsoever.

The direction by Mike Nichols provides a fascinating contrast with Nichols' handling of his previous service comedy *Catch-22* (see **Chapter 19**). Divesting himself of the bravura *nouvelle-vague* grandstanding of the earlier film, in *Biloxi Blues* Nichols deliberately harks back to the old pre-*auteur* days in which directors were content to set up the camera and record the action without drawing attention to themselves. In fact, Nichols' directorial hand is all but invisible, with many of the best moments—Eugene's bunkmates giving him a drubbing after finding his secret journal, the USO dance with Eugene and Daisy—filmed in lengthy, unedited takes. So accomplished are the young performers and so expertly handled are the dialogue exchanges that one is never consciously aware that the camera has barely moved and no cutaways of any kind have taken place. *Biloxi Blues* represents the perfect marriage between Mike Nichols the stage director and Mike Nichols the filmmaker.

Not all of Nichols' creative choices met with universal approval. In conveying the *zeitgeist* of the mid–1940s, the director went for what he described as a "Norman Rockwell" look, collaborating with cinematographer Bill Butler and production designer Paul Sylbert to desaturate the colors in order to convey the appearance of an old, faded family album. This nostalgic approach worked better with the lay public than the professional critics, many of whom felt that both Nichols and Simon had softened the original play "not just visually, but *dramatically*," as noted by David Denby. Some complained that the bittersweet quality of Simon's stage prose had most of the "bitter" squeezed out in the transition to film, and not to the property's benefit. Unlike the Eugene of the play, argues Denby, "our hero undergoes no very great traumas. Eugene Morris Jerome enters the wartime army a nice boy. He becomes a slightly wiser nice boy."

This writer can't entirely agree. One of the protagonist's most traumatic experiences—in which Pvt. Hennessy, the only non–Jew to defend Eugene and Arnold from the racist barbs of their fellow rookies, is revealed to be homosexual and placed under arrest—has a far more shattering impact on film than on stage. In the original play, Hennessy's outing is startling but perfunctory; in the film, the event is made infinitely more shocking and humiliating by having a pair of MPs nab the unfortunate rookie during an outdoor maneuver exercise, in full view of everyone in camp. It is clear from his body language that bystander Eugene will never forget this outrage ... and neither will anyone else.

But no one really goes to a Neil Simon film for the gnashing of teeth and the rending of garments. The laughs in *Biloxi Blues* are generously distributed by a uniformly superb ensemble, with two standout performances. As the blasé prostitute Rowena, cult-movie perennial Park Overall exhibits nary a whit of intimidation over being in a big-budget movie that a mainstream audience will want to see. No director is better at staging clumsy seduction scenes than Mike Nichols (remember *The Graduate*?), and he rises to the occasion with the screamingly funny deflowering of the nerdish Eugene under the skilled tutelage of veteran boudoir strategist Rowena. And on the off-chance that Park Overall's brilliant performance might fade from the audience's memory, the script makes certain that Rowena's essence lingers on long past her one big scene. Possessing an even keener business sense than Pvt. Mulvehill in *See Here, Private Hargrove*, Rowena supplements her income by selling her own special brand of perfume to her customers. The payoff to this setup arrives a few minutes later during a USO dance, as innocent little Daphne expresses wide-eyed astonishment that all the men in the room smell so nice.

The best performance we've saved for last: Christopher Walken as the truly bizarre drill instructor Sergeant Merwin Toomey. The original play provides Toomey with plenty of exposition regarding the steel plate that the doctors have imbedded in his skull. Christopher Walken hardly has to say anything beyond the fact that the plate is there: We can "see" that cranial implant as clearly as we see the fiery car crash that the actor fantasizes over (but never pulls off) in Woody Allen's *Annie Hall*. Resisting the temptation to take large bites out of the scenery, Walken is twice as effective by underplaying the flaky Toomey, delivering such loaded lines as "It was my intention of getting Epstein in here, and putting a pistol to his ear, and blowing a tunnel through his head, but you'll do just as well" with the casual air of asking a dinner companion to pass the salt.

Observers who regard Walken's Sgt. Toomey as a full-throttle madman are missing the author's point. Throughout the story, Toomey has tried and failed to impress upon Eugene and Arnold the non-negotiable importance of their boot camp training. Asking Eugene what he'd do if the whole Japanese army was standing behind him, Toomey is in no mood for the boy's wimpy rejoinder "Surrender and get some sleep"; nor does the Sergeant have much sympathy for Arnold's insistence that the training process could be a loss less tough and a lot more sensitive. Thus it is that in the film's climax, a drunken Toomey staggers into the barracks brandishing a pistol, threatening to kill both Eugene and Arnold on the spot if they don't perform one final drill entirely to his liking. World War II veteran Neil Simon clearly understands that Toomey is *not* exhibiting uncontrollable insanity. There's only one way to shake wise-ass kids like Eugene out of their cocoons and make them understand that war is a life-or-death proposition in which they must be prepared for anything lest they get killed the minute they step into battle—and that way is to literally scare the crap out of them. If Eugene isn't prepared to handle a liquor-crazed Sergeant with a piece of steel in his head and an itchy trigger finger, how on earth will he be prepared to handle an assault from the enemy? Though Sgt. Toomey would never dream of using the term, what he's practicing on the terrified Eugene is his own peculiar version of Tough Love.

Whether *Biloxi Blues* is a better film than *See Here, Private Hargrove* is beside the point. Asked which film makes a bigger impression on them, contemporary audiences will choose *Biloxi Blues* hands down. Funny though *Hargrove* is in its best moments, we are so distantly removed from the era which spawned the piece that its original impact can never be recaptured. But you don't have to have been alive during World War II to be touched by the profoundly timeless and universal philosophy expressed by Eugene Morris Jerome's final monologue in *Biloxi Blues*:

> As I look back now ... I realize my time in the Army was the happiest time of my life. God knows not because I liked the Army, and there sure was nothing to like about a war. I liked it for the most selfish reason of all. Because I was young ... I didn't really like most of those guys then, but today I love every damn one of them. Life is weird, you know.

10

Stranger Than Fiction

While there's a kernel of truth in every military comedy, there are some that contain the whole ear of corn. This chapter features four comedies which despite the most ludicrous situations and unbelievable plot convolutions were all inspired by well and thoroughly documented true stories. We begin our journey into the "stranger than fiction" realm with a 20th Century–Fox production that was shipped out under two different titles within the same year.

The genesis for this film was published in the January 21, 1950, edition of *The New Yorker*: "The Flying Teakettle," a humorous article written by John W. Hazard, executive editor of *Changing Times* magazine. During World War II Hazard had been skipper of the PC-452, a small diesel-operated warship designed to sink enemy submarines. The article recounted how Hazard's crew was comprised of "90-day wonders" like himself: Recently activated naval reservists, few of whom had ever been to sea. This in itself was not unique in that 95 percent of the wartime Navy was made up of reservists and civilians. The angle here was that Hazard and his crew had been chosen to participate in an experimental Navy program, in which a steam turbine rather than a diesel engine was installed in their ship — hence the vessel's nickname, "The Flying Teakettle." The experiment was a resounding failure, abandoned by the Brass with this terse comment: "If a small ship can't be handled by the average Reserve crew, it is no good to the Navy."

When 20th Century–Fox purchased the movie rights to Hazard's story, the studio altered the title to *U.S.S. Teakettle*, changing the protagonist's name to John W. Harkness. Initally, Fox planned to cast studio contractee William Lundigan in the lead, but when the film's budget was expanded to accommodate location shooting at the Navy facilities in Hampton Roads, Virginia, it was decided to use a more bankable star, Gary Cooper. Casting the 49-year-old Cooper instead of the 35-year-old Lundigan guaranteed wider audience identification with the plight of a lifelong landlubber who is suddenly thrust into the command of a Navy war vessel. Clearly relishing the assignment, Cooper used his familiar onscreen truculence to perfectly convey the quizzical queasiness of Lt. John Harkness, whose only "qualification" for his assignment was that he'd earned a degree in engineering — 18 years before the war.

Scriptwriter Richard Murphy was no comedy specialist, having previously labored on the likes of *Slattery's Hurricane* and *Panic in the Streets*. Nor did director Henry Hathaway, who had collaborated with Cooper on such essentially straight-faced efforts as *Lives of a Bengal Lancer* and *The Real Glory*, have much of a comedy background. Evidently, Fox's strategy was to offset the potential absurdities of the film's storyline, wherein 50 inexperienced reservists must face the responsibility of guiding an unreliable vessel through treacherous waters, by hiring a creative team grounded in more realistic film fare. For the most part, this strategy worked.

Once placed in command of Patrol Craft 1168 ("played" by an actual sub chaser first commissioned in 1943), Lt. Harkness is dismayed to discover that with the exception of his grizzled chief bosun's mate Larrabee (Millard Mitchell), everyone on board is as green as he is. The vessel's shakedown cruise does not bode well, with the crew nearly smashing into a mooring and winding up drifting aimlessly at sea. No one on board can figure out why they've been picked for this mission, nor why the diesel sub has been outfitted with a new steam engine. Christened "The Thing," the engine appears as unseaworthy as the crew, hissing, sputtering and exploding with sickening regularity. Many more mishaps occur before the "U.S.S. Teakettle" is slated to participate in an official test for the Admiral's Board. To say the test is a disaster would be giving it a break: The engine's valves become frozen, causing the "Teakettle" to careen insanely out of control. Angered over what he regards as a monumental snafu in assigning his ragtag crew to such a delicate assignment, Harkness storms into the office of Captain Elliot (Harry Von Zell), fully prepared to give his commanding officer a piece of his mind and to tender his resignation. Imagine Harkness' surprise when Elliot bestows a commendation on the officers and crew of the "Teakettle," at the same time explaining that the Navy had deliberately put a bunch of novices in charge of the patrol craft to test the viability of steam engines over diesel motors without the input of maritime experts tipping the scale in steam's favor. Though the "Thing" was a bust, the mission was a success: Faced with impossible odds, the inexperienced crew rose to the occasion with courage and resourcefulness. The film implies that the real purpose of the Navy experiment was not to verify the practicality of steam engines but to test the resilience of the reservists (sounds like a bit of "CYA" on the part of the higher-ups, but we'll let that pass).

Gary Cooper receives solid support from such reliable players as Millard Mitchell, Eddie Albert, John McIntire, Ray Collins, and a pre–*Dragnet* Jack Webb in a marvelous turn as a fatalistic crewman who anticipates calamity at every turn. Several newcomers also acquit themselves nicely, including Lee Marvin, Charles Bronson and Harvey Lembeck in their collective screen debut and Jack Warden in his second film appearance. Only *film noir* icon Jane Greer seems like a fish out of water in her very minor role as Cooper's supportive wife (Greer was a last-minute replacement for Joanne Dru, who'd been dropped from the project when she refused to sign a long-term studio contract).

Fox did a bang-up job promoting *U.S.S. Teakettle*, with Gary Cooper enthusiastically participating in a nationwide promotional tour and lending his star clout to the film's promotional trailer. The New York critics responded to the hoopla with almost uniformly glowing reviews: Bosley Crowther of the *Times* declared the film "the best comedy of the year," while Otis L. Guernsey Jr. of the *Herald-Tribune* cited Fox's wisdom in casting Cooper in the lead: "His acting is of the economical and yet clear and versatile type that would make any audience identify itself with his frustration." Even the columnists, traditionally more jaded than critics, got behind the film, notably Walter Winchell. But the public wasn't buying: During its initial run in February 1951, *U.S.S. Teakettle* barely made a dime. Under normal circumstances, this would mean that the film would be returned to Fox for a re-editing job, but the studio merely reissued the film *without* cuts under a new title, *You're in the Navy Now*. Business improved somewhat, but not enough to encourage Gary Cooper to ever participate in another service comedy. (It was a different matter with screenwriter Richard Murphy, as we shall see.) Viewed today, *You're in the Navy Now*

You're in the Navy Now (20th Century–Fox, 1951): Stars Gary Cooper and Jane Greer grace the cover of a British film magazine.

doesn't seem quite as funny as so many observers thought it was in 1951, hampered by the cut-and-dried "factory" look common to most 20th Century–Fox releases of the era. It's an amusing effort, but hardly in the same league as the next fact-based Navy comedy on our docket, 1959's *Operation Petticoat*.

Two separate wartime incidents were folded into this film. The first incident sounds like something that has improved with the telling over the years, but it has been confirmed as 100 percent fact by the Snopes.com website, which specializes in determining the veracity of "urban legends." Here's the story: On July 30, 1941, J.W. Coe, commanding officer of the U.S.S. *Skipjack*, submitted a requisition to the supply ship U.S.S. *Holland*, anchored at Mare Island, California, for 150 rolls of toilet paper. Not until June 10, 1942, did the *Skipjack* receive a response: No toilet paper, but instead an invoice, dated November 26, with the stamped notation "Cancelled—Cannot Identify."

Captain Coe's reaction to this reply was truly one for the ages: "During the 11¾ months elapsing from the time of ordering the toilet paper and the present date, U.S.S. *Skipjack* personnel, despite their best efforts to await delivery of the subject material, have been unable to wait on numerous occasions, and the situation is now quite acute, particularly during depth-charge attacks." Enclosing a sample square of bathroom tissue "for the information of the Supply Officer," Coe added that he could not "help but wonder what is being used at Mare Island in place of this unidentifiable material, once well known to this command." Giving the *Holland* the benefit of the doubt by suggesting that the "Cannot Identify" notation was an error prompted by a shortage of this "strategic war material," Captain Coe wrapped up with a master stroke of stinging sarcasm: "In order to cooperate in the war effort at a small local sacrifice, the *Skipjack* desires no further action be taken until the end of the current war, which has created a situation aptly described as 'War is Hell.'"

Presently occupying a place of honor at the USS *Bowfin* Submarine Museum and Park in Honolulu, Captain Coe's celebrated "toilet paper memo" is the stuff of which service legends are made. During the 1950s, several writers tried to adapt the incident as a television play, but this wasn't possible at a time when American network television avoided scatological humor. Finally came the bright idea of building a theatrical feature around Coe's memo—but once the memo is read aloud on-screen, what does one do for an encore? The solution arrived at by scenarists Paul King and Joseph Stone was to formulate a Navy comedy in which the toilet-paper incident was but one of many frustrations heaped upon a world-weary C.O.—and rather than leave the outcome of the incident dangling, the decision was made to provide that C.O. with a wheeler-dealer junior officer adept at sidestepping Navy bureaucracy, who was not above staging a phony commando raid in order to steal the necessary tissue rolls from a heavily fortified Navy warehouse. From this tiny acorn grew the mighty oak known as *Operation Petticoat*.

Casting about for other wartime anecdotes that might fit into this framework, the writers came up with a doozy involving the crew of the submarine *Seadragon,* who when ordered to paint their vessel were forced to use a combination of red and white lead paint as the undercoat because there were no other colors available. Before the job could be finished, the *Seadragon* was ordered to set sail for the Philippines—still covered only in a luminiscent shade of pink. This story found its way into *Operation Petticoat,* expanded from a potential one-off sight gag into a crucial plot device which determines the outcome of the story.

The film's title sprang from the fertile minds of screenwriters Stanley Shapiro and Maurice Richlin, who'd recently struck gold with the popular Universal-International sex comedy *Pillow Talk*. With the studio anxious to cash in on the team's previous success, Shapiro & Richlin spiced up King & Stone's military comedy with liberal doses of female pulchritude and sexual innuendo. This required a method of bringing women into the all-male milieu of a submarine, a problem solved when the writers contrived to have the sub's junior officer arrange transport for five Navy nurses, evacuees from a recent enemy attack, to another port—only to be stuck with the ladies when no other port can accommodate them (the film is set during the first weeks of World War II, a time when "safe harbor" space was at a premium).

Operation Petticoat director Blake Edwards and star Tony Curtis had recently registered well with another Universal military comedy, *The Perfect Furlough* (see **Chapter 16**). Curtis later claimed that it was he who urged the studio to film the submarine story, and to cast Cary Grant as his costar: Tony had idolized Grant since he first saw the older actor play a *serious* sub commander in 1943's *Destination Tokyo*. That Blake Edwards was also a longtime Grant devotee is demonstrated by his casting of Cary Grant sound-alikes Craig Stevens and John Vivyan in his TV series *Peter Gunn* and *Mr. Lucky*. Approached by Lew Wasserman of MCA (which had recently purchased Universal), Grant agreed to participate in the production so long as his own production company had a controlling interest, and he himself received 75 percent of the net profits or 10 percent of the gross, whichever was higher. The hiring of Cary Grant boosted the film's budget from one to three million dollars, prompting Universal's decision to film the picture in color (incredibly, the film had been planned for black & white—pink sub or no pink sub).

Framed in flashback to assure the audience that the star won't pull a "Mister Roberts" and get killed in the end, *Operation Petticoat* is the story of the *Sea Tiger*, a Navy submarine skippered by Lt. Cmdr. Matt Sherman (Cary Grant). Three days after Pearl Harbor, the *Sea Tiger* is about to set sail for battle in the Philippines when a surprise raid all but destroys the sub while it is still docked (this opening scene is also based on fact). Matt pleads with superior officer Henderson (Robert F. Simon) to be allowed to make some repairs so he can take the sub to the nearest port for a complete overhaul. Henderson gives Sherman a mere two-week window, assigning Matt a bare-minimum crew and a prissy-looking junior officer, Lt. Nick Holden (Tony Curtis). Though he carries himself like a Park Avenue socialite, Holden is actually a streetwise sharpster and natural-born scavenger, proving his worth by using his own "special methods"—and his special team of fellow reprobates—to supply the *Sea Tiger* with toilet paper and other necessities whenever the Proper Channels fail to do so. Though the hardened Sherman looks askance at Holden's *nouveau riche* airs (the Lieutenant dresses immaculately in civilian-tailored "whites" and brings a custom-made set of golf clubs on board), the C.O. must admit that his new junior officer is indispensible, especially when appropriating the equipment necessary to repair the *Sea Tiger*'s inner workings—which since the attack have been groaning and wheezing like a asthmatic old man. Holden wants the sub restored to seaworthiness as much as Sherman, but for a different reason: While Matt is itching to get into the War, Nick must return stateside to wed a wealthy and well-connected debutante.

Both men's anxiousness is heightened when the *Sea Tiger*, still a long way from being totally up to code, takes on a shapely "cargo" of stranded Navy nurses: Maj. Edna Hayward (Virginia Gregg) and lieutenants Dolores Crandall (Joan O'Brien), Barbara Duran (Dina Merrill), Claire Reid (Madlyn Rhue) and Ruth Colfax (Marion Ross). A crimson-faced Sherman orders his men to ignore the ladies' presence, which is something akin to spreading sugar on the ground and ordering the ants to stay away. The plot rolls merrily along until the final reel, when urgency dictates that the *Sea Tiger* head out to sea covered in nothing but pink primer. The Allied forces have no way of knowing if the pink submarine is friend or foe—and with the sub's radio out of commission, Sherman is unable to set the Allies straight. All that saves the *Sea Tiger* from being sunk by friendly fire is Holden's last-minute inspiration to jettison the nurses' undergarments through the torpedo tubes. As wave after wave of bras and panties float to the surface, the Allies are finally convinced that the *Sea Tiger* is on their side—"The Japanese have nothing like this!"—and agree to hold their fire. By film's end, Sherman has fallen in love with cute-but-klutzy Dolores Crandall, Holden has given up his rich fiancee in favor of Barbara Duran, and even the ship's misogynistic Chief Mechanic's Mate Sam Tostin (Arthur O'Connell) has found a kindred spirit in Edna Hayward, who hits upon the perfect method of muffling the engine's noisy valves with the strategic application of a girdle.

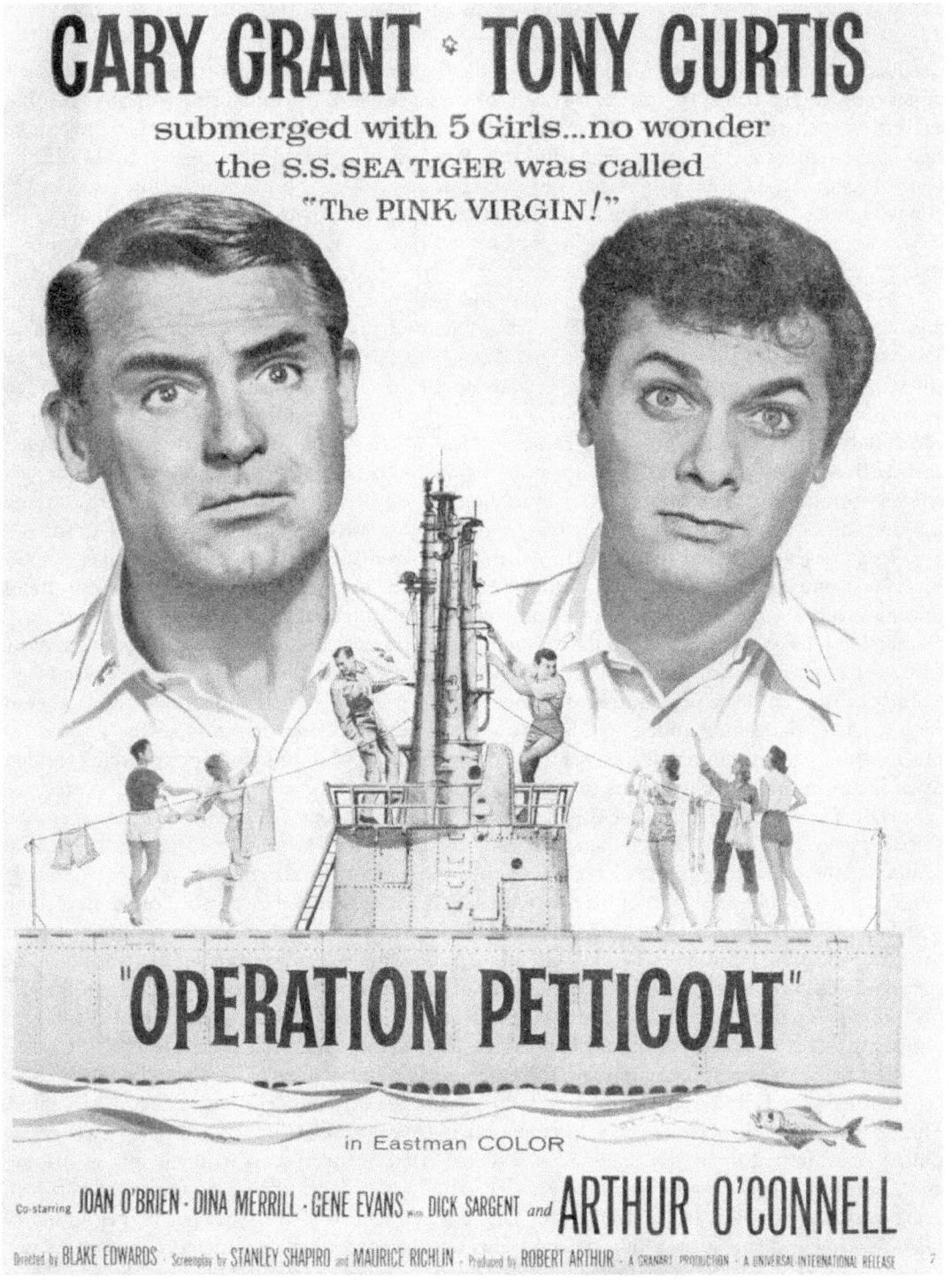

Here's a magazine advertisement for Universal-International's 1959 service comedy *Operation Petticoat*. Keep reading.

Most of *Operation Petticoat's* location scenes were filmed at Boca Chica and Key West in Florida, with additional footage at the San Diego Naval Base. Except for the interior shots, three genuine submarines were used during filming: The *Queenfish* (SS-393) in the wraparound "modern" scenes, the *Archerfish* (SS-311) in most of the underwater scenes, and the *Balao* (SS-285) for the climax in which the *Sea Tiger* is painted pink. To emphasize the embarrassment of a bunch of nervous seamen trying to squeeze through the passageways of the submarine without brushing against the well-rounded nurses, Blake Edwards arranged for those passageways to be built some four inches narrower than on a regulation sub. Edwards also placed the collision button in the control room at a different height than normal to set up the classic bit in which Dolores Crandall clumsily sets off the alarm with her *derriere*. The endless parade of anatomical jokes was allegedly the reason that actress Tina Louise, who took herself *very* seriously, turned down an opportunity to appear in the film.

In keeping with the film's factual premise, the best moments in *Operation Petticoat* are based on well-circulated Navy anecdotes, though the authenticity of these stories is difficult to confirm. The brilliant sight gag in which another of Dolores' blunders causes a torpedo to fire prematurely, whereupon the shell skids onto the shore of a Japanese-held island and "sinks" a truck, was regarded as such a winner that it was not only included in the film's promotional trailer, but also later excerpted for the Universal-produced TV series *McHale's Navy*—for which Cary Grant demanded and received a hefty fee. Nearly twenty years later, the torpedo gag was refilmed (with far less effective miniature work) for the TV-series version of *Operation Petticoat* (ABC 1977–79), starring John Astin in the Grant role and Tony Curtis' daughter Jamie Leigh Curtis as Nurse Duran.

Another legend-based sequence, in which Lt. Holden (Curtis) and seaman Henkle (Gavin MacLeod) smuggle a stolen pig on board the *Sea Tiger* by dressing the porker in a uniform and passing it off as the besotted "Seaman Hornsby," was originally designed as a setpiece for Cary Grant, who refused to participate in the pig-napping portion of the escapade. In this, Grant demonstrated that he had a firm understanding of his true appeal as a film star. By absenting himself from the caper until the pig's outraged owner shows up to register a complaint, Grant reserved for himself a wonderfully undeplayed bit of humor as Lt. Cmdr. Sherman eloquently "covers" for Lt. Holden — while simultaneously settling a score with his flippant junior officer by forcing Holden to exchange his precious golf clubs for "Seaman Hornsby."

Described by historian Jeanine Basinger as a feminized version of *Destination Tokyo*, *Operation Petticoat* proved to be the biggest box-office success in Universal's 47-year history, earning $6.8 million at the box office. It was also Cary Grant's most lucrative assignment to date, personally netting him $3 million. As part of his deal with MCA, Grant retained ownership of the film along with two other Universal releases, *The Grass Is Greener* and *That Touch of Mink*, enabling the actor to accrue additional millions when he sold all three films to NTA for television distribution. The success of *Operation Petticoat* did not pass unnoticed by other Hollywood studios, specifically Columbia, who happened to have a similar property already in the works—and in fact had been preparing this particular project for nearly three years before *Petticoat*'s December 1959 release.

The true story behind Columbia's *The Wackiest Ship in the Army?* (1960) can be found in an article titled "Big Fella Wash-Wash," first published in the July 1956 edition of *Argosy* magazine. The story involves the Army's seafaring force during World War II, specifically the oldest active sailing vessel in that force: the U.S.S. *Echo*, a twin-masted wooden scow with a length of 104 feet and a beam of 26 feet. First registered to New Zealand in 1905, with a diesel engine installed fifteen years later, the *Echo* was transferred to the U.S. government for a two-year period beginning in 1942. Serving as a supply ship in the New Hebrides, the somewhat dilapidated *Echo* and its raw but willing fifteen-man crew were assigned to deliver cargo and personnel through shipping lanes too narrow and coral reefs too treacherous for a larger craft. One of the tiny scow's most offbeat assignments was to deliver a grand piano to an Australian plane spotter who'd been a musician in civilian life, an incident highlighted in the magazine story. Just before the *Echo* was decommissioned in 1944, the crew of the vessel received a commendation from the Army for their bravery. The title of the *Argosy* piece was based on native slang for "crazy ship"—which the antiquated *Echo* definitely was in appearance if not in performance.

Inspired by the reminiscences of the *Echo*'s former commander Meredith "Rip" Riddle, "Big

Fella Wash-Wash" was written by Columbia University grad-school student Herbert Carlson. *Argosy* liked the story but felt it was "rambling" and "overlong." Marion Hargrove of *See Here, Private Hargrove* fame (see **Chapter 9**) was brought in to refine and tighten Carlson's prose — and it was hoped, to make the story more attractive for a potential movie sale. The cover of the July 1956 *Argosy* advertised the story with the headline "The Wackiest Ship in the Army," and it was under this title that the piece was purchased by Columbia the following year. The studio saw the property as a potential vehicle for their new contract comedian Ernie Kovacs, who was scheduled to play the *Echo*'s reluctant new skipper Lt. Rip Crandall. Kovacs' close friend and frequent costar Jack Lemmon was slated to portray Crandall's eager-beaver junior officer, Ensign Tommy Hanson. A proposed third major role, the ship's hopelessly inept cook, was reserved for a movie newcomer: ex-cowboy and ex-bartender Bill Stebbins, whom Columbia evidently hoped to develop into the next Aldo Ray.

Lemmon and Kovacs' prior commitments prevented the studio from starting production until the spring of 1960. Inasmuch as Kovacs had not yet demonstrated that he could carry a picture and Lemmon had outgrown the ensign role, Ernie was diverted to other assignments and Jack was promoted to the lead role of Lt. Crandall. At the same time, Bill Stebbins was let go and the now-diminished role of the cook went to Alvy Moore. Richard Murphy, the screenwriter for 1951's *You're in the Navy Now*, signed on as both scripter and director for *Wackiest Ship in the Army?* (the question mark, introduced in the film's animated opening titles, was often ignored by studio publicists). Murphy proceeded to knead the film into a partial reworking of the earlier Gary Cooper vehicle by manning the U.S.S. *Echo* — here depicted as an old garbage scow — with a crew of bumbling Army misfits, none of whom has had any experience on the high seas. Nor do these guys even know the proper Navy terminology for the various components of their own ship, freezing on the spot when the word "foc'sle" is mentioned. Rip Crandall himself has been assigned the *Echo* only because he'd been a yachtsman in civilian life and was thus familiar with shallow-draft vessels, while Ensign Hanson has requested the duty to make up for a grievous rigging error he'd committed as a deckhand on Crandall's yacht. Convinced that his longtime rival Lt. Cmdr. Vanderwater (John Lund) has given him the *Echo* to settle an old grudge, Crandall is all for demanding a transfer, but eventually warms up to both the ship and its crew, who may be stumblebums but certainly aren't shirkers or cowards. What Crandall doesn't know until halfway through the film is that his apparently pointless mission is of vital importance to Joint Operations, and in fact the *Echo*'s commission was personally ordered by General Douglas MacArthur.

There is slapstick and gaggery aplenty during the film's establishing scenes, with Crandall bumping his head on a low ceiling no fewer than three times within the first eight minutes, and sundry comic bits involving the *Echo*'s outmoded equipment and the near-nonexistent maritime skills of the crew. All this is evocative of *You're in the Navy Now*, right down to the bizarre sound effects accompanying the faulty diesel engine and a near-collision with another, larger ship (actually *two* ships this time, in a sight gag that would have done Mack Sennett proud). But for all its frivolity, *Wackiest Ship in the Army?* contains moments of stark drama and edge-of-seat suspense that would do credit to many a serious war picture. For every scene in which the Spike Jones–like musical score by George Duning playfully "comments" on the action (as the *Echo* tries to maneuver its way out of a heavily mined port, we hear the strains of "Here We Go 'Round the Mulberry Bush"), there are such sobering moments as Ensign Hanson's nauseated reaction upon finding the befouled corpse of an Australian soldier, or the brutally efficient murders of two Japanese sentries by a solemn-faced Aborgine. An amusing bit involving a pair of girl-starved Japanese pilots bandying about such American colloquialisms as "Broad" and "Dog" is neutralized a few minutes later when a ruthless enemy officer endeavors to undermine the morale of the *Echo*'s crew in letter-perfect English. And while Jack Lemmon is his usual funny, flibbertygibbet self throughout most of the action, it's no joke at all when Rip Crandall is seriously wounded less than ten minutes before the final fadeout. Writer-director Richard Murphy's remarkable ability to keep the audience

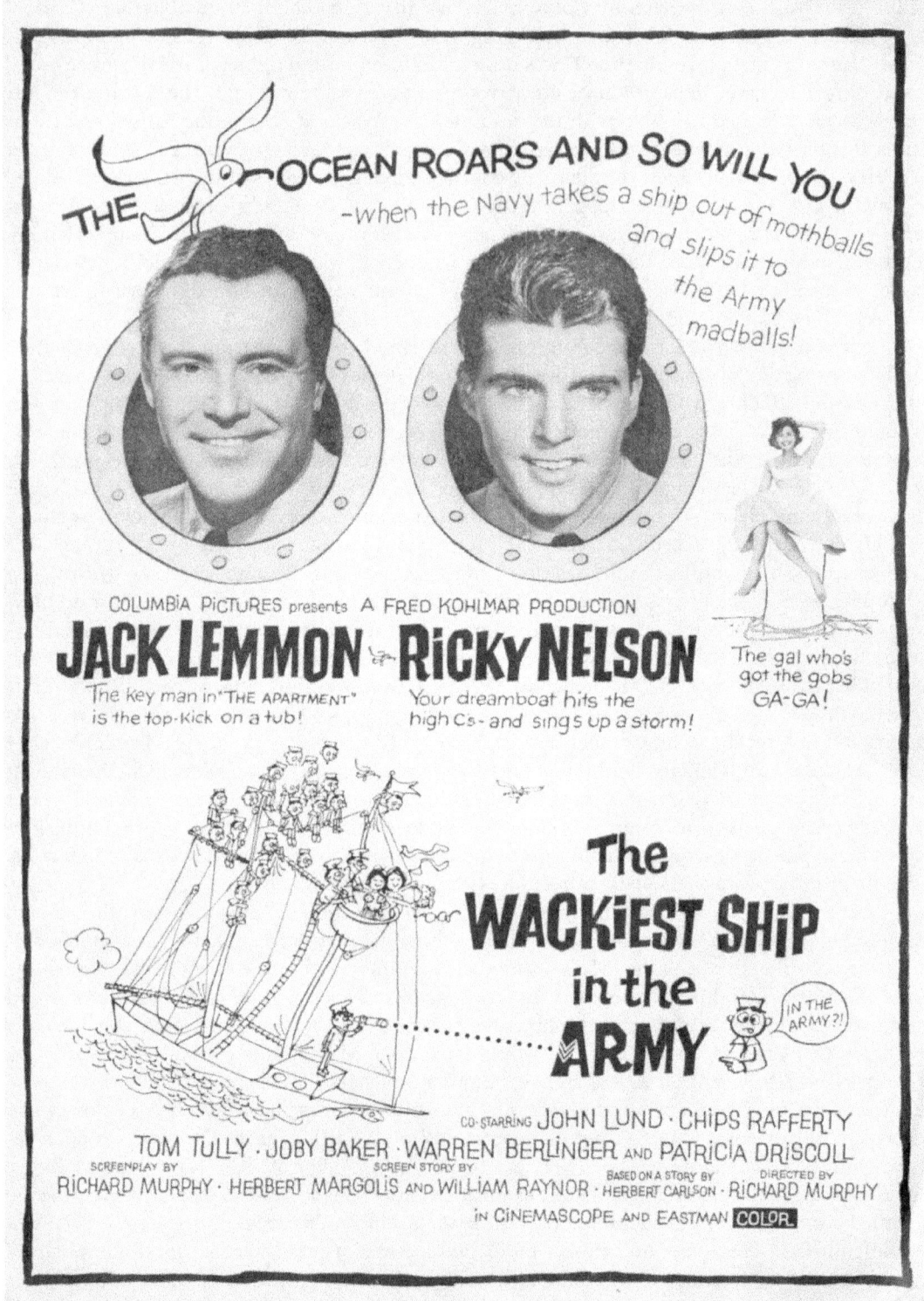

Here's a magazine ad for the 1960 service comedy *The Wackiest Ship in the Army.* Can it be that Columbia Pictures was trying to capitalize on the popularity of Universal's *Operation Petticoat?* Such a suspicious nature you have!

guessing whether the film is a mere studio-confected comic charade or a no-nonsense recreation of historical events naturally makes for a more compelling moviegoing experience.

The grand-piano anecdote spotlighted in the *Argosy* article was hardly substantial enough to support an entire feature film, so the *Echo*'s precious cargo was changed to a human being. Murphy expands the material by having Lt. Crandall ordered to transport the rickety *Echo* across 400 miles of open water to Port Moresby, New Guinea. Upon arrival, Crandall is informed that he is to hand over his command to priggish Lt. Foster (Richard Anderson), who disdainfully refers to the *Echo*'s crew as "a USO tour." Though not particularly fond of Foster (indeed, no one is!), Captain McClung (Tom Tully) has assigned him to accompany crusty Australian coast-watcher Patterson (Chips Rafferty) to enemy-held New Britain, where Patterson is to keep an eye on Japanese troop movements until relieved by Foster. By now convinced that he is the only man capable of skippering the *Echo*, Crandall leaves Foster cooling his heels in New Guinea and escorts Patterson to New Britain himself, with the *Echo* disguised as a native fishing boat and the crew similarly camouflaged (two of them in female drag).

Once on dry land, Ensign Hanson (played by pop singer Ricky Nelson) spots a distant Japanese convoy and rushes back to report to Crandall, only to find that the *Echo* has been captured by UCLA-educated Japanese officer Shigetsu (George Shibata), leaving the frustrated skipper with little recourse other than cracking wise about the Rose Bowl game. (At one point, Shigetsu was to have been an alumnus of the University of Alabama, complete with Southern accent, but Jack Lemmon was able to talk the director out of this foolish fancy.) Using their knowledge of the *Echo*'s eccentricities to their advantage, Crandall and Hanson manage to subdue their captors and retake the vessel. Under heavy enemy fire the crew is forced to abandon ship, but manage to return to Port Moresby in time to file a report about the approaching convoy. The intelligence gathered during the *Echo*'s secret mission contributes mightily to the Allied victory at the Battle of the Coral Sea in March of 1943 — and one year later, a highly decorated Rip Crandall takes charge of a brand-new destroyer, bringing every man-jack of his loyal crew along for the ride. In reality, the *Echo* had little do with the outcome of the aforementioned battle: The enemy convoy was actually spotted by an American bomber crew. But since this movie isn't titled *The Wackiest American Bomber Crew in the Army*, we can allow Murphy some dramatic license.

With the exception of a few exteriors filmed in Long Beach, much of *Wackiest Ship in the Army?* was shot in Hawaii, using many of the heavily-foliaged locations previously seen in the 1958 film version of *South Pacific*. The versimilitude of these exterior scenes is unfortunately mitigated by the film's clumsy overuse of stock footage and process work, the latter particularly unconvincing whenever the actors, filmed in the proper 24 frames-per-second sound speed, stand before a process shot that has been stretched-framed at 16 fps. Also lessening the film's effectiveness is the script's tendency to spend a great deal of time establishing certain characters, only to suddenly lose all interest in them. Cast as Lt. Cmdr. Vanderwater's placidly efficient Australian secretary Maggie, nominal leading lady Patricia Driscoll serves an important expositional purpose in her few scenes, only to totally disappear from view at the very moment that the audience begins to warm up to her. As the insufferable Lt. Foster, Richard Anderson throws a hilarious hissy-fit when Crandall takes over his assignment without permission — but once his ranting voice fades from the soundtrack, that's the last we see of Foster. The most regrettable waste of talent and character potential involves Australian superstar Chips Rafferty, who in his few minutes' screen time makes an indelible impression as the leathery, laconic transport spotter Patterson. Alas, the moment the *Echo* drops Patterson at his secret New Britain outpost, the script drops him as well.

Conversely, the one element of the film that the viewer might expect to come up short actually plays quite well: The performance of Ricky Nelson as the shavetail Ensign Hanson. Though not a particularly skillful actor, Nelson's awkwardness is exactly right for the callow, inexperienced character he is playing. One marvelous moment occurs when Hanson, too timid to exert his authority as junior officer, mumbles an order to the *Echo*'s Chief Mate McCarthy (Mike Kellin) — who dutifully relays that order to the crew in loud, ratchetlike tones. (When Hanson finally works up the cojones to yell "Shut up!" at a lumpish crewman, the viewer is hard pressed not to stand up and cheer.) Even the obligatory scene in which Ricky satiates his fans with an "impromptu" song isn't as cringeworthy as it might have been, as the young hearthrob delivers a thoroughly respectable rendition of "Do You Know What It Means to Miss New Orleans?" accompanied on piano by a tipsy-looking Jack Lemmon.

While *The Wackiest Ship in the Army?* technically predated *Operation Petticoat* as a movie property, the fact that it was filmed and released after the popular Cary Grant–Tony Curtis comedy invited the inevitable comparisons. That there is barely even a surface resemblance between the two pictures didn't prevent Columbia from capitalizing on *Petticoat*'s success by dropping a few hints here and there that *Wackiest Ship* was more of the same. Many of Columbia's print ads were virtual carbon copies of the graphics employed by Universal to promote *Operation Petticoat*— even with a suggestion that the sex-farce trappings of *Petticoat* would be duplicated in *Wackiest Ship* by including a tantalizing body-shot of Patricia Driscoll, neglecting to mention that the actress' contribution to the Columbia feature was only half a step above marginal.

In one respect, the two films shared a common bond: Both were destined to be adapted as weekly television series. Airing on NBC during the 1965–66 season, the TV version of *Wackiest Ship in the Army* (no question mark in the title) was unlike the film played almost entirely straight. The series was more an espionage yarn than a war saga, with the titular two-masted scow— rechristened the *Kiwi*— disguised as a neutral Swedish fishing ship so that the crew could take on various undercover missions against the Japanese. Jack Warden led the cast as Army major Simon Butcher, with Gary Collins as the *Kiwi*'s Navy skipper Lt. Rip Riddle (restoring the name if not the rank of the real-life person upon whom Jack Lemmon's character was based). The strongest link between film and series was the presence in the both casts of Mike Kellin; though contemporary articles suggested that he was recreating his film role as Chief Mate McCarthy, Kellin in fact played CPO Willie Miller on TV. Marion Hargrove, whose doctoring job on the original *Argosy* story that inspired the filmization of *Wackiest Ship in the Army* was never mentioned in any of the film's publicity, contributed a handful of scripts to the TV series—one of them featuring Chips Rafferty, so woefully underused in the film version, in a colorful guest appearance.

While *You're In the Navy Now*, *Operation Petticoat* and *The Wackiest Ship in the Army?* will never be mistaken for documentaries, each film is backed up by enough factual information to bring credibility to even the most incredible moments. But consider for a second or two this plot synopsis: "A disillusioned reporter searching for the scoop of a lifetime finds what he's looking for when he meets a man claiming to be a former member of an elite corps of psychic soldiers, who use paranormal powers to help American win the War on Terror—and, hopefully, to prevent all future wars." Your first reaction might be something like "Oh, spare me! That's tin-foil-hat stuff, the sort of weirdo gobbledygook you hear on all-night talk shows. It could never happen in a million years." Except that maybe it did.

Welshman Jon Ronson describes himself on his website as "journalist, humorist and documentary maker." Ronson doesn't mention, possibly because it's common knowledge, that he specializes in TV documentaries about political extremists, conspiracy theorists and other such wackos. His most celebrated project is a three-part documentary titled *Crazy Rulers of the World*, originally shown by Britain's Channel 4 from November 7 through 21, 2004. To set up Ronson's premise that America is in the hands of madmen, the opening episode "Men Who Stare at Goats" begins its narrative in 1983, the year that Major General Albert Stubblebine startled his Army colleagues by attempting to walk through the wall of his office. It is explained that like many others who lived through the Vietnam years, Stubblebine had been psychologically "bruised" by armed warfare and was seeking out a less lethal means of achieving victory. Dr. Ray Hyman, the first of Ronson's on-camera interviewees, recalls that Stubblebine was fascinated by self-styled psychic Uri Geller and regularly held "spoon-bending" parties. From Geller's thesis that metal can be bent by mind control, Stubblebine theorized that it is possible to stare at animals and, with psychic concentration, cause their hearts to stop beating.

The second interviewee is former Green Beret Glenn Wheaton, who claims that in the 1980s he'd been in charge of a secret psychic-force operation called "Project Jedi," for reasons obvious to anyone who's ever seen the *Star Wars* films. Wheaton further insists that he knew of a Sergeant Michael Echanis, who was reportedly able to kill a goat merely by staring at it. Why a goat, you ask? Because Special Ops was using goats for medical experiments, and they happened to be handy. Though Wheaton didn't witness Echanis' fatal staredown first-hand, he is certain that it occurred at Fort Bragg, indicating to him that the Army was actively pursuing Stubblebine's theories. Ronson moves on to Jim Channon, identified as the creator of Fort Bragg's psychic-solider program. Resembling a *Dragnet* caricature of a overaged hippie burnout—flowing hair, love beads, Technicolor dreamcoat and all—Channon tells Ronson that while serving as an officer in Vietnam he'd witnessed the *en masse* killing of a group of soldiers who seemed incapable of aiming their weapons at a female sniper. Sensing that this tragedy occurred because the victims had never developed mental "cunning," Channon began searching for that cunning and found it in California's New Age Movement. In 1979 he published *The First Earth Manual*, dedicated to incapacitating the enemy with such mesmerizing tactics as "sparkly eyes." Channon also came up with the strategy of gently lulling the enemy into docility by repeatedly playing the same discordant song. With Stubblebine's blessing, Channon established the First Earth Battalion, espousing the philosophy "Be all that we can be! The right to think the unthinkable, dream the possible, bring it about for others." Included in the training program were fasting sessions, massages and chanted mantras.

Though Channon insists that his methods were merely intended to improve the morale of his charges, there were those at the top of the military food chain who wanted to use the First Earth Batallion as a force of aggression (or so says Ronson). We learn some more about alleged goat-killer Michael Echanis—who died years earlier in a helicopter crash—and meet the late sergeant's Army pal Pete Brusso, a martial-arts teacher who seems to take great pleasure inflicting pain on Ronson while demonstrating "kinetic energy." Next, former general John Alexander is interviewed by the documentary's producer John Sergeant. The conversation is largely unproductive save for Alexander's insistence that the "goat-killer" wasn't Echanis at all, but instead another ex-sergeant named Guy Savelli, presently running a combination dance studio and martial arts school. Savelli is famous in paranormal circles as the man who claims to have killed a hamster by (yes) staring at it. What's more, he has the videotape to prove it. The tape does indeed show the hamster slumping to the bottom of his cage, only to get up again moments later—but it sure *looked* stiff for a while there. Eventually Savelli gets around to discussing the goat ... or rather, goats. I picked out thirty of 'em, he says, and stared 'em all down—and the goat *next* to the one I was staring at dropped dead! (No videotape this time, though he does have footage of another staring session which ends with the goat still up and braying.) Back we go to Pete Brusso, who dismisses goat-staring as a party trick but offers to show Ronson how to "project" himself to another location without moving a muscle. Jim Channon floats in again just before the fadeout, claiming that Secretary of Defense Donald Rumsfeld has invited him deploy his paranormal powers in the War on Terror.

Most of the interviewees in this episode of *Crazy Rulers of the World* seem to be struggling to keep a straight face. The sequence with the funkadelic Jim Channon suggests that he's put on this dog-and-pony show many times before, and that he might be laying it on a bit thicker than usual because Ronson is such an easy mark. One is left with the impression that everyone whom Jon Ronson interviews is as big a huckster as Albert Stubblebine's beloved Uri Geller. The whole episode comes off like a prolonged spoon-bending trick.

This sideshow atmosphere is not sustained in the two remaining episodes, where the tone is grimmer and more accusatory. Episode Two, "Funny Torture," chronicles the controversial methods used by Special Ops to coerce information from Iraqi and Al-Quaida prisoners, suggesting that these harsh techniques are perversions of the benign psychological procedures espoused by the First Earth Batallion — including the breaking down of captives by playing the theme song of the TV kiddie show *Barney and Friends* over and over again. Ronson theorizes that the *Barney* story was deliberately leaked to the American media by the government, who hoped that its surface ridiculousness would defuse the bad press surrounding the Army's extreme interrogation tactics and the prisoner abuse at Abu Ghraib. Episode Three, "Psychic Footsoldiers," is a disturbing dissection of the Army's experiments with ESP and mind control, focusing on the death of interrogator Frank Olson from an alleged LSD overdose. Blisteringly biased from first frame to last, *Crazy Rules of the World* may not win any new converts to Jon Ronson's viewpoint, but he certainly makes a trenchant argument.

Ronson incorporated much of the documentary's material in a 2005 book published by Simon & Schuster, *The Men Who Stare at Goats*. The impression in the TV series that the interviewees may have occasionally been pulling the author's leg isn't quite as pervasive in the book; minus the visuals, the saga of the First Earth Batallion seems to take on added plausibility. While Ronson never states outright that the paranormal phenomena he describes actually occurred, many of his editorial decisions seem calculated to lead the reader to just such a conclusion. For example, though it is obvious in the documentary that Pete Brusso is shifting his body from side to side while claiming to "project" himself, in the book Ronson says that he did not see Brusso move. Even so, the TV and literary versions of *Men Who Stare at Goats* have two things very much in common: Ronson's outrage over the extreme coercion tactics used by interrogators during the Second Gulf War, and the author's skepticism regarding the Army's official story of Frank Olson's LSD-related death.

No one in Hollywood was surprised when the movie rights for *The Men Who Stare at Goats* were optioned by actor George Clooney and his producing partner Grant Heslov. As an outspoken opponent of President George W. Bush's Iraq policy, Clooney would have been entirely in character had he filmed the property as a deadly serious propaganda piece and retained Ronson's bitter indictment of the American power structure. Instead, the actor opted to dwell upon the lighthearted (and lightheaded) tone of the book's earlier chapters concerning the First Earth Batallion. Jon Ronson had described these passages in a 2005 interview: "I think *The Men Who Stare at Goats* shows that insane conspiracies happen, but quite often in slightly buffoonish human ways (like Major Generals trying to walk through walls)." This buffoonery was the ball that Ronson passed along to Clooney, who ran with it all the way. Scripted by Peter Straughan, directed by co-producer Grant Heslov (his first such assignment) and released in 2009 by Overture Films, *The Men Who Stare at Goats* is one of the falling-down-funniest Army comedies ever made.

Ronson's book opens with the pithy statement "This Is a True Story." The film version begins with "More of this is true than you would believe." Though the actual participants in the story are readily recognizable, all the names have been changed. The cast includes George Clooney as Lynn Cassady, a character based on "Project Jedi's" head man Glenn Wheaton; Jeff Bridges as Bill Django, the film's Jim Channon counterpart; Stephen Root as Gus Lacey, inspired by Guy Savelli; and Stephen Lang as Brigadier General Avery Hopgood, who like his real-life role model Albert Stubblebine sets things in motion by attempting to walk through a solid wall. As will be seen in the following synopsis, practically all the factoids set forth in the earlier versions of *The Men Who Stare at Goats* show up in the film, though seldom in the same context.

The story is told from the P.O.V. of narrator Bob Wilton, a reporter from Ann Arbor, Michigan. After his wife dumps him, the disillusioned Bob determines to "find himself" by becoming a war correspondent in Iraq. Once in the Middle East, he chances to meet Lynn Cassady, a sales rep for a Halliburton-like business firm. Having heard Cassady's name before, Bob mentions their mutual acquaintance Gus Lacey, whom he'd once interviewed. Lacey's tirades about psychic spies and animals killed with brain-waves had struck Bob as funny, but the mere mention of Gus's name has a disturbing effect on Cassady. Gradually unwinding, Cassady tells Bob about his participation

George Clooney is without question one of *The Men Who Stare at Goats*, from the 2009 Overture Films release of the same name.

in the "New Earth Army," a special unit created by the charismatic Bill Django to experiment with psychic-warfare tactics under the benevolent guidance of General Hopgood. Cassady explains that in order to properly harness the unit's paranormal skills, one must become a "Jedi"—thereby triggering a huge laugh from the audience, inasmuch as Bob Wilton is being played by Ewan McGregor, only four years removed from his portrayal of the young Obi-Wan Kenobi in the three *Star Wars* prequels. Agreeing to drive Bob to Iraq, Cassady continues to reveal bits and pieces of his military past, occasionally showing off his psychic powers to prove he isn't just another crackpot. In each such case, these "powers" can be chalked up to illusion or coincidence, and Bob remains unpersuaded. He also begins to seriously question his companion's sanity: While attempting to conjure a cloudburst out of the sky, Cassady smashes up his vehicle, forcing himself and Bob to trudge through the desert on foot—all the while insisting that he has the situation well in hand.

Kidnapped by bandits and locked in a cell, Bob is now convinced that he was better off in Michigan, but Cassady assures him that they were both destined for their current fate. The two men are rescued by defense contractor Todd Nixon (Robert Patrick) who intends to "westernize" the war-torn region for fun and profit. Before long, Bob and Cassady are caught in the crossfire between two rival American contracting firms (arguably the film's most blatant anti–Gulf War statement), whereupon they determine that the only honorable person in these here parts is a local named Mahmud (Walee Zuaiter). Cassady later declares that he's been "reactivated" to straighten out the Iraq crisis via an ESP message from his former comrade-in-arms Bill Django, and is compelled to obey because he feels responsible for the downfall of the New Earth Army after a tragedy involving a bad drug trip. The incident was actually the handiwork of another New Earther, a mean-spirited Uri Geller wannabe named Larry Hooper (Kevin Spacey), who after precipitating the suicide of a spaced-out soldier during an unauthorized LSD experiment managed to heap all the blame on Django. Taking charge of the unit, Hooper ordered Cassady to start working on "offensive" tactics, beginning with staring down and killing a goat. Forced to use his powers for eee-vil, Cassady has carried his shame with him ever since.

Arriving at a secret base near the Iraqi border (actually and appropriately filmed near Roswell, New Mexico!), Bob and Cassady find out that Hooper is now head of a private firm called Psi-Security (read: Blackwater), specializing in such enhanced-interrogation techniques as the aforementioned repetition of the *Barney* theme; among the prisoners subjected to this fiendish torture is the wholly innocent Mahmud. Even worse, the once-proud Django is a pathetic husk of his former self, reduced to toadying for Hooper. Angling for a double redemption, Bob begs Django to use his old black magic to lift Cassady out of his depression and foil Hooper. Ultimately, Bob must assume the "Jedi" role by taking charge of the situation, sneaking into the base's mess tent and lacing the scrambled eggs with LSD—which, thanks to Django, is also poured into the drinking water (the filmmakers are well versed in their hippie mythology). With Hooper and his minions too stoned to put up a defense, Cassady atones for past failures by freeing all the Iraqi prisoners, as well as the hundreds of experimental goats that Psi-Security has kept penned up. Safely back in Michigan, Bob gets word that Cassady and Django had crashed while making their getaway in a helicopter (Michael Echanis, remember?) In their honor, he writes an exposé of Hooper's diabolical experiments, only to be disillusioned twice in the same movie when the Media ignores most of his story—but latches on to the *Barney* part just to get a few easy laughs.

Virtually all of the sinister and conspiratorial aspects of Jon Ronson's original book are sacrificed for the sake of sheer unadulterated looniness in the film version of *The Men Who Stare at Goats*. Even when the pace begins to lag midway through the picture, the virtuoso performance of George Clooney and the flashy retro-sixties direction of Grant Heslov keep the audience's interest at high pique. Surprisingly, Jon Ronson did not object at all to the film's cartoonlike approach. Interviewed by the UGO website's Jordan Hoffman, the author noted: "The funny stuff from the first half of the book is all there. The second half of the book is very dark, and much of this is only hinted at in the film, but I think that makes sense—the movie has to have its own logic. I'm not sure focusing any more on the torture stories would have been appropriate." Less supportive was Ronson's TV producer John Sergeant, who'd spent three years doing the leg work and arranging all the interviews for the documentary series *Crazy Rulers of the World*, only to be "airbrushed" (his own word) out of the subsequent book and film. The crowning insult came when Sergeant was not invited to the picture's premiere at the London Film Festival. This contretemps might make a good movie in itself, should George Clooney ever be in the mood to stare at something again.

While acknowledging that *The Men Who Stare at Goats* is a gut-buster, many military-comedy fans prefer the more conventional fact-based films referenced in this chapter, with *Operation Petticoat* usually cited as the best of the batch. But even those with no special affection for *Goats* must admit that it contains a humdinger of a closing disclaimer: "Although this film is inspired by John Ronson's book *The Men Who Stare At Goats*, it is a fiction, and while the characters Lynn Cassady and Bill Django are based on actual persons, Sergeant Glenn Wheaton and Colonel Jim Channon, all other characters are invented or are composites and are not portrayals of actual persons. The filmmakers ask that no one attempt walking through walls, cloudbursting while driving, or staring for hours at goats with the intent of harming them ... invisibility is fine."

11

The Wheeler Dealers

The term "wheeler dealer" originated in the American West of the 19th century, referring to a high-stakes gambler who preferred roulette (a "wheeler") or poker (a "dealer"). Gradually the term came to describe not the gambler but the man who controlled the wheel or dealt the cards—usually to his own crooked advantage. Initially a compliment, "wheeler dealer" eventually became a pejorative, synonymous with cheating, finagling and taking advantage of suckers.

They may have been called "big dealers," "smooth operators" or "high rollers," but from World War I onward there always seemed to be at least one bonafide wheeler-dealer at every Army barracks, on every Navy vessel and in every Marine platoon — at least in the movies. You've seen 'em all: The lucky stiff who somehow manages to roll a seven or deal himself four aces with stunning regularity, collecting everyone else's bankroll after only putting up a buck or two of his own dough; the habitual speculator who gulls new recruits into betting on a thing so "sure" that it can't lose, but always does; the self-styled Romeo who monopolizes all the good-looking girls in town with a basketful of promises he has no intention of keeping. Seldom is it a game of chance with these guys: They've staked out the territory, covered all bets, weighed all risks and figured out all angles way ahead of time.

A variation of this type is the camp entrepreneur who never lets anything as trivial as a war stand in the way of good old American enterprise. These are the fellows who run the camp laundry or recreation hall at a tidy profit; who despite officer-imposed restrictions somehow scare up enough cigarettes, chocolate bars and nylons to exchange with civilians for financial and/or sexual services rendered; who sneak liquor and even girls into the barracks for various nocturnal shindigs without ever awakening a single top sergeant or M.P.; and who, upon discovering that their best pal possesses unique talents, will move heaven and earth to promote that pal to stardom — after first reserving for themselves a generous percentage of all future profits. A singularly resourceful form of wheeler-dealer can be found wearing the uniform of a supply sergeant or the apron of a camp cook. Need a few extras jeeps, radios, rifles or rounds of ammo that you've previously been denied by HQ? No problem. Want to make sure that the regular "grunts" get fed just as well if not better than the officers? No sweat. The credo of these seasoned scavengers is always the same: "The difficult we do immediately. The impossible takes a little bit longer."

Until the mid–1950s, the wheeler-dealers of service films were by and large limited to supporting roles in comedies (Keenan Wynn as the glib self-appointed "agent" of soldier-author Robert Walker Sr. in *See Here, Private Hargrove*), or as comedy relief in serious films (Jay C. Flippen as Major John Wayne's light-fingered line chief in *Flying Leathernecks*). Their transition to stardom occurred in the fall of 1955 with the premiere of the CBS television sitcom *You'll Never Get Rich*. Also known as *The Phil Silvers Show*, this popular weekly starred comedian Silvers as Master Sergeant Ernest T. Bilko, resident wheeler-dealer *nonpareil* of fictional Fort Baxter in Rosewell, Kansas (and later of Camp Fremont in Gopher City, California). Bilko was an extension of Harrison Floy, the early–20th-century scam artist portrayed by Silvers in the 1948 Broadway musical *High Button Shoes*. A brilliant creation (thanks largely to the star, who wrote much of his own dialogue), Harrison Floy burst onto the stage stocked with a limitless supply of schemes and scams — and if one of his cons didn't work, he would instantly conjure up another one on the spot. Even when exposed as a charlatan and surrounded by minions of the law, Floy was never at a loss for a new strategy, often switching gears in mid-sentence: Sternly threatening to sue for false arrest, then gushing praise on the cops for the smartness of their uniforms and the neatness of their haircuts, and finally offering to purchase tickets for the policeman's ball. If ever an award was issued for Thinking Fast on Your Feet, Harrison Floy would haved copped the prize three years running.

Following *High Button Shoes*, Phil Silvers headlined another Broadway hit, *Top Banana*. When this show folded in 1954, Silvers found himself "at liberty" fo the first time in a decade. Out of boredom, he approached CBS program manager Hubbell Robinson and offered his talents for a TV series. Robinson paired the comedian with Nat Hiken, a writer who had previously created funny situations for Milton Berle, Fred Allen and Martha Raye. A fan of *High Button Shoes*, Hiken felt that the Harrison Floy character was a "natural" for television, but not in the same period setting as the musical. After discussing dozens of potential series premises with Silvers, Hiken suggested casting the actor as a flim-flamming Army sergeant named Bilko. According to TV historian Ted Thomey, Silvers was at first resistant: "Bilko and bilk. The name and the guy's money schemes are too apparent. It has a kind of phony ring to it. A show like that can get tiresome pretty fast." Hiken eventually persuaded the comedian that Bilko was the ideal character for his patented sharpster persona.

As Silvers himself described his character in a 1955 *TV Guide* interview, Sgt. Bilko "is a composite picture of all the great goldbrick artists who ever made good in the army. He's king of the motor pool, of the mess hall, scourge of the orderly room.... He runs poker games, baseball pools, and bedmaking contests. He also sells embroidered pillows. He even rents his car at 10 cents a mile — with a group plan available at special rates." *You'll Never Get Rich* was perfectly attuned to a 1950s TV audience largely comprised of ex-servicemen. After enduring years of inequities regarding regulations and rank, these veterans reveled at the sight of a rule-bending noncom who so effortlessly outfoxed his superior officers. What World War II or Korea veteran could *not* live vicariously through the escapades of Sgt. Bilko, wishing that he'd had the guts and gall to pull off Ernie's elaborate hoaxes while simultaneously hoodwinking the Brass? The decision by Nat Hiken to balance Bilko's buffoonery with a realistic depiction of a typical American military post further strengthened audience identification with the series, adding a much-needed touch of authenticity to the wacky goings-on. Bilko also endeared himself to viewers (particularly the ladies) by coming off as the proverbial Scoundrel with a Heart, a soft touch who would invariably relent if one of his schemes threatened to victimize someone who didn't truly deserve it, or who would use his mountebank skills to help the downtrodden. Silvers' concern that *You'll Never Get Rich* would "get tiresome pretty fast" turned out to be unfounded: The series lasted four years and 142 episodes.

Contractual obligations prevented Phil Silvers from starring in a feature-film version of *You'll Never Get Rich* while the show was still running (the property wouldn't make it to the Big Screen until long after Silvers' death, but we'll get to that in due time). Still, the wheeler-dealer spirit of Sgt. Ernie Bilko was manifested in several other characters appearing in service comedies from 1957 onward. These Bilko derivations were generally driven by one of two motivations. The nobler of the two was to deploy their con-artist talents for the common good, to save the lives of their fellow soldiers and expeditiously defeat the enemy. The less noble (but often more enjoyable) motivation was simply to have as much fun and make as much money as possible despite the joyless, profitless strictures of military life. For the sake of chronology we'll discuss that second motivation first, beginning with the earliest of the major "wheeler dealer" comedies, Columbia's *Operation Mad Ball* (1957).

Immediately after Jack Lemmon won an Academy Award for his performance as Ensign Pulver in Warner Bros.' *Mister Roberts* (see **Chapter 8**), the logical response of the actor's home studio Columbia should have been "Let's get Lemmon into another service comedy FAST!" Instead, the studio awkwardly wedged the actor into a brace of musical remakes, *My Sister Eileen* and *You*

Can't Run Away from It (the latter derived from Capra's *It Happened One Night*). Only after both films died at the box office did Columbia wise up and put Lemmon back in uniform for *Operation Mad Ball,* based on a stage farce written by Arthur Carter and originally produced by Jed Harris. Though the theatrical version never got to Broadway, Harris wielded enough clout to produce the film version as well, and even receive a cowriting credit, though the bulk of the scriptwork was handled by Richard Quine (who also directed) and Blake Edwards.

Opening with a theme song performed over the credits by an unbilled Sammy Davis Jr, *Operation Mad Ball* takes a place a few months after VE Day at an American Hospital Division base near Le Havre, France. The story details the various authority-tweaking scams hatched by one Private Hogan, who has the brains to qualify as an officer but prefers to remain a single-striper because it's more fun that way. No matter how often Hogan gets into hot water, he manages to avoid the stockade with his encyclopedic knowledge of Army regulations; it also helps that he has the confidence of the camp's easygoing commanding officer Colonel Rousch. The thorn in Hogan's side is Captain Locke, a modern-day Malvolio with but two goals in life: To prevent anyone from enjoying himself, and to entrap Hogan in an act of insubordination that will ensure our hero a speedy court-martial.

Among Hogan's barracks buddies is Cpl. Berryman, who happens to be in love with a pretty nurse. Berryman is downhearted for two reasons: All nurses are officers, and enlisted men are not allowed to fraternize with officers; and even if he was allowed to dally with his girlfriend, he is due to be shipped to the South Pacific in 72 hours. Hogan makes it his mission to arrange a romantic rendezvous for Berryman and the nurse at a nearby inn, gradually expanding this tête-à-tête into a lavish "mad ball" where all the GIs and nurses can dance, drink and socialize without fretting over protocol — and without tipping off the troublesome Captain Locke. Hogan's increasingly complex "operation" involves the top-to-bottom renovation of a rundown inn at the Army's expense; an attractive nurse named Betty Bixby, who inspires Hogan to feign an ulcer to enjoy the pleasure of her company; a jive-talking transportation sergeant named Yancy Skibo who is cajoled into shipping an entire regiment out to sea without official sanction; a pair of maleable German POWs who'll take orders from anyone with a loud voice; and some deft sleight-of-hand involving a pilfered set of X-rays and an unusually mobile cadaver. No matter what unforeseen obstacle crosses his path, Hogan always manages to pull a new rabbit out of his hat and dream up a strategy even more inspired than the last one.

Though *Operation Mad Ball* occasionally betrays its stage origins with protracted dialogue sequences played out on single sets, director-writer Richard Quine and collaborator Blake Edwards effectively cinematize the property with a number of sight-gag setpieces and running gags. Highlights include a delightful exercise in black humor as Hogan tries to pass off a very-much-alive POW as a corpse in his efforts to keep Captain Locke from tumbling to his party plans; and some harmlessly sadistic physical humor when nurse Betty Bixby discovers that Hogan has not been entirely honest and above-board with her. But despite the input of Quine and Edwards, the pace tends to falter from time to time, especially in the film's midsection. Also, after nearly two hours of colorful characterizations, breathless crosstalk and zany plot twists, *Operation Mad Ball* arrives at a disappointingly limp conclusion, the titular "ball" coming off as square and sedate as a high school prom. But let's move on to the good stuff.

Previously limited to standard leading-man roles opposite such female luminaries as Judy Holliday and June Allyson, Jack Lemmon is positively dazzling in his first genuine starring role as Private Hogan, carrying the film and its thousand-and-one plot machinations through sheer force of personality. Never overplaying his hand, Lemmon is charmingly cunning and deliciously duplicitous from first frame to last. Too, Jack's scenes with leading lady Katherine Grant (a busy Columbia starlet who ultimately became the second Mrs. Bing Crosby) proved that he didn't need the star power of a Holliday or an Allyson to convincingly play a romantic lead, despite Richard Quine's assertion that Lemmon's "boyish quality" precluded him from becoming one of the immortal lovers of the screen. (Undoubtedly Quine said this just to get the goat of his good friend Lemmon, who was so "offended" that he continued to work with the director in such projects as *Bell Book and Candle*, *The Notorious Landlady* and *How to Murder Your Wife*.) Lemmon himself would list *Operation Mad Ball* as one of his favorite films, not because it was a box-office smash (it wasn't) but because director Billy Wilder was sufficiently impressed by the actor's performance to offer him a leading role in a little trifle called *Some Like It Hot*.

Several of the casting choices in *Operation Mad Ball* were made to keep members of the Columbia payroll busy. Contract players Roger Smith, James Darren and Dick York are seen to excellent advantage, with York a standout as a resentful corporal who helps Hogan undermine the hateful Captain Locke, all the while doing a Uriah Heep act as Locke's loyal toady. Arthur O'Connell, fresh from his triumph as the erstwhile fiance of old-maid schoolteacher Rosalind Russell in Columbia's *Picnic*, makes every one of his scenes count as the befuddled Colonel Rousch, at times scoring bigger laughs than star Lemmon. Best of all is Mickey Rooney, at the tail end of a Columbia contract that had included two previous service-comedy collaborations with Richard Quine and Blake Edwards, *Sound Off* (see **Chapter 12**) and *All Ashore* (see **Chapter 6**). Though Rooney's character Sgt. Yancey Skibo doesn't appear until the final third of the film, the actor so dominates the proceedings that the other players virtually melt into the background. Scampering around like a squirrel on steroids and rattling off his lines in a manic hipster lingo peppered with rhymed couplets ("Skiddle-dee-dee, not for me!"), Rooney is almost impossibly hilarious. As Richard Quine recalled years later: "Mickey never did the scene twice in the same way; every time he'd add a new touch, Jack would just fall over backwards. It was the only time I ever saw Lemmon unable to handle an acting chore. He only had one line and I don't think he ever got it out."

No, we haven't forgotten that *Operation Mad Ball* represents the screen debut of Ernie Kovacs. This is not the time or place to rhapsodize over Kovacs' genius in the field of television comedy in the 1950s, nor to itemize the many technical innovations he brought to the medium during his tragically brief lifespan. Suffice to say that by 1957, the mustachioed, cigar-chomping comedian's reputation was so exalted that Columbia was willing to offer him $100,000 (considerably more than Jack Lemmon took home!) to costar in *Operation Mad Ball*. The studio also permitted Ernie to write and appear in the film's coming-attractions trailer, the closest *any* movie ever came to being a true "Kovacs Production." Striking a casual pose while leaning against a prop fireplace (which immediately collapses), Kovacs graciously explains that *Operation Mad Ball* is based on *Webster's New Collegiate Dictionary*: "Everything you've read in the dictionary is in this picture. 'Love' ... 'Hate' ... 'Fear' ... 'Passion' ... 'Xylophones.'" Offering to show a few "exciting scenes" from the film, he holds up a set of 8X10 glossies well out of viewing range, flipping each photo to the ground as he leers over its contents. Next he discusses the cast, beginning with a "gripping" scene featuring Glenn Ford: "Not in this picture, but it's a good scene." Each of the actual stars of *Operation Mad Ball* is dismissed with a seconds-lasting snippet except for Katherine Grant, who is revealed in her underwear. "Sorry, kid," Ernie apologizes to the mortified actress. "Thought you were ready." Finally Kovacs gets around to showing one of his own scenes in *Mad Ball*, consisting of an extreme long shot minus Ernie or any other recognizable human being. In closing, our host assures us that the picture is "adult ... mature ... astute." (Astute?)

This trailer primed filmgoers to assume that Kovacs was one of the instigators of the wackiness in *Operation Mad Ball*, instead of the beady-eyed villain who works so diligently to spoil the fun. It's likely that Ernie's fans were disappointed to find him consigned to a bad-guy role; Ernie himself later noted that Captain Locke was just the sort of intractable authority figure that he had hated and tirelessly battled throughout his TV career. It is to the actor's credit that he transcends his role's limitations with some inspired bits of comic business. Whether licking his chops over the prospect of a cushy post-military political career, barely suppressing his animal instincts while exchanging small talk with luscious nurse Betty, or mapping out his campaign to destroy Pvt. Hogan while noisily

Judging from this irreverent studio portrait, you'd think that Ernie Kovacs was the hero of Columbia's 1957 Army comedy *Operation Mad Ball*, instead of the villain of the piece.

inhaling nasal spray, no one but Ernie Kovacs could so brilliantly combine ruthless ambition with rank vulgarity.

Richard Quine has described Jack Lemmon and Ernie Kovacs as "a sophisticated Laurel and Hardy," though the actors were never actually teamed in any of their three costarring films. Nonetheless, the two became close friends during filming of *Operation Mad Ball*—another reason beyond the aforementioned *Some Like It Hot* connection that Jack regarded the movie as one of his favorites. For Kovacs, the film was both blessing and curse. Though it established the comedian as a bankable screen presence, it also typecast him in military roles. Of the ten films in which Kovacs appeared before his death in 1962, he would play captains in four of them, an artistic rut that prompted Ernie to post a plaintive full-page ad in the Hollywood trade papers: "NO MORE CAPTAINS — PLEASE!" (See **Chapter 8** for another of Kovacs' Komic Kaptains in 1960's *Wake Me When It's Over*.)

The year following *Operation Mad Ball*, audiences were introduced to another form of military wheeler-dealer: The clever soldier who stages an elaborate ruse not for personal gain but to save his own life and those of his comrades. This character, the spiritual descendant of cagey POW Sgt. Sefton in Billy Wilder's wartime drama *Stalag 17*, blossomed forth comedically with Glenn Ford's portrayal of Master Sergeant Murphy Savage in *Imitation General* (MGM, 1958), the first of the actor's collaborations with director George Marshall.

Imitation General is one of several Army comedies written by former *Life* magazine staffer William Bowers, who in 1944 had put his embryonic Hollywood screenwriting career on hold to enlist in the Civilian Pilot Training Program, with the promise of an officer's commission in the Army Air Corps. He quickly learned that, contrary to the entreaties of eager recruiting officers, men who were too old to fly fighter planes and too inexperienced to pilot bombers were a glut on the market — and also that the only available training planes were an assortment of obsolete clunkers that hadn't flown since the days of Von Richtofen. Denied his commission and shunted off to a dismal stateside Army camp that had been set aside for "the overaged, overweight, undesirable and underappreciated," Bowers found himself in the company of several other college-educated enlistees for whom the Service had no real use beyond perpetual KP and endless twenty-mile hikes. All that alleviated the boredom of barracks life was Bowers' friendship with the incredible Archie Hall, an ex-cowboy, ex-radio announcer, ex-movie stuntman and ex-just-about-everything else, who at age 36 was even more of a square peg than his fellow would-be flyboys— not that he had any burning desire to actually fly a plane. Fascinated by the smooth-talking Hall's ability to avoid regular duties and secure privileges and creature comforts that were out of reach for most buck privates—frequently by dropping hints that he was actually an officer in disguise, a scam Hall was able to pull off with remarkable finesse — Bowers quietly catalogued Archie's various escapades for future literary use.

By the late 1950s, Bowers was an established screenwriter with two Oscars to his credit. Though he hadn't yet immortalized Archie Hall on celluloid, vestiges of his silver-tongued Air Force buddy can be found in *Imitation General*. In fact, this curious film offers *two* accomplished wheeler-dealers, each presumably representing a different aspect of Archie's personality.

Imitation General is set "Somewhere in France" just after D-Day. Several American soldiers, cut off from their units without officers, are trapped in a pocket surrounded by Germans. Accompanied by his driver Murph Savage and radioman Cpl. Chan Derby (Red Buttons), Brigadier General Charles Lane (Kent Smith) arrives and takes charge of the bedraggled troops, straightening out their aimlessness and confusion within seconds. A tough-but-kindly Omar Bradley type, Lane explains to Murph that men under pressure perform best when they know they have a strong leader, further emphasizing how important it is for the troops' morale to actually see a general walking among them. Alas, no sooner is this said than Lane is killed by enemy sniper fire. Ruminating over the General's loss, Murph and Derby sit disconsolately in a farmhouse owned by fiery mademoiselle Simone (Taina Elg). Suddenly in barges Cpl. Terry Sellers (Dean Jones), panicking over the current crisis. Spotting General Lane's helmet in Murph's lap, Sellers assumes that the Sergeant is himself the General, but before Murph can set him straight the battle-fatigued corporal breaks down in sobs. Remembering Lane's words about putting up a strong front to sustain morale, Murph assumes the role of General and sternly but compassionately orders Sellers to pull himself together. Impressed by the positive effect he has on the corporal, and knowing that the chances of any other high-ranking officers showing up in the near future are slim to none, Murph decides to continue his impersonation, much to the dismay of the nervous Derby.

Within the span of a single day, general-by-necessity Murph has molded the marooned troops into a high-functioning combat machine, mostly by repeating the patriotic platitudes he'd previously heard from the lips of General Lane. By now accustomed to bluffing his way through any situation — so impressively that a shavetail lieutenant (John Clayton) takes it for granted that the "General" is a West Pointer — Murph passes along this talent to the men in his command, successfully gulling the Germans into mistaking a jeep covered in scrap metal for an armored vehicle and halting two enemy tanks in their tracks simply by posting a sign saying that a bridge is mined (which of course it isn't). Meanwhile back at the farmhouse, Derby exercises his *own* sharpster skills by outwitting the odious Pvt. Orville Hutchmeyer (Tige Andrews) — who'd been Master Sergeant Orville Hutchmeyer until Murph had gotten him busted for dealing in stolen Army supplies. Itching to get even with Murph, Hutchmeyer must be prevented from finding out that the Sergeant has spent the last several hours impersonating an officer. Derby pulls this off by (a) convincing Hutchmeyer that Murph was killed at Normandy, fabricating a heartrending account of the Sergeant's sacrificial heroics; and (b) keeping Hutchmeyer from bursting in on an argument between Murph and Simone by telling the private that "General Lane" is subject to crazy spells, especially whenever anyone tries to move in on "his" girlfriend. The last and silliest strategy to flummox Hutchmeyer occurs at the end of the film, when the stewed-to-the-gills private is led to believe that Murph's ghost is haunting him!

Despite such advertising tags as "The wildest SNAFU the Army ever knew," *Imitation General* is an uncertain and unstable mixture of comedy and drama. The film has moments of warmth, grace and gentle humor — especially the scenes with Finnish actress Taina Elg, who plays her role entirely in French — that are thoroughly mitigated by appalling lapses in taste, with Glenn Ford and company having *way* too much fun slaughtering Germans in a variety of ways. This left MGM at a loss over how to properly promote the picture, though at the time of its release most observers, still basking in the rosy glow of the star's recent *Teahouse of the August Moon* and *Don't Go Near the Water*, accepted *Imitation General* as a comedy pure and simple. In his review for the New York *Herald Tribune*, Paul V. Beckley wrote that William Bowers "is obviously familiar with the particular brand of sardonic conversation typical of American GI's.... Although it never rises to satire, and the variant of mistaken-identity gambit so dear to farce is far from fresh, the charm

11. The Wheeler Dealers

of Ford's and Buttons' performances gives it a sprightly, good-humored air.... Although their styles are hardly identical, each exudes in his own way a sort of exuberant and wry confidence that is largely responsible for the picture's charm."

Around the same time that *Imitation General* was being hooked together, Bill Bowers dusted off his old "Archie Hall" project and approached TV actor-producer-director Jack Webb, who was anxious to sever ties with his long-running *Dragnet* series and concentrate on theatrical features. Though amused at the prospect of directing a comedy, Webb put Bowers' project on the back burner and set the screenwriter to work on the director's current film project, the newspaper drama *-30-*. Once that epic was in the can, Webb turned his attention to the earlier Bowers script, now titled *The Last Time I Saw Archie*. To cinch a release deal, Webb assured United Artists that he'd land a major star and assemble a top-notch cast for his new picture. Among the big names approached by Webb was Robert Mitchum, who hadn't appeared in an American film for nearly two years. Mitchum agreed to make the picture for $100,000 per week, four weeks guaranteed; he also demanded full script approval. When asked by columnist Sheila Graham why he regarded *The Last Time I Saw Archie* as his favorite film, Mitchum's reply couldn't have been more characteristic: "It's the first time I made $100,000 a week ... plus the keys to the ignition."

Mitchum of course played Archie Hall, while Jack Webb wore two hats as director and costar, essaying the role of William Bowers (Webb and Bowers were by now close friends). True to his word, the director stocked his supporting cast with some of the best comic talents available. Louis Nye and Don Knotts were just coming off a long hitch with *The Steve Allen Show*; Joe Flynn and Del Moore were established TV-sitcom second bananas; and Robert Strauss and Harvey Lembeck had stolen everything but the cameras with their supporting antics in *Stalag 17*. Richard Arlen, a

Robert Mitchum (left) and Jack Webb try to dead-pan their way past a couple of MPs in *The Last Time I Saw Archie* (United Artists, 1961).

35-year movie veteran who'd costarred in the first Oscar-winning picture *Wings,* was hired for "acting relief," as was former *Henry Aldrich* star James Lydon, who went on to join the Warner Bros. production staff when Jack Webb took over the studio's television unit in 1963. Unabashed sports fan Webb also found small (but prominently billed) roles for two pro athletes, Don Drysdale of the Los Angeles Dodgers and Bill Kilmer of the San Francisco 49ers. And since a Robert Mitchum picture demanded an attractive leading lady, Webb obligingly hired *two*: Martha Hyer, a svelte blonde hitherto specializing in sultry roles, and Eurasian actress France Nuyen, star of the recent Broadway hit *The World of Suzie Wong.*

Filmed at the old Republic Studios in glorious black & white, *The Last Time I Saw Archie,* set in the last months of 1944, wastes no time establishing Archie Hall as a wheeler-dealer *par excellence,* with Bill Bowers as his best pal and softest touch. Assigned to Buckley Field in Colorado, Hall is determined to renew his acquaintance with a local girl named Peggy, and to take Bowers along, ostensibly on a double-date basis but in reality to finance Archie's night on the town. This, however, requires a one-day pass. Nonchalantly strutting around the camp with a clipboard in his hand and making comments like "very good" and "carry on" to everyone he passes, Archie strides into the office of duty sergeant Greenbriar (Lembeck), and without overtly offering a bribe in exchange for a pass, does exactly that. Greenbriar wonders why Archie appears to be such a take-charge guy, especially since he's only a private. Doltish master sergeant Erlenheim (Strauss) has a theory: According to an article he once read, Military Intelligence officers have been known to show up at certain bases unannounced, posing as privates in order to gather information. Before long, Greenbriar and Erlenheim have convinced themselves that not only is Archie Hall a member of G-2, but also a general in disguise! It's *Imitation General* redux, only this time the protagonist merely intimates that he's an officer without resorting to flat-out lies—and of course the stakes aren't as high as in the earlier film.

Once they've secured their pass, Hall and Bowers commiserate with local lovelies Peggy Kramer (Hyer) and Cindy Hamilton (Nuyen). When it turns out that she's not the same Peggy with whom Archie had an affair before the war, Miss Kramer gravitates to Bowers, while Archie snuggles with Cindy. The fact that Miss Hamilton is a Japanese-American who asks all sorts of probing questions about the boys' previous military activities, coupled with her limitless bankroll of outdated 20-dollar bills (the sort usually carried by foreigners newly arrived in the U.S.), prompts Bowers to suspect that Cindy is an enemy spy. At the same time, Greenbriar and Erlenheim, believing that there is an illicit relationship between Ellie and camp commander Colonel Martin (Arlen), jump to the same conclusion—and also presume that Archie is either working undercover or has sold out to the Japanese. Another subplot involves a trio of middle-aged privates (Nye, Flynn and Moore), who are jealous over the amazing Mr. Hall's ability to avoid grunt duty, hobnob with officers, and wine and dine beautiful women. To mollify his resentful buddies, Archie periodically sets them up with girls and booze, hosting several parties at Cindy's apartment. All this extracurricular activity makes Bowers, Greenbriar and Erlenheim even more suspicious of Archie and Cindy.

It is revealed that Cindy is indeed involved in espionage, but on behalf of the United States. With the blessing of Col. Martin—*not* her boyfriend, but her legal guardian—she has been behaving suspiciously on purpose to bring a genuine nest of Japanese spies out in the open. In love with Archie, Cindy sees to it that he is not punished for misleading everybody to assume that he's something he isn't, though in fact Archie has never once actually claimed to be an officer, spy or anything else. A postwar postscript shows Bowers back at work as a Hollywood writer in the employ of Archie Hall, who has somehow sweet-talked his way into a production job at a major studio— with the former Sgt. Erlenheim as his chauffeur. (In real life, Arch Hall *did* go into film production, mostly turning out such cut-rate dreck as *Eegah!* and *Wild Guitar,* both starring the uniquely ungifted Arch Hall Jr.)

Released in 1961, *The Last Time I Saw Archie* is yet another example of a movie that reads better than it plays. Jack Webb directs comedy as if he was still directing *Dragnet*, with all the trademarks of that classic TV cop show in attendance: The laconic offscreen narration, the lengthy tight-closeup dialogue exchanges, the heavy-handed musical cues, and the pantomimic "punch lines" at the end of each scene. One half expects Bill Bowers to deliver an impassioned anti-drug speech to Blue Boy.

As usual, Webb's acting is as stiff as a mackerel, never more so than when he is trying to be relaxed and casual. In contrast, the usually low-key Robert Mitchum is positively giddy in several scenes, mugging and mincing as never before and never again. It's hardly his best performance, but it has enough novelty value to sustain interest during the otherwise sluggish expositional sequences. Perhaps Mitchum was overcompensating for the fact that his character is never as funny or compelling as Bill Bowers seems to think he is. Moreover, we never get to see Archie Hall in full fettle as a scam artist because his victims are such pushovers that he barely has to exert himself to pull the wool over their eyes.

Most of the talented supporting cast is ill served. Harvey Lembeck and Robert Strauss go through their usual paces, while Louis Nye and Joe Flynn work much too hard to breathe life into their lackluster characters. Only Don Knotts manages to sparkle as a 90-day-wonder Army captain, delivering a hilariously hackneyed welcome speech to the new recruits. It's little more than a variation on one of Knotts' nightclub monologues, but the actor manages to pack more comic punch into three minutes than the rest of the players in the remaining ten reels. Alas, once Knotts finishes his routine, he all but disappears from the film, except for a seconds-lasting closeup in a PX scene that is more interesting for its surfeit of product placement (Coca-Cola machines, neatly arranged boxes of Kellogg's Corn Flakes) than its narrative content.

Because of its failure at the box office — a $1.5 million gross on a $2 million budget — most of the participants of *The Last Time I Saw Archie* preferred to put the experience behind them. Outside of Mitchum's aforementioned comment that it was his favorite film, the nicest words about *Archie* were spoken by leading lady France Nuyen, who described it as a "wonderful experience." Less positive was the reaction of the real-life Archie Hall, who apparently was so offended that he sued United Artists for invasion of privacy. This turn of events hardly fazed Bill Bowers, who later remarked that the legal action was totally consistent with Archie Hall's character — especially since Hall knew full well what was going into the film before shooting started, and claimed to be flattered by Bowers' portrayal.

Another 1961 wheeler-dealer comedy, MGM's *The Honeymoon Machine*, had like *Archie* been intended for an established middle-aged star: Cary Grant, who'd enjoyed enormous success with the 1959 service comedy *Operation Petticoat* (see **Chapter 10**). But in the end MGM decided to go with a younger and less expensive leading man, and to fill the rest of the cast with equally young and equally economical supporting players.

The Honeymoon Machine was based on Lorenze Semple Jr.'s 1959 Broadway comedy *The Golden Fleecing*. The single-set stage version concerned a trio of U.S. Navy men sequestered in a posh Venice hotel. Disguised as civilians, the tricky trio have devised a plan to win a fortune at the roulette table of the hotel's casino by using their ship's state-of-the-art computer MACS — an acronym for Magnetic Analyzer Computer Synchotron — to predict each turn of the wheel. Since MACS is supposed to be a top-secret project, the protagonists must carry out their moneymaking scheme with the precision of a covert military operation, planting one of their conspirators on board ship to relay MACS's data via semaphore. The unforeseen arrivals of the admiral's daughter and a snoopy signalman, plus the third-act intrusion of Venetian gangsters who are anxious to find out why the three seamen are enjoying such a lucky streak at the roulette wheel, add up to a frenetic farce of the door-slamming, phone-ringing, "I demand an explanation!" variety. The *Time* magazine reviewer complained that *The Golden Fleecing* was farcical "without being farcical enough," adding that the play was "into the second act before it explodes into laughter. Then it expires in the third. Playwright Semple cannot solve the author's great problem of getting his people into trouble while staying out of it himself. He is too laborious tying his yarn in knots, too predictable untying it. Amid director Abe Burrows' sharp whipcracking, there is too much forced wisecracking; amid a great many antics, there is never quite enough fun."

Though drubbed by critics and ignored by theatergoers (it opened the last week of October and closed the last week of December), *The Golden Fleecing* yielded a couple of benefits. One was long-ranging, involving the play's stars Tom Poston and Suzanne Pleshette, who during the play's run enjoyed a very brief backstage romance; four decades later, Poston and Pleshette jump-started their relationship and became husband and wife. The other benefit was considerably more short-term: In 1958, a year before its Broadway debut, *The Golden Fleecing* was purchased by MGM. The studio chose Steve McQueen, then just coming off his long-running TV series *Wanted: Dead or Alive* and the blockbuster western film *The Magnificent Seven*, to head the cast of the movie version of *The Golden Fleecing*, which was filmed and released in 1961 under its new title *The Honeymoon Machine*.

With McQueen set for the role of high-rolling Lt. Ferguson "Fergie" Howard, MGM grabbed their contract roster and checked off the names of Jim Hutton, cast as civilian computer wizard Jason Eldridge; Hutton's perennial costar Paula Prentiss, cast as the *very* nearsighted millionairess Pam Dunstan, whom Eldridge refuses to marry until he's as rich as she is; former Chicago kiddie-show hostess Brigid Bazlen as Julie Fitch, who despite the fact that she's the Admiral's daughter eagerly participates in Fergie's break-the-bank scheme; and Jack Mullaney as the conspirators' feckless ship-to-shore liason man, Lt. Beau Gilliam. Others in the cast were freelancers: Dean Jagger, looking more like President Eisenhower than ever in the role of short-fused Admiral Fitch, who must be kept in the dark about the casino caper lest Fergie be instantly court-martialed; William Lanteau as Pam's stuffy diplomat fiance Tommy Dane; and Jack Weston as Signalman Burford Taylor, whose tipsy tiptoeing along a dizzyingly high window ledge provides the film's biggest laughs.

The film needed all the laughs it could get. Under the antediluvian direction of Richard Thorpe, *The Honeymoon Machine* is a "photographed stage play" in the most negative sense. Virtually the only changes made to the theatrical original by Lorenzo Semple Jr. and scriptwriter George Wells are a few establishing scenes set on the USS *Providence*, standing in for the film's Mediterranean–based U.S.S. *Elmyra*; and a climactic slapstick melee at the casino. In a lame attempt at topicality, the play's gangsters have been replaced by Russians, with the Soviet hierarchy suspecting that the roulette-related messages sent out by MACS are some sort of espionage code (we know *exactly* the year this film was made when we see a Russian emissary banging his shoe on the table). Astonishingly, one of the few laudatory reviews given *The Honeymoon Machine* was from *Time* magazine, the same periodical that had taken *The Golden Fleecing* to the cleaners two years before. Hailing the film as a return to the screwball comedies of yore, *Time* gushed, "*The Honeymoon Machine* is the Hollywood machine in a rare moment of felicitous clank, turning out the slick, quick, funny film for which it was designed.... It produces a satisfyingly idiotic conclusion."

Though most of the cast goes through its farcical paces with aplomb — especially Paula Prentiss, who got all the best reviews — Steve McQueen is woefully out of his element as a light comedian; it should come as no surprise that he considered *The Honeymoon Machine* to be his worst film. In addition to openly clashing with director Thorpe throughout the shooting, McQueen was never able to establish a satisfactory working relationship with his 17-year-old leading lady Brigid Bazlen. Reports differ as to the source of the problem: Either McQueen and Bazlen detested each other on sight, or they were so enamored of one another that they could never be left alone. Whatever the case, McQueen's agent had to act as mediator between the two stars — and also as a buffer between MGM and Brigid Bazlen's mother, powerful Chicago columnist Maggie Daly.

Critics were brutal to the point of sadism towards Steve McQueen, some having the temerity to advise the actor to forget about movies and return to television. Happily McQueen would ignore such advice and achieve film superstardom, but before scaling the heights with such blockbusters as *The Thomas Crown Affair* and *Bullitt* the actor would make a return visit to the military-comedy genre in the 1963 Allied Artists release *Soldier in the Rain*, adapted by Blake Edwards (who also produced the film) and Maurice Richlin from a novel by William Goldman (*Butch Cassidy and the Sundance Kid*). The film also marked a re-enlistment of sorts for costar Jackie Gleason, two decades after his last brush with Army humor in *Tramp Tramp Tramp* (see **Chapter 4**). At the time of production, Gleason was a bigger name than McQueen, thus he received preferred billing—his name to the left of his co-star's—in the print ads and the film itself. (Allied Artists' original plan to bill the actors as simply "THE GLEASON" and "THE McQUEEN" was thwarted by threats of legal action from the mayors of Gleason, Tennessee, and McQueen, Montana!) Cashing in on the popularity of Jackie's concurrently produced CBS TV variety series, the photo ads depicted the comedian in his typically jaunty "How sweet it is!" pose—considerably at odds with the complex character he plays in the film.

Filmed at Paramount studios and on location in Monterey, *Soldier in the Rain* takes place in the Southern army camp that has become the permanent residence of Master Sergeant Maxwell Slaughter (Gleason), aging bon vivant, heavyweight highbrow and seasoned sharpie. Expending as little physical energy as possible unless he can extract a few extra bucks from his subordinates, and surrounded by such non–GI fringe benefits as an air conditioner and a personal soda machine, the sanguine Sergeant has already served six hitches in the Army and harbors no desire to return to civilian life. Max Slaughter is the idol of gumptious young supply sergeant Eustace Clay (McQueen), who in collaboration with Slaughter keeps busy with innumerable moneymaking schemes and scams, trading government property for personal gain without arousing the suspicions of commanding officer Lt. McGee (Tom Poston)—who for his part spends more time pouring sauerkraut juice on his aching feet than fulfilling his leadership duties. Convinced that he could make a financial killing by leaving the Service and going into private business, Clay urges Slaughter to retire from the Army and become his partner. But Slaughter keeps Clay at arm's length with his pet catchphrase: "Until that time, Eustace, until that time." For all his bluster, bravado and big words, Slaughter is terrified of venturing into the Outside World, convinced that his age and weight would make him an object of ridicule.

Hoping to cheer up his moody role model, Clay arranges a date between Slaughter and vivacious high school senior Bobby Jo Pepperdine (Tuesday Weld). Though Bobby Jo can't resist describing Slaughter to his face as "a fat Randolph Scott," she truly enjoys his company; the feeling is mutual for Slaughter, who takes a paternal interest in the ditsy teenager. This annoys Slaughter's longtime enemy, sadistic MP sergeant Lenahan (Lew Gallo), who regards the nubile Bobby Jo as his personal property. After being forced to publicly apologize to the girl for his brutish behavior, Lenahan exacts vengeance by picking a fight with Slaughter's loyal hanger-on Clay in a local tavern, with fellow MP sergeant Priest (Ed Nelson) joining the fracas. Coming to Clay's rescue, Slaughter beats up both MPs, bringing the battle to a spectacular conclusion by holding Priest aloft and tossing him across the room — a remarkable feat achieved by rigging actor Ed Nelson with a wire (both Nelson and Gleason waived the use of stunt men for this scene). Alas, this gallant gesture has tragic consequences, and the film ends with an echo of *Mister Roberts,* eloquently described by critic Marcia Eaton as "a strange kind of sadness."

This could also serve as a description for all 88 minutes of *Soldier in the Rain*, which though structured and marketed as a comedy contains isolated moments that are every bit as dark and melancholy as the film's title. This odd, unsettling blend of happiness and heartache is encapsulated in a scene near the end of the film, in which, to win a $1000 photography prize, Eustace Clay has persuaded his hyperactive Private pal Jerry Meltzer (well played by future studio executive Tony Bill) to dress up as a woman. Just as Meltzer has slipped on a dress and applied lipstick, Lt. McGee walks into the room — and of course the audience eagerly anticipates a shocked reaction or smarmy

"Mmmm ... a little travelling music, please!" Tuesday Weld and Jackie Gleason are an unlikely twosome indeed in *Soldier in the Rain* (Allied Artists, 1963).

reference to Meltzer's sexual inclination. But McGee's reaction is cut short when another soldier arrives to inform Clay that Sgt. Slaughter is dying from injuries sustained in that barroom brawl.

Echoing his behavior during the making of *Honeymoon Machine*, Steve McQueen was contrary and contentious throughout the filming of *Soldier in the Rain*, to the extent that the traditionally temperamental Jackie Gleason came off as benign and well-mannered, winning the hearts of the entire production crew with his casual kindnesses and generous gifts. The normally abrasive Jackie also took pains to say nice things about McQueen to the press, though this courtesy was not reciprocated. The ill-will between the two stars led to McQueen refusing to show up on the set until after Gleason arrived, and vice versa — a stalemate that took quite a few expensive days to resolve. Director Ralph Nelson (who'd previously collaborated with Gleason on 1962's *Requiem for a Heavyweight*) tried to determine the source of McQueen's animosity, finally tracking it down to the actor's jealousy over Gleason's expensive motorized golf cart. (One can guess to whom author William Goldman was referring when he made his famous observation, "Never underestimate the insecurity of a star.") Personal differences aside, the two stars work together beautifully on screen, their combined charisma mining laughs from even the corniest material: When, for example, Gleason admits to being a narcissist, McQueen exclaims, "I thought you liked girls like everyone else." But the film's best reviews were garnered by Tuesday Weld as Gleason's unlikely vis-à-vis — another in a gallery of inspired performances by this still very young actress.

Though it proved to be a popular film among servicemen, *Soldier in the Rain* failed to click with general audiences. Ralph Nelson has chalked up the film's financial loss to the fact that it opened only five days after the assassination of John F. Kennedy, but it may also have been due to Allied Artists' misleading ad campaign, which did nothing to prepare filmgoers for the movie's doleful passages and downbeat finale. Steve McQueen would have to wait until 1965's *The Cincinnati Kid* before his name alone could be guaranteed to open a picture—and one might take note that he never again appeared in a comedy, military or otherwise.

For producer Blake Edwards, the failure of *Soldier in the Rain* was cushioned by such subsequent successes as *The Pink Panther* and *The Great Race*; besides, one setback could hardly dampen Edwards' enthusiasm for the military-comedy genre, certainly not with such hits as *The Perfect Furlough* and *Operation Petticoat* under his belt. In 1965 the producer again collaborated with Maurice Richlin to pen the screenplay for the big-budget ($5 million) service farce *What Did You Do in the War, Daddy?*, directed by Edwards, bankrolled by the Mirisch Brothers and released in 1966 by United Artists. The idea for the film had originated with screenwriter William Peter Blatty, who had previously worked with Edwards on *A Shot in the Dark* (this was of course several years before Blatty's meteoric ascent to international acclaim as the author of *The Exorcist*). Blatty had written the first draft and submitted it to Edwards, who filed it away for future reference and promptly forgot all about it. Only when the director's then-wife began laughing her head off while skimming through Blatty's manuscript did Edwards realize he had an uncut diamond on his hands. Keeping everything in the family, it was Blake Edwards' young son Geoffrey who came up with the film's title.

An expansion of themes previously explored in both *Imitation General* and Blake Edwards' own *Operation Mad Ball*, *What Did You Do in the War, Daddy?* involves a company of American combat veterans led by the infinitely resourceful Lt. Christian (James Coburn) and rugged Italian-American Sergeant Rizzo (Aldo Ray), who in late 1943 are ordered by grandstanding General Bolt (Carroll O'Connor) to capture the strategic Sicilian village of Valerno. Placed under the command of persnickety by-the-book West Point grad Captain Cash (Dick Shawn), the soldiers charge into the village and promptly "invade" a friendly game of soccer. The Americans are relieved to find that the war-weary citizens and military personnel of Valerno are happy to surrender—but only if they are first allowed to hold their annual wine festival. Over Cash's protests, Christian agrees to these terms, obliging him to explain the delay in capturing the town by sending reports back to General Bolt about "minor resistance" from the locals. As the festival flourishes into the wee hours of the morning, Americans and Sicilians alike are fully surfeited by wine, women and song. Unfortunately, the town's military leader Captain Oppo (Sergio Fantoni) is outraged that a drunken Captain Cash has spent the night with Oppo's sweetheart Gina (Giovanna Ralli), who also happens to be the daughter of the town mayor (Jay Novello). The Italian officer huffily withdraws his surrender ... and then the fun begins.

What follows is a vast and vertiginous variety of farcical entanglements and ridiculous running gags, far too numerous to describe in detail or in context. Key situations involve a game of strip poker in which the Americans lose their uniforms to the Italians; a pair of bungling bank robbers (Vito Scotti, Johnny Seven) with a talent for tunneling into every building *but* the bank; a packet of aerial recon photos that mislead both Allies and Germans to conclude that a minor fistfight is a deadly armed confrontation; a mock battle stage-managed by Lt. Christian, with men from both sides "dying" on cue and a coterie of local whores acting as cheerleaders; a ferret-like PR officer named Potts (Harry Morgan) who gets lost in the catacombs beneath the village and goes progressively (and hilariously) insane; the inconvenient arrival of a no-nonsense German colonel (Leon Askin) who orders that the Americans be shot at sunrise, forcing Christian to formulate a daring mass-escape plan that requires Cash to dress up as a woman and "seduce" an amorous enemy captain (Kurt Krueger); and an equally bold scheme by members of the local Communist party to capture a high-ranking Nazi and hold him hostage—cheerfully oblivious to the fact that they've kidnapped a corpse.

It was Blake Edwards' original plan to film on location in Italy, but personal domestic problems forced the director to remain in the States and build the village of Valerno at Lake Sherwood Ranch in the San Fernando Valley. Edwards had also intended to honor William Peter Blatty's request that the film open in a black & white documentary fashion, played with utmost seriousness for the first reel or so and then blossoming into full color when the comedy took over. In an interview for the Screenwriters on Film website, Blatty recalled, "We had made a pact in blood that there was not to be a single smile or chuckle in the course of the first twenty minutes of this film"—shattering the mood only when Capt. Cash, standing in a chow line, gets a ladleful of beans plopped into his hand. Instead, Edwards chose to play the opening pre-credits scene between the

"For the good of the service": Dick Shawn dons drag at the behest of temporary comrade-in-arms Sergio Fantoni in order to vanquish their common Nazi foe in *What Did You Do in the War, Daddy?* (United Artists, 1966).

uptight Cash and the hard-drinking General Bolt as a combination of straightforward exposition and surreptitious chuckles, tipping off the audience that they were in for a comedy long before that pile of beans found its way into Cash's open palm.

Edwards focuses so intently on the film's farcical machinations (mistaken identity, the blurred line between artifice and reality, obtuse authority figures who see only what they want to see, female impersonation) and his own predilection for black humor (the increasingly unhinged Potts, the ubiquitous Nazi corpse) that he often neglects the individual characterizations. Although James Coburn's Lt. Christian is firmly established as a garrulous, quickwitted con artist in the best Bilko tradition, we never truly find out anything about the man or his background. Has he always been a wheeler-dealer, or has he become one overnight out of necessity? Has he ever used his skills as a sharpster for personal gain, or only to bail out his buddies and outwit the Germans? Blake Edwards never tells.

In contrast, we know everything we need to know about the rule-bound Capt. Cash: His neurotic intractability in the early scenes, his drunken confession to the lovely Gina that he's never been anything in his life other than a glorified "gopher," his borderline-hysterical reaction to Christian's labyrinthine "explanation" of all the idiotic events that transpired while he was sleeping it off, and his "I'm dead already, what can I lose?" attitude when he is persuaded to don female attire in the climactic scenes. Though not always seen to best advantage in his film appearances, Dick Shawn's work in *What Did You Do in the War, Daddy?* is superb, ranking only slightly lower than his unforgettable "hippie Hitler" in Mel Brooks' *The Producers*. Even impossible-to-please film critic Andrew Sarris was moved to write that Shawn's drag scene was "the funniest I have ever seen in a narrative context."

Like most of Blake Edwards' films, *What Did You Do in the War Daddy?* benefits enormously from the director's hand-picked supporting cast: Harry Morgan, Vito Scotti, Leon Askin, Jay Novello and especially Carroll O'Connor as the clueless General Bolt, who never quite catches on that the "heroics" of his men are mostly fabricated for his benefit. Though he only had a handful of scenes, O'Connor made such a vivid impression on producer Norman Lear that four years later the actor was invited to star in Lear's groundbreaking TV sitcom *All in the Family*. But before this career milestone took place, Carroll O'Connor essayed another General Bolt-like role — named General *Colt*— in another expensive World War II comedy, *Kelly's Heroes* (MGM, 1970).

Set in France but location-filmed in Yugoslavia, *Kelly's Heroes* (working title: *The Warriors*) is as much a "caper" film as a war flick, a sort of combination *Ocean's Eleven* and *The Dirty Dozen* (with two of *that* film's leading players, Telly Savalas and Donald Sutherland, joining the fun). The screenplay by British writer Troy Kennedy-Martin was inspired in part by a true story, adding a few dashes of Dashiel Hammett's fictional detective yarn "The Gutting of Couffinall," in which a bank robbery is planned and executed with the cunning of a military offensive. We are introduced to the film's protagonist Private Kelly (Clint Eastwood) during a tense action sequence in which he kidnaps a German colonel (David Hurst) right from under the enemy's nose. Lest we mistake this picture for a drama, we next see Master Sergeant "Big Joe" (Telly Savalas) pumping the captured German for information as to where to find the best hotels and whorehouses in the vicinity. Kelly, however, is more interested in the two gold ingots that he finds in the colonel's pocket. The German reveals the existence of 14,000 additional ingots valued at $16 million, locked in a bank vault in the town of Clairemont — thirty miles behind enemy lines. The wheels start turning in Kelly's head, and before long he has talked Big Joe into using the three-day absence of their slightly detached commanding officer Capt. Maitland (Hal Buckley) — who is in Paris to find spare parts for his personal yacht!— as an opportunity to sneak past the Germans and into Clairemont, there to rob the bank and emerge as millionaires. Despite foreknowledge of Kelly's checkered past (once a lieutenant, Kelly was demoted for fatally fouling up an important mission), Big Joe goes along with the plan, as does the rest of the Sergeant's platoon, figuring that if they must face certain death they may as well do it for profit.

In the *Mission: Impossible* tradition of fitting the right men to the right jobs, Kelly arranges for a fidgety artillery sergeant (George Savalas) with a habit of using too much ammunition to provide the fire cover necessary for the "heroes" to make their foray into occupied territory. For the requisite walkie-talkies, rounds of ammo and other equipment, Kelly contacts an ethically challenged supply sergeant named Crapgame (Don Rickles). And when the need arises for three Sherman tanks, Kelly calls upon the aptly named Sgt. Oddball (Donald Sutherland), a bearded, long-haired hippie type long before such a type had been invented. If the viewer hasn't yet tumbled to the fact that *Kelly's Heroes* is not *Saving Private Ryan*, the presence of Oddball—who barks like a cocker spaniel, plays country-western songs through loudspeakers mounted on his tanks, and habitually puts down his chief technician Moriarty (Gavin MacLeod) for emitting "negative waves"—will remove all doubt. (Sutherland's puckish performance belies the fact that the actor was deathly ill through much of the shooting.)

As Kelly's mercenary mission rolls on, the men are repeatedly forced to engage the enemy in combat, winning each skirmish and progressively liberating German-held territory that up to now has been beyond the reach of General Colt, the area's commander of operations. Monitoring Kelly's radio messages, Colt mistakes such names as "Oddball" and "Crapgame" for code words and jumps to the conclusion that a fearless maverick unit has taken upon itself the task of smashing the enemy stronghold on behalf of the Allied war effort. Colt's rah-rah enthusiasm over this apparent demonstration of Yankee pluck (he never does figure out what's really happening) quickly develops into a running gag, as does the fact that Kelly and company are forced to cut more people into their $16 million heist—a bridge-building unit, a drum-and-bugle corps—the more elaborate and complex the caper becomes. Arriving in Clairemont, the "Heroes" are compelled to challenge a formidable ememy Panzer division. When the smoke clears, the last standing German tank commander (Karl-Otto Alberty) agrees to surrender, and even allows the Americans to use his big guns to blast through the bank's walls—but only if *he* gets a piece of the action as well.

Donald Sutherland (left) and Clint Eastwood in *Kelly's Heroes* (MGM, 1970). And you thought Tuesday Weld and Jackie Gleason were an odd couple.

In later years, star Clint Eastwood would bemoan the fact that director Brian Hutton (with whom he'd previously collaborated on *Where Eagles*

Dare) was denied the right of final cut by MGM president James Aubrey, who in Eastwood's opinion made several damaging excisions, including the removal of the screenplay's subliminal anti-war message. Nonetheless, MGM's publicity flacks took full advantage of 1970's prevailing pacifist sentiments by stocking the ad campaign for *Kelly's Heroes* with such establishment-taunting tags as "They had a message for the Army: 'Up the Brass.'" The PR boys also played up the participation of Donald Sutherland ("of *MASH* fame"), whose mind-blown demeanor is hardly the most glaring of the film's calculatedly "hip" anachronisms.

Despite an attenuated length of 145 minutes, *Kelly's Heroes* was a hit in the United States and a megahit in Great Britain, later toting up even more mazumah as a perennial TV favorite. This writer must confess to enjoying the film more in 1970 than while catching up with it over forty years later. It now seems incredibly slow, with the random serious moments—notably the deaths of three of Kelly's Heroes in a minefield, and the carnage leading up to the climactic siege of Clairemont—losing impact by being paced in the same leisurely fashion as the comic highlights. Still, it's tough to dislike a picture containing the splendiferously sadistic spectacle of Oddball's tank crew mowing down German soldiers like dogs while a recording of Hank Williams' "Sunshine" wafts gently through the air, or the self-satire inherent in the Mexican standoff between a heavily armed Clint Eastwood and the last remaining Panzer tank—as a reasonable facsimile of Ennio Morricone's theme from *The Good, the Bad and the Ugly* is heard in the background.

Our next wheeler-dealer comedy represents a 26-year step forward in chronology and a 100-year leap backward in quality. The only theatrical feature ever directed by actor Bert Convy, the R-rated *Weekend Warriors* (Moviestore Entertainment, 1986) takes place in 1961, just before the Berlin Crisis. With the assistance of protagonist-narrator Vince Tucker (played by Chris Lemmon, son of Jack), we are introduced to the members of the Hollywood National Guard's "Fighting 73rd," comprised of underemployed actors, writers and stuntmen who can't afford to be drafted. In the spirit of Mort Sahl's catchphrase "Is there any group I haven't offended?" Tucker's fellow Guardsmen include a duncical Polish private, a flaming queen, and a he-man who talks like Elmer Fudd. Appalled by the 73rd's slacker attitude and all-around incompetence, blowhard congressman Balljoy (Graham Jarvis) and gung-ho Sergeant Burge (Vic Tayback) conspire to activate Tucker and his fellow Hollywoodites and ship them overseas—not to Berlin (after all, that might make sense!) but to Rockland Island, the most godforsaken outpost on the planet. The only way our heroes can avoid this fate is to pass a grueling inspection before an audience of American and Eastern-bloc dignitaries. To do this, they employ all the glitz-and-glamour artifice that Hollywood has at its disposal, creating an illusion of adequacy via special effects, prop weaponry and choreographed stunt work.

Despite its seemingly surefire comic premise, *Weekend Warriors* is about as funny as a colonoscopy. It's the sort of picture in which people keeping saying "Things are getting crazy" when they clearly aren't. The humor is on the aesthetic level of third-graders scribbling on a bathroom wall, with the members of the Fighting 73rd calling themselves "The Mouse Farts," insults like "anus-eyed idiot!" volleyed about with abandon, military code words referring to various body parts and bodily functions, and a sniggering eulogy for the late Colonel Lingus. The long-in-coming "inspection" finale is especially disappointing, with setups and sight gags so weak and underdeveloped that one suspects this is precisely the moment where the film's already low budget ran out completely. Only the dependable Lloyd Bridges transcends the climactic mediocrity in the role of Colonel Archer, an ex-cowboy star who dazzles the dignitaries by rescuing a little girl from certain death (never guessing that the "child" is actually a stunt midget in drag). Otherwise, we must squirm through such negligible highlights as the scene in which an arrogant officer is persuaded that he is suffering from "African Shrinking Sickness" when he is surrounded with oversized furniture. Just before attending the film's opening in San Antonio, director Bert Convy confessed "I'm as apprehensive as hell." As well he should have been: Earning a piddling $350,000 during its initial run, *Weekend Warriors* was almost instantly exiled to VHS under the title *Hollywood Air Force*.

Illustrating Dorothy Parker's adage that the only "ism" Hollywood practices is plagiarism, *Weekend Warriors* was blatantly conceived as a hybrid of two earlier comedy hits, *Stripes* (see **Chapter 12**) and *Police Academy*. Hollywood continued feeding upon itself well into the next decade with additional ripoffs of past successes, along with a spate of theatrical features inspired by popular TV shows of the 1950s, 1960s and 1970s, reflecting the cultural frame of reference of the young turks running the movie industry. This video-to-movie trend resulted in such films as *The Addams Family*, *The Brady Bunch Movie*, *Mission: Impossible*, *The Beverly Hillbillies*, *Dragnet*, *Car 54, Where Are You?* and others of varying quality and success. And in a reversal of the procedure which had previously brought forth TV-series versions of such Army-comedy films as *MASH* and *Private Benjamin*, the 1990s offered a brace of theatrical films based on two of television's most popular military sitcoms—the first of these harking back to the series that started the "wheeler-dealer" ball rolling way back in 1955.

Though Phil Silvers had passed away in 1985, this didn't stop Imagine Entertainment and Universal Pictures from assembling a 1996 feature-length adaptation of Silvers' signature series

Steve Martin finds his "inner Phil Silvers" as the title sharpster in *Sergeant Bilko* (Imagine/Universal, 1996).

You'll Never Get Rich, appropriately retitled *Sergeant Bilko*. In addition to the title character, the film resuscitates many of the continuing characters from the old series, albeit played by different actors. The sole direct link to the original TV show is Phil Silvers' daughter Cathy Silvers, cast as bespectacled computer wonk Lt. Monday (her fellow wonk is played by Chris Rock, in a distressingly small part).

The starring role of enterprising motor-pool sergeant Ernest T. Bilko was offered to Michael Keaton, Robin Williams and Billy Crystal before Steve Martin agreed to take on the formidable task of stepping into Phil Silvers' custom-made boots. In the film, Bilko is still stationed at Fort Baxter, still under the command of Colonel Hall, who as played by Dan Aykroyd is much more compliant and easygoing than Paul Ford's blustery interpretation of Hall in the TV series. Replacing Maurice Gosfield as stumpy, slovenly Pvt. Duane Doberman is Eric Edwards; Max Casella is seen as Spc. Dino Paparelli, previously portrayed by Billy Sands; John Marshall Jones takes over from Allan Melvin as Bilko's chief conspirator Henshaw, here promoted from corporal to sergeant; Mitchell Whitfield portrays Pfc. Zimmerman, succeeding the TV version's Mickey Freeman; and Brian Leckman rather than Herbie Faye is cast as Pfc. Fender. In a nod to political correctness, the role of Cpl. Rocco Barbella, which had made a TV favorite out of Harvey Lembeck in 1955, undergoes both a gender switch and an increase in rank, emerging as Sgt. Raquel Barbella and played by Pamela Segall (later known as Pamela Adlon).

As before, Bilko has his fingers in a multitude of moneymaking pies at Fort Baxter, so much so that he has no time left to follow military protocol or tend to his assigned duties. Everyone else at Fort Baxter conspires with Bilko to put on a charade of "spit-and-polish" whenever Col. Hall or another high-ranking officer shows up at the Motor Pool, with the camp's resident disc jockey playing pre-chosen songs like Chuck Berry's "No Particular Place to Go" to warn Ernie of approaching Brass. Dropped unprepared into this casual atmosphere is Pfc. Holbrook (Darryl Mitchell), a young "regular army" type of unbesmirched character who is appalled by Bilko's lackadaisical attitude and larcenous nature. Because Holbrook is a nice kid, we know he will be humanized (or is it corrupted?) by the equally genial Bilko before the film ends. But no such redemption is in store for the film's principal heavy Major Thorne (Phil Hartman), a longtime enemy of Bilko who is aching to get even with Ernie for a snafu at Fort Dix involving a fixed boxing match (*both* fighters were bribed to take a dive) that ended up getting Thorne transferred to Greenland. It is Thorne who assigns Bilko's platoon the sure-to-fail mission of testing the experimental HTX1 Hovertank, a $70 million all-terrain assault vehicle which the motor pool is supposed to have been working on for months. Trouble is, they *haven't* been working on it, so they must get the device — and themselves— up to code with a bare minimum of time or else face dire consequences. Bilko also has problems with his fiancee Rita Robbins (Glenne Headly), who despite being left at the altar innumerable times by the scampish Ernie remains faithful because she enjoys gambling as much as he does. Even so, she has given him 30 days to marry her or she'll break off the relationship permanently — another plot peg that fits into Thorne's vengeance scheme. It would be cumbersome to reveal everything that happens next, though the general tenor of the picture is summed up by its closing disclaimer: "The filmmakers gratefully acknowledge the total lack of cooperation from the United States Army."

Diehard fans of the original *You'll Never Get Rich* who had braced themselves for a graceless travesty of the original property were pleasantly surprised by *Sgt. Bilko*, which for the most part manages to capture the essence of the 1950s series while fashioning its best comic turns to satisfy a wider 1990s audience. The difference between Phil Silvers' portrayal of Bilko and Steve Martin's spin on the character is the difference between "How *dare* you question my honesty?" and "Aw, c'mon. Would I lie to you?" Both interpretations are viable, and both are perfectly attuned to the actor in question. Though Steve Martin can't match Phil Silvers' nervous incandescence when performing such treasured "Bilko bits" as flattering Col. Hall's wife by pretending to mistake her for a movie star, Martin skillfully conveys the character's genius for instantly concocting a new strategy whenever the current one falls flat. And while the film's script prevents Martin from convincing us, as Silvers did so effortlessly, that Bilko actually *could* be an efficient soldier when the need arose, Steve has it all over Phil as a viable romantic lead, establishing a wonderful rapport with actress Glenne Headly (with whom Martin had previously worked in *Dirty Rotten Scoundrels*). Ironically, the sharpest criticism leveled at Steve Martin came not from Phil Silvers aficionados but from Martin's fans in the press, who were disappointed that he didn't indulge in the "Wild and Crazy" antics of his earlier standup-comic days. (Reviewers of this stripe should be drummed out of the profession anyway. These retrogressive fatheads who can't make a reference to Martin without dredging up the "Wild and Crazy" business that hasn't been cutting-edge since 1978 are the red-headed stepchildren of those jerk journalists of the 1960s who just couldn't resist ending every news item about the Beatles with a patronizing "Yeah, Yeah, Yeah!")

Beyond the performance of Steve Martin, *Sgt. Bilko* offers many more delights: Rita Robbins arguing with a bunch of eighth-graders over "motivation" while directing a junior-high production of *Guys and Dolls*, Bilko serenading Rita with a backup military chorus singing "Only You," Pvt. Doberman's tug-of-war with a horse, Pfc. Holbrook's remote-control rigging of the Hovertank so that it can blow up a target even before it fires a shot, Austin Pendleton's inspired performance as the Hovertank's neurotic inventor, the obligatory obstacle-course scene to the tune of the Dirty Dozen Brass Band's "My Feet Can't Fail Me Now," and the protagonist's endless stream of such character-defining homilies as "We don't need to be holding four aces if they think we're holding four aces." With this in mind, it pains us to report that *Sgt. Bilko* did not perform according to expectations, posting only a $30 million gross on a $39 million investment. Conversely, it is not at all painful to report the financial failure of another TV-inspired military comedy. We refer to the 1997 release *McHale's Navy*, which cost $31 million and took in a pathetic $4 million. It's astonishing that it made *that* much.

The original TV-series version of *McHale's Navy*, which ran on ABC from 1962 through 1966, is generally regarded as a knockoff of *You'll Never Get Rich*, even by the series' star Ernest Borgnine. While this is true, the property didn't start out as a "Bilko" wannabe. As written by Albert Aley and directed by Bernard Girard, the series' hour-long pilot episode "Seven Against the Sea" was a cold-sober World War II action drama with scattered moments of comic relief, set on the fictional South Pacific island of Taratupa in the spring of 1942. After enduring heavy bombardment by the Japanese, only 18 of the 150 men stationed at Taratupa's PT base have survived. Led by Lt. Commander Quinton McHale (Borgnine), the survivors have remained in hiding since the attack, forming strong friendships with the indigenous islanders and in general enjoying the Life of Riley. Waited on hand and foot by native maidens and operating such going concerns as a laundry service and a moonshine still, McHale and his men have no intention of emerging from their sanctuary and returning to active combat. Into this tropical paradise parachutes young Lt. Durham (Ron Foster), a by-the-book type (again!) who has been assigned to reactivate Taratupa in order to help evacuate a Marine battalion pinned down on a nearby island by an enemy cruiser. Unwilling to lose any more of his men, McHale initially resists Durham's entreaties, but eventually relents and pulls off the capture of a Japanese PT boat. Rather than merely evacuate the Marines per instructions, the newly energized McHale and six carefully selected crew members use the captured vessel to destroy the incoming enemy cruiser, sailing under cover of the Japanese flag to sneak up on their quarry.

Originally telecast April 3, 1962, as an episode of the ABC anthology *Alcoa Premiere*, "Seven Against the Sea" was advertised as the test film for the proposed Ernest Borgnine TV series *McHale's Men*, though in recent interviews Borgnine has indicated that he was only a guest star and that the series was intended to spotlight Ron Foster as Lt. Durham. Mostly filmed on the same backlot exteriors seen in the 1953 Universal-International horror film *The Creature from the Black Lagoon*, the 60-minute drama made little impression on the executives at Universal's TV arm Revue Productions. It was agent-turned-producer Jennings Lang, a man enshrined in Hollywood folklore for his infallible ability to make lemonade from lemons, who suggested reformatting *McHale's Men* as a situation comedy. According to legend, the inspiration came to Lang when a pre-telecast screening of "Seven Against the Sea" in the Universal projection room invoked loud laughter in the all the wrong places, though a recent viewing of the pilot film doesn't entirely support this allegation.

Carried over into the retitled half-hour sitcom version *McHale's Navy* were Ernest Borgnine as McHale, the wartime Taratupa setting, the crew's various non-regulation business enterprises, and one of the supporting actors from "Seven Against the Sea," Gary Vinson as quartermaster Christy Christopher. The new crew of the PT 73 included a holdover from Universal's popular 1959 service comedy *Operation Petticoat*, Gavin MacLeod, as seaman "Happy" Haines; and a veteran of *You'll Never Get Rich*, Billy Sands, as machinist "Tinker" Bell. Also on hand were comic magician Carl Ballantine as torpedoman Lester Gruber, Edson Stroll as gunner's mate Virge Edwards and John Wright as radioman Willy Moss. The premise of the original was altered so that McHale and his authority-defying "pirates" continued to be a source of frustration and embarrassment for the Brass, but were tolerated because of their intimate knowledge of Taratupa and its environs and their uncontested skill at chasing down and destroying enemy vessels. The character of straight-arrow Lt. Durham was burlesqued on the TV series in the form of bumbling Ensign Charles Parker (Tim Conway), who was originally assigned by McHale's eternal adversary Captain Wallace Binghamton (Joe Flynn) to whip the PT-73 into shape and up to Regulation, but who quickly became one of McHale's most reliable co-conspirators. Once Parker was lost to him, Captain Binghamton's single overriding ambition was to throw McHale and his fellow reprobates in the brig, and in this pursuit he was aided by the ultra-obsequious Lt. Elroy Carpenter (Bob Hastings). Adding to the farcical ambience was Yoshio Yoda as Fuji, a Japanese POW whom the crew of the 73 kept hidden from the authorities because of his expertise as a gourmet chef. Habitually confusing his "L"s with his "R"s and prone to such non-oriental expletives as "Oy veh!" and "Mama Mia!" the stereotypical Fuji tends not to play well with modern-day viewers, though Yoshio Yoda himself always seemed to take his role in stride. (The actor retired from show business not long after *McHale's Navy* to launch a new and considerably less demeaning career as a software executive.)

Whereas in *You'll Never Get Rich* Phil Silvers' Ernie Bilko was always the driving force and *agent provocateur* behind the series' schemes and scams, in *McHale's Navy* Ernest Borgnine's Quinton McHale generally played straight to the grifters and mountebanks under his command, justifying his top billing by dreaming up brilliant eleventh-hour strategies to straighten out the messes his men had created, or to convince the Brass that the scam-at-hand was actually devised for the benefit of the War Effort. The formula remained workable for 138 episodes, faltering only in Season Four when some genius at Universal decided to freshen the property by moving McHale, the crew, Binghamton, Carpenter and even Fuji from the South Seas to the fictional Italian village of Volta Fiore. In truth, this massive troop movement merely involved busing the production unit a half-mile or so across the Universal lot, from the Creature's Black Lagoon to the venerable "Frankenstein Village" standing set. Even in its fourth and final season, *McHale's Navy* remained one of the least expensive TV sitcoms ever filmed.

Likewise penurious in concept and execution was Universal's 1964 theatrical-feature version of *McHale's Navy*, which differed from its TV source only in that it was longer and in color. All the series' regular cast members were still in attendance, with the show's producer Edward J. Montagne doubling as director and series stalwart Si Rose contributing to the script. The plot was also the mixture as before, with the crew of the 73 conniving to square a $2000 gambling debt. Accidentally acquiring the famous Australian racehorse Silver Spots, the boys enter the steed under an assumed name in a high-stakes race in New Caledonia, using a variety of inventive subterfuges (glued-on fur, smoke screens, etc.) to prevent the judges from discovering that Silver Spots is a ringer. During the final scenes, Tim Conway gets to show off his propensity for comic dialects as he impersonates an Australian "digger"; and as usual, it is up to McHale to bail out his boys and foil Captain Binghamton before fadeout time. Claudine Longet, then the wife of singer Andy Williams, appears as nominal female lead Andrea Bouchard, while two actors who frequently popped up on the TV series, George Kennedy and Jean Willes, are cast respectively as Andrea's suitor Henri Le Clerc and McHale's erstwhile girlfriend Margo Monet (since this was pre–*Cool Hand Luke*, there's every likelihood that George Kennedy took home a smaller paycheck than even Joe Flynn). Flying in the face of conventional Hollywood wisdom that TV fans will think twice about spending money for something they can get at home for free, this cinemazation of *McHale's Navy* was a success, inspiring Universal to produce a 1965 sequel-of-sorts, *McHale's Navy Joins the Air Force*—minus Ernest Borgnine, for reasons discussed in our analysis of the sequel in **Chapter 12**'s overview of "Misfit Makes Good" comedies.

The purpose of this long-winded preamble is to provide background for the 1997 theatrical-feature version of *McHale's Navy*, filmed on location in Mexico, which was neither a remake of the 1964 film nor a literal translation of the old TV series. What it *was* was a bid by Universal Pictures to leech off the anticipated success of Steve Martin's *Sgt. Bilko*—and when *Bilko* fell short of expectations, Universal was still stuck with *McHale's Navy*, and so were we. Let this be a lesson to us both.

The project was developed by former Universal CEO Sid Sheinberg, best known as the man who recommended *Schindler's List* to director Steven Spielberg. With his sons Bill and Jon, Sheinberg had created a new production company, The Bubble Factory. By rights, the Bubble should have burst after the company's inaugural effort *The Pest* (1997), a flaccid John Leguizamo comedy which earned back only one-sixth of its cost. But the turnover time between concept and production in Hollywood is often so lengthy that it takes a couple of years for the rot to set in, so as far as Universal was concerned the Bubble Factory still had earning potential when Sheinberg approached them with *McHale's Navy*—a project that seemed particularly attractive because the studio already owned the TV series and wouldn't have to bargain over movie rights. Hired to direct *Navy* was Bryan Spicer, fresh from 1996's *Mighty Morphin Power Rangers*. The talented Spicer (who also plays a cameo role) did the best he could with a script cowritten by Peter Crabbe, whose past credits included the stupefyingly awful 1994 movie version of another classic sitcom, *Car 54, Where Are You?*

When Jason Alexander took a pass on the role of Lt. Cmdr. Quinton McHale, the script was offered to Tom Arnold. Transforming a standup comedian into a movie star can be a risky proposition. Sometimes it pays off in huge dividends, as with *Sgt. Bilko*'s Steve Martin; and sometimes you end up with Tom Arnold. A variable performer capable of fine supporting work in such films as Arnold Schwarzenegger's *True Lies* (1994), Arnold has proven somewhat less effective in leading roles, as demonstrated by his two failed TV sitcoms of the early 1990s. Even so, Sid Sheinberg apparently believed that Tom Arnold could carry *McHale's Navy*—but to hedge all bets, the actor was surrounded by a supporting cast of proven film and TV-series favorites, including Debra Messing (*Will and Grace*), David Alan Grier (*Martin*), Tim Curry (*The Rocky Horror Picture Show*), Dean Stockwell (*Quantum Leap*), French Stewart (*Third Rock from the Sun*) and Bruce Campbell (*Army of Darkness*), plus counterculture comedian Tommy Chong of "Cheech and Chong" fame.

The original series' World War II backdrop was forsaken for a modern-day setting in the 1997 film version, not only robbing the movie of the series' narrative urgency but also depriving us of the TV version's charming anachronisms, including references to tape recorders, tranquilizer pills and bikini bathing suits—none of which existed in the early 1940s. The film's plot finds the future of mankind jeopardized by the malevolent Major Vladikov (Tim Curry), who bristles whenever anyone reminds him that he is only "The Second Most Dangerous Terrorist in the World." (The Second Most Dangerous Terrorist in the World. The Second Most Dangerous Terrorist in the World. The Second Most Dangerous Terrorist in the World. Getting sick of reading that phrase? Wait until you see the movie.) Not only does Vladikov jockey to be Number One with a top-secret

11. The Wheeler Dealers

Given a choice between Ernest Borgnine, seen here in Universal's 1964 film version of *McHale's Navy,* and Tom Arnold in the same studio's 1997 remake, it's gotta be Ernie every time.

plan for mass destruction, but he also has a score to settle with Quinton McHale, now retired from the Navy and thriving as a small-time smuggler and black marketeer on the Caribbean island of San Ysidro. McHale's a scoundrel, yes, but a lovable one, as proven by his benevolence toward the local kids and his contributions to the island hospital (this is the sort of sentimental treacle that Pauline Kael used to characterize as tipping the blind beggar for luck. Ernie Borgnine never had to pet little kids on the head or sneak aspirin to native doctors to convince us that he was a Good Guy). The knowledge that McHale is out of circulation is ambrosia to another longtime nemesis, Captain Wallace Binghamton (Stockwell), who is struggling to rebuild his Navy career after accidentally sinking the Love Boat. On orders from a high-ranking Pentagon official known only by the code name Cobra, McHale is reactivated and restored to his former rank to cross swords with Vladikov. Upset that *he* hasn't been given this mission, Binghamton determines to discredit McHale by having two officers keep tabs on him: His own second-in-command Lt. Carpenter (now Lt. *Penelope* Carpenter, played by Messing), who falls in love with McHale; and incurably inept Ensign Parker (Grier), who somehow always manages to do the wrong thing right. Reels and reels later, McHale and Vladikov have their final showdown on the high seas.

Only occasionally are we treated to McHale wheeling and dealing in the grand tradition, notably an extended sequence in which he sneaks his crew into Cuba to purchase some vital materiel from good-natured smuggler Tommy Chong. Another fond harkback to the TV series finds David Alan Grier channeling Tim Conway as Ensign Parker in a lengthy disguise scene, wherein he poses as Fidel Castro. And to be fair, some of the film's newer gags have merit: A PT-73 crewman opening a beer bottle with his eye, Parker's misadventures with an inflatable wetsuit, and Vladikov's psychiatrist (Scott Cleverdon) calmly advising his patient that there are more effective ways to deal with people than killing them. Otherwise, we'll have to go along with critic Chris Hicks of the *Deseret News*, who described *McHale's Navy* as "a lot like its star, Tom Arnold—big and bombastic, but with no substance."

Supporting player Bruce Campbell has revealed in his autobiography that no one other than Tom Arnold was given much in the way of direction. It looks that way. In addition to the film's erratic pacing, misfire laugh-lines and distressingly sloppy handling of the climactic chase scene (one wonders if anyone ever consulted the 100-plus storyboards prepared for this finale), it's a toss-up as to which of the film's two villains gives the most obnoxiously out-of-control performance. For all his eyebrow-arching and lip-curling, and despite the script's continuous references to his previous atrocities, Tim Curry's Vladikov conveys no genuine menace whatsoever, not even when resorting to the normally surefire device of threatening a youngster. As the for film's Captain Binghamton, Dean Stockwell can't seem to make up his mind from one scene to the next whether to imitate Joe Flynn, Jackie Gleason, or Dean Stockwell.

One of the few participants who emerges from this fiasco without egg on his face is the only carryover from the original *McHale's Navy*: None other than Ernest Borgnine himself, cast as the shadowy Pentagon official Cobra (whose true identity will come as no surprise to anyone who's seen the similar last-act revelation in Mel Gibson's 1994 filmization of *Maverick*). While Tim Conway turned down the opportunity to play a cameo in the picture because he didn't want to fly to Mexico for a single day's shooting, Borgnine happily accepted the offer, though he wasn't happy with the results. "I was in it," he told interviewers David Fantle and Tom Johnson. "They paid me well for it and I can't say another word about it. In the TV series, I had a chemistry with these guys that spewed forth a sense of comedy. I'm sorry to say in the film they made, there was just nothing there." That said, the 79-year-old actor was a thorough professional both on and off the screen. Compared with Tim Curry's overacting and Tom Arnold's non-acting, the deftly underplayed *McHale's Navy* vignette in which Borgnine expresses embarrassment over having to pin a medal on Debra Messing's chest is a minor masterpiece of comic credibility.

Bad though it is, at least we're never in doubt that *McHale's Navy* is supposed to be a comedy. Such is not always the case with the final wheeler-dealer film in this chapter, the 2003 Miramax release *Buffalo Soldiers*. True, the film is based on a perversely hilarious 1993 novel by Robert O'Connor. True, the film was promoted and reviewed as a comedy. And true, the film's costar Anna Paquin has commented that she found certain scenes funny in performance that didn't amuse her at all in cold print. But if you can get any more than three laughs from this 98-minute cure for insomnia, you're a better man than I.

11. The Wheeler Dealers

The title *Buffalo Soldiers* is an allusion to the famous post–Civil War Cavalry regiment largely comprised of newly freed slaves, who in Robert O'Connor's words were charged with "fighting a war of extermination" against Native Americans. "This is the way Armies work," O'Connor explained in a newspaper interview. "The people fighting and dying aren't the ones benefiting." The reference is symbolic: The novel does not take place in the late 19th century but in the early 1980s, a time when American military morale was at an all-time low and the Army was overrun with losers and outcasts. Described by one wag as "Sgt. Bilko on Smack," *Buffalo Soldiers* is set at a U.S. Army base in Stuttgart, Germany. The hero (for lack of a better word) is 57th Division battalion clerk Ray Ellwood, who narrates the story in a stream-of-consciousness, second-person-singular fashion, referring to himself as "You" in the manner of the old radio series *The Whistler*. Having joined the Army because he had no other job prospects, Ellwood is as bored and mired in defeatism as any other soldier on the base. Trusting no one and trusted by no one, Ellwood passes his time and fills his pockets by trading stolen supplies with the local black market, keeping himself and his fellow soldiers in a perpetually stoned state by consuming and dealing heroin. With ineffectual camp commander Col. Berman oblivious to what's going on outside his office, Ellwood is able to lead a cushier lifestyle than Sgt. Bilko could ever have imagined, stocking his barracks with expensive TVs and stereo equipment and cruising around in a brand-new Porsche. To be sure, there are minor distractions in Ellwood's life — the camp's thuggish and corrupt MPs, the recent "accidental" death of another uniformed grifter, and Ellwood's own lack of compunction over killing anyone who crosses him — but in general this is as good as it's ever going to get.

Everything changes with the arrival of psychopathic topkick Sgt. Lee, whose Vietnam record indicates that murder is the kindest act he is capable of. Lee is bound and determined to smash Ellwood's drug-trafficking empire and make the clerk's life Hell on Earth. Ellwood exacts vengeance by seducing and corrupting Lee's underage daughter Robyn, who for her part is willing to double-cross her father because it was his drunken dereliction which resulted in the amputation of her right arm. Throughout the novel, Ellwood has premonitions of an unhappy and untimely demise, yet he still clings to the fragile hope that he will somehow escape the inevitable, comparing his mindset to that of the equally foredoomed inmates at the Dachau death camp. Fatalism and irony abound in *Buffalo Soldiers*, right up to the morbidly existential finale, which occurs just after a mammoth drug deal arranged by Ellwood goes horribly awry.

But hold on there. We said the book is *funny*. Incredibly, the bleaker and more meaningless life becomes for Ray Ellwood, the more one feels the urge to laugh out loud, with Ellwood's deadpan articulation of his miserable lot in life possessing a witty, Salingeresque sense of self-awareness. The novel boasts some surprisingly uproarious passages involving Ray's night of kinky passion with a French prostitute, a crash course on how to properly bake and package a fresh shipment of smack, and a bawdy barracks discourse regarding a sappy American TV sitcom. But here's the rub: The harder one laughs at the author's twisted brilliance, the more difficult it is to envision these passages being recreated on film. There is, for example, absolutely no way to effectively film the aforementioned sex scene unless the filmmaker is willing to produce a full-length pornographic cartoon. The quicksilver humor in *Buffalo Soldiers* works best — and for the most part *exclusively*— on paper. One could say of Robert O'Connor the same thing that a frustrated Hollywood screenwriter exclaimed while attempting to adapt an F. Scott Fitzgerald novel: "The son-of-a-bitch writes in water!"

Shot on location in Germany with the barracks scenes staged in an abandoned Army base near the town of Karlsruhe, the film version of *Buffalo Soldiers* stars Joaquin Phoenix as Ray Ellwood, Anna Paquin as Robyn Lee, Scott Glenn as Sgt. Lee and Ed Harris as Col. Berman (the two last-named actors decided to switch roles just before shooting started). The film's director and co-screenwriter was Gregor Jordan, who had himself grown up on a Royal Australian Air Force base; though groomed for a military career in the tradition of his fighter-pilot father, Jordan pursued moviemaking instead. Steeling himself against criticism that *Buffalo Soldiers* was like the novel an anti-military tract, Jordan described the film as a "black comic Cold War thriller," adding that that it was intended as a period piece. "The Army's a very different place now," noted Jordan in a 2003 interview. "They realized that crime and drug use were prevalent and got rid of the bad apples." With these words in mind, it is curious indeed that the film moves the action of the story forward from the Dark Days of the early '80s to the autumn of 1989, just as the Berlin Wall was being demolished — at which time, according to most credible historians, Army morale was at its highest point in years, and many of the "bad apples" had already been crated up and shipped out.

Avoiding the headache of attempting to film the book's more unfilmable passages, Jordan used only those elements of the novel that would work on screen, notably the bizarre sight gag in which Sgt. Lee demonstrates that he's not to be trifled with by forcing Ellwood to "execute" his own Porsche. Elsewhere, the director comes up with his own ideas of what constitutes irreverent military humor, concocting a spectacular opening sequence in which a doped-up tank crew obliterates a gas station (with dialogue and imagery straight out of *Reefer Madness*), inventing an adulterous romance between Ellwood and Col. Berman's restless wife (Elizabeth McGovern), and suggesting that the base's soldiers are so ill-suited to their mission, and so detached from reality, that they don't even know if they're stationed in East or West Germany. In view of these alterations, some critics compared *Buffalo Soldiers* to *MASH*. We'll accept that — except *MASH* was funny.

The novel's Ray Ellwood is utterly unsympathetic, unlikable and unmotivated in his antisocial behavior. So as not to totally alienate a mass movie audience, the character as rewritten by Gregor Jordan is slightly softened. For starters, Ellwood is given a compelling reason for his rebellious attitude: Instead of joining the Army for lack of anything better to do, the film's Ellwood has been forced into military service lest he be sent to prison for his civilian crimes. Stuck in a place he doesn't want to be and with no means of escape, Ellwood's lashing out against the System is understandable if not entirely forgivable. The film also purges the character of his homicidal tendencies, and modifies his revenge-driven seduction of Robyn Lee (who, incidentally, is no longer an amputee) by having him fall in love with her in spite of himself—and by demonstrating that Robyn likes to live as dangerously as Ray does, at one point introducing *him* to the date-rape drug Ecstasy.

On the other hand, the film's hero occasionally exhibits behavior even more sociopathic than his counterpart in the novel. Beyond his illicit affair with Col. Berman's wife, the movie version of Ray Ellwood has no qualms about trading American weaponry with emissaries from unfriendly nations, and in one scene arranges for his platoon to lose a crucial war-games exercise for his own benefit, a defeat that all but wrecks the military career of the bumbling but good-natured Berman (outside of a cameo appearance by Dean Stockwell as a nail-spitting general, Ed Harris is the only actor in the film truly capable of extracting humor from humorless situations). One suspects the filmmakers were hoping that Joaquin Phoenix's inherent charm would counteract his character's unsavory qualities. Evidently no one told Phoenix, who plays most of his scenes with a disengaged screw-you hauteur that seems calculated to turn off even his staunchest fans. Bill Murray in *Stripes* (see **Chapter 12**) can get away with this sort of slacker smugness: Joaquin Phoenix can't.

And not only did Phoenix's fan base feel let down by *Buffalo Soldiers*. Devotees of the original novel were equally disappointed that the film weeded out O'Connor's complex, intertwined story structure, most conspicuously by dismissing the mysterious death of one of Ellwood's confederates as a throwaway gag, effectively killing the full significance of the Sgt. Lee character. The biggest letdown is reserved for the final scene: After an intensely violent buildup which seems to hold out promise that the novel's marrow-chilling last paragraph will be faithfully recreated on-screen, the filmmakers contemptuously tack on an imbecilic happy ending that makes *Rebecca of Sunnybrook Farm* look like *Sophie's Choice*.

Even if *Buffalo Soldiers* had been a better picture, its doom would have been sealed by an unforeseen quirk of history. Completed in 2001, the film was previewed at the Toronto Film Festival beginning on September 8 of that year — three days before terrorists brought down the Twin Towers in New York. It goes without saying that festival attendees were not in the proper mood to enjoy a film that trashed the American military as a dumping ground for "soldiers with nothing to kill but time," who "know that war is hell, but peace ... peace is fuckin' boring." With measured understatement, *Variety*'s Todd McCrary assessed the initial viewer response to *Buffalo Soldiers*: "This looks like the wrong place at the wrong time." The film was shelved for nearly two years, re-emerging at the Sundance Film Festival on January 21, 2003, where audience reaction ranged from hushed indignation to outright violence. It might have been a wise diplomatic gesture if Miramax had at least removed the film's opening scene, which shows a group of soldiers marching over a pavement painting of the American flag. Mirroring the self-absorption of his screen character, star Joaquin Phoenix hardly helped matters by issuing such statements as "I don't know why anyone would be offended.... If we don't show things as they really happen, then what's that about?" The film finally received limited theatrical release in the spring of 2003, just as America was gearing up for the Second Gulf War — again the wrong place, the wrong time. Figuring that they couldn't market the picture as a comedy any more, Miramax labelled *Buffalo Soldiers* a "satire," which in the literal sense doesn't *have* to be funny. The film cost $15 million; it earned $350,000; and my arm is getting sore from beating this dead horse.

Undoubtedly some future Army comedy built around a wheeler-dealer will expunge the bitter aftertaste of *Buffalo Soldiers*. Comic dynamos like Phil Silvers and Jack Lemmon may no longer be among us, but the spirit of the wheeler-dealer will endure as long as there's a quick buck to turn, a weapon or supply to "requisition" without bothering with red tape, and a pompous superior officer in dire need of having the wind taken out of his sails.

12

It Ain't Stupid If It Works
The "Misfit-Makes-Good" Comedy

Of the many plot gimmicks used in military comedies, few are more popular than the "misfit makes good" device. The spectacle of a luckless goofball or a perpetual screw-up bucking the odds and achieving success as a member of the armed forces works with audiences on one of two levels (and sometimes both). The viewer can either smugly assure himself "I could *never* be as dumb as that guy," and laugh at the protagonist's failures and setbacks from a safe and superior distance; or, the viewer can shed all self-deception and confess, "Hey, I *have* been as dumb as that guy," experiencing a vicarious thrill as the protagonist perseveres and triumphs.

One could argue that all of the service comedies featuring professional comedians (Chaplin, Laurel & Hardy, Jerry Lewis, etc.) fall into the misfit-makes-good category, with the star comic proving his mettle by summoning up reserves of spunk and resourcefulness that he never knew he had, or by emulating the legendary Good Soldier Schweik, succeeding purely through the grace of God or sheer idiot luck (Harry Langdon immediately comes to mind here). You will find many such examples throughout this book, especially in **Chapter 3**. In this chapter, we offer a roundup of films that haven't been classified elsewhere.

A familiar service-comedy misfit is the arrogant wiseacre who considers himself smarter than anyone else in uniform, figures that rules were made for other people, and exerts himself only when there's something in it for him. A character of this type is invariably chastened when his insubordination results in misfortune for his fellow servicemen — a lost wager, a serious injury — at which point the person whom the protagonist cares about more than anyone else in the world — his best pal, his mother, his sweetheart — tells him off in no uncertain terms. From this low point, the smart-aleck misfit can only make amends by proving conclusively that he is worthy of his uniform. During the World War II years, this particular character was seldom the lead comedian, but rather the straight romantic lead. In Columbia's 1952 service comedy *Sound Off*, however, comedian and leading man are rolled into one in the form of the effervescent Mickey Rooney.

The film's title was taken from a serviceman's marching song that had gained popularity in civilian circles via its usage in MGM's 1949 war drama *Battleground*. Though the song may seem as if it has been around forever, "Sound Off" was actually written in 1944 by a GI named Willie Duckworth, earning him a fat royalty check whenever it was performed on screen. In addition to "Sound Off," five new tunes by George Duning were showcased in the course of the Mickey Rooney picture: Since it is established in the opening scene that Rooney's character Mike Donnelly is a popular nightclub entertainer, it's only natural that he and the other characters would burst into song once in a while (at times it appears that the Army has limited the draft exclusively to chorus boys).

A brazen young bucko who is used to receiving preferential treatment by dint of his celebrity, Mike Donnelly gets off to bad start with the military when, during his nightclub act, he deliberately deposits a tossed salad on the noggin of fuming Sgt. Crockett (Gordon Jones). Upon receiving his draft notice, Mike breezes into camp assuming that he'll be handled with kid gloves, only to come face to face with Crockett, who is now his topkick. Unlike his counterparts in such World War II comedies as *Buck Privates* (see **Chapter 4**), Sgt. Crockett isn't really a bad sort at all; though irritated by Mike's conceited attitude, the sergeant genuinely hopes to make a decent soldier out of the little jerk. Commanding officer Maj. Whiteside (John Archer) and camp psychologist Capt. Karger (Marshall Reed) are on the same page as Crockett, combining forces to help straighten Mike out. The notion that so many authority figures would pool their resources for the sake of one solitary private stretches the film's credibility to the snapping point—but then, one doesn't expect stark reality from a picture that begins with Mickey Rooney cavorting on stage with a bunch of dancers dressed up as cavemen and Amazons. For all that, Rooney delivers a sincere, believable performance throughout, especially in his scenes with Anne James as Mike's WAC sweetheart Lt. Colleen Rafferty, and Sammy White as long-suffering talent agent Joey Kirby.

Getting back to the picture, Pvt. Donnelly continues to circumvent Sgt. Crockett's orders by expending the least possible amount of dedication to his basic-training duties, and by making a joke out of everything. In so doing, Mike comes off as a *deliberate* misfit, rather than the inadvertently incompetent numbskulls in other service comedies. Mike finally realizes the folly of his attitude with a little prodding from his agent Joey, who urges the boy to tackle the challenge of military life in the same spirit as the old backstage adage "the show must go on." In the end, Mike emerges as a topnotch soldier, at which point he is assigned to Special Services to entertain the other troops. (Since this sort of work is ideally suited to his talents, why didn't the Army put him in Special Services in the first place? Oh, never mind.)

For the most part, *Sound Off* works as a modest, unpretentious comedy with music, an excellent showcase for Mickey Rooney during his transitional period between child star and adult character actor. Only a climactic slapstick speedboat chase falls flat thanks to the mannered direction by Richard Quine, who evidently assumed that it was enough to merely establish that none of the characters can properly operate a speedboat without bothering to milk the situation for its full value. Filmed in the cost-conscious Cinecolor process, *Sound Off* was popular enough for producer Jonie Tapps to reassemble the same creative team—star Rooney, director/screenwriter Quine, coscripter Blake Edwards and composer George Duning—for another service comedy, the 1953 Technicolor production *All Ashore* (see **Chapter 6**).

In contrast with the cavalier attitude exuded by Mickey Rooney in *Sound Off*, the Army-officer hero in *The Horizontal Lieutenant* (MGM 1962) wants with every fiber of his being to perform his duties well and efficiently, only to be continually frustrated—not so much because of his own clumsiness (which, admittedly, is considerable) but by a quirk of fate that replicates itself throughout the story. The film is adapted from *The Bottletop Affair*, a 1959 novel by Gordon Cotler based on his own wartime travails (or so he claims on the dustcover). Cotler's first choice for the novel's title, and the ultimate title of the film, was *The Horizontal Lieutenant* for the simple reason that the hero repeatedly finds himself in a horizontal position after being rendered unconscious in various nonsensical ways.

The film begins in late 1945, with 2nd Lt. Merle Wye (Jim Hutton) serving in Army Intelligence despite the fact that he has never been able to see an assignment through without bungling it. During an Army baseball game in Honolulu, Merle is knocked cold by a foul ball. Awakening in the infirmary, he renews his acquaintance with childhood sweetheart Molly Blue (Paula Prentiss), now an Army nurse. Of no further use to his team, Wye is exiled to the remote Japanese island of Rotohan, presently occupied by the Allies. Since the local residents have put up no resistance to the American invaders—in fact, they seem quite content to be conquered—it is hoped that Merle has at last found a safe haven where he won't get into trouble. Unfortunately, Rotohan is currently under siege from an elusive Japanese soldier (Yuki Shimoda), whose habit of stealing such requisitioned items as razor blades and matzoh balls has become a great source of irritation for Merle's C.O. (Jim Backus). Nicknamed "Bottletop" because of his fondness for American soft drinks, the renegade soldier must be captured before he robs the island blind. Incredibly, Army

Intelligence has decided that Merle Wye is the right man for this mission, despite the objections of exasperated Col. Korotny (Charles McGraw). Hoping to succeed in his assignment, not only to prove his worth but also to impress Molly Blue, Merle enlists the aid of local interpreter Sgt. Tada (Yoshio Yoda), who has troubles of his own with his meddlesome girlfriend Akiko (Miyoshi Umeki). As things develop, it is fortunate indeed that the two leading ladies are involved in the search for the light-fingered enemy soldier. It is Akiko who recognizes and points out "Bottletop" while he is disguised as an acrobat during a local variety show; and after Merle is knocked unconscious *again* while pursuing his quarry, it is Molly who ends up capturing "Bottletop"—but not before arranging the evidence so that Merle receives all the credit.

The Horizontal Lieutenant represents the fourth and final screen teaming of Jim Hutton and Paula Prentiss, who'd previously costarred in the MGM service comedy *The Honeymoon Machine* (see **Chapter 11**). Though they enjoyed working together, Hutton had grown so weary of being pigeonholed as half of a romantic team that he took a 15-month suspension rather than work with Prentiss again. Perhaps his discomfiture is the reason that the usually reliable Hutton seems so detached throughout the film, allowing Prentiss to dominate the proceedings and scoop up all the good reviews. Further hampered by George Wells' by-rote screenplay and Richard Thorpe's plodding direction, *Horizontal Lieutenant* is of interest today primarily for its supporting cast of reliable second bananas: Jack Carter in his first screen role, Marty Ingels in his second movie appearance, and Yoshido Yoda, soon to be cast as the cheerful POW Fuji on the TV series *McHale's Navy*, as Sgt. Tada. Arguably more amusing than the film itself is the backstory of Yoshido Yoda, a UCLA student who spoke impeccable English and had to be coached by a professional dialectitian in the questionable art of conversing in a stereotypical "flied lice" Japanese accent.

Yoda was seen in his familiar "Fuji" guise—Pidgin-English and all—in the 1965 Universal production *McHale's Navy Joins the Air Force*. As the nominal sequel to the sitcom-inspired theatrical feature *McHale's Navy* (1964), which featured a merry band of maritime con artists operating in the South Pacific during World War II, the 1965 film might on the basis of its title seem more suited to our analysis of military-movie "wheelers and dealers" in **Chapter 11**. But the plotline of *McHale's Navy Joins the Air Force* has little in common with either its TV source or the wheeler-dealer genre: Instead, it is just as much a "misfit triumphant" exercise as *Horizontal Lieutenant*.

Shot on the Universal back lot in a fast 17 days, this slapped-together sequel was adapted from a single anecdote in William J. Lederer's best-selling novel *All the Ships at Sea* (see **Chapter 17** for notes on Lederer's *The Skipper Surprised His Wife*). The book, which covers nearly twenty years in the life of a Naval officer, had originally been optioned by entertainer Ray Bolger in 1951 as a potential film or TV series. After Universal bought the rights from Bolger, the studio retained only a tiny portion of the Lederer original, and even that was barely recognizable on-screen. Its title notwithstanding, *McHale's Navy Joins the Air Force* made do without the services of eponymous *McHale's Navy* star Ernest Borgnine—who, depending on the source, was either too busy making *Flight of the Phoenix* to appear in the *McHale's* sequel, or had turned the assignment down because the money wasn't good enough. Catapulted to star billing in Borgnine's absence was the first film's costar Tim Conway, here essaying his familiar TV role as Ensign Charles Parker, the dutiful but hopelessly inept junior officer placed in charge of the carefree crew of PT-73. Said crew was played by Conway's fellow *McHale's Navy* returnees Gary Vinson (Christy), Billy Sands (Tinker), Edson Stroll (Virgil), John Wright (Willy), and Gavin MacLeod (Happy); the only missing "regular" outside of Ernie Borgnine was Carl Ballantine as Gruber.

Once again, Ensign Parker is bedevilled by bespectacled, blustery Captain Wallace B. Binghamton (Joe Flynn) and the Captain's toadying assistant Lt. Elroy Carpenter (Bob Hastings). This time, the plot doesn't involve any sort of con job: rather, the story is motivated by mistaken identity, as Ensign Parker is forced by an incredible set of circumstances to take the place of flight lieutenant Wilber Harkness (Ted Bessell), son of a high-ranking Army Air Corps officer (Tom

12. It Ain't Stupid If It Works   243

Ensign Parker (Tim Conway, left) involuntarily lends an ear to Captain Binghamton (Joe Flynn) as Lt. Carpenter (Bob Hastings) bears witness. From the McHale-less *McHale's Navy Joins the Air Force* (Universal, 1965).

Tully). Through a series of misunderstandings and coincidences, the more Parker messes up, the higher he is promoted. A typical scene occurs in a USAF control tower, where while conversing with a pretty WAC corporal (Susan Silo) Parker accidentally sets off the air raid alarm — thereby alerting the base of an actual air strike and earning himself one more stripe. By the final reel, Parker holds the rank of Major, and in this capacity is ordered to serve as navigator on a cargo plane. Through still another blunder, Parker and Captain Binghamton find themselves stuck in a jeep suspended in midair beneath the plane, allowing Parker to spot an approaching Japanese fleet, warn the American Navy and secure a crucial victory for the Allies. The combined comic energy of Tim Conway and Joe Flynn almost — but not quite — compensates for the tinker-toy special effects and the glaringly obvious process screen in this climactic sequence.

Though John Fenton Murray's slapsticky screenplay reaches mighty low for laughs, *McHale's Navy Joins the Air Force* is one of those silly but likeable comedies that never fails to come to life in front of an audience (it was originally released in tandem with a compilation film, *The World of Abbott and Costello*). The ending is a beautiful example of a running gag that pays off in spades. Flown to the White House to be decorated by President Franklin D. Roosevelt, Parker is asked by a newsreel crew to stand in for the absent President while they focus their cameras and test the sound levels. Meanwhile, Captain Binghamton cools his heels in the hallway, grumbling over Parker's recent elevation to the rank of Lieutenant Colonel and wondering how much higher the "little fathead" can possibly be promoted. Stepping into the Oval Office, Binghamton practically has a coronary when he sees Parker sitting behind the President's desk, playing with Roosevelt's pet dog Fala and accommodating the newsreel boys with a dead-on FDR imitation!

While *McHale's Navy Joins the Air Force* hardly qualifies as a classic, it looks like *Mister Roberts* when compared to another misfit-hero farce from 1965. Having made a bundle with their popular teen-oriented "Beach Party" films, American-International Pictures decided to use the same format and studio personnel in an entirely different setting. The result was *Sergeant DeadHead*, with singer Frankie Avalon in the title role. The klutziest soldier at Smedley Missile Base, Sgt. O.K. Deadhead surpasses himself when he accidentally blows up a rocket during a parade. Escaping from the guardhouse with the help of two other prisoners (played by "Beach Party" perennials Harvey Lembeck and John Ashley), Deadhead hides in another rocket, which is promptly launched into space with himself and a chimpanzee aboard (let's not quibble over who gives the better performance). Through the sort of fluke that could only happen when the writer has run out of all the good ideas, Deadhead undergoes a personality change during his brief space flight, transforming from a shy bumbler to a girl-chasing egomaniac. Returning to a hero's welcome on earth, the "new" Deadhead threatens to tell the world that he was launched into space accidentally unless he's given a huge payoff. Base commander Gen. Rufus Fogg (Fred Clark) locks our hero up *again* and orders a look-alike, Sgt. Donovan (also Avalon), to take Deadhead's place at public events. By the time the film enters the home stretch, it looks as if Donovan will be marching down the aisle with Deadhead's fiancee Lucy Turner (Deborah Walley, in the role usually assigned to Annette Funicello in these things), forcing the real Sergeant — now back to his subnormal self — to escape yet once more and race to his own wedding before it's too late.

Casting Frankie Avalon in a double role gives him the opportunity to be twice as dreary as usual. Curiously, the film is practically over before American-International truckles to Avalon's teeny-bopper fan base by allowing their idol to sing. Most of the film's forgettable tunes are warbled by Deborah Walley, while one extended number is performed by "special guest star" Eve Arden! The presence in *Sergeant DeadHead* of such distinguished actors as Arden, Fred Clark, Cesar Romero, Gale Gordon and Reginald Gardiner was standard operating procedure for the "Beach Party" pictures, an attempt to attract older audiences to what was essentially a juvenile franchise. But here as in the series' previous films, the veteran performers are ill served by the mediocrity of their material, and worse still are encouraged by director Norman Taurog to mug and bellow like a bunch of varsity-show amateurs. The saddest waste of talent in *DeadHead* is Buster Keaton in the role of a dessicated handyman; outside of resurrecting a gag originally written for his 1930 feature *Doughboys* (see **Chapter 3**), Buster would have been better off staying home and collecting sick pay. Amazingly, American-International not only trumpeted the collection of stellar personalities debasing themselves in *Sgt. DeadHead*, but the studio actually seemed pleased with the results. Interviewed by the AP's Bob Thomas, Frankie Avalon was as giddy as a schoolgirl: "Being in a picture with people like these can only make me look good.... You can't help but come off well when you're with fine talent." That's what *he* thinks.

Bad as *Sergeant DeadHead* is, we can take heart in the fact that it's only one picture. The same cannot be said of the much-later "misfit" comedy *Best Defense* (Cinema Group/Paramount, 1984), which is essentially two movies in one. We'd say it is two movies for the price of one, except that it's hardly worth the price of the coming-attractions trailer.

Based on Robert Grossbach's novel *Easy and Hard Ways*, *Best Defense* started out as a solo vehicle for Dudley Moore, cast as underachieving civilian engineer Wylie Cooper. In fine tradition, Cooper is hosannaed as a genius when he is falsely given credit for inventing the "DYP," a gyroscope designed for a new fleet of military assault vehicles. As originally conceived, the plot would focus on Wylie's efforts to protect the DYP from those who'd stop at nothing to steal it, notably neurotic KGB agent Jeff (David Rasche); and in a development reminiscent of Moore's earlier comedy *10*, Wylie would also be kept busy avoiding his whiny wife Laura (Kate Capshaw) while trying to win the heart of sexy coworker Clair Lewis (Helen Shaver).

That's the film as it stood when *Best Defense*, written by Gloria Katz and Willard Hyuck (*American Graffiti*) with Hyuck doubling as director, was previewed for test audiences in early 1984. The negative feedback bade fair to consign the film to the ever-growing list of cinematic fiascos starring Dudley Moore (dubbed "The Seven Dudley Sins" by *New York* magazine in 1996). In a desperate effort to save the project, the producers turned to Eddie Murphy, then the hottest comic actor in Hollywood, offering him $15 million to appear in a handful of new scenes filmed in Israel. A secondary plot was hastily contrived whereby Murphy's character T.M. Landry, an Army lieutenant specializing in armored tanks, is assigned to try out the marvelous new DYP gyroscope in his own vehicle. Almost as much of a foul-up as Wyatt Cooper, Landry accidentally drives his tank into the middle of a war between Iraq and Kuwait, where the DYP enables him to not only evade both armies but also rescue a group of captured American soldiers.

In a later interview with *Jet* magazine, Eddie Murphy was remarkably candid: "I knew the script for *Best Defense* was horrible, but I got talked into the movie by Paramount. They started offering me all of this money. I was 21 years old. I said to hell with it and went for it. It was a mistake, but we all make mistakes in our career." Murphy could afford to shoulder some of the blame for the picture's failure, since there was so much blame to go around. The final version of *Best Defense* proved not only unfunny and confusing ("An Artistic Offense" was the headline of the *Boston Globe* review), but downright infuriating. Dudley Moore fans were upset that their favorite was bound hand and foot by lousy material: "Moore may find himself doing commercials by Tuesday," predicted the *Pittsburgh Press*. Eddie Murphy fans were angry that Eddie appeared only in the first and last reels of the picture, totaling approximately 12 minutes' screen time: "You see more of Murphy in the average *Saturday Night Live*," grumbled critic Roger Ebert. And fans of both comedians were incensed that Dudley and Eddie never appeared together in the same scene (actually, a meeting between the two stars had been shot at the last minute, but was excised before release; it couldn't have been because the scene failed to live up to the standards of the rest of the picture). Several exhibitors joined the chorus of catcalls, some threatening to sue Paramount for false advertising. This whole sorry mess was neatly summed up by *The Onion*'s Nathan Rabin: "*Best Defense* makes *Stripes* look like *Dr. Strangelove*."

Oh, haven't we mentioned *Stripes* yet? No, this isn't an oversight. It was first necessary to discuss *en masse* the various service comedies which featured a single misfit protagonist. Released by Columbia Pictures in 1981, *Stripes* takes us into a new realm: The misfit-makes-good comedy in which a entire group of dolts and doofuses are galvanized to excellence under the guidance of an habitual loser, for whom this daunting mission is the proverbial Last Chance.

Stripes was originally pitched to Paramount Pictures as *Cheech and Chong in the Army*, a proposed vehicle for the counterculture comedy team whose funky "doper" humor had won over a huge mainstream audience in such films as *Up in Smoke* and *Cheech and Chong's Next Movie*.

Attached to the project from the word "go" was Ivan Reitman, who had recently produced and directed the incredibly profitable Canadian-made *Meatballs*, starring Bill Murray as the head counselor in a summer camp comprised of clods, klutzes and other assorted nuts. Reitman liked the idea of transferring the "loser wins all" format of *Meatballs* to a military setting, and began angling for permission to film at an actual Army base, just as *Meatballs* had been shot at a real summer camp and Reitman's earlier lovable-misfit comedy *Animal House* (which he produced but did not direct) was lensed on a genuine college campus. Quoted by the AP in July 1981, Reitman explained: "I think filming in real places contributes to the feeling and atmosphere of the comedy, whereas shooting in a studio provides a plastic, phony sheen."

When Cheech & Chong's agent demand that Reitman turn over 25 percent of the profits from his next five films in exchange for the team's services, the director turned him down, whereupon the two comedians were dropped from the cast. Barely pausing for breath, Reitman moved the project — now retitled *Stripes* — from Paramount to Columbia, instructing scriptwriters Daniel Goldberg and Len Blum to rewrite the script to suit the talents of *Meatballs* star Bill Murray, and further hiring comedian Harold Ramis (also a *Meatballs* alumnus) to coscript the picture and add a meaty role for himself. With the comparatively "straight" Murray and Ramis in the leading roles, all that remained of Cheech & Chong's peculiar brand of stoner humor was concentrated in a supporting character named Elmo Blum, played in the film by newcomer Judge Reinhold.

Now that he didn't have the "drug" angle to worry about, Reitman redoubled his efforts to obtain Pentagon approval to film on a real Army base. The Brass objected at first, but Reitman argued that showing a band of screw-ups overcoming their stupidity and working together as a finely-honed unit could only enhance the military's then somewhat tarnished image, serving as an excellent recruiting tool in the bargain. Reitman further offered to make several technical changes for the sake of accuracy, promised to tone down the mud-wrestling scene that dominated the middle portion of the picture, and agreed to get rid of the more objectionable military characters or make them expendable to the plot (only the obnoxious officer played by John Larroquette survived to the final script). This may explain why the R-rated-raunchy *Stripes* received full cooperation from the military, while the less outrageous *Private Benjamin* (see **Chapter 14**), which placed heavy emphasis on a dishonest Army recruiter and a lecherous colonel, was given a thumbs-down by the Pentagon.

In his first starring role in a major motion picture, Bill Murray plays John Winger, a part-time cabdriver and full-time slacker who loses his job, his car, his girlfriend and his pizza within the first 15 minutes of the film. Commiserating in the company of his best friend Russell Ziskey (Harold Ramis), who is also dissatisfied with his lot in life, John happens to see a TV ad for the Army ("Be all that you can be!"). Deciding that they need a change in life — and some easy money — John and Russell head to the nearest recruiting station. After a quick introduction to the two female MPs who will be the ladies in their lives, Louise (Sean Young) and Stella (P.J. Soles), our heroes arrive at Fort Arnold, where they meet several other rookies, losers all: Dewey "Ox" Oxberger (played by Harold Ramis' former *SCTV* colleague John Candy), Francis "Psycho" Soyer (Conrad Dunn), Cruiser (John Diehl) and the aforementioned Elmo Blum. Hard-ass drill sergeant Hulka (Warren Oates, slyly satirizing his established tough-guy image) is determined to whip this very raw material into shape, despite Winger's habit of scoffing at authority figures and using every aspect of basic training as an excuse for a wisecrack. During their first leave, the platoon precipitates a riot at a mud-wrestling bar (where another *SCTV* veteran, Dave Thomas, is the emcee), prompting uptight Captain Stillman (John Larroquette) to threaten them with a top-to-bottom repeat of "basic," with no likelihood of ever graduating to Private First Class status. The situation worsens when Sgt. Hulka is injured and unable to participate in the platoon's eleventh-hour shakedown.

Rising to the occasion, John Winger takes charge of the motley crew and delivers an inspiring speech to his fellow rookies — one which has been committed to memory by every fan of *Stripes* and doesn't need repeating here. (For the benefit of the uninitiated, we note that the speech includes such talking points as "Wretched Refuse" and "Old Yeller.") Under Winger's sterling leadership, the "loser" platoon practices all through the night for the next morning's graduation ceremonies. (This wasn't just acting, either: The cast members drilled for an hour each morning before filming started — virtually the only aspect of the picture that didn't grow out of Bill Murray and Harold Ramis' on-set improvisations.) To everyone's amazement, Winger's oddly-uniformed warriors emerge as the ceremony's star attraction, performing a dazzling close-order drill which brilliantly blends standard Army procedure with their own special brand of deadpan subversiveness. By the time the platoon has come to attention ("That's the fact, JACK!"), General Barnicke (Robert J. Wilke) is completely won over by Winger's unorthodox methods, declaring that the misfits are exactly the kind of men he needs for a top-secret project in Italy.

Had *Stripes* been made back in the 1930s or 1940s, when it was perfectably acceptable to release a 60-minute feature film on a top-of-the-bill basis, the picture would have been over at this point, and the audience would have gone home satisfied. But with another 46 minutes to go, the patchwork starts showing and the film begins moving in short spurts rather than the full frontal assault needed to sustain the comic momentum. The job at hand for John Winger and his fellow rookies is to guard the newly developed assault vehicle EM-50, which looks suspiciously like a late-1970s RV. The ever-insubordinate Winger and Ziskey decide to "borrow" the EM-50 to visit Louise and Stella in West Germany. When Capt. Stillman finds the vehicle missing, he leads the rest of the platoon on an unauthorized recovery mission. The stupidly stubborn Stillman accidentally crosses the border into Communist Czechoslovakia, where he and the other men are seized by the East German army. Managing to avoid capture, Sgt. Hulka sends out a "Mayday" which is picked up by the EM-50. With their girlfriends in tow, Winger and Ziskey embark upon a rescue mission, leading to the big slapstick climax that audiences had been looking forward to all evening — and would have torn down the theater if they hadn't received. (During this sequence, yet another of Harold Ramis' *SCTV* compadres, Joe Flaherty, shows up as a German border guard.) Happily, this grand finale is uproarious enough to make up for the raggedness of *Stripes*' second half.

In addition to posting an $85 million gross in North America, *Stripes* proved a bountiful revenue source for the state of Kentucky, with ex–Miss America Phyllis George Brown, wife of the state's governor, providing services and facilities to Ivan Reitman in her capacity as director of the Kentucky Film Commission. Most of the "Fort Arnold" scenes were filmed at Fort Knox, with other locations representing New York and Italy photographed in and around nearby Louisville. During the climactic "Czechoslovakia" sequence, the building complex standing in for East German headquarters was actually part of the Jim Beam Whiskey distillery in Bardstown. And as an added fillip for the hometown press, two of the film's costars, Warren Oates and Sean Young, were Kentucky natives.

The creative team responsible for *Stripes* was able to parlay the "triumphant loser" format into an even bigger success a few years later with the blockbuster comedy-fantasy *Ghostbusters*. But though Bill Murray et al. had abandoned the service-comedy format (none too soon for Murray, who felt antsy about carrying firearms and was not ashamed to admit it), the concept of a group of woebegone washouts truly "being all they can be" in the modern American military continued to thrive in other films. Unlike *Stripes*, not all of these were classifiable as comedies pure and simple. There were many observers who regarded director Penny Marshall's *Renaissance Man* (Touchstone, 1994) as a drama with humorous undertones, along the lines of the 1989 Robin Williams vehicle *Dead Poet's Society*. Perhaps this was an accurate assessment: Though initially marketed as a comedy, *Renaissance Man* is rather wanting in the laugh department.

Reportedly based on the actual experiences of its screenwriter Jim Burnstein, *Renaissance Man* stars Danny DeVito as Detroit-based insurance man Bill Rago, who like John Winger in *Stripes* turns to the Military only after running out of all other options. Having gone through a

"THAT'S THE FACT, JACK." Bill Murray in *Stripes* (Columbia, 1981).

messy divorce, Rago receives an additional blow to his self-esteem when he loses his job and is unable to find another because he possesses no marketable skills. Finally, the local unemployment agency finds Bill a temp position teaching a remedial English class at the nearby Fort McClane army training base (actually Fort Jackson, South Carolina). If Bill is underwhelmed by this assignment, his lack of enthusiasm is matched by his surly students, a group of low-achieving privates known as "squeakers" because they have only gotten this far by earning barely-passing grades in their previous schooling. Among these habitual losers are wisecracker Jamaal Montgomery (Kadeem Hardison), ex-gang member Donnie Benitez (Lillo Brancato Jr.), ultra-reclusive Roosevelt Hobbs (Khalil Kain, who drops out of the story when his character is revealed to be an undercover drug dealer), annoyingly obsessive Brian Davis Jr. (Peter Simmons), redneck child-abuse victim Melvin Melvin (Gregory Sporleder), foul-mouthed "trailer trash" Tommy Lee Hawood (pop singer Mark Wahlberg in his first dramatic role), and the sole female student — and the only one who seems to have any real ambition — Miranda Myers (Stacey Dash). Since this is officially a comedy, each of the Squeakers has a personal eccentricity that not only sets him or her apart from "normal" people but is also good for a few cheap laughs: Melvin Melvin, for example, is forever falling asleep, even while standing up.

Once all of the requisite remedial-classroom clichés have been exhausted, Bill Rago must needs be given the standard-issue antagonist, in this case drill sergeant Cass (Gregory Hines), who regards Rago's efforts to teach a bunch of "Double Ds" ("dumb as dog shit") as a waste of the Army's time and money. More sympathetic to Rago's challenge is Capt. Tom Murdoch (James Remar), who is intensely critical of a public-school system that cheats its marginal students by "handing out high school diplomas like they were toilet paper." In case you haven't caught on by now, the Army is not only a last chance for Bill Rago, but also for the Squeakers.

After several frustrating days of trying to teach his charges the fundamentals of simple comprehension, Rago starts quoting from his favorite Shakespearean play *Hamlet*. Having never heard 16th-century iambic pentameter before, the Squeakers are mesmerized. Rago brings more Shakespeare into the curriculum, contemporizing the material by relating it to the students' own experiences (by a stupendous coincidence, each of the kids' backstories is a Cliffs Notes synopsis of a major play in the Bard's canon). He also takes the class to a outdoor production of *Henry V*, during which the black students react so enthusiastically to the St. Crispin's Day speech ("Once more into the breach, dear friends") that they nearly get kicked out of the theater. As the story trudges onward to its oh-so-predictable climax, Rago's students pull a *Stripes* on the parade grounds, using the plot and characters of *Hamlet* as lyrics in a rap marching song ("Hamlet's Mother, She's the Queen/Buys It in the Final Scene")—an admittedly lively sequence that earned the praise of at least one Shakespearian scholar, who likened it to the absurdities of the "Pyramus and Thisbe" finale in *A Midsummer Night's Dream*! By the time one of the Squeakers delivers an almost letter-perfect rendition of the St. Crispin's Day speech during a practice drill in a driving rainstorm, even the skeptical Sgt. Cass is persuaded that Rago's students are "Double-Ds" no more.

We're all supposed to be profoundly moved by *Renaissance Man*, and perhaps it might have actually worked had we not seen this story so many times before. The average filmgoer who'd enjoyed Danny DeVito in his previous movie incarnations was probably more kindly disposed to the film than the professional critics. "Not to put too fine a point on it, Penny Marshall ... has become a hack," wrote David Denby of *New York* magazine. "She works the audience over, producing easy emotions and easy laughter; her directing has a shrewd, can-do rhythm and pace, but you can't see anything of life peeking through the movieish tensions, climaxes and resolutions." Roger Ebert of the *Chicago Sun-Times* complained that "we are subjected once again to the dishonest fiction that academic knowledge can somehow be gained by enthusiasm and osmosis." And here's Hal Hinson of the *Washington Post*: "*Renaissance Man*, Penny Marshall's intellectually ambitious new comedy, is an extravagant and all-too-familiar Hollywood contradiction — a movie that celebrates the life of the mind and the uniqueness of the individual but does so in glib slogans and is, itself, a sort of knockoff ... *Hamlet* may be the most indestructible of Shakespeare's plays, but *Renaissance Man* pounds it into politically correct dust..." But when all is said is done, the best critique was offered 394 years earlier by Hamlet himself: "I had as lief the town-crier spoke my lines."

Distressed by the film's poor box office, Touchstone decided to stop advertising *Renaissance Man* as a comedy, promoting it instead as a "feel-good" drama with the new title *By the Book* (in

Renaissance Man (Touchstone, 1994): Civilian teacher Danny DeVito (standing) brushes up his Shakespeare in a classroom of slow-learning soldiers. The student body includes, clockwise from right, Kadeem Hardison, Mark Wahlberg (his back to the camera, something that would *never* happen today!), Lillo Brancato Jr., Khalil Kain and Stacey Dash.

Australia, it was released under its working title, *Army Intelligence*). This strategy helped not at all, and the film joined the ranks of *Cabin Boy*, *Tank Girl* and *The Scarlet Letter* as one of the biggest bow-wows of 1994. The lesson that Penny Marshall and her coworkers had failed to take away from *Stripes* was that audiences who normally respond to multiple-misfit comedies don't *want* an Important Message along with the mindless laughs. Popular "lovable loser" films like *Police Academy* and *Major League* are proof enough that most filmgoers prefer to put their brains on hold as they sit down and prepare to laugh their heads off.

It was in fact the combined creative forces behind *Police Academy* (screenwriter Hugh Wilson) and *Major League* (director David Ward) who were chiefly responsible for the final comedy in this chapter, *Down Periscope* (20th Century–Fox, 1996). Accordingly, the film adheres slavishly to the formula jointly established by its predecessors: The talented professional who has never reached full potential because of his noncomformist behavior, given one final chance to prove his worth by molding a ragtag band of weirdos, deadbeats, addlebrains and bunglers into a team of champions. At the same time, the film avoids the pretentious pitfalls of *Renaissance Man* by delivering no weightier message than "Who needs to think when you can laugh?" This does not necessarily make *Down Periscope* a good film — it is far from that — but it is definitely a more entertaining one than *Renaissance Man*.

In a game attempt to finesse his TV success vis-à-vis *Cheers* and *Frasier* into a film career, Kelsey Grammer stars as Lt. Cmr. Thomas Dodge, a lifelong Navy man who at the outset of the picture is serving as second in command on the nuclear submarine U.S.S. *Orlando*. Dodge yearns to be assigned a sub of his own, but his loose-cannon behavior and non-regulation methods, coupled with the animosity of longtime nemesis Rear Admiral Graham (Bruce Dern), have caused him to be passed over time and again. Unexpectedly, the selection committee decides to grant Dodge his wish, but Graham sees to it that our hero is assigned the 40-year-old U.S.S.

Stingray—the only diesel sub in the fleet, so rundown and antiquated that it fully lives up to Dodge's description as "an ad for Rustoleum." To make the going all that much tougher, Graham hands Dodge the crummiest crew in the Navy, a sorry lot who can't even rise to the level of "misfit."

With the tools at hand, Dodge must participate in a brace of war games, in which he must first complete a successful evasive maneuver at Charleston Harbor, then stage a mock attack on his former sub *Orlando* at Norfolk Harbor. Going over Graham's head, Dodge makes a deal with Vice Admiral Winslow (Rip Torn) that he will be assigned a nuclear submarine if he wins the two-pronged war games. Harboring mysterious motives of his own, Winslow agrees. The rest of the picture charts the transition of the *Stingray* crew from a loose gathering of goofuses into a super-efficient unified whole, with Dodge and his female diving operator Lt. Emily Lake (Lauren Holly)—whose only prior "experience" has been theoretical and on dry land—overseeing the metamorphosis. Periodically setting up roadblocks for Dodge and Lake are Rear Admiral Graham, whose grasp of the "fair play" concept is tenuous at best, and the *Stingray*'s by-the-book executive officer Marty Pascal (Rob Schneider), who much to the relief of the crew (and the audience) is disposed of early in the proceedings.

As you have probably deduced by now, there are very few surprises in *Down Periscope*, nor is the film a likely candidate for the Library of Congress Preservation List. Many of the gags and routines calculated to reduce the audience to tears of laughter tend to fizzle out like a bottle of flat soda pop. The revelation early in the film that Thomas Dodge has the words "WELCOME ABOARD" tattooed on his penis works as a comedy device precisely once, as an appropriate excuse for the puritanical Graham to despise Dodge. Repeated over and over, the references to Dodge's decorated deal become so tiresome that even the sniggling 12-year-olds in the back row will get sick of them. And when the *Stingray* crew gets even with the insufferable Marty Pascal by holding a "pirate trial" and forcing him to walk the plank, there's no denying that this is an apt punishment

Submarine skipper Kelsey Grammer's confidence is not matched by his wide-eyed second in command Lauren Holly in *Down Periscope* (20th Century–Fox, 1996).

for this obnoxious character, but the scene goes on *way* too long to keep the audience amused throughout.

Conversely, some of the most obvious humor in *Down Periscope* is the stuff that works best with a large crowd. The film's obligatory "fart" joke is not only handled with astonishing dexterity, but is also entirely relevant to the storyline (the gastric indiscretion is picked up by sonar and mistaken for a depth-bomb explosion); not since *Blazing Saddles* has flatulence been exploited so creatively. In the same vein, the individual peculiarities of the various crew members, while never remotely credible, are expertly harnessed to push the plot forward. For example, the *Stingray*'s literally burned-out electrician Nitro (Tony Huss), who has withstood so many shocks from his jerry-built equipment that he could probably illuminate Times Square by rubbing his hands together, proves to be an excellent "conductor" during a potentially disastrous power outage. And while all the characters are service-comedy stereotypes, they possess an almost Descartian self-awareness. In his introductory scene, shiftless 1st Engineman Stepanek (Bradford Tatum) cheerfully admits to being "a pain in the butt," "detrimental to the whole operation" and "a total morale crusher." You won't get that sort of candor in a well-written movie, we guarantee you that.

An occasional unanticipated moment is allowed to emerge from the cliché festival known as *Down Periscope*. When the misogynistic crew of the *Stingray* hazes Lt. Emily Lake by stealing her bra and undershirt, she emerges on deck with her barely-concealed attributes bulging blimplike beneath her blouse. But just as the audience has braced itself for a string of vulgar "boob" jokes, the customarily irreverent Thomas Dodge grimly informs the crew that he will clean all their clocks personally if they ever try a trick like that again, or if they ever for a single moment neglect to treat Lt. Lake with the respect due her. For a PG-13 comedy made in A.D. 1996, this is quite a novelty.

The best aspect of *Down Periscope* is the filmmakers' decision to stage even the most ridiculous comedy sequences against a totally believable military backdrop. Several exteriors were filmed on such actual Naval installations as the "mothball fleet" in Benicia California, while the U.S.S. *Stingray*, which could easily (and more economically) have been conveyed by a CGI special effect, is a genuine diesel submarine: The U.S.S. *Pampanito*, which sank six Japanese subs during World War II, and at the time of filming was serving with dignity as a perfectly preserved tourist attraction at San Francisco's Maritime Museum. The restoration of the *Pampanito* had been so thorough that sculptor Thomas Richardson and his crew were hired to scrape off all the new paint, sand and prime the hull, and apply fake rust on the vessel from stem to stern so it could convincingly double as the woebegone *Stingray*.

A legend has arisen that *Down Periscope* was an unmitigated failure, and that the critics were merciless in their condemnation. Actually, while the film was not a huge hit, it earned back its cost and made a small profit internationally. And though many reviewers concurred with *Entertainment Weekly*'s "D" rating, others were quite benign: Chris Hicks of the *Deseret News* called the film "a generally pleasant surprise," while *Variety* regarded it a "good-natured, innocuous frivolity." If one were rating the films cited in this chapter on a scale of 1 to 10, *Down Periscope* would probably score around "5," halfway between the nirvana of *Stripes* and the nadir of *Sergeant DeadHead*. (Sorry I can't come up with a better closing paragraph, but I'm *such* a misfit and foul-up....)

13

The Children's Crusade
Military-Academy Comedies

Military academies were an essential part of upper-class European life long before they were introduced to the United States. Never pretending to be bastions of democracy, these academies were established as training grounds for the sons of royalty and aristocracy, who for centuries were the only men permitted to serve as officers. Though accustomed to giving rather than receiving orders, the privileged few admitted to academies were expected to follow the orders of schoolmasters and upperclassmen unswervingly, the better to prepare them to lead others into battle without flinching or second-guessing. The academy cadet also learned the character-building value of endurance to pain: There was no greater source of pride for an ex-cadet than a prominent dueling scar. Above all, these fledgling warriors were relentlessly drilled in the edicts of Honor— and were not only encouraged but often ordered to take their own lives should they ever breach that honor. Is it any wonder that European novelists and playwrights did not regard military academies as a rich source of humor?

The same lack of frivolity held true in America, at least until the early 20th century. Though being born into a family of bluebloods was no longer a prerequisite of admission to such institutions as the Army's West Point (established 1802) or the Navy's Annapolis (established 1845), it helped if the cadet happened to be descended from a long line of military men, or if the cadet's family had strong political connections. Unlike their European counterparts, American cadets were discouraged from dueling, either in sport or in earnest (though dueling certainly did occur, often over the most trivial of insults), but the old traditions of strict discipline, blind loyalty and rigid honor codes were still very much in play. Since most cadets had entered the academy by choice, the average "plebe" (a nickname for underclassmen, derived from "plebian") knew better than to complain about persecution from upperclassmen who demanded that they recite obscure rulebook paragraphs from memory or face humiliating consequences. Nor were any objections raised about the no-exception adherence to such regulations and restrictions as West Point's famous "No Horse, No Wife, No Mustache."

The disillusionment that followed World War I tended to place an onus on the tradition of training young Americans to be "officers and gentlemen." Where formerly the military-academy system was hailed the Builder of Men, certain reactionary authors now regarded that system as a breeding ground for fascism. Typical of this line of thinking were two plays that opened on Broadway in the fall of 1936. Joseph M. Viertel Shapiro's *So Proudly We Hail* told of a sensitive young cadet transformed into a bullying beast by the sadistic commandant of "Stone Ridge Academy," while Henry Misrock's *Bright Honor* focused on a pacifistic English teacher who was hounded out of "Newtown Military Academy" by his warmongering students.

Since both of these plays had failed spectacularly, the smart money during the 1936–37 Broadway season was *not* on a brand-new show about life in a military academy, this one written by a pair of 26-year-old newcomers named John C. Monks and Fred Finklehoffe, both 1932 graduates of the Virginia Military Institute. Founded in 1839, the VMI was best known for training several top officers of the Confederacy during the Civil War (General Stonewall Jackson had once been an instructor), and for being the only military academy to form a separate fighting unit. The traditions of stiff-necked discipline and austerity established at VMI during the 19th century were still in place in 1936. All cadets, no matter the rank, slept on cots (or "hays") rather than beds. The trainees, here known as "rats," were not only deprived of all creature comforts during their plebe year, but also forced to march along a prescribed barracks line at an exaggerated attitude of attention known as "straining." Each upperclassman, or "dyke," was assigned as mentor to a specific plebe, and while the dyke was allowed to indulge in the standard hazing and hassling of his charge, he was also expected to protect the designated plebe from all harm — until that plebe was finally awarded fourth-class-student status during "Breakout Week." Every student was subject to an Honor Court which strictly enforced the VMI code: "A rat does not lie, cheat, steal, nor tolerate those who do." Finally, every man was required to participate in one or more of VMI's athletic teams.

While this may sound like fodder for another searing dramatic exposé of academy life, Monks and Finklehoffe's play was a comedy concentrating on the lighter aspects of "rat-hood" at VMI. Well known on campus as jokesters and cut-ups, the two aspiring authors had dreamed up their play while sitting in a civilian jail after a weekend fracas. With the encouragement of their English professor Raymond E. Dixon, the boys worked on their play during their off-hours, incorporating as many real-life anecdotes as they could remember while carefully casting the Academy in a respectful light. Originally titled *When the Roll Is Called*, the play zeroed in on three cadets named Bing Edwards, Billy Randolph and Dan Crawford. Bing is secretly married to Kate Rice, an infraction of VMI rules that could get him drummed off campus. Billy and Dan spend most of the play helping Bing keep his secret (thereby risking defiance of VMI's Code of Honor), which becomes problematic when Kate announces that she's pregnant. They also endeavor to aid Bing in his efforts to win a $300 prize as the school's best all-around athlete. Along the way, Bing's pals pursue their own romances: Billy is sweet on college girl Joyce Winfree, while Dan is enamored of Joyce's bookish roomie Claire Adams, little suspecting that Claire is the daughter of his commanding officer. Providing punctuation to the proceedings is long-suffering plebe Misto Bottome, the fall guy for many of the upperclassmen's schemes.

Briefly going their separate ways after graduation, Monks and Finklehoffe linked up again a few years later to pitch their student collaboration, retitled *Stand at Ease*, to a potential New York producer. By the time it was optioned by Broadway tyro George Abbott, the play had undergone 32 revisions— and yet another name-change. As *Brother Rat* (VMI slang for a freshman), the show opened at the Biltmore Theater on December 16, 1936, having received the blessing of Monks and Finklehoffe's former classmates and officers, who were undoubtedly relieved that the play was not a harsh condemnation of the academy system as *So Proudly We Hail* and *Bright Honor* had been.

Producer-director George Abbott sensed that the essential appeal of *Brother Rat* was its youthful exuberance. Unlike other plays of the period in which actors well into middle age were passed off as teens and twenty-somethings, none of the six principal players of *Brother Rat* was over the age of thirty. The most experienced member of the main cast, Hollywood veteran Frank Albertson (best known for his supporting work in such films as *Just Imagine* and *Alice Adams*), was a mere tot of 27, while his costars, a pair of beardless whippersnappers named Eddie Albert and José Ferrer, were respectively 30 (but just barely) and 24. Also in the cast as the beleagured Misto was 19-year-old Ezra Stone, an Abbott protege who later became an excellent director on his own, helming the original stage version of the postwar comedy *At War With the Army*— the film version of which, starring Martin & Lewis, was produced by *Brother Rat* co-author Fred Finklehoffe (see **Chapter 3**). Abbott also helped another kid chart a course for a profitable future: Hired as a publicist for *Brother Rat* was VMI graduate Frank McCarthy, who went on to become Assistant Secretary of State during the Truman Adminstration and later established himself as a top Hollywood producer, winning an Oscar for the decidedly *non*-comic military epic *Patton*.

13. The Children's Crusade

After his misbegotten *Uncle Tom's Cabin* adaptation *Sweet River* had laid an egg in early 1936, Abbott promised to deliver one hit comedy per season to Broadway audiences: *Brother Rat* fulfilled that promise to the tune of 577 performances. Having helped finance the stage production, Warner Bros. secured the rights for the 1938 film version, which like the play served as a showcase for promising young talent. Of the original Broadway cast, Eddie Albert was carried over to the film to recreate the role of Bing Edwards, while William Tracy, who'd played Misto in one of the play's touring companies, was hired to essay the same part on screen (Tracy would later headline a series of military comedies for producer Hal Roach, as noted in **Chapter 5**). Other primary cast members were drawn from Warners' contract roster. Wayne Morris, fresh from an auspicious starring debut in 1937's *Kid Galahad*, was cast as Billy Randolph. Former sportscaster Ronald Reagan, hitherto limited to Warners' B output, landed his first role of consequence in an "A" picture as Dan Maxwell. The extraordinarily gifted Jane Bryan was given brief respite from such tragic roles as Bette Davis' kid sister in *Marked Woman* to play Bing's secret wife Kate. Priscilla Lane, who with her sisters Rosemary and Lola had just finished work on the popular tearjerker *Four Daughters*, was assigned the role of Joyce. And sporting blonde tresses and a fashionable pair of horn-rimmed glasses in the role of Claire was up-and-coming starlet Jane Wyman.

Throughout the 1930s, Warner Bros. had a disturbing habit of filming their Broadway adaptations in the same stagebound manner as the original productions, with lengthy scenes played out in single sets and characters providing detailed descriptions of events that had occured off-camera (This is particularly true of two other acquisitions from George Abbott, *Three Men on a*

The Broadway hit ***Brother Rat*** came to the screen courtesy of Warner Bros. in 1938. Here we see Eddie Albert (left), the lone carryover from the original stage production, sharing a scene with Wayne Morris, Jane Wyman, and a young fellow who later retired from acting to take a government job (with benefits).

Horse and *Boy Meets Girl*). *Brother Rat* director William Keighley avoided this claustrophobia by filming several important scenes on location in and around the actual VMI campus in Lexington, Virginia. Quoted by Ronald Reagan biographer Lou Cannon, newspaperman and Lexington native Charles McDowell recalled that the Warners unit took over the small Southern town for an entire week, commandeering the town's only taxicab — thus preventing the VMI professors from sneaking off-campus to purchase liquor! One of the funniest scenes in the film does not appear in the play, and for full comic effectiveness could *only* have been staged on the VMI parade grounds: In anticipation of fatherhood, Bing Edwards breaks rank while marching with his company to practice funny faces and "kitchy koos" on a stranger's baby.

Other changes in the play were made to satisfy the Hollywood censors: some of the language was toned down, while the pregnant Kate never "shows," not even in the third trimester. Gratifyingly, one element of the play was left untouched by Warner Bros. In the original *Brother Rat*, the three separate romantic subplots are given equal time, none of the couples given precedence over the others. Resisting the temptation to build up Wayne Morris and Priscilla Lane, the two most prominent performers in the cast, at the expense of their costars, the Morris-Lane romance is given no more emphasis than the Albert-Bryan marriage or the Reagan-Wyman relationship. Critics applauded the studio's decision to retain the balance of the Broadway version by turning out a genuine ensemble piece rather than a contrived "star" vehicle.

A hit with civilian and military audiences alike (Warners' Virginia exchange kept a print of the film in circulation for decades by popular demand of the VMI cadets), *Brother Rat* was also a huge career boost for its talented young cast. Given this fact, Warners had no problem persuading the principals to reunite for the 1940 sequel *Brother Rat and a Baby*. Following the three cadets and their ladies into civilian life, the sequel lacks the newness and novelty of the military-academy setting, coming off as a bland situation comedy with too much emphasis on the destructive behavior of Bing and Kate's troublesome progeny.

Nonetheless, Warners felt the original property still had enough value to warrant a Techicolor musical remake in 1952 (a project that had actually been in the works since 1948). Retitled *About Face*, this version stars Gordon MacRae, Eddie Bracken and Dick Wesson in the roles previously played by Ronald Reagan, Eddie Albert and Wayne Morris; each character bears a new name in the remake, just as VMI now goes by the alias "Southern Military Institute." The three leading ladies this time out are Virginia Gilmore, Phyllis Kirk and Aileen Stanley, Jr., a hasty rewrite blending elements of two separate *Brother Rat* characters so that Gilmore is now both the pregnant wife *and* the colonel's daughter. The role of plebe-patsy Misto is rechristened "Bender" and expanded to showcase the talents of 20-year-old Joel Grey in his film debut. Similarly, a secondary character from *Brother Rat*, the irritatingly rule-bound cadet "Lacedrawer" Rogers (played in the earlier film by Gordon Oliver), is built up to accommodate another specialty performer, dancer Cliff Ferre. Of the seven songs written for *About Face* by Charles Tobias and Peter DeRose, the only one worth mentioning is Joel Grey's character number "I'm Nobody," in which the young *toomler* rattles off several celebrity impersonations, including a stunningly accurate Jerry Lewis. Cliff Ferre is likewise given opportunity to shine with a running gag in which his hair continually changes color, the result of a chemically altered lotion bottle. By the time the "End" credit rolls around, Ferre's hair has turned blue, which somehow inspires him to launch into a energetic dance solo. Though generally unimpressed by *About Face* (the consensus was that the principals were much too old for their roles), critics were unified in their praise for Cliff Ferre, predicting that he'd be the film's "breakout" star. As for Joel Grey — well, give the kid a little time and he might amount to something ...

Like *Brother Rat and a Baby*, *About Face* lacked the freshness and uniqueness that had made *Brother Rat* a hit; it was too much in the familiar vein as other, better military-academy musicals like *Best Foot Forward* (1943) and *The West Point Story* (1950) to stand out on its own. The same is true of the later Pat Boone vehicle *Mardi Gras* (20th Century–Fox, 1958), which like *Brother*

Rat was filmed in great part on the VMI campus. Because of its overabundance of music at the expense of comedy, *Mardi Gras* doesn't really belong in this book beyond mentioning that several of the film's cast members would be reassigned to the subsequent 20th Century–Fox military comedies *A Private's Affair* and *All Hands on Deck* (see **Chapter 16**).

Up to now we've been discussing films spotlighting military academies designed for college-age recruits, who in general enrolled at their own free will. It was a different story with military schools catering to adolescents and pre-college-age students. Though quite a few enrollees genuinely want to be in such schools, for the most part these institutions are classified as "therapeutic boarding schools," designed for youngsters with academic and behavioral issues that the mainstream education system is not equipped to handle. Read any weekend edition of the *New York Times* and you'll find page after page of classified ads for military academies which promise to "straighten out" difficult children and invest in them the values of self-discipline and the desire to excel in the "real" world.

Unmentioned in these advertisements are those wealthy parents of children *without* profound behavioral or learning problems, parents who nonetheless shunt their kids off to military institutions because they simply haven't the time, patience or desire to deal with the kids themselves. In Hollywood, actor Earle Foxe helped establish just such an institution for the sons of busy studio executives and employees, the Black-Foxe Academy. The grownups who sequestered their youngsters in Black-Foxe patted themselves on the back for exposing their pampered offspring to the character-building regimen of Army life. Reflecting this, the studios churned out such fictional military-school films as *Dinky*, *On Dress Parade* and *Military Academy* (the latter filmed on location at Black-Foxe), which stressed the positive aspects of teenage and pre-pubescent kids wearing uncomfortable uniforms, performing close-order drills and punishment duty for hours on end, submitting to the barked orders of imperious student officers who weren't much older than they were, and slavishly adhering to a dizzying variety of intractable honor codes (Billy Wilder's 1942 effort *The Major and the Minor* was one of the few films with an academy setting that de-emphasized these clichés, focusing instead on the comic possibilities of an attractive female—in this case Ginger Rogers—plunked in the middle of an all-male environment). Needless to say, many real-life military school students regarded the experience less glowingly than their parents. Years after the fact, Samuel Goldwyn Jr. described his tenure at Black-Foxe as "sheer fucking hell."

The most memorable film comedy dealing with a pre-adult military institution soft-pedaled the negatives of the aforementioned story elements, though this didn't mean that the characters were free from trauma or discontent. *The Private War of Major Benson* (Universal-International, 1955) was the first theatrical-feature project for the radio/TV writing team of Joe Connelly and Bob Mosher, filmed halfway between their lengthy hitch on *Amos 'n' Andy* and their creation of the imperishable sitcom *Leave It to Beaver*. Connelly got the idea for the project after listening to his son relate his experiences as a parochial-school student. Together with Mosher, Connelly felt that the comic potential of such a setting would be enhanced if the church-controlled school also sponsored an ROTC program—and to add suspense and "heart appeal," if that program was in danger of losing its accreditation. At the same time, actor Charlton Heston was just coming off a grueling dramatic assignment as Moses in DeMille's *The Ten Commandments*, and was of the mind that he "needed a comedy" not only to unwind from the rigors of leading the Chosen People out of Egypt, but also to boost his fan following. Heston had become interested in *Private War of Major Benson* while the property was in the hands of his home studio Paramount, but by the time he was free from his DeMille commitment the Connelly-Mosher script had been sold to Universal. Unable to convince Paramount to buy the script back, Heston brokered an independent alignment with Universal, agreeing to waive his salary in exchange for a percentage-of-profits deal. (The studio had previously struck similar mutually beneficial deals with James Stewart and Errol Flynn.)

The Private War of Major Benson was directed by Jerry Hopper and location-filmed in Anaheim, California on the campus of St. Catherine's, a genuine Catholic military school originally

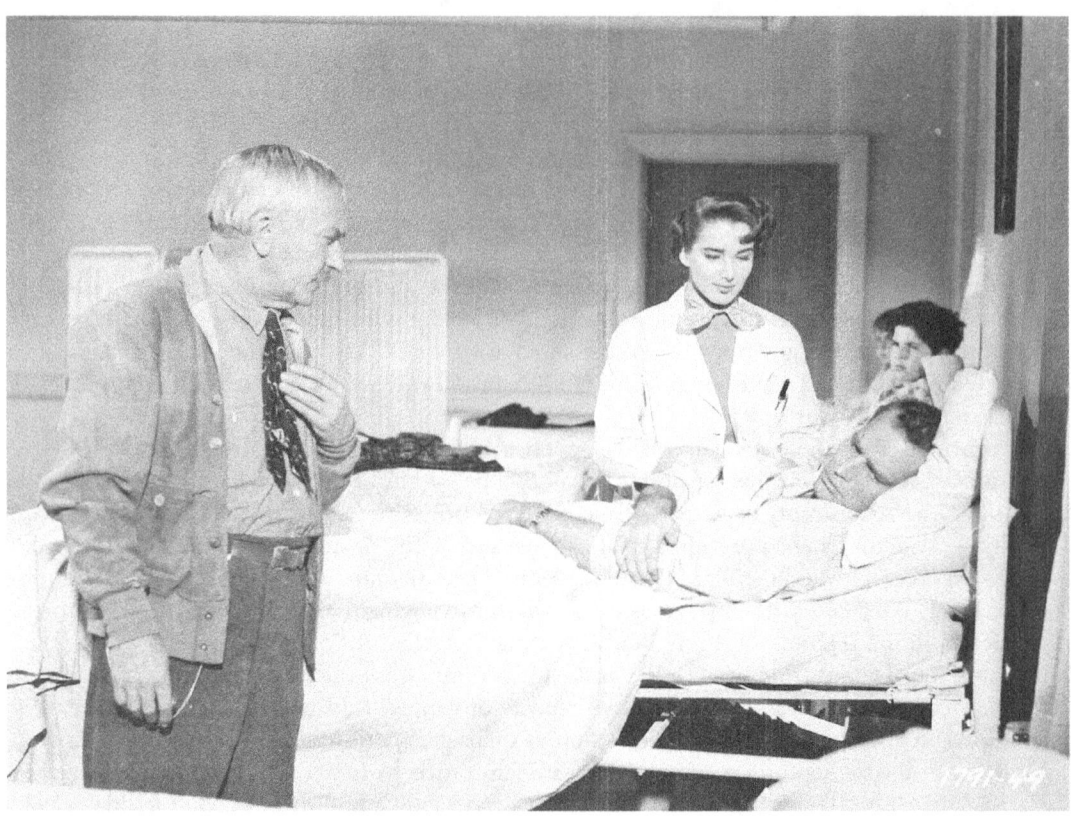

An uncharacteristically passive Charlton Heston reposes in bed while William Demarest and Julie Adams do the heavy acting in this scene from *The Private War of Major Benson* (Universal-International, 1955). Please note the avoidance of "Moses" and "Ape" jokes.

built as an orphanage in 1889. Heston stars as Army major Bernard "Barney" Benson, a merciless martinet and notorious "loose cannon." When his oft-repeated complaints that the modern Army is comprised of weaklings in need of round-the-clock training are quoted in *Newsweek*, Benson is called on the carpet by Major-General Ramsey (Milburn Stone), who warns Barney that he could very well be dishonorably discharged for his careless words. In consideration of Benson's brilliant combat record, Ramsey gives the Major a chance to escape punishment with a forced assignment at cash-poor Sheraton Military Academy — without telling him that the institution is headed by a formidable nun named Mother Redempta (Nana Bryant), and that the school's ROTC program is comprised of kids ranging in age from 6 to 14. Benson's hard-driving, hard-drinking lifestyle does not endear him either to Mother Redempta or the school's attractive doctor Kay Lambert (Julie Adams), nor does he exactly hit it off with the students, whose sloppiness on the parade grounds is unrivaled in military annals. The Major's spartan training methods further alienate him from his coworkers and cadets, with the exceptions of the school's only Private, little Thomas "Tiger" Flaherty (Tim Hovey), and impressionable teenage Cadet Colonel Sylvester Dusik (Sal Mineo in his second film). While Benson pays lip service to exerting a more benign "fatherly" influence on the kids, it is only to impress Kay, on whom he obviously has designs.

Even though Benson's no-quarter regimen yields positive results — especially with Sheraton's perennial-underdog football team — the youngsters can't overcome their hatred of the man and sign a petition to have him ousted. Preparing to leave Sheraton in defeat, Benson has a lengthy soul-searching conversation with fellow "outcast" Tiger Flaherty, who has run away from campus. The two lost souls suddenly realize that they've misunderstood each other throughout the picture, and when Benson covers up for the AWOL Tiger, the boy becomes his biggest fan, an attitude that spreads throughout the student body. Eventually Benson and the kids learn to meet each other halfway, and the end result is a promotion for the Major and a reprieve for the school's imperiled ROTC program. The climactic parade-ground sequence, in which the boys prove on their own initiative that Benson's tough training methods have not been in vain while the Major himself is bedridden with the measles, is in the best Connelly-Mosher *Leave It to Beaver* tradition of simultaneously tickling the funnybone and touching the heart.

Aside from the occasional double take, "pain" reaction and pratfall, Charlton Heston wisely opts to play his character straight, allowing the situation and the secondary characters to provide the biggest laughs (he would use this Jack Benny-like passivity to equally good advantage in his next service comedy *The Pigeon That Took Rome*). Supporting players William Demarest (as Sheraton's crabby caretaker) and Milburn Stone (as Benson's C.O.) bring their own reservoir of acting tricks to the proceedings, with Stone particularly enjoyable in a role that led directly to his 20-year run as the misanthropic "Doc" on TV's *Gunsmoke*. Of the younger cast members, 9-year-old Tim Hovey is a standout as the lonely Tiger Flaherty, a characterization that resulted in a brief spate of stardom beginning with the exploitatively titled *The Toy Tiger* (a 1955 remake of the 1938 Deanna Durbin musical *Mad About Music*), also set in a boy's school. Though there are few surprises in *The Private War of Major Benson*, there are few dull spots either; and thanks to his percentage deal, Charlton Heston earned more money for this box-office winner than any of his previous films.

The virtues of *Major Benson* stand out in sharper relief when the film is compared to its 1995 remake *Major Payne*, which eschews a "dramatic" leading man in favorite of professional comedian Damon Wayans, who collaborated on the screenplay with Dean Lorey and Gary Rosen (original scenarists Connelly, Mosher, William Roberts and Richard Allan Simmons receive a "based on" credit), and whose Wife 'n' Kids production company packaged the film for Universal release. Though several of the films described in this book are so bad as to be insulting, *Major Payne* is the only one that actually made this writer physically ill.

The plot of the 1995 film is similar enough to the 1955 original that there's no need to go into detail. Significant changes include the fact that the leading character is now a Marine, rechristened Major Benson W. Payne (the "W" stands for Winifred, ha ha ho ho); and the setting, no longer a Catholic institution but a non-denominational private school called Madison Academy ("played" by the Miller School of Albermarle in Charlottesville, Virginia), presided over by a senile septuagenarian (William Hickey) instead of an fully functional Mother Superior. Also, the school is not in danger of losing its ROTC accreditation as in the earlier picture; thus the main focus is shifted to the uncertain military future of the protagonist and his burgeoning romance with the school's prosocial female guidance counselor ("Ellen Walburn" rather than "Kay Wilbanks").

We will attempt to break down the film's failure with three salient points. Though in *Private War of Major Benson* the title character runs his charges ragged and imposes harsh penalties on those who fail to live up to expectations, we are never for one minute worried that the kids are in any real physical danger. In *Major Payne*, we learn within the first five minutes that the protagonist is a combat-crazed veteran of Iraq, Panama and Kuwait — by his own admission a "trained weapon of destruction"— and that he's been yanked from active duty because of the high number of casualties on *both* sides incurred by his commando tactics. In his efforts to adjust to civilian life, Major Payne displays the same reckless, near-homicidal streak that he did on the battlefield — and to top it off, he's dumb as a box of rocks, a dangerous dimwit. By the time that an old officer pal arranges for Payne to take charge of the ROTC kids at Madison Academy, we have every reason to fear that not only will the youngsters not survive the program, but they probably won't even survive to adulthood. Placing children in jeopardy on-screen only works when the villains do it, or the kids do it to themselves; putting them in peril at the hands of the hero is just plain irresponsible.

Irresponsible *and* mean-spirited — and that's the second point of contention with *Major Payne*. Given the necessity of instilling discipline, endurance and teamwork in ROTC cadets, we're able to accept the dictatorial behavior of Charlton Heston's Major Benson: Yes, he's a stern taskmaster, but he isn't cruel or sadistic. Damon Wayans' Major Payne is both. Called upon to punish his charges, he forces them to march around the campus while wearing girls' dresses. Not content with simply teaching them a lesson, Payne insists upon publicly humiliating a bunch of pre-teen boys in a manner that the other students will never let them live down, and which will very likely leave enough emotional scars to last a lifetime. Interviewed in *Jet* magazine, Damon Wayans declared that *Major Payne* is "about tough love and treating children with respect but treating them like children.... It's a movie the entire family can enjoy because aside from the big laughs it shows how the characters learn to respect themselves and respect each other's differences." Can't argue with that: Dressing boys as girls is a sure sign of respect, and assaulting the viewer with gratuitous jokes about fat kids, deaf kids and bedwetters is ideal family entertainment — if you happen to be the Borgia family.

Above and beyond the film's serious scriptwriting flaws, blame for *Major Payne*'s failure as a comedy must alas rest with star Damon Wayans, a particularly depressing assessment in view of Wayans' creative genius in most other aspects of his career. Though Charlton Heston was never the most versatile or flexible of actors, he was skilled enough to persuade audiences that there was a living, breathing human being behind all those false beards and Biblical proclamations. In contrast, Damon Wayans doesn't even seem to be trying to be believable, relying instead on a shallow, grating characterization that comes off as a fourth-rate Eddie Murphy imitation. Unlike Major Benson, who manages to mellow and mature as a person without sacrificing his core principles, Major Payne remains the same repulsive S.O.B. from beginning to end. The script tries to force-feed some humanity into the character by introducing an even more abhorrent piece of humanity, the abusive-drunkard father of the school's most troubled cadet. "See folks?" the writers seem to be saying. "Even Payne isn't as rotten as *this* guy!" We remain unconvinced.

A few very minor pleasures can be found in *Major Payne*. The performance by leading lady Karyn Parsons is appealing, as is the work by child actor Orlando Brown as pint-sized cadet Tiger, the role originally played by Tim Hovey. (For reasons unexplained, Tiger is the only black member of Madison's ROTC.) Also, there's a wonderful comic setpiece which indicates the direction the film *could* have taken with a little more imagination and ingenuity. While reading *The Little Engine That Could* to Tiger, Major Payne begins embellishing on the material, "reimagining" the familiar children's fable as if it were a bloody Vietnam reconnaissance mission — with the wide-eyed youngster hanging on Payne's every word! Come to think of it, the biggest and most appreciative audience for *Major Payne* whenever it shows up on cable TV is comprised almost entirely of boys between the ages of 6 and 13. Go figure.

Building a comedy on a realistic foundation worked for *Private War of Major Benson* but not for *Major Payne*. Perhaps it would have been the other way around if that foundation had been totally unrealistic, almost to the point of fantasy. Which brings us to the 1980 Warner Bros. release *Up the Academy*, which is so far removed from anything resembling Real Life that it might as well have been a cartoon. Matter of fact, the film was inspired by a periodical that was filled with nothing *but* cartoons — hence its original title, *MAD Magazine Presents Up the Academy*.

Having elevated sophomoric humor to an art form in the 1950s and 1960s, the satirical magazine *MAD* faced its first serious competition in the early 1970s from *National Lampoon*, developed and nutured by such Harvard-bred iconoclasts as Doug Kenny, Michael O'Donoghue, Sean Kelly, Tony Hendra and P.J. O'Rourke. Appealing to an older and hipper audience than *MAD*, *National Lampoon* broke new ground with its take-no-prisoners irreverence and freewheeling profanity, eviscerating the sacred cows of the Left and Right alike with deadly precision. Among the upstart publication's lasting cultural contributions was an ancillary "High School Yearbook" parody published in 1974, purporting to chronicle the 1964 graduating class of Estes C. Kefauver High as seen through the eyes of its least distinguished student Larry Kroger. Some of the characters and jokes introduced in this special issue were folded into *National Lampoon*'s first theatrical-movie venture, 1978's *Animal House* (written by *Lampoon*ers Kenny and O'Donoghue), the success of which fostered a whole new cycle of "teen-raunch" comedies like *Meatballs* and *Porky's*.

Uncomfortably aware that *National Lampoon* was leaving them eating dust by the late 1970s, the "usual gang of idiots" at *MAD* hoped to beat *Lampoon* at its own game with another teen-raunch movie comedy. Ironically, though *MAD* had through the years skewered its many imitators (*Sick, Cracked,* etc.) for not having the wit and invention to come up with fresh ideas of their own, the magazine's maiden movie effort *Up the Academy* copies the *Animal House* format to the minutest detail. The misfit protagonists are placed in an institution of higher learning, where their nutty behavior becomes a chancre for the authorities: In *Animal House*, the institution is ivy-league Faber College, while in *Up the Academy* it's an upscale military school, Sheldon R. Weinberg Academy. Along the way, the misfits make a dangerous enemy of the institution's head man: The malevolent, mob-connected Dean Wormer in *Animal House*, the sadistic and lecherous Major Vaughn Liceman in *Up the Academy*. On the verge of being shipped home in disgrace, the misfits stage a spectacular counteroffensive guaranteed to make their foes look like fools: The outcasts of *Animal House*'s Delta House pile into a pimped-up roadster and destroy a downtown parade, while *Up the Academy*'s lovable losers inflict pain, humiliation and exploding rockets on Liceman and his flunkies during the annual student-faculty soccer game. The basic plotline of *Up the Academy* is also a derivation, not of *Animal House* but of the vintage British comedy *The Happiest Days of Your Life*: The all-male Weinberg Academy and the all-female Butch Academy are about to merge, resulting in an outbreak of raging hormones. However, one doesn't have to be familiar with *Happiest Days of Your Life* to determine that the earlier film was not the point of origin for *Academy*'s "showcase" gag involving a piece of excrement floating in a punch bowl.

The script for *Up the Academy* was written by Tom Patchett and Jay Tarses, who in happier times worked on such TV series as *The Bob Newhart Show* and *Alf*. The film's four principal teenagers have been unjustly classified as delinquents and forced to attend Weinberg for disciplinary reasons. Oliver (J. Hutchinson) is a rube from Ohio; Chooch (Ralph Macchio) is the rebellious scion of a Mafia family; Ike (Wendell Brown) is the jive-talking offspring of a black preacher; and Hash (Tom Citera)—short for El Hashid Amir Jr—is the son of an Arab shiek. (So we don't miss the point, Hash always wears a *keffiyah* on his head. Try getting away with a gag like *that* nowadays.) Unlike *Animal House*, there isn't a "John Belushi" breakout performer among them, though 18-year-old Ralph Macchio, making his screen debut as Chooch, would hit it big four years later with *The Karate Kid*. In a 1984 *People* magazine interview, Macchio confessed that he treated acting as a lark until *Up the Academy*, but when play became work he decided to quit college and concentrate fulltime on his craft. To give him his due, he's not bad at all in *Academy*, and it's easy to see why he survived in show business while his costars faded from view.

Though *MAD Magazine Presents Up the Academy* is no epic, it wasn't cheap or slipshod either, its budget hovering above *Animal House*'s $2.7 million. Nor was it a total hack job, not with a director the caliber of Robert Downey Sr. in charge. The *auteur* of the underground favorites *Putney Swope* and *Greaser's Palace* has in the ensuing years carefully distanced himself from *Academy*. Quoted by Gerald Duchovnay in *Film Voices*, Downey recalled that he was opposed to the studio's original "wacky teenager" concept, feeling that the story would work better if the academy students were all nine or ten years old. Told "You can't work kids all day," Downey replied, "Well, then, work them half a day, but don't use fifteen and sixteen years old, because it's not going to work." According to the director, the discussion broke down at this point: "They basically said, 'If you don't like it, you can get the fuck out of here.' No, I'm not really involved in the film at all.... Not a pleasant experience." As minor compensation Downey was permitted to cast his then 14-year-old son Robert Jr. in a bit part. And no, Robert Downey Jr. doesn't include the picture in *his* current resume either.

In the *Animal House* tradition of supporting the younger players with experienced pros, *Up the Academy* features Ian Wolfe as Weinberg's doddering commandant, Barbara Bach as local "fast lady" Bliss, and Tom Poston as a gay dance instructor, among others. Cast in the central role of Major Liceman was Ron Leibman, an actor for whom the word "intense" isn't intense enough. Judging by his *con brio* performance — which includes a Faulknerian-idiot Southern accent and a scene in which he shows up for a romantic rendezvous dressed in Frederick's of Hollywood lingerie — you'd never guess that Leibman was just as out of sorts as Robert Downey Sr. during filming. There was no question that *something* was bothering Leibman when he took Warner Bros. to court, demanding that his name be removed from the credits. "It's a complicated legal situation I'm not allowed to go into," the actor told the *Pittsburgh Press*. "It's in litigation. As far as I know, it has never happened in the history of movies that the star is mentioned nowhere. Interesting. We'll see what happens." Ultimately *Up the Academy* was shipped out with no mention of Leibman either on screen or in the ads. Could he *now* reveal the whole story behind this unorthodox demand? "To be quite honest, I didn't want to have billing over the title of the movie in which I play a Southern major who's so mean his students feel a chilling wind every time I walk by," he explained to the *New York Times*. "I thought the young kids in the film should have credit. Anyway, the boss, when he heard this, said, 'OK. No one will have billing.' Then he must have said to himself, 'Wait a minute. That's bad business.' Well, I found out that it was legally possible to be non-existent in the movie. Then the head of the studio said, 'Ah, come on, Ron, we were only kidding.'" (Research has not revealed if Ron Leibman also returned his salary.)

Nor were Downey and Leibman the only ones who wished to pretend that the film never hap-

A motley band of military-school cadets — played by (from left) Wendell Brown, Tom Citera, J. Hutchinson and Ralph Macchio — are given a dressing down by their sadistic C.O. in *MAD Magazine Presents Up the Academy* (Warners, 1980). The adult in the room is Ron Leibman, who at his own request received no billing either in the film or on this still.

pened. Dissatisfied with the end result, the editors of *MAD* demand that all references to the magazine and its moronic mascot Alfred E. Neuman be removed from the non-theatrical prints. Thus, *MAD Magazine Presents Up the Academy* was issued to TV and home video as simply *Up the Academy*, with graceless jumpcuts eliminating all shots of the plaster-of-Paris Alfred E. Neuman statue that originally dominated the exterior scenes, as well as the anonymous extra who wandered through the campus wearing a form-fitting mask of the "What? Me worry?" kid.

The nicest thing one can say about *Up the Academy* is that it's better than *Major Payne*. Of the reviewers, only *The New York Times* was willing to describe the film as "cheerful and zany." Others were in agreement with *Film Bulletin*: "Dull comedy designed for brief playoffs." Michael Kulp of the Penn State University *Collegian* cut closer to the bone, pinpointing exactly why the film was such a disappointment: "[*MAD*]'s usual mix of parody and wry satire, which has made their magazine so popular and enjoyable, has failed to make the transformation into film." How true: If only the filmmakers had gone full-court and produced a *MAD* magazine come to life, allowing Don Martin and Mort Drucker to draw the storyboards, featuring characters like Joe Fonebone and Roger Kaputnick, and seasoning the dialogue with such colorful catchwords as "Fershlugginer" and "Potrzebie." In closing, Kulp noted that the problems with the film were "so abundant" that they would make an "excellent target" for *MAD*'s "own brand of humor." And that's just what happened when *MAD* published a biting parody of the film that had once borne the magazine's name in their October 1980 issue — mainly, "Throw Up the Academy."

That might also have been an apt title for the final entry in this chapter, though its actual title, *Getting Wasted*, will do just as well. Completed in 1978 and released (barely) by Diversified Film Distribution in 1980, *Getting Wasted* not only demonstrated the sad disrepair into which the military-school comedy had fallen since 1938's *Brother Rat*, but was also a portent of things to come for the raunchy-teen genre in the next few years.

Director Paul Frizler was a college literature professor who decided late in life to become a filmmaker; clearly he wasn't influenced by *Potemkin* or *Citizen Kane*, but rather by *Easy Rider* and *American Graffiti*. Written by Frizler and John Flaherty, *Getting Wasted* is set in 1967 (there's a banana-smoking scene to confirm the date) at California Armed Forces Academy, a seedy military school whose teachers profess to be "liberal" even while imposing Torquemada-like penalties on anyone who shows a trace of individuality. Lead character Brad Carson (Brian Kerwin), forced to attend the Academy after being booted out of high school, bonds with a bunch of other student malcontents, all of whom have been exiled to a single dorm room. He also pals around with some artistic hippie types who hang out at a nearby beach — especially the stunning Paula (Wendy Rastatter), who makes macrame plant holders. The recent suicide of Brad's favorite high school teacher, likewise a rebel against the Establishment, has already given the boy ample reason to disdain the Academy's conformist values, but he really goes overboard in his hatred of The Pig Power Structure when he learns of the sadistic hazing prank that has permanently damaged the psyche of his train-obsessed roommate Choo-Choo (Stefan Angrim).

The film is supposed to be a comedy, and perhaps someone can sift a chuckle or two from these sample snippets: The requisite fat cadet (inevitably played by Steven Furst) infuriates a group of Chicanos by doing a parody of Alfonso Bedoya in *Treasure of the Sierra Madre* ("We don't got to show you no stinkin' matches!"); the heroine "gets off" on watching whales mate; a strung-out hippie tries to make conversation with a dead parrot named Leary; the local hangout is called The Roach's Clip Joint; bull manure is mixed with confetti at a homecoming dance; Brad's clueless mother (Ronnie Clare Edwards) dries off a wet dog in her new microwave; and in a scene that will have you rolling on the floor, a very small kid toddles onto the beach peddling pot.

Almost like an oasis in a desert of dull direction and sloppy scriptwriting, one truly hilarious scene emerges: A school hygiene class in which the teacher screens a gloriously hideous anti-VD cartoon wherein "Sammy Semen" and "Olivia Ovum" are menaced by the evil "Gona Coccus" (who sounds like Edward G. Robinson). Specially made for *Getting Wasted* by Lyon-Lamb Animation, this little gem was directed by future DePatie-Freleng stalwart John Lamb and animated by onetime *Yellow Submarine* in-betweener Russ Mooney. From the looks of things, half the film's budget must have gone into the cartoon segment, with the other half going to music clearance for such period-flavor tunes as "Mellow Yellow," "Monday Monday" and "Somebody to Love."

Unfortunately, this scene is missing from the currently available public-domain video version of *Getting Wasted*, which was transferred from a splicy, grainy, color-faded and heavily censored TV print. While the other military-school comedies in this chapter have long been in circulation — you can even find *Up the Academy* if you really want to — it's a safe bet that *Getting Wasted* would have sunk into total obscurity but for one fortuitous piece of casting: Billed 34th in the microscopic role of a drunken punk who torches tires and rolls them into the street is 22-year-old David Caruso. Once Caruso skyrocketed to stardom with TV's *NYPD Blue*, this early embarrassment rose from the ashes and received a VHS release, with a head shot of Caruso prominently displayed on the dust jacket. The name of the enterprising video distributor was Miracle Pictures — and forgive me if I abstain from repeating *that* tired old wheeze.

14

"Holy Smokes! A Dame!"
Women in the Military

Prior to World War II, the issue of women in the U.S. military never came up in films for the simple reason that there were no women in the U.S. military. If a uniformed female showed up in a service picture, she was either a member of the Salvation Army or a nurse in the Red Cross. Out of respect for the latter group's selfless ministrations on the battlefield, these "angels of mercy" were seldom figures of fun, with such conspicuous exceptions as Marie Dressler in *The Cross-Red Nurse* (1918) and ZaSu Pitts and Thelma Todd in *War Mamas* (see **Chapter 3**). In general, women in uniform were spared the indignities of slapstick and pratfalls, allowing the male comedians to handle the funny stuff. Even when leading ladies Madeline Hurlock (in Billy Bevan's *Over There-abouts*) and Sally Eilers (in Buster Keaton's *Doughboys*) were active participants in wartime comedies, they never precipitated the humor. Occasionally the script would contrive to have the heroine disguise herself as a male soldier, but this was not always played for laughs: There are precious few yocks in such somber efforts as D.W. Griffith's *The House with Closed Shutters* (1909) or Henry King's *She Goes to War* (1929).

In the "Everybody Pitch In" spirit of World War II, two all-female military units were formed in 1942: The Women's Army Corps (WACs), and the Navy's "Women Accepted for Volunteer Emergency Service" (WAVES). Neither was a combat unit, and in fact women were expressly forbidden to participate in the fighting; both units were limited to clerical, secretarial, technical, transport and intelligence personnel. Also in 1942, the Army Air Corps established the Women's Auxiliary Ferrying Squadron (WAFS), a group of female transport pilots, and Women's Flying Training Detachment (WFTDs), an amalgam of two older auxiliary units; the WAFS and WFTDs flew on non-combat assignments, freeing male pilots for fighting. By 1943, the two units had merged into one, the Women Airforce Service Pilots (WASPs); and when the United States Air Force was officially formed in 1947, the women's division was renamed the WAFs, which now stood for Women in the Air Force. Army and Navy nurses were also active throughout World War II, with all members attaining officer status upon completion of training—thereby theoretically banning the non-commissioned male troops from fraternizing with the nurses. (This "How dare you make a pass at an officer?" set-up would be a fertile source of material for comedy films.)

Though contemporary feminists may be put out that it took a World War for the Military to appreciate the value of women enlistees, in one respect it was fortunate that the WACs, WAVES and WAFs were *not* formed a few decades earlier, when the notion of "girls in khaki" would likely have been treated with chauvinistic derision by the boys-club movie industry. Consider the ridicule heaped upon suffragettes in films made prior to passage of the 19th Amendment, or the treatment of female business executives in Depression-era films, wherein "boss ladies" were invariably tamed into domesticity upon falling in love with one of their handsome subordinates.

Once the War made women in the military "acceptable," the concept was taken seriously by filmmakers—perhaps too seriously. While the Office of War Information grew less tolerant of training-camp comedies as the 1940s wore on, they grudgingly accepted misfit-private and tough-sergeant humor because it could not possibly affect the rate of male conscription. But since women were not subject to the draft, they needed extra enticement and encouragement. Comedies satirizing the negatives in the military — the sacrifice of personal freedoms and creature comforts, the grueling rigors of training, the harshness of sergeants and superior officers— might be counterproductive to female enlistment. Also, politicians who disapproved of women in the military would hardly have their minds changed if life in the WACs or WAVES was depicted as a barrel of laughs. "Why should we approve all that appropriation money if those dizzy dames are gonna behave like a bunch of overaged Campfire Girls?" the argument might have gone. Any filmic treatment of the auxiliary female units would *have* to be presented with a straight face — maybe a dab of comedy relief here and there, but that's all.

This mindset resulted in such dramatic films as MGM's *Keep Your Powder Dry* (1944), starring Lana Turner, Laraine Day and Susan Peters as three women from disparate backgrounds who join the WACs. The focus is on Turner, playing a spoiled debutante who has signed up for selfish reasons: the only way she will receive her inheritance is if she can prove her maturity in a worthwhile cause. Intending to resign from the WACs the moment the inheritance goes through, Turner is ultimately inspired to persevere by the shining example of her dedicated comrades-in-arms Laraine Day (the strictly-business daughter of a military family) and Susan Peters (the devoted wife of a serviceman). By film's end, Turner has truly matured, but the inheritance now means far less to her than Duty, Honor and County. Given its frivolous double-edged title (referring to both ammunition and cosmetics), *Keep Your Powder Dry* might well have been treated comedically, but the times—and the OWI — wouldn't countenance such irreverence.

Nor was there much laughter raised by Monogram's earlier *She's in the Army* (1942), even though it was promoted as a comedy in the trade ads. Veda Ann Borg is cast as a pampered nightclub singer who volunteers for the Women's Ambulance and Defense Corps merely to win a $5000 bet with a snide newspaper columnist (John Holland), who has wagered that she won't survive the six-week shakedown period. In two words, she does—and she also lands her Captain (Lyle Talbot) as a husband. (Another Monogram epic, 1943's *A WAVE, a WAC and a Marine*, is more backstage musical than comedy, despite the presence of Henny Youngman in the cast and Lou Costello in the producer's chair. Incidentally, the WAVE is played by Anne Gillis and the WAC by Elyse Knox — but neither lady joins up until the tail end of the picture.)

By the 1950s, the OWI had been disbanded and the future prospects of women in the military were not likely to be endangered by a lighthearted film treatment. Still, a measure of respect and reverence was necessary if any filmmaker embarking on such a project hoped to secure Army cooperation. Produced by Frederick Brisson as a vehicle for his actress wife Rosalind Russell, *Never Wave at a WAC* (Independent Artists/RKO, 1953) turned out to be so Army-friendly that the real-life Women's Army Corps allowed the production unit to film many of the key scenes on location at WAC training headquarters in Fort Lee, Virginia, and even to use actual WACs in bit and supporting roles.

Scripted by Don Mankiewicz from an idea by William Dozier, *Never Wave at a WAC* was optioned by Freddie Brisson under the title *The Private Wore Skirts*, a title changed to avoid giving away a crucial plot point. To gauge audience reaction, the property was tried out as a live one-hour TV play, originally broadcast October 19, 1951 on *Schlitz Playhouse of Stars*. This also represented the TV debut of Rosalind Russell, cast as flighty Washington socialite Jo McBain, daughter of an influential U.S. senator played by Charles Dingle. Recently divorced, Jo wants to be near her new boyfriend, an Army major stationed in France. When her father suggests that she join the WACs as a means of being reunited with her sweetheart, she goes along with the idea, smugly assuming that dear old dad will use his pull to get her an officer's commission. But after swearing in and donning uniform, Jo finds that she is, and will likely remain, an ordinary private — and as if this isn't embarrassing enough, Jo's top sergeant is her own daughter (played by Betty Lynn, best known as "Thelma Lou" on *The Andy Griffith Show*). Beyond this setup, there were few surprises in *Never Wave at a WAC*. Initially treating military service as a lark, Jo ends up taking even her toughest duties seriously, "assailed by a wave of *esprit de corps* which turns her into an efficent rookie," to quote a contemporary *Life* magazine article. She also returns to her former husband, a scientist working as an Army consultant. Of course, this was her dad's plan all along: Weary of Jo's diva behavior and firmly on the side of her ex-hubbie, the cagey senator figured that a dose of WAC discipline, minus any sort of preferential treatment, would be just the right medicine to straighten her out (feminists *please* note: this was, after all, 1951).

The positive response to the TV production of *Never Wave at a WAC* was enough to warrant a feature-film version, adapted for the screen by Ken Englund, with Rosalind Russell and Charles Dingle repeating their roles. Paul Douglas and William Ching were respectively cast in the expanded parts of Jo's ex-husband Andrew McBain and Army-officer fiance Sky Fairchild. No one was cast as Jo's daughter, since the role was eliminated from the film version; in her stead, Jo was given a non-relative sergeant, briskly played by Arleen Whelan.

While the TV original concentrated on the evolution of Jo McBain from vapid social butterfly to dedicated soldier, the film is more a "battle of the sexes" romp, with Andrew McBain using his position as a scientist to get even with Jo for past humiliations. Knowing that his former spouse is willing to volunteer for anything that will earn her an officer's commission, Andrew pushes her patience and endurance to the limit with a rigorous series of simulated stress tests (The spectacle of the elegant Rosalind Russell shivering in her boots and collapsing under the weight of a heavy snowsuit during a phony Arctic blizzard is worth the price of admission in itself). When Jo finally cracks under the strain, Andrew realizes that he's gone too far and tries to make amends. But by this time Jo is so fed up with the WACs that she raises a ruckus which gets her separated from the service. By film's end, however, that aforementioned *esprit de corps* has kicked in and Jo decides to re-enlist — and there's every indication that she will be reunited with the now-contrite Andrew.

Rosalind Russell manages to invest the brittle, imperious Jo McBain with charm and likeability, making it easier for the viewer to accept her last-act character conversion. Perhaps audiences sensed that the real-life Russell was as hard-working and devoted to her craft as her screen character. In her syndicated column of January 11, 1970, Hollywood reporter Joyce Haber revealed the extent to which Russell was willing to give her all to her art. According to Haber, during filming of *Never Wave at a WAC* Roz was required to jump into a moving Army truck: "On the first take she cut her leg so badly that it later needed seventeen stitches. 'Keep the cameras rolling,' she screamed. 'She passed out two minutes later,' her husband says. 'But she knew she could never do it again.'"

Russell was also secure enough in her stardom to graciously permit another actress to steal several scenes away from her, and even dominate the proceedings at times. Cast in a role that didn't appear in the original TV play but was added to pep up the film's marquee value, Marie Wilson delivers one of her best-ever performances as exotic dancer "Danger O'Dowd," who after being ogled and pawed by one predatory male too many opts for a career change and joins the WACs under her given name Clara Schneidermann. Though Wilson had risen to prominence as one of Hollywood's favorite dumb blondes (and was cast as such in the earlier *She's in the Army*), her character in *Never Wave at a WAC* isn't dumb at all, just a shade naïve about the world outside show business. While scriptwriter Ken Englund fashions several jokes around the actress' impressive bustline, he compensates for this chauvinism by showing Pvt. Clara Schneidermann cheerfully carrying out her military duties with diligence and dedication. At one point, she is held up to the lackadaisical Jo McBain as an example of what a good WAC should be!

The rest of the cast is an amalgam of familiar Hollywood character faces and amateur performers drawn from the ranks of the real-life WACs at Fort Lee. Director Norman Z. McLeod was either very persuasive or very patient in extracting relaxed, non-self-conscious performances from these novice actresses. Cast as "herself," Sgt. Norma Bussey proved so adept at deadpan comedy in an extended dialogue exchange with Marie Wilson that it's a shame she didn't pursue an acting career when her hitch was up.

Rosalind Russell and Marie Wilson are prominently featured on the cover of this souvenir program from Danish release of RKO's 1953 service comedy *Never Wave at a WAC* (The title shown here translates as *Don't Shoot with a Female Soldier*. Words to live by.)

Painting an attractive picture of the WACs while still warning potential enlistees that life in uniform was no bed of roses, *Never Wave at a WAC* not only earned full military approval, but also the endorsement of General Omar Bradley, who makes a fleeting guest appearance in the film. On January 28, 1953, RKO staged the world premiere of *Never Wave at a WAC* in Washington DC, inviting the Fort Lee drill team to stage a precision march for the benefit of the opening-night crowd. The team was under the direction of Lt. Col. Ruby E. Herman, head of the Fort Lee training center, who soon afterward resigned her commission to marry *Never Wave at a WAC*'s art director William Flannery.

While the Rosalind Russell picture was praised for its sophistication and avoidance of "easy" laughs, no such accolade was given to 1952's *A WAC from Walla Walla*, a rustic comedy with music starring Republic Pictures' resident soubrette Judy Canova. In *WAC from Walla Walla* (British title: *Army Capers*), Judy finds herself in the Army by accident and indirection. Once she has adjusted to life in the WACs, the hillbilly hoyden foils an attempt by enemy agents to steal the plans for a new guided missile; she also sings four songs with titles like "Boy, Oh Boy." Though big-city critics and filmgoers were unimpressed, the film was a success with Judy Canova's small-town and rural fan base.

The two above-mentioned films have been discussed out of sequential order in order to permit the author the privilege of a segue. A decade prior to *Wac From Walla Walla*, Judy Canova had briefly assumed male drag as "Private Yoo Hoo" in Paramount's *True to the Army*, a musical remake of the 1934 Bing Crosby starrer *She Loves Me Not*. The same property was filmed again in 1955 as the 20th Century–Fox musical *How to Be Very Very Popular*, costarring Betty Grable and Sheree North. Immediately following this effort, Ms. North was headlined in the service comedy *The Lieutenant Wore Skirts* (1956), likewise a Fox release.

Unlike her previous sisters in uniform, North's character Lt. Katy Whitcomb does not join the service to earn an inheritance, win a bet or solidify her relationship with a faraway fiancée; nor has she signed up by mistake. It is established early in the screenplay by Frank Tashlin (who also directed) and Albert Beich that Katy is a World War II veteran who'd served for love of country. It was during her tour of duty that she met and married Air Force officer Gregory Whitcomb (Tom Ewell), who after the war gained universal renown as a best-selling author. As the story proper gets under way in the mid–1950s, Gregory is a successful TV writer and Katy is a complacent Hollywood wife. Peeking at a letter summoning her Reservist husband to active duty, Katy persuades Gregory's agent Hank Gaxton (Les Tremayne) to arrange a deferment. Later during the Whitcombs' anniversary party, an increasingly besotted Gregory seethes with jealousy as Katy appears to bask in the attentions of Korean war hero Barney Sloan (Rick Jason). To assert his masculinity, Gregory waives his deferment and agrees to show up for his Air Force physical, prompting Katy to likewise re-enlist. While Katy is accepted for active service, Gregory is rejected because of a bum knee. Hence the film's working title, *I Lost My Wife to the Army*.

When Katy is stationed in Hawaii, Gregory rents an apartment near the base, a cat amongst a flock of Army-wife pigeons. The fact that Barney Sloan has been stationed at the same base prompts Gregory to goad Katy into resigning her commission by making her jealous of all the ladies around him. When this fails, he formulates a scheme to have her kicked out of the service on a Section Eight, stage-managing a scenario based on one of his own TV plays to convince a psychiatrist (Edward C. Platt) that Katy has gone off her chump. This also fails, whereupon the humiliated Katy tells Gregory that she is leaving him and transferring to Germany. Upholding a tradition as old as Hollywood itself, the Whitcombs' marriage is saved — and the dilemma of a uniformed wife with a civilian husband instantly resolved — when Katy discovers that she's pregnant.

Under the direction of Frank Tashlin, *The Lieutenant Wore Skirts* turns out to be a misnomer. Spending a generous amount of screen time wearing tight slacks, hip-hugging shorts, form-fitting pajama bottoms, revealing swimsuits and even a flimsy hula costume, Sheree North is almost never seen in anything as mundane as a skirt. Add to this the presence in the cast of Rita Moreno in a backless sunsuit and dancer Sylvia Lewis in a snug sarong, and what might have been an ordinary service comedy is elevated to a veritable voyeur's banquet. Surprisingly, Tashlin does not go the same route as such films as *Francis Joins the WACs* and its 1961 remake *The Sergeant Was a*

Lady (both covered in **Chapter** 5) by having his camera dwell upon Sheree North's bulging military blouse (and remember, this is the guy who made a movie star out of Jayne Mansfield).

Tashlin of course would have never admitted to being the King Leer of 20th Century–Fox, insisting that his films featured big-breasted, long-stemmed ladies because he thought big breasts and long stems were funny. Other typical Tashlin touches in *Lieutenant Wore Skirts* include several broad swipes at the entertainment industy: Describing her husband, Katy confesses, "Maybe he isn't exactly an author — he writes for television. But I knew that before I married him. I love him anyway." And what would a Tashlin movie be without a few quickie parodies of other directors' movies? The sequence in which Gregory Whitcomb tries to convince Katy that she's crazy is an extended lampoon of 1944's *Gaslight*, right down to the wife turning the tables on the husband. More blatant is the scene in which temporary bachelor Gregory has a brief encounter with a breathless movie starlet played by Rita Moreno — a scene so transparently inspired by a similar situation in the Marilyn Monroe picture *The Seven Year Itch* (which also costarred Tom Ewell) that the same background music is heard. This little vignette is even funnier in retrospect, since we now know that it was *Lieutenant Wore Skirts* star Sheree North, and not supporting player Rita Moreno, whom 20th Century–Fox was grooming as a potential Marilyn Monroe replacement.

Though its predecessor *Never Wave at a WAC* is the better film, *The Lieutenant Wore Skirts* received more attention from moviegoers of the period, partly because Frank Tashlin enjoyed a wider critical following than Norman Z. McLeod. The Tashlin cult had already extended beyond the United States thanks to such French *auteuristes* as Jean Luc-Godard. In his *Cahiers du Cinema* review of *Skirts*, Godard compared the film to Alfred Hitchcock's 1932 domestic drama *Rich and Strange*: "The misadventures of a couple of idiots are brought by too much love to domestic squabbles and then to the point of break-up ... trying to prove they love each other and only succeeding in hating each other. Happiness is not gay, says Max Ophuls; because gaiety is the opposite of happiness, caps Tashlin.... With Tashlin there is no starting point, and this is precisely his originality. Only the point of arrival matters, a scene at the very limits of absurdity...." Godard also likened *The Lieutenant Wore Skirts* to Voltaire's *Candide*. Mon Dieu!

Tashlin's obsession with the female anatomy, considered daring in 1956, was kid's stuff compared to later women-in-uniform efforts that took advantage of a relaxed movie-ratings system and a more permissive society. Curiously, even in the let-it-all-hang-out 1970s there were "jiggle" films that promised more than they delivered. Case in point: *Chesty Anderson, U.S.N.* (Cinefilm, 1976), with Shari Eubank, a protegée of skin-flick king Russ Meyer, in the title role. Advertised as "a tidal wave of comedy" despite its lurid storyline about a young WAVE determined to avenge the Mafia-ordered murder of her sister, *Chesty Anderson*'s cup runneth over with voluptuous starlets in a variety of revealing outfits, not to mention reams of double- and single-entendre dialogue referring to the heroine's two "deadly weapons." And yet, very little of a prurient nature really happens; in fact, the leading lady remains fully clothed for most of the picture — even during the obligatory physical-examination scene.

While the "sexploitation" genre remained on the snickering level of kindergarteners peeking into their dad's *Penthouse* collection, by the early 1980s mainstream movies had advanced dramatically in their treatment of women. Filmmakers in this progressive period would have rejected the heroines of *Never Wave at a WAC* and *The Lieutenant Wore Skirts* as dimensionless stick figures, invented by men who had but minimal understanding of what really makes a woman tick. Despite having a male director (Howard Zieff, replacing Arthur Hiller) and two male scriptwriters (Harvey Miller, Charles Shyer), *Private Benjamin* (Warner Bros., 1980) is definitely a female-oriented service picture, reflecting the viewpoint of its coproducer and cowriter Nancy Meyers, as well as its star and executive producer Goldie Hawn. The film also reflected the positive changes made since the Women's Army Corps was disbanded in 1978 and its members — now designated as "specialists" — were absorbed into the regular Armed Forces.

Though she had come a long way from her salad days as the resident giggling gamine on

Rowan and Martin's Laugh-In, and despite an Oscar win for her first major screen appearance in *Cactus Flower* (1969), Goldie Hawn was in 1980 at a low point in her film career, her successful pictures (*Butterflies Are Free, Foul Play*) imbalanced by the misfires (*There's a Girl in My Soup, The Duchess and the Dirtwater Fox*). She was in dire need of a good vehicle to prove anew that her ditsy-blonde image, which film critics still insisted upon invoking, was a thing of the past. Hawn also wanted a clean break from playing characters whose destinities were determined by the men in their lives. Describing *Private Benjamin* to journalist Skip Sheffield in 1980, Goldie insisted: "It's a statement about the patriarchy that still pervades our culture. The man is still considered the king and provider. Good little girls grow up to depend on that patriarch. I wanted to show that even a sheltered, pampered woman could find herself and become independent."

In the opening scenes of *Private Benjamin*, Hawn's character Judy Benjamin is the quintessential Jewish American Princess, groomed by her overprotective parents to be nothing more nor less than the wife of a wealthy man who will take care of her for the rest of her life. But Judy's first marriage has ended in divorce, and her second union with lawyer Yale Goodman (Albert Brooks) is over before it begins when he drops dead on their wedding night. With no frame of reference beyond her pampered upbringing, Judy regards this tragedy as a personal affront: "I did everything right. And now I feel like I'm being punished." Judy decides to change the direction of her life, so like Marie Wilson's character Clara Schneidermann in *Never Wave at a WAC*, she enlists in the Army. But unlike Clara, Judy has no idea what she's getting into, thanks to a duplicitous recruiting sergeant (Harry Dean Stanton) who sweet-talks the vulnerable young widow into joining the "Army of the '80s"— the one with condos, private rooms and sauna baths.

Bypassing the all-too-familiar promotional still from *Private Benjamin* (Warners, 1980) showing a miserable, mud-caked Goldie Hawn, we offer a closeup of our Goldie relishing a moment of military triumph (*MOVIE STAR NEWS*).

It doesn't occur to Judy that the recruiter may have been a double-dyed deceiver until her first night in the barracks, and even then she can't believe that anyone would be so impudent as to fill her full of fibs. With the same condescending tone that she might use on a counter clerk at Bloomingdale's, Judy informs Captain Dorene Lewis (Eileen Brennan) that there's obviously been a mistake, and that she's actually joined a "different Army." With a sharkish smile on her face, Lewis lets Judy drone on about the crowded accommodations, the smelly latrine and the lack of curtains on the walls, then lowers the boom on the prattling private, telling her in no uncertain terms that this the only Army there is and she'd better get used to it.

For the next several weeks, Captain Lewis and topkick Sgt. Ross (Hal Williams) subject Judy to the same dehumanizing "basic" as all the other grunts. At first glance, our little princess seems a hopeless prospect for an Army career ("I wanna wear my sandals! I wanna go to lunch! I wanna be *normal* again!") Gradually, and for the first time in her life, she develops a genuine sense of self-esteem through her military accomplishments. This growth process notwithstanding, Judy still tends to rely upon the men in her life for guidance and security. When Col. Clay Thornbush (Robert Webber) personally selects Judy for paratrooper training, she is thrilled to have at last found a nurturing father figure, only to be abruptly disillusioned when Thornbush turns out to be just another dirty old man. Judy finally learns to stand on her own feet without a man around to keep her from stumbling — yet she must pass one more test of her newfound independence when suave French physician Henri Tremont (Armand Assante) enters her life.

Everyone who has seen *Private Benjamin* retains the famous poster-art image of a grimy, stringy-haired Judy Benjamin suffering through the rigors of training, and of her frequent tiltings with the slow-simmering Captain Lewis. It is harder to conjure up memories of the male cast members — and even if this *wasn't* a conscious choice by the filmmakers, the strength of the female supporting cast tips the scales in favor of the ladies. Despite being cast as adversaries, longtime friends Goldie Hawn and Eileen Brennan exhibit such a marvelous rapport that one might logically conclude that each actress was responsible for the other's Academy Award nomination. Also well represented are Mary Kay Place, P.J. Soles and the other actresses cast as Judy Benjamin's comrades in arms. All reports indicate that these women developed a strong mutual bond during filming, frequently delaying set-ups by giggling hysterically over some private joke. According to P.J. Soles, it was Goldie Hawn, whose career was founded upon a high-pitched giggle, who invariably had to step in and calm everyone down so they could get some work done.

Private Benjamin might have been a flawless piece of entertainment were it not for its awkward construction. Approximately 55 minutes into the film, Judy Benjamin has firmly proven herself as a topnotch soldier. There is really nowhere for the story to go at this point — but with 55 minutes left, the scripters must drag things out with the romance between Judy and Dr. Tremont, the outcome of which merely reiterates what we already know about the heroine. (As noted in **Chapter 12**, this same structural flaw is duplicated in 1981's *Stripes*, though that film makes up for its narrative shortcomings with a dynamite slapstick finale). Audiences in 1980 didn't really care if *Private Benjamin*'s plotline came to an end long before the film itself; they had fallen in love with Goldie Hawn all over again, and that was enough for the picture to earn a $70 million domestic gross. The only people who weren't entirely enchanted with the film were the higher ranks of the U.S. Army, who withheld their official cooperation because the scriptwriters refused to make changes in the negative characters of the prevaricating recruiting sergeant and the libidinous Col. Thornbush. (A TV-sitcom version of *Private Benjamin*, starring Lorna Patterson as Judy with Eileen Brennan and Hal Williams reprising their screen roles as Capt. Lewis and Sgt. Ross, ran for 39 episodes on CBS from April 6, 1981, to September 5, 1983. And as of this writing, a theatrical-movie remake is in the works.)

For every small step forward like *Private Benjamin*, there will always be a giant leap backward like *Basic Training* (Playboy/Moviestone 1985), a pathetic skin flick that makes one pine for the days of *Chesty Anderson U.S.N.* Also known as *Up the Military,* this alleged comedy ("You CAN do it in the Army!" screamed the ad copy) stars Ann Dusenberry as Melinda, a minor Pentagon employee who is fired for resisting the sexual overtures of a horn-dog lieutenant. She gets even by publicly exposing the hanky-panky going on in the uppermost circles of the military, taking time out to search for some missing files on Russia's defense system. Infiltrating a party for the Soviet ambassador, Melinda is kidnapped and spirited away to the North Pole. She saves both herself and Democracy through the charmingly simple expedient of removing her clothes and baring her breasts. Featuring a top-secret mission labelled "Operation Sky Beaver," belly dancers and senile generals wandering the halls of the Pentagon, and a guest appearance by Rhonda Shear (the flimsily garbed hostess of the USA Network's *Up All Night*), *Basic Training* is not likely to be confused with a movie one would actually pay money to see.

Horrible though it was, *Basic Training* was not so horrible as to expunge memories of the better women-in-uniform films like *Private Benjamin*. Certainly the people responsible for the 2006 comedy variously known as *Private Valentine: Blonde and Dangerous* and *Major Movie Star* were so impressed by the Goldie Hawn film that they used it as their template — and managed to squeeze out all the entertainment value in the process.

On paper, *Major Movie Star* (the title by which it is best known) seems to hold at least a hint of potential; on screen, this potential dies the death of a thousand cliché cuts. Heroine Megan Valentine is a coddled young movie actress whose fame rests upon the talking-dog epic *Rupert and Alice*, which has won her the "most popular star" award from the inmates of Leavenworth prison. Megan's naïvete is in such an advanced state that she fails to notice that all her closest associates are leeching off her fame. Life catches up with the stunned starlet when, in one fell swoop, she loses her $15 million fortune and discovers that her boyfriend is gay. Drunk and depressed, she impulsively joins the Army—"From A-List to En-list," as the film's ads proclaim — where she quickly learns that shouting "Where's my stunt double?" won't spare her the indignities of the obstacle course. Female drill sergeant Morley is rough on Megan, but only because she thinks the girl isn't fulfilling her potential. Our heroine's barracks-mates include two supportive pals and one vengeful bitch, the latter ripe for repeated humiliation. Megan perserveres and becomes the best soldier in her platoon, though a temporary field promotion goes awry when, while trying to issue orders, she is stopped cold by the Vengeful Bitch's rejoinder "Ooh! You must be Scary Spice." During the requisite awards ceremony, Sgt. Morley gazes at Megan's khaki-covered bosom (all swelled up with pride) and says "Congratulations, Private Valentine. I knew you had it in you."

While the film's production unit was on location at Camp Minden in Louisiana, an observer was heard to remark "This may be one of the worst movies ever made" — and that was one of the actors. It is tempting to advise the reader to avoid any film made after 1990 costarring Steve Guttenberg, but he isn't the real problem with *Major Movie Star*; in truth, he's pretty good in the role of Megan's pseudo-hip agent. Nor can blame be laid at the feet of Vivica A. Fox as Sgt. Morley, Cheri Oteri as Megan's nemesis, or Olesya Rulin and Keiko Agena as her best friends (Andy Milonakis also appears briefly as a member of the *paparazzi*). The two primary weaknesses of *Major Movie Star* are the "just shout 'Action!' and hope for the best" direction of Steve Miner, and the performance of the Major Movie Star herself. Megan Valentine is played by Jessica Simpson, a modestly talented pop singer whose comedy skills can be charitably described as underdeveloped. Not that Ms. Simpson didn't extensively prepare for her role: one press release affirms that she spent two days in a real boot camp learning how to salute. But dear Jessica's portrayal of Megan is so shaky and inconsistent that it is hard to conceive of any producer shelling out good coin to put this film together. On second thought, we can conceive it. One of the film's producers was Jessica Simpson's father.

Like Simpson's first starring feature *Blonde Ambition*, *Major Movie Star* was offered to several theatrical distributors but rejected hands down by everyone. It looked for a while that, also like *Blonde Ambition*, the picture would have to go direct to video; had this been the case, the reader wouldn't have been subjected to the above synopsis. No such luck. *Major Movie Star* eventually did get a theatrical release, but not in the United States; in fact, it played in practically every other country in the world *except* the U.S., moving comedian Conan O'Brien to remark that the picture was so bad it would never be released "in any country where English is the primary language." But neither O'Brien nor anyone else could have foreseen what would happen next: On October 8, 2008, *Major Movie Star* premiered in the former Soviet Union, where it became that nation's Number One smash hit! (Seems like a fair enough cultural exchange. Russia gives us Tchiakovsky, Chekhov, Eisenstein and Nureyev; we give them Jessica Simpson.)

Ironically, one of the funniest films involving the female branches of the Military is built around a male protagonist. This production was inspired by a 1947 *Baltimore Sun* article written by Belgian physician Roger Charlier, using the pen name Henri Rochard. The article was later reprinted by *Reader's Digest* under the title "I Was a Male War Bride," which was also the name of the film version (except in Great Britain, where it was known as *You Can't Sleep Here*).

Both article and film were based on Dr. Charlier's real-life experiences as an officer in postwar Europe. Involved in a car accident, Charlier was tended to by an American nurse, with whom he fell in love. Planning to settle in the United States upon Charlier's discharge, the engaged couple were stymied by "Public Law 271," enacted by the 79th congress in 1945. Put simply, Law 271 stated that Charlier could only be admitted to the U.S. under provisions regulating the entry of "War Brides." Charlier of course qualified as a War Husband, but this fact did not enable him to cut through the red tape until it was determined that the law technically referred to "spouses," with no gender specified. Charlier's story was purchased by 20th Century–Fox's Darryl F. Zanuck, who passed it along to director Howard Hawks as a potential romantic comedy starring Rex Harrison as the beleagured "Henri Rochard." Hawks seized upon the opportunity to re-explore the comedy of frustration and humiliation as laid out in his 1938 screwball farce *Bringing Up Baby*, and also to delve into the humor arising from sexual role reversals, previously touched upon in the director's 1940 comedy *His Girl Friday*. Both these films had starred Cary Grant, and it was Grant whom Hawks ultimately selected for the title role in *I Was a Male War Bride*.

Making the project especially attractive to Zanuck and Hawks was the fact that most of the story was set in Germany, which would give them an excuse to film overseas; Hawks had long wanted to ply his trade in a foreign locale, while Zanuck looked forward to utilizing the studio's "frozen funds," cash that had been impounded in Europe during the war and could only be spent in that continent. Unfortunately, the decision to lens several scenes in such German cities as Heidelberg and Frankfurt had negative consequences for stars Cary Grant and Ann Sheridan, both of whom contacted pneumonia because of their unfamiliarity with the German climate. Things got worse when Sheridan also came down with pleurisy and Grant with a near-fatal case of hepatitis, causing him to lose a great deal of weight (in the film, one can see his weight fluctuating dramatically from scene to scene, and even from shot to shot). The fact that Cary was earning $100,000 plus 10 percent of the gross was undoubtedly his chief motivation to see the project through. The situation was considerably improved when production moved to England, a friendlier clime to the Bristol-born actor.

To hype the film's laugh potential, it was decided to carry the implications of Law 271 to their logical extreme. Hacking through a jungle of confusing and self-contradictory regulations, Henri Rochard (Grant) and his American sweetheart Catherine Gates (Sheridan) are finally married. Alas, Rochard is barred from accompanying his wife to America because the powers-that-be have concluded that "271" applies only to brides. Catherine decides to circumvent the rules by disguis-

Cary Grant in *I Was a Male War Bride* (20th Century–Fox, 1949). Put a dress on him and you can take him anywhere.

ing her husband as a WAC named Florence, a situation that is amusing in itself but truly hilarious only after "Florence" is assigned to an all-female troop ship.

The image of Cary Grant in WAC drag with an ill-fitting "dutch bob" wig was made so indelible by the film's press coverage that many moviegoers have convinced themselves that Grant appears in women's clothing throughout the picture. In truth, the drag scenes occur only in the final ten minutes; the bulk of the film is devoted to the initially antagonistic relationship between Henri and Catherine, who are thrown together by circumstance so often that they can't help but fall in love, and the subsequent bureaucratic nightmare surrounding their marriage. Once he assumes his "Florence" guise, Grant plays straight in every sense of the word, never resorting to limp wrists or a falsetto voice to get laughs — which is less a testament to Grant's artistic discipline than to the restraint of Howard Hawks, who early on ordered the actor not to behave in an effeminate manner. (Those who choose to believe the anecdotal assertions that Cary Grant swung both ways in real life have argued that, by *not* playing up the femininity, Grant merely "proved" that he was comfortable in female duds. Imagine their reaction if Cary had gone with his first impulse and camped up the role.)

I Was a Male War Bride clocked in as the third most profitable film of 1949, and was inargurably one of the funniest pictures of that year; Cary Grant would later remark that he never hear an audience laugh louder at any of his other films. A happy ending to this particular chapter? Well, it *might* have been, except that Dr. Roger H. Charlier, the man who started it all, went and spoiled everything by suing 20th Century–Fox for breach of contract — which explains why, for all its popularity, *I Was a Male War Bride* was never adapted for radio or television.

15

Special Ops

One would think that at the height of the James Bond-driven "spy craze" in the mid–1960s, there would have been scores of military comedies built around an espionage or covert-operation theme. Surprisingly, only a smattering of such films were ever produced, and only one of them during the aforementioned spy cycle. While there are individual examples elsewhere in this book, here are four otherwise unclassifiable films in which the characters went the trenchcoat route as undercover agents.

Charlton Heston was deep into his "epic" period when, in 1961, he thought it would be a nice change of pace to star in another comedy — and since *The Private War of Major Benson* (see **Chapter 13**) had done so well back in 1955, Heston chose another service comedy, this one based on Donald Downes' novel *The Easter Dinner*. Making the prospect especially enticing was the fact that it would be filmed in Europe, permitting Heston the same income-tax break that had allowed him to pocket most of his earnings from *Ben-Hur* and *El Cid*, also lensed abroad. Too, the film was slated for completion in twelve weeks, the shortest production schedule he'd had in years.

Adapted for the screen and directed by Mel Shavelson, *The Easter Dinner* cast Heston as Paul MacDougall, an Infantry captain dispatched to occupied Rome shortly after the fall of Mussolini. MacDougall's mission is to find out why the Nazis have reversed their "open city" policy and are planting mines in the Roman streets. Though protesting that they know nothing about espionage or undercover activities, MacDougall and Italian-speaking sergeant Joseph Contini are ordered to disguise themselves as priests and infiltrate the Nazi stronghold. They are further ordered to send messages back to the Allies, using the several hundred carrier pigeons that had previously been smuggled into Rome by submarine. MacDougall and Contini move into the home of middle-aged Resistance leader Ciccio Massimo, where Contini falls in love with Ciccio's pregnant daughter Rosalba. In anticipation of a wedding, Rosalba's older sister Antonella, who has been kept in the dark about her father's Resistance activities because of her pro–German sentiments, prepares a lavish Easter feast that obliges her to kill, dress and cook all but one of those precious carrier pigeons. Antonella's kid brother Livio tries to make amends by "borrowing" some fresh pigeons from German headquarters, meaning that the birds will instinctively wing their way to Berlin the moment they're released. To confuse the enemy, MacDougall composes ridiculous and contradictory messages to be delivered by the pigeons. One of these subverise missives is inadvertently affixed to the leg of the sole remaining American bird, who heads straight to the Allies in Anzio. A potential disaster is averted when MacDougall's "crazy" message prompts the Americans to mount a big offensive, resulting in the liberation of Rome and a Congressional Medal of Honor — for the pigeon. Throughout all the fuss and feathers, MacDougall strives to win the loyalty and love of the anti-American Antonella, eventually succeeding on both counts. (Early in the film, MacDougall and Antonella unwillingly share a shower bath, but the circumstances are so chaste that the restraint exhibited by the actors is laughable in itself.)

The first major change from script to screen was the title: Paramount, the studio releasing the film, reasoned that audiences acclimated to Charlton Heston's Biblical epics might assume that *The Easter Dinner* was all about the Last Supper. Overruling Heston's preferred alternate title

Americans Go Home, Paramount chose *The Pigeon That Took Rome*, which not only made sense in context but also allowed the studio's promotional department to aim for the family trade with a trailer featuring an animated-cartoon pigeon. Once the title was settled upon, the matter of a suitable leading lady came up. Heston had wanted the part of Antonella to go to Sophia Loren, with whom he'd just finished filming *El Cid*, or Greek actress Melina Mercouri, then in great demand thanks to *Never on Sunday*. When both ladies proved unavailable, director Mel Shavelson chose the comparatively unknown Italian actress Elsa Martinelli, hoping that Heston alone could carry what the actor described as "the marquee weight." Next on the cast list was the important role of Antonia's lovably bombastic father Ciccio. Heston and Shavelson briefly considered changing the film's locale to France and hiring either Maurice Chevalier or Charles Boyer, but in the end they opted to remain in Rome and to cast the brilliant Italian opera singer Salvatore Baccaloni. Having switched to character acting in the late 1950s, Baccaloni had already pulled off the daunting task of stealing scenes from Jerry Lewis in *Rock-a-Bye Baby* and Danny Kaye in *Merry Andrew*. In *Pigeon That Took Rome*, Baccaloni himself was given a run for his money by 14-year-old Carlo Angelletti (here billed as Marietto), the appealing young actor cast as Ciccio's light-fingered son Livio. Rounding out the cast were Italian starlet Gabriella Paloma as Rosalba, and Hollywood veterans Harry Guardino as Sgt. Contini, Brian Donlevy as MacDougall's C.O. and Arthur Shields as the priest who instructs MacDougall in the ways of the Cloth. (Though Charlton Heston cut an impressive figure in collar and frock, he didn't fool his old friend Orson Welles, who while visiting the set declared that Heston was "the most Lutheran-looking priest I've ever seen.") The titular pigeon was played by "Geronimo II," who receives special billing in the closing credits — quite an honor for an actor in his first (and last) picture.

It had been decided early on to keep the budget under control by filming *Pigeon* in black and white, though the lighthearted nature of the story seems to cry out for Technicolor. Even so, an extra million dollars was tacked onto the budget when, at Charlton Heston's insistence, the production unit moved from Italy to Hollywood to film the major interior scenes. Having made this move for the sake of convenience (he had several American film and TV commitments to fulfill at the same time), the actor later admitted it was a mistake, since the added expenditure cut deeply into the film's profits. A box-office disappointment in its initial 1962 release, *The Pigeon That Took Rome* nevertheless remains an agreeable blend of situation comedy and espionage thriller, with Heston effectively playing straight and allowing the supporting players and the basic premise to provide the laughs. The actor's avoidance of gratuitous clowning enhances the credibility of the film's isolated serious moments, notably the climactic scene in which MacDougall, outraged when little Livio is seriously wounded by German machine-gun fire, charges into the enemy camp to wreak vengeance — only to be stopped short by the realization that the baby-faced Germans aren't all that much older than Livio.

Like Charlton Heston, Paul Newman excelled in intense dramatic roles in the 1960s, though he occasionally leavened the solemnity with such comedies as *A New Kind of Love* and *What a Way to Go!* Unlike Heston, who retained his clenched-teeth stoicism throughout the silliest complications in *Pigeon That Took Rome*, Newman had a disturbing habit of shouting and grimacing his way through comedy parts, a technique that proved tedious and irritating to all but the actor's most loyal fans. In the 1968 military-espionage comedy *The Secret War of Harry Frigg*, Newman is so far over the top that one has serious concerns about the man's sanity.

Assembled by Universal Pictures in a manner suggesting that the studio already had a TV sale in mind, *The Secret War of Harry Frigg* casts Newman as a rascally American Army private who has gained fame for the number of times that he has successfully (and creatively) escaped from the guardhouse. With World War II raging all about him, Harry Frigg is determined to avoid combat duty, but Gen. Homer Prentiss (James Gregory) of Army Public Relations has other plans for our hero. It seems that five Allied brigadier generals (Andrew Duggan, John Williams, Tom Bosley, Jacques Roux and Charles Gray) have been captured by the Germans. Imprisoned in a

Paul Newman (left) gets himself captured by the Germans in order to rescue a group of Allied generals (among them Jacques Roux and Tom Bosley, at right) in *The Secret War of Harry Frigg* (Universal, 1968). Considering how the picture turned out, Sylva Koscina could well be saying, "There's the door to the street, Paul. Run while you have a chance!"

lavish Italian villa, the high-ranking quartet would probably have figured out a means of escape long ago had they not wasted time bickering over strategy and protocol. Besides, they rather enjoy their palatial surroundings, as well as the hospitality provided by their Italian captor Col. Ferucci (Vito Scotti), who behaves more like a concierge than a commandant. With Allied prestige deteriorating every day that the generals remain under guard, Prentiss orders Frigg to come up with a heroic — and foolproof — escape plan that will impress the American media. Bitching and moaning every inch of the way, Harry is rapidly promoted to the rank of major general, on the theory that none of the captive generals would demean himself by taking orders from a lowly private. Parachuting into enemy territory, he deliberately gets himself captured and is whisked off to the luxurious villa, where he is instantly smitten by Contessa Francesca di Montesore (Sylva Koscina), owner of the estate. Reluctant to tear himself away from Francesca, Harry is gratified to learn that his "fellow" generals have grown so fond of Col. Ferucci that they don't want to spoil his impending promotion with an embarrassing mass escape — at least not right away. But by the time the generals are in a mood to be rescued, the pesky Germans show up and transport all the prisoners to a maximum-security POW camp. (In one of the film's few genuinely funny moments, a long shot of the German trucks bearing the prisoners is accompanied by a rumbling rendition of Bach's "Toccata and Fugue in B Minor.") Forced to be the grown-up in the room, Harry engineers an escape so spectacular that he wins a permanent promotion — and also the love of Francesca, who up until now has regarded Harry as merely a charming ne'er-do-well.

Coscripted by Peter Stone of *Charade* fame and directed by Jack Smight, *The Secret War of Harry Frigg* has potential, but is sabotaged by the frenzied performance of Paul Newman — though in fairness to the actor, the rest of the cast isn't much better. Perhaps because of the good will engendered by Newman's earlier work (including the private-eye drama *Harper*, also directed by Smight), the film received a few charitable reviews; for the most part, however, critical reaction was on a par with Pauline Kael's plaintive "What is Paul Newman doing in *The Secret War of Harry Frigg*?" Though reportedly everyone had a ball making the picture, the studio knew that the project was in trouble from the outset; the numerous — and overpublicized — title changes (*Meanwhile Far from the Front, The Best-Kept Secret of the War* et al.) that transpired before the dubious "winner" was chosen are evidence of that. The film was such a conspicuous failure that Paul Newman refrained from discussing it in later interviews, except to say that he had borrowed his character's walk from a fellow he'd known in the Navy. The actor would have been better off if he'd used that walk to distance himself from the film the moment it was offered him — but weep not for Mr. Newman, inasmuch as within a year of *Harry Frigg*'s release, the bad taste was washed from the collective mouth of the public with *Butch Cassidy and the Sundance Kid*.

While both *The Pigeon That Took Rome* and *The Secret War of Harry Frigg* had a modicum of novelty value by virtue of the espionage angle and the presence of two dynamic leading players, both were basically traditional war comedies. The same can hardly be said of 1964's *The Incredible Mr. Limpet*: in fact, until plans were drawn up to remake the property in the early 21st century, *Mr. Limpet* could truly be classified as a *sui generis* among military and spy films.

The project's starting point was a 1942 novel written by Theodore Pratt, who though born in Minnesota spent the last half of his life in Florida, writing historical fact and fiction about his adopted state; his novel about Miami's first postal service was filmed in 1951 as *The Barefoot Mailman*. Pratt also wrote on a variety of contemporary topics unrelated to Florida: Another of his novels optioned by Hollywood was *Mr. Winkle Goes to War* (published 1943, filmed 1944), the semiserious story of a middle-aged nonentity who becomes a hero when he enlists in the early months of World War II, a time when the Army was still accepting recruits in their early forties (Pratt himself was 42 when the novel was published). A year before *Mr. Winkle*'s appearance, the author had penned a more whimsical tale about a thirty-something wimp who contributes heroically to the War effort. The title character of *Mr. Limpet* is a henpecked husband who yearns for the glory of combat, but is trapped by his 4F status in a go-nowhere job as a Brooklyn bookkeeper. While on a weekend excursion to Coney Island with his wife, Henry Limpet falls into the ocean and is miraculously transformed into a fish. Though technically no longer an American (*does* a fish have a nationality?), Limpet is still a patriot, and he uses his newly acquired swimming skills to help the U.S. Navy seek and destroy Nazi submarines. Soon the whole world knows of the piscatorial Limpet's accomplishments: At one point, Adolf Hitler tries to buy the hero's loyalty by offering Limpet a commission and full reign over the Mediterranean and Caspian Seas. Though fantastic in nature, and provided with Disneyesque illustrations by artist Garrett Price, *Mr. Limpet* is *not* a children's story. Pratt was aiming at a grown-up audience, especially with his treatment of the adulterous (and implicity bestial!) relationship between the very-married Mr. Limpet and his underwater paramour, the seductive Ladyfish. Well reviewed at the time of its publication, *Mr. Limpet* sold only 3500 copies, perhaps because the reading public of 1942, none too confident that America would win the war, was put off by the notion that the fate of the free world rested in the fins of a talking fish.

Once the war was won, *Mr. Limpet* became a more palatable property, especially where Hollywood was concerned. But unlike Theodore Pratt's other novels, it hardly lent itself to a traditional screen treatment: Even the most versatile of actors would be hard pressed to convincingly impersonate a fish. When Warner Bros. optioned *Mr. Limpet* some two decades after its publication, the immediate assumption was that it would result in an animated cartoon feature. However, only Walt Disney had ever enjoyed any real success in this genre: Such earlier non–Disney cartoon features as Max Fleischer's *Gulliver's Travels* (1939) and *Mr. Bug Goes to Town* (1941) were only marginally profitable, while UPA's more recent *1001 Arabian Nights* (1959) and *Gay Pur-ree* (1962) had floundered in a sea of red ink.

Producer John C. Rose, a longtime Disney associate engaged by Warner Bros. to supervise the studio's family-oriented productions, opted to enhance the novelty value of the film version of *Mr. Limpet* by combining live action with cel animation. This in and of itself was not an innovation: Animators had been "co-starring" live actors with cartoon characters since the days of Fleischer's *Koko the Clown*, Disney's *Alice in Cartoonland* and Walter Lantz' *Dinky Doodle*. But these had all been short-subject series. In feature films, the mixture of "live" and animated had always been regarded as a stunt, an extended special effect. Fox's *Servant's Entrance*, MGM's *Anchors Aweigh*, Disney's *Song of the South* and Warners' *My Dream Is Yours*, to cite four examples, boasted highlights in which flesh-and-blood actors commiserated with pen-and-ink characters, but these were isolated dream or fantasy sequences. Up until 1963, no one in Hollywood had put together a feature-length film in which cel animation and live-action were combined from start to finish in a credible fashion — nor in which the basic storyline and its outcome were dictated by this combination. By declaring that *Mr. Limpet* — or *The Incredible Mr. Limpet*, as it was ultimately released — would blend "live" and "cartoon" into a unified whole, John C. Rose was taking quite an artistic gamble.

Finding the right actor to portray the "pre-fish" Henry Limpet proved easier than expected; in fact, the choice was so obvious that this writer will be surprised if a future researcher discovers that anyone else was considered for the role. Since making his movie debut in *No Time for Sergeants* (see **Chapter 8**), goggle-eyed, liver-lipped comic actor Don Knotts had achieved television stardom as the "Nervous Man on the Street" in NBC's *Steve Allen Show* and Deputy Barney Fife in the CBS sitcom *The Andy Griffith Show*. In films, the actor continued to essay small supporting roles, notably in the military comedies *Wake Me When It's Over* (see **Chapter 8** again) and *The Last Time I Saw Archie* (see **Chapter 11**), where his scrawny frame and tremulous voice provided amusing contrast to the muscular machismo surrounding him. *The Incredible Mr. Limpet* was Knotts' first starring feature, and he makes an excellent impression despite the fact that he is physically offscreen for all but twenty minutes of the film, literally phoning in the role of his animated counterpart. Much was made by the Warners publicity department of Knotts' startling resemblance to the "fishy" version of Mr. Limpet. The actor seemed flattered by the comparison, telling *Life* magazine that the first time he saw his animated alter ego, "I thought it was actually me."

Don Knotts may have looked like a fish, but it was no cinch for the animators to come up with a fish who looked like Don Knotts. In his autobiography, the actor recalled that the producer "hired and fired" several artists before he was able to settle on a picturization that satisfied him

Don Knotts compares lips with his animated alter ego in *The Incredible Mr. Limpet* (Warners, 1964) (*MOVIE STAR NEWS*).

(a slightly skinnier version of the Mr. Limpet created by Garrett Price in the original novel). Knotts also remembered that it was less of a challenge to appear on camera than to convey a fully formed character using only his voice. It didn't help matters when studio head Jack Warner complained that the cartoon version of Mr. Limpet wasn't as funny as the real Don Knotts. Defending both himself and the animators, Knotts has noted that "Mr. Limpet was not supposed to be funny. Quaint and amusing, yes, but not funny." Still, Don Knotts managed to score quite a few chuckles in both his screen incarnations, simply by being his own quaintly amusing self.

The film follows the basic plotline of the book, with a few variations and expansions. Shy, bespectacled bookkeeper Henry Limpet is so obsessed with his collection of tropical fish that he has all but driven his long-suffering spouse Bessie (Carole Cook) to the looney bin. Mr. Limpet harbors two fervent desires: To serve in the Navy alongside his friend and neighbor George Stickles (Jack Weston), even though he has already been rejected for active service because of an equilibrium problem; and to somehow metamorphose into one of his beloved fish. Once Henry takes his plunge into the Atlantic—at which point we switch from live action to animation—his second wish is granted. At first, he is as much a misfit as he'd been in human form because, in the words of his hermit-crab companion Crusty (voice provided by Paul Frees), he is an "unknown species"; certainly no other fish of Crusty's acquaintance requires a pair of thick glasses to see where he's swimming. The lovely Ladyfish (voiced by Elizabeth MacRae), rescued from a shark by the quick-thinking Limpet, is attracted to the "new" Henry and invites him to spawn with her, but he remains faithful to Bessie—who, for her part, is convinced that Henry has drowned, making her a most eligible widow in the eyes of the amiably wolfish George (this carryover element from the novel is a bit unsettling, considering the family audience to whom the film is purportedly aimed).

Apprised of the attack on Pearl Harbor, Limpet seizes the opportunity to do his bit for the war effort by using his newly-developed sonic powers—an eerie wail described as the "thrumm"—to guide U.S. Navy subchasers toward the Atlantic hiding places of Nazi U-boats. (It is this peculiar talent that has led some movie historians to describe Mr. Limpet as a dolphin rather than a fish, though this is not specified in the film.) When he swims to the surface to offer his services to Commander Harlock (Andrew Duggan) on a full-time basis, the Commander, unable to see the source of the disembodied voice, refuses to believe Henry's fish story. Only when the name of George Stickles is invoked does the Navy find a "liason" who can pass along Henry's reconnaissance information, though the Admiralty still has trouble swallowing the idea that a mere fish is their most powerful secret weapon. Limpet's remarkable success in locating enemy subs finally convinces Harlock's superior Adm. Spewter (Larry Keating, in his final film role) that Henry is precisely who he says he is—and despite his initial protests, the irascible Spewter bestows a lieutenant's commission upon Citizen Limpet. After V-E Day, Henry surfaces one last time to bid farewell to his confused human wife Bessie ("Let's be logical. You can't very well keep me in the bathtub, can you?") before swimming off to parts unknown in the company of the devoted Ladyfish.

Though total credibility was out of the question, the makers of *Incredible Mr. Limpet* strove for at least a superficial reality by hiring Arthur Lubin to direct the live-action sequences. As proven by his "Francis the Talking Mule" comedies (see **Chapter 5**), Lubin was an expert at bringing plausibility to the most implausible situations by having his actors react as normal people would *genuinely* react when confronted by the Unbelievable. Thus, astonished exclamations and farcical double-takes are at a minimum; even so unsubtle an actor as Jack Weston is kept in check. Equally effective is the film's straightforward, non-satirical treatment of World War II, especially the handling of the German characters. Avoiding the temptation to hoke up the proceedings with *Hogan's Heroes*-style clowning and comic-opera dialects, the Germans play their scenes seriously—and in their own language.

The cartoon sequences represented the last hurrah of the venerable Warner Bros. animation unit, soon to be disbanded in an economy move. In his first and only assignment at Warners, Vladimir "Bill" Tytla, who a quarter of a century earlier had overseen the "Sorceror's Apprentice" and "Night on Bald Mountain" segments in Disney's *Fantasia*, was hired as *Mr. Limpet*'s supervising animation director. Unfortunately, he fell ill early in the proceedings and was replaced by Warners stalwarts Robert McKimson and Hawley Pratt, though Tytla still receives screen credit. Along with McKimson and Pratt, studio regulars Gerry Chiniquy, Maurice Noble and Don Peters handled what were billed as the "special piscatorial effects," while Disney veterans Art Babbitt and Hugh Fraser, and future TV-cartoon producer Phil Roman (*Garfield, The Simpsons*), made uncredited contributions as well. The animation admittedly falls short of Disney standards, but Warners had always faltered when attempting to imitate Disney, and were at their best when sticking to their *own* distinctive style. The character design is consistently amusing, the background art eyecatching without being ostentatious, the movement smooth and adroit, and the blending of gags with story values every bit as felicitious at it had been in Warners' glory days.

And while the matching of live action and animation is not altogether seamless—certainly not to modern-day audiences weaned on *Who Framed Roger Rabbit?* and the more recent CGI and Pixar festivals—cinematographer Harold C. Stine and his lab technicians wisely employed a heavily saturated form of Technicolor, so that the bright tints in the "live" scenes would perfectly match the lush hues in the cartoon sequences. The filmmakers also avoided the risk that the scenes in which the live and animated characters appeared together on screen would come off as clumsy by making certain that there was as much distance between the "real" and "unreal" actors as possible. One unavoidable blend of live-action and cartoon—the animated Henry Limpet bobbing up and down in a genuine ocean—was handled magnificently by the studio's special-effects department, and is perhaps the film's most memorable aspect.

Though Jack Warner was less enthused over *The Incredible Mr. Limpet* than the people who made it, the studio spared no expense in promoting what they hoped would be a bright spot in the otherwise disappointing 1963–64 movie season. Two months before the official release date, the world press premiere was held on January 17, 1964, at Weeki Wachee Springs, a Florida theme park 70 miles north of St. Petersburg. More specifically, the premiere was held some 20 feet *under* Weeki Wachee Springs. Echoing a stunt dreamed up by Howard Hughes for the premiere of his 1955 Jane Russell vehicle *Underwater!*, *Mr. Limpet* was projected on a submerged screen on the ocean floor, with the audience watching from the dry comfort of the park's new underwater theater, shielded by fifteen plate glass windows. (All this hype was dutifully dispensed by Warners' national publicity director Joe Hyams, who for the benefit of photographers dived into the ocean to sign a contract with the "Weeki Wachee Mermaids.") Among those present for the inaugural showing were the film's stars and production staff, novelist Theodore Pratt and his wife, 200 members of the international press, and radio personality Arthur Godfrey—who also appeared in *Limpet*'s theatrical trailer, shamelessly plugging his own 45-rpm recording of one of the film's songs.

Approximately twenty minutes too long for its own good, and bogged down with a batch of unmemorable tunes by Sammy Fain and Harold Adamson, *The Incredible Mr. Limpet* is nonetheless still capable of entertaining children and adults alike. Well, not *all* adults: A few writers of the Christian Fundamentalist persuasion have carped that, by illustrating the various "stages" Mr. Limpet passes through as he transforms from human to fish, the film is a unabashed endorsement of the Evolution theory!

If these religious commentators were capable of finding fault with something as innocuous as *The Incredible Mr. Limpet*, God only knows what they would have made of the final espionage-themed World War II comedy in this chapter. *All the Queen's Men* (Strand Releasing, 2001) was an American/British/German/Hungarian coproduction with an Austrian director (Stefan Ruzowitzky) and an international cast. The last time so many diverse cultures collaborated on anything this disastrous, it was called The Hundred Years' War.

All the Queen's Men is based (it says here) on the true story of an OSS commando team comprised of British and American males, who went behind Nazi lines disguised as women to infiltrate a factory manufacturing German cipher machines. The commandos were to blend into the all-female working staff for the purpose of either stealing or sabotaging the machines—a mission ultimately rendered pointless when the Allies cracked the enemy code on their own. Faced with the challenge of treating a story about soldiers in drag seriously, the scriptwriters threw in the towel early on and decided to go for laughs. Since one of the writers was Digby Wolfe, cocreator of the landmark TV series *Rowan and Martin's Laugh-In*, it is likely that there was never any intention of telling the story "straight" (as it were). It is equally likely that, since neither Wolfe nor his cowriters had been active in filmmaking for several decades, the script for *All the Queen's Men* was completed long before the film's 2001 production date. This may explain why many of the script's comedy setpieces and one-liners are of a vintage even older than *Laugh-In*—and why the entire film looks like an acid flashback to the 1970s, complete with pop-art opening credits, ultra-low-tech special effects and retro gay jokes (the commandos are nicknamed "The Poof Patrol").

Exercising the same sort of brilliant career move that prompted him to accept the leading role in *Ed*, a "comedy" about a baseball-playing chimpanzee, former *Friends* regular Matt LeBlanc stars as maverick OSS operative O'Rourke, who is teamed with professional drag queen Tony (Eddie Izzard), sexually ambivalent cipher expert Johnno (David Birkin) and overaged British adjutant Archie (James Cosmo). O'Rourke and his compatriots are directed to parachute into Germany, don women's clothing and cosmetics, then worm their way into Marchenland, a combination toy factory and amusement park where the cipher machines are being assembled. The team's contact is beautiful librarian Romy (Nicolette Krebitz), who spends much of the film carrying on a combative romance with O'Rourke. Problems arise when Tony, a self-described "bisexual lesbian in a man's body," is confronted by his ex-wife Paloma (Sissi Berlinger), a popular Berlin cabaret singer who is unswerving in her loyalty to Der Fuhrer. Tony also has an awkward reunion with his former male lover Franz (Oliver Korittke), who happens to be Paloma's current boy-toy.

In a separate development alternating between comedy and pathos (and failing spectacularly on both counts), an obnoxious little war orphan latches on to the female-garbed Archie in the belief that "she" is the kid's mother.

Played entirely for laughs in its early reels, *All the Queen's Men* switches gears just before the end with several gore-encrusted onscreen deaths; but the film is neither workable nor believable at either dramatic extreme. Let's get beyond the notion that German soldiers could be so starved for sexual gratification that they find the disguised commandos irresistably attractive. And let's not dwell on the fact that the British stereotypes are even more exaggerated and artificial than the gay stereotypes. The film is a failure for one huge, gorilla-in-the-room reason: Never in a million years could the four male progagonists successfully pass themselves off as women — not even Eddie Izzard, the only cast member with practical gender-bending experience in his resume. In a feeble effort to explain why the OSS would select four operatives so obviously unsuited for such a delicate mission, we are informed in the closing scenes that the mission was *supposed* to fail, a diversionary tactic to prevent the Germans from finding out that the British have already broken their code. The willingness by the higher-ups to sacrifice four "expendables" for the Greater Good is depicted as callous and inhuman rather than a wise strategic move — further indication that the script may have been originally aimed at the anti-military crowd of an earlier decade.

For all the script's derisive quips about homosexuals and cross-dressers, *All the Queen's Men* is sympathetic and nonjudgmental in its treatment of gay characters. This was small compensation for such gay-friendly publications as the *San Francisco Chronicle* and *The Village Voice*. Edward Guthman of the *Chronicle* wrote: "Who knows why nifty ideas bomb? I'd wager that the goulash of nationalities that worked on the film ... was so scrambled that they never found a cohesive, unified style ... Ought to be funny, but this overreaching hybrid of farce, action and wartime tragedy never finds its groove." Michael Atkinson of the *Voice* dismissed the picture as "a graceless, witless attempt at mating *Some Like It Hot* with the World War II espionage thriller ... what you see is a bloody, hair-yanking contest between the most deplorably staged action scenes and the lamest trannie jokes of the last decade."

It was Scott Tobias of the satirical weekly *The Onion* who provided *All the Queen's Men* with the perfect epitaph: "A cheap Europudding production toplined by Matt LeBlanc, the most cursed of the cinematically luckless *Friends* cast, the film gives new hope to bad ideas the world over: If a high-heeled World War II drag farce starring LeBlanc and Eddie Izzard can get made, then keep those monkeys chained to their typewriters."

16

PR/CYA

Not all wars are fought on the battlefield. In the ongoing struggle to win the hearts and minds of American civilians and politicians, the Armed Services must put aside weapons of mass destruction and rely instead upon the subtler methods of public relations. Anyone who's ever seen a newsreel or propaganda short from the World War II years will notice the tireless exhortations to invest in war bonds and stamps ("Buy YOURS at this theatre!") or to support the second, third or fourth War Loan Drive (the 1945 two-reel extavaganza *All-Star Bond Rally*, for example). Even when engaged in deadly combat for the inarguably worthwhile cause of destroying fascism and preserving democracy, it was necessary to solicit donations.

To guarantee that money would continue pouring in, the men and women of the Army, Navy and Marine public relations divisions had to put the most positive face on how the money was being spent, and to shed the best possible light upon the troops who relied most heavily upon the cash flow. It was for this reason as much as for public morale that the victories of war were always afforded more print and screen space than the defeats, and why the average fighting man of World War II was invariably depicted as a paragon of youthful virtue and nobility, with character flaws softpedalled and the grim emotional side effects of battle injuries downplayed to the point of nonexistence. Virtually every civilian theater in America was encouraged to screen the War Department-produced short subject *Diary of a Sergeant* (1945), a relentlessly upbeat account of soldier Harold Russell's healthy adjustment to losing both of his hands in a training accident. But John Huston's somber documentary *Let There Be Light* (1946), chronicling the rehabilitation of 75 soldiers suffering from severe psychoneurosis, was withheld from civilian audiences until 1980.

After the war there were quite a few movies, plays and novels of the *Command Decision* variety which revealed how the military had to walk on eggshells while currying favor with politicians and the home folks to make certain that the billion-dollar appropriations would continue unabated. Uniformed negotiators not only had to be adept at "PR" (public relations), but also experts in the realm of "CYA" (Cover Your Ass) to sweep under the rug anything that might cause civilians to think twice about providing funds. The earliest service comedy to deal with this highwire act was director Billy Wilder's *A Foreign Affair* (Paramount, 1948).

While serving as a United States Army colonel in the immediate postwar era, the Austria-born Wilder oversaw a program which barred former Nazis from working in the German entertainment industry. Touring the war-ravaged American sector of Berlin, Wilder came across a bedraggled, emaciated young woman who told him that she was anxious for the Occupation forces to turn on the gas in her apartment — not because she was cold, but because she planned to commit suicide. Touched by her plight, Wilder conceived a bittersweet film scenario in which a demoralized *fräulein* is given a new lease on life when she befriends a confused Jewish-American GI, who by championing the girl's cause comes to appreciate the necessity of World War II and his own importance in the scheme of things.

By the time Wilder's concept had taken screenplay form in collaboration with Charles Brackett, Richard Breen, and Irwin and David Shaw, *Foreign Affair* (working titles: *Up in the Air* and *Operation Candy Bar*) had morphed into a comedy, albeit retaining the bleak postwar–Berlin setting. The suicidal German waif was now a jaded cabaret singer named Erika von Schluetow, played by Marlene Dietrich; similarly, the simon-pure GI had coarsened into a world-wise Army captain named John Pringle, portrayed by John Lund. The film fades in as a Congressional committee arrives in Berlin to investigate shocking allegations that the black market has been thriving despite official Army attempts to crack down on its operation — and even worse, that American GIs have been fraternizing with the local females. Straitlaced Iowa congresswoman Phoebe Frost (Jean Arthur) is persuaded that her constituent Captain Pringle can be relied upon to help her identify and expose the mysterious American officer who has been trading black-market goods for sexual favors with Erika Von Schluetow. Phoebe is also on the verge of discovering that the same officer has been tampering with official Army records to protect Erika, a suspected Nazi collaborator, from internment in a Russian prison camp. This places Pringle in quite a pickle, inasmuch that he himself is the rogue officer who is both protector and paramour of Fraulein von Schluetow.

The "PR" specialist in this melange is Pringle's commanding officer, Colonel Rufus Plummer (Millard Mitchell). It is Plummer's job to not only ride herd over the men in his command and curb local black marketeering, but also de–Nazify the civilian population — and he knows only too well that he'll never gain the confidence and cooperation of the Berliners if he bears down too hard on enforcing the rules. At the same time, if Plummer doesn't fulfill his duties to the letter, the committee will undoubtedly turns thumbs-down on future appropriations. The last thing the Colonel needs is a self-righteous Iowa congresswoman rocking the boat, to say nothing of a reckless American officer who may well be sharing his bed with an ex–Nazi.

Once Plummer has verified what Pringle is up to, he orders the Captain to keep his romance with Erika aflame as a means of flushing out her insanely jealous former lover, a high-ranking Nazi official who up to now has successfully evaded capture. In the spirit of "CYA," the amorous Pringle must also keep Phoebe Frost preoccupied lest she connect the dots between the Captain and Erika, thereby creating a public-relations nightmare. Meanwhile, prissy Phoebe has become so enamored of Pringle that she makes a public spectacle of herself and winds up in the custody of the German police. The poor woman is further humiliated when it appears that Pringle has merely been stringing her along, though the audience knows that the chastened Captain is now genuinely in love with her. A burst of melodrama in the final reel resolves everyone's problems, most of them satisfactorally.

Bearing traces of Billy Wilder's previous scripts for *Ninotchka* (a humorless female idealogue humanized by love) and *Double Indemnity* (a man forced to track himself down for past crimes), *A Foreign Affair* was one of the first postwar Hollywood efforts to be partially filmed on location in Berlin, exposing Wilder to a barrage of adverse criticism for using the devastated city, and the collective German "war guilt," as backdrops for a romantic comedy. Influential critic James Agee commended Wilder for the "sharp, nasty, funny stuff at the expense of investigatory Americans," at the same time chastising the director for the "rotten taste" of allowing Marlene Dietrich to warble a caustic *Threepenny Opera*-style song poking fun at black market activities. This was typical of the impish Wilder, who loved to raise the hackles of prudish filmgoers by skirting the edges of decency and decorum. In *Foreign Affair* he actually reduces the black market to a running gag, beginning when Phoebe Frost presents John Pringle with a cake baked by one of his hometown sweethearts— which Pringle promptly sells to purchase a mattress for Erika Von Schleutow, thereby setting the plot in motion. Similarly, the near-insurmountable task of de–Nazifying the millions of German children born and raised during the Hitler regime (a dilemma dramatized with stark seriousness in the play and film *Tomorrow the World*) is treated as a throwaway gag, with an unreconstructed *Hitlerjugend* merrily scribbling swastikas on any available space. Billy Wilder was of course enough of a showman to counteract the bitter taste of this scene with an extended audience-pleasing sequence showing a bunch of "democratized" German kids playing baseball (in a letter to the military government film office, Wilder insisted that the film should strike a happy medium between propaganda and entertainment). And though both Wilder and his German-born star Marlene Dietrich were outspokenly anti–Nazi, the director and the actress nonetheless softened the callous opportunism of Erika Von Schleutow, providing rationalization if not justification for her Nazi collaborations.

Harold V. Cohen, critic for the *Pittsburgh Post-Gazette*, was among those willing to overlook Wilder's lapses of taste in building comedy upon tragedy: "The overall vein here is frankly one of such wry humor that a chuckle always immediately dissolves a pin-prick. And don't think that doesn't require some pretty quick fingers. For there are many times in *A Foreign Affair* when the idea of treating basically serious matters so flippantly threatens to rub the wrong way, but Mr. Brackett and Mr. Wilder know exactly when to stop and just when to begin winking their way out of it. That kind of a skill must be swift and sure; otherwise reason might be outraged and taste offended. This never happens here, however, and the note of high comedy stays constantly on key."

Seen today, *Foreign Affair* seems infinitely more tasteful and less shocking than some of Wilder's later excesses (*Kiss Me, Stupid* immediately comes to mind), though at least one example of the director's audacity can still take one's breath away. As Captain Pringle heads for a rendezvous with Erika, his jeep passes by several city blocks of the most appallingly bombed-out ruins of Berlin — while the soundtrack blossoms forth with a lush rendition of "Isn't It Romantic?"

Though not schooled in the field of public relations, *Foreign Affair*'s Col. Plummer was forced by the pressures of his job to become a PR expert. The first screen comedy devoted to an entire department of military public-relations specialists was 1957's *Don't Go Near the Water*, based on the best-selling novel by former *Life* magazine staffer William Brinkley. When first presented to Random House editor Bennett Cerf, Brinkley's book was a loose gathering of anecdotes based on the author's wartime experiences while toiling away in the Navy's PR division in the South Pacific, thousands of miles removed from battle. The central character is Lt. Max Siegel, described as the most "spectacularly ugly" man in the Navy; but what Siegel lacks in looks he makes up for in wit and cunning. Under the less than sterling command of Lt. Cmdr. "Marblehead" Nash, a former Merrill-Lynch stockbroker who suffers from delusions of grandeur, Siegel and his fellow "typewriter warriors"—all Madison Avenue advertising geniuses—work round the clock to compose press releases that will shower prestige and glory upon the Navy.

The challenges facing these "dry-land sailors" include an effort to humanize mean-spirited Admiral Boatwright in the eyes of the public by providing the old curmudgeon with a pet dog; making certain that gorgeous but troublesome Deborah Aldrich, a correspondent from *Madame* magazine, doesn't foul up a combat mission with her predilection for self-serving stunts; and transforming a stupid, foul-mouthed, obscenely tattooed sailor with the incongruously heroic moniker of Farragut Jones into a clean-cut, straight-arrow "Typical Young Navy Man" for the purposes of a stateside lecture tour. Max Siegel's other adventures involve persuading a group of articulate, well-educated island natives to pose as stereotypically monosyllabic savages for the benefit of the newsreel cameras; arranging a romantic rendezvous between Navy nurse Lt. Alice Tomlen and lowly seaman Adam Garrett while simultaneously squelching lecherous Lt. Ross Pendleton; using a phony tryst and a wire recorder to blackmail waspish war correspondent Gordon Ripwell into financing a new schoolhouse for the local islanders; and building a lavish officer's club without the input (or the expertise) of the Seabees. In each of these episodes, William Brinkley's waggish "wink-wink nudge-nudge" prose carries the day, the humor augmented by combining traditional Navy slang with ad-executive jargon ("Think Big").

Bennett Cerf liked the material but felt it was too hit-and-miss to qualify as a novel. He recommended that William Brinkley choose the ten best anecdotes and organize them into chapters, which were then both separated and unified (a neat trick!) by "interludes" involving Siegel's romance with sexy schoolma'rm Melora Alba, the daughter of Tulara Island's wealthiest citizen. Cerf also advised Brinkley to use certain isolated incidents as set-ups for boffo punchlines in the final chapter. The author obliged by building "Marblehead" Nash's inability to figure out the mechanics of a simple Navy sextant into a running joke; and by divesting the haughty Deborah Aldrich of her black lace panties, literally "running them up the flagpole to see if anyone salutes," then framing and mounting the undergarments on the wall of the officer's club.

MGM paid $355,000 for the movie rights to *Don't Go Near the Water*, outbidding actor-director Dick Powell, who'd wanted to make the film at 20th Century–Fox. Ernest Borgnine was a front-runner for the part of Max Siegel until MGM decided to ignore the author's unflattering description of the character in favor of the handsomer and more bankable Glenn Ford, who'd just come off the successful service comedy *Teahouse of the August Moon* (see **Chapter 8**). When it appeared that Ford would be tied up costarring with Rita Hayworth in Columbia's *The Notorious Landlady*, MGM briefly considered the actor's *Teahouse* costar Marlon Brando as Siegel. But *Landlady* was shelved (it wouldn't be filmed until 1962, and then with Jack Lemmon and Kim Novak) and Ford was back on deck, with Brando's then wife Anne Kashfi initially cast as Melora Alba. What happened next depends on which source one reads: Either Ford demanded that Kashfi be replaced because of his personal dislike for Brando, or she was fired after infuriating Ford by taking advice on how to play a comedy scene from an "outsider," Spencer Tracy. Whatever the case, Melora was recast with Gia Scala, who later identified the role as her all-time favorite.

The rest of the actors were selected through the usual typecasting and contract-player channels: Fred Clark as the bombastic "Marblehead" Nash, with Russ Tamblyn as his maltreated valet Ensign Tyson; Keenan Wynn as the acidulous Gordon Ripwell, who also narrates the film; Eva Gabor as the imperious Debbie Aldrich, who assumes that Siegel can introduce her to the Admiral because "you're both in the same war"; Anne Francis as good-natured nurse Alice Tomlen (less promiscuous than her literary counterpart), with Jeff Richards as her would-be seducer Lt. Pendleton and Earl Holliman as her true love Seaman Garrett; Howard Smith as the truculent Admiral Boatwright, a characterization similar to the actor's portrayal of publicity-conscious Major General Bush in 1958's *No Time for Sergeants* (see **Chapter 8**); and in the role of a lifetime, Mickey Shaughnessy as profanity-spewing Farragut Jones.

Under the prosaic direction of Charles Walters, the film version of *Don't Go Near the Water* lacks the snappy pace and jaunty irreverence of the novel. Still, the movie contains two "money scenes" which guaranteed positive word-of-mouth from 1957 audiences. The first such scene is the lengthy slapstick passage in which the all-thumbs PR personnel attempt to build a rec center, with several painful indignities heaped upon the overbearing "Marblehead" Nash. Glenn Ford himself cited this as the film's highlight, expressing regret that his character was only peripherally involved in the shenanigans. The second sure-fire sequence, and the one for which the film is best remembered, involves Max Siegel's Pygmalion-like efforts to transform the foul-mouthed Farragut Jones into a prototypical Navy hero and the squeaky-clean idol of millions.

The comedy in this sequence is almost totally reliant upon Jones' endless barrage of curse words—in particular the one Anglo-Saxonism that to this day almost invariably results in an "R" rating. Though we've printed that word in its proper context elsewhere in this book, when *Don't Go Near the Water* was first published in 1956 Bennett Cerf could not drop the F-bomb without the risk of being hauled into Federal Court on obscenity charges. The solution in the novel was to use dashes, as in "_____ing" and "____er." Obviously this would not work on screen: Jones had to make *some* sort of sound or his scenes would fall flat. Thus, MGM harked back to a gimmick used in the 1951 baseball comedy *Angels in the Outfield*, in which the main character's obscenities were obscured by playing the soundtrack backwards. In *Don't Go Near the Water*, every time Farragut Jones cuts loose with the Forbidden Word, the blare of a ship's foghorn is heard on the soundtrack—whether he's anywhere near a ship or not. This was considered the pinnacle of hilarity back in 1957: If the horn effect doesn't play as well today, it is only because we've heard the actual word spoken so often on-screen that even its own comic value has all but evaporated.

Though falling short of perfection, *Don't Go Near the Water* at least has the virtue of scrupulous fidelity to its source novel. Such is not the case with an earlier service comedy in the "PR/CYA"

Visting journalist Eva Gabor attracts a great deal of attention while strolling the deck of a Navy cruiser in *Don't Go Near the Water* (MGM, 1957). Small wonder that she needs an armed escort.

vein, *Top Secret Affair* (Warner Bros., 1957). This one was inspired by *Melville Goodwin, U.S.A.*, a 1952 novel written by John P. Marquand, whose other works include the "Mister Moto" mystery yarns and the Pulitzer-winning *The Late George Apley*. Marquand's title character is the son of a small-town druggist, who after graduation from West Point rises to the rank of Major General, lauded as a legend in his own time for his valor and resourcefulness. Trouble is, Melville Goodwin has been a soldier so long that he knows nothing about the world outside the military, and even less about predatory females like Dottie Peale, the wealthy widow of a powerful and influential publisher. When his fellow generals get wind of Goodwin's plan to leave his wife Muriel in favor of the glamorous Dottie, they combine forces to save him from himself—and, incidentally, save the Pentagon from a maelstrom of bad press.

Goodwin's colleagues will have to move as quickly as possible to keep the General's peccadilloes from going public. Sidney Skelton, a successful radio–TV news analyst, has begun a series of interviews with General Goodwin to get the story behind the story of the Great Man. Uncomfortable with his own wealth and fame, Skelton (the novel's narrator) finds in Goodwin a kindred spirit, a man who would be more comfortable leading an ordinary life instead of wrestling with the responsibilities of being a public figure. The Pentagon's surreptititious efforts to bust up Goodwin's clandestine romance turn out to be for naught when Dottie decides to break things off herself, whereupon Melville returns to Muriel, who all along has been complacent in the knowledge that she was in no real danger of losing him. As for Sidney Skelton, he has plenty of dirt to dish about Goodwin but chooses not to use it, figuring that America needs all the heroes it can get. At the same time, Goodwin's example inspires Skelton to rethink his own life and give up the synthetic trappings of celebrity in order to devote more time to his wife and children.

There was a lot of speculation as to whom Melville Goodwin was based upon. Many assumed that the character was inspired by George C. Patton, who was known to have kept a mistress during the final days of World War II, or Douglas MacArthur, whose spotty marital record had caused him a lot of PR grief over the decades. A few "in the know" observers believed that Goodwin was a thinly-disguised Dwight D. Eisenhower, who for many years had been dogged by unsubstantiated rumors of an extramarital affair with his wartime chauffeur Kay Summersby. There was less mystery regarding the basis for the character of Dottie Peale, who was transparently patterned after Claire Boothe Luce, the well-connected wife of *Time* magazine poobah Henry Luce. While writing *Melville Goodwin, U.S.A.*, Marquand had made several exploratory visits to *Time* headquarters in New York; after *Goodwin*'s publication, the author publicly apologized to one of the magazine's female researchers for what she perceived as an unflattering fictional portrait of her in the novel.

Despite a reasonably faithful 1952 adaptation of *Melville Goodwin, U.S.A.* on the TV anthology *Pulitzer Prize Playhouse* (with Paul Kelly, Margalo Gillmore and Jayne Meadows), Warner Bros. felt that Marquand's original story was unsuitable for filming when the studio bought the movie rights in 1955. Warners instructed screenwriters Roland Kibbee and Allan Scott to ignore everything but Marquand's main characters and concoct a plotline of their own. In one respect, this made perfect sense. The studio had purchased the property as a vehicle for Humphrey Bogart and his wife Lauren Bacall, and there was no way that Bogie could have conveyed the unworldly ingenuousness of the novel's Melville Goodwin—nor would audiences have warmed to seeing Hollywood's premier tough guy playing a character so easily manipulated by the women in his life.

So many changes were made between book and screen that even Marquand's title was nixed in favor of *Their Top Secret Affair*, soon streamlined to *Top Secret Affair*. Acknowledging this total overhaul, the opening credits state outright that the script is merely based on *characters* from *Melvin Goodwin, U.S.A.*, rather than the novel itself. The film version of Dottie Peale remains a high-profile publisher who has inherited a media empire (avoiding too close a likeness to Claire Booth Luce, the character is a liberal rather than a conservative), but Melville Goodwin is now a lifelong bachelor. Rather than pursue him romantically, Dottie goes after Maj. Gen. Goodwin with vengeance in her heart: He has just landed a prestigious appointment to the Joint Atomic Energy Commission that Dottie had hoped to secure for a man of her choice. Summoning all her feminine wiles, she goes out of her way to discredit the General, either by manipulating him into public embarrassment or by digging up a few unsavory secrets from his past. Nothing like the cloistered *naif* of the novel, Goodwin is completely savvy to the ins and outs of media manipulation and has a pretty good idea of what Dottie is up to—and to make certain that nothing goes awry, he is accompanied practically everywhere by diligent Army PR officer Homer Gooch. Small wonder that every effort by Dottie to catch Goodwin making a fool of himself backfires. When goaded into singing his favorite song during Amateur Night at a hipster hangout, the General brings the patrons to their feet in patriotic fervor with a robust rendition of "The Caissons Go Rolling Along." And when Dottie attempts to get Goodwin drunk, it is she who ends up totally blotto, falling fully clothed into a swimming pool.

All Dottie has left in her arsenal is a "scandal" dating back to the Korean War involving Goodwin and an alluring enemy spy named Yvette de Fresnay. Facing disgrace, humiliation, and a possible term in Leavenworth, Goodwin is hauled before a Senate investigating committee, where he remains stoically silent while his reputation is dragged through the mud. Only the last-minute intervention of the White House enables Goodwin to reveal a top-secret Army document that clears up everything. Yes, he did have a romance with Yvette, and yes, he did reveal to her some highly classified military information. But the General goes on to explain that he was aware of Yvette's Communist connections and had been ordered by his superiors to supply her with false information—and once the mission was completed, he put his personal feelings aside and ordered Yvette's execution. Totally exonerated, Goodwin rescues Dottie from an angry mob of American Legionnaires, declaring that he's fallen in love with the chastened publisher with a magnificent double-entendre closing line. (Just in case you're wondering, the novel's narrator Sidney Skelton has been split into two secondary characters, Dottie's top researcher Phil Bentley and her ace photographer Lotzie.)

In the advanced stages of the cancer that would ultimately kill him, Humphrey Bogart was forced to bow out of *Top Secret Affair*, and Lauren Bacall followed suit; they were replaced by Kirk Douglas and Susan Hayward. Two other members of the announced cast, Keenan Wynn as Phil Bentley and Walter Matthau as Col. Homer Gooch, were replaced by Paul Stewart and Jim Backus. Hyped to theater managers as "your biggest happiness-maker since *Mister Roberts*," the film premiered on January 30, 1957, sixteen days after Bogart's death.

J.P. Marquand's low-key satire of celebrity and public relations is only marginally intact, with a handful of harpoons aimed at the arrogance of the newsmagazine business and Col. Gooch's manic efforts to keep the Military from losing face with the fickle public. A golden opportunity to use humor as a weapon against the presumptuousness of civilian investigating committees grilling military officers—the Army-McCarthy hearings were still fresh in the minds of 1957 filmgoers—is unfortunately bungled in the climactic scene. Saving *Top Secret Affair* from middling mediocrity are the delightful performances by Kirk Douglas and Susan Hayard, two traditionally serious actors adapting quite nicely to the script's surfeit of slapstick, farce and witty rejoinders.

Melville Goodwin may not have been comfortable having his life and personality constantly exposed to public view, but he had learned to live with the necessity. The principal characters in *Kiss Them for Me* (20th Century–Fox, 1957) not only resent having to traffic with military Public Relations, but also derive a great deal of pleasure from causing the PR boys as much grief as possible.

While convalescing in a Navy hospital in 1944, Frederick Wakeman (best known as the author of that devastating attack on Madison Avenue known as *The Hucksters*) dashed off his first novel *Shore Leave*. No relation to the 1922 Broadway play of the same name, *Shore Leave* was a bitterly funny tirade against the Military's insistence upon parading war heroes before the public as if they were show horses, and against civilian opportunists who exploit those heroes for their own benefit. Wakeman's protagonists were three highly decorated Navy pilots, likewise hospitalized after performing Above and Beyond. Cognizant of the brass' plans to send them on a stateside lecture tour, the men use their "hero clout" to wangle an extended shore leave, in which Booze and Broads are scheduled as the main events. The Navy PR flacks are dispatched to discourage any behavior that might cast aspersions upon the moral fibre of America's fighting forces, but the three funsters elude the bloodhounds at every turn. *Shore Leave* was quite popular with real-life Navy personnel, who embraced the work for its hilarious accuracy. The main characters' come-on line to impressionable females—"There I was on my back at 30,000 feet"—was briefly adopted as a catchphrase by genuine Navy pilots.

Less harsh and more military-friendly than the Wakeman original, Luther Davis' theatrical adaptation of *Shore Leave* made its Broadway debut on March 20, 1945, under the title *Kiss Them for Me*. Most of the play's action transpires in a lavishly appointed suite at San Francisco's St. Mark Hotel, where Navy flyboys Crewson, Mac and Mississipp, contemptuous of the "hero act" they will soon be performing on behalf of their superiors, intend to hold a wild and drunken party during a four-day leave. As a means of luring women to the festivities, the boys issue an advertisement claiming that they're holding a sale on nylons. The trio's tagalong PR officer Walter Wallace has a vested interest in keeping the revelry from getting out of hand: Wallace hopes to use the public's adulation of the three heroes as a springboard for a lucrative postwar position as head publicist for powerful shipping magnate Eddie Turnbill. But Crewson threatens to throw a monkey wrench in Wallace's plans by falling in love with Turnbill's fiancee Gwinneth Livingston.

Though popular enough to warrant 110 performances, *Kiss Them for Me* was chided by critics for a limp third act in which the hilarity was slowed down by Crewson's angry tirade against the war-profiteering Turnbill, then totally halted by the pilots' decision to throw away the opportunity to sit out the rest of the war when they learn that while they've been enjoying themselves, their cruiser has been torpedoed with heavy loss of life. While the play was picked apart for its failings, critics were unanimous in their admiration for the cast, which included Richard Widmark as Crewson, Dennis King Jr. as Mississipp, Richard Davis as Mac and future TV director Daniel Petrie (*Eleanor and Franklin, My Name Is Bill W*) in a minor role. Singled out for special praise was a 24-year-old nightclub entertainer named Judy Holliday, cast as a sweet-natured hooker named Alice (euphemistically described as a "victory girl" by *Life* magazine), who tries to pass herself off as an intellectual by showing up at the party with a copy of *Fortune* magazine tucked under her arm. The scene in which Alice systematically seduces Mac as he wistfully reminisces about his wife at home was lauded as the play's highlight.

The cynicism directed at the exploitation of wartime heroics in *Kiss Them for Me,* to say nothing of the play's tawdrier aspects, proved too raw and randy for postwar Hollywood, and as a result, no film version of the property emerged until 1957. While some of the pungent commentary in the novel and play was carried over to the film—notably Mac's willingness to capitalize on his heroism by running for Congress, having deliberately put himself in harm's way on the battlefield for the sole purpose of becoming a hero to guarantee his election—scripwriter Julius Epstein toned down several of the play's dicier elements. Epstein did a particularly careful laundering job on the character of the prostitute Alice, here transformed into an innocuously flirtatious "Rosie the Riveter" type.

Richard Widmark was briefly in line to recreate his stage role of Crewson before 20th Century–Fox contractee Dan Dailey was floated as a possibility. Both Widmark and Dailey were forgotten when Cary Grant expressed interest in the part, turning down an opportunity to work with Billy Wilder in *Love in the Afternoon*. This resulted in the first of four collaborations between Grant and director Stanley Donen, the best of these 1963's *Charade*. Fox filled the principal female roles with two of the studio's resident starlets, actress-model Suzy Parker and that structural phenomenon Jayne Mansfield. More model than actress in 1957, Parker allegedly had so much trouble delivering lines that some of her dialogue was dubbed by another actress (some sources claim it was Deborah Kerr). Mansfield comes off better in the role originated by Judy Holliday, though she seems to be straining to imitate Holliday rather than developing her own characterization. Cary Grant's fellow pilots are well played by Ray Walston (Mac) and Larry Blyden (Mississipp), while Leif Erickson adroitly blends subtle menace with stuffed-shirt arrogance as the mercenary shipbuilder. The film's most surprising characterization, that of prissy PR officer Wallace, is offered by Werner Klemperer, with nary a trace of the actor's "Colonel Klink" accent or bearing.

The movie version of *Kiss Them for Me* suffers from the same narrative flaw as the play version, the comic airiness of its first two-thirds dragged down by the sloshy soul-searching and sentimentality of the final third. Despite the star power of Cary Grant, the film was a box-office disappointment domestically, though for reasons unknown (but worth researching in another book) it was one of Fox's biggest moneymakers in Australia.

The year following *Kiss Them for Me*, Cary Grant's future *Operation Petticoat* costar Tony Curtis was cast as Cpl. Paul Hodges, a soldier slated to embark on a promotional tour of his own in *The Perfect Furlough* (Universal-International, 1958). Stationed at an Arctic radar base, Hodges is one of 104 unmarried servicemen who are about to go out of their gourds for lack of female companionship. Army psychiatrist Lt. Vicki Loren (played by Curtis' then-wife Janet Leigh) suggests a morale-boosting stunt that will also be a boon to public relations. The men will be invited to describe their "perfect furlough," then hold a lottery to choose one of their ranks for this three-week idyll. Cpl. Hodges pulls the lucky number, winning an all-expense-paid trip to Paris and a date with South American movie queen Sandra Roca (Linda Cristal). Knowing Hodges' reputation as a womanizer, his superiors are terrified that the Corporal will despoil the starlet and bring down the full wrath of the civilian and Hollywood community alike—especially since Sandra's agent (Elaine Stritch) and producer (Keenan Wynn) have fashioned a gigantic publicity campaign around the dream date. Lt. Loren is ordered to accompany Hodges on his furlough to make certain that Sandra is returned to her studio unsullied. By the time the three weeks have run their course, *both* the corporal and the lady psychiatrist have made international fools of themselves thanks to a

Jayne Mansfield (standing) tries to arouse Cary Grant from his sickbed with a little drinkie-poo in *Kiss Them for Me* (20th Century–Fox, 1957). Suzy Parker is the lady very much in the background.

staggering series of farcical mishaps. And surprise of surprises, Corporal and Lieutenant have also fallen in love.

Directed by Blake Edwards and written by Stanley Shapiro, who like Tony Curtis would both also move on to *Operation Petticoat*, *The Perfect Furlough* is a typical tickle-and-tease sex comedy of the era, in which much is inferred but little actually happens. Exhibiting his genius for combining slapstick with situational humor, Edwards contrives to draw laughs from a plaster body cast, a "frozen" man, and a messy free-for-all in a wine vat, this last bit anticipating the director's mammoth pie fight in *The Great Race* (1965). Another foretaste of the Blake Edwards to come is personified by a bumbling Gallic police officer who breaks his pointer-stick, trips after issuing orders to his minions, and gets drunk while stripped to his underwear—an embryonic Inspector Clouseau.

Edwards would ever after regard *The Perfect Furlough* as a milestone in his career, at least insofar as its physical-comedy content was concerned. It was also the film that earned Edwards his *auteur* stripes with the French film critics. In his review of *Furlough*, Jean-Luc Godard regretted that Edwards didn't fully stamp the picture as his own by writing the screenplay as well as directing. Godard also indicated that his enjoyment of the film may have had something to do with the presence in the cast of cult figure Marcel Dalio, the star of Jean Renoir's *Le Grande Illusion* and *Rules of the Game*: "Given a Tony Curtis in good form, Edwards could surely have made something more out of this banal comedy.... This said, the direction still manages an idea per shot, often charming (Tony Curtis behind a curtain as Janet Leigh takes a bath), sometimes funny (Tony Curtis worrying about the meaning of the word *ampoule*), and occasionally remarkable (Janet Leigh falling into a wine-vat under the gaze of a sublimely eccentric Dalio)."

It isn't known whether Godard saw 20th Century–Fox's 1959 service yarn *A Private's Affair*, even though the film was directed by another darling of the French *cineastes*, Raoul Walsh. Point of fact, virtually none of the book-length analyses of Walsh's work have even acknowledged the existence of *A Private's Affair*. "Typical auteurist procedure," notes John Reid in his book *Cinemascope Two*. "If you come across a film from one of your idols that simply doesn't fit into your sublime theories, just drop it. Just pretend it doesn't exist." Especially if the film is lousy.

A Private's Affair (working title: *The Love Maniac*) almost didn't make the cut in this book because it's hard to tell if it's supposed to be comedy. Starting as a musical, it abruptly shifts to a romance, then suddenly becomes a farce before reverting to a musical again (following Oscar Levant's definition of a musical as "a series of catastrophes ending in a floor show"). The film's immediate predecessor *Mardi Gras* was *definitely* a musical, starring Pat Boone as a military-academy student who like Tony Curtis in *Perfect Furlough* wins a date with movie star Christine Carère. As with most major studios in the late 1950s, 20th Century–Fox felt obliged to make youth-oriented films with popular recording artists to keep apace of the Elvis Presley films at Paramount. Released in November 1958, *Mardi Gras* was among the earliest efforts to cash in on the furor surrounding Elvis' recent induction into the Army. In addition to Pat Boone, two other pop-music stars were in the cast, Tommy Sands and Gary Crosby (son of Bing). Both Gary Crosby and Christine Carère would be carried over to *A Private's Affair*, in which the main drawing card was another teen fave, 19-year-old Sal Mineo. Like Pat Boone, Mineo was an accomplished musician. Unlike Pat Boone, Sal could act.

The top-billed Mineo plays a tenement-bred beatnik named Luigi, who after receiving his draft notice reports to a New Jersey training camp along with millionaire's son Jerry (Barry Coe) and Oregon-born lothario Mike (Gary Crosby). While pulling KP duty, the three draftees break spontaneously into the Jay Livingston-Ray Evans tune "Same Old Army," with Luigi playing the trashcan lids like bongos. Evidently this scene is all that Raoul Walsh chose to remember about making *A Private's Affair*, griping that Sal Mineo's incessant drumming between takes drove him bonkers. Be that as it may, "Same Old Army" will figure prominently in the rest of the film thanks to the quick thinking of the platoon's resident technogeek (Bob "Gilligan" Denver in his movie

A Private's Affair (20th Century–Fox, 1959): G.I.s Barry Coe, Gary Crosby and Sal Mineo (left to right) don't know it yet, but one of them is about to find himself waist-deep in bureaucratic quicksand.

debut), who transcribes the impromptu number on his homemade tape recorder. Along the way, the boys find time for *l'amour*, with Luigi wooing Jerry's wealthy next-door neighbor Marie (Christine Carère), Jerry squiring Luigi's childhood friend Louise (Terry Moore) and Mike trying to make time with sarcastic WAC Katey, who keeps the would-be Romeo at bay with her judo skills (Katey is played by Barbara Eden, replacing a pregnant Sheree North).

If you're wondering what all this has to do with Public Relations, keep reading. Katey happens to work in the camp's PR division, which is prepping for a visit from Elizabeth Chapman (Jessie Royce Landis), the nation's first female Secretary of the Army. Upon arrival, Chapman is apprised of the plight of a little girl whose Dutch-born mother was killed in an accident, and whose father lies near death in the same Army hospital where Jerry (Barry Coe, remember?) is being treated for laryngitis. In a clumsily constructed sequence, the middle-aged Chapman offers to secretly marry the young father on his deathbed, thereby providing the orphaned child with a relative who can sign papers necessary to keep her out of a Dutch orphanage. As these things are wont to happen in the movies, the room numbers get confused and Elizabeth Chapman ends up marrying the heavily sedated Jerry — at which point nominal star Sal Mineo cedes the leading role to Barry Coe, hardly a fair trade by any means.

Meanwhile, TV host Jim Gordon (Jim Backus), auditioning talent for an all-military variety show, has heard the tape of the three rookies performing "Same Old Army" (recorded by a microphone so sensitive that it even picks up the 20th Century–Fox orchestra). So now the gears are primed for the hectic final reels, as poor Jerry tries to make it to the variety show on time while simultaneously jumping through hoops to extricate himself from his marriage to Ms. Chapman — providing he can prove to a skeptical Army shrink (Alan Hewitt) that the mariage ever took place.

The climactic scenes are a crazy quilt of running gags, "CYA" doublespeak, and production numbers with lots of leggy chorines. The only real laughs are provided by the Marquis Chimps, who don't even receive the courtesy of a screen credit.

The final public-relations comedy in this chapter is another youth-oriented semimusical from 20th Century–Fox, this one teaming *Mardi Gras*' Pat Boone with *Private's Affair*'s Barbara Eden. Released in 1961, *All Hands on Deck* was based on the gently humorous service novel *Warm Bodies* (Simon & Schuster, 1957), written by Donald R. Morris, a career Navy officer, CIA specialist in psychological warfare, and author of the remarkable *Washing of the Spears* (1965), a history of the African war between the British and the Zulus told from the natives' viewpoint. The title *Warm Bodies* was taken from a familiar serviceman's phrase referring to the Navy's undiscerning habit of recruiting any male human being with "at least one arm and two fingers who can pick something up when he is told to." Morris helpfully provides this definition in the book's foreword, adding: "Warm bodies can carry boxes, count small objects, turn on lights, chip paint, and sweep."

The author cast himself as the book's protagonist, an accident-prone lieutenant (j.g.) possessed of what the *New York Times* described as "a fine flair for the ludicrous," who after graduating 409th in an Annapolis class of 410 takes his own warm body to a peacetime LST. The episodic plotline extracts humor from the little things in Navy life, ranging from the "perfect" method of chipping rust from the ship's hull to substituting a sock for a white glove during a surprise inspection. The hero regards himself as a confirmed bachelor, content to while away his idle hours on board ship while his married fellow officers link up with their wives during holidays and shore leaves. But by the end of the story, the lieutenant has traded the solitary tranquility of Navy life for suburban domesticity as the husband of fetching Southern belle Sally Hobson. There's very little rancor in the narrative, and surprisingly nothing of a bawdy nature. Donald Morris scores his biggest laughs with thumbnail sketches of his more eccentric shipmates, notably enlisted man S.E. Garfield. A full-blooded Chickasaw Indian (his initials stand for "Screaming Eagle"), Garfield can neither read nor write, insists on speaking only in his native tongue, and gets into heap big trouble every time he goes ashore; but he is indispensible to the LST because of his genius with all things mechanical.

What little satire there is in *Warm Bodies* is manifested in the characters of the hero's superior officers, including an easygoing captain who'd rather go fishing than play skipper, and an anal-retentive investigating officer who issues demerits for obscure, antiquated infractions that haven't been enforced by any reasonable Navy man since the days of John Paul Jones. The film version *All Hands on Deck* tries to substitute belly laughs for the novel's quiet chuckles, pumping up the comedy content with sledgehammer gags related to the Navy's morbid obsession with Public Relations. The script was by Jay Sommers, who later had a lot fun at the expense of pompous authority figures in the TV sitcom *Green Acres*.

Pat Boone stars as Lt. Victor Donald, executive officer of the LST *St. Clair County* (playing "herself") out of Long Beach. Inasmuch as the unmarried Donald has already offered to sub for his married comrades as they head out for shore leave, he is ordered to keep close watch on "Screaming Eagle" Garfield, played by Buddy Hackett (who can explain Hollywood's fascination with casting Jewish comedians as Native Americans?) After the war-whooping Garfield trashes a movie theater during the screening of a western picture in which the Cavalry defeats the Indians, reporter Sally Hobson (Barbara Eden) shows up to get the whole story behind the incident, turning her Southern accent on and off like a faucet to charm her way into the Navy's confidence. It so happens that the oil-rich Garfield is the wealthiest member of the Chickasaw tribe, and as such has V.I.P. status with Bureau of Indian Affairs, whose representatives insist that under no circumstances is Screaming Eagle to be punished for any infraction at any time. Thus it is Lt. Donald's burden in life to drag Garfield along wherever he goes, the better to keep the impetuous Indian from stirring up any more negative publicity.

Falling in love with Sally, Donald wants to propose marriage, but his LST is ordered to the

Aleutians for a trial run. At the same time, Garfield smuggles his pet turkey Owasso aboard ship (the Indian explains that the turkey's name is the Chickasaw word for "affection," though anyone who's ever taken first-year French will recognize *oiseau* as the Gallic word for "bird"). Efforts to hide Owasso from the ship's commanding officer O'Gara (Dennis O'Keefe) come acropper when the bird takes a liking to the skipper. The feeling isn't mutual, however, and O'Gara is more than somewhat peeved when the Navy orders him to keep the turkey on his ship as a morale-boosting mascot. All occasions inform against Donald and O'Gara when nit-picky Cmdr. Bintle (Gale Gordon) shows up for one of his dreaded inspections—and to make things worse, lovelorn Sally has sneaked on board disguised as a sailor (the only occasion when the well-upholstered Barbara Eden *doesn't* wear an outfit at least one size too small). Things look bleak until Sally reveals that her uncle is the chairman of the Navy Appropriations Committee, whereupon Bintle supplicatively offers to waive all demerits on this occasion. As a bonus, Garfield's turkey mates with a pelican, resulting in a bonanza of positive PR when the bird's egg hatches into the world's first "Pelikey."

Pat Boone will never be mistaken for Sir John Gielgud, but he's agreeable enough in the leading role, his singular highlight occurring when he croons a love song to the heroine which is overheard by the entire crew courtesy of the ship's PR system (admittedly, 1970's *MASH* would do this gag better—and dirtier). Barbara Eden is cute, Dennis O'Keefe is appropriately flustered, TV-sitcom stalwarts Gale Gordon and Ann B. Davis (as Eden's roommate) deliver TV-sitcom performances, and Warren Berlinger and Joe E. Ross do a lot with the little they're given. Under the perfunctory direction of Norman Taurog, *All Hands on Deck* was accepted as harmless, inoffensive entertainment by audiences in 1961. That's not likely to happen these days, thanks to Buddy Hackett's enthusiastic but insulting portrayal of Screaming Eagle Garfield. We know that Buddy is a Native American because he brandishes a tomahawk and wears a feather in his cap. Enough said.

Because of its racist underpinnings, *All Hands on Deck* has not worn as well as the other films in this chapter. There is, however, one element common to all these films that has not dated at all: The warriors in charge of the military establishment continue to kowtow to the noncombatants in charge of the Public Relations Brigade—and they still continue to depend upon the delicate art of "CYA" whenever the truth catches up with them.

17

The Home Front

The time: shortly after America's entry into World War I. The place: a rundown farmhouse in Pennsylvania Dutch country. Sitting on the sun porch, vainly trying to repair an old sock, is young Johanna Renssaller. Fed up with her humdrum existence, her insensitive mother, her hoggish grandfather, and the cacophony of barnyard noises emanating from the livestock, Johanna glances heavenward and murmurs a desperate prayer: "Oh, Lord, You promised often to come to our help. Now is Your chance. Send me a beau!" As if in answer, the sound of a distant bugle is heard. Johanna glances down a long and dusty road. An endless column of mounted artillery troops are marching forward in preparation of establishing a training camp near the Renssaller farm. Johanna smiles as she's never smiled before.

Thus begins the 1918 Mary Pickford vehicle *Johanna Enlists*, one of the earliest comedy films to comment upon how the war affected civilians on the "home front." The film also shows the effect that civilians had on the troops, as the long-ignored Johanna suddenly finds herself the center of attention amidst hundreds of eligible bachelors. This results in a feud between Johanna's most ardent swains, Private Vibbard (Monte Blue) and Lieutenant LeRoy (Emory Johnson), but their quarrelling becomes a moot point when our heroine chooses Captain Van Renssaller (Douglas MacLean)—no relation, of course—to be her husband. All of which was fine with real-life Army officials, who like everyone else in the known world were enamored of actress Mary Pickford. According to *Motion Picture News*, the film was "produced with full cooperation of the 143rd Artillery Regiment, under the command of Captain Faneuf, and of which Miss Pickford is an honorary captain."

Released a scant two months before the Armistice, *Johanna Enlists* was fairly realistic, but within certain boundaries. The film was careful not to suggest that the relationship between the soldiers and the home folks was strained or uncomfortable. If anyone showed resentment towards being in close proximity with men in uniform, that person was depicted as an obnoxious jerk; and though the action in the film includes a scene in which Johanna is surprised in her bath by Lt. LeRoy, the byplay around the scene makes it abundantly clear that the outrage is an accident and the lieutenant is as shocked as the heroine. It was only during the years between the two World Wars, a time when it was no longer necessary to deify either civilians or military, that Hollywood films began featuring servicemen with selfish motives or untoward thoughts on their minds—and also began featuring non-service personnel (mostly pretty young girls and disgruntled oldsters) who regarded soldiers, sailors and marines as predatory beasts who couldn't be trusted any farther than they could be thrown.

But after Pearl Harbor the pendulum swung back, and the Hollywood version of military-civilian relationships returned to their previous level of mutual respect and tolerance. One compelling reason for this was the widespread sentiment that "we're all in this together," much more so than in 1918. Some modern-day social historians have theorized that the U.S. government really didn't *have* to impose its draconian rationing system on such goods as gasoline, rubber, coffee, sugar and meat; nor were all those scrap-iron and paper drives entirely necessary. But whether justified or not, such things were essential to sustaining civilian morale, convincing the folks at home that their contributions and sacrifices to the war effort were as vital and indispensible as those made by the fighting forces. (Of course, quite a few civilians balked at "pitching in," preferring to circumvent governmental strictures via hoarding rationed items and trafficking with the black market, but such people were *never* shown in a sympathetic light on the movie screen during World War II — certainly not in the same way that bootleggers and their customers were given a pass in Prohibition-era films.)

Another reason that the relationship between civilians and the military was generally depicted as harmonious was because such organizations as the Office of War Information and the Bureau of Censorship strongly advised against any negative depiction. While participation with both of these organizations was voluntary and there were few serious repurcussions against studios who balked at following their suggestions, other government agencies could and did lower the boom if they saw something on-screen that they didn't like. A classic example of this sort of interference occurred during filming of the Laurel & Hardy vehicle *Air Raid Wardens* (MGM, 1943). Ideally, the film could have scored laughs by using Stan and Ollie's customary incompetence as a method of teaching actual air raid wardens how *not* to do their job, thereby improving their own performance. Alas, the on-set presence of a genuine civil defense representative as technical advisor discouraged this type of harmless nonsense. The representative insisted that Laurel & Hardy's best comedy material be deleted so as not to cast aspersions on the efficiency of his operation, resulting in a plethora of desultory setpieces which never live up to their potential. The government-vetted script also forces the boys to admit that they are hopeless failures, with Stan delivering a lachrymose monologue in which he says that Uncle Sam would be better served if he and Ollie weren't air raid wardens at all. To be sure, the film ends on a upbeat note as ex-wardens Laurel & Hardy foil a Nazi plan to blow up a magnesium plant, but the bitter aftertaste of "official" interference lingers long after the final fadeout.

Some films harked back to *Johanna Enlists* by dramatizing the romantic entanglements between cloistered small-town girls and love-starved servicemen. Many of these films danced delicately around the possibility that the boys' intentions may not have been entirely honorable, but by and large the soldiers and sailors seen on film were basically decent sorts, and the girls in their lives equally blameless. Warner Bros. 1944's cinematization of Josephine Bentham and Herschel Williams' 1942 Broadway hit *Janie* is a case in point. When impulsive teenager Janie Conway (Joyce Reynolds) falls for Dick Lawrence (Robert Hutton), a private stationed at a nearby Army base, she forgets all about the other boys in town. Taking advantage of her parents' absence, Janie throws a small party at her home for Dick and a few of their friends, but things get out of hand when several dozen more uniformed men swarm into *chez* Conway. The revelry gets so noisy that the cops and the MPs are summoned, and when the dust settles the house is littered with empty bottles, dirty dishes and upended furniture. Janie's newspaper-editor father (Edward Arnold) is appalled, having warned the community that permitting the establishment of an Army base would only lead to trouble — and most likely, to a passel of teenage girls *in* trouble. But as it turns out, none of the military personnel has taken undue advantage of the female partygoers, allowing Janie to preserve her reputation and prevent Dick from being tossed in the stockade with an emotional third-act speech in defense of the soldiers. Once Dick has departed for overseas duty, Janie's life returns to normal — until the Marines come marching down Main Street! The film version of *Janie* was hardly an accurate reflection of real life, but audiences in 1944 preferred to believe that it was — and besides, it was in Warners' best interest to curry favor with the Army by avoiding any actual hanky-panky between Janie and Dick.

In stark contrast, Paramount's tyro producer-director-writer Preston Sturges had both the guts and the clout to suggest that something salacious might be lurking beneath the veneer of World War II respectability. Casting the innocence of *Janie* to the four winds, Sturges came up with the screamingly funny *The Miracle of Morgan's Creek* (Paramount, 1944), which dared to set forth on screen what audiences had known all along: The traditional moral values of small-town life would relax to the point of narcolepsy the moment that an Army camp moved into the neighborhood. As timid 4-F Norval Jones (Eddie Bracken) suffers in quiet desperation, his vivacious sweetheart Trudy Kockenlocker (Betty Hutton) spends her nights out on the town with practically every G.I. she meets—much to the dismay of her police-chief father (William Demarest), who has threatened lethal consequences to any man brazen enough to take advantage of his daughter. After one particularly boisterous *soiree*, Trudy awakens with a monster hangover and vague memories of having gone through a wedding ceremony with a soldier named Ratskywatsky or something. A few months later, Trudy discovers that she's pregnant, a fact she must hide from her dad because she has no evidence of her marriage — if indeed such a marriage took place. The hysterical heroine prevails upon true-blue Norval Jones to see her through this crisis, the upshot being that Officer Kockenlocker (I *could* have commented on that censor-baiting surname, but every other film historian has beaten me to it) is convinced that poor Norval has defiled his daughter. The hero's disgrace miraculously turns to triumph when Trudy becomes the world's first "octo-mom," the multiple birth transforming her into a national heroine and compelling the state's genially corrupt governor (Brian Donlevy) to annul her marriage to Ratskywatsky-or-something and cook the books to make Norval the "legitimate" daddy. So overwhelming was the impact of *Miracle of Morgan's Creek* that critic James Agee was famously moved to comment, "The Hays Office has either been hypnotized into a liberality for which it should be thanked, or it has been raped in its sleep."

Another home-front comedy, *Kiss and Tell* (Columbia, 1945), contains elements from both *Janie* and *Miracle of Morgan's Creek*, though in fact the property was in development at virtually the same time as those two films, having been derived from playwright F. Hugh Herbert's mildly risqué 1943 Broadway success. In one of her best grown-up roles, 17-year-old Shirley Temple plays flirtatious teenager Corliss Archer, a character who would enjoy a vigorous afterlife as a sitcom heroine on radio and television (incredibly, 27-year-old Rita Hayworth had been Columbia's first choice for the movie version of *Kiss and Tell*). Corliss' popularity with the locally-stationed GIs is established at the very beginning at the film, when on the advice of her best friend Mildred Pringle (Virginia Welles) she sets up a kissing booth at a USO bazaar. In the tradition of *Janie*'s Mr. Conway, Corliss' mother (Katherine Alexander) is outraged by her daughter's public displays of affection, accusing Mildred of "corrupting" the girl. This ignites a feud between the Pringle and Archer families, forcing Mildred to marry her Air Force officer sweetheart, Corliss' brother Lenny (Scott Elliott), in secret. Corliss agrees not to tell her parents about the marriage, which becomes a difficult assignment several months down the line when Mildred has a baby. In a variation of the *Morgan's Creek* situation, Corliss covers for Mildred by allowing everyone to

No one embodied the attitude of the "typical" middle-aged civilian better than Robert Benchley during the World War II years. Here he is seen in a rare uniformed role in **Kiss and Tell** (Columbia, 1945); he would remain in civvies for such other wartime comedies as **Janie** and **Snafu**, also covered in this chapter.

assume that the baby is hers—and that nonplussed Army private Jimmy Earhardt (Scott McKay) is the father. By the time this one is straightened out, the baby is practically ready for nursery school.

Miracle of Morgan's Creek and *Kiss and Tell* have sometimes been described as screwball comedies because they contain two essential screwball elements, deception and mistaken identity. These elements also fueled the many comedies in which hero and heroine carry on a pen-pal romance, with one of the correspondents misleading the other by pretending to be someone else and/or enclosing a photograph of a more attractive friend or relative. Two service-related comedies were cut from this familiar pattern: *A Letter for Evie* (MGM, 1946) and *Dear Ruth* (Paramount, 1947), the latter adapted from the long-running Broadway play by Norman Krasna, who based three of the main characters on his friend Groucho Marx, Groucho's first wife Ruth, and their daughter Miriam (the screenplay was written by another Marx crony, Arthur Sheekman). In *Letter for Evie*, bashful GI John McPherson (Hume Cronyn) develops a long-distance crush on clothes-factory employee Evie O'Connor (Marsha Hunt) after reading an affectionate letter that Evie has slipped into a size 16½ shirt. Convinced that a girl like Evie would never be interested in an undersized wimp like himself, John pretends to be his brawny soldier pal Wolf Larson (John Carroll), so named because of his reputation as a lady-killer. John sends Evie a picture of Wolf to sustain her interest — and what happens next is, paradoxically, both totally predictable and completely out of left field (and *too* good a plot convolution to give away here). In *Dear Ruth*, it is teenager Miriam Wilkins (Mona Freeman) who pulls off the deception, pretending to be her older sister Ruth (played by Broadway's original Corliss Archer, Joan Caulfield) while writing passionate letters to sailor William Seacroft (William Holden)—never dreaming that Seacroft would one day show up at the Wilkins' doorstep to meet his sweethheart in the flesh. The resolution of *Dear Ruth* is more conventional than that of *A Letter for Evie*, but equally as mirth-provoking. (And just to satisfy your curiosity, the "Groucho" character is Miriam and Ruth's father Harry Wilkins, played in the film by *Janie*'s Edward Arnold.)

Another durable service-comedy cliché involved the trials and tribulations attending military marriages. The most frequent plot device relied upon what the Latins called *coitus interruptus*—the marriage that cannot be consummated or is otherwise interfered with by the husband's military obligations. The frustration of the Army or Navy wife left home alone while hubby is off defending Democracy was good for laughs throughout the war years and beyond. A prime specimen of this subgenre is the obscure 1945 Monogram comedy *G.I. Honeymoon*, starring Gale Storm as the new bride of Army officer Peter Cookson. In his classic tome on B-movies, Don Miller has recounted the film's highlight: "One of those rare moments of perfect comic timing occurs as Miss Storm, seductively attired in a revealing negligée, awaits Cookson's return to their apartment from duty. She opens the door to behold him, out on his feet, grimy and in full field uniform — he delivers the line 'Hello, honey ... I just got back from a thirty-seven mile hike,' while falling to the floor."

Variations on the matrimonial angle include the "marry in haste — repent in leisure" theme, focusing on the all-too-true wartime dilemma of young couples who impulsively wed just before the husband is shipped overseas, without ever truly getting to know one another — and subsequently suffering buyer's remorse when they are reunited. Most often treated seriously (as in MGM's 1944 Lana Turner starrer *Marriage Is a Private Affair,* or the Dana Andrews-Virginia Mayo relationship in Goldwyn's 1946 *The Best Years of Our Lives*), this situation was given a farcical going-over in *The Impatient Years* (Columbia, 1944), told in flashback as war bride Jean Arthur and her soldier husband Lee Bowman stand before a divorce-court judge. The singular comic brilliance of Jean Arthur helps guide this one over its many rough spots, particularly a protracted sequence in which a stupid hotel clerk is convinced that Bowman has poisoned his wife!

Another favorite plot device involves the well-meaning civilian wife who causes her military husband embarrassment with her non-regulation behavior. A good postwar example of this brand of humor can be found in *It Started with a Kiss* (MGM, 1959), in which newlywed model Debbie

Reynolds shows up in Spain for a reunion with her husband, Air Force sergeant Glenn Ford. Debbie has already informed Glenn that he's in for a "big surprise," and naturally he assumes that she's pregnant. Instead, Debbie brings forth a flaming red Lincoln Futura prototype car that her husband has won in a charity raffle. The complications arising from the presence of both his flighty young bride and his flashy new car end up getting Ford in deep doo-doo with commanding officer Fred Clark. (That troublesome bubble-topped Futura would later be painted black and recycled as the Batmobile on the 1960s TV series *Batman*.)

In Warner Bros.' 1966 sex farce *Not with My Wife, You Don't*, the above-mentioned formula was flipped. This time it is Virna Lisi, the wife of Air Force colonel Tony Curtis, who suffers embarrassment at the hands of her husband — especially near the end of the picture, when Curtis goes AWOL from an Arctic survival course and shows up in Rome disguised as a middle–Eastern potentate. Perhaps an explanation is in order. It seems that while stationed in Korea in 1952, the cagey Curtis was able to woo Virna away from rival USAF officer George C. Scott by leading her to believe that Scott had been killed in action. Fourteen years of wedded bliss later, Scott suddenly reappears, proof incarnate that reports of his death were slightly exaggerated. In order to have a clear field with with his old flame Virna, Scott draws upon his influence with the Pentagon and orders that Curtis be bundled off to the North Pole. Once everything is straightened out, the unflappable heroine declares that she still loves Curtis—though she encourages Scott to pay her a visit once in a while and say hello to her new twin sons, who don't look much like twins.

Returning to the war years, another marriage-related theme explored by filmmakers was the culture shock suffered by GI brides when they were yanked out of their comfortably spacious family surroundings and penned up in cramped, inadequate housing facilities in order to be near their husbands. Otto Preminger's *In the Meantime, Darling* (20th Century–Fox, 1945) finds spoiled rich girl Jeanne Crain causing friction for all concerned — especially her husband — when she moves into a boarding house crowded with several other Army wives. While the drama in Preminger's film outweighs the comedy, Columbia's *Over 21* (1945) is played almost entirely for laughs, lapsing into seriousness only in the final reel.

Over 21 was adapted from the Broadway play by actress Ruth Gordon, who based a goodly portion of the story on the experiences of her writer-director husband Garson Kanin, who as an Army lieutenant during World War II was assigned to the Office of Strategic Services. Accustomed to the lavishness of his New York apartment, the urbane Mr. Kanin had quite a time adjusting to his spartan military digs. Ruth Gordon felt that this situation might be even funnier on-stage if an officer's wife, likewise a Broadway sophisticate, would have to adjust to such mean surroundings as well. Gordon also drew from military anecdotes related by her playwright friend Thornton Wilder; then in his mid-'40s, the Pulitzer Prize-winning Wilder sweated and strained to qualify for an officer's commission, experiencing great difficulty absorbing technical information that the much-younger candidates had no trouble memorizing.

Gordon cast herself as star of the 1944 theatrical version of *Over 21*, playing glamorous novelist Paula Wharton, a character inspired by celebrated wit Dorothy Parker. Paula's husband Max is a successful New York newspaper editor who gives up his job for the duration to join the Army and apply for OCS, feeling that he can better write about the war by actually experiencing it. Max's "desertion" infuriates his ulcerated publisher Robert Drexel Gow (a character patterned after real-life print mogul Herbert Bayard Swope), who vows to keep after Max to fulfill his editorial duties despite his relocation. Though she herself is under pressure to finish a screenplay for a David O. Selznick-like movie producer, Paula elects to follow Max to his military base, setting up housekeeping in a dismal little bungalow where none of the utilities work properly. While the indefatigably upbeat Paula manages to make the best of things, her middle-aged husband agonizes over retaining the mass of military minutiae necessary to earn his commission. When Gow tries to strong-arm Max into writing a series of flag-waving editorials from his vantage point in camp, Paula secretly begins composing the editorials herself, signing Max's name. This deception leads to unexpected complications and consequences, all happily resolved in time for the stage manager to signal the final curtain.

Though Ruth Gordon's play was a typically insubstantial star vehicle, the actress managed to land the powerful Max Gordon (no relation) as producer. Max in turn engaged playwright George S. Kaufman as both director and unofficial script doctor, in hopes of glossing over the play's many faults. Kaufman's principal contribution was a running gag involving the absurd physical contortions that Paula Wharton had to undergo to perform such picayune tasks as closing a screen door or turning off the lights in her shabby bungalow. This elegant slapstickery was successfully carried over to the screen version of *Over 21*, which stars Irene Dunne as Paula, Alexander Knox as Max and Charles Coburn as Gow (the once-important character of the Selnickesque producer was reduced to a bit part and played by an uncredited Pierre Watkin). At the time, Dunne was criticized for patterning her performance on Ruth Gordon's interpretation of Paula, but this is not readily obvious to modern-day viewers who are more familiar with Gordon's crazy-old-coot portrayals in such films as *Rosemary's Baby* and *Harold and Maude*. Alexander Knox had just come off the expensive biopic *Wilson*, so it was not surprising that critics like James Agee quipped that he was merely resuming his imitation of President Woodrow Wilson in the role of Max. This was unfair to Knox, who does a marvelously understated job extracting humor from the plight of a 39-year-old Manhattanite struggling to keep apace both physically and intellectually with the uniformed whippersnappers surrounding him. In his final scene, Knox manages the near-miraculous feat of bringing both sincerity and credibility to a pretentiously pontificating speech (tacked on by screenwriter Sidney Buchman, Columbia's resident liberal voice) in which he compares the establishment of the United Nations to the baking of an apple pie.

The hero and heroine of *Over 21* do their best to adapt themselves to their surroundings; in contrast, the Naval-officer protagonist of *The Skipper Surprised His Wife* (MGM, 1950) labors mightily to make his surroundings adapt to him. The film was based on a 1948 magazine article written by Navy commander William J. Lederer and inspired by his efforts to run his home in a truly "ship-shape" manner, rigidly adhering to maritime procedure and discipline within a civilian milieu. This was nothing out of the ordinary for Bill Lederer, whose friends and intimates knew him as a bit of an eccentric given to such whimsies as keeping pet goats in his house to save on milk prices. Lederer's other works include the humorous wartime novel *Ensign O'Toole and Me*, later adapted as a 1962 TV sitcom starring Dean Jones. And on a more somber note, Lederer wrote or cowrote several books that were highly critical of American foreign policy, most memorably *The Ugly American*.

During pre-production of *The Skipper Surprised His Wife*, Vincente Minnelli was scheduled to direct and Van Heflin was slated to star. By the time the film got under way, Elliott Nugent was calling the directorial shots and Heflin had been replaced by Robert Walker, doing a complete about-face from his irreverent "Private Hargrove" persona as Cmdr. William "Bill" Lattimer. After several months overseas, Lattimer returns to his home town of Coronado, California, to begin a new sonar study program. No sooner has Bill settled in than his wife Daphne (Joan Leslie) slips on one of her sons' roller skates and breaks her ankle. With Daphne laid up indefinitely, Bill takes charge of the domestic chores, quickly finding himself exhausted and unable to concentrate on his sonar classes due to a complete lack of organization in his house, to say nothing of a total absence of cooperation from his two youngsters. To remedy this, the baby-faced martinet imposes Navy-style rules and regulations in his domicile, installing an intercom system and automatic labor-saving devices for utmost efficiency. While Bill's methods make him quite popular with his fellow husbands and something of local celebrity, Daphne is unable to live up to her husband's exacting standards and threatens to walk out on him. Only the intervention of the Lattimer family doctor convinces Bill to lighten up and defer all domestic duties to Daphne, despite her pronounced aversion to "The Navy Way." (It would be churlish to observe here that author William Lederer ended up being married and divorced twice. If you want a Hollywood ending, go to Hollywood.)

Sophisticated novelist Irene Dunne (standing) improvises a truly intimate dinner party in the cramped living quarters of her officer-candidate husband Alexander Knox (seated at right, in uniform) in *Over 21* (Columbia, 1945). Others in the gathering include (from left) Lee Patrick, Cora Witherspoon, Charles Coburn (standing next to Dunne) and Charles Evans (back to camera).

Additional laughs were wrung from a situation that was generally treated dramatically in such films as *The Best Years of Our Lives* and *Til the End of Time*: The difficulties encountered by returning GIs in readjusting to civilian life. This problem was exacerbated to the limits of its comic possibilities in Columbia's 1945 film version of Louis Solomon and Harold Buchman's 1944 Broadway comedy *Snafu*. The plot revolves around 15-year-old runaway Ronald Stevens, who lies about his age and enlists in the Army. When they spot their son in a newsreel, Ronald's parents Madge and Ben contact the War Department and demand he be returned home. But now that he's had a taste of adult life (and as a sergeant to boot), Ronald finds his civilian surroundings dull, confining and childish. Adding to Ronald's plight is the unexpected arrival of his worldly solider buddy Danny Baker, armed with all sorts of sensational stories about Ronald's wartime exploits which drive his parents into a state of near-apoplexy. Misunderstandings fomented by journalism student Laura Jessup, who mistakes Danny for Ronald, lead to an embarrassing situation in a girl's dormitory and a severe strain on Ronald's relationship with his next-door sweetheart Kate Hereford. The third-act intervention of Ronald's former colonel reveals that everyone has misjudged the boy, and that his overseas experiences have not jaded him to the point of depravity.

Like the aforementioned *Kiss and Tell*, the Broadway version of *Snafu* had been produced by George Abbott, who wangled a Columbia Pictures contract that allowed him full creative control over both film versions, with no interference from Columbia chieftan Harry Cohn. This may explain why the two pictures look like photographed stage plays, with little effort to "open up" the action: Even the exteriors are wholly artificial, while certain devices that were frankly more

The Skipper Surprised His Wife (MGM, 1950): Naval officer Robert Walker (standing) delivers a ladies' club lecture about running a "tight ship" in his own home. Kathryn Card is the lady holding the microphone; seated on either side of Walker at the daïs are Spring Byington and Jan Sterling.

effective on stage than on film (notably, in the case of *Snafu*, the presence of one character who is heard but never seen) are transferred intact. This isn't an altogether bad thing: despite the expected excision of "racy" dialogue, the movie version of *Snafu* manages to save some of the better lines from the theatrical original, notably the heroine's defense of the beleaguered teenage hero: "How'd you feel if right in the middle of a battle, the CO sends for you and says 'your mother wants you?'" But the filmization of *Kiss and Tell* has the advantage cinematically, with veteran Hollywoodite Richard Wallace in the director's chair. *Snafu*'s director Jack Moss, formerly associated with Orson Welles' Mercury Theater (he'd also been drafted to play the voluminous villain in Welles' 1942 film production *Journey Into Fear*), apparently had no grasp of movie technique, and this deficiency was all too glaring on screen. When Harry Cohn complained to George Abbott that Moss was ruining the picture, Abbott replied flippantly, "Well, it's only money." Years later in his autobiography the producer admitted, "I had made a complete fool of myself. The picture was a mess, Cohn was right, and I had behaved inexcusably."

Well, *Snafu* isn't a *total* mess, and credit for that must be given the wonderful ensemble cast. In one of his last screen appearances before his death, humorist Robert Benchley (who'd previously appeared in both *Janie* and *Kiss and Tell*) delivers perhaps the finest and warmest performance of his acting career as Ronald Stevens' befuddled father, while comedienne Barbara Jo Allen — billed onscreen as Vera Vague, a scatterbrain character she'd created for radio — drops her traditional movie zaniness to provide an equally effective portrayal of Ronald's mom (Allen was a last-minute replacement for Mary Astor). Admirably carrying his weight in the difficult central role of Ronald is Conrad Janis, then only 17 years old and galaxies removed from his best-known characterization as Pam Dawber's middle-aged dad on TV's *Mork and Mindy* (to say nothing of his wide renown in musical circles as a brilliant jazz trombonist). Janis Wilson, who'd played Paul Henreid's troubled daughter in *Now Voyager* and would go on to portray Barbara Stanwyck as a child in *The Strange Love of Martha Ivers*, enjoys one of her meatiest screen assignments as Ronald's hometown girl Kate; and recreating her stage role as the hero's Aunt Emily is silent-screen star Enid Markey, here making a movie comeback that would prolong her career well into the 1960s.

Snafu ran into difficulty upon its original release thanks to its acronymic title, which Columbia insisted was comprised of the initials for "Situation Normal, All Fouled Up" but was already notorious as a thinly-veiled obscenity (see the notes on the *Private Snafu* cartoons in **Chapter 21** for further details). Though the studio tried to work around potential censorship problems with such advertising tags as "Even spelled backwards it's fun for U FANS!" in some communities the local bluenoses insisted that the title not be posted on movie marquees. A few newspapers refused to list the picture by name, resorting to the standard subterfuge of advising readers to phone the local theater for full information. Those movie patrons who were lured into the theater on the expectation that they would be indulging in some sort of forbidden delight were sorely disappointed by the vanilla-flavored Hollywood confection that greeted them.

Another plot device that has done yeoman movie duty concerns the military widow whose husband has died in the service of his country, and who is understandably wary of embarking on a new romance with a man in uniform for fear that she'll eventually lose him as well. This traditionally dramatic device served as the foundation for the frothy 1963 MGM production *A Ticklish Affair*. The property was based on Barbara Luther's short story "Moon Walk," first published in the February 1962 edition of *Ladies Home Journal*. The title had nothing to do with either Neil Armstrong or Michael Jackson. Instead, it referred to an unusual game played by the youngest son of a Navy widow, whose airline-pilot brother brought large weather balloons home from his flights, filled them with helium, attached them to a harness around his nephew's waist and allowed the youngster to float several feet above the ground in the safety of his backyard. The central character of "Moon Walk" was the high-tripping kid's mom, who lived in Point Loma, Calfornia, just across the channel from the North Island Naval Air Station. Courted by most of the unattached Navy pilots in the vicinity, the widowed mom stubbornly spurned their attentions, still not sufficiently recovered from the death of her aviator husband.

The story was optioned by MGM producer Joe Pasternak, a Hungarian emigré who had built his Hollywood reputation on a string of popular musicals starring such teenage sopranos as Deanna Durbin and Jane Powell. Though frequently written off as corny and old-fashioned by critics of the 1960s, Pasternak nonetheless continued posting profits for MGM with such films as *Where the Boys Are* and *Please Don't Eat the Daisies*, the latter film attracting adult moviegoers with its sexual implications while also appealing to youngsters with its plethora of child actors and family-oriented comedy situations. The producer sensed the same potential in "Moon Walk" and set the wheels in motion for its production, first securing cooperation from the U.S. Navy by contacting that service branch's busiest Hollywood technical advisor and liason man, former child star Frank Coghlan Jr. By 1963 Coghlan had risen to the rank of lieutenant commander, much respected by both his superior officers and the Hollywood elite for his tireless efforts to present the Navy in the best and most positive light on screen, and his diplomacy in obtaining full Naval cooperation for movie production units. Coghlan agreed with Pasternak that "Moon Walk" was a delightful story that could do no harm to the Navy's public image, and arranged for the producer to film exterior scenes at the Naval Air Station near San Diego and a few location shots on a genuine aircraft carrier.

Directed by George Sidney from a screenplay by Ruth Brooks Flippen, "Moon Walk" reached the screen under the title *A Ticklish Affair*. Shirley Jones stars as fetching young widow Amy Martin, with Gig Young as Navy commander Key Wheedon, who is brought into the story when he and an armed boarding party show up at Amy's house to investigate the distress signals emantaing from an upstairs window. It turns out that the S-O-S's are being transmitted by Amy's youngest son Grover (played by Peter Robbins, who later voiced the title character in *A Charlie Brown Christmas*), using an old blinker light given to him by his Uncle Cy (Red Buttons), a commercial pilot. Once this is straightened out, Wheedon begins to squire Amy, who though she enjoys Key's company turns down his proposal of marriage. Her reluctance is not just because of her husband's death: Having spent her childhood as a "Navy brat," she doesn't want her three sons to grow up being dragged from one remote base to another. Hoping to bring Amy and Key together with a manufactured crisis, little Grover prevails on Uncle Cy to tether him to a bunch of helium-filled balloons for a Moon Walk to end all Moon Walks — whereupon the kid cuts the rope holding him to the ground. The climax finds Grover drifting high above the California coastline, with both the Navy and the Coast Guard mobilized into action to rescue the airborne youngster. It is Key Wheedon who manages to snatch Alex from the clouds by commandeering a Navy blimp — and with this act of selfless courage fresh in her mind, what choice does Amy have but to say "Yes!" the next time Key pops the question? Despite an overreliance upon cutesy background music, this thrilling finale makes up for the pokier stretches of *A Ticklish Affair*, which in sum total confirms the critical consensus that producer Joe Pasternak was a few years past his prime.

Amidst the many formula-driven "home front" comedies discussed in this chapter, at least one picture is in a class by itself. *When Willie Comes Marching Home* (20th Century-Fox 1950) was inspired by the real-life experiences of screenwriter Sy Gomberg, who during World War II served with the Air Force Motion Picture Unit in Hollywood. On one particular Friday morning, Gomberg left home for the airport and flew directly to the South Pacific, was strafed by a Japanese plane over the weekend, and came back to the safety of his own home by Monday. He refashioned this dizzying sequence of events into a short story for *Collier's* magazine, which was purchased by 20th Century-Fox after the war and adapted for the screen by Richard Sale and Mary Ann Loos (though only Sale received screen credit).

Interviewed years later by Ronald L. Davis, Loos recalled that the film version — known variously as *Rise and Shine, Front and Center* and *When Leo Comes Marching Home* before the final title was chosen — was planned as a medium-budget comedy and assigned to director John Ford as punishment for his refusal to work on the Darryl F. Zanuck production *Pinky*. Though not keen on doing a comedy at this point in his career, Ford acquiesced, requesting permission to direct the Dan Dailey musical western *A Ticket to Tomahawk*. But Zanuck wasn't about to accommodate the recalcitrant Ford, assigning *Tomahawk* to another director and ordering "Pappy" to make *When Willie Comes Marching Home* or pay the penalty. There was some compensation in that both films starred Dan Dailey, whom Ford admired for his song-and-dance skills. The director intended to use Dailey's talents to peak advantage by refashioning *Willie* as a musical, but all that remains of this intriguing concept is an outtake of a dance number involving Dailey and leading lady Colleen Townsend — the only scene of its kind ever directed by John Ford. (Incidentally, Townsend was a replacement for actress June Haver, who like Ford had balked at participating in the film, but who unlike the director was willing to go on suspension.)

At base, *When Willie Comes Marching Home* is a satire of homegrown wartime patriotism, the obtuseness of small-town civilians who have no idea what it's like to be in uniform, and the anal stick-to-the-program mindset of military authorities. Upon hearing about the Pearl Harbor attack, young collegiate Willie Kluggs (Dailey) is the first citizen of Punxatawney, West Virginia, to sign up for military service. After a huge sendoff from his fellow townsfolk and a lingering farewell kiss from his girlfriend Marge (Townsend), Willie is chagrined to discover that he has been assigned as a gunnery instructor at the army base located in his home town of Puxatawney. Itching for overseas duty, Willie makes numerous requests for a transfer but is repeatedly turned down, leading his friends and family to assume that he is just a malingerer who really doesn't want to get into the shooting war. Months of enduring the scornful glances of people who'd previously lauded him as a hero follow before Willie is allowed to take the place of an aerial gunner

When Willie Comes Marching Home (20th Century–Fox, 1950): Dan Dailey (front, center) prepares to begin training for active war duty, little imagining that he'll be stationed in his own home town.

who has fallen ill. While flying to his new assignment, Willie is forced to bail out over France, where he is rescued by gorgeous resistance fighter Yvonne (Corinne Calvet) and her compatriots. Before long he has embarked on a reconnaissance mission to pinpoint the location of several Nazi rocket emplacements. Escaping to his own lines and reporting this vital information to his superiors, Willie is sworn to secrecy lest the Germans be tipped off. Thereupon he is flown right back to Punxatawney, a scant four days after his departure. Unable to tell anyone what has happened, our hero must continue to suffer the slings and arrows of doubt and derision from his cloddish neighbors until he is decorated for his actions by the President himself.

Many reviewers have compared *When Willie Comes Marching Home* to Preston Sturges' *Hail the Conquering Hero*, which offers a reversal of Willie's situation by featuring a 4-F protagonist who is mistaken for a war hero by his worshipful fellow citizens and can't persuade anyone that he is nothing of the sort. (Coincidentally, Sturges "regular" William Demarest appears in both films.) This has given rise to the opinion of many *auteur* theorists, notably Andrew Sarris, that *Willie* would have been a better and funnier film had it been directed by Sturges and invested with his distinct satirical style. Instead, John Ford handles the material in a sour, mean-spirited fashion, with both the small-town characters and the military authorities coming off as clueless, insensitive knuckleheads. Possibly this was because Ford was a dyed-in-the-wool Navy man with an inbred contempt for the Army, but more likely it was because the cantankerous old poop didn't want to make the picture in the first place.

Though it scored points for uniqueness, *When Willie Comes Marching Home* failed to live up to its expectations as either a comedy or a box-office attraction. Audiences promised a rollicking laughfest were disappointed by its long arid stretches of seriousness, while Ford cultists were let down by the conspicuous absence of the director's "signature" (our only clue that this is a John Ford picture is the presence in the cast of several of the director's pet supporting players, including Mae Marsh and Jack Pennick). The film's indifferent reception led Fox to scuttle its plans to use *Willie* as the vanguard of a new series of program pictures starring Dan Dailey as the same character.

In 1958, 20th Century–Fox offered another satirical slant on small-town attitudes and military bombast from another prestigious filmmaker. Directed by Leo McCarey and based on the novel by Max Shulman, *Rally 'Round the Flag, Boys!* was set in the post–World War II, post–Korea era, accurately pinpointing the chill that inevitably sets in between civilians and the military whenever there is no common cause to unite the two factions. The plot is motivated by the Army's decision to build a missile base in the tiny New England town of Putnam's Landing. The locals are dead set against the establishment of the base for two reasons: They are staunchly opposed to any sort of change in their Rockwellian lifestyle, and they are convinced that the influx of young soldiers will pose a dire threat to the virtue of every teenage girl within a radius of twenty miles. In the original novel, this cloistered attitude was but one of many targets at which Max Shulman took satirical aim. Others included the modern sexual mores of status-seeking suburbanites and harried commuters; the abundance of pointless civic activities and self-serving "good works" indulged in by bored housewives; the frustrations of being a 1950s teenager trapped in an adult world informed by hopelessly outdated attitudes and restrictions; the culture shock experienced by city-bred outsiders (especially those with foreign-sounding names or "radical" ideas) when confronted with the clannishness and closed minds of small-town society; and the overbearing demeanor and deliberately confusing doublespeak of contemptuous military officials when dealing with the civilian population.

The first writer hired to work on the script for *Rally 'Round the Flag, Boys!* was like Max Shulman a seasoned satirist: George Axelrod, author of the Madison-avenue lampoon *Will Success Spoil Rock Hunter?* In a later interview with Patrick McGilligan, Axelrod admitted, "*Rally 'Round* was a very hard book to beat, and I was never able to beat it, and neither was anybody else." The writer had come up with the concept of staging the film in a manner of a "Pete Smith Specialty" short subject, with the action playing out more or less in silence while an offscreen narrator — "somebody like Fred Allen" — provided dry and sarcastic commentary. This, argued Axelrod, was quite in keeping with the tone of the novel: "It would work very well that way, I thought, and Leo [McCarey] liked that approach." Unfortunately, Fox executive producer Buddy Adler didn't understand or appreciate Axelrod's concept and insisted upon a more traditional treatment. "Leo eventually had to go the other way. I thought the final script had nothing to do with what I wrote, so I took my name off."

McCarey brought in his old friend Claude Binyon to help rewrite the film. Between them, the two men selected what they felt were the novel's highlights, placing heavy emphasis on a plot thread involving the sexual dalliances of neglected husband Harry Bannister, who while his wife Gracie is preoccupied with leading a group of Putnam's Landing residents in opposing the missile base, briefly takes up with seductive "grass widow" Angela Hoffa. (In the book, this extramarital affair is consummated; in the movie, it isn't, but comes awfully close.) Other carryovers from the novel include the simmering feud between a bunch of countrified soldiers, among them an Elvis-type troubadour named Opie Dalrymple, and the local teenage boys headed by Grady Metcalf, who in a risible effort to pass themselves off as Rebels Without a Cause have adopted the "J.D." mannerisms of Marlon Brando in *The Wild One.* The major bone of contention between Opie and Grady is the town's resident heartbreaker, a 15-year-old cutie with the gloriously Shulmanesque moniker of Comfort Goodpasture. Another of the novel's characters who made the cut in the screenplay is the obnoxiously undiplomatic Major Hoxie, whose open hostility towards the civilian "feather merchants" runs counter to the Army's frantic efforts to convince the community that the missile site is for their own good. The animosity between soldiers and civilians comes to a head during a disastrous Fourth of July pageant, with the locals and the military personnel waging open warfare while performing in a re-enactment of the founding of Putnam's Landing. McCarey and Binyon change the theme of the pageant to the arrival of the Mayflower, but the end result — a slapstick rumble between "Pilgrims" (Opie and the soldiers) and "Indians" (Grady and his gang) — remains the same.

One of the novel's more entertaining subplots involves the romance between two new arrivals in town: Guido Di Maggio, the Army PR man who accepts the challenge of winning over the local populace as a means of avoiding overseas duty; and elementary-school teacher Maggie Larkin, a virginal "progressive" who nearly destroys her academic career before it begins by delivering a lecture on sex (with illustrations!) to a class of second-graders. The decision by McCarey and Binyon to eliminate the role of Maggie Larkin and combine the characters of Guido Di Maggio and Harry Bannister (who is called back to active Naval duty for this purpose) precluded the studio's original plan to cast Frank Sinatra as Guido and Deborah Kerr as Maggie in the film version of *Rally 'Round the Flag, Boys!* Several other high-profile actors were proposed and abandoned before Fox decided upon Paul Newman and Joanne Woodward as Harry and Gracie Bannister, Joan Collins as the vampish Angela Hoffa and Jack Carson as Captain Hoxie. Among the younger and less renowned members of the cast were Tuesday Weld as the fickle Comfort Goodpasture and Dwayne Hickman as Brando wannabe Grady Metcalf. Max Shulman was so impressed by both of these youngsters that he arranged to have them starred in another of his projects, the TV sitcom *Dobie Gillis.*

In discussing director Leo McCarey, George Axelrod chose his words carefully: "Leo was a kind of genius, although I caught him at the end of his career." The film's star Paul Newman was less guarded, carping in later years over having been forced to work with a director "in his dotage." It must be admitted that McCarey had seen better days by the time he made *Rally 'Round the Flag, Boys!*; it must also be admitted that he didn't receive much help from Paul Newman, who as demonstrated in such films as *The Secret War of Harry Frigg* (see **Chapter 15**) could never be accused of possessing a light comic touch. As observed by Lawrence J. Quirk in *The Films of Paul Newman,* "He tended to be sardonic when he should have been fey; he would use his entire body, complete with heavy-handed gestures and mannerisms, trying several shades too hard for laughs when a flick of the eyebrow or the gentlest of double-takes would have done the trick." Newman's leaden performance, coupled with McCarey's flabby direction, effectively blunts the edge of Max Shulman's satire. The one moment where Newman shines is the 4th of July sequence, as he steadfastly remains perched on the mast of the fascimile *Mayflower* while the vessel sinks slowly into

Some things are well worth fighting for: Joan Collins as suburban mantrap Angela Hoffa in Leo McCarey's *Rally 'Round the Flag, Boys!* (20th Century–Fox, 1958).

Long Island Sound. As for McCarey, most of his "improvements" on the source material are seldom as funny as they should be, save for the climactic scene in which, while loading a lab monkey onto a guided missile, the bullheaded Captain Hoxie is accidentally launched into space himself. On the whole, *Rally 'Round the Flag, Boys!* is at its best when concentrating on the younger cast members. Especially delightful are the scenes featuring Tom Gilson as the guitar-strumming, amiably rakish Cpl. Opie Dalrymple — though the mechanics of the script and the infallibility of the Hollywood star system never allow Opie to emerge as the true hero of the story, which much to everyone's surprise is exactly what happens in the novel.

If military-civilian relationships came off as curdled in *Rally 'Round the Flag, Boys!*, they were positively rancid by the time *Suppose They Gave a War and Nobody Came?* was released by the Cinerama Corporation in 1970. The title, based on an anonymous graffiti message first reported in the mid–1960s, seems calculated to suggest that the film was one of the several anti-war screeds (*Catch-22, MASH*) from the same period. The producers encouraged audiences to assume that the film bore a pacifistic, anti–Vietnam message by incorporating a "peace" sign in the poster art. To put it as nicely as possible, this ad campaign was a bald-faced lie. *Suppose They Gave a War and Nobody Came?* is one of the most ardently *pro*-military comedies of the 1970s, and as such received the full cooperation of the U.S. Army, who allowed the production unit to film several exteriors at Fort Huachuca in Arizona. If the film is "anti" anything, it is stridently anti-civilian.

The story is set at a small-town Army base located in an unidentified Southern state; the film was supposed to have taken place in Mississippi, but all references to that state were removed in the release print, prompting screenwriter Don McGuire to grouse, "If it were *my* picture, I'd damn well call it Mississippi." Brian Keith plays Army community-relations officer Michael Nace, who is forced to grit his teeth and hold his gut whenever dealing with the hostile locals and the town's sanctimonious leaders. The civilians' attitude toward the Army has hit an all-time low, and vice versa. The hypocritically self-righteous town authorities have prohibited the GIs from enjoying themselves at such respectable functions as high school dances and church socials, forcing the boys to spend their off-hours at either the local brothel or the rundown tavern where faded belle Ramona (Suzanne Pleshette) tends bar. The GIs must also put up with bigoted town sheriff Harve (Ernest Borgnine), who revels in levying huge fines for the most minor of infractions. Another cross to bear is xenophobic billionaire Joe Davis (Tom Ewell), a self-anointed "General" in charge of his own private militia. If this doesn't exactly sound like surefire comic material, it may be because the producers were unable to decide whether the film would play better as a comedy or drama, a debate that raged on until shooting was nearly over.

Despite intense provocation, Michael Nace has promised himself not to lose his cool, partly because he feels a sense of security as a career soldier, but mostly because his commanding officer Col. Flanders (Don Ameche) wants to retire with a clean record and doesn't need any hassles with the civilians to bollix up his plans. Bemused by the self-contradictory standards of the "new" Army, Nace is the proverbial Warrior without a War, a status he shares with two other "lifers": Sgt. Gambroni (Tony Curtis), a womanizing hellraiser, and Sgt. Jones (Ivan Dixon), a don't-make-waves type who wants nothing more from life than to own a small gas station. When Jones is denied a bank loan on orders from the town's lard-butt mayor (Robert Emhardt), it is nearly the last straw for Nace; but the camel's back isn't completely broken until Sheriff Harve slaps Gambroni in jail with the intention of beating him black and blue while no one is looking (the producers obviously hadn't forgotten Ernie Borgnine's similar treatment of Frank Sinatra in *From Here to Eternity*). Blowing both his stack and his pension, Nace vows to "do the right thing" by stealing a Sherman tank and charging into town to force Gambroni's release. The resultant havoc has the positive effect of exposing the village elders ("General" Joe Davis in particular) for the useless poltroons that they are, and also bringing about the resignation of the quivering sheriff. As icing on the cake, Nace manages to settle a personal score with the insufferably snobbish Captain Myerson (Bradford Dillman), the film's only truly negative military caricature.

Though *Suppose They Gave a War and Nobody Came?* was completed well before *MASH*, the former film seems to be channeling the latter by featuring a "Radar O'Reilly"–style information wonk (John Fiedler) and an ineffectual clergyman (Grady Sutton) . Otherwise, and despite the aforementioned efforts by the producers to hoodwink the public into mistaking it for an anti-war picture, *Suppose They Gave a War ...* bears absolutely no resemblance to the Robert Altman picture, either in content or quality. The direction by Hy Averback is on a par with your average made-for-TV movie; one can almost see the commercial breaks. Don McGuire and Hal Captain's script likewise seems better suited to the small screen, its occasional profanities notwithstanding. Curiously, though the film seems to be building up to a climactic confrontation between the African American Sgt. Jones and the redneck Sheriff Harve, nothing of this sort ever occurs—possibly because the "friendly" banter between Jones and his pal Sgt.Gambroni is so laden with offensive racial epithets that anything Harve could have said or done to further denigrate Jones would have been superfluous.

Generally restricted to drive-ins and budget theaters during its initial release, *Suppose They Gave a War and Nobody Came?* would not appear to have been a likely candidate for a big-budget remake — yet remade it was (albeit unofficially) as the 1984 Lorimar/Universal release *Tank*. Once again, a veteran military officer finds himself locked in a war of wills with a vicious Southern lawman: In *Tank*, the antagonists are James Garner as newly retired Sgt. Major Zack Carey and G.D. Spradlin as Sheriff Cyrus Buelton. Once again, the breaking point comes when the sheriff jails one of the officer's closest associates; on this occasion, the stakes are raised when Buelton frames Carey's own son Billy (C. Thomas Howell) on a drug charge that will condemn the kid to a brutal prison farm. And once again, the military man takes matters in his own hands by commandeering a tank and threatening to blow the Sheriff's office to smithereens unless the prisoner is freed; *Tank* expands upon this by having Carey race his tank (which is his own personal property!) to the state line, with Buelton in hot pursuit and the combined news media of the United States covering the epic chase every inch of the way.

Location-filmed at Fort Benning, Georgia, *Tank* was originally given an R rating but managed to bargain down to a PG with a few minor cuts. Some observers wished that the producers had edited out even more footage, leaving only the opening and closing titles. There is some fun to be had in the film's depiction of a hamstrung military establishment that has no jurisdiction over a civilian who owns a Sherman tank; and it is mildly amusing when Zack Carey explains that he has purchased a tank because "it's very hard to shoot yourself while you're cleaning it." But these isolated chuckles aren't enough to compensate for the film's numerous flaws, notably its gaping logic holes. To cite one example among many: Since the media is obviously rooting for Zack Carey to make good his escape from Sheriff Buelton, why has no investigative reporter questioned the severity of the sentence imposed upon Carey's son — nor even the fact that the boy was sentenced in the first place?

Not even half as enjoyable as *Suppose They Gave a War and Nobody Came?* (and *that* wasn't much), *Tank* is worth noting only as a measure of how far the relationship between the military establishment and the "home front" had deteriorated by the mid–1980s. If Mary Pickford's *Johanna Enlists* had been filmed in 1984 instead of 1918, it's likely that sweet Johanna would have greeted the arrival of an artillery regiment with a shotgun in her dainty little hands and several rounds of ammunition in the pockets of her gingham apron.

18

No Laughing Matter?
*Comedies About the
Civil War and Vietnam*

Notwithstanding the abundance of war comedies turned out by Hollywood, there's nothing really funny about a war—and some wars are so tragic and wasteful that it's nearly impossible to imagine any filmmaker wanting to extract laughs from them. Even so, there have been a handful of film comedies inspired by the two most divisive and devastating armed conflicts in American history: The Civil War of 1861–1865, and the Vietnam War, which dragged on from the mid–1950s to the mid–1970s.

Let's get the standard argument about the Civil War out of the way here and now. You can invoke "state's rights," you can bring up the tariffs imposed by the North on the South, you can play all the usual games of denial and obfuscation, but you can't alter the fact that the slavery issue was the biggest and most compelling reason that the Confederate States of America declared war on the United States of America in April of 1861. Not that some historians haven't tried hard to downplay slavery, especially during those years in which it was expedient for the North to curry favor with the South (presidential elections, advertising campaigns and the like), or when certain Northern interests were trying to "justify" their own prejudicial treatment of the African American population ("So what if we practice housing discrimination and impose quotas? After all, that's not the *real* reason the Civil War was fought"). Conveniently ignoring 300 years of black oppression and the self-serving political compromises that led up to the bloodiest war in American history (over 620,000 dead), the mythology of the "Lost Southern Cause" and the "nobility" of the Antebellum plantation aristocracy was perpetuated in novels, plays and films for over eight decades after the war ended. This is one case in which history was written by the losers.

By the time the manufacturers of film comedy got around to the Civil War (approximately half a century after cessation of hostilities), it was considered prudent to merely show the war without dwelling upon the cause. So far as these comedies were concerned, once upon a time there was a four-year period of unpleasantness in which Americans wearing blue uniforms fought Americans wearing gray uniforms, and that's all we care to say on the subject. Only in one curious instance, noted later in this chapter, was the issue of Slave vs. Free states even touched upon. As for most of the Civil War comedies, the few black characters depicted on screen were little more than atmosphere players, on hand just to remind us that we're in the South.

The earliest known examples of cinematic Civil War humor were produced in 1913 by Mack Sennett's Keystone studio, intended as satires of the more serious essays on the conflict produced by D.W. Griffith and Thomas H. Ince. After turning out a number of "split-reel" comedies running about 500 feet each, Sennett released his first full one-reeler, *The Battle of Who Run*, on February 6, 1913. The audacity of using a title that poked fun at the Battle of Bull Run when it was within living memory—and when many survivors of *both* battles bearing that name were among the moviegoing public—was typical of Mack Sennett's nothing-sacred comic philosophy (Imagine someone in 1997 producing a slapstick farce about the invasion of Okinawa). *The Battle of Who Run* starred Sennett himself as a Union soldier, with Ford Sterling as his commanding officer, Fred Mace as his Confederate counterpart, and Mabel Normand as the girl he left behind. Sennett was able to obtain some spectacular battle scenes without paying a cent, simply by setting up his cameras near the same locations concurrently being used for one of Thomas H. Ince's elaborate Civil War dramas—not only "stealing" long shots of the dozens of extras hired for the Ince film, but also borrowing costumes and props.

Sennett pulled the same trick with his subsequent 1-reel Civil War comedy *Cohen Saves the Flag*, released November 27, 1913. A follow-up to the 1912 split-reeler *Cohen Collects a Debt*, the film features a pair of grotesque Jewish caricatures named Cohen and Goldberg, who carry their lifelong rivalry onto the battlefield. To get rid of Cohen (Ford Sterling) so he can claim the heroine (Mabel Normand) for himself, Yankee officer Goldberg sends his rival on a suicide mission—and when Cohen manages to survive this death trap, Goldberg trumps up some espionage charges and orders Cohen to be shot at sunrise. Once the news is out that Cohen has saved the flag (from the motion picture of the same name), all ends happily. As with *The Battle of Who Run*, Sennett kept his budget under control by filming *Cohen Saves the Flag* concurrently with the lavish Thomas Ince production *The Battle of Gettysburg*, utilizing the same Malibu, California locations. By setting up his unit just outside of Ince's camera range, Sennett was able to use the other film's realistically staged battle scenes as a backdrop for his own actors' buffoonery. Inasmuch as *The Battle of Gettysburg* is now a lost film, the brief glimpses seen in the Sennett comedy are all that remain of what must have been an impressive production. Historian Frank Thompson has noted: "As comedy, *Cohen Saves the Flag* is almost entirely dreadful. But because of the massive scenes of battle taken from the Ince production, it has a great deal of value." (One assumes that Ince, unlike Sennett, was able to keep the Pacific coastline from creeping into his long shots.)

A few short comedies of the talkie era were also set during the Civil War. Released by Columbia in early 1935, the Three Stooges' *Uncivil Warriors* casts the bumbling trio as Northern undercover agents, posing as Southern officers "Duck, Dodge and Hyde" to obtain information about Confederate troop movements. Lacking the budget for any sort of battle scenes (save for a few explosions and one climactic shot of a cannon), director Del Lord concentrates on the absurdities of three disreputable-looking comics posing as refined Southern gentlemen. The film's centerpiece gag has nothing to do with the War, but is instead the first of several instances in which the Stooges inadvertently eat a potholder instead of a cake, then spend the next few minutes coughing up feathers. Another Columbia 2-reeler, 1939's *Mooching Through Georgia*, opens with star Buster Keaton (of whom more later) in old-age makeup as a Confederate veteran, reminiscing with an equally decrepit ex–Union soldier (Ned Glass) over his wartime experiences. The rest of the film finds Buster and his brother (Monty Collins) continually changing from blue to gray uniforms and back again to avoid being killed by *both* Armies. Hardly worthy of Keaton's talents, *Mooching Through Georgia* worked rather better when it was remade by the Three Stooges as *Uncivil Warbirds* in 1946.

Feature-length comedy treatments of the Civil War are sparse, with Harold Lloyd the first to step gingerly into the genre with a flashback sequence in his 5-reel *Grandma's Boy* (Hal Roach/Pathé, 1922). The film's main story involves a coward who is elevated to bravery with the aid of a magic talisman, handed down from his Confederate-hero grandfather. Some historians have theorized that the Civil War flashback had originally been filmed as a stand-alone 2-reeler, with the rest of the picture built around it; others insist that the 1860s sequence was an afterthought, added to extend *Grandma's Boy*'s running time. Whatever the case, despite its period trappings and vintage uniforms the sequence is typical Lloyd material, as the protagonist defeats the Northerners with an even balance of brains and brawn. Disguised as a Union orderly, Harold spikes the bluecoated officers' punch with whiskey, then calmly circles their table and knocks them out one by one with a pistol butt, making it appear that their unconsciousness is the result of

No stranger to Civil War comedies, Buster Keaton headlined this middling Columbia 2-reeler from 1939 (*courtesy James L. Neibaur*).

overindulgence. When finally exposed as a Johnny Reb, Harold takes on the last standing officer in a sword duel, distracting his opponent by throwing apples at him and finally emerging triumphant with a well-placed kick in the midriff.

The first silent comedy feature to fully exploit a Civil War setting was Paramount's *Hands Up!* (1926). It was also the first starring comedy for sophisticated "silk-hat" comedian Raymond Griffith, who'd been awarded his own production unit after his excellent showing as a debonair jewel thief in the 1925 Betty Compson vehicle *Paths to Paradise*. Since most of Griffith's silent films are lost, we are fortunate indeed that a film as consistently hilarious and inventive as *Hands Up!* has survived. While it is hard to determine if the film represents a "typical" Griffith feature, it most certainly is entirely in keeping with the actor's trademarked screen persona: An unquenchably cheerful man-about-town who cares about nothing, is fazed by nothing, and is always the master of any given situation. Though Griffith makes no effort to elicit audience sympathy — he has been described by critic Walter Kerr as "heartless," though not in a negative sense — the viewer is pulling for him every step of the way, eager to see what new strategy he'll come up with to wriggle out of his next tight spot. A great deal of credit for this must be given director Clarence Badger, who'd proven in *Paths of Paradise* that he knew best how to invest humanity in the otherwise *sang-froid* Raymond Griffith, and to scriptwriters Monte Brice and Lloyd Corrigan.

Subtitled "An historical incident, with variations," *Hands Up!* begins in late 1864, with president Abraham Lincoln (played by perennial Old Abe impersonator George Billings) dispatching his ace undercover agent Capt. Edward Logan (Montague Love) to Nevada, there to arrange a deal with mine owner Silas Woodstock (Mack Swain) to obtain a huge gold supply that will secure a

Northern victory. Simultaneouly, Southern general Robert E. Lee orders *his* best espionage agent, the aristocratic Jack (Raymond Griffith), to head to Nevada on the same gold-seeking mission. En route via stagecoach, Jack meets Woodstock and his lovely daughters Mae (Marion Nixon) and Alice (Virginia Lee Corbin), earning their undying gratitude when he rescues them from hostile Indians—though Woodstock remains unaware that Jack is working for the Confederacy. Arriving in Nevada, Jack comes face to face with Logan, and for the next reel or so the two men take turns gaining the upper hand of one another, with Jack temporarily winning the contest when he accuses Logan of being General Lee's elusive Southern spy. Along the way, both of Woodstock's daughters fall in love with Jack, and he with them, to the extent of separately proposing marriage to each girl, using the exact same words on each occasion. Jack's mission comes to an abrupt end when news arrives of Lee's surrender at Appomattox—and though he takes this setback in his usual stride, he must now confront the dilemma of loving two girls equally and not being able to choose between them.

The best military-related gags in *Hands Up!* occur early in the film. The one gag that is always cited by film historians represents the epitome of Raymond Griffith's unflappable screen image: Sentenced to die by firing squad, Jack calmly pulls a plate from under his cloak and tosses it in the air, whereupon the sharpshooters instinctively swing their rifles upward and bring the plate down—as Jack politely applauds their excellent marksmanship. A less famous but equally characteristic vignette occurs when Jack arrives at a small shack in the middle of a battlefield, there to discuss his secret mission with Robert E. Lee and his adjutant. Suddenly a cannonball blows the shack to bits—and when the smoke clears, Jack and the General are still exchanging pleasantries as if nothing has happened. Finally, Lee turns to Jack and the adjutant and warns (via subtitle), "This is a secret between the three of us." At that instant, a shot is fired and the adjutant falls dead. Without missing a beat, Jack respectfully corrects the General: "The *two* of us, Sir."

Dauntless, debonair Raymond Griffith, star of the classic silent Civil War comedy *Hands Up!* (Paramount, 1926).

The film's most memorable gag has nothing to do with *la guerre* and everything to do with *l'amour*. Upon hearing that the war is over, Jack turns his attention to the apparently insoluble problem of having proposed to two equally desirable damsels. Just when all seems hopeless, a stagecoach pulls up and out steps an old friend of the Woodstock family: Mormon leader Brigham Young (Charles K. French) and his retinue of wives. This gives Jack his best idea yet ... and as the film fades, we see our hero and the two heroines riding toward the horizon in a coach bearing the sign "Salt Lake City or Bust!" (This delectably irreverent closing gag is missing from a few existing censored prints of *Hands Up!*, including those originally circulated in Utah; ironically, Griffith's costar Mack Swain was himself a native of Salt Lake City.)

As was customary in films of the 1920s, the sociopolitical issues that had sparked the Civil War remain unmentioned in *Hands Up!*, though there's a hint of historical accuracy when Jack's cover is nearly blown by the unanticipated arrival of his faithful old black servant, fresh from the family plantation in Virginia. While it is all too easy for contemporary critics to pooh-

pooh the notion of a slave displaying loyalty and affection to his master, silent film historian Glenn Mitchell has correctly observed: "The elderly black servant ... is in fact precisely the sort of character who existed in Virginia in the 1860s." (Moviegoers in 1926 were probably unaware that this was not the only black man appearing in the film: Famed African American actor/filmmaker Noble Johnson shows up in the Indian camp scene as Chief Sitting Bull!) Not that Raymond Griffith and his collaborators were terribly concerned with authenticity. Throughout the narrative, Griffith winks at the audience with a variety of deliberate anachronisms, such as his holding a strap in a 19th-century stagecoach in the style of a 20th-century subway commuter, and later teaching an Indian tribe how to dance the Charleston.

Described in its advertising as "The *Covered Wagon* of Comedy" (a reference to Paramount's popular 1923 western epic) and showered with such critical accolades as "a ludicrously funny farce" (from the *New York Times*), *Hands Up!* proved to be a major moneyspinner for its home studio. Released in January 1926, the film was still accruing profits well into 1927, by which time Buster Keaton had brought forth his own silent Civil War comedy feature, *The General*, as his inaugural release for United Artists.

Having recently made two stage adaptations (*Seven Chances*, *Battling Butler*) that had been urged upon him by his producer and brother-in-law Joseph Schenck, Keaton was anxious to come up with a picture that was wholly his own conception, made totally under his own control. The comedian's head gagwriter and co-director Clyde Bruckman delivered the goods by loaning Buster his copy of William Pittenger's *The Great Locomotive Chase*, a Civil War memoir originally published in 1887 as *Daring and Suffering, a History of the Great Railroad Adventurers*.

On April 12, 1862, Pittenger, then a sergeant in the Union Army, participated in the famously futile "Andrews Raid" under the command of civilian spy James J. Andrews. Accompanied by some two dozen Northern volunteers, Andrews sneaked into the Georgia town of Big Shanty and hijacked the Confederate locomotive *General*, proceeding to Chattanooga while disrupting Southern troop movements and communications all along the way. Though many telegraph lines were felled and numerous obstacles were left in the wake of the *General* to slow down the pursuing Confederates, Andrews was unsuccessful in carrying out his master plan to destroy a series of strategic railroad bridges. Within three days, Andrews' raiders were captured and the leaders sentenced to hang. Pittenger avoided this fate but remained in the custody of the Confederates until he was sent back North in a prisoner exchange, whereupon he was promoted and awarded the Congressional Medal of Honor. In the two decades preceding his death in 1904, Pittenger not only wrote and lectured extensively on the Civil War but also became a staunch campaigner against the Darwin theory — but of course this latter aspect of Pittenger's life was of no interest to Buster Keaton, who'd already gotten monkeys out of his system by posing as a trained chimp in his 1921 film *The Playhouse*. It was the Civil War setting and the ongoing-chase angle that inspired Keaton to produce an 8-reel comedy adaptation of the Pittenger memoir, titling his film *The General* after the "abducted" Southern locomotive.

A one-reeler based on the Andrews raid had been produced by Kalem in 1911; 45 years later, Walt Disney tackled the same story with his Technicolor feature *The Great Locomotive Chase*. Like Pittenger's book, Disney's film (actually based on another account of the raid, Charles O'Neill's *Wild Train*) was told from the Northern viewpoint, with Fess Parker as James J. Andrews and John Lupton as William Pittenger. Jeffrey Hunter costarred as William Allen Fuller, the young civilian conductor of the *General* and the film's most sympathetic Southern character. At the time of the original raid, the Confederacy fêted Fuller as a hero for his relentless one-man pursuit of the stolen *General*, during which he not only chased after the locomotive by foot and handcar, but also briefly commandeered a Northern train. Though in *The Great Locomotive Chase* we see Fuller and Andrews shaking hands after the latter's capture, the real-life William A. Fuller became jealously possessive of the Andrews Raid legend, issuing scores of angry letters to newspapers and lecturers who hadn't told the "true" story as he saw it.

The Disney film made money, but not as much as the studio had hoped. In a 1965 interview with Kevin Brownlow, Buster Keaton attributed the disappointing box office to Disney's "mistake" of "putting Fess Parker in the lead as a Northerner," effectively making villains of the Confederates: "Well, you can't do that with a motion-picture audience—they resent it. And the same goes if I was in Michigan, Maine, Massachussetts. They lost the war anyhow, so the audience resents it. We knew better; when the story ended, the South was winning. This was correct. All this took place in 1862, and the South lost in 1864." Keaton expanded upon this point in another 1965 interview with John Gillett: "When my picture ended the South was winning, which was all right with me."

Are we to take this comment as some sort of "proof" that Keaton was an unreconstructed Confederate sympathizer, thereby "explaining" why he never touches upon the subject of slavery in *The General*? Not really. Unlike Chaplin, Keaton never injected any sort of political ideology into his films. If the reasons behind the Civil War are ignored in *The General*, it's simply because Buster didn't regard them as essential. The story involving the train, and the gags arising from that story, were all that mattered. Buster's "all right with me" probably had no further significance than indicating that it was "all right" with him to give *The General* a happy ending—as opposed to the final chapter of Pittenger's book, in which eight of the Northern conspirators are simultaneously hanged from the same horizontal pine tree.

As for telling his story from the Southern point of view, Keaton had sensed that the only character he could logically play in a film version of *The Great Locomotive Chase* was William A. Fuller, the lone Southern conductor who never gave up pursuit of "his" beloved locomotive. So Buster essentially became Fuller, renamed "Johnnie Grey" and promoted from the *General*'s conductor to the engineer. Johnnie Grey is very much in keeping with Keaton's established screen image: The resourceful little guy, somewhat detached from the rest of the world, who single-mindedly perseveres despite any and all roadblocks that might be strewn in his path, using whatever means necessary—including in this case borrowing another train, the *Texas*, to chase after the raiders—to accomplish his goal. And as was *de rigueur* in the cinema world of Buster Keaton, Johnnie Grey is so focused on the job at hand that he often fails to notice what's transpiring around him; see the classic scene in which Johnnie, chopping firewood on the tender of the speeding *Texas*, is totally oblivious to the massive Northern advance and Confederate retreat taking place in a clearing right behind him.

Although *The General* was meant to be a comedy, Keaton was adamant that the basic Pittenger story be told as realistically as possible—and with so many other books and articles devoted to this film, it isn't necessary to reiterate the multitude of details surrounding Buster's famous edict to his production crew, "It's got to be so authentic it hurts." These words may seem contrary to Buster's avowed desire that *The General* be a film entirely of his own making. But while readily admitting to John Gillett that the events occurring in the first half of the film, during Johnnie Grey's pursuit of his stolen train, were "staged exactly the way they happened," Keaton added: "The original locomotive chase ended when I found myself in Northern territory and had to desert. From then on it was my invention, in order to get a complete plot. It had nothing to do with the Civil War." In his book *The Silent Clowns*, Walter Kerr expresses admiration for Keaton's instinctive "geometric patterns" in *The General*, and the manner in which the film "turns on itself" once Johnnie recovers his engine: "He must take it back over the very same route he has traveled, repeating along the way *every bit of business* that has been done on the way out.... It is a controlled and challenging design for an epic film." That Keaton was able to meet that challenge, and score even bigger laughs while making the same trip over the same territory, is the essence of *The General*'s greatness.

If one wants to be nit-picky, it's possible that *The General* doesn't belong in a book about military comedies. Despite the presence of literally thousands of Northern and Southern soldiers (most of them actually members of the Oregon National Guard), Keaton's Johnnie Grey is like his

An exquisitely designed trade ad for Buster Keaton's *The General*, which appeared in the pages of *Film Daily* two months before the picture's general release in February of 1927.

role model William A. Fuller a civilian throughout most of the film, receiving a uniform and commission only in the last five minutes. Keaton's non-military status is part and parcel of the film's comic throughline of misconception and misunderstanding: Virtually everyone *except* Johnnie Grey spends the bulk of the film jumping to the wrong conclusions. Unaware that Johnnie has been rejected for military duty because he is of more value to the Confederacy as an engineer, the father and brother of Johnnie's sweetheart Annabelle Lee (Marion Mack) assume that he never even tried to enlist — and so does Annabelle. Later on as Johnnie chases after his stolen locomotive, the Northern raiders become convinced by circumstances that they are being pursued not by one solitary civilian, but by the entire Confederate army. Still later, when Johnnie stumbles into Union headquarters, he finds Annabelle Lee locked in a bedroom, having previously been kidnapped by the Raiders to keep her from tipping off their scheme. Up to this moment, Johnnie hasn't even had an inkling that Annabelle has been a reluctant passenger of the *General* all throughout the chase — but when the girl expresses gratitude that Johnnie has risked life and limb for the purpose of rescuing her, who is *he* to argue? Finally returning to the Southern lines, Johnnie avoids getting shot by donning the Confederate tunic previously used to disguise one of the Northern spies. While thus garbed, he manages to get the drop on a Union officer, who takes one look the tunic and immediately surrenders; only after handing over his sword does it dawn on the officer the Johnnie had no real authority to capture him.

This may be the only analysis of *The General* that doesn't dwell upon the endearing stupidity of heroine Annabelle Lee or the spectacular sight gag involving a collapsing bridge. Well, *almost* the only analysis: We are compelled to cite the aforementioned sight gag, which cost $40,000, to illustrate Keaton's willingness to spare no expense in bringing his vision to the screen. While most of Buster's silent features were budgeted at around $250,000, *The General* came in at three times that amount. United Artists trumpeted the film as "the costliest comedy spectacle ever made," which might lead one to assume that the releasing company was preparing to make back its cost many times over. But this was during a period in which UA was rumored to be among Hollywood's foremost practioners of "creative bookkeeping," with many another independent producer sensing that something was amiss when their films didn't make as much money as audience turnout seemed to indicate: William S. Hart in fact took UA to court over the company's mishandling of his 1925 western feature *Tumbleweeds*. While no one will ever know for certain if UA was shortchanging Keaton (after all, company president Joseph Schenck *was* Buster's producer), it does seem odd that a film which played to capacity houses during the regional preview process in late 1926, and which enjoyed an excellent opening week at New York's Capitol Theater in February 1927, would end up in the red with an official domestic gross of only $454,000. Though Keaton would go to his grave insisting that *The General* was a success — as did leading lady Marion Mack — the picture has entered Hollywood folklore as one of those inexplicable flops that had to wait until its latter-day "rediscovery" to finally post a profit and take its proper place as an enduring classic.

Fueling the mythology surrounding *The General* are the many stories of how the film's reviews were uniformly negative, though even a casual perusal of contemporary publications proves that this wasn't the case. Among the many critical bouquets that have been reprinted on Steve Webster's *General* website include: "Excellent comedy for first class houses. It cannot fail to please a discriminating audience" (*Bioscope*, January 1927); "It's a pleasure to laugh continuously but comfortably" (*Motion Picture*, March 1927); "Capital entertainment" (*Picutregoer*, April 1927); "Good satire on war melodrama and excellent comedy thrills" (*Picture Play*, May 1927); and, from part-time *Chicago Daily News* film critic Carl Sandburg, "If they'll put Buster Keaton at the head of the armies next time there's a war his maneuvers will bring that war to a pleasant, painless and prompt conclusion, because the belligerents will simply die laughing.... If you want a good laugh, don't miss *The General*." Unfortunately, many critics were (and are) sheep, content to regurgitate the sentiments of *Life* magazine's Robert E. Sherwood, who was normally one of the comedian's biggest boosters: "Buster Keaton shows signs of vaulting ambition in *The General*; he appears to be attempting to enter the 'epic' class. That he fails to get across is due to the scantiness of his material as compared to the length of his films; he has also woefully bad judgment in deciding just where and when to stop." Sherwood seems to have been especially annoyed by the brief comic scene in which Johnnie Grey accidentally kills a Northern sniper, the punchline being that he is never aware of his lethal act: "Someone should have told Buster that it is difficult to derive laughter from the sight of men being killed in battle." Paradoxically, the critic goes on to say that *The General* is "not nearly so good" as Raymond Griffith's *Hands Up!* Evidently Sherwood had stepped out to the lobby for a lemonade during the scene in which Griffith managed to derive *lots* of laughter from the battlefield death of General Lee's adjutant.

Whether a blockbuster or merely a bust, *The General* would for many years to come serve a vital Hollywood function as a bountiful source of stock "battlefield" footage for several subsequent Civil War pictures. Both *The General* and D.W. Griffith's *Abraham Lincoln* (1930) are amply represented by the stock shots used in the only feature-length Civil War comedy of the 1930s, Hal Roach's *General Spanky* (working title: *Colonel Spanky*).

By 1936, Roach was easing out of 2-reel comedies and concentrating his energies on feature films, testing his most popular short-subject stars in the longer format. While Laurel & Hardy had already passed the test and gone on to even greater popularity in features, Charley Chase was fired by Roach after his inaugural 6-reeler *Bank Night* ran into legal entanglements and resistance from Roach's distributor MGM, forcing the producer to release the picture in a compressed 2-reel version titled *Neighborhood House*. That left the team of Patsy Kelly and Lyda Roberti, whose amusing 1937 feature *Nobody's Baby* might have kept the duo in clover had not Roberti died suddenly the following year; and the Our Gang kids, who after churning out dozens of 2-reelers over a 14-year-period (with various necessary changes in personnel) were bumped up to the 7-reel class with *General Spanky*, released at the tail end of 1936. Not only was this Our Gang's first feature, but it was also the first film in which the kiddie contingent was yanked out of its contemporary surroundings and plunked into a period setting.

Per its title, the film's central character was the most popular member of the troupe, 8-year-old George "Spanky" McFarland, here cast as an orphaned shoeshine boy plying his trade on a Mississippi riverboat in the weeks just prior to the firing on Fort Sumter. In the course of his duties, Spanky makes a loyal friend of handsome Southern aristocrat Marshall Valient (Phillips Holmes) and a powerful enemy of crooked gambler Simmons (Irving Pichel). The kid also reluctantly acquires a pint-sized "slave" named Buckwheat (played by 5-year-old Billie Thomas), who out of fear of being hanged for accidentally escaping his slavemaster has attached himself to the little bootblack. Jumping overboard to avoid Simmons' wrath, Spanky and Buckwheat make their way to Marshall Valient's palatial home, just before Valient marches off to war under the Confederate flag. Instructed to "protect the womenfolk" in Valient's absence—said womenfolk being Marshall's sweetheart Louella Blanchard (Rosina Lawrence) and her mammy Cornelia (Louise Beavers)—Spanky takes his duties quite seriously. Gathering together a group of neighbor kids including the cowlick-haired Alfalfa (9-year-old Carl Switzer), Spanky organizes an underground army called the Royal Protection of Women and Children, Regiment Club of the World and the Mississippi River—or the RPWCRCWMR for short.

When an invading Northern regiment under the dubious leadership of Spanky's old nemesis Simmons marches into view, Spanky's junior army successfully fights off the enemy with a variety of makeshift weapons, convincing the cowardly Simmons that he is vastly outnumbered and his doom is nigh. Once it is revealed that the Union forces have been held off by a mere bunch of tots, a kindly Northern general (Ralph Morgan) congratulates Spanky for his bravery and promises that his men will not bother Louella. In an effort to wreak vengeance against practically everybody, Simmons captures the wounded Marshall Valient and sentences him to be shot as a spy, but thanks to Spanky's quick thinking the General intervenes at the very last moment. Marshall and Louella are reunited, and a grateful Spanky makes the General an honorary member of the RPWCRCWMR, complete with ottoman hat and antimacassar robe. (Question: If the film's story commences just before the outbreak of the war and concludes sometime in 1862, why aren't Spanky and Buckwheat any older at the end of the picture than they are at the beginning? Answer: Who cares?)

Though in later interviews Hal Roach seemed to take pride in the fact that his beloved Our Gang kids (or at least three of them) had once headlined a feature titled *General Spanky*, he was slightly vague regarding the reasons behind his radical decision to place the youngsters in a Civil War setting. The logical answer would seem to be that Shirley Temple had recently scored a hit in her own Civil War–based vehicle *The Littlest Rebel*, but Roach apparently never referenced the Temple picture. Interviewed by Our Gang historians Leonard Maltin and Richard Bann, the producer explained: "Well, the idea was the kids had a play fort, then the Northern Army came along and thought the thing was on the square, so they attacked." This would seem to suggest that the "fort" scene, a variation on Our Gang's 1923 army spoof *Dogs of War* (see **Chapter 2**) was the idea that set *General Spanky* in motion. But in stating this, Roach also acknowledged the main reason that the 1936 feature played to tepid box-office response: "The audience wouldn't believe it and so it just didn't work. The comedy part of the picture, involving the kids, was all right.... But putting in the other story, the North-South conflict, was a mistake, and it was this dramatic part of the picture that slowed it way down. Besides, as I say, it was unconvincing too. So I was basically unhappy with it."

There are other reasons that *General Spanky* displeased audiences in 1936 and remains an unsatisfactory experience to this day. Given the novelty of its setting, it would have been nice if

"Little Rascals" Alfalfa Switzer, Buckwheat Thomas and Spanky McFarland defending the Confederacy with grit, determination and scrap iron. From *General Spanky* (Hal Roach, 1936).

Roach's scriptwriters had come up with some fresh material rather than leaning so heavily on tried-and-true gags that had previously been put to better use in such Our Gang 2-reelers as *Stage Fright* (1923), *Every Man for Himself* (1924) and *Rainy Days* (1928). Even the best of the film's comic setpieces, Spanky's portentiously named underground military organization, pales in comparision with the immortal "He-Man Woman Hater's Club" in 1937's *Mail and Female*. Also, as pointed out by Maltin and Bann, the film's "sympathetic" adult characters treat the youngsters with the sort of condescension that seems calculated to alienate and offend the kids in the audience. As for the bland, monotonous villainy by the usually dependable Irving Pichel, Roach would have been far better off casting one of his old reliable stock-company players instead: Imagine what pop-eyed Jimmy Finlayson or sneering Richard Cramer could have brought to the role!

The most painful aspect of the film for present-day viewers is the treatment of black youngster Buckwheat, who in addition to being referred to throughout as a "pickaninny" is forced to endure the humiliating scene in which, to avoid possible hanging as a fugitive slave, he toddles up to one white adult after another, begging each man to be his "master"! Yet in a curious way, this weakness turns out to be the picture's one discernable strength. Standing apart from the other films in this chapter, *General Spanky* is the only Civil War comedy to address the issue of slavery head-on — and beyond that, to perfectly encapsulate the warped values of the typical Antebellum Southern aristocrat. Nowhere is this more pronounced than in an early dialogue exchange between two Southern gentlemen as they discuss the friction between the North and the South:

> FIRST MAN: I was in Washington a while back, and to hear them talk you'd think we treated our slaves something awful.
> SECOND MAN: I'd like to see them find any discontented ones on *my* plantation.
> FIRST MAN: Nor mine either. Why, my slaves get better food and shelter than most white men.
> SECOND MAN: It's those runaways which cause all this war talk.
> FIRST MAN: Sure it is. Slaves have to be kept in tow. Every slave has to have a master.
> SECOND MAN: And any slave that *doesn't* have a master ought to be shot!
> FIRST MAN: Hmmm ... shootin's too good for 'em. They ought to be hamstrung.

To use a phrase not in common coinage during the Civil War, the mind boggles.

So, is there anything else left to say about this misbegotten effort to promote Our Gang to the feature-film class? Well, *General Spanky* is magnificently photographed by Walter Lundin and Art Lloyd, with California's Sacramento River doing its usual excellent job of standing in for the Mississippi. The sound recording by Elmer A. Raguse and William Randall was deemed worthy of an Academy Award nomination, one of several such honors received by Roach's production staff in the late 1930s. And though the film tanked at the box office, Roach's distributor MGM insisted that he continue producing Our Gang one-reelers for the next two seasons, with Mighty Metro ultimately taking over the still-lucrative franchise in 1938.

Finally, *General Spanky* represents an audition of sorts for supporting players Phillips Holmes and Louise Beavers. As reported by Kasper Monahan in the February 3, 1937 edition of *The Pittsburgh Press*, a number of movie-magazine popularity polls had chosen Phillips Holmes as a front-runner for the role of Ashley Wilkes in the forthcoming film version of Margaret Mitchell's blockbuster novel *Gone With the Wind*, while Louise Beavers was the odds-on favorite for the role of Mammy. It's possible that the screenwriters for *General Spanky* were trying to give Mr. Holmes a little leg-up by adding a scene in which his character Marshall Valient discusses the futility of the upcoming Civil War—a scene that bears a stunning similarity to Clark Gable's introductory speech as Rhett Butler in the 1939 filmization of *Gone with the Wind*. If indeed this was an effort to boost Holmes' chances, the strategy failed to pay off: in case you haven't read a paper in a couple of days, Leslie Howard ended up playing Ashley, while Hattie McDaniel landed the Oscar-winning part of Mammy.

Though *Gone with the Wind* was the single biggest movie hit of the 1930s, that didn't prevent Hollywood pundits from writing off Civil War films as box-office poison — which, for the most part, they were. Not until 1948 would another comedy use the North-South conflict as a backdrop for a star comedian. MGM's *A Southern Yankee* has sometimes been inaccurately described as a talkie remake of Buster Keaton's *The General* (even by Keaton scholars who should know better!), principally because Buster, then working as a comedy consultant for the studio, contributed several of the film's best gags. But outside of their common Civil War setting, *The General* and *A Southern Yankee* couldn't be farther apart in concept and execution. Certainly if MGM *had* intended to do a remake of *The General,* their protagonist would not have been a Damn Yankee!

Throughout the 1940s Buster Keaton had begged MGM head man Louis Mayer to give him a separate production unit to nurture the talents of the studio's Number One comedy star Red Skelton: "Let me take Skelton, and work as a small company within Metro—do our stories, our gags, our production, our directing. Use your resources to do it our way—the way I did my best pictures. I'll guarantee you hits. I won't take a cent of salary until they have proved themselves at the box office." But control-freak Mayer wasn't about to give anyone an autonomous unit at his studio, so Keaton had to be content with providing individual sight gags for Skelton's films, brilliantly carried out by the young comedian with the occasional assistance of Red's favorite stunt double Gil Perkins (In a 1970 interview, Perkins commented: "With a red hairpiece on, I look quite a bit like Red Skelton—in *his* hairpiece.") It must have been some satisfaction to Keaton that two of Red's MGM vehicles, *I Dood It* and *Watch the Birdie,* were remakes of Buster's silent features *Spite Marriage* and *The Cameraman,* with exactly-repeated gags and situations.

Despite the harmonious working relationship between Keaton and Skelton, Red originally balked at appearing in *A Southern Yankee.* The comedian was unhappy with the way that MGM was trying to transform him into a conventional leading man in such unsuitable vehicles as *The Show-Off,* and also with the studio's ongoing habit of casting him as comedy relief in films starring "bigger" names like Ann Sothern and Eleanor Powell. While on loan to Columbia in late 1947, Red was given his most fulfilling assignment in years: *The Fuller Brush Man,* a 100 percent undistilled example of the comedian at his pantomimic best. *Fuller Brush Man* was directed by S. Sylvan Simon, with whom Skelton had been working copacetically since 1941's *Whistling in the Dark,* and Red had hoped that Simon would be assigned his next MGM project. Instead, *Southern Yankee* was given to Edward Sedgwick, a longtime Keaton crony who by 1948 had lost much of the energy and panache that had distinguished his earlier comedies.

There was also the matter of the film's proposed leading lady, Ava Gardner. Then on the ascendancy to superstardom, Gardner was being carefully groomed by MGM with flashy roles and extended showcase scenes—the same sort of treatment afforded Esther Williams in *her* breakthrough picture *Bathing Beauty,* which had started out as a Red Skelton vehicle but ended up with the comedian's footage considerably reduced. Hollywood gossip columnists began sending out reports of how Skelton was taking lengthy absences from the studio instead of commencing work on *Southern Yankee* (the film's cowriter Harry Tugend has gone on record insisting that Skelton "deliberately dogged" his obligation to MGM). There was even speculation that Red was prepared to buy up his contract rather than appear in the film. Ultimately, however, Skelton returned to work, albeit opposite leading lady Arlene Dahl, a considerably lesser light than Ava Gardner. And after a few days of filming, Edward Sedgwick was removed and S. Sylvan Simon brought in to complete the picture. Though Sedgwick still gets full directorial credit, Skelton would always insist in later interviews that the unbilled Simon (who asked that his name be removed from the credits when denied the opportunity to do some needed retakes) was responsible for the entire film, with none of Sedgwick's footage remaining in the final release print.

Buster Keaton's contributions likewise went unheralded on-screen, though his participation in *Southern Yankee* was well publicized by MGM, and would continue to take up plenty of print space in subsequent books on Keaton's career, including his autobiography *My Wonderful World of Slapstick.* It is well documented that Buster's first advice to MGM was to make Skelton's character more believable and less imbecilic in his introductory scenes, lest audiences lose sympathy for him (in the finished film, Red is more accident-prone than stupid.) Also cited over and over is the famous Keaton-created gag in which Skelton, caught in the crossfire between Northern and Southern troops, keeps himself alive by hastily stitching together two different uniforms and two different flags. As he marches down the middle of the battlefield with the opposing forces on either side, Red is cheered madly by both armies. The reason? His uniform is now one-half blue and one-half grey, while his flag bears the Union's Stars and Stripes on one side and the Confederacy's Bars and Stripes on the other. Alas, the wind suddenly changes direction, exposing our hero's deception at the worst possible moment. Curiously, only a few of Keaton's chroniclers have noted that this classic gag was lifted from one of Buster's earlier talkie 2-reelers, *Jail Bait*. Equally curious is the fact that few of the comedian's devotees have bothered to mention the *other* distinctly Keatonesque gag in *Southern Yankee*, in which Skelton sidetracks his Confederate pursuers by disguising the rear end of a cow with a woman's sunbonnet (a gag borrowed from Buster's 1923 silent feature *Our Hospitality*).

It's about time we got around to the plot of *A Southern Yankee*, so here goes. The year is 1865: Aubrey Filmore (Skelton), a bumbling bellboy at the Palmer Hotel in St. Louis, continually pesters Union secret service officer Col. Clifford Baker (Art Baker) for an espionage assignment. To get Aubrey out of his hair, Baker tells him that his wish will be granted if he manages to capture an elusive and dangerous Southern undercover agent known as the Gray Spider—something that could never happen in a million years. Well, time sure flies when you're having fun, and by sheer accident Aubrey manages to waylay the Gray Spider, aka Major Jack Drumman (George Coulouris), turning his prisoner over to the astonished Baker. Enter gorgeous Southern belle Sallyann Weath-

Bogus Confederate officer Red Skelton is close to completing his mission on behalf of the Union in *A Southern Yankee* (MGM, 1948)—providing that his startled expression doesn't betray his allegiance to the North. Charles Dingle is seen at left; Forbes Murray is holding the map.

arby (Arlene Dahl), who though she has never met Drumman is one of the dashing spy's most ardent admirers. Mistaking Aubrey for the Gray Spider, Sallyann passes along vital information to the befuddled bellhop. Taking advantage of this turn of events, Baker orders Filmore to continue posing as the Gray Spider—after all, if Aubrey is killed, what has the North got to lose?—and in this guise the "Southern Yankee" infiltrates Confederate headquarters in order to deliver phony Union war plans and thus assure a Northern victory. Threatened with exposure at every turn—especially after the real Gray Spider escapes custody—Aubrey manages to pull off his charade through a combination of circumstance and providence. Complicating matters is Aubrey's growing fondness for loyal Southerner Sallyann, but this problem is solved in virtually the same abrupt manner as in Raymond Griffith's *Hands Up!*

While the bulk of the comedy material was devised by Buster Keaton and veteran gagsmith Harry Tugend (an unbilled Nat Perrin also contributed to the fun), much of the credit for *A Southern Yankee*'s success must be attributed to screenwriters Norman Panama and Melvin Frank, acknowledged masters of building comedy upon a firm foundation of credible and coherent story values. As previously demonstrated in their Bob Hope vehicles *My Favorite Blonde* and *Monsieur Beaucaire*, Panama and Frank knew instinctively that the antics of their lead comic would be doubly funny, and have more point, if that comic is placed in a truly perilous and life-threatening situation. Red Skelton hiding in a flea-infested doghouse near the end of *A Southern Yankee* is good for a few chuckles at most; showing him a few minutes later scratching and squirming as he stands before a firing squad is an absolute scream.

Movie-comedy historians who have performed calisthenics comparing *A Southern Yankee* to *The General* have often overlooked the fact that *Southern Yankee* is essentially a dry run for another masterpiece of mirth, Panama and Frank's 1956 Danny Kaye vehicle *The Court Jester*. Though *Yankee* takes place in the 1860s and *Jester* is set in medieval times, the basic storyline, individual situations, plot intrigues and key characters are remarkably similar in both pictures, right down to the tongue-twisting instructions that the hero is forced to memorize if he wants to stay healthy. Whereas in *The Court Jester* Danny Kaye must bear in mind that "the pellet with the poison's in the vessel with the pestle; the chalice from the palace has the brew that is true," in *A Southern Yankee* Red Skelton's survival hinges on the deathless admonition "The paper's in the pocket in the boot with the buckle; the map's in the packet in the pocket of the jacket."

In keeping with Buster Keaton's theory that audiences resented it when moviemakers tried to make heavies out of the Confederates, there are few out-and-out villains in *A Southern Yankee*. Though ruthless and cold-blooded, the Gray Spider is motivated by patriotism rather than malice, while the least sympathetic of the "rebel" characters, mercenary vigilante Jed Callahan (John Ireland) and war profiteer Kurt Devlinn (Brian Donlevy), are depicted as exceptions to Southern gallantry rather than the rule. With this in mind, a modern-day viewer should not expect a penetrating exposé of slavery and slaveholders from this essentially lighthearted effort. One of the film's few prominent black characters, a female domestic played by Louise Beavers, exists merely as a foil for one of Skelton's best sight-gag sequences, as the hero tries to hide behind a laundry line while Beavers progressively removes each article of clothing. The film's other noteworthy black performer is 9-year-old tapdancer Drexie Haywood, whom Skelton had discovered while the boy was waiting for an autograph outside Red's radio studio. Haywood's brief sequence is the only "musical" moment in *A Southern Yankee*, and like the film's comedy highlights the youngster's specialty number is smoothly integrated into the plotline.

Sixteen years would pass between *A Southern Yankee* and Hollywood's next (and as of this writing, last) Civil War comedy—which, if it had remained faithful to its source novel, wouldn't have been a comedy at all. Published in 1957, *Company of Cowards* was written by Jack Schaefer, best known today as the author of *Shane*. Schaefer's inspiration was a 1956 *Saturday Evening Post* article by William Chamberlain which recounted the apocryphical Civil War stories of "Company Q," a unit comprised of Northern soldiers who had been court-martialed or otherwise disgraced

("Company Q" was 19th-century army slang for the sick list). According to legend, this group was exiled to the wilds of New Mexico and given a chance to redeem themselves by defending the Union against hostile Indians. In Schaefer's novel, among the eight convicted cowards dispatched to this hellhole is former officer Jared Heath. Much to his own amazement, the self-loathing Heath summons the intestinal fortitude to lead his fellow outcasts to victory during an Indian attack. In the end, all eight members of Company Q have their commissions restored, some posthumously. Critics in 1957 compared *Company of Cowards* favorably to another novel of wartime redemption, Stephen Crane's *The Red Badge of Courage*.

Even though their 1951 screen adaptation of the Crane novel was one of the studio's most conspicuous failures, MGM bought the rights to *Company of Cowards* and announced plans to make a movie version during the 1958–59 season. There is every indication that the studio planned to film the novel as a serious western, the attendant publicity sent out by staff producer Edmund A. Grainger listing several prominent action stars as candidates for the leading role of Jared Heath. It isn't clear why MGM chose instead to shelve the project, though one suspects that their decision was forced by rival Columbia Pictures, who beat Metro to the punch with 1959's *They Came to Cordura*. This rugged quasi-western starred Gary Cooper as an accused coward assigned to lead a band of disreputable soldiers during the Mexican border insurection of 1916, for the purpose of finding potential Medal of Honor winners amongst this motley crew. By film's end, Cooper has atoned for his own past sins in a manner quite similar to the conversion of Jared Heath. After *They Came to Cordura*, anything MGM could have come up with vis-à-vis *Company of Cowards* would have looked like warmed-over stew.

With the Civil War Centennial in full swing during the early 1960s, MGM reactivated their plans to cinematize *Company of Cowards*. Assigned to adapt the property for the screen were Samuel A. Peeples, a specialist in literary and TV westerns, and William A. Bowers, who as mentioned in our notes on *The Last Time I Saw Archie* (see **Chapter 11**) preferred to use the military genre as a source of humor. Somewhere along the line Bowers' comic approach to the material superceded Peeples' more straightforward interpretation, and it was as a comedy western that *Company of Cowards* was brought to life by the film's new producer Ted Richmond. The choice of Glenn Ford as leading man was motivated less by the actor's track record in such westerns as *The Fastest Gun Alive* and *3:10 to Yuma* than by his prior success in such service comedies as *Teahouse of the August Moon* and *Imitation General* (the latter also scripted by Bowers).

Once Glenn Ford was set for the picture, the actor's favorite director George Marshall was also signed up. Not only was Marshall well versed in the service-comedy format, but he had also acquitted himself nicely in the comedy-western field with *Destry Rides Again*, *Fancy Pants* and *The Sheepman*, among others. The Ford-Marshall combo proved to be a wise economy move for MGM, which at the time was undergoing another of its chronic financial crises. Though a proven commodity with a strong fan following, Glenn Ford was one of Hollywood's least expensive freelance stars, his films (especially those directed by Marshall) almost invariably coming in on schedule and frequently under budget. Despite its Civil War trappings, *Company of Cowards* was a corner-cutter every inch of the way, beginning with the decision to film in black & white rather than color. Though a few location jaunts were necessary, many of the big outdoor action scenes were filmed right on the MGM backlot, using leftover sets from such pictures as *Showboat* (the 1951 version), *Raintree County*, *Cimarron* and *How the West Was Won*, and even from such TV shows as *The Twilight Zone*.

We won't expend any energy comparing the novel and film versions of *Company of Cowards*, except to say that virtually all they have in common are the name of protagonist and the Civil War background (the film is set in 1862). The first character we see in the movie is Colonel Claude Weatherby (Melvyn Douglas) who despite his West Point background is the dictionary definition of "incompetent." Every morning, Weatherby's 5th Ohio Artillery Volunteers and their Confederate counterparts exchange 30 token rounds of fire, each side taking care not to hurt anybody lest they may actually have to do some real fighting. Captain Jared Heath (Glenn Ford) objects to this lackadaisical attitude, but the phlegmatic Weatherby advises him not to upset the status quo. When ordered to charge the Southern lines, Weatherby grumpily agrees, but thanks to the "magnetic attraction" of Cpl. Silas Greeley (Jesse Pearson) the Colonel's horse races off in the wrong direction—and so do the men under his command. During the subsequent court martial, presiding judge Gen. Willoughby (Jim Backus) has trouble swallowing the 5th Ohio Artillery's garbled explanation for their retreat, but decides against a mass execution because it would make President Lincoln queasy. Instead, the entire 5th Ohio, along with a fresh batch of misfits and screw-ups, are shipped off to Ft. Hooker in New Mexico, far enough removed from the shooting war to avoid any further Public Relations headaches. When the Confederate high command sees the brand-new "Company Q" heading westward, they assume that the Union has formed an elite corps of specialists for the purpose of protecting a valuable gold shipment from both the Rebs and a guerrilla band led by mercenary Hugo Zattig (James Griffith). Dispatched to spy on Company Q and undermine their "mission" (which of course doesn't exist) is sexy Southern undercover agent Martha Lou Williams (Stella Stevens), who poses as one of a group of "working girls" being transported to New Mexico by blowsy madam Easy Jenny (Joan Blondell). It doesn't take Jared Heath long to figure out that Martha is working for the enemy, but he really doesn't care since he intends to marry the girl and take her away from all this.

Once everyone has arrived in New Mexico, Martha Lou contacts Zattig, who is in cahoots with erudite West Point–educated Indian chief Thin Elk (Michael Pate). Using some skinny-dipping maidens as bait, Thin Elk captures Company Q and strips them to their undies, handing their uniforms over to Zattig so his guerrillas can steal the Union gold. Again harnessing Cpl. Greeley's "magnetic attraction" to stampede the Indians' horses, Heath and his men manage to escape, at approximately the same moment that Zattig is double-crossing Martha Lou for his own gain. With no horses of their own, Company Q descends upon the mercenaries using barrel staves as skis. (How do you ski down a *dry* hill?) In retaliation, Zattig stages a raid on the nearby town of Sioux Landing, but is foiled again with the help of an improvised catapult designed by Col. Weatherby in emulation of the ancient Greeks.

I have gone into some detail for a couple of reasons. First, to illustrate the utter inappropriateness of the film's original title *Company of Cowards.* Under the harebrained leadership of Col. Weatherby, the men of Company Q may be indigents, dimwits and klutzes, but as can plainly be seen there isn't a coward among them. Once MGM finally glommed onto this, the studio changed the title to *Advance to the Rear* in late March of 1964, six months after the film's completion and approximately three months ahead of its New York premiere. Nevertheless, the film was copyrighted as *Company of Cowards* and released under that title in Great Britain, while the original title song is still performed by the New Christy Minstrels during the opening and closing credits.

Secondly, by recounting the plot in detail one can see how the film is brimming with comic possibilities—which, alas, are for the most part unrealized. Director George Marshall's usually infallible comic timing is off by at least half a beat in every scene, while the seemingly surefire script material is seldom played out for full value. Company Q's personnel includes several men with bizarre character traits: One soldier suffers from a case of permanent hiccups; another insists upon placing everyone he meets in a bonecrushing bear-hug; yet another is a pyromaniac; still another is constantly causing gunpowder to explode prematurely; yet still another is an habitual flagpole sitter; and so on and so forth. In most "misfit" service comedies, the audience can confidently predict that each and every one of the characters' personal peculiarities will be brought into play in a positive manner, enabling the misfits to triumph in the closing scene: Even a so-so effort like 1996's *Down Periscope* (see **Chapter 12**) does a great job milking this cliché. But once the characters' individual eccentricities are established in *Advance to the Rear*, virtually nothing is done to exploit them. It's as though someone had spent 45 minutes building up a joke and then suddenly left town before delivering the punchline. Nor is this the film's only example of opportunity wasted:

Southern spy Stella Stevens is about to be disarmed by Northern officer Glenn Ford in *Advance to the Rear* (MGM, 1964).

When supporting actor Whit Bissell's character is identified as "Captain Queeg," the *least* we can expect is a close shot of Bissell rolling a pair of steel balls in his hand — yet again, nothing comes of this. The desultory nature of *Advance to the Rear* may be due to extensive recutting after the film's completion. Evidence of this is the surprising brevity of the roles played by well-known actors Preston Foster and Yvonne Craig, neither of whom receives screen credit.

In contrast with the undeveloped comedy elements, other aspects of the film are way too overdeveloped, most conspicuously the performance of Melvyn Douglas as the dunderheaded Col. Weatherby. Most of the veteran supporting players do quite well with the material they're given, notably Joan Blondell, Jim Backus, Michael Pate and Alan Hale, Jr., whose oafish-yet-sincere portrayal of Sgt. Beauregard Davis was reportedly the deciding factor in landing him the role of the Skipper in the TV sitcom *Gilligan's Island*. But if Melvyn Douglas' turgid, boorish interpretation of Weatherby is not the worst performance in the actor's long and distinguished career, it is certainly the silliest. During the early 1960s, Douglas was often quoted as bemoaning the disappearance of the sophisticated comedies that had been his forte in the 1930s and 1940s, at the same time admitting that such films were out of date and declaring his determination to avoid being forever typecast as an urbane, witty roué. In *Advance to the Rear* he definitely succeeded in shattering his old image: No way could we confuse *this* Melvyn Douglas with the sleek continental Romeo who wooed and won Greta Garbo in *Ninotchka*.

Perhaps Douglas overplayed his hand because he didn't have much confidence in the script. This might also explain MGM's ruinous post-production decision to hoke up *Advance to the Rear* with asinine cartoon-style sound effects: Tweety-tweet birdies following a blow on the head, a kettle drum marking a punch in the stomach, slide whistles accompanying a barrage of flying rocks, a "twang" sound whenever a character does a double-take, *ad nauseam*. This artless application of the sound-mixing process extends to the appalling lack of showmanship in the presentation of what would emerge as the film's big song hit, "Today" (aka "A Million Tomorrows"). Performed only once in the film as a vocal by the New Christy Minstrels, the song is thrown away as background music for a scene between Glenn Ford and Stella Stevens, whose dialogue effectively drowns out both the lyrics *and* the melody. Apparently the same guys who thought that "Over the Rainbow" should have been cut from *The Wizard of Oz* were still on the loose in the MGM sound department.

For all its faults, *Advance to the Rear* is admittedly great audience material—provided it isn't an audience of one dour film historian sitting alone in his living room. The missed comic opportunities, clumsy technical aspects and total lack of historical accuracy (since the actors never bother to convince us that they're living in the 1860s, there's no point in citing the film's unwillingness to broach the subject of slavery) can all be forgiven in the light of the first-rate stunt work by a hand-picked team of professionals including Charles Horvath, Hal Needham, Chuck Roberson, Buzz Henry and Frank Mitchell. The stunts are both funny and believable, especially in the scene where each and every member of Company Q falls from his horse at precisely the same time. Equally gratifying is the willingness by several members of the starring cast to perform their own stunts, with Stella Stevens in particular giving her all to her art with a spectacular climactic dunking in MGM's backlot brook.

In attempting to mine laughs from tragedy and devastation, the Civil War comedies cited in this chapter had the advantage of distance. During the 10-year period in which *Hands Up!*, *The General* and *General Spanky* were released, the superannuated veterans of the War were inclined to wax nostalgic rather than dwell upon the horrors of combat whenever they gathered for reunions or media interviews. When *A Southern Yankee* was made in 1948, the ranks had thinned to but a few thousand veterans, mostly in convalescent homes. And by the time *Advance to the Rear* showed up in 1964, there was not one man left standing from the Civil War: The last survivor, a former Confederate drummer boy, passed away in 1959. Had Bob Newhart created his classic monologue on Abraham Lincoln's presidential campaign in 1865 or even 1875, he most likely would have been jailed on sedition charges for his famous punchline: "Say Abe—why don't you take in a play?" But Newhart developed his Lincoln routine in 1959, and the final line was invariably greeted with huge gales of laughter. Time heals all wounds, even those administered by John Wilkes Booth.

From the vantage point of the early 21st century, one wonders if this adage will ever apply to the long, frustrating and ultimately pointless war in Vietnam. Too many veterans still retain bitter memories of a muddy, bloody war in which no one had a clear idea why they were fighting—nor *whom* they were fighting on any given day. Worse still was the indifference and sometimes raw hatred these gallant warriors encountered upon returning home from the war, when they were vilified as "baby killers" for doing fundamentally the same job that had made heroes of their World War II counterparts. Even those of us who never set foot in Southeast Asia would find it difficult to chuckle over a disturbing mosaic of images including an American serviceman casually setting fire to a thatched hut with a cigarette lighter, a Vietnamese police official coldly executing a bound prisoner in the middle of a bustling urban street, and a throng of desperate refugees scrambling aboard an American helicopter as it ascends from the roof of a Saigon apartment building just before the Vietcong takeover in April 1975.

And yet, less than four years after the American pullout at least one war veteran believed that a degree of humor could be sifted from the Vietnam experience. It turned out he was a bit premature, which he subsequently acknowledged: "I guess it was just a little too close in time; nobody believed you could do a comedy about Vietnam." This man was former Air Force sergeant and radio personality Adrian Cronauer, who in May 1965 arrived in Saigon to launch a morning musical program, "The Dawn Buster," for the American Forces Vietnam Network. Though he adhered faithfully to the Service's regulations, Cronauer's fast-paced melange of popular music, deejay chatter and quirky humor breathed new life into the AFVN's notoriously outdated format. "I tried to make AF radio sound like a stateside radio station" was Cronauer's typically modest summary. Even after he left AFVN in April 1966, his trademark sign-on — a loud, extended "Gooooooood MORNING, Vietnam!"— was carried on by his successors, leading many troopers to assume that they were still listening to the long-departed Cronauer. (To this day, he never accepts compliments from fans without carefully advising them of the likelihood that they never actually heard him at all.)

Though he did not regard himself as a crusader during his Vietnam gig, Adrian Cronauer waged an ongoing battle against AFVN's policy of soft-pedalling and censoring potentially volatile war reports. His contention was that the guys in the field had a right to be treated as adults and be apprised of what was really happening, the better to prepare them for future dangers. It was this aspect of his AFVN work, peppered with amusing anecdotes of his experiences in and out of the radio studio, that Cronauer felt had potential as either a feature film or a *M*A*S*H*–like TV sitcom. Six years and several rejections later, this project — titled *Good Morning, Vietnam*— had entered the third circle of Development Hell, and might have remained there had not Larry Brezner, the agent of comedian Robin Williams, optioned the property in 1985.

After undergoing five script revisions, the movie version of *Good Morning, Vietnam* finally went before the cameras in April 1987, with Brezner producing, Barry Levinson directing, and Robin Williams starring as Adrian Cronauer. "From the very inception of the project," Brezner is quoted by historian Lawrence H. Suid as saying, "The dream was to make *Good Morning Vietnam* as a metaphor for the war. In early 1965, no one was taking the Vietnam situation very seriously, but by the end of the year, the number of troops had increased by the thousands. 1965 was the year that Jekyll became Hyde." Touchstone Films executive Jeffrey Katzenburg was a bit more pragmatic: As cited in Henry A. Giroux's *Disturbing Pleasures*, Katzenberg's primary motivation for okaying the film had less to do with making a statement about Vietnam than with providing Robin Williams full range for his raw comic brilliance. The film's subsequent success (a $124 million domestic gross) can safely be attributed to the drawing power of its star rather than its anti-war message. All audiences needed and wanted were those long, unencumbered closeups of Robin Williams sitting in front of a microphone, adlibbing and stream-of-consciousness-ing to his heart's content.

Robin Williams as Adrian Cronauer, signing on his daily AFVN platter party in *Good Morning, Vietnam* (Touchstone/Buena Vista, 1987).

According to the storyline concocted by screenwriter Mitch Markowitz, irreverent young madcap Adrian Cronauer is yanked from obscurity and transferred to Saigon, there to enliven AFVN's morning lineup at the behest of good-ole-boy General Taylor (Noble Willingham). The arrival of this upstart sparks the jealousy of cloddish AFVN programmer Lt. Hauk (Bruno Kirby), who labors under the misapprehension that he is a natural-born comedian, and incurs the downright hostilty of station manager Sgt. Maj. Dickerson (J.T. Walsh), a borderline psycho who regards AFVN as a battlefield and his subordinates as so much cannon fodder. On the brighter side, Cronauer finds a pair of kindred spirits in chubby Pvt. Garlick (Forrest Whitaker) and eternally guffawing engineer Dreiwitz (Robert Wuhl).

Cronauer immediate shakes things up by rejecting AFVN's "approved" playlist of Ray Coniff, Perry Como and Lawrence Welk, replacing them with such cutting-edge artists as the Beach Boys and James Brown. He also stakes out his territory with his clarion call "Gooooood MORNING, Vietnam!" and his ceaseless cannonades of political, sexual and scatological humor between records. The more popular he becomes with the troops, the more aggravating he becomes to Hauk and Dickerson. They jump at the opportunity to suspend the irrepressible Cronauer when, in a fit of pique, he breaks AFVN rules by delivering a censored news report of a Saigon restaurant bombing which he himself has witnessed. Though restored to his job by popular demand (his replacement Houk proves to be about as funny as a land mine), the disenchanted Cronauer is all for packing it in and leaving AFVN — until he comes face to face with several soldiers to whom his daily program is the sole ray of sunshine in the dark void of Vietnam. "War wipes the grin off [Cronauer]'s face," notes film critic Roger Ebert. "His humor becomes a humanitarian tool, not simply a way to keep him talking and us listening."

But not for long. While pursuing a romance with Trinh (Chintara Sukapatana), a Vietnamese girl he met while teaching an English-language class, Cronauer comes in contact with Trinh's brother Tuan (Tung Than Tranh), who unbeknownst to our hero is a Vietcong terrorist. This finally gives Dickerson an excuse to permanently banish Cronauer from the airwaves and have him discharged, but a protacted climax indicates that the hero-worshipping Pvt. Garlick will pull an "Ensign Pulver" and carry on Cronauer's mission (and radio format) for many years to come.

Yes, Adrian Cronauer had been in Saigon; yes, he had broadcast for AFVN in 1965 and 1966; and yes, he was a staunch opponent of radio censorship. Beyond that, *Good Morning, Vietnam* has so little to do with the real Cronauer that when asked why the film even used his name, he replied, "It beats me." For starters, none of his superior officers ever objected to his on-air behavior or the music he played. "In the film it shows that I was constantly being pushed around by the brass, which wasn't really the case." On those rare occasions when his superiors expressed an opinion of his work, it was one of apathy rather than hostility. They simply couldn't understand why he went to so much trouble to make his daily broadcast so entertaining: With nothing else to listen to, the troops would have tuned in every morning regardless of what Cronauer said or did. Nor was he discharged for insubodination and sent home in disgrace. Cronauer left AFVN simply because his tour of duty was over.

The situation might have been different had Cronauer really indulged in the sort of edgy free-association comedy that was Robin Williams' forte. But instead of launching into extended rants about such hot-button issues as bureaucratic stupidity, race relations, drug use and copulation, Cronauer preferred subtle one-liners and mild situational humor ("If I had done half of what Robin Williams did, I would have been in jail.") And although his "Goooooooood MORNING, Vietnam!" sign-on is portrayed as an act of defiance in the film, Cronauer actually used this drawn-out salutation to give himself enough time to set up his turntables and tape cartridges so that he could get his show off and running without any "dead air."

The funniest scene in *Good Morning Vietnam* is the one that deviates farthest from the facts. Forced to air a prerecorded pro-war speech by former Vice President Richard Nixon, Cronauer puckishly re-edits the tape in the form of an interview, using loaded questions to make it sound as if Nixon has been smoking weed. Sidesplitting though it may be, this sequence is a fabrication from top to bottom. For one thing, Richard Nixon was completely off the political radar in 1965, a non-person so far as professional jokesters were concerned. For another thing, Adrian Cronauer was, and is, a staunch Republican.

It would be wearisome to rattle off the many other departures from the truth in *Good Morning, Vietnam* (To cite one among many: Cronauer did indeed conduct an English-language class for the locals, but he certainly didn't teach them Anglo-Saxon profanities and black street jargon!) Nor would it serve any purpose to annotate the script's many anachronisms, inevitable in a film wherein a comedian with 1980s sensibilities is cast as a 1960s deejay. The main consideration in discussing *Good Morning, Vietnam* is whether or not it succeeds as a comedy. The answer is a resounding "Yes"—but only so long as Robin Williams is on screen. Whenever the star is absent, the pace lags and the plot contrivances begin to show, most glaringly in the overwrought sequences involving Cronauer's principal antagonists Hauk and Dickerson. These two humorless twits are so unremittingly despicable (if Dickerson had a mustache, he'd have twirled it) that the audience is *forced* to hate them—and simultaneously forced to pull for a protagonist who, as written and played, is little more than a shallow, self-righteous windbag.

Outside of Williams' brilliant radio monologues, the film scores highest in its distressingly authentic depiction of 1965 Saigon and its environs, an authenticity confirmed by veterans of the war. (Politicial expediency required the filmmakers to use Thailand as a substitute for Vietnam.) Especially powerful in conveying the confusion and ambiguity of the entire Southest Asian experience is the scene in which Cronauer tries to save his girlfriend's terrorist brother from being shot on sight by the Americans. Stumbling into a squalid, war-ravaged jungle village, Cronauer finds himself surrounded by stone-faced civilians who glower at him with barely concealed contempt. Though Robin Williams says very little in this scene, the benumbed expression on his face speaks volumes: Who exactly *is* the Enemy here? Could it possibly be Cronauer himself?

Described by *Time* magazine as "the best military comedy since *MASH* disbanded," *Good Morning, Vietnam* doesn't entirely hold up when seen today, but this is due more to changing tastes than the film's content. Contemporary audiences indoctrinated in the gospel of Political Correctness may be disinclined to laugh unreservedly at Robin Williams' constant African American dialect jokes and incessant jibes at homosexuality. These same audiences have, however, responded positively to the *Good Morning Vietnam* derivations in which Williams has starred since 1987. Take a close look at both *Dead Poets Society* and *Patch Adams* and you'll notice that both films are constructed in precisely the same manner as *Vietnam*: The wacky-but-sincere maverick invading an ultra-conservative environment, provoking his resentful colleagues to the point that they must "destroy" him—but not before he has made the world around him a better place.

The real Adrian Cronauer has nothing but praise for Williams and *Good Morning Vietnam*, despite the screenplay's careless handling of the facts. The film's success has bestowed celebrity status upon Cronauer, providing the broadcaster-turned-lawyer with a bully pulpit to carry on his work as a spokesman for free speech in the media and for fair and equitable treatment of military veterans. It has also enabled him to tolerate those confused fans who insist upon accosting him and gushing about how much they enjoyed *Dead Poets Society*. At least, Cronauer chuckles, they don't tell him how much they enjoyed *Mrs. Doubtfire*.

Though *Good Morning Vietnam* upholds the *MASH* tradition of playing its comedy against the backdrop of a terrible and controversial war, this is hardly the case with another Vietnam comedy, 1995's *Operation Dumbo Drop*. Rather than address any of the serious or troubling issues that would normally arise from a cinematic dissection of Vietnam, *Operation Dumbo Drop* goes along its merry way as if none of these issues exist. It is altogether appropriate that the film was a Disney project, since its depiction of the Vietnam war is about as historically accurate as the Pirates of the Caribbean ride at the Magic Kingdom.

Operation Dumbo Drop was inspired by a true story, first related in print by former U.S. Special Forces officer Jim Morris. The events occurred in the late 1960s, a time when many pro–American Vietnamese villagers were acting as unofficial intelligence agents by reporting enemy troop movements along the Ho Chi Minh Trail. To secure the villagers' loyalty, Special Ops went to great lengths to honor and respect all local customs, traditions and religious beliefs. According to Morris, who served three tours in Vietnam, the villagers' elephants were especially prized and sacrosanct, not only used as beasts of burden but also worshipped as demigods. In certain areas

Bo Tat the elephant and his young mascot Linh (Dinh Thien Le) are escorted through the jungles of Vietnam by Green Berets Cahill (Danny Glover) and Doyle (Ray Liotta) in *Operaton Dumbo Drop* (Disney/Buena Vista, 1995). Bringing up the rear are specialists Ashford (Doug E. Doug), Poole (Denis Leary) and Farley (Corin Nemec).

where the pachyderm population had been scattered or killed off, it was necessary for Special Ops to bring in fresh supplies of healthy elephants. It has been claimed by Morris and other first-hand sources that in the spring of 1968, one such elephant was winched into the cargo hold of a C-130 transport plane and then parachuted into a remote village.

Scripted by *Police Academy* veteran Gene Quintano and future *Ghost Whisperer* producer Jim Kouf, *Operation Dumbo Drop* was directed by Simon Wincer, who had previously helmed the PETA–friendly moneyspinner *Free Willy*. Danny Glover and Ray Liotta star respectively as Sam Cahill and T.C. Doyle, two Green Beret captains of vastly different temperaments. In charge of a native village bordering the Ho Chi Minh Trail, Doyle has become so immersed in the local culture that he seems positively zenlike in comparision with his stiff-necked replacement Doyle, who never moves a muscle without consulting the rulebook. Accidentally precipitating the death of the village's beloved elephant, Doyle is ordered to find a replacement and bring it back to the natives. To this end, Cahill and Doyle assemble a team of operatives including scared-and-superstitious SP4 Ashford (Doug E. Doug), animal-phobic SP5 Farley (Corin Nemec), and shady requisitions officer Lt. Poole (Denis Leary). Through ways of his own, Poole manages to dig up an elephant named Bo Tat, who unfortunately is a near-rogue that can only be controlled by its youthful trainer, an orphan named Linh (Dinh Thien Le) who harbors a deep distrust of Americans. Inevitably — and what's a Disney flick without a dewy-eyed kid?— Linh is allowed to go along with Doyle and company as they carry out their mission. Also inevitably, Doyle shakes off his rules-are-rules rigidity and becomes warm and likable, while Linh loses the chip on his shoulder and becomes ardently pro–U.S.A. (The film tactfully ends before we can ascertain Linh's fate after the Communist takeover.)

A few isolated moments in the film suggest that the director and scriptwriters *might* have been inclined to rise above the usual Disney formula trappings. When at one point Bo Tat is transported across a river on an ancient barge, the film unexpectedly segues into a spoof of Robert

Duvall's *Die Walküre*-loving helicopter pilot in *Apocalypse Now*, as the scruffy barge captain lustily sings along to a recording of "Queen of the Night" from *The Magic Flute*. And there's an unusually tense and thrilling finale, blending superb aerial photography with flawless process work as the parachute-equipped Bo Tat bails out of the C-130 with enemy aircraft bearing down from all sides (here as in several earlier scenes, the elephant is extensively "doubled" by an animatronic replica.)

Otherwise, the filmmakers take the easy and predictable way out at every turn. In the tradition of such earlier Disneys as *Sammy the Way-Out Seal* and *The Ugly Daschund,* no opportunity for gratuitous slapstick arising from the presence of an oversized animal is ever wasted. During the first leg of their trek into the jungle, the Specialists load Bo Tat onto a cargo plane, where a disgruntled Doyle must explore the animal's rectal regions to apply a tranquilizer — which of course wears off at the least opportune moment, whereupon the aroused elephant shimmies and shakes so much that the human passengers are tossed to and fro like rag dolls. Later, Bo Tat is led onto a flatbed truck and driven through a crowded village square. On cue, the elephant escapes and runs amok, leading to the time-honored Disney "mayhem in the marketplace" sequence with sundry produce carts smashed to bits, fruits and vegetables flying in all directions. Too bad that the village population didn't include a well-dressed dowager who could take a headlong dive into a three-tiered wedding cake.

Beginning with the producers' decision to film the location scenes in some of the prettiest and least threatening patches of Thailand real estate imaginable, the overall lack of credibility in *Operation Dumbo Drop* is mind-numbing. The film may set a record for the least amount of casualties in *any* Vietnam picture. Other than a flashback in which Linh's father is caught in the crossfire of a jungle skirmish, and the offscreen death of the elephant whom Bo Tat replaces, no one is killed or even wounded. This shouldn't be too surprising, since throughout the film the Viet Cong is characterized as the Gang That Couldn't Shoot Straight. It is even suggested that the enemy forces don't really *want* to use their weapons; near the end of the picture, an NVA anti-aircraft gunner refuses to open fire upon Bo Tat, exclaiming, "I did not join this Army to shoot elephants—especially ones that fly." And we *lost* this war?

More astonishing still is the fact that there is virtually no profanity in the film — and keep in mind that we're talking about a 1995 movie set in 1968 Vietnam, featuring Ray Liotta from *Wiseguy*, Denis Leary from *The Ref* and Danny Glover from every violent action flick since Mankind began to walk upright. The near-total absence of cuss words might not have been so obvious were it not for the moment in which Ray Liotta reacts to an unexpected setback by exclaiming, "My word!" It is conceivable that the filmmakers threw Denis Leary a bone by allowing him a single scene in which he "damns" and "hells" with abandon and ruminates over a past clandestine affair with a superior officer's wife; but notice that this scene does nothing to advance the plot, and can easily be removed for future family-hour network telecasts. Otherwise, it would appear that the film earned its PG rating not from its mild profanity, but from its repeated references to elephant poop.

Many observers are disturbed by *Operation Dumbo Drop*'s stubborn refusal to invest its Vietnam setting with even a modicum of reality. Disturbing for different reasons is the film's depiction of SP4 Ashford, the character played by African American comedian Doug E. Doug. Bulging his eyes, trembling in his boots and frantically rubbing a rabbit's foot, Ashford comes uncomfortably close to winning the Stepin Fetchit Award away from *Star Wars: The Phantom Menace*'s Jar Jar Binks. All that saves the film from being labelled as implicitly racist is the balancing presence of cool-and-confident Capt. Cahill (Danny Glover), and Ashford's last-reel heroics when he overcomes his terror and rescues his comrades from the VC.

Good Morning, Vietnam falls a few yards short of perfection; *Operation Dumbo Drop* misses the target completely. The fact that the Vietnam war has as of this writing inspired only two comedy films would seem to verify Adrian Cronauer's theory: It may be "just a little too close in time" for laughter.

19

"One, Two Three, What Are We Fighting For?"
Anti-War and Anti-Military Comedies

It isn't necessary to launch into a history of anti-war and anti-military films to declare with some authority that most such films have been dramas: *All Quiet on the Western Front, J'Accuse, Paths of Glory, The Naked and the Dead, The Victors, Casualties of War, Redacted,* et al. In the years bordering the two World Wars, such "anti" films were born from a general disillusionment and a feeling that shedding blood on behalf of an imperfect national philosophy might well be a futile or even meaningless sacrifice. Only during the period between 1961 and 1971, the years covering the "progress" of the Vietnam War from an obscure foreign skirmish to a voracious monster devouring thousands of young lives for no clear or discernable purpose, did the anti-war/anti-military/anti-establishment *comedy* film gain prominence. While an attempt to provide an succinct explanation for this phenomenon would be presumptuous, here's a modest suggestion: Faced with the worst life has to offer, some people prefer laughing hysterically to sobbing uncontrollably— especially the talented people who made these "anti-" comedies possible. And it takes a lot of talent, to say nothing of a lot of nerve, to generate laughter while whistling in a graveyard.

The films given the most space in this chapter are the three most often cited as the definitive anti-war and anti-military comedies: *Dr. Strangelove, Catch-22* and *MASH*. Also included are three others that aren't as famous or celebrated—among them at least one film you've probably never heard of. Certainly *I'd* never heard of it until I started this book.

Dr. Strangelove grew from a novel written by former RAF intelligence officer Peter George and inspired by an incident that occurred while George was serving at a United States military base in 1957. As a B-47 soared overhead, the vibration caused a coffee cup to crash to the floor, whereupon a startled onlooker declared "That's the way World War III will start!" Within three weeks, George had fashioned a nightmare scenario about a suicidal American general named Quinlen who becomes obsessed with the belief that the only way to prevent the Soviet Union from bombing the United States into the stone age is to stage a pre-emptive strike, nuking the Russians before they have a chance to blink. Asking himself if an American bombing crew would be willing to embark on such a mission, Quinlen answers his own question: If he were to *personally* order the strike, his crew would be duty-bound to follow his orders without question. Tipped off to Quinlen's mad scheme by a plot device as trivial as that smashed coffee cup, the American President has only two hours to stop the general's bombers from destroying Moscow. Quinlen alone possesses the secret code needed to bring the bombers home, but when the general commits suicide it is up to one of his aides to decipher the near-incomprehensible code words. Meanwhile, the President has given the Soviet premier full authority to shoot down the American bombers—and if this fails, the Soviets will be allowed to destroy a major American city in retaliation. On the very brink of Apocalypse, the lead bomber is brought down by the Russians and the world is saved. Except for the lunatic Quinlen, there is little of an anti-military nature in the novel. Peter George's message is that the fate of Mankind should never be in the hands of any single man, but instead must depend upon a permanent balance of power between the United States and the USSR.

Using the pseudonym Peter Bryant, George published his novel in England in 1958 under the title *Two Hours to Doom*; not long afterward, it appeared in America as *Red Alert*. One of several doomsday thrillers of the late 1950s (*On the Beach, Alas Babylon,* et al.), *Red Alert* might have been forgotten had it not been referenced in an early-1960s article written by Thomas Schelling for *The Bulletin of Atomic Scientists.* Around that same time, filmmaker Stanley Kubrick was deep into research on the subject of thermonuclear warfare. Reading Schelling's article, Kubrick dug up a copy of *Red Alert*, then contacted Peter George with an offer to transfer the novel to film. As Kubrick and his producer Jack H. Harris labored on a preliminary screenplay, the two men came down with an attack of giggles when one of them wondered aloud what would happen if, during a tense conference on the impending destruction of the world, a delivery boy from the local deli calmly ambled into the War Room to take sandwich orders. Thereafter, Kubrick was incapable of thinking of *Red Alert* in anything but comic terms. He decided to transform the work into a satire of nuclear paranoia, jettisoning the novel's original upbeat ending in favor of one of the blackest and funniest finales in the annals of screen comedy.

This decision scotched any further screenplay collaboration between Kubrick and Peter George, who saw nothing amusing in the concept of global annihilation. Kubrick then turned to humorist Jules Feiffer, who likewise did not share the director's vision. At this point, the film's proposed star Peter Sellers took a hand in matters. Enchanted by Terry Southern's wickedly hilarious novel *The Magic Christian*, Sellers convinced Kubrick that Southern was just the man to bring the film version of *Red Alert* to full satiric fruition. It was Southern who, despite his late entry into the proceedings, set the film's absurdist tone by providing the characters such *MAD*-magazine monikers as General Jack D. Ripper, General Buck Turgidson, Major "King" Kong, Colonel "Bat" Guano, and President Merkin Muffley (this last name a dirty joke we won't explain here). And it was Southern who promoted the film's thesis that Mankind's primitive urge to kill is joined at the hip with his primal urge for unbridled sex.

In the earliest stages, the filmmakers had come up with the nominal hero of the piece, to be played by Peter Sellers: A bookish American science professor who becomes intoxicated with power when he turns out to be the only man qualified to save the world from nuclear devastation. This character would evolve into a demented ex–Nazi scientist named Dr. Strangelove, who upon realizing that the Apocalypse is unavoidable droolingly outlines a plan whereby the post-nuclear world will be repopulated through the mating of a select group of middle-aged political and military leaders with a carefully chosen harem of voluptuous young women (this sort of May-December carnality had been at the heart of Kubrick's earlier *Lolita*). While some latter-day "experts" have suggested that the thickly accented Strangelove was based on future Nixon adviser Henry Kissinger (a virtual unknown in the early 1960s), he was actually inspired by nuclear expert Edward Teller. The character's German dialect came from a truly out-of-left-field source: The legendary Austrian tabloid photographer "Weegee" (nee Arthur Fellig), whom Peter Sellers had met on the set of *Red Alert*. By that time, however, the film wasn't called *Red Alert* any more: To clue the audience in on its comic nature, the filmmakers had come up with the delightfully cumbersome *Dr. Strangelove or: How I Learned to Stop Worrying and Love the Bomb.*

According to both Peter Sellers and Terry Southern, *Strangelove* was a tough sell for potential financiers, who agreed to invest in the project only when assured that the versatile Sellers would play *all* the principal male roles *a la* Alec Guinness in *Kind Hearts and Coronets*. When this proved unwieldly, Sellers was limited to playing Strangelove, President Muffley (whom the actor patterned after Adlai Stevenson), RAF group captain Lionel Mandrake, and lead bomber pilot Major "King" Kong. An injury forced Sellers to surrender the role of Kong to American actor Slim Pickens (after *Bonanza*'s Dan Blocker turned down the part), but it's likely that Kubrick would have politely asked Sellers to forsake Kong due to the actor's inability to master a broad Texas accent.

The rest of the cast was filled by a matchless ensemble. Having seen George C. Scott and James Earl Jones in Joseph Papp's Central Park production of *The Merchant of Venice*, Kubrick cast Scott as xenophobic General Buck Turgidson and Jones (in his film debut) as aerial navigator Lothar Zogg (one of Southern's cleaner inside jokes: the "original" Lothar was the hulking African assistant of comic-strip hero Mandrake the Magician — and note the aforementioned Lionel Mandrake). The part of General Jack D. Ripper (the equivalent of the novel's General Quinlen) was played by Sterling Hayden, whom Kubrick had previously directed in *The Killing* (1956). Military-comedy stalwart Keenan Wynn proved to be a tower of strength in the cameo role of Col. "Bat" Guano, who sees "deviated preverts" everywhere. Finally, when Kubrick was informed that the only way he'd be permitted to shoot *Strangelove* in England (per Peter Sellers' contractual demands) was to cast at least one more British actor in a major part, Peter Bull was signed on as Soviet ambassador De Sedesky, who grimly reveals the existence of the "Doomsday Device" that will trigger an unstoppable nuclear chain reaction should Moscow be destroyed.

Kubrick had wanted to play the film totally straight and allow the laughs to grow from the situation, but with Peter Sellers improvising to his heart's content this proved impossible. The director compensated by allowing the actors full head to bellow and posture while staging the plot itself in as straightforward a manner as possible, with the help of production designer Ken Adam's realistically austere sets and Gilbert Taylor's documentary-style monochrome photography. Terry Southern went along with this approach, offsetting the script's absurdities with the ominous "grounding" of the Doomsday Device. The only time Kubrick deviated from his kidding-on-the-square approach was the intended climax for the film, which was to occur just before the closing montage of mushroom clouds and the syrupy strains of Vera Lynn's "We'll Meet Again." As conceived and filmed, the War Room personnel vented their frustrations over the world's impending doom with a Mack Sennett-style pie fight. A lot of time and money was expended on this sequence, but ultimately it was removed from the release print. Kubrick later said that the pie-hurling melee shattered the film's delicate balance between hilarity and horror; Terry Southern stated that the pie fight fell flat because the actors were obviously having too much fun; and those who have seen the fully edited version of the original finale at the British Film Institute have opined that the sequence was dropped simply because it wasn't funny. No matter: Film purists are willing to forgo a "director's cut" of *Dr. Strangelove*'s final scene as long as they are blessed with the spectacle of the crippled Strangelove, galvanized by the prospect of breeding with dozens of nubile maidens, standing erect and screaming, "Mein Fuhrer! I can walk!"

Dr. Strangelove (Columbia, 1964): The titular doctor (Peter Sellers) ponders the possibilites of a post-apocalyptic world populated by dirty old men and ripe young women.

It was not Kubrick's avowed intention to create an anti-military film. He had clearly hoped that the level-headed Lionel Mandrake and the quietly efficient Lothar

Zogg would compensate for the grotesquely caricatured Jack D. Ripper, Buck Turgidson, Major Kong and Bat Guano. But the scales were tipped in favor of the grotesques, and *Dr. Strangelove* stands as one of the most devastating attacks on the military mindset ever filmed. This is especially true in the film's depiction of Jack D. Ripper, who comes off as a lampoon of über-conservative General Edwin D. Walker. A favorite *bête noire* of American liberals, Walker made no secret of his anti–Kennedy and anti–Civil Rights sentiments, prompting the U.S. Army's decision to relieve the General of his command shortly before *Strangelove*'s release. (Another Edwin Walker clone appears in John Frankenheimer's *Seven Days in May*, played by Burt Lancaster.)

Ripper's twisted rationale for attacking the Soviets—his delusion that the Communists have poisoned America's "precious bodily fluids"—is based on another 1960s platform of the Extreme Right: the addlepated theory that the fluoridation of America's drinking water was somehow a sinister Commie plot. Ripper's ramblings also feed into *Dr. Strangelove's* correlation between warfare and sex, which is further underlined by the iconic image of a yahooing Major Kong ecstatically riding to his death astride a very phallic-looking bomb, and the apelike leer on Turgidson's face as Strangelove maps out his "Playboy Philosophy" scenario to repopulate the Earth. Surprisingly, *Dr. Strangelove* encountered only minor problems with the Production Code over the smirking eroticism of the dialogue. The censors seemed more preoccupied with such piffle as the number of "hells" and "damns," and the brevity of the bikini worn by Gen. Turgidson's mistress (Tracy Reed, billed in the studio ad copy—but not on screen—as "Miss Foreign Affairs").

Columbia Pictures served as distributor when *Dr. Strangelove* went into general release in January 1964, but not without a few bumps along the road. It wasn't that Columbia was hesitant to promote an anti-military film: the studio already had such a project in circulation, producer Carl Foreman's all-star World War II epic *The Victors*. A far costlier production than *Strangelove*, Foreman's film was heavily promoted to the extent that the studio's PR department went around advising theater owners to tell their patrons that *Strangelove* was sold out, and to go see *The Victors* instead. Also, *Red Alert* author Peter George had brought legal action against Eugene Burdick and Harvey Wheeler, co-authors of the alarmingly similar doomsday novel *Fail-Safe*. It didn't take long for several concerned parties to point out that George hadn't said Word One about *Fail-Safe* when it was published, nor even when it was serialized in *The Saturday Evening Post*, but only after director Sidney Lumet announced his intention to film the property. Nonetheless, to mollify George's attorneys Columbia agreed to take over distribution of the 1963 movie version of *Fail-Safe*, with the assurance that *Dr. Strangelove* would be released first. Not unexpectedly, the promotional blitz surrounding the Kubrick film cut deeply into *Fail-Safe*'s profit potential, and Columbia was forced to absorb the loss. There were also a few uncomfortable moments now and then when moviegoers who had already seen *Strangelove* began laughing in the wrong places during *Fail-Safe*. These isolated incidents gave film critic Andrew Sarris, who has spent many a waking hour tearing down Stanley Kubrick, the opportunity to quip that "*Fail-Safe* is funnier unintentionally than *Dr. Strangelove* is intentionally."

Both films wound up providing unintentional laughs thanks to a preemptive move made by Columbia to deflect criticism from government and military officials. *Dr. Strangelove* and *Fail-Safe* were originally released with a disclaimer tacked onto the opening credits, assuring the public that the nuclear blunders occuring on-screen could never, *ever* happen in real life, Scout's Honor. Funnier still was an extra precaution taken by the Strategic Air Command to dispell any fears raised in the public's consciousness by the plotlines of *Strangelove* (war triggered by rogue general) and *Fail-Safe* (nuclear attack launched by computer glitch). Briefly going into the movie business, the organization commissioned a 17-minute propaganda film titled *SAC Command Post*. In one sequence, stock footage of row upon row of nuclear bombers, followed by scenes of uniformed men comandeering a deck of telephones, is accompanied by the soothing words of an offscreen narrator: "World War Three can't be triggered by an unauthorized launching of a nuclear bomb.... Positive and authentic voice instructions originating at the presidential level are required to commit the SAC forces to their target." Civilian translation: We're never wrong, it can't happen, shut up, go back to sleep. (For reasons unknown, *SAC Command Post* was never released, remaining buried until researcher William Burr dug up the only surviving copy in 2010.)

The excitement over *Dr. Strangelove* overshadowed the *other* significant military satire of 1964, MGM's *The Americanization of Emily*. Adapted from a 1959 novel by William Bradford Huie, *Emily* was originally the second installment in a trilogy devoted to the "private and uncensored" memoirs of United States Naval Reserve officer James Monroe Madison, a character largely based on Huie himself (the first novel in the Madison "series," 1951's *The Revolt of Mamie Stover*, had been filmed in 1956 with Jane Russell and Richard Egan). A public relations specialist, Lt. Jimmy Madison is what is known as a "dog-robber," a master at keeping himself and his superior officers well fed, well clothed, and well loved by willing damsels. Stationed in wartime London as an aide to Admiral William Jessup, Madison manages to requisition the best food, liquor, accommodations and other perks despite severe shortages and tight rationing. As flippant about women as he is about military protocol, Madison regards the entire female population of London as candidates for "Americanization," referring not to bringing the Yankee brand of democracy to Merrie Olde England but to bribing girls into granting sexual favors by offering fresh fruit, candy and cigarettes.

Such is Madison's philosophy when he tries to put the moves on his WAAF chauffeur Emily, a young war widow with a grudge against Americans. Plied with rationed strawberries during her first dinner with Madison, Emily protests that the tasty treat is "too forbidden, too expensive," not at all the reaction to which the lieutenant is accustomed. Later admitting that she has occasionally shared her affections too easily *without* being bribed, Emily feels guilty about accepting gifts and responding in kind: "Am I behaving like a whore?" she asks Madison. "Whoring is a peacetime action," he replies, setting the cynical tone of their relationship. In a secondary plotline, Adm. Jessup demands that the upcoming D–Day invasion be exploited for morale purposes with an on-the-spot documentary film, which Madison has been ordered to supervise. (In real life, William Bradford Huie had been among the first Americans to land on Normandy.) Though he regards the documentary mission to be as ludicrous as it is dangerous, Madison is fully prepared to risk his life for the sake of pro–American propaganda — much to the dismay of Emily, who doesn't need any more dead lovers in her life.

In book form *The Americanization of Emily* is a straight romantic yarn with very few laughs. It was the decision of screenwriter Paddy Chayefsky to reshape the story into a satire of empty patriotism and military stupidity, transforming the character of Lt. Madison into a craven — and self-admitted — coward, who goes to extreme lengths to avoid combat duty. As the Madison of the screenplay explains to Emily's mother: "Wars are always fought for the best of reasons.... So far this war we've managed to butcher some ten million humans in the interest of humanity.... As long as valor remains a virtue we shall have soldiers. So I preach cowardice. Through cowardice we shall be saved." Having lost a husband and a brother in the war, Emily finds this philosophy disgusting, but can't help falling in love with a man who has no pretensions about himself.

Chayefsky also savagely skewers the military higher-ups, anticipating his own Oscar-winning script for *Network* (1977) by placing a madman in charge of the D-Day documentary. Having suffered a nervous breakdown a few days before the invasion, the normally rational Adm. Jessup is in the grip of dementia, hysterically raving that there is only one way to make certain the Navy will continue getting Congressional appropriations: "The first dead man on Omaha Beach *must* be a sailor!" Jessup goes so far as to assign a Navy cameraman to capture this "glorious" death on film. Though well aware that Jessup hasn't got all his pencils in a straight row, overambitious Navy officer "Bus" Cummings carries out the Admiral's orders to the letter, pulling strings to push the reluctant Madison directly into the line of fire on D-Day — then forcing him at gunpoint to scramble onto the shore of Omaha Beach before any of the other troops have shown up! The situation is beyond absurd, but Paddy Chayefsky had no qualms about abandoning credibility to drive home his anti-war and anti-military manifesto.

Had *Americanization of Emily* possessed the courage of *Dr. Strangelove*'s convictions, the film would have ended with Madison's death and Adm. Jessup going on to greater glories without anyone suspecting how dangerously demented he really was. Possibly because it was felt that Chayefsky had already pushed the envelope with an American war film built around an acknowledged coward, a cop-out coda was devised in which Madison is only presumed to be dead — and upon turning up alive, he is sent on a stateside "victory tour" as the first hero of the Invasion. At the same time, Jessup has fully recovered from his breakdown, expressing contrition for having come up with such a ridiculous scheme and anger at Bus Cummings for acting upon orders that had obviously been issued by a crackpot. As for Emily, her initial contempt for Madison's yellow streak has given way to respect for his lack of intestinal fortitude: "Every man I ever loved was a hero and all I got was death." Nevertheless, she encourages him to continue posing as the hero he's supposed to be, because that's what the World happens to need at the moment.

When the movie version of *The Americanization of Emily* was first announced in 1962, Martin Ritt was slated to direct. Having recently emerged from the exile of Hollywood blacklist, Ritt was a risky choice for a film that cast a disparaging light upon the Military. Producer Martin Ransohoff fended off criticism by circulating a statement from author William Bradford Huie: "[It] is not subversive or unpatriotic to depict an Amercan admiral playing bridge in London before D-Day or drinking whisky or eating steak or bathing with Palmolive soap or enjoying the company of a beautiful woman." But by the time production began, Ransohoff had replaced Martin Ritt with the less controversial William Wyler — and when Wyler insisted upon a complete script overhaul, he himself was dropped in favor of Arthur Hiller.

The first choice for the role of Lt. Madison was William Holden; when he took a pass the studio signed James Garner, who'd originally been in line for the part of Bus Cummings. Garner proved to be a perfect selection, having previously established himself with his portrayal of a charming coward in the TV series *Maverick* (his casting may be the reason that Madison's first name was changed from "James" to "Charley"— too much identification with a specific character type could be harmful to an actor's career). In her second film — and her only one in black&white — Julie Andrews is positively radiant as Emily, a role that her agents would probably have vetoed a few years later as being counter to her goody-goody *Sound of Music* image (during one scene with Garner, Julie exclaims, "Oh, I hope to God I'm pregnant!"— a far cry from getting all aflutter over raindrops on roses and whiskers on kittens). Melvyn Douglas treads a fine line between lucidity and lunacy as Adm. Jessup; James Coburn is a quiet riot conveying Bus Cummings' casual callousness as he feeds into Jessup's craziness; and Keenan Wynn carves another notch in his "war movie" handle as the drunken old salt who is assigned to film Madison's death throes at Normandy. Seen briefly as Bus Cummings' *au naturel* bedmate is a pre–*Laugh-In* Judy Carne, identified in the closing credits as one of "Three Nameless Broads." •

Despite its watered-down finale, *The Americanization of Emily* proved disturbing to moviegoers with preconceived notions of how wartime heroics should be depicted on screen. A few observers who hadn't yet learned to appreciate the *Strangelove* brand of dark humor were offended by the zaniness of the final reels, with one critic condemning the "pretty deadly joke of making a comedy episode of the D-Day landing and having laughs at the expense of an admiral who has had a nervous breakdown." Though it earned two Oscar nominations, the film failed to make back its cost, and might have remained in MGM's red-ink column had it not been reissued a few years later under the simplified title *Emily*, cashing in on the popularity of both Julie Andrews and the theme song written for the film by Johnny Mandel and Johnny Mercer.

Three years after *Emily*, MGM bankrolled another comedy that poked fun at the military, with even less success. *The Extraordinary Seaman* was intended to be an anti–Vietnam satire, or so director John Frankenheimer would always claim when the topic of the film came up. But when pressed for details, Frankenheimer would become vague and evasive, either promising to someday tell the "whole story" behind the project or huffily refusing to discuss the film because the memory

Taking advantage of Julie Andrews' post–*Sound of Music* superstardom, MGM reissued their 1964 comedy-drama ***The Americanization of Emily*** with a streamlined title and new poster graphics, deliberately obscuring the film's trenchant antiwar message. In the process, supporting player James Coburn — who like Andrews had become a box-office magnet since the film's initial release — was elevated to costar status.

was too painful. Critics and historians are divided into two camps, with devotees of Frankenheimer citing the director's best films—*The Birdman of Alcatraz, The Manchurian Candidate, Seven Days in May*—as "proof" that the mediocrity we now know as *The Extraordinary Seaman* was butchered beyond all recognition by those philistines at MGM, utterly destroying its creator's "vision." Less worshipful observers, noting that Frankenheimer was also responsible for such train wrecks as *Prophecy* and *The Island of Dr. Moreau*, are of the opinion that *Seaman* pretty much represents what the director had in mind from the get-go, and that MGM's culpability in its failure was marginal.

Scripted by Philip Rock and Hal Dresner, *Extraordinary Seaman* is the Flying Dutchman legend updated to World War II. Detached from their ship during a lifeboat drill, four blundering American sailors—Lt. Morton Krim, Cook 3rd Class W.J. Oglethorpe, Gunner's Mate Orville O'Toole and Seaman 1st Class Lightfoot Star—are marooned on an uncharted Philippine island. Before long the quartet comes upon the *H.M.S. Curmudgeon*, a World War I–vintage gunboat stuck in a sandbar. The *Curmudgeon* is skippered by Lt. Commander Finchhaven, an eccentric Britisher garbed in an immaculate white uniform and guzzling from a seemingly bottomless whiskey bottle. During a later forage into the island for supplies to repair the gunboat, the sailors are shot at by Jennifer Winslow, the attractive American who runs the local trading post. Jennifer agrees to give them supplies in exchange for passage off the island, but Finchhaven seems reluctant to set sail. Only after a group of Filipino refugees are added to the passenger roster is it revealed that Finchhaven is a ghost, doomed to remain on board the *Curmudgeon* until he can make amends for disgracing his family (war heroes all) when he got drunk and fell overboard during his first battle in 1914. The Commander is bent upon proving his worthiness to enter admiralty heaven by ramming the *Curmudgeon* into a nearby Japanese cruiser, unaware that this happens to be the same ship where the Americans and Japanese are about to sign the treaty ending World War II. The cruiser is destroyed, the "live" characters are forced to tread water until they are rescued, and Finchhaven is condemned to remain earthbound on the *Curmudgeon*—which by film's end has been transformed into a tourist attraction—until the *next* war comes around.

The original plan was to film *The Extraordinary Seaman* on location in the Philippines, but when this didn't work out the cast and crew moved to the Mexican coastal outpost of Coatzacoalos, somewhere between Mexico City and the Yucatan Peninsula. A tough three-month shoot in the Spring of 1967 was made tougher by oppressive heat, bad weather, inadequate local facilities and periodic invasions from wild horses, stray chickens and rampaging cockroaches. Faye Dunaway, who in her fourth feature film was cast as rifle-toting Jennifer Winslow, has very few pleasant memories of the film in her autobiography except for the actor cast as the dotty spectre Finchhaven, David Niven—whom she recalls as gracious, charming, and an endless source of hilarious Hollywood anecdotes. Alan Alda, in his *second* feature film cast as the inexperienced Lt. Krim, has likewise noted that the overall experience was unpleasant—except for David Niven, who was gracious, charming, and an endless source of hilarious Hollywood anecdotes. David Niven himself could not conjure up any hilarious Hollywood anecdotes about the film in his own memoirs, except to comment in a gracious, charming manner that he was once directed by John Frankenheimer.

Which leaves Frankenheimer as the sole reliable source on the film ... maybe. In the years immediately following its production, the director would tell anyone who'd listen that *The Extraordinary Seaman* was conceived as a "quiet little anti-war story," a commentary on the foolish fatuousness of the military establishment. "Unfortunately," wrote Ray Bennett in a 1970 article for *The Windsor* [Ontario] *Star*, "the subtleties of the thing went over the heads of the people who take over when the director's job is done." Clarifying this point in a 1971 interview with Roger Ebert, Frankenheimer said "MGM hated it. They wanted changes, and I wouldn't make them." You may have noticed that these comments were made several years after the film's completion. That's because *Extraordinary Seaman* remained on the shelf for nearly two years after Frankenheimer called a wrap in June of 1967 — and what *really* happened during those two years has always been shrouded in a fog of contradictions.

According to Frankenheimer's disciples, MGM hacked huge chunks out of the film, deliberately obscured the "point" of the ending, hoked up the remaining footage with campy subtitles borrowed from Winston Churchill's multivolume history of World War II — "The Gathering Storm," "Their Finest Hour," "The Hinge of Fate" and "Triumph and Tragedy" — and padded the running time with newsreel footage, including an endlessly repeated shot of Mrs. Bess Truman trying to christen an ambulance plane with a champagne bottle that refuses to break. Ending up with a shapeless farrago that ran just short of 80 minutes, MGM added insult to injury by refusing to give *Extraordinary Seaman* an official release. The studio sat on the picture until the fall of 1969, at which time it was furtively sneaked into a handful of U.S. and European theaters as a throwaway filler for overlong double bills. (In Milwaukee, *Seaman* was screened as a companion feature to the 179-minute musical *Camelot*, itself already two years old and relegated to the grindhouse circuit.)

Other sources indicate that once Frankenheimer put the final touches on his version of *The Extraordinary Seaman*, the film was no longer than 70 or 75 minutes — hardly an acceptable length for a major studio release in 1967. The inclusion of wartime newsreel footage to extend the running time may have actually been Frankenheimer's own idea, rather than a clumsy post-production brainstorm by MGM. This theory is supported by a March 1969 article in the Australian periodical *The Age*: "MGM, feeling that some documentary footage of troop inspection during the second world war is likely to offend their public, have demanded that Frankenheimer either remove the scene, or obtain the permission of the hundreds of troops shown in the scene to leave it in." While MGM's impossible demand feeds into the theory that the studio despised the film and was doing everything it could to render it unreleasable, the *Age* article also suggests that the gratuitous stock footage — regarded by many observers as the worst aspect of *The Extraordinary Seaman* — was not entirely the studio's doing. In a 1969 *Monthly Film Bulletin* review (reprinted in John Reid's *Movie Mystery and Suspense*), Richard Combs opined that the stock shots and the Churchillian subtitles constituted an attempt by old-schooler Frankenheimer to be hip and trendy: "the film often takes on the appearance of a pop art collage, a variegated comic strip of farce, fantasy and romantic comedy spiced with some happily spoofed newsreel titles and a mock histrionic collection of chapter titles, as if Frankenheimer had done a deliberate about-turn and was making his way, admittedly against some resistance, towards something akin to decelerated Richard Lester."

Despite Frankenheimer's bitter complaints about how the film was mangled by MGM, the studio's film exchanges insisted "that the print was distributed as they received it," according to the *Windsor Star*'s Ray Bennett. While the editing is hopelessly chaotic at times (especially the climactic assault on the Japanese cruiser, with two prominently billed actors reduced to nonspeaking extras), the existing version of *The Extraordinary Seaman* also includes several long, uninterrupted takes, most of them dialogue exchanges between David Niven and Alan Alda, which could not possibly have been tampered with by the MGM cutting department — and which, sad to say, are every bit as dreadful as the rest of the film.

Difficult though it is for Frankenheimer's acolytes to admit, *The Extraordinary Seaman* may simply be an example of Hamlet wanting to play the Clown: A serious director of serious subjects who, just this once, thought it might be "fun" to tackle a comedy. Like many another comedy novice, Frankenheimer makes all sorts of rookie errors, such as assuming that simply by casting Mickey Rooney and Jack Carter in the roles of Oglethorpe and O'Toole, you don't have to bother feeding them good material to get laughs. Further, Frankenheimer imagines that it is uproarious to transform these two characters into Johnny One-Notes, with each of them obsessing on a single comic idea — Oglethorpe thinks that everyone he meets is Japanese, O'Toole can't stop talking about automobiles — presumably on the theory that if you repeat something often enough, it's bound to get a laugh *sometime*.

Though Frankenheimer insisted for the remainder of his life that both he and *The Extraordinary Seaman* were screwed by the studio—"MGM didn't like it. They didn't want a quiet little anti-war story. That was that"—a few interviews indicate a suppressed desire to perform a belated *mea culpa*. "That's probably the worst movie I ever made," he is quoted as saying by *Videohound's Groovy Movies*. "I did it for all the wrong reasons. I did it for the money." Still, the film has adherents, just as it had back when it was given its limited theatrical release. In 1970, Ray Bennett lauded the picture for its "bizarre, Joseph Hellerish commentary on the military and war"—words not chosen randomly, but as a deliberate comparison to a genuine "Joseph Hellerish" comedy that was then being prepared for release by Paramount Pictures: The long-awaited, much-debated cinemadaptation of Joseph Heller's bestselling 1961 novel *Catch-22*.

At first glance, the original *Catch-22* seems to be a random, non-chronological collection of satiric anecdotes (a "giant roller-coaster of a book," according to the *New York Herald Tribune*), recounting the near-surrealistic occurrences at an American air base in the Mediterranean during the last years of World War II. Amidst a wealth of offbeat and sometimes lunatic characters bearing such colorful cognomens as Milo Minderbinder, Doc Daneeka, Captain Aardvark, Major Major Major Major, General Dreedle, Chaplain Tapman and Lieutenant Scheisskopf, a protagonist gradually emerges: Captain John Yossarian, a B-25 bombardier who is sick of risking his life and hopes he'll be rotated home after completing the requisite number of missions. But Yossarian and his fellow pilots are at the mercy of a military hierarchy that keeps increasing the number of obligatory missions with seemingly no rhyme or reason. In desperation, Yossarian tries to get a ticket home by proving he is insane and unfit for duty. Alas, there's a catch to this strategy, Catch-22: Anyone who asks to be relieved from duty isn't *really* crazy, and thus can't be classified as such. Or, as Heller put it so eloquently, a bomber "would be crazy to fly more missions and sane if he didn't, but if he were sane he had to fly them. If he flew them he was crazy and didn't have to; but if he didn't want to he was sane and had to." Apprised of this airtight arrangement, "Yossarian was moved very deeply by the absolute simplicity of this clause of Catch-22 and let out a respectful whistle." He will become less respectful and more desperate during the climactic chapters—during which the novel's Alice-in-Blunderland insanity soars to epic proportions.

Catch-22 was a bestseller in the tradition of *War and Peace* and *Ulysses*—the sort of book everybody bought because they "had to," but which few people actually read from start to finish. Joseph Heller cheerfully admitted that many readers told him they had never gotten past the first few chapters: "But that didn't bother me, because I get the royalties anyway—people don't have to read it, just buy it." Those that actually waded through the entire novel were amply rewarded for their efforts, many of them feeling like members of an exclusive club of "in the know" bibliophiles who could quote whole passages from memory or dazzle their friends with in-depth details about the dozens of characters who weave in and out of the narrative. Still, as a "popular" entertainment *Catch-22* was for many years relatively unfamiliar to the average American reader, to the extent that when William K. Zinsser referenced the novel in his brilliant 1966 *Horizon* magazine article on American humor, he found it necessary to quote verbatim the passage in which Heller (via a conversation between Yossarian and Doc Daneeka) explains the perverse logic behind Catch-22. It was not until after the film version was released in 1970 that the phrase "Catch-22" entered the common lexicon as a description of *any* dilemma which no one can escape from or resolve because of "mutually conflicting or dependent conditions." For this, Heller was eternally grateful to director Mike Nichols and the other creative forces behind the filmization of *Catch-22*, which the author would praise unflinchingly: "I can't think of any American film I've ever seen before, or any I've ever seen since, that I would put on a higher level."

Rather than risk serious damage to my already overloaded word processor, I'll assume that the reader has at least a nodding familiarity with the book and/or movie version of *Catch-22* and its multitude of intersecting characters and subplots. That said, we begin with the observation that the film rights to the novel were originally secured by Columbia Pictures in 1962, around the

19. "One, Two Three, What Are We Fighting For?"

A naked Yossarian (Alan Arkin) is encouraged to sample a chocolate-covered cotton ball, currently being marketed by the mercenary Milo Minderbinder (Jon Voight). From Paramount's 1970 adaptation of Joseph Heller's *Catch-22*.

same time that Joseph Heller was occupied elsewhere working on the pilot episode of the TV series *McHale's Navy* (eventually filmed — but not as the pilot — under the title "PT 73, Where Are You?"). In the wake of *Dr. Strangelove*, Columbia evidently felt that two military satires would glut the market, and allowed their rights to lapse. A few years later, Orson Welles was making noises about possibly buying the novel and directing it himself, but at that time no major studio was willing to finance any sort of project helmed by the increasingly erratic *auteur* of *Citizen Kane*. By 1966, *Catch-22* was in the hands of Paramount, who first approached Richard Lester to direct — a logical choice, inasmuch as the novel's *Monty Python*-esque warped logic and deadpan nihilism was very much in keeping with Lester's work on the satirical British TV series *A Show Called Fred* and his two Beatles films. But Lester said no, preferring to direct an anti-military comedy of his own invention, the British *How I Won the War*.

Paramount next went to Mike Nichols, then Hollywood's fair-haired boy by virtue of his scalding cinematization of Edward Albee's *Who's Afraid of Virginia Woolf?* Though he agreed to direct *Catch-22*, Nichols was so worn out by *Virginia Woolf* that he asked Paramount to push the Heller adaptation forward a couple of years. By that time, the director had completed another hit film, *The Graduate*, scripted by satirist Buck Henry. At Nichols' request, Henry was assigned to adapt *Catch-22*, and was also cast in the role of Lt. Col. Korn. Chosen to play the central role of Yossarian was Alan Arkin, whose expertise at conveying an aura of barely controlled hysteria had made him the toast of Broadway in such stage comedies as *Enter Laughing* and *Luv*, but who up to this point had never carried a big-budget motion picture. Though Joseph Heller was unaware that either Nichols or Arkin were involved in the project until he read the studio press announcement, he heartily approved both selections.

It was Buck Henry's herculean task to tackle a novel that if filmed faithfully would run twice as long as *Gone with the Wind*, and pare it down to an acceptable length without upsetting its flow or disappointing its fans. The first shooting script ran 187 pages, which would have added up to a three-hour picture; this was eventually whittled down to a length of 122 minutes. Along the way, several of the novel's best characters were eliminated, including the anal-retentive Lt. Scheisskopf, whose obsession with military parades was second only to his habit of carrying personal grudges to the *n*th degree; and intelligence officer Captain Black, who demanded that everyone sign loyalty oaths at the drop of a hat (the removal of Black was one of the few decisions with which Heller disagreed; he'd created the character as a brutal attack on Senator Joseph McCarthy). Other characters were combined, such as Kid Sampson and Hungry Joe, with Joe (played in the film by Seth Allen) "inheriting" Sampson's gruesomely spectacular death scene. The surviving characters were every bit as broadly caricatured as Heller had intended, foremost among them the publicity-hungry Colonel Cathcart (a role intended for George C. Scott but ultimately played by Martin Balsam), who continues increasing the number of bombing missions in order to get a favorable write-up in *The Saturday Evening Post*; and capitalist-in-khaki Lt. Milo Minderbinder (played by Jon Voight, taking over from first choice Gene Wilder), Heller's personification of the "Military Industrial Complex," whose enterprises included "borrowing" parachutes from the bomber planes in order to peddle the silk on the black market, and coating a surplus of Egyptian cotton with chocolate so he can sell it as candy.

To attract as wide an audience as possible, Paramount decided to go the "all-star" route, casting the many principal roles with such big names as Jack Gilford (Doc Daneeka), Anthony Perkins (Chaplain Tapman), Art Garfunkel (Capt. Nately) Dick Benjamin (Maj. Danby), Paula Prentiss (Nurse Duckett) and Bob Newhart (Major Major)—resulting in a starting budget estimated at $15 million, which would balloon to $18 million before shooting ended. Filming commenced in January 1969 at an enormous temporary airfield designed by Richard Sylbert and constructed some thirty miles from Guayama, Mexico. The sets were all "practical," serving as both interiors and exteriors; the actors lived in the fabricated baracks and took meals in the ersatz mess hall, cultivating the ensemble mindset that was vital to a film of this nature. As with *The Extraordinary Seaman*, the decision to film in a remote area of Mexico, linked to the nearest city only by a single telephone that didn't work half the time, was not without its difficulties, which in this case included the close proximity of bandits, the loss of several Mexican extras in various drug busts, and an occasional bout of *turista*. Too, there were a lot of abrupt firings, angry resignations and costly technical malfunctions in the course of filming, creating an overall insecurity that was hard for the participants to suppress (some of this uneasiness shows up onscreen, though several of the actors, especially Martin Balsam, insisted that the experience was a hoot from start to finish).

Despite difficult working conditions both in Mexico and later when production moved across the ocean to Rome, Mike Nichols was able to establish and maintain a rapport with the cast—with the exception of Orson Welles, cast as the thick-eared General Dreedle. Still fuming over being denied the opportunity to direct the picture himself, Welles was even more imperious than usual, insisting upon dispensing advice to his fellow actors whether they wanted it or not. Austin Pendleton, cast as Dreedle's wimpy adjutant (and son-in-law) Lt. Col. Moodus, won the eternal gratitude of his beleaguered colleagues by ordering the Great Orson to mind his own damn business. Outside of Welles, Nichols' biggest challenge involved the realistic bomber-mission scenes, utilizing a fleet of B-25s and other vintage aircraft supplied by stunt pilot and aviation expert Frank Tallman (some of the second-unit flying sequences were handled by Andrew Marton, fresh off another service comedy, *Kelly's Heroes*).

Joseph Heller's novel is not an attack on war or militarism *per se*. He himself has said that certain wars are necessary not only for the welfare of Mankind but as a steam valve to relieve humanity's frustrations; and he has proudly observed that among the novel's biggest fans were officers of the U.S. Air Force. Heller's avowed purpose was to use *Catch-22*'s fictional air base as an allegory for "the contemporary regimented business society" of the early 1960s, and this is made obvious by the constant sloganeering and the relentless pursuit of specific *idées fixes* by the novel's grotesquely drawn authority figures. And though there is a modicum of truth in everything he writes, Heller did not intend the events of the novel to be taken for Real Life. Carefully establishing a burlesque tone early in the proceedings, the author hoped that by the time the novel arrived at its most ludicrous passages the reader would have become so accustomed to the absurdities that nothing would seem impossible. With the consistency of an allegory, the novel creates its own logic; it doesn't *have* to bear any relation to the real world to be believable on its own terms.

Mike Nichols and Buck Henry had different ideas. With anti-war and anti-military sentiments attaining hitherto unscaled heights during the Vietnam era, the filmmakers invested Heller's prose with these same sentiments. Henry in particular saw Heller as a visionary, anticipating the mass Canadian emigrations of draft-age American males in the novel's depiction of Capt. Orr (played in the film by Bob Balaban), who continually cracks up his plane in the Atlantic Ocean, farther and farther away from his home base on each occasion, as preparation for his climactic desertion from the Air Corps. As Henry told interviewer Nora Ephron, Heller "was writing about a man who had finally decided to opt out and who in the end ends up in Sweden. That was a total absurdity when he wrote it, a really far-out kind of insanity. Well, it's come true."

To retain Heller's narrative device of presenting isolated incidents out of chronological order, Nichols and Henry framed the film as an hallucinatory nightmare, suffered by Yossarian after being stabbed by a mysterious assailant. This allowed the filmmakers to counterpoint the "real" incidents in Yossarian's past with nightmarish exaggerations, continuity and logic be hanged. Again quoting Buck Henry: "The film's center of consciousness is the delirium of Yossarian ... induced by a wound he received at the beginning of the picture and that activates the jumps backward and forward in time." Like Heller, the director and scriptwriter use Yossarian's repeated flashbacks to the death of his young navigator Snowden (Jon Korkes) as a continual reference point—but with a different narrative purpose. In the novel, Snowden's grisly, gut-splattered demise is but one of many horrors visited upon Yossarian, the last in a long line of straws. As depicted in the film, Snowden is Yossarian's "Rosebud," the entire *raison d'etre* for the protagonist's frustration and his ultimate decision to follow Orr's example by escaping to Sweden.

Though most of the film is as absurdist as the novel, in some instances the filmmakers chose to take a starkly realistic approach. For example, Joseph Heller did not expect readers to swallow whole the notion that Milo Minderbinder was willing to arrange for the Germans to attack his own air base simply to pick up a few extra bucks on the black market—and that the American higher-ups would permit Milo to get away with his treachery. This was one of the many moments in the novel that was meant to invoke laughter with its utter ridiculousness. Interviewed by Paul Krassner in 1962, Heller insisted: "Now, I sincerely think that this is an impossibility; this is the one thing that could not happen—literally. I don't think that in time of war a man could get up and actually drop bombs deliberately on his own people and then escape without punishment, even in our society. I think people in every country commit *actions* which would cause infinitely more damage to the national strength, to national survival, to their fellow citizens; even commit actions which result in more deaths, physical deaths, as well—and be *lionized* for it; be made into heroes for it. But I don't think the actual *act* of killing would be allowed to escape punishment with everybody's approval." You'd never be able to discern Heller's satiric intent in the film version of *Catch-22*, wherein Minderbinder's overt act of treason is not only staged in an utterly plausible fashion, but also appears to be nothing more than business as usual for the duplicitous military establishment, carried out with the full approval of the craven Col. Cathcart.

Only occasionally do the filmmakers successfully capture Heller's "playful prose" (Mike Nichols' description) with fleeting, almost missable moments of insanity, such as the white sidewall tires on General Dreedle's staff plane, and the lengthy single-take sequence in which the deer-in-the-headlights Major Major (Bob Newhart) orders his sergeant (Norman Fell) to tell everyone who wants to see him to wait outside the office until he can escape through the back door (Sergeant: "And then what do I do with them?" Major: "*I don't care!*"). To represent Major Major's short-circuited thought patterns, the camera occasionally pans past a photograph on the wall, which changes each time it is shown—beginning with a photo of President Roosevelt and ending with a portrait of Josef Stalin. While Joseph Heller himself would have avoided this sight gag ("whimsical, arbitrary humor. It's not something I would have recommended"), it remains one of the film's few guaranteed belly-laughs.

Such comparative subtleties are rare in *Catch-22*, which can be described as either too much of a good thing or an object lesson in overkill. Though Mike Nichols insists that the only time he indulged himself in the picture was by using Richard Strauss' "Thus Spake Zarathustra" (aka the theme from *2001: A Space Odyssey*) to herald the arrival of a buxom Italian hooker, several of the film's key scenes are so cluttered with directorial gimcrackery that they're a chore to sit through. The long, uninterrupted tracking shot of Yossarian and Doc Daneeka carrying on a conversation while behind them the airfield is abuzz with activity is undeniably impressive on a technical and logistical level, but the point of the scene—Daneeka's explanation of "Catch-22" to the incredulous Yossarian—is virtually lost amidst the hustle-bustle and background noise. Nichols seems to function best when he allows the camera to relax and Heller's words to be heard without adornment, such as the marvelous Roman brothel sequence wherein a world-weary Italian centenarian (the matchless Marcel Dalio) gently shatters Capt. Nately's illusions about decency and Democracy.

In one respect, Mike Nichols succeeds admirably in capturing the tone of the novel, in which Heller starts things rolling with hilarity before gradually unfolding a darker and less frolicsome scenario somewhere around Chapter 39. The film conveys this unsettling shift of mood when Yossarian ventures into a bombed-out Roman neighborhood, where Milo Minderbinder has set up a corporate empire by regimenting the town's prostitutes. It is as if one movie suddenly ends and a new one begins, and though the transition isn't quite as graceful as in the novel, Nichols is to be credited for his effort to translate a purely literary device into cinematic terms. But while Heller switches from "dark" back to "light" again before the end of the novel, Nichols chooses not to do so in the film. Instead, the director stages Yossarian's climactic escape as a sop to the antiwar movement, symbolically giving a thumbs-up to all the draft-age American males who had chosen to flee to Canada. The pretentiousness of the finale is exacerbated by the utilization of Sousa's "Stars and Stripes Forever" as background music (Compare the heavy irony of a patriotic tune counterpointing an unpatriotic act with Stanley Kubrick's brilliant deployment of "When Johnny Comes Marching Home" to underline the scenes of the American bombers preparing to trigger the end of the world—all in the name of patriotism—in *Dr. Strangelove*).

Paramount's promotional campaign for *Catch-22* played up both its pacifistic message and the provocative elements that had earned the film an "R" rating. A great deal of attention was afforded the scene in which Yossarian shows up stark naked to receive a medal for valor; one suspects, however, that most viewers were more interested in the *other* nude scene (and full frontal at that) involving Paula Prentiss. But neither of these skin displays was sufficient to prevent *Catch-22* from posting a $10 million loss. This has often been attributed to the extremely mixed press reviews (opinions ranging from "brilliant" to "abysmal"), but it is equally likely that its failure was a matter of bad timing. The film's creators knew they were in trouble when, during the post-production process, they happened to catch an early showing of another, less prestigious and far less expensive military satire from 20th Century–Fox. As this rival film unspooled, Mike Nichols recognized that it "was much fresher and more alive, improvisational, and funnier than *Catch-22*. It just cut us off at the knees." Production designer Richard Sylbert agreed: "We sat there afterwards in a mild state of shock, knowing that the crowd-pleaser we had just seen was going to make a huge dent in our audience."

You've already guessed that this upstart military comedy was Robert Altman's *MASH*, filmed in 1969 and released in January 1970. With shelves of books and entire college courses devoted to Altman's films, what can one says about *MASH* that hasn't already been said? For the uninitiated — both of you out there — we note that the film was based on a novel by Richard Hooker, the pen name of former Army doctor H. Richard Hornberger, who had been attached to a Mobile Army Surgical Hospital (M.A.S.H.) unit during the Korean War. After eleven futile years trying to peddle his novel, Hornberger finally signed a contract with William Morrow & Company in 1968, a year in which any book with even a hint of an anti-establishment message was considered a saleable commodity. In his foreword to *MASH*, the author writes: "The surgeons in the MASH hospitals were exposed to extremes of hard work, leisure, tension, boredom, heat, cold, satisfaction and frustration that most of them had never faced before. Their reaction, individually and collectively, was to cope with the situation and get the job done. The various stresses, however, produced behavior in many of them that, superficially, at least, seemed inconsistent with their earlier, civilian behavior patters. A few flipped their lids, but most of them just raised hell, in a variety of ways and degrees...."

Like the paratroopers of World War II, the military doctors of Korea were given a wide berth by their superiors. The medicos' lackadaisical attitude towards rules and regulations and their zany off-duty antics were tolerated because of their indispensibility. Little could be gained and much could be lost — especially lives— if higher-ranking officers went around disciplining doctors for every trivial breach of protocol. Thus the three leading lights of the novel's fictional 4077th MASH unit — Captains Duke Forrest, Hawkeye Pierce, and Trapper John McIntyre — are able to drink, gamble, carouse, play unauthorized golf games and pull practical jokes with impunity, secure in the knowledge that the Army needs their combined brilliance and expertise in the operating room more than it needs to obsess over such mundane matters as saluting, saying "sir" to their superiors and addressing subordinates by rank rather than their first names. The novel's tone was neither anti-war nor anti-military, but rather anti-authority and anti-decorum (H. Richard Hornberger's personal politics leaned in the direction of Conservative Republican). This cheekiness was something with which every ex-servicemen could empathize, just as there was strong audience identification with the end of the novel, in which, after cutting quite a swath in Korea (and most of the way back home), Doctors Forrest and Pierce return to their loving families and respectable civilian practices with all malfeasance purged from their systems.

Excessively episodic in nature, the novel covers a year in the life of the 4077th, detailing the various means by which Duke, Hawkeye and Trapper John retain their sanity and stave off boredom. Our heroes down martinis by the gallon, womanize promiscuously and play 12-hour poker games between 12-hour shifts. They confound such enemies as the rule-bound Colonel Merrill and Nurse Margaret Houlihan — nicknamed "Hot Lips" after she is caught in a comprising position — as well as the imperious Major Frank Burns and obnoxious Bible-thumper Major Hobson. They reward such friends as Korean houseboy Ho-Jon (an aspiring physician) and chronically suicidal Army dentist Waldoski (aka "The Painless Pole"). And they obtain vital medical equipment without bothering to wade through the so-called proper channels. The book's climax is a down-and-dirty football game between the MASH unit and a team of "ringers" brought in by money-grubbing General Hammond, with the 4077th coming out on top thanks to the gridiron wizardry (and creative cheating) of former NFL star Wendell "Spearchucker" Jones. Other prominent characters include the unit's easygoing CO, Lt. Col. Henry Blake; Cpl. Radar O'Reilly, so named because of his remarkable ability to recite Blake's commands in unison with his superior officer; and camp chaplain Father Mulcahy, whose shock of red hair (and not, as might be assumed, his flask of Communion wine) has earned him the soubriquet "Dago Red."

After his "overnight" success with *MASH*, Hornberger turned out a brace of sequels, *MASH Goes to Maine* and *MASH Mania*, which followed the "Swamp Gang" from the 4077th into civilian life. There would be a dozen more *MASH* novels published between 1975 and 1977, purportedly cowritten by "Richard Hooker" and William E. Butterworth but actually penned by Butterworth alone. We can ignore these follow-ups and concentrate on the original, which went out to the public with a dust-jacket endorsement by Hollywood screenwriter Ring Lardner Jr.: "Not since *Catch-22* has the struggle to maintain sanity in the rampant insanity of war been told in such outrageously funny terms."

At the suggestion of his former agent Ingo Preminger, Lardner had read the novel while it was still in galley form, at roughly the same time that 20th Century–Fox purchased the movie rights for *MASH* and assigned Preminger to produce. Blacklisted as one of the "Hollywood Ten" in 1947, Lardner's exile was finally lifted in 1965 when he received his first screen credit in nearly two decades for *The Cincinnati Kid*. Anxious to sustain the momentum, the author planned a full-scale comeback by adapting *MASH* for the screen. Though Lardner's strong antiwar sentiments seeped into the source material, his adaptation was quite faithful to the novel, using all the key dialogue, comic highlights and major characters (with a few exceptions like Maj. Hobson, whose negative character traits were transferred to the equally repellant Frank Burns); he also retained Hornberger's sentimental "homecoming" finale. In this form, the script was similar to previous mainstream Hollywood comedies featuring devil-may-care soldiers who derived pleasure from bypassing rules and tweaking the noses of the higher-ups. The film version of *MASH* was envisioned as a traditionalist Army comedy with a traditionalist cast headed by Jack Lemmon and Walter Matthau, and with a "safe" old-guard director at the helm.

Unfortunately, the studio had trouble attracting a director of any kind because the script was so loosely structured. The tally varies from source to source, but it appears that as many as 18 directors turned down *MASH*, among them George Roy Hill, Sidney Lumet and Bud Yorkin. With Ingo Preminger busy on the production end, Lardner had taken a new agent, George Litto, whose top directorial choices were Stanley Kubrick and Robert Altman, the latter having generated positive critical response for his 1969 film *That Cold Day in the Park*. Kubrick wasn't interested, so Preminger reluctantly went with Altman, whose unorthodox methods, fondness for on-set improvisations and violent aversion to front-office interference had lost him several plum jobs in the past. Fox wasn't enthused about Altman either, remembering all too well how the director had incurred the wrath of a Congressional committee with his notoriously sadistic 1961 episode of the studio's TV series *Bus Stop,* in which pop idol Fabian played a charming serial killer. The main reason that Altman was hired was his willingness to accept a flat fee of $75,000, minus any percentage points.

With only a $3 million budget to play with, Altman couldn't afford to use Fox's first-choice stars Lemmon and Matthau, nor such suggested alternates as James Garner and Burt Reynolds (none of whom wanted to be in the picture anyway). Frankie Avalon was a relatively inexpensive choice for the role of Radar O'Reilly, but he turned it down, as did Austin Pendleton. Elaine Stritch was originally scheduled to play "Hot Lips" Houlihan—a more sensible choice than it seems, since in the novel Hot Lips is in her forties—but she, like several other actresses, felt the part was too small as written. Fox was finally able to land Elliott Gould, a rising star by virtue of his performance in the recent *Bob & Carol & Ted & Alice*, for the role of Duke Forrest (keep reading—this isn't an error!), and Donald Sutherland, who had developed a strong following for his work in such films as *The Dirty Dozen* and *Joanna*, as Hawkeye. The role of Radar went to Gary Burghoff, a movie newcomer who had starred in the off–Broadway musical *You're a Good Man Charlie Brown*, and who would be the only member of the *MASH* cast to repeat his role in the long-running TV series version. Called in to read for the two principal female roles of Nurse Dish and Hot Lips Houlihan, up-and-coming Sally Kellerman felt that the latter part wasn't big enough to be worth her time, but agreed to give it a try when Altman assured her that it would be expanded during production; meanwhile, Jo Ann Pflug, who'd worked with Altman in television, was hired for Nurse Dish.

Several other members of the director's "talent trust"—those whom he'd worked with elsewhere and had responded well to his methods—were cast in *MASH*, among them Robert Duvall as Frank Burns, Michael Murphy as "Me Lai" Marston and Tom Skerritt as Trapper John McIntyre. Or at least, Tom Skerritt *was* Trapper John, until Elliott Gould insisted that he and Skerritt switch roles. Among the other actors were two soon-to-be Altman regulars, Rene Auberjonois (replacing Malachi McCourt) as Father Mulcahy and Bud Cort as Pvt. Boone. Additional roles were filled by John Schuck (making his film debut as Waldoski), Fred Williamson ("Spearchucker" Jones), Bobby Troup (Sgt. Gorman), Roger Bowen (Henry Blake), G. Wood (General Hammond), David Arkin (Sgt. Maj. Vollmer), Kim Atwood (Ho-Jon), and future *Jaws* screenwriter Carl Gottlieb (Ugly John).

Altman set up his production unit at the Fox Ranch in the Lake Malibu district, which had previously stood in for the Far East in such films as *The Left Hand of God* and *Satan Never Sleeps*. Like Mike Nichols in *Catch-22*, the director encouraged his cast and crew to spend as much time together as possible in the film's makeshift tents and portable quonset huts, the better to develop the ensemble "feel" that he desired. What ultimately developed was more of a party atmosphere, late-'60s style, with liquor, drugs and casual sex in abundance. As was his custom, Altman used Ring Lardner Jr.'s script as merely a skeleton, encouraging his actors to ad-lib fresh lines and improvise new bits of business during their communal read-throughs. "We'll try things," he was fond of telling his players. "They'll work." To this end, Altman recruited his extras from various California comedy-improv ensembles, each of whose members had to be assigned at least one line of dialogue in order to qualify as "actors" and thus avoid legal action from the Screen Extra's Guild.

Altman's freewheeling approach to his source material occasionally led him to paint himself in a corner. Having chosen to completely dispense with the lachrymose homecoming finale, the director suddenly found himself without a proper ending for the picture. It was only during the three-month postproduction period that Altman and his editor Danford B. Greene hit upon the idea of closing the film with a spoken cast-and-credits roster, delivered via loudspeaker by the 4077's public-address announcer: "Attention. Tonight's movie has been *MASH*. Follow the zany antics of our combat surgeons as they cut and stitch their way along the front lines.... Starring Donald Sutherland, Elliott Gould, Tom Skerritt, Sally Kellerman..." etc., etc., etc. This is turn led to the expanding of the never-seen P.A. voice into a brand-new supporting character, whose laconic, detached commentary (frequently accompanied by sugary pop tunes) proved the perfect counterpoint to the doctors' wacky behavior and the horrific carnage they had to deal with on a round-the-clock basis. The disembodied voice also provided the film with the strong sense of unity that Ring Lardner, Jr., for all his talent, had never quite been able to bring to the novel's rambling prose.

Eleventh-hour inspirations of this nature (the camp P.A. appears nowhere in either the novel or the screenplay) would generate a great deal of ill will between Altman and Lardner. Though the essential plot points were retained in the film, along with many of the original script's best dialogue exchanges ("I wonder how such a degenerate person ever reached a position of authority in the Army Medical Corps?" "He was drafted!"), so much of the material was developed by the actors themselves during rehearsals that Lardner would ever after complain that Altman had ruined his work. The air became so thick that the Fox executives had to pull teeth to prevent Lardner from removing his name from the credits (ironically, the writer would end up winning the film's only Academy Award). The situation wasn't improved by the insistence of *auteur* theorists that the end result was Altman's and Altman's alone, with Lardner a mere cog in the wheel.

Nor was the writer the only person who challenged the director's methods. Both Elliott Gould and Donald Sutherland tried to have Altman removed from the picture, their official complaint being that although he would never give them any direction, he would mercilessly tear them down in front of everyone if they didn't perform to his satisfaction. The two stars' displeasure actually went deeper than that: Eager to assert their new-found stardom, they didn't enjoy being treated as part of an ensemble, nor were they happy when Altman would capriciously build up a bit player's role at their expense. Though Gould eventually reconciled with Altman and continued to collaborate with him on such films as *The Long Goodbye* and *California Split*, Sutherland never worked with the director again.

Altman's blithe disregard for the feelings of others (at least for the "others" who bitched the most) spilled over into his relationship with the studio executives. It didn't seem to faze him in the least that his picture was four days behind schedule within the first week of shooting, but this gnawed away at the front office until the director finally wrapped up *MASH* three days *under* schedule and some $500,000 under budget. Having been occupied elsewhere with bigger Fox projects like *Patton* and *Hello Dolly*, certain executives were appalled when they first laid eyes on Altman's finished product, worrying that the excess of profanity (including the first F-word in a mainstream American film), the nude shower scene with Sally Kellerman, and the rivers of blood and entrails in the operating-room scenes would invoke outrage rather than laughter from audiences. There was also some concern that the director's deliberately untidy camerawork, slapdash editing patterns and overlapping mumbled dialogue would confuse filmgoers accustomed to the neatness and decorum of standard Hollywood pictures (the gospel according to the French *nouvelle vague* had still not caught on with the beardless prophets of Old Hollywood, despite the recent success of such unorthodox American films as *Bonnie and Clyde* and *Easy Rider*). However, all fears were quelled by a single preview showing of *MASH* in San Francisco, in which the patrons, already primed for comic irreverence by a screening of Fox's *Butch Cassidy and the Sundance Kid*, howled with laughter throughout the Altman picture.

MASH (20th Century–Fox, 1970). Director Robert Altman extended his "ensemble" approach to this production still, in which stars Elliott Gould (bearded, waving) and Donald Sutherland (wearing glasses and floppy hat) are given no more prominence than any of the other actors. If you look closely, you'll also find John Schuck, Rene Auberjonois and Fred Williamson among the crowd.

There is no question that despite its total absence of battle scenes, *MASH* is an anti-war picture. Whether *MASH* is a blatantly anti–Vietnam picture, as has often been claimed, is something else again. Those who worked on the film have insisted that the war in Southeast Asia was barely mentioned on the set, and that Altman never came out and said that he was using Korea as an analogy for Vietnam. The argument that the film's setting was intentionally vague so as to lead audiences to assume that it *was* Vietnam has been bolstered by the claims of producer Ingo Preminger and writer Ring Lardner Jr. that they had early on toyed with the idea to update and relocate the action of the original novel to make it more relevant to the 1970s. Also, in the finished film Altman neglected to firmly establish the locale as Korea and the time as the early 1950s, necessitating the last-minute addition of an introductory title. This might have been a deliberate attempt by Altman to equate Korea with Vietnam, but more likely it was a typical example of the director's disdain for "conventional" storytelling techniques, as shown by his habit of introducing the main characters in bits and pieces rather than with huge chunks of expository dialogue. One might also observe that never once in the film does Altman clarify the meaning of the acronym *MASH*. There doesn't seem to be any special significance to *this* omission: Explaining the initials simply wasn't that important to him.

In fact, many of the film's participants felt that Altman invested more importance in the climactic football game — on which he lavished nearly a third of the production schedule — than in any other aspect of the picture, save for his calculatedly savage attacks on organized religion. A lapsed Catholic, Altman never lets slip an opportunity to ridicule the rituals of Catholicism, beginning with the scene in which the ineffectual Father Mulcahy is shown blessing a jeep, continuing with the simpering psalmistry of Major Burns and climaxing with the blasphemous Last Supper parody attending the "suicide party" for the melancholy Waldoski. It was this element as much as the film's sex and profanity that nearly caused the MPAA to impose an "X" rating on *MASH*, and it was only Altman's impassioned assurances that the film's wild comedy would gloss over its more questionable aspects that secured a less stringent "R." (The popularity of the subsequent *M*A*S*H* TV series — the asterisks don't appear between the letters in the original film's titles — encouraged Fox to reissue the picture in the early 1970s; now aimed at a less restricted audience, the film was re-edited to qualify for a "PG," and it is this version that is generally shown today.)

To the dismay of those who had labored so mightily on the more expensive and more generously publicized *Catch-22* only to see it nosedive at the boxoffice, little insignificant *MASH* ended up as the third highest-grossing film of 1970, ringing up $36,720,000 in the U.S. alone. Practically the only adult filmgoers who didn't see the picture during its first release were those recruits on the Army and Air Force bases where *MASH* was banned from exhibition (conversely, the Navy had no problem with the picture and allowed it to be screened for its personnel without limit). It has since been theorized that the film's success was due in great part to a general wave of anti-war sentiment, though if this were entirely the case *Catch-22* would have been equally as popular. *Catch-22* was in its own way irreverent and iconoclastic, but in sum total it was just another slick, factory-sealed Hollywood product. Even its funniest scenes had a cut-and-dried look to them, with any feeling of spontaneity scuttled by the impression that what we were seeing had been laboriously sorted out from dozens of repeated takes, filmed from a multitude of angles by a bored camera crew. *MASH* on the other hand looks as if it is being made up on the spot, shot by a rogue cameraman lucky enough to capture the moment before it evaporates never to be seen again. The immediacy of Altman's directorial approach is as fresh and vibrant now as it was forty years ago. Seen today, so far removed from the political climate of the spring of 1970, *MASH* remains an enormously entertaining, rewarding and *living* experience. The film may even play better than when it first came out, simply because so many of Altman's groundbreaking techniques — the quivery newsreel-style photography, the fragmentary continuity, the seemingly garbled soundtrack in which we hear only what the director wants us to hear — have since been absorbed into the moviemaking mainstream.

But like many another film from a bygone era, *MASH* has its share of cringeworthy moments. Particularly troubling for 21st century observers is the film's undercurrent of sadism, manifested early in the proceedings by the punishment meted out to Maj. Frank Burns after he is goaded into striking Hawkeye. Even allowing for the character's negative influence on the 4077th, the image of a glassy-eyed Burns being led off to the psych ward in a straitjacket seems unduly harsh, and seldom provokes laughter today. Also problematic is the film's demeaning treatment of Hot Lips Houlihan, especially during the celebrated shower scene. Actress Sally Kellerman has defended Altman's depiction of Army nurses as sex objects, repeating the director's assertion that this is how women in uniform were treated in the mid–1950s and that he was merely reflecting truth. Minus this frame of reference, however, the film's cavalier attitude towards its distaff characters now seems to mirror the 1970s as much as it does the Korean war — and if you doubt this, just ask some of the female activists of the era who were expected to remain barefoot, pregnant and in the kitchen while their male soulmates were out doing the "man's work" of protesting the Establishment. (On a related PC topic, let's not even get into the unlikelihood that any contemporary filmmaker could get away with naming a black character "Spearchucker.") Robert Altman was always the first to admit that *MASH* is a cruel film: "That's what it was. That's what I see constantly. Certainly that time and certainly that situation breeds that." While the Comedy of Cruelty has its adherents, you won't find all that many of them among the generations of fans who have grown up on the sweeter, kindlier, Alan Alda-ized TV version of *M*A*S*H*.

A book on military comedy *films* has no business analyzing the already-overdocumented TV *M*A*S*H*, nor for that matter the obscure unsold pilot film for a 1973 TV-series spinoff of *Catch-22*, starring Richard Dreyfuss as Yossarian. It would be nice to close this chapter on the high note of the movie *MASH*, but there's still one loose end to deal with: a *very* obscure 1971 anti-military comedy described in its newspaper ads as "The picture that insults everyone regardless of race, creed or color" and by Columbia Pictures historian Clive Hirschhorn as "a mega-bomb."

Scripted by Clement Biddle Wood from his own 1966 novel, Columbia's *Welcome to the Club* is set at an American occupational base in 1945 Hiroshima, a few months after the Bomb. Comedian Brian Foley (who also composed the film's rancid theme song) stars as Lt. Andrew Oxblood, a virginal 19½-year-old Quaker who has been appointed the base's morale officer. In an idealistic effort to see to it that the African Americans under his command receive equitable treatment, Oxblood tries to have a black USO singing group quartered in the Officer's Club, only to bang his skull against the stone wall of intolerance as personified by the flagrantry racist Colonel Ames (Lionel Murton). Nor does Oxblood receive much support from his roommates Robert E. Lee Fairfax (Andy Jarrell) and Harrison W. Morve (Kevin O'Connor), who betray their own prejudices by their shabby treatment of female Japanese housekeeper "Hogan" (Francesca Tu). The only man on the base who makes even a token effort to assist Oxblood in his noble mission is General Strapp (Jack Warden), but even he cannot overcome his inbred bigotry. The story's outcome is triggered by a rehash of an old urban legend: Though she detests Robert E. Lee Fairfax, black singer Leah Wheat (Marsha A. Hunt) agrees to sleep with him, but upon awakening Fairfax finds a note scrawled on his mirror in lipstick, informing him that he's been infected with gonorrhea. Disillusioned that one of his idealized "Negroes" would act in this spiteful fashion, Oxblood gets drunk, just as Hogan tries to come on to him. Feeling rejected, Hogan sleeps with one of the male black singers, Marshall Bowles (Lon Sutton). Now at a complete loss as to his own racial attitudes, Oxblood slaps Hogan, sobering himself to the realization that he's just as bigoted as any other white soldier. The Big Epiphany Climax arrives right on schedule, as Oxblood summons the rest of the troops to inform them that they, and he, have all been infected with the "social disease" of prejudice.

In one of the few pre-release articles on *Welcome to the Club*, columnist Earl Wilson suggested that the film was made to cash in on the newly popular TV series *All in the Family*, with costar Jack Warden doing what amounted to an Archie Bunker imitation. However, the film had been started in 1969 and completed in 1970, long before *All in the Family* burst onto the American scene. Other observers were closer to the mark when they tagged *Welcome to the Club* as a rank imitation of both *Catch-22* (with such character names as "Betsy Wholecloth") and *MASH* (a tradition-trashing rebel against the venal Military Establishment). The picture was produced by Walter Shenson, whose credits included *The Mouse That Roared* (1959), a good political satire, and *A Hard Day's Night* (1964), a good establishment-baiting musical. Shenson evidently didn't recognize that the reason these two films *were* good had a lot to do with directors Jack Arnold and Richard Lester, else he wouldn't have chosen to make his own directorial debut with *Welcome to the Club*. Aside from one funny confrontation between a Jewish officer and a German-American noncom, the film lives up (?) to the aforementioned description by Clive Hirschhorn. Catching a rare theatrical screening of *Welcome to the Club* in 1972, *Cue* magazine's William Wolf remarked: "At least Hiroshima was spared further atrocity—the film was shot in Denmark."

20

"The Mother of All Movies"
Satires and Parodies

At ease, ladies and gentlemen. You don't have to brace yourselves for an excruciatingly detailed history of *all* military satires dating back to Aristophanes' *Lyisistrata*. In fact, if we take in account the dictionary definition of "satire" as "ridicule intended to expose the truth," the word is not entirely applicable to every film mentioned in the forthcoming chapter. For the most part we'll rely upon such interchangeable designations as "parody," "lampoon," "burlesque," "spoof," "travesty," "takeoff" and "send-up," with maybe a sidetrip or two to the world of the pastiche ("a work of art formed from disparate sources").

Movie parodies are as old as the movies themselves, so it should be no surprise that the military-movie parody is hardly a bold new concept. In previous chapters we have referenced such examples as 1918's *The Geezer of Berlin*, a 2-reel takeoff on the serious anti–German picture *The Kaiser—Beast of Berlin*; 1926's *The Heavy Parade*, a semi-spoof of the previous year's *The Big Parade*; and 1933's *War Babies*, a dismal travesty of 1926's *What Price Glory?* featuring a cast of children. To get this chapter rolling, we have until now held in reserve our discussion of the 1931 MGM 2-reeler *So Quiet on the Canine Front*, the fifth in a series of nine "Dogville" comedies produced and directed by Jules White and Zion Myers.

Per their blanket title, the "Dogville" films featured a cast of trained dogs costumed as humans, walking around on their hind legs (often with the aid of strategically hidden wires) and fed chunks of toffee so that it would appear that their mouths were forming words, with professional voice actors dubbing the dialogue. These comedies were originally intended to feature a cast of horses, but as Jules White explained to interviewer David N. Bruskin: "I said to them, 'Dress dogs up as people. The most beloved thing on earth, next to a baby, is a pet dog. All these women that have cute little dogs—you see those dogs dressed up and cavorting and doing their stuff—are a ready made audience.'" To extend the films' appeal beyond those women, each "Dogville" entry was a spoof of a popular movie or movie genre. Typical of the series was 1930's *Dogway Melody*, which not only kidded the backstage intrigues of the 1929 Oscar-winning feature *Broadway Melody* but also used portions of that film's soundtrack.

With this in mind, one might expect *So Quiet on the Canine Front* to be a direct takeoff on another Oscar-winning film, the 1930 World War I drama *All Quiet on the Western Front*. Though Jules White's grasp of good taste was shaky at best, even he was not so insensitive as to ridicule the plot and characters of the unremittingly tragic and fatalistic *All Quiet on the Western Front*—save for a near-perfect replica of the earlier film's opening classroom sequence, wherein a xenophobic schoolmaster exhorts his students to throw down their books and march off to battle. Otherwise, the "all-barkie" *So Quiet on the Canine Front* is less a specific parody of a specific film than a free-for-all takeoff of war dramas in general. The script makes light of such stock setpieces as the "Let me be the first to die" nobility of the officers, the shell-shocked rookie driven berserk by the constant bombardment, and the incongruity of enemy soldiers speaking Pidgin-English with German accents rather than conversing in their own language. So as not to leave any stone unturned, White and his co-conspirator Zion Myers also poke fun at the standard clichés of wartime *comedies*, including the never-ending "Sez You-Sez Me" banter of *What Price Glory?* and its sequels, and the overworked device of having the lead comic (in this case, a white bulldog) disguise himself as a woman to divert the enemy officers.

While it is undeniably funny to see a canine barbed-wire party stringing a line of frankfurters alongside the trenches keep the enemy at bay, to witness a doggie firing squad dispersed by "flea grenades," and to hear such dialogue as "I didn't raise my boy to be a sausage!" one's enjoyment of *So Quiet on the Canine Front* is hampered by the same queasiness one experiences while watching the rest of the "Dogville" comedies. Despite Jules White's assertions that no animals were ever harmed in the making of these pictures, one cannot help but be disturbed by the sight of dogs being manipulated in so un-doglike a fashion — and looking for all the world as if they'd rather be anywhere else than a hot, stuffy movie studio. That said, *So Quiet on the Canine Front* is to be praised for its application of the three essential ingredients of a good parody film: A storyline which banks on the audience's familiarity with a specific genre, a collection of ridiculous verbal and visual gags lampooning that genre's timeworn clichés, and above all an ever-present veneer of authenticity. For all its foolishness, *So Quiet on the Canine Front* is filmed on surprisingly realistic-looking sets (especially the studio recreation of No Man's Land) and photographed in the same grim, ominously shadowed style that one normally associates with serious wartime epics. It is somehow aesthetically satisfying when a comedy filmmaker takes the extra time and care to provide a parody film with the same visual dynamics as the film it is parodying.

So Quiet on the Canine Front also has the advantage of brevity; running 16 minutes, the film fades out before its humor and novelty has a chance to wear thin. Few filmmakers of the 1920s, 1930s or 1940s were willing to take the risk of making a feature-length parody, sensing that audiences would tire of the kidding somewhere around Reel Three. Early efforts to make longer parodies bear this out: The 1951 western spoof *Skipalong Rosenbloom* gets its biggest laughs in the first 20 minutes; unfortunately there are still 52 minutes to go, and the material simply can't sustain the premise. Only during the 1960s and 1970s, a period when many old cast-in-stone "truths" about filmmaking finally began to erode, were audiences willing to accept parody films that ran more than two or three reels. All this started with the "camp" craze of the mid-1960s, in which television and film producers amused themselves by mocking through exaggeration the sort of material that people had once (allegedly) taken seriously: That's how we ended up with the *outré* TV series *Batman* and such feature-length spy spoofs as *Our Man Flint* and *Casino Royale*. Though the public's fascination with "camp" eventually died out, writer-director Mel Brooks was able to firmly establish the commercial viability of the long-form parody with his star-studden western burlesque *Blazing Saddles* (1974) and his comic horror-film homage *Young Frankenstein* (1975). Brooks' success inspired his former *Your Show of Shows* colleague Neil Simon to try his hand at cinematic send-ups with *Murder by Death* (1976) and *The Cheap Detective* (1978). By the end of the 1970s, the spoof film was a proven bankable commodity, enabling a talented band of youthful funsters to stake their own claim in this lucrative field.

The bards of Shorewood, Wisconsin, brothers Jerry and David Zucker and their best friend Jim Abrahams had assembled a comedy revue called *Kentucky Fried Theatre*, consisting of quickie movie and TV parodies. Moving their troupe from Wisconsin to Los Angeles, the Zuckers and Abrahams enjoyed such popularity that they decided to gather together nearly two dozen of their best skits into a feature film, which ended up being directed by John Landis under the title *Kentucky Fried Movie*. Released in 1977, the film returned a $20 million gross on a $700,000 investment, emboldening the trio to assemble a second feature under their own joint direction (despite resistance from the Directors' Guild over billing three people as director of a single film). For their inspiration, the boys referred to a videotape they'd made of the 1957 airline-disaster film *Zero Hour!*, laughing hysterically throughout what was supposed to be an intensely serious melodrama. The result was the 1980 Paramount release *Airplane!*, which took in $80 million at the box office—and made it impossible for anyone to ever again watch *Zero Hour!* with a straight face.

The basic formula of the Zucker-Abrahams-Zucker films (the team will be henceforth referred to as Z-A-Z for brevity's sake), so brilliantly set forward in *Airplane!*, should be familiar enough to the reader to preclude the necessity of going into meticulous detail or providing a laundry list of famous dialogue quotes. Suffice to say that each and every scene in a typical Z-A-Z laughfest is jam-packed with visual and verbal gags, in emulation of the "chicken-salad" technique popularized by such *MAD* magazine artists as Mort Drucker and Wally Wood; and just to make certain that every gag in this packing process was a surefire laugh, Z-A-Z videotaped each take, allowing them to make decisions instantly on the set rather than later in the editing room. The team had a special fondness for puns and lexical ambiguities (words with multiple meanings depending on context); when feeling particularly ambitious, the filmmakers indulged in what linguists refer to as the "paraprosdokian," in which the latter part of a sentence is so unexpected as to force the listener to reevaluate the sentence's beginning. (Please save your notes. This will all be on the final exam.) Trusting that the audience was as pop-culture-savvy as they were, the three directors also threw in "flash" parodies of films that had nothing to do with the plot at hand, yet somehow arose naturally from the action, such as *Airplane!*'s quotations from *Jaws, Saturday Night Fever, From Here to Eternity, Since You Went Away* and *Knute Rockne—All American*. And in the old vaudeville tradition of "always leave 'em laughing," even the closing credits crawl in a Z-A-Z effort was chock full of unexpected jokes, puns and nonsequiturs.

Most importantly, the team built their comedy on a firm foundation of solid story values—in the case of *Airplane!*, by recreating virtually every dramatic highlight of *Zero Hour!* and using the film's "straight" dialogue exchanges as launching pads for the laugh lines. In the world of Z-A-Z, the story *always* came first: The boys never even started dreaming up gags until the plot and character arcs were firmly in place, providing an aura of credibility and coherence to the zany goings-on. Any halfway decent comedy writer can spew out joke after joke, but it takes time and talent to provide those jokes with the substance of a moderately believable chain of events, making the comedy all the funnier in contrast. To maintain their films' surface sheen of authenticity, Z-A-Z made a practice of casting prominent dramatic actors and action-film regulars who could be counted on to recite the most idiotic of dialogue with the utmost gravity—and who were good enough sports to lampoon their own screen images. Peter Graves, Lloyd Bridges, Robert Stack and Leslie Nielsen were among the distinguished performers comprising *Airplane*'s Self-Mockery Brigade.

A decade into Z-A-Z's reign as Hollywood's premiere spoofmeisters, Jim Abrahams splintered off to tackle the military genre with the 1991 20th Century–Fox release *Hot Shots!* Like *Airplane!*, the film was inspired by a "straight" genre piece, the phenomenally popular 1986 Tom Cruise vehicle *Top Gun*. This cliché-ridden but highly entertaining yarn concerned a group of young and fabulous-looking students at an elite United States fighter-pilot school, with emphasis on the aptly named Maverick (Cruise of course), a reckless lone wolf who must not only learn the value of teamwork in the air, but also absolve an infamously fatal error committed years earlier by his jet-pilot father. It was comedy writer Pat Proft, who'd joined the Z-A-Z team during their early–1980s TV series *Police Squad!*, who first floated the idea of sending up *Top Gun;* and it was 20th Century–Fox CEO Joe Roth who recommended Charlie Sheen, heretofore almost exclusively associated with nonhumorous action films like the Oscar-winning *Platoon*, for the role of *Hot Shots!* protagonist Lt. Topper Harley (a play on Harley Topper, a popular 1960s motor scooter). Roth had been impressed by Sheen's ability to score big laughs with a rare comedy part in the 1988 baseball film *Major League*, simply by being his own taciturn self and allowing the material to carry the humor. The beauty of Charlie Sheen's characterization in *Hot Shots!* is the actor's utter sincerity: his Topper Harley would have been a perfectly legitimate romantic lead in any serious aviation epic. It is simply one more illustration of Z-A-Z's genius for providing their off-the-wall comedy with a sturdy inner lining of credibility.

Hot Shots! uses just enough of the plot, characters and situations from *Top Gun* for audiences to recognize the source of the parody; for example, though the climactic flying scenes in *Hot Shots!* are gloriously unbelievable, they are but slight exaggerations of what audiences were expected to swallow whole in the purportedly "realistic" *Top Gun*. Fleshing out the material, Jim Abrahams and Pat Proft took a cue from such earlier parodies as *So Quiet on the Canine Front* by incorporating as many tried-and-true aviation movie clichés as they could recite from memory. Particularly well handled are the stock genre stereotypes, notably the would-be pilot whom the audience knows from the outset will be washed out, and the foredoomed flyboy who is destined to meet an untimely end while flying his last scheduled mission. *Hot Shots!* wastes no time in outing these familiar characters (here played by Jon Cryer and William O'Leary), audaciously saddling the poor saps with the nicknames "Wash-Out" and "Dead Meat." The latter character figures into one of the film's best gag-cluster sequences, with chuckles building to belly laughs and belly laughs to howls in a matter of seconds. It isn't enough that Dead Meat has all but signed his own death warrant by having a lovely young wife and several cute children; the scriptwriters contrive to pile on virtually *every* time-honored portent of doom — a black cat, a broken mirror, a lost lucky charm, an unsigned insurance policy — then top it all off by revealing that not only has Dead Meat formulated a secret plan to solve global warming, but he has also unearthed the shocking truth behind the Kennedy assassination!

Unlike the *Zero Hour!*-*Airplane!* situation, in which Z-A-Z was at liberty to use exact quotes from *Zero Hour!* because both the earlier film and *Airplane!* were Paramount properties, *Hot Shots!* was barred from a word-for-word dissection of *Top Gun* because the latter film was not a 20th Century–Fox release. Undaunted, Abrahams and Proft concocted a fairly solid scenario of their own, incorporating the *Top Gun* elements into a plotline involving an avaricious weapons manufacturer, and climaxing with a military air strike on Iraq which the bad guy tries to sabotage for his own gain. This provided the filmmakers the opportunity to once again populate the supporting cast with veteran film and TV favorites, with Efrem Zimbalist Jr. cast against type as the villainous manufacturer and *Airplane!* alumnus Lloyd Bridges (replacing first-choice George C. Scott) having the time of his life in the role of Navy admiral Thomas "Tug" Benson, a senescent Six Million Dollar Man whose entire body has been prosthetically reconstructed — even the space between his ears. Also, by not being tightly bound to their *Top Gun* source material, Abrahams and Proft were permitted to go off on innumerable flights of quickie-parody fancy, with seemingly gratuitous but actually well-integrated lampoons of such films as *Dances with Wolves, Nine and a Half Weeks, An Officer and a Gentleman, The Godfather* and *Marathon Man*.

In writing of Laurel & Hardy's seemingly improvisational comedy technique, John McCabe observed: "This form is attained by sweat." The same is true of the creative forces behind *Hot Shots!* Though the film seems to overflow with spontaneous hilarity, Abrahams and Proft worked hard to make it look easy. The scene in which Topper Harley and several other pilots land on the deck of an aircraft carrier is a veritable cornucopia of throwaway gags: One pilot jumps out of his plane to feed a parking meter, another pulls two bags of groceries from the cockpit, a third removes his helmet to reveal that he's wearing curlers, and a fourth is accosted by an angry man in a wheelchair after his plane taxis into a handicapped space. One marvels at the seamless virtuosity of this scene, but it probably doesn't dawn on the casual viewer that a lot of very hard labor went into each and every gag — and that none of these gags was the first (or even the second) one the writers came up when they sat down at the conference table. Later in the film, the pilots involved in the Iraqi air strike are told that their principal target is the palace of Sadam Hussein: Failing that, they are given the choice of two alternate targets— an accordion factory and a mime school. It's safe bet that the writers spent the better part of a working day determining which two "alternates" would prompt the biggest laugh from a general audience. It is this sort of painstaking, trial-and-error dedication to the art of comedy that sets *Hot Shots* apart from the flood of generic "spoof" films (*Epic Movie, Date Movie, Dance Flick*) turned out by Z-A-Z's many imitators.

Charlie Sheen is worth at least two and a half men as reckless Navy pilot Topper Harley in the action-flick parody *Hot Shots!* (20th Century–Fox, 1990).

For an example of a military-movie parody that demonstrates the value of the Abrahams-Proft creative process by refuting it, we refer you to the 1990 Cannon Pictures release *A Man Called Sarge*. Though it came out before *Hot Shots!*, it really doesn't matter: *A Man Called Sarge* would never have existed were it not for the worldwide success of such previous Z-A-Z genre takeoffs as *Airplane!* and *The Naked Gun: From the Files of Police Squad* (1988). *A Man Called Sarge* was produced by Gene Corman (Roger's brother) and written and directed by Steward Gilliard, who has since gone on to such loftier projects as the TV series *Charmed* and *One Tree Hill*. Acknowledging that the picture earned only $97,000 during its initial release, Gilliard has observed that "Maybe three people saw it." Make that four.

A Man Called Sarge is an undisciplined takeoff of such wartime "hero squad" films as *Raid on Rommel* and *Tobruk*—and in fact is set in Tobruk, though actually filmed in Israel. The story takes place during "World War Eye Eye," or so says offscreen narrator Don LaFontaine (the ubiquitous "In a world..." voice of Hollywood movie trailers), who plays so large a role in the film that he should have received star billing. However, that honor was reserved for onetime *Saturday Night Live* regular Gary Kroeger, cast as "American Good Guy" Sgt. Duke Roscoe. Assigned to destroy a German-held oil reserve, "Sarge" Roscoe leads a ragtag band of Foreign Legion deserters to ultimate victory. There. That's the whole plot. So much for building comedy on a solid narrative base.

The philosophy of the brain trust behind *A Man Called Sarge* would seem to be as follows: "*Airplane!* uses sophomoric humor? *We* use sophomoric humor! *Airplane!* pokes fun at movie clichés? *We* poke fun at movie clichés! *Airplane!* has funny character names? *We* have funny character names! *Airplane!* features outrageous sexual jokes? *We* feature outrageous sexual jokes! *Airplane!* has anachronisms and nonsequiturs? *We* have anachronisms and nonsequiturs! *Airplane!* is full of puns and plays on words? *We're* full of puns and plays on words! What has *Airplane!* got that we haven't got?" Feast your eyes upon the following examples of humor from *A Man Called Sarge* and you'll have no trouble answering that question.

At the outset, the narrator informs us that "this is not an important story, but it's a darn good way to kill 90 minutes." Sgt. Roscoe's commando team includes a swarthy-looking Mafia type, a Native American who talks like Tonto "because you white guys think it's cool," a "goy kind of guy" redneck and a token Jew (identified as such) who at one point is held up to the Nazis as bait. "Five brave Americans against one Kraut"— who indeed is named Von Kraut, "a German bad guy with a small schnitzel." We are also introduced to a pair of foreign commandos, designated "a British stupid guy" and "a French poodle," the latter because he barks like a dog at the mention of his ex-sweetheart, "a French spy with big boozoombahs." The film's heroine Sadie (Gretchen German) is, we are helpfully informed, a "horny American schoolteacher" who reads to her children from "The Hitite Report" (it took me a couple of minutes to realize that this was a play on the bestselling sex treatise *The Hite Report*). In the course of events, the British commando comments, "I shall have to rely strictly on my wits," to which Sarge replies, "Then you're halfway there, sir." Tiptoeing into a dangerous situation, Sarge mutters, "I got a bad feeling about this. It's like a hickey on your dick. It just won't go away." A couple of Englishmen perform what I assume is meant to be a Monty Python takeoff involving the words "Duck" and "Dump." Key North African strongholds are given names like BenCasey-BenCasey and Berri-Berri. Must I go on?

Okay, I can take it if you can. When we see a stock shot, the narrator intones "A stock shot." After the mandatory fart joke, the narrator chimes in with "Mandatory fart joke." So it goes throughout the film, with jokes explained, commented upon and apologized for. Whereas the *Hot Shots!* team uses clusters of anachronisms and nonsequiturs as throwaways, in *A Man Called Sarge* the filmmakers take such great pride in showing a modern-day stewardess on a World War II bomber and a Panzer tank in a valet parking slot that they linger on these images for what seems like eons. As for Abrahams and Proft's clever and inventive deployment of famous actors and celebrity cameos, there's a world of difference between Charles Barkley and Bill Laimbeer recreating their infamous basketball-court brawl in *Hot Shots!* and Bruce Jenner appearing in *A Man Called Sarge* simply because he's Bruce Jenner. Then there's the matter of quickie movie parodies. In *Airplane!* and *Hot Shots!* we don't see any of these mini-spoofs coming, and that's why we laugh. In *A Man Called Sarge*, we can see those takeoffs of *Casablanca, The Godfather, The Third Man* and *The Good, the Bad and the Ugly* coming a mile away, and that's why we writhe in agony. In the same vein, the one-liners and puns in the Zucker/Abrahams/Proft comedies are never funnier than when they catch the audience by surprise (e.g., *Hot Shots!* leading lady Valeria Golino, in the thick of a tense confrontation with the hero, suddenly asking how you handle an elephant with three balls). Conversely, can you guess way ahead of time the payoffs to such *Man Called Sarge* straight lines as "Take your chairs," "Check your weapons," and "Everyone pipe down"? Or do I have to spell it out for you? (That's another of the set-ups, by the way. Surely you've guessed the payoff to *that* one. And don't call me Shirley.)

Hot Shots! and its Z-A-Z predecessors were meticulously crafted by men dedicated to the craft of comedy, willing to go that extra mile to make their product as funny and fullfilling as possible for an audience whom they clearly loved and respected. *A Man Called Sarge* is a cheesy, cynical ripoff, hastily conceived in pursuit of the fast buck by filmmakers who evidently regarded their target audience with contempt and operated on the theory that those stupid yokels will laugh at anything if it's loud, obvious and dirty. *Hot Shots!* is a good parody of military films; *A Man Called Sarge* is a bad parody of good parodies.

We could also add that *A Man Called Sarge* was very cheaply made with a cast of unknowns, but that shouldn't be held against it: The same could be said of Z-A-Z's first cinematic effort *Kentucky Fried Movie*, and look at the wonderful results. Besides, it's entirely possible to make a parody film on a decent budget with a cast of well-known performers and still come up with a clunker. A case in point is the Warner Bros. comedy filmed in 1990 as *Dive!* and released the following year as *Going Under*. For a while, it looked as if I would be spared the inconvenience of discussing *Going Under* in this chapter, for two reasons. First, though definitely a parody film, this 80-minute tale of an incompetent submarine crew has a closer kinship to the *Police Academy* "misfit makes good" school of filmmaking as discussed in **Chapter 12**; indeed, the film's German release title *Das Boot Akademie* deliberately suggests some kind of familial relationship with the interminable *Police Academy* series of the 1980s and 1990s. Second, a number of sources—including the film's star Bill Pullman—have indicated that *Going Under* was never released theatrically, instead going directly to video; had that been the case we wouldn't be talking about it now. But this last point has been refuted by firm evidence of big-screen showings throughout late August and early September of 1991. One such exhibition was reviewed by Adrian McCoy of the *Pittsburgh Press*: "This leaden comedy sinks quickly and never resurfaces.... Next to this sophomoric, silly stuff, *McHale's Navy* looks like *Das Boot*."

No, *Going Under* isn't a parody of the classic German submarine thriller *Das Boot*. It *might* have been intended as a specific send-up of the 1990 American nailbiter *The Hunt for Red October*, though in performance it comes off as a catch-all spoof of the entire "submarine" genre. Produced and written by Darryl Zarubica and Randolph Davis, and directed by TV veteran Mark W. Travis (*The Facts of Life, Family Ties*), the film stars Bill Pullman as Navy officer Biff Banner, who has not only run the last few subs under his command aground, but also suffers from claustrophia. Nonetheless, Banner is placed in charge of the submarine U.S.S. *Standard* (Sub Standard. *Sub Standard!* That's a joke, son!). The sorriest vessel in the fleet, the *Standard* is manned by a crew of foul-ups and dimwits, the dregs of the "silent service." Since it would be cheaper to sink the defective submarine than repair it, the Department of Defense sends the *Standard* and its expendable personnel on the certain-death mission of hunting down a Soviet nuclear sub. Fortunately, Banner and his crew are able to throw the Russians off the track by camouflaging the *Standard* as a gigantic whale!

Unlike *A Man Called Sarge*, *Going Under* actually indicates that some thought and money went into its preparation. While the production values are not lavish, they are at least up to 1990s theatrical-feature standards. Avoiding the amateurish mugging and joke-underlining of *A Man Called Sarge*, Bill Pullman is well suited to his stoic reluctant-hero role; likewise sidestepping the temptation to make faces and hop about are villains Ned Beatty and Robert Vaughn, the former as a corrupt military officer and the latter as a crooked industrialist. Also making the most of their limited screen time are cameo players Roddy McDowall as the namby-pamby Secretary of Defense, *Police Academy* regular Michael Winslow (aka "the human sound-effects machine") as an inquiring reporter, and Joe Namath as the *Standard*'s athletic coach. Finally, the submarine-to-whale special effects are smoothly and convincingly rendered by Fantasy II, the same brilliant technicians who worked on such excursions into the fantastic as James Cameron's *The Abyss* and *Terminator 2*.

There's only one problem with *Going Under*. It isn't funny.

Shall we go through the same sort of bullet-list that we used to itemize the least amusing moments of *A Man Called Sarge*? This time around, it should be enough to observe that among the character names in *Going Under* are General Malice (Ned Beatty) and his fellow officers General Confusion, General Alert, General Telephone, General Air Quality and General Lee Good. And on this occasion we can skip the rundown of laughless laugh lines merely by quoting the very first "joke" in the picture, in which a WAC tour guide effusively welcomes a group of Girl Scouts to Washington, D.C., by chirping "Here's where our nation's leaders take mommy and daddy's tax dollars and turn them into machines of global destruction." As with *A Man Called Sarge*, it appears that the people responsible for *Going Under* opted to use the first joke they came up with rather than expending time and energy weighing *all* the joke possibilities—which is why the Z-A-Z parodies still stand head and shoulders above the rest.

The saddest aspect of *Going Under* is that much of the comedy material had real potential. A scene between General Malice and the Secretary of Defense is staged in the manner of *Mister Rogers' Neighborhood*; the *Standard*'s navigator is a surly ex-cab driver, while the sonar operator is a fussy old lady; and whenever the sub is disguised as a whale, the crew must steer clear of some *very* determined Japanese whale hunters. Unfortunately, these and other tantalizing comic setups are either underbaked or stretched far beyond their worth. The film's biggest laugh occurs in the first 60 seconds, when the avaricious General Malice accepts a huge bribe to purchase the blueprints for a state-of-the-art "communications device"—which at closer glance turn out to be detailed sketches of a carrier pigeon. Alas, the promise held out by this clever gag is unfulfilled by the dull 79 minutes which follow.

Inasmuch as the filmmakers were incapable of sustaining the humor of *Going Under*'s premise, it is astonishing that they would have the gall to try their hand at satire. Up until now, we've been talking about parodies, which don't have to be satirical (as defined in the beginning of this chapter) or even contain any satirical content to be effective. But *Going Under* has loftier ambitions, using its humor as a savage attack on that old bugaboo of the anti-war movement, "The Military-Industrial Complex." Not only is General Malice a bribe-taking reprobate, but he is the loyal toady of venal industrialist Wedgewood (Robert Vaughn)—and *both* men are in cahoots with the entire U.S. Government, shown to be peopled almost exclusively by criminals and incompetents. We've already established that hero Biff Banner has been set up to fail by taking command of the *Standard*, but that's only half of the story. It isn't merely a matter of the government spending less on sinking a submarine than paying for its repairs: Everyone in authority *knows* that the *Standard* has been built with shoddy materials purchased at the least possible cost by General Malice, so it is to everyone's advantage that no evidence of their collusion remain. But you ain't heard nothin' yet! By failing in his mission, Banner will unavoidably trigger the nuclear reactor hidden on the Russian sub, thereby starting a third World War from which the greedy Wedgewood will reap enormous profits. Not even *Dr. Strangelove* (see **Chapter 19**) was so vicious in its indictment of the Powers That Be—but then, the creators of *Dr. Strangelove* were restrained by such intangibles as talent, taste and judgment. "Sophomoric" is too grandiose a term for the satirical pretensions of *Going Under*. This is kindergarten stuff.

Ned Beatty seems to be warning Michael Winslow not to swallow his microphone without chewing it in this scene from the submarine-movie spoof *Going Under*. (Warner Bros., 1991). Incidentally, this still is labelled with the film's original title, *Dive!*

Of course, one could take the "apologist" stance by suggesting that *Going Under* is a purer form of satire than *Dr. Strangelove*, of the sort that doesn't *have* to be funny to make its points. Those of us who slogged through *Animal Farm* and *Gulliver's Travels* back in high school without ever cracking a smile are painfully aware that the label "satire" is no guarantee of a laugh riot. So maybe *Going Under* isn't funny because it wasn't supposed to be funny. And you don't believe that any more than I do.

At any rate, for an example of a military-movie satire that was definitely intended to get laughs, let us turn to the final entry in this chapter, the Pax-Americana Pictures effort *Military Intelligence and You!* As in the case of *Going Under*, this film just barely qualifies for inclusion in this book. Though never given a full theatrical release in the United States, it began making the film-festival rounds at Austin, Texas in October of 2006, and *has* been shown commercially on a one-time-only basis; thus, technically it rises above the "direct-to-video" class.

Written and directed by Dale Kutzera, *Military Intelligence and You!* falls somewhere between a "mockumentary" and a pastiche. Lensed in black and white, the film employs the mockumentary style previously seen in such efforts as Christopher Guest's *This is Spinal Tap* and Woody Allen's *Zelig*, presenting fictional events in the form of a documentary, complete with pretentious offscreen narration. It is also a pastiche in that it weaves excerpts from earlier films into a new comic scenario, in the manner of Carl Reiner's *Dead Men Don't Wear Plaid*, wherein contemporary comedian Steve Martin exchanged dialogue with such film noir icons as Humphrey Bogart and James Cagney with the aid of 1940s-vintage filmclips.

In the case of *Military Intelligence and You!*, vignettes from various military training and propaganda films from the World War II era are bundled together to form a parody of that particular genre. Among the films cannibalized for this purpose are several produced at Fort Roach (the former Hal Roach Studios) by the Armed Forces' First Motion Picture Unit: *Resisting Enemy Interrogation*, featuring Lloyd Nolan, Arthur Kennedy, Kent Smith, Carl Esmond, Peter Van Eyck and Steven Geray; *Ditch and Live*, again with Arthur Kennedy; *Recon Pilot*, with William Holden; *Photo Analysis for Aerial Bombardment*, with Alan Ladd; *Identification of a Japanese Zero*, with Ronald Reagan; and *Target for Today*, directed by William Keighley. Also included is a morale-boosting short subject produced by the United States Army and released stateside by Warner Bros.: *Baptism of Fire*, featuring Elisha Cook Jr. and Russell Arms. Adroitly edited by Joseph Butler, these snippets are expertly matched with newly filmed scenes lensed at Los Angeles' ShowBiz Studios by cinematographer Mark Parry in the precise photographic style of the earlier footage, which itself was digitally enhanced to bring it up to 21st-century standards. Though the matching isn't entirely seamless, overall it is quite impressive.

Produced under the title *At War with Military Intelligence*, the film was originally much longer than its present 78-minute running time. As explained by creator Dale Kutzera on his own web log, he had a huge selection of World War II battle scenes culled from old training films at his disposal, and had planned to "stuff all this cool footage" into *Military Intelligence*. But Kutzera had to forsake some of the most exciting material because he found it was impeding the film's overall pace: "Imagine that ... action becoming boring."

Opening with a faux "declassified" title, *Military Intelligence and You!* is identified as Training Film #125 in the "Give Them Liberty" series. Set in March of 1944, the narrative involves the 950th Bomber Group's Able Squadron in their efforts to seek out and destroy the dreaded German Ghost Squadron. We are introduced to Major Nick Reed (Patrick Muldoon), an Army Intelligence analyst whose job it is to locate the Ghost Squadron's secret base. The action alternates between military headquarters, the cockpit of the bomber piloted by Major Mitch Dunning (Mackenzie Astin), and the on-the-ground adventures of fuzzy-cheeked PFC Jimmy Ryan, "played" by Russell Arms in footage culled from *Baptism of Fire*. In a plot wrinkle that would not normally have been included in an actual training film, Major Reed and Major Dunning are rivals for the affections of WAC lieutenant Monica Tasty (Elizabeth Ann Bennett).

One cannot help but marvel at the care, effort and ingenuity that went into *Military Intelligence and You!* On a purely technical level, the film can be regarded a success. But as a comedy-parody-satire, it doesn't quite cut it. Whereas the *Hot Shots!* team garnered laughs by playing its most ludicrous material entirely straight, as if the actors involved truly believed the nonsense they were uttering, there is an air of smug superiority throughout *Military Intelligence and You!* with everyone involved so pleased with themselves that they become rather cloying. Explaining the necessity of demoralizing the German army, bombastic narrator Clive Van Owen says, "It's not enough just to beat them, we want to do it in front of their girl friends and mothers to embarrass them"—and that's only one of many such ham-handed remarks. Similarly, the actors in the new footage are so busy "commenting" on the campiness of 1940s-era acting techniques they fail to deliver credible performances. In this respect, the performers seen in the old filmclips are far more believable (and likeable!) than anyone in the new scenes.

Then there's the matter of anachronisms, which as demonstrated by earlier movie spoofs can be quite funny. In *Military Intelligence and You!*, the deployment of such post–Production Code expletives as "shit" and "pissed" are evidently meant to be an amusing contrast with the straitlaced strictures of 1940s fimmaking; instead, this sort of badinage comes across as self-conscious and a bit childish. Also, one gets the impression that some of the anachronisms weren't even intentional. The presence in Army Intelligence Headquarters of a map showing Germany carefully divided into Eastern and Western sectors—a partition that didn't occur until well after World War II—seems more like carelessness than a deliberate attempt at time displacement. Likewise, the narrator's reference to a cure for polio might well have been the result of the filmmakers' lack of awareness that such a cure didn't exist until the 1950s.

None of this is terribly important, however, since *Military Intelligence and You!* aspires to be much, much more than merely a parody of a 1940s training film. Its primary reason for being is to satirically skewer the foreign policy of President George W. Bush—specifically the war on Iraq in the wake of 9/11, which the filmmakers obviously regard as an act of blind and brutish American chauvinism. We are told by the narrator that the mission of military intelligence is to "spread the secular love of our Christian democracy," and that "it is military intelligence that distinguishes the dangerous enemies from merely annoying foreigners." This xenophobia is parroted by Major Mitch Dunning: "It's not our fault we're better and smarter than anyone else. It's just the way God made things." The misdeeds and prevarications allegedly perpetrated by Bush's White House are endlessly invoked in the film: American forces are rallied into battle with promises from "The National Security Officer" that victory will be quick and easy; hatred for the enemy is ginned up with rumors of Germans "peddling opium in the mean streets of Dusseldorf" (an allusion to "yellow cake," perhaps?); and a wholly unnecessary air strike is staged so as not to deprive the pilots of an opportunity to show off their training. On the slim chance that we might miss the point, throughout *Military Intelligence and You!* the attack on Pearl Harbor is referred to as "12/7," the Vice President of the United States is identified as "the most powerful man in the free world" (Take *that*, Dick Cheney!), such talking points as "War on Evil" and "Axis of Generalities" are bandied about, and the government-dictated "threat levels" are given such colors as Tangerine, Butterscotch and Autumn Blossom. Even the film's publicity packet gets into the act: "Finally, a training film that dramatizes the importance of knowing what we're attacking—before we attack it!"

The last time we looked, this is a free country, and if a filmmaker wants to use a military-movie parody as a political forum, more power to him. If Z-A-Z alumnus David Zucker has a right to make a strident, one-joke Conservative comedy like *American Carol* (2008), a mean-spirited attack on documentarian-*provocateur* Michael Moore, certainly Dale Kutzera has a right to make a strident, one-joke Liberal comedy like *Military Intelligence and You!*, an equally mean-spirited attack on "W." And if, like David Zucker, Dale Kutzera came up with an appallingly unfunny effort guaranteed to alienate half its potential audience and bore the other half, that was a risk he was clearly willing to take. In all fairness, not everyone was put off by the Kutzera film. Kenneth Turan of the *Los Angeles Times* praised it as "both a loving spoof of World War II films and a pointed satire on America's involvement in Iraq," while *Box Office* magazine declared the picture "laugh out loud hilarious." This, however, was the minority opinion. Most observers, even the most partisan, went along with *Variety*, which noted that the film "belabors the obvious."

The most damning criticism against *Military Intelligence and You!* has less to do with politics than with judgment. If, as has been claimed, Robert Altman used the Korean War as an analogy for Vietnam in *MASH*, he was in good company: Many historians have drawn comparisons between the two conflicts, citing their lack of clear purpose and their long-range tragic consequences. But by using World War II as an analogy for the Iraq War, *Military Intelligence and You!* both stumbles and crumbles. In contrast with the vagaries and contradictions attending Iraq, there was both a strong purpose and sound logic behind the Second World War, and the goals couldn't have been better defined: The utter destruction of European fascism and Japanese militarism and the liberation of the victims of both. Even if you don't agree with this thesis, consider another indictment against *Military Intelligence and You!* In the excitement of making a joke out of the Bush policy, Dale Kutzera has by extension also made a joke out of World War II, which is flat-out unfair to the millions of soldiers and civilians who sacrificed, bled and died to win that war.

Is this assessment too harsh? Well, take a gander at Kutzera's manipulation of two lengthy excerpts from the wartime propaganda films *Baptism of Fire*, in which a GI played by Elisha Cook Jr. delivers a impassioned monologue about facing death, and *Resisting Enemy Interrogation*, in which a group of American POWs are subjected to the Nazis' insidiously sophisticated information-gathering techniques. Though these scenes may be a bit corny, there is nothing inherently ridiculous about them. But when placed within the framework of *Military Intelligence and You!*, the anxiety of the GI in *Baptism of Fire* and the plight of the prisoners in *Resisting Enemy Interrogation* are tastelessly held up for ridicule — a fatal error from which the film never recovers.

This writer laughed exactly once while watching *Military Intelligence and You!*, when in an excerpt from *Identification of a Japanese Zero* a confused-looking Ronald Reagan shrugs and sighs, "Wish I could apologize from here." It's a guaranteed howl, as well it should be: If you can't raise a laugh from an out-of-context shot of Ronald Reagan, you have no business making comedies. Which brings to mind another film, which since 1980 has been endlessly plundered by political satirists on the strength of a single sequence in which All-American fighter pilot Ronald Reagan is forced to don a Nazi uniform. That film is the 1943 Warner Bros. release *Desperate Journey*, and it's a curiously appropriate title with which to end this chapter. In his 1964 book *The Bad Guys*, film historian William K. Everson makes a perceptive observation which casts this purportedly serious war melodrama in a whole new light: "One of the most exhilarating and action-packed of all war films, *Desperate Journey* was actually a tongue-in-cheek spoof of its own genre, something that nobody seemed to realize at the time...."

A whole new chapter could be added to this volume highlighting the "straight" films, military or otherwise, which on closer examination contain subtle elements of self-satire and self-parody. But to again quote (or rather, paraphrase) William K. Everson, that belongs in another book.

21

Extra Added Attractions
The Cartoons

This being a book devoted to live-action military comedies, any discussion of animated cartoons will have to be brief and comparatively superficial. Of the thousands upon thousands of theatrical and non-theatrical cartoons released in the past century, a few hundred can be classified as military-themed, beginning with a group of seven animated shorts produced by Charles Bowers and Raoul Barré, commissioned during the World War I era for training purposes by the U.S. War Department. Of these, only the cautionary *A.W.O.L.*, released after the Armistice, appears to have survived.

Typical of the pre–World War II talkie cartoons which relied upon military humor were a pair of Max Fleischer productions. The 1932 "bouncing ball" sing-along *Oh, How I Hate to Get Up in the Morning* is a series of spot gags about barracks life combined with a live-action performance of the title song by vaudevillians Reis & Dunn. And the 1934 Betty Boop vehicle *There's Something About a Soldier* imagines a savage battle on land, air and sea between the human race and a swarm of giant mosquitoes (the notion of anthropomorphic insects or animals deploying the tools of mechanized warfare was a popular cartoon theme, as in Warner Bros.' *What Price Porky* and *The Fighting 69½*, among many others). One of the strangest Army cartoons from this period is Warners' *Bosko the Doughboy* (1931), a jaw-dropping exercise in death and devastation set to bouncy jazz music. Animation historians Jerry Beck and Will Friedwald sum it all up neatly: "In this cartoon, you realize these cartoon characters are devising funny and cute li'l ways to kill each other, [and] it becomes morbid humor. It almost seems like a parody when inanimate objects mimic the human act of dying." Equally as whimsical in its treatment of battlefield bloodshed is Warners' 1936 Porky Pig cartoon *Boom Boom*, which would become a favorite on the college-revival circuit in the 1970s.

Upon the establishment of the peacetime draft in 1940, the cartoon industry responded with such timely efforts as *The Cute Recruit* (Columbia, 1941), in which an Army and a Navy recruiter aggressively compete for the attentions of a potential conscriptee, only to discover that they've wasted their powers of persuasion on a three-year-old child. Other cartoons released just prior to Pearl Harbor include the faux newsreel *Meet John Doughboy* and the basic-training farce *Rookie Revue*, both from Warner Bros. As indication of how close to home the Draft hit Hollywood's animation studios—most of them staffed by men under the age of 35—*Rookie Revue* features caricatures of the "Termite Terrace" staffers (Tex Avery, Henry Binder, et al.) as various officers and enlistees. In a similar vein, the production credits for Warners' non-military cartoon *Of Fox and Hounds* (1940) list "Draft No. 1312" as screenwriter and "Draft No. 6102" as animator.

The bulk of the war-related cartoons produced between 1941 and 1945 have been so thoroughly covered by other film and animation histories that anything said here would be redundant. It's worth noting that many of today's most distinguished World War II historians grew up in the 1950s and 1960s, a time when youngsters were exposed to endless TV reruns of Hollywood cartoons

This frame capture represents one of the less family-friendly moments from the 1931 "Looney Tunes" entry *Bosko the Doughboy*.

from the early 1940s. These baby boomers were inundated with constant references to such despots as Hitler, Mussolini and Tojo; to curfews, blackouts, and travel restrictions; to the rationing of rubber, shoes, silk, sugar and thick juicy steaks; to A-Cards and Meatless Tuesdays; to gremlins, fifth columnists and food hoarders; to scrap-iron and paper drives; to defense plants and their female employees; and to the "V for Victory" opening notes of Beethoven's Fifth. Forget your junior-high history class; these cartoons were as powerful and potent a history primer as any dusty old textbook. Even today, youngsters who were born decades after World War II can confidently pinpoint an old cartoon's production date upon hearing such catchphrases as "Hey, you! Put out that light!" and "Is this trip really necessary?" This remains true despite the fact that children of the 21st century are not always permitted to reap the full cultural benefits of wartime cartoons, especially those banned titles like *Tokio Jokio* and *Bugs Bunny Nips the Nips,* both featuring offensive Japanese stereotypes—films all too often taken out of context by self-styled experts to "prove" that Hollywood has always been rife with racial intolerance. (These come-lately social critics might also take a peek at the vicious racial slurs in such pro–Nazi cartoons of the 1940s as *Die Störenfried* and *Nimbus Libéré*. A different time, a different world.)

But while there was an abundance of war-related animated shorts, the number of military-themed theatrical cartoons was comparatively small. It's hard to say why this was true, except to hypothesize that the largest fan following for cartoons during this era was comprised of servicemen who preferred escapist film fare like comedies, musicals and westerns, and were not all that hepped up over Army and Navy pictures. Even so, it was impossible to ignore the fact that a goodly percentage of the American male population was in uniform, and cartoons acknowledged this. Warner Bros.' Daffy Duck enlisted in the fight against Fascism in *Daffy — The Commando*

(1943) and *Plane Daffy* (1944); Walter Lantz' Woody Woodpecker joined the Army Air Corps in *Ace in the Hole* (1942); and Walt Disney paid tribute to the K-9 corps with *Private Pluto* (1943), as did MGM's Hanna-Barbera (albeit without an established cartoon "star") in *War Dogs* (1943). And following in the bootsteps of Disney's animated features, the 1-reel service cartoons of the 1940s plundered the world of fables and fairy tales. The Three Little Pigs organize a well-armed batallion against a Hitlerized wolf ("Go ahead and hiss—who cares?") in Tex Avery's *The Blitz Wolf* (MGM, 1943), while the Seven Dwarfs, redrawn as outrageous black caricatures, proclaim in song that they're "in the Army now!" in Bob Clampett's *Coal Black and de Sebben Dwarfs* (Warners, 1943).

Most of these titles were one- or two-shots; seldom were the more familiar cartoon characters regularly cast as military personnel. Exceptions to this rule include Terrytoons' Gandy Goose, Disney's Donald Duck and Max Fleischer/Paramount's Popeye the Sailor. The Terrytoons efforts were the most disappointing of the lot, though they got off to a good start with 1942's *Sham Battle Shenanigans*, in which Gandy Goose (an Ed Wynn sound-alike) appears on the "Dunker's Donuts" radio program to relate his training-camp experiences with top sergeant Sourpuss (a Jimmy Durante-type cat) while participating in an elaborate mock battle. Also worth noting, if for no other reason than its impressive (by Terrytoons standards) variety of gags, is 1943's *The Last Round-Up*, wherein Pvt. Gandy and Sgt. Sourpuss make short work of Hitler and Mussolini, respectively caricatured as a pig and a monkey. Thereafter it was all downhill, as Gandy and Sourpuss went through their all-too-typical paces without taking any sort of comic advantage of their military surroundings. Such entries as *Lights Out* (1942) and *Aladdin's Lamp* (1943) were unambitious potboilers that might just as well have been made before or after the War with the two stars in mufti.

Far better was a brief spate of wartime Disney cartoons in which Donald Duck went through the trials and tribulations of the era's real-life conscriptees. *Donald Gets Drafted* (1942) set the pattern for these six films, its traditional "sunburst" closeup of Donald in the opening credits showing the plucky duck wearing a Army hat instead of his standard sailor's cap. As an offscreen chorus belts forth the semi-satirical tune "The Army's Not the Army Anymore," Donald is impressed by a series of recruiting posters promising recreation, luxuries, pretty girls and friendly generals to anyone willing to sign up for a hitch. Presenting his draft notice (dated March 24, 1941) to the recruiting officer, Donald is rushed through a cursory physical exam ("What color is this red card?" queries the eye doctor) and issued a voluminous uniform that becomes form-fitting only when doused with a bucket of water. Arriving at boot camp, Donald finds himself at the mercy of the requisite tough sergeant, portrayed by Disney's all-purpose cartoon villain Black Pete. "I'm gonna give you a SPECIAL trainin'!" Pete growls ominously, and the last shot shows draftee Donald peeling a mountain of potatoes. As the unseen chorus launches into a final refrain of "The Army's Not the Army Anymore," the disgruntled duck uses a potato peel to spell out the word "Phooey!" (Often accused of blindly marching in lockstep with the government in his propaganda films of the 1940s, Disney had no qualms about speaking Truth to Power in *this* cartoon.)

Donald gets even with Pete in his next Army cartoon *The Vanishing Private* (1942), rendering himself invisible with camouflage paint and driving the surly sergeant to the psych ward. Back to peeling potatoes in *Sky Trooper* (1942), Donald, newly relocated to Mallard Field Air Training Base, yearns to be a flyboy. Our hero finally takes to the air as a paratrooper, though not by choice. As is his custom, Donald briefly stands suspended in mid-air before realizing how high above ground he really is. You would think he'd know by now that no one in a Disney cartoon *ever* falls until he looks downward.

Next up is *Fall Out—Fall In* (1943), a plotless pottage of marching and tent-pitching gags. Though the weakest of Donald Duck's service cartoons, *Fall Out—Fall In* served a valuable purpose as a "teaching moment" for the Disney staffers, who used the marching sequence to experiment with animating an oversized rainstorm. Virtually all of Donald's "Army" vehicles were in a sense rehearsals for the more sophisticated techniques that Disney would utilize in his increasingly ambitious feature-length cartoons. *Donald Gets Drafted* is highlighted by some impressive "perspective" gags as an ant crawls onto Donald's beak; *Vanishing Private* boasts an abundance of unique color combinations; and *Sky Trooper* effectively combines the caricatured Donald Duck and Black Pete with realistically rendered human characters.

The weirdest of Donald's military escapades is *The Old Army Game* (1943). Returning from an unauthorized night on the town, Donald must figure out a way to sneak back into camp without alerting Sgt. Pete. After briefly impersonating a rabbit (and admirably resisting the temptation to quack "What's up, doc?") Donald hides in one of three packing crates conveniently abandoned on the campground. Now Pete must choose which crate contains Donald, a task complicated when the duck begins rapidly switching them around (hence the film's title, an arcane reference to the "old shell game"). In the confusion, Donald's crate is cut in half—and when he can't locate his feet, the horrified duck assumes that he too has been cleft in twain (an assumption bolstered by a grotesque sight gag in which the lower half of Donald's body is shown ascending to heaven, complete with wings and halo!) Instantly remorseful, Pete helps Donald hold an impromptu funeral for his lower extremities—but when it turns out that Donald is merely buried waist-deep in mud, the chase resumes, albeit in slow motion ("Keep it Under 30," remember?) Never had Walt Disney's singular fondness for "butt humor" been so bizarrely played out as in *The Old Army Game*.

The sixth and final entry in this animated mini-series is *Commando Duck* (1944), which finds Donald parachuting into an enemy-held jungle to destroy a Japanese air base. The principal gag involves a water-filled raft which grows in size until it totally submerges Donald's target ("Contacted Enemy—Washed Out Same"). Unseen for decades because of its crude Japanese caricatures, *Commando Duck* reemerged in the early 21st century as part of a Disney DVD collection, with cartoon expert Leonard Maltin issuing a disclaimer for the easily offended.

Less artistically adventuresome but more prolific were the wartime service comedies featuring Max Fleischer/Paramount's celebrated spinach-eater Popeye. Though identified in the credits and his theme song as a "sailor man," Popeye was essentially a landlubber in most of his prewar cartoon adventures. He even expresses interest in trading his nautical garb for khaki and boots in 1936's *I'm in the Army Now*, one of several Fleischer "cheaters" in which new wraparound footage was used to bracket excerpts from previous Popeye cartoons.

Once the nation began gearing up for war, Popeye dutifully returned to sea, going so far as to forsake the "skipper" costume he'd been wearing since his comic-strip inception in 1929 in favor of traditional Navy whites—a uniform he'd retain, with occasional switchovers to Navy blues, until the end of his theatrical-cartoon career in 1957. The first Popeye vehicle to depict him as a *genuine* sailor is *The Mighty Navy*, originally released November 14, 1941. Reflecting the plight of many an "old salt" of the period, Popeye has trouble adjusting to the highly regulated and mechanized modern Navy, infuriating his superiors by fouling up both a gunnery and a dive-bombing practice. He redeems himself by using his spinach-fueled muscle power to sink a fleet of enemy vessels (an unidentified enemy, since America was still neutral). The now-famous closing scene shows a circled caricature of Popeye (in his original costume) being adopted as the official insignia of the U.S. Navy's Bomber Squadron—which actually happened shortly before this cartoon went into production.

Amidst a few "Navy" shorts in which servicemen Popeye and Bluto vie for the attentions of the eternally fickle Olive Oyl (*Kickin' the Conga Around*, *Olive Oyl and Water Don't Mix*, *Many Tanks*), Popeye returned to battle-station mode in *Blunder Below* (1942), wherein the stalwart sailor single-handedly destroys a Japanese submarine, and *Fleets of Stren'th* (1942), in which after a few miscalculations with a torpedo boat he makes amends by personally knocking several enemy planes out of the sky. The final "Popeye" entry produced by Fleischer Studios was *Baby Wants a*

Bottleship (1942), which though containing no combat scenes includes such contemporary quippery as "It should happen to Hitler."

Once production of the Popeye shorts was taken over by Paramount's "house" animation unit Famous Studios, the squint-eyed tar went to War on a grand scale, beginning with the much-maligned but undeniably hilarious *You're a Sap, Mr. Jap* (1942), which concludes with a Japanese battleship sinking beneath the waves to the sound of a flushing toilet. *Scrap the Japs* (1943) is likewise very much a product of its times, with Asian caricatures so shameless that the cartoon was withdrawn from TV showings a far back as the 1950s, *before* the P.C. era. *Spinach fer Britain* (1943) pits Popeye against the Nazis for a change, as he endeavors to deliver a shipment of spinach all the way to the doorstep of Number 10 Downing Street. And backtracking a bit in *Seein' Red White and Blue* (1943), Popeye returns to the States as a recruiting officer, determined to convince draft-dodger Bluto to join the battle against the Axis. Highlights of this lively little flag-waver include Emperor Hirohito morphing into a horse's ass, and Adolf Hitler delivering a speech consisting entirely of the foghorn-like "BEEEE-OHHHH!" as heard in the old Lifebuoy soap commercials.

Even when he wasn't fending off the enemy, Popeye was cast as a bonafide sailor in most of his wartime vehicles. A few of these —*Happy Birthdaze, The Marry-Go-Round, Moving Aweigh*— team Popeye with a fellow gob named Shorty (voice provided by Arnold Stang), who joins the star in various misadventures on shore. The most intriguing of Popeye's Navy comedies is *The Hungry Goat* (1943), intended as the pilot for a spinoff series featuring the ravenous title character, who here spends most of his screen time chowing down on Popeye's all-metal battleship — until the Admiral, who in a cute Pirandellian touch happens to be watching *The Hungry Goat* in a movie theater, figures out what's going on. Other war-related "Popeye" entries include *A Jolly Good Furlough* (1943), *Spinach-Packin' Popeye* (1944), *Service with a Guile* (1946), and best of all, 1943's *Ration fer the Duration*, an updated version of "Jack and the Beanstalk" featuring a sugar-hoarding giant and a tantalizing closeup of a brand-new rubber tire, underscored by an orchestral rendition of "Thanks for the Memory."

Arguably the most famous of the World War II–themed cartoons were not intended to be shown to the general public, but instead were produced between 1943 and 1945 for the weekly newsreel *The Army-Navy Screen Magazine* and shown exclusively to American military personnel. It was Major Frank Capra, then in charge of the First Motion Picture Unit of the Army Signal Corps, who came up with the idea of using humorous animation as an educational tool, the better to teach soldiers and sailors the proper use and maintenance of equipment and weaponry, and also emphasize the importance of learning new technology, understanding maps and codes, adapting to new climates, staying healthy at all times, saving instead of squandering paychecks, avoiding the spreading of rumors, and maintaining utmost secrecy when conversing with civilians. Capra dreamed up the character of a goofy "everyman" soldier as an example of how *not* to follow proper military protocol, passing his concept along to magazine illustrator and children's-book author Theodore "Dr. Seuss" Geisel, who headed the Corps' animation branch.

Geisel and future UPA scripter Phil Eastman wrote the lion's share of the four-minute, black & white *Private Snafu* cartoons, submitting their storyboards to the Pentagon for final approval; some of these were written in Seuss-like rhyme, notably 1944's *The Chow Hound*. Several Hollywood animation firms were approached to handle production, with the Leon Schlesinger unit at Warner Bros. turning out the bulk of the shorts (Disney was Capra's first choice, but Walt's asking price was too high). Chuck Jones is credited — though not on screen — with directing the first of the *Private Snafu* series, while others in the group were helmed by Frank Tashlin, Friz Freleng and Bob Clampett. Longtime Schlesinger "regular" Mel Blanc provided most of the voices (with assistance from such character actors as Marjorie Rambeau and Harold "Great Gildersleeve" Peary), with house orchestrator Carl Stalling handling the musical scores, not only utilizing such well-worn compositions as Raymond Scott's "Powerhouse" but also several popular songs written by the likes of Rodgers & Hammerstein and Cole Porter — expensive tunes that could not be used in the standard Warners theatrical releases because of budget considerations, but here were donated *gratis* by their creators.

The most pathetically incompetent soldier in the Army, Private Snafu nearly always manages to do the wrong thing, sometimes out of stupidity, sometimes out of sheer orneriness. Occasionally he will heed the advice of the unshaven, diapered, implicitly gay "Technical Fairy First Class" and get things right; but it's much funnier (and more instructive) when Snafu lives up to his acronymic surname, which of course stands for "Situation Normal, All Fucked Up." In one 1944 episode our hero was given a pair of brothers: Tarfu, an acronym for "Things Are Really Fucked Up"; and Fubar, which translates as "Fucked Up Beyond All Recall." The word "Fouled" is substituted for the one they couldn't use when these names are "explained" on screen, but otherwise the *Snafu* cartoons, carefully calculated to establish a rapport with an audience comprised of young servicemen, are gloriously uninhibited in their use of scatological and sexual humor. Choice examples include Snafu's frequent exclamation "Ah, the hell with it!"; the mockingly "safe" sight gag accompanying the phrase "So cold it could freeze the nuts off a jeep!"; and endless visual and verbal references to the female anatomy, especially the mammary glands. Cartoons like 1945's *It's Murder She Says*, in which the scourge of malaria is personified by a female mosquito drawn to resemble a haggard old prostitute, would hardly get past the projection booth in a civilian theater, but were much appreciated and cherished by their target audience.

Frame capture of the opening title card for the *Private Snafu* cartoons, used even when Snafu didn't appear.

Some of the *Snafu* shorts utilized animation that had already appeared in Warners' mainstream cartoons; for example. *Private Snafu vs. Malaria Mike* (1944) lifts the entire "air strike" climax from *The Fighting 69½*. Conversely, the *Snafu* entry *Booby Traps* (1944) is highlighted by a brand-new gag in which Private Snafu plunks out "Those Endearing Young Charms" on a piano, unaware that one of the keys is rigged to explode. This gag would be repeated verbatim in two of Warners' postwar theatrical cartoons, *Ballot Box Bunny* and *Show Biz Daffy*, and was affectionately reprised several decades later by Matt Stone and Trey Parker on a episode of the animated TV series *South Park*.

As mentioned, not all the *Snafus* were Schlesinger-Warner productions. Some installments were handled by a maverick animation unit that would soon develop into UPA, the innovative firm responsible for the *Mr. Magoo* and *Gerald McBoing-Boing* cartoons of the 1950s. These seminal UPA efforts, not all of which featured Private Snafu, were shorter than the Warners product, each running between 60 and 90 seconds and given the blanket title "A Few Quick Facts." Less amusing and more preachy than the "Termite Terrace" efforts, they were distinguished only by a boldness in design, especially *A Few Quick Facts About Fear* (1945), which artfully uses a "knighthood" motif to explain how fear can be channeled into positive energy on the battlefield.

Near the end of the war, when evidence arose that Leon Schlesinger had been fraudulently padding his budgets, the U.S. Navy bypassed Warner Bros. in favor of Harman-Ising productions to launch an extension of the Signal Corp's *Snafu* series, aimed specifically at Navy personnel. The first and last effort in this project, *Private Snafu Presents Seaman Tarfu In the Navy* (1946), contains no propaganda but plenty of raucous entertainment — and if one didn't know better, one would swear that Tex Avery was in the director's chair.

A lesser-known cluster of *Army-Navy Screen Magazine* cartoons represented a joint effort by the United States Navy and the War Allotment Department, and featured a character developed by future *Dennis the Menace* creator Hank Ketcham. "Seaman Hook" was an animated sailor, a man with but a single purpose: To persuade his fellow tars to invest their hard-earned cash in war bonds, thus preparing them for a financially secure postwar existence. Seaman Hook made his first appearance in *Take Heed, Mr. Tojo* (1943), the only series entry produced by Walter Lantz Studios and the only one filmed in color. Set in the future — specifically, 1953 — the story finds the pug-nosed Mr. Hook in civilian garb, explaining (with the voice of *Blondie* star Arthur Lake) the wisdom of investing in the future to his young son, using as example a wartime adventure in which government bonds helped the Fleet vanquish a villainous Japanese pilot. The cartoon has none of the raciness or rough edges of the Warner *Snafus*, but it conveys its message effectively, finding time for such throwaway gags as the compact helicopter parked in Mr. Hook's futuristic driveway. The remaining *Seaman Hook* cartoons were produced in black & white by the old Warner Bros. gang, restoring the vigorous vulgarity of the *Snafus*. Though the "Buy Bonds" message was a constant throughout the *Hook* series, the subsequent films (at least, those that still exist) have a wider range of gags and situations. The best of the batch is Bob Clampett's *Tokyo Woes* (1945), with the penny-wise Hook locked in an ideological battle against a Tokyo Rose-style propaganda merchant (voiced by Bea Benaderet) who is introduced while perched on a toilet seat!

The scattered military-themed cartoons produced after the war were for the most part pleasant but undistinguished. A noteworthy exception was a one-shot produced by William L. Snyder, directed by Gene Deitch and released by Paramount in September 1961. *Munro* is a faithful adaptation of the Jules Feiffer story about a 4-year-old boy who through a bureaucratic blunder is drafted into the Army. A devastating attack on military groupthink, the story grows more maddeningly absurd as it goes along. Nobody takes time to notice that Munro is a child as they rush him through his medical and psychological exams. Classified 1A, Munro's only comment upon being issued a uniform approximately twelve sizes too large is "Button me, mister." Sent to boot camp, the kid assumes that everyone around him is playing one of two mysterious games: "Face" (as in "about face" and "right face") and "Take This Man's Name."

When someone finally figures out that Munro isn't your typical conscript, the Brass declares that he can't possibly be only four years old because it's against regulations, so he must instead be sick. Using this logic, the boy is sent to sick call, where all he gets for his protestations is an aspirin. Next Munro toddles into the office of the camp psychatrist, who also refuses to believe the evidence of his own eyes and proclaims that the boy is bucking for a Section Eight. Giving up trying to make sense of things, Munro agrees to play soldier so long as he's able, and as the new recruits pour into the camp the compliant 4-year-old is held up as an example of what a "real soldier" ought to be. Finally Munro bursts out crying, which proves so embarrassing that the General is called in. After much pontification, the General declares, "I rule ... that he's a little boy." Munro is sent home to a ticker tape parade with a congratulatory message from the President in his sticky little hand — but since no one is willing to admit that Army has been in error, Munro's parents are able to control his future behavior by threatening to get him re-drafted.

The casual cruelty of the story is offset by the charming vocal performances of Gene Deitch's son Seth as Munro and adult actor Howard Morris as Everybody Else, and by the disarmingly simple visual design. *Munro* received an Academy Award as the best animated short subject of

1961, and also earned William Snyder and Gene Deitch several other commissions for Paramount, including a group of made-for-TV cartoons based on comic-strip icon *Krazy Kat*. Alas, the one batch of strip-inspired TV 'toons that could have benefited most from Deitch's light satirical touch, Paramount-King Features' *Beetle Bailey* series, was farmed out to other animators who were never quite able to capture the special appeal of this most popular and durable of all pen-and-ink military protagonists.

Filmography

The following filmography covers all the feature-length military comedies described in this book. As a rule, "feature length" refers to any silent film running 5 reels or longer (a "reel" consisting of 1000 feet of film), and to any sound film exceeding a length of 50 minutes. There are, however, a few exceptions. *Shoulder Arms*, a 3-reel Charlie Chaplin comedy, is included in the list for its historical importance, as is the 4-reel Harold Lloyd comedy *A-Sailor Made Man*. The 4½-reel "streamliners" (running between 43 and 50 minutes) comprising Hal Roach's "Sgt. Doubleday" series of the 1940s (see **Chapter 5**) are also listed.

Individual films are listed chronologically, beginning with the film's title in **Bold**, followed by the production company and/or releasing organization. "RL" refers to the original release date; "D" refers to the film's director (or directors). The writing credits are generally broken down as follows: "Sc" means "Screenplay," "St" means "Story," "Dlg" means "Dialogue," "Addl. Dlg." means "Additional Dialogue," and "T" refers to "Titles" (in the silent films only). "RT" refers to the film's length, or "Running Time." This information is followed by a cast list, generally comprised of those performers who receive on-screen credit. Production and cast credits have been kept as brief and succinct as possible.

Unless otherwise indicated, all titles listed were filmed in black & white and in standard-aspect ratio (1:33-to-1 in films made prior to 1953, 1:85-to-1 in most films made after that year). Exceptions are noted by such designations as "Technicolor," "Metrocolor," "Eastmancolor," "Cinemascope," "Panavision," "Super 35," etc. For films produced after 1968, the MPAA ratings (G, PG, R, etc.) are included. Reissue titles are also noted when applicable.

You got all that, or are you just nodding to be polite?

Silent Films

Johanna Enlists. Pickford Films/Artcraft. Rl: 9/15/1918. D: William Desmond Taylor. Sc: Frances Marion. St: Rupert Hughes. RT: 5 reels. Cast: Mary Pickford, Anne Schaefer, Fred Huntley, Monte Blue, Douglas MacLean, Emory Johnson, John Stepping, Wallace Beery, Wesley Barry, June and Jean Prentis.

Shoulder Arms. Chaplin Prod./First National. Rl: 10/20/1918. D/Sc: Charles Chaplin. RT: 3 reels. Cast: Charles Chaplin, Edna Purviance, Syd Chaplin, Jack Wilson, Henry Bergman, Albert Austin, Tom Wilson, John Rand, Park Jones, Loyal Underwood.

Yankee Doodle in Berlin. Sennett/Sol Lesser-Gardiner Syndicate. Rl: 3/2/1919 (press showing); 6/29/1919 (official premiere). D: F. Richard Jones. St: Mack Sennett. RT: 5 reels. Cast: Bothwell Browne, Ford Sterling, Malcolm St. Clair, Bert Roach, Ben Turpin, Charles Murray, Marie Prevost, Eva Thatcher, Chester Conklin.

Hay Foot, Straw Foot. Ince/Paramount. Rl: 6/22/1919. D: Jerome Storm. St: Julian Josephson. RT: 5 reels. Cast: Charles Ray, Doris Lee [Doris May], William Conklin, Spottiswoode Aitken, J.P. Lockney.

23½ Hours' Leave. Ince/Paramount. Rl: 11/16/1919. D: Henry King. Sc: Agnes Christine Johnson. St: Mary Roberts Rinehart (novel). RT: 5 reels. Cast: Douglas MacLean, Doris May, Tom Guise, Maxfield Stanley, Wade Boteler, Alfred Hollingsworth, N. Leinsky, Jack Nelson.

A Sailor-Made Man. Hal Roach/Associated Exhibitors-Pathé. Rl: 12/25/1921. D: Fred Newmeyer. Sc: Hal Roach, Sam Taylor. RT: 4 reels. Cast: Harold Lloyd, Mildred Davis, Noah Young, Dick Sutherland.

Grandma's Boy. Hal Roach/Associated Exhibitors-

Pathé. Rl: 9/22/1922. D: Fred Newmeyer. Sc: Hal Roach, Sam Taylor, Jean Havez, Thomas J. Crizer. St: Hal Roach, Harold Lloyd, Sam Taylor. T: H. M. Walker. RT: 5 reels. Cast: Harold Lloyd, Mildred Davis, Anna Townsend, Charles Stevenson, Noah Young, Dick Sutherland.

Shore Leave. Inspiration/First National. Rl: 9/6/1925. D: John S. Robertson. Sc: Josephine Lovett. St: Hubert Osborne (play). T: Agnes Smith. RT: 6 reels. Cast: Richard Barthelmess, Dorothy Mackaill, Ted McNamara, Nick Long, Marie Shotwell, Arthur Metcalfe, Warren Cook, Samuel S. Hinds.

Hands Up! Paramount. Rl: 1/11/1926. D: Clarence Badger. Sc: Monte Brice, Lloyd Corrigan. St: Reginald Morris. RT: 6 reels. Cast: Raymond Griffith, Mack Swain, Montagu Love, Virginia Lee Corbin, Marian Nixon, George A. Billings.

Behind the Front. Paramount. Rl: 2/22/1926. D: A. Edward Sutherland. Sc: Monte Brice, Ethel Doherty. St: Hugh Wiley. T: Ralph Spence. RT: 6 reels. Cast: Wallace Beery, Raymond Hatton, Mary Brian, Richard Arlen, Hayden Stevenson, Chester Conklin, Tom Kennedy, Frances Raymond, Melbourn MacDowell.

The Strong Man. Langdon Corp./First National. Rl: 9/19/1926. D: Frank Capra. Sc: Hal Conklin, Robert Eddy. St: Arthur Ripley. T: Reed Heustis. RT: 7 reels. Cast: Harry Langdon, Priscilla Bonner, Gertrude Astor, William V. Mong, Robert McKim, Arthur Thalasso.

The Better 'Ole. Warner Bros. Rl: 10/23/1926. D: Charles "Chuck" Reisner. Sc: Darryl F. Zanuck, Charles "Chuck" Reisner. St: Bruce Bairnsfather, Arthur Eliot (play). T: Robert Hopkins. RT: 10 reels. Cast: Syd Chaplin, Harold Goodwin, Jack Ackroyd, Edgar Kennedy, Charles K. Gerard.

Private Izzy Murphy. Warner Bros. Rl: 10/30/1926. D: Lloyd Bacon. Sc: Philip Lonergan. St: Raymond L. Schrock, Edward Clark. RT: 8 reels. Cast: George Jessel, Patsy Ruth Miller, Vera Gordon, Nat Carr, William H. Strauss, Spec O'Donnell, Gustav von Seyffertitz, Douglas Gerrard, Tom Murray.

We're in the Navy Now. Paramount. Rl: 11/6/1926. D: A. Edward Sutherland. Sc: John McDermott. St: Monte Brice. T: George Marion Jr. RT: 6 reels. Cast: Wallace Beery, Raymond Hatton, Chester Conklin, Tom Kennedy, Donald Keith, Lorraine Eason, Joseph W. Gerard, Max Asher.

What Price Glory. Fox. Rl: 11/23/1926. D: Raoul Walsh. Sc: James T. O'Donohoe. St: Laurence Stallings, Maxwell Anderson (play). T: Malcolm Stuart Boylan. RT: 12 reels. Cast: Edmund Lowe, Victor McLaglen, Dolores del Rio, William V. Mong, Phyllis Haver, Elena Jurado, Leslie Fenton, Barry Norton, Sammy Cohen, Ted McNamara, August Tollaire, Mathile Comont, Pat Rooney.

Tin Hats. MGM. Rl: 11/28/1926. D/St: Edward Sedgwick. Sc: Donald W. Lee, Albert Lewin, Lew Lipton. T: Ralph Spence. RT: 7 reels. Cast: Conrad Nagel, Claire Windsor, George Cooper, Bert Roach, Tom O'Brien, Eileen Sedgwick.

The General. Keaton Prod.-Joseph M. Schenck Prod./United Artists. Rl: 12/23/1926 (World Premiere: Tokyo); 2/5/1927 (New York premiere). D: Buster Keaton, Clyde Bruckman. Sc: Buster Keaton, Clyde Bruckman, Al Boasberg, Charles Smith. RT: 8 reels. Cast: Buster Keaton, Marion Mack, Glen Cavender, Jim Farley, Frederick Vroom, Charles Smith, Frank Barnes, Joe Keaton, Mike Donlin, Tom Nawn.

Let It Rain. MacLean Prod./Paramount. Rl: 2/12/1927. D: Eddie Cline. Sc/St: Wade Boteler, George Crone, Earle Snell. RT: 7 reels. Cast: Douglas MacLean, Shirley Mason, Wade Boteler, Frank Campeau, James Bradbury Jr., Lincoln Stedman, Lee Shumway, Jim Mason, Eddie Sturgis, Ernest Hilliard. Part-Technicolor.

Spuds. Semon Prod./Pathé. Rl: 4/10/1927. D/Sc: Edward I. Luddy [Edward Ludwig]. RT: 5 reels. Cast: Larry Semon, Dorothy Dwan, Edward Hearn, Kewpie Morgan, Robert Graves, Hazel Howell, Hugh Fay.

Rookies. MGM. Rl: 4/30/1927. D: Sam Wood. Sc/St: Byron Morgan. T: Joe Farnham. RT: 7 reels. Cast: Karl Dane, George K. Arthur, Marceline Day, Louise Lorraine, Frank Currier, E.H. Calvert, Tom O'Brien, Charles Sullivan, Lincoln Stedman, Gene Stone.

Lost at the Front. John McCormick Prod./First National. Rl: 5/29/1927. D: Del Lord. Sc: Hampton Del Ruth, Frank Griffin. Comedy Construction: Clarence Hennecke. T: Ralph Spence. RT: 6 reels. Cast: George Sidney, Charles Murray, Natalie Kingston, John Kolb, Max Asher, Brooks Benedict, Ed Brady, Harry Lipman, Nita Martan, Nina Romano.

Two Arabian Knights. Caddo/United Artists. Rl: 9/23/1927 (Los Angeles premiere); 10/22/1927 (New York premiere). D: Lewis Milestone. Sc: Wallace Smith, Cyril Gardner, James T. O'Donohoe. St: Donald McGibeny. T: George Marion Jr. RT: 9 reels (restored version: 92 minutes). Cast: William Boyd, Mary Astor, Louis Wolheim, Ian Keith, Michael Vavitch, M. Visaroff, Boris Karloff, DeWitt Jennings, Nicholas Dunaew, Jean Vachon, Denis D'Auburn [David Cavendish].

A Sailor's Sweetheart. Warner Bros. Rl: 9/24/1927. D: Lloyd Bacon. Sc: John Farrow, Harvey Gates. St: George Godfrey. RT: 6 reels. Cast: Louise Fazenda, Clyde Cook, John Miljan, Myrna Loy, William Demarest, Dorothea Wolbert, Tom Ricketts.

The Gay Retreat. Fox. Rl: 9/25/1927. D: Benjamin Stoloff. Sc: Eddie Moran, Murray Roth, J. Walter Ruben. St: William M. Conselman, Edward Marshall. RT: 6 reels. Cast: Gene Cameron, Betty Francisco, Judy King, Sammy Cohen, Jerry the Giant [Jerry Madden], Holmes Herbert, Ted McNamara, Edward Fulton, Pal the Dog.

Sailor Izzy Murphy. Warner Bros. Rl: 10/8/1927. D: Henry Lehrman. Sc: Edward T. Lowe. St: Henry Lehrman, Edward T. Lowe. RT: 7 reels. Cast:

George Jessel, Audrey Ferris, Warner Oland, John Miljan, Otto Lederer, Theodore Lorch, Clara Horton.

Now We're in the Air. Paramount. Rl: 10/22/1927. D: Frank R. Strayer. Sc: Thomas J. Geraghty. St: Monte Brice, Keene Thompson. T: Ralph Spence, George Marion Jr. RT: 6 reels. Cast: Wallace Beery, Raymond Hatton, Russell Simpson, Louise Brooks, Emile Chautard, Malcolm Waite, Duke Martin.

Ham and Eggs at the Front. Warner Bros. Rl: 12/24/1927. D: Roy Del Ruth. Sc: Robert Dillon, James A. Starr. St/T: Darryl Francis Zanuck. RT: 6 reels. Cast: Tom Wilson, Heinie Conklin, Louise Fazenda, Myrna Loy, William Irving, Noah Young, Tom Kennedy.

Sharp Shooters. Fox. Rl: 1/25/1928. D: John G. Blystone. Sc: Marion Orth. St: Randall Faye. T: Malcolm Stuart Boylan. RT: 6 reels. Cast: George O'Brien, Lois Moran, Noah Young, Tom Dugan, William Demarest, Gwen Lee, Josef Swickard.

Top Sergeant Mulligan. Morris R. Schlank Prod./Anchor. Rl: 1/25/1928. D: James P. Hogan. Sc/St: Francis Fenton. T: De Leon Anthony. RT: 6 reels. Cast: Donald Keith, Lila Lee, Wesley Barry, Gareth Hughes, Wade Boteler, Arthur Thalasso, Sid Smith, Sheldon Lewis.

A Girl In Every Port. Fox. Rl: 2/26/1928. D/St: Howard Hawks. Sc: James K. McGuinness, Reginald Morris, Seton I. Miller. T: Malcolm Stuart Boylan. RT: 6 reels (review print: 78 min.). Cast: Victor McLaglen, Louise Brooks, Robert Armstrong, Maria Casajuana [Maria Alba], Francis McDonald, Leila Hyams, Natalie Joyce, Gretel Yoltz, Michael Visaroff.

Tillie's Punctured Romance. Christie/Paramount. Rl: 3/3/1928. D: A. Edward Sutherland. Sc: Monte Brice, Keene Thompson. RT: 6 reels. Cast: W.C. Fields, Louise Fazenda, Chester Conklin, Mack Swain, Doris Hill, Grant Withers, Tom Kennedy, Babe London, William Platt, Mickey Bennett, Kalla Pasha, Mike Rafetto, Baron von Dobeneck.

Why Sailors Go Wrong. Fox. Rl: 3/25/1928. D: Henry Lehrman. Sc: Randall H. Faye. St: William M. Conselman, Frank O'Connor. T: Delos Sutherland. RT: 6 reels. Cast: Sammy Cohen, Ted McNamara, Sally Phipps, Nick Stuart, E.H. Calvert, Carl Miller.

Buck Privates. Universal. Rl: 6/3/1928. D: Melville W. Brown. Sc: Melville W. Brown, Albert DeMond. St: Stuart N. Lake. T: Albert DeMond. RT: 7 reels. Cast: Lya De Putti, Malcolm McGregor, ZaSu Pitts, James A. Marcus, Eddie Gribbon, Capt. Ted Duncan, Bud Jamison, Les Bates.

The Good-Bye Kiss. Sennett/First National. Rl: 7/8/1928. D: Mack Sennett. Sc: Jefferson Moffitt, Mack Sennett. St: Jefferson Moffitt, Phil Whitman. T: Carl Harbaugh, John A. Waldron. RT: 8 reels. Cast: Johnny Burke, Sally Eilers, Matty Kemp, Wheeler Oakman, Irving Bacon, Lionel Belmore, Alma Bennett, Carmelita Geraghty, Eugene Pallette, Jean Laverty, Andy Clyde.

The Fleet's in. Paramount. Rl: 9/15/1928. D: Malcolm St. Clair. Sc/St: Monte Brice, J. Walter Ruben. T: George Marion Jr. RT: 8 reels. Cast: Clara Bow, James Hall, Jack Oakie, Bodil Rosing, Eddie Dunn, Jean Laverty, Dan Wolheim, Richard Carle, Joseph W. Girard.

Heart Trouble. Langdon Corp./First National. Rl: 10/1/1928. D: Harry Langdon. Sc: Harry Langdon, Clarence Hennecke, Earl Rodney. St: Arthur Ripley. T: Gardner Bradford. Ph: Frank Evans, Dev Jennings. RT: 6 reels. Cast: Harry Langdon, Doris Dawson, Lionel Belmore, Madge Hunt, Bud Jamison, Mark Hamilton, Nelson McDowell.

All at Sea. MGM. Rl: 2/9/1929. D: Alfred Goulding. Sc: Byron Morgan, Ann Price. St: Byron Morgan. T: Robert E. Hopkins. RT: 6 reels. Cast: Karl Dane, George K. Arthur, Josephine Dunn, Herbert Prior, Eddie Baker.

Sound Films

Sailor's Holiday. Pathé. Rl: 9/14/1929. D: Fred C. Newmeywer. Sc: Joseph F. Poland, Ray Harris. St: Joseph F. Poland. RT: 58 min. Cast: Alan Hale Sr., Sally Eilers, George Cooper, Paul Hurst, Mary Carr, Charles Clary, Jack Richardson, Natalie Joyce, Phil Sleeman. Also released in a silent version.

The Cock-Eyed World. Fox. Rl: 10/20/1929. D: Raoul Walsh. Sc: Raoul Walsh. St: Maxwell Anderson, Laurence Stallings, Wilson Mizner, Tom Barry. Dlg: William K. Wells. RT: 113 min. Cast: Victor McLaglen, Edmund Lowe, Lili Damita, Leila Karnelly, El Brendel, Bob Burns, Jeanette Dagna, Joe Brown, Stuart Erwin, Ivan Lindow, Jean Bary [Jean Laverty], Soledad Jiménez, Albert "Curley" Dresden.

Hit the Deck. RKO Radio. Rl: 2/2/1930. D/Sc: Luther Reed. St: Luther Osborne (play), Herbert Fields (musical adaptation). RT: 103 min. Cast: Jack Oakie, Polly Walter, Roger Gray, Franker Wood, Harry Sweet, Marguerita Padula, June Clyde, Wallace MacDonald, George Ovey, Ethel Clayton, Nate Slott, Andy Clark, Dell Henderson, Charles Sullivan. Part-Technicolor.

Dames Ahoy. Universal. Rl: 2/9/1930. D: William James Craft. Sc: Albert DeMond, Matt Taylor. St: Sherman L. Lowe. RT: 64 minutes (silent version: 51 min.) Cast: Glenn Tryon, Helen Wright, Otis Harlan, Eddie Gribbon, Gertrude Astor.

Anybody's War. Paramount. Rl: 7/10/1930. D: Richard Wallace. Sc: Lloyd Corrigan, Hector Turnbull. Add. Dlg: Walter Weems. RT: 90 min. Cast: Moran & Mack [Bert Swor, Charles Mack], Joan Peers, Neil Hamilton, Walter Weems, Betty Farrington, Walter McGrail.

Doughboys. MGM. Rl: 8/30/1930. D: Edward Sedgwick. Sc: Richard Schayer. St/Dlg.: Al Boasberg, Sidney Lazarus. RT: 79 min. Cast: Buster Keaton, Sally Eilers, Cliff Edwards, Edward Brophy, Victor Potel, Arnold Korff, Frank Mayo, Pitzy Katz,

William Steele. [Spanish-language version: **De frente, marchen.** D: Salvador de Alberich, Edward Sedgwick. Cast: Buster Keaton, Conchita Montenegro, Romualdo Tirado, Juan de Landa, Victor Potel, Martin Garralaga, Francisco Madrid, Hans von Morhart, Gabry Rivas, Rosita Granada, Lothar Méndez].

Leathernecking. RKO Radio. Rl: 9/12/1930. D: Eddie Cline. Sc: Alfred Jackson, Jane Murfin. St: Herbert Fields (musical play). Ph: J. Roy Hunt. RT: 79 minutes. Cast: Irene Dunne, Ken Murray, Louise Fazenda, Ned Sparks, Lilyan Tashman, Eddie Foy Jr., Benny Rubin, Rita La Roy, Fred Santley, Wilhelm von Brincken, Carl Gerard, Werther and Wolfgang Weidler. Part-Technicolor.

Half Shot at Sunrise. RKO Radio. Rl: 10/4/1930. D: Paul Sloane. St: James Ashmore Creelman. Dlg: Anne Caldwell, Ralph Spence. RT: 78 min. Cast: Bert Wheeler, Robert Woolsey, Dorothy Lee, George MacFarlane, Edna May Oliver, Leni Stengel, Hugh Trevor, Robert Robinson, Jack Rutherford, The Tiller Sunshine Girls.

A Devil with Women. Fox. Rl: 10/18/1930. D: Irving Cummings. Sc: Henry Johnson, Dudley Nichols. St: Clements Ripley (novel). RT: 64 min. Cast: Victor McLaglen, Mona Maris, Humphrey Bogart, Luana Alcañiz, Michael Vavitch, Soledad Jiménez, Mona Rico, John St. Polis, Robert Edeson, Joe De La Cruz.

A Soldier's Plaything. Warner Bros-First National. Rl: 11/1/1930. D: Michael Curtiz. Sc: Perry Vekroff. St: Viña Delmar. Dlg: Arthur Caesar. RT: 57 min. Cast: Ben Lyon, Harry Langdon, Lotti Loder, Noah Beery Sr., Fred Kohler Sr., Lee Moran, Marie Astaire, Frank Campeau. Filmed in both standard 35mm and 65mm Vitascope process.

Sea Legs. Paramount. Rl: 12/1/1930. D: Victor Heerman. Sc: Marion Dix. St: George Marion Jr. RT: 63 min. Cast: Jack Oakie, Eugene Pallette, Lillian Roth, André Cheron, Albert Conti, Harry Green, Jean Del Val, Charles Sellon, Tom Ricketts.

Women of All Nations. Fox. Rl: 5/31/1931. D: Raoul Walsh. Dlg: Barry Conners. RT: 72 min. Cast: Victor McLaglen, Edmund Lowe, El Brendel, Greta Nissen, Fifi D'Orsay, Marjorie White (uncredited on screen, billed in trade ads), Bela Lugosi (uncredited).

Goldie. Fox. Rl: 6/28/1931. D: Benjamin Stoloff. Sc: Gene Towne, Paul Perez. RT: 68 min. Cast: Spencer Tracy, Warren Hymer, Jean Harlow, Jesse Devorska, Leila Karnelly, Ivan Linow, Lina Basquette, Eleanor Hunt, Maria Alba, Eddie Kane.

Sky Devils. Caddo/United Artists. D/St: A. Edward Sutherland. Sc: A. Edward Sutherland, Robert Benchley, Carroll Graham, Garrett Graham, James A. Starr. Rl: 3/12/1932. RT: 90 min. Cast: Spencer Tracy, William "Stage" Boyd, George Cooper, Ann Dvorak, Billy Bevan, Yola d'Avril, Forrester Harvey, William B. Davidson, Jerry Miley.

Pack Up Your Troubles. Hal Roach/MGM. Rl: 9/17/1932. D: George Marshall, Raymond McCarey. Dlg: H. M. Walker. RT: 68 minutes. Cast: Stan Laurel, Oliver Hardy, Donald Dillaway, Mary Carr, Jacquie Lyn, James Finlayson, Richard Cramer, Adele Watson, Tom Kennedy, Charles Middleton, Richard Tucker, Muriel Evans, Grady Sutton, Montague Shaw, Billy Gilbert.

Sailor Be Good. Jefferson/RKO Radio. Rl: 3/7/1933. D: James Cruze. Sc: Ralph Spence, Ethel Doherty, Viola Brothers Shore. RT: 58 min. Cast: Jack Oakie, Vivienne Osborne, George E. Stone, Lincoln Stedman, Max Hoffman Jr., Gertrude Michael, Huntley Gordon, Gertrude Sutton, Charles Coleman.

Sailor's Luck. Fox. Rl: 3/17/1933. D: Raoul Walsh. Sc: Charles Miller, Marguerite Roberts. St: Bert Hanlon. RT: 79 min. Cast: James Dunn, Sally Eilers, Victor Jory, Sammy Cohen, Frank Moran, Esther Muir, Will Stanton, Curley Wright, Jerry Mandy, Lucien Littlefield, Buster Phelps, Frank Atkinson.

Her First Mate. Universal. Rl: 8/3/1933. D: William Wyler. Sc: Earle Snell, Clarence Marks, H.M. Walker. St: Frank Craven, John Golden, Daniel Jarrett (play). RT: 66 min. Cast: Slim Summerville, Zasu Pitts, Una Merkel, Warren Hymer, Berton Churchill, George F. Marion Sr., Henry Armetta, Jocelyn Lee, Herbert Clifton.

Son of a Sailor. First National-Warner Bros. Rl: 12/23/1933. D: Lloyd Bacon. Sc: Alfred A. Cohn, Paul Girard Smith. Addl. Dlg: Ernest Pagano, H.M. Walker. RT: 73 min. Cast: Joe E. Brown, Jean Muir, Frank McHugh, Thelma Todd, Johnny Mack Brown, Sheila Terry, George Blackwood, Merna Kennedy, Kenneth Thomson, Samuel S. Hinds, Noel Francis, Arthur Vinton, George Irving.

Come On, Marines. Paramount. Rl: 3/23/1934. D: Henry Hathaway. Sc: Joel Sayre, Byron Morgan. St: Philip Wylie. RT: 70 min. Cast: Richard Arlen, Ida Lupino, Roscoe Karns, Grace Bradley, Fuzzy Knight, Monte Blue, Edmund Breese, Virginia Hammond, Emile Chautard, Toby Wing, Julian Madison, Roger Gray, Clara Lou [Ann] Sheridan, Gwenllian Gill, Lona Andre.

She Learned About Sailors. Fox. Rl: 6/29/1934. D: George Marshall. Sc: William M. Conselman, Henry Johnson. St: Randall Faye. RT: 78 min. Cast: Alice Faye, Lew Ayres, Harry Green, Frank Mitchell, Jack Durant, Ernie Alexander.

The Marines are Coming. Mascot. Rl: 11/20/1934. D: David Howard. Sc: James Gruen. St: Colbert Clark, John Rathmell. RT: 74 min. Cast: William Haines, Esther Ralston, Conrad Nagel, Armida, Edgar Kennedy, Hale Hamilton.

Bonnie Scotland. Hal Roach/MGM. Rl: 8/23/1935. D: James W. Horne. Sc: Frank Butler, Jeff Moffitt. RT: 80 min. Cast: Stan Laurel, Oliver Hardy, June Lang, William Janney, Anne Grey, Vernon Steele, James Finlayson, David Torrence, Maurice Black, Daphne Pollard, Mary Gordon, Lionel Belmore.

Miss Pacific Fleet. Warner Bros.-First National. Rl: 12/14/1935. D: Ray Enright. Sc: Peter Milne, Lucille

Newman, Patsy Flick. St: Frederick Hazlitt Brennan. RT: 66 min. Cast: Joan Blondell, Glenda Farrell, Hugh Herbert, Allen Jenkins, Warren Hull, Eddie Acuff, Marie Wilson, Minna Gombell, Guinn "Big Boy" Williams.

Follow the Fleet. RKO Radio. Rl: 2/20/1936. D: Mark Sandrich. Sc: Allan Scott, Dwight Taylor. St: Hubert Osborne (play). RT: 110 min. Cast: Fred Astaire, Ginger Rogers, Randolph Scott, Harriet Hilliard, Astrid Allwyn, Betty Grable, Harry Beresford, Russell Hicks, Brooks Benedict, Ray Mayer, Lucille Ball.

Sons O' Guns. Warner Bros.-Cosmopolitan. Rl: 3/20/1936. D: Lloyd Bacon. Sc: Jerry Wald, Julius J. Epstein. St: Jack Donohue, Fred Thompson (play). RT: 75 min. Cast: Joe E. Brown, Joan Blondell, Beverly Roberts, Eric Blore, Craig Reynolds, Wini Shaw, Joseph King, Robert Barrat, G.P. Huntley Jr., Frank Mitchell, Bert Roach, Dave Worth, Hans Joby, Michael Mark, Otto Fries, Mischa Auer.

Lady Be Careful. Paramount. Rl: 9/4/1936. D: J.T. [Theodore] Reed. Sc: Dorothy Parker, Alan Campbell, Harry Ruskin. St: Kenyon Nicholson, Charles Robinson (play). RT: 72 min. Cast: Lew Ayres, Mary Carlisle, Larry [Buster] Crabbe, Grant Withers, Irving Bacon, Barbara Barondess, Sheila Bromley, Wilma Francis [Marlo Dwyer], Ethel Sykes, Murray Alper, Jack Chapin, Wesley Barry, Nick Lukats, Purnell Pratt, Jack Adair, Josephine McKim, Jennifer Gray, Barbara [Bobbie] Koshay, Irene Bennett, Terry Ray [Ellen Drew], Louise Stanley.

General Spanky. Hal Roach/MGM. Rl: 12/11/1936. D: Gordon Douglas, Fred C. Newmeyer. Sc: Richard Flournoy, John Guedel, Hal Yates, Carl Harbaugh. RT: 71 min. Cast:George "Spanky" McFarland, Phillips Holmes, Ralph Morgan, Irving Pichel, Rosina Lawrence, Billie "Buckwheat" Thomas, Carl "Alfalfa" Switzer, Hobart Bosworth, Robert Middlemass, James P. Burtis, Louise Beavers, Willie Best.

23½ Hours' Leave. Grand National. Rl: 3/21/1937. D: John G. Blystone. Sc: Henry McCarty, Harry Ruskin, Samuel J. Warshawsky. St: Mary Roberts Rinehart (novel). RT: 72 min. Cast: James Ellison, Terry Walker, Morgan Hill, Arthur Lake, Paul Harvey, Wally Maher, Andy Andrews, Murray Alper, Pat Gleason, John Kelly, Russell Hicks, Ward Bond.

Navy Blues. Republic. Rl: 3/29/1937. D: Ralph Staub. Sc: Gordon Kahn, Eric Taylor. RT: 68 min. Cast: Dick Purcell, Mary Brian, Warren Hymer, Joe Sawyer, Edward Woods, Horace McMahon, Chester Clute, Lucille Gleason, Ruth Fallows, Alonzo Price, Mel Ruick, Carleton Young.

Sweetheart of the Navy. B.F. Zeidman Films/Grand National. Rl: 6/8/1937. D: Duncan Mansfield. Sc/St: Carroll Graham, Jay Strauss. St: Garrett Graham. RT: 61 min. Cast: Eric Linden, Cecilia Parker, Roger Imhof, Bernadene Hayes, Don Barclay, Etta McDaniel, Reed Howes, Edward Waller, Jason Robards Sr., Cully Richards, John T. Murray, Art Miles, Henry Roquemore, Fred Murray, Vance Carroll, Benny Burt.

Swing It Sailor. B.F. Zeidman Films/Grand National. Rl: 2/4/1938. D: Raymond Cannon. Sc/St: Clarence Marks, David Diamond. RT: 57 min. Cast: Wallace Ford, Ray Mayer, Isabel Jewell, Mary Treen, Max Hoffman Jr., Cully Richards, George Humbert, Tom Kennedy, Alexander Leftwich, Kenneth Harlan, James [Archie] Robbins, Kernan Crips, Rex Lease

Give Me a Sailor. Paramount. Rl: 8/19/1938. D: Elliott Nugent. Sc:Frank Butler, Doris Anderson. St: Anne Nichols (play). RT: 80 min. Cast: Martha Raye, Bob Hope, Betty Grable, Jack Whiting, Clarence Kolb, J.C. Nugent, Bonnie Jean Churchill, Nana Bryant.

Brother Rat. Warner Bros. Rl: 10/29/1938. D: William Keighley. Sc: Jerry Wald, Richard Macauley. St: Fred F. Finklehoffe, John Monks Jr. (play). RT: 89 min. Cast: Priscilla Lane, Wayne Morris, Johnnie Davis, Jane Bryan, Eddie Albert, Ronald Reagan, Jane Wyman, Henry O'Neill, Gordon Oliver, Larry Williams, William Tracey [Tracy], Jessie Busley, Olin Howland, Louise Beavers, Isabel Withers.

Pack Up Your Troubles. 20th Century–Fox. Rl:10/20/1939. D: H. Bruce Humberstone. Sc: Lou Breslow, Owen Francis. RT: 75 min. Cast: Jane Withers, The Ritz Brothers, Lynn Bari, Joseph Schildkraut, Stanley Fields, Fritz Leiber, Lionel Royce, Georges Renavent, Adrinee D'Ambricourt, Leon Ames, William [Wilhelm] Von Brincken, Edward Gargan, Robert Emmett Keane, Henry Victor.

The Flying Deuces. Boris Morros Productions/RKO Radio. Rl: 11/3/1939. D: A. Edward Sutherland. Sc/St: Ralph Spence, Charles Rogers, Alfred Schiller, Harry Langdon. RT: 69 min. Cast: Stan Laurel, Oliver Hardy, Jean Parker, Reginald Gardiner, Charles Middleton, Jean Del Val, Clem Wilenchik [Crane Whitley], James Finlayson.

Sailor's Lady. 20th Century–Fox. Rl: 7/5/1940. D: Allan Dwan. Sc: Frederick Hazlitt Brennan. St: Frank Wead. Addl. Dlg: Lou Breslow, Owen Francis. RT: 67 min. Cast: Nancy Kelly, Jon Hall, Joan Davis, Dana Andrews, Mary Nash, Larry [Buster] Crabbe, Katherine [Kay] Aldridge, Harry Shannon, Wally Vernon, Bruce Hampton, Charles D. Brown, Selmer Jackson, Edgar Dearing, Edmund MacDonald, William B. Davidson, Lester Dorr, George O'Hanlon, Matt McHugh, Peggy Ryan, Ward Bond, Barbara Pepper, Steve Pendleton, Eddie Acuff, Edward Earle, Pierre Watkin, Paul Harvey, Emmett Vogan.

Buck Privates. Universal. Rl: 1/31/1941. D: Arthur Lubin. Sc: Arthur T. Horman. Special Material: John Grant. RT: 84 min. Cast: Bud Abbott, Lou Costello, Lee Bowman, Alan Curtis, The Andrews Sisters, Jane Frazee, Nat Pendleton, Samuel S. Hinds, Harry Strang, Nella Walker, Leonard Elliott,

Shemp Howard, Mike Frankovich, Dora Clement, Jeanne Kelly [Jean Brooks], Elaine Morey [Janet Warren], Kay Leslie, Nina Orla, Dorothy Darrell, The World Champion Boogie Woogie Dancers.

In the Navy. Universal. Rl: 5/30/1941. D: Arthur Lubin. Sc: Arthur T. Horman, John Grant. St: Arthur T. Horman. RT: 86 min. Cast: Bud Abbott, Lou Costello, Dick Powell, Claire Dodd, The Andrews Sisters, Dick Foran, Butch and Buddy [Billy Lenhart, Kenneth Brown], Shemp Howard, The Condos Brothers.

Caught in the Draft. Paramount. Rl: 7/4/1941. D: David Butler. Sc/St: Harry Tugend. Addl. Dlg: Wilkie C. Mahony. RT: 82 min. Cast: Bob Hope, Dorothy Lamour, Lynne Overman, Eddie Bracken, Clarence Kolb, Paul Hurst, Ferike Boros, Phyllis Ruth, Irving Bacon, Arthur Loft, Edgar Dearing.

Tanks a Million. Hal Roach/United Artists. Rl: 9/12/1941. D: Fred Guiol. Sc: Edward E Seabrook, Paul Girard Smith, Warren Wilson. RT: 50 min. Cast: William Tracy, James Gleason, Noah Beery Jr., Joe Sawyer, Elyse Knox, Douglas Fowley, Knox Manning, Frank Faylen, Dick Wessel, Frank Melton, Harold Goodwin, William Gould, Norman Kerry.

Navy Blues. Warner Bros. Rl: 9/13/1941.. D: Lloyd Bacon. Sc: Arthur T. Horman, Richard Macaulay, Jerry Wald, Sam Perrin. St: Arthur T. Horman. RT: 108 min Cast: Ann Sheridan, Jack Oakie, Martha Raye, Jack Haley, Herbert Anderson, Jack Carson, Jackie C. Gleason, William T. Orr, Richard Lane, John Ridgely, Navy Blues Sextette (Katherine [Kay] Aldridge, George Carroll, Marguerite Chapman, Peggy Diggins, Lorraine Gettman [Leslie Brooks], Claire James).

Sailors on Leave. Republic. Rl: 9/23/1941. D: Albert S. Rogell. Sc: Malcolm Stuart Boylan, Art Arthur. St: Herbert Dalmas. RT: 71 min. Cast: William Lundigan, Shirley Ross, Chick Chandler, Ruth Donnelly, Mae Clarke, Cliff Nazarro, Tom Kennedy, Mary Ainslee, Bill Shirley, Garry Owen, William Haade, Jane Kean.

Great Guns. 20th Century–Fox. Rl: 10/10/1941. D: Montague Banks. Sc: Lou Breslow. RT: 74 min. Cast: Stan Laurel, Oliver Hardy, Sheila Ryan, Dick Nelson, Edmund MacDonald, Charles Trowbridge, Ludwig Stossel, Kane Richmond, Mae Marsh, Ethel Griffies, Paul Harvey, Charles Arnt, Pierre Watkin, Russell Hicks, Irving Bacon.

Top Sergeant Mulligan. Monogram. Rl: 10/17/1941. D: Jean Yarbrough. Sc: Edmond Kelso. RT: 70 min. Cast: Nat Pendleton, Carol Hughes, Sterling Holloway, Marjorie Reynolds, Tom Neal, Frank Faylen, Charlie Hall, Betty Blythe, Dick Elliott, Maynard Holmes, Wonderful Smith.

Keep 'Em Flying. Universal. Rl: 11/28/1941. D: Arthur Lubin. Sc: True Boardman, Nat Perrin, John Grant. St: Edmund L. Hartmann. RT: 86 min. Cast. Bud Abbott, Lou Costello, Martha Raye, Carol Bruce, William Gargan, Dick Foran, Charles Lang, William [B.] Davidson, Truman Bradley, Loring Smith, William Forrest, Freddie Slack, The Six Hits.

You're in the Army Now. Warner Bros. Rl: 12/25/1941. D: Lewis Seiler, Sc: George Bentley. St: Paul Girard Smith. RT: 79 min. Cast: Jimmy Durante, Phil Silvers, Jane Wyman, Regis Toomey, Donald MacBride, Joe Sawyer, Clarence Kolb, Paul Harvey, George Meeker, Paul Stanton, William Haade, John Maxwell, Etta McDaniel, Navy Blues Sextette (Kay Aldridge, Peggy Diggins, Marguerite Chapman, Georgia Carroll, Lorraine Gettman [Leslie Brooks], Alice [Alix] Talton), Matty Malneck, Armando and Lita.

Hay Foot. Hal Roach/United Artists. Rl: 1/2/1942. D: Fred Guiol. Sc: Edward E. Seabrook, Eugene Conrad. RT: 48 min. Cast: William Tracy, Joe Sawyer, James Gleason, Noah Beery Jr., Elyse Knox, Douglas Fowley, Harold Goodwin.

Private Snuffy Smith. Capitol/Monogram. Rl: 1/16/1942. D: Edward Cline. Sc: Jack Grey, Jack Henley, Lloyd French, Doncho Hall. RT: 67 min. Cast: Bud Duncan, Edgar Kennedy, Sarah Padden, J. Farrell McDonald, Doris Linden, Jimmy Dodd, Andraia [Andria] Palmer, Pat McVeigh [McVey], Frank Austin.

The Fleet's in. Paramount. Rl: 1/24/1942. D: Victor Schertzinger. Sc: J. Walter Ruben, Sid Silvers, Ralph Spence, Walter DeLeon. St: Kenyon Nicholson, Charles Robinson (play); Monte Brice (short story). RT: 93 min. Cast: Dorothy Lamour, William Holden, Eddie Bracken, Betty Hutton, Cass Daley, Gil Lamb, Leif Erickson, Jimmy Dorsey and His Orchestra, Bob Eberly, Helen O'Connell, Betty Jane Rhodes, Lorraine and Rognan, Jack Norton, Barbara Britton.

Call Out the Marines. RKO Radio. Rl: 2/13/1942. D: William Hamilton, Frank Ryan. Sc: Frank Ryan. RT: 67 min. Cast: Victor McLaglen, Edmund Lowe, Binnie Barnes, Paul Kelly, Robert Smith, Dorothy Lovett, Franklin Pangborn, Corinna Mura, George Cleveland, The King's Men, Six Hits and a Miss.

Tramp Tramp Tramp. Columbia. Rl: 4/2/1942. D: Charles Barton. Sc: Harry Rebuas [Sauber], Ned Dandy. St: Hal Braham, Shannon Day, Marion Grant. RT: 68 min. Cast: Jackie Gleason, Jack Durant, Florence Rice, Bruce Bennett, Hallene Hill, Billy Curtis, Mabel Todd, Forrest Tucker, James Seay, John Tyrrell, John Harmon, Eddie Foster, Al Hill, Borrah Minnevitch and His Harmonica Rascals.

About Face. Hal Roach/United Artists. Rl: 4/16/1942. D: Kurt Neumann. Sc: Eugene Conrad, Edward E. Seabrook. RT: 43 min. Cast: William Tracy, Joe Sawyer, Jean Porter, Marjorie Lord, Margaret Dumont, Veda Ann Borg, Joe Cunningham, Harold Goodwin, Frank Faylen, Dick Wessel, Charles Lane.

Hillbilly Blitzkrieg. Capitol/Monogram. Rl: 8/14/1942. D: Roy Mack. Sc: Ray S. Harris. RT: 63 min. Cast: Bud Duncan, Edgar Kennedy, Cliff Nazarro, Lucien Littlefield, Doris Linden, Alan Baldwin, Jimmy

Dodd, Frank Austin, Nicolle Andre, Manart Kippen, Jerry Jerome, Jack Carr, Teddy Mangean.

Fall in. Hal Roach/United Artists. Rl: 3/5/1943. D: Kurt Neumann. Sc: Eugene Conrad, Edward E. Seabrook. RT: 48 min. Cast: William Tracy, Joe Sawyer, Robert Barrat, Jean Porter, Arthur Hunnicutt, Rebel Randall, Frank Faylen, Clyde Fillmore.

Air Raid Wardens. MGM. Rl: 3/18/1943. D: Edward Sedgwick. Sc: Martin Rackin, Jack Jevne, Charley Rogers, Harry Crane. RT: 67 min. Cast: Stan Laurel, Oliver Hardy, Edgar Kennedy, Jacqueline White, Horace [Stephen] McNally, Nella Walker, Donald Meek, Henry O'Neill, Howard Freeman, Paul Stanton, Robert Emmet O'Connor, William Tannen, Russell Hicks, Phil Van Zandt, Frederick Worlock, Don Costello.

Yanks Ahoy. Hal Roach/United Artists. Rl: 6/29/1943. D: Kurt Neumann. Sc: Eugene Conrad, Edward E. Seabrook. RT: 58 min. Cast: William Tracy, Joe Sawyer, Marjorie Woodworth, Minor Watson, Frank Faylen, Walter Woolf King, Romaine Callender, Robert Kent.

Let's Face It. Paramount. Rl: 8/5/1943. D: Sidney Lanfield. Sc: Harry Tugend. St: Russell G. Medcraft, Norman Mitchell (play); Dorothy Fields, Herbert Fields (musical adaptation). RT: 76 min. Cast: Bob Hope, Betty Hutton, ZaSu Pitts, Phyllis Povah, Dave Willock, Eve Arden, Cully Richards, Marjorie Weaver, Dona Drake, Raymond Walburn, Andrew Tombes, Arthur Loft, Joe Sawyer, Grace Hayle, Evelyn Dockson.

Adventures of a Rookie. RKO Radio. Rl: 8/20/1943. D: Leslie Goodwins. Sc: Edward James. St: William Bowers, M. Coates Webster. RT: 64 min. Cast: Wally Brown, Alan Carney, Richard Martin, Erford Gage, Margaret Landry, Patti Brill, Rita Corday, Robert Anderson.

Hi'ya Sailor. Universal. Rl: 10/8/1943. D: Jean Yarbrough. Sc: Stanley Roberts. St: Fanya Foss. RT: 63 min. Cast: Donald Woods, Elyse Knox, Eddie Quillan, Frank Jenks, Phyllis Brooks, Jerome Cowan, Matt Willis, Florence Lake, Charles Coleman, Mantan Moreland, Jack Mulhall, Ray Eberle's Orchestra, Wingy Malone and His Orchestra, Delta Rhythm Boys, Mayris Chaney Dance Trio, Leo Diamond Quintet, Hacker Duo, The Nilsson Sisters, George Beatty.

Rookies in Burma. RKO Radio. Rl: 12/16/1943. D: Leslie Goodwins. Sc: Edward James. RT: 62 min. Cast: Wally Brown, Alan Carney, Erford Gage, Joan Barclay, Clare Carleton, Ted Hecht.

The Miracle of Morgans Creek. Paramount. Rl: 1/5/1944 (New York premiere) 1/19/1944 (general release). D/Sc: Preston Sturges. RT: 99 min. Eddie Bracken, Betty Hutton, Diana Lynn, William Demarest, Porter Hall, Emory Parnell, Al Bridge, Julius Tannen, Victor Potel, Brian Donlevy, Akim Tamiroff.

Sailor's Holiday. Columbia. Rl: 2/24/1944. D: William Berke. Sc: Manuel Seff. RT: 60 min. Cast: Arthur Lake, June [Jane] Lawrence, Bob Haymes, Shelley Winter[s], Lewis Wilson, Edmund MacDonald.

See Here, Private Hargrove. MGM. Rl: 3/22/1944. D: Wesley Ruggles. Sc: Harry Kurnitz. St: Marion Hargrove (novel). RT: 100 min. Cast: Robert Walker Sr., Donna Reed, Keenan Wynn, Robert Benchley, Bob Crosby, Grant Mitchell, Ray Collins, Chill Wills, Grant Mitchell, Marta Linden, George Offernan Jr., Edward Fielding, Donald Curtis, William "Bill" Phillips, Douglas Fowley.

Up in Arms. Goldwyn/RKO Radio. Rl: 3/27/1944. D: Elliott Nugent. Sc: Don Hartman, Allen Boretz, Robert Pirosh. St: Owen Davis Sr. (play). RT: 106 min. Cast: Danny Kaye, Dinah Shore, Dana Andrews, Constance Dowling, Louis Calhern, George Mathews, Benny Baker, Elisha Cook Jr., Lyle Talbot, Walter Catlett, George Meeker, Tom Keene, Margaret Dumont, Donald Dickson, Charles Arnt, Charles Halton, Tom Dugan, Sig Arno, Harry Hayden, Charles D. Brown, Maurice Cass, Fred Essler, Rudolf Friml Jr., The Goldwyn Girls. Technicolor.

Abroad with Two Yanks. Edward Small Prod./United Artists. Rl: 8/4/1944. D: Allan Dwan. Sc: Wilkie Mahoney, Ted Sills, Edward E. Seabrook, Charles Rogers, Tedwell Chapman. St: Fred Guiol. RT: 80 min. Cast: William Bendix, Helen Walker, Dennis O'Keefe, John Loder, George Cleveland, Janet Lambert, James Flavin, Arthur Hunnicutt, Steve Dunhill, Herbert Evans, William Forrest, John Abbott.

Janie. Warner Bros. Rl: 9/2/1944. D: Michael Curtiz. Sc: Charles Hoffman, Agnes Christine Johnson. St: Josephine Bentham, Herschel V. Williams (play). RT: 102 min. Cast: Joyce Reynolds, Robert Hutton, Edward Arnold, Ann Harding, Alan Hale Sr., Robert Benchley, Clare Foley, Barbara Brown, Hattie McDaniel, Richard Erdman, Jackie Moran, Ann Gillis, Russell Hicks, Ruth Tobey, Virginia Patton, Colleen Townsend, William Frambes.

The Impatient Years. Columbia. Rl: 9/10/1944. D: Irving Cummings. Sc: Virginia Van Up. RT: 91 min. Cast: Jean Arthur, Lee Bowman, Charles Coburn, Edgar Buchanan, Charley Grapewin, Phil Brown, Harry Davenport, Jane Darwell, Grant Mitchell, Bob Haymes.

G.I. Honeymoon. Monogram. Rl: 4/6/1945. D: Phil Karlstein [Karlson]. Sc: Richard Weil Jr. St: A.J. Rubien, Robert Chapin, Marion Page Johnson (play). Addl. Dlg: Tim Ryan. RT: 70 min. Cast: Gale Storm, Peter Cookson, Arline Judge, Frank Jenks, Jerome Cowan, Jonathan Hale, Andrew Tombes, Virginia Brissac, Ruth Lee, Ralph Lewis, Earle Hodgins, Lois Austin, John Valentine, Claire Whitney, Frank Stephens, Jack Overman.

Over 21. Columbia. Rl: 8/8/1945. D: Charles Vidor. Sc: Sidney Buchman. St: Ruth Gordon (play). RT: 102 min. Cast: Irene Dunne, Alexander Knox, Charles Coburn, Jeff Donnell, Loren Tindall, Lee

Patrick, Phil Brown, Cora Witherspoon, Charles Evans.

Kiss and Tell. Columbia. Rl: 10/4/1945. D: Richard Wallace. Sc/St: F. Hugh Herbert. RT: 90 min. Cast: Shirley Temple, Jerome Courtland, Walter Abel, Katherine Alexander, Robert Benchley, Porter Hall, Virginia Welles, Tom Tully, Darryl Hickman, Mary Philips, Scott McKay, Scott Elliott, Kathryn Card, Edna Holland.

What Next, Corporal Hargrove? MGM. Rl: 11/21/1945. D: Richard Thorpe. Sc: Harry Kurnitz. RT: 95 min. Cast: Robert Walker Sr., Keenan Wynn, Jean Porter, Chill Wills, Hugo Haas, William "Bill" Phillips, Fred Essler, Cameron Mitchell, Ted Lundigan, Dick Hirbe, Arthur Walsh, Maurice Marks, Paul Langton, James Davis, Jack Carlyle, Walter Sande, Theodore Newton, Robert Kent, Matt Willis, Richard Bailey.

Snafu. Columbia. Rl: 11/22/1945. D: Jack Moss. Sc/St: Louis Solomon, Harry Buchman. RT: 85 min. Cast: Robert Benchley, Vera Vague [Barbara Jo Allen], Conrad Janis, Nanette Parks, Janis Wilson, Jimmy Lloyd, Enid Markey, Eva Puig, Ray Mayer, Marcia Mae Jones, Winfield Smith, John Souther, Byron Foulger, Kathleen Howard.

A Letter for Evie. MGM. Rl: 1/28/1946. D: Jules Dassin. Sc: DeVallon Scott, Alan Friedman. St: Blanche Brace. RT: 89 min. Cast: Marsha Hunt, John Carroll, Hume Cronyn, Spring Byington, Pamela Britton, Norman Lloyd, Percival Vivian, Donald Curtis, Esther Howard, Robin Raymond, Therese Lyon, Lynn Whitney.

Buck Privates Come Home. Universal-International. Rl: 4/4/1947. D: Charles Barton. Sc: Frederic I. Rinaldo, Robert Lees, John Grant. St: Richard Macaulay, Bradford Ropes. RT: 77 min. Cast: Bud Abbott, Lou Costello, Tom Brown, Joan Fulton [Joan Shawlee], Nat Pendleton, Beverly Simmons, Don Porter, Donald MacBride, Don Beddoe, Charles Trowbridge, Russell Hicks, Joe Kirk, Knox Manning, Milburn Stone.

Dear Ruth. Paramount. Rl: 6/10/1947. D: William D. Russell. Sc: Arthur Sheekman. St: Norman Krasna. RT: 95 min. Cast: Joan Caulfield, William Holden, Mona Freeman, Edward Arnold, Billy De Wolfe, Mary Philips, Virginia Welles, Kenny O'Morrison, Marietta Canty, Irving Bacon.

A Southern Yankee. MGM. Rl: 8/5/1948. D: Edward Sedgwick*. Sc: Harry Tugend. St: Norman Panama, Melvin Frank. RT: 90 min. Cast: Red Skelton, Brian Donlevy, Arlene Dahl, George Coulouris, Lloyd Gough, John Ireland, Minor Watson, Charles Dingle, Art Baker, Reed Hadley, Arthur Space, Joyce Compton. *See **chapter 18** for details on this film's directorial credit.

A Foreign Affair. Paramount. Rl: 8/20/1948. D: Billy Wilder. Sc: Billy Wilder, Charles Brackett, Richard L. Breen, Robert Harari. St: David Shaw. RT: 116 min. Cast: Jean Arthur, Marlene Dietrich, John Lund, Millard Mitchell, Peter von Zerneck, Stanley Praeger, Bill Murphy, Raymond Bone, Boyd Davis, Robert Malcolm, Charles Meredith, Michael Raffetto, Damian O'Flynn, Frank Fenton, James Larmore, William Neff, George Carleton, Gordon Jones, Fred Steele.

I Was a Male War Bride. 20th Century–Fox. Rl: 8/19/1949. D: Howard Hawks. Sc: Charles Lederer, Leonard Spigelgass, Hagar Wilde. St: Henri Rochard. RT: 105 min. Cast: Cary Grant, Ann Sheridan, Marion Marshall, Randy Stuart, William Neff.

Francis. Universal-International. Rl: 12/13/49 (Los Angeles premiere) 2/1/1950 (general release). D: Arthur Lubin. Sc/St: David Stern. RT: 90 min. Cast: Donald O'Connor, Patricia Medina, ZaSu Pitts, Ray Collins, John McIntire, Eduard Franz, Howland Chamberlain, James Todd, Robert Warwick, Frank Faylen, Anthony [Tony] Curtis, Mikel Conrad, Loren Tindall, Charles Meredith.

On the Town. MGM. Rl: 12/30/1949. D: Stanley Donen, Gene Kelly. Sc/St: Adolph Green, Betty Comden, from an idea by Jerome Robbins. RT: 98 min. Cast: Gene Kelly, Frank Sinatra, Betty Garrett, Ann Miller, Jules Munshin, Vera-Ellen, Florence Bates, Alice Pearce, George Meader. Technicolor.

When Willie Comes Marching Home. 20th Century-Fox. Rl: 2/17/1950. D: John Ford. Sc: Richard Sale. St: Sy Gomberg. RT: 82 min. Cast: Dan Dailey, Corinne Calvert, Colleen Townsend, William Demarest, Jimmy Lydon, Lloyd Corrigan, Evelyn Varden.

The Skipper Surprised his Wife. MGM. Rl: 6/29/1950. D: Elliott Nugent. Sc: Dorothy Kingsley. St: William J. Lederer (article). RT: 85 min. Cast: Robert Walker Sr., Joan Leslie, Edward Arnold, Spring Byington, Leon Ames, Jan Sterling, Anthony Ross, Paul Harvey, Kathryn Card, Tommy Myers, Rudy Lee, Finnegan Weatherwax.

Abbott and Costello in the Foreign Legion. Universal-International. Rl: 9/25/1950. D: Charles Lamont. Sc: John Grant, Martin Ragaway, Leonard Stern. St: D.D. Beauchamp. RT: 80 min. Cast: Bud Abbott, Lou Costello, Patricia Medina, Walter Slezak, Douglass Dumbrille, Leon Belasco, Marc Lawrence, Wee Willie Davis, Tor Johnson, Sam Mancker [Menacker], Jack Raymond, Fred Nurney, Paul Fierro, Henry Corden.

At War with the Army. Finklehoffe-Screen Associates-York/Paramount. Rl: 12/31/50(San Francisco premiere) 1/17/1951 (New York premiere). D: Hal Walker. Sc: Fred F. Finklehoffe. St: James B. Allardice (play). RT: 93 min. Cast: Dean Martin, Jerry Lewis, Mike Kellin, Jimmy Dundee, Dick Stabile, Tommy Farrell, Frank Hyers, Dan Dayton, William Mendrek, Kenneth Forbes, Paul Livermore, Ty Perry, Jean Ruth, Angela Greene, Polly Bergen, Steve Roberts, Al Negbo, Dewey Robinson.

Bowery Batallion. Monogram. Rl: 1/24/1951. D: William Beaudine. Sc: Charles R. Marion. RT: 69 min. Cast: Leo Gorcey, Huntz Hall, Donald

MacBride, Virginia Hewitt, Russell Hicks, Bernard Gorcey, William Benedict, Buddy Gorman, David Gorcey, John Bleifer, Al Eben, Frank Jenks, Selmer Jackson.

You're in the Navy Now. 20th Century–Fox. Rl: 2/23/1951 (under the title **U.S.S. Teakettle**). D: Henry Hathaway. Sc: Richard Murphy. St: John W. Hazard (article). RT: 93 min. Cast: Gary Cooper, Jane Greer, Millard Mitchell, Eddie Albert, John McIntire, Ray Collins, Harry Von Zell, Jack Webb, Richard Erdman, Harvey Lembeck, Henry Slate, Ed Begley Sr.

Up Front. Universal-International. Rl: 3/5/1951. D: Alexander Hall. Sc: Stanley Roberts. St: Bill Mauldin (book). RT: 92 min. Cast: David Wayne, Tom Ewell, Martina Berti, Jeffrey Lynn, Richard Egan, Maurice Cavell, Vaughn Taylor, Silvio Minciotti, Paul Harvey, Roger De Koven, Grazia Narciso, Tito Vuolo, Mickey Knox.

Let's Go Navy. Monogram. Rl: 7/29/1951. D: William Beaudine. Sc: Max Adams. RT: 68 min. Cast: Leo Gorcey, Huntz Hall, Allen Jenkins, Tom Neal, Charlita, Richard Benedict, Paul Harvey, Jonathan Hale, William Benedict, Bernard Gorcey, Buddy Gorman, David Gorcey, Emory Parnell, Douglas Evans, Frank Jenks, Dave Willock, Ray Walker, Tom Kennedy, Murray Alper, Dorothy Ford.

Leave It to the Marines. Tom Prod./Lippert. Rl: 9/28/1951. D: Sam Newfield. Sc: Orville H. Hampton. RT: 65 min. Cast: Sid Melton, Mara Lynn, Gregg Martell, Ida Moore, Sam Flint, Douglas Evans, Margia Dean, Richard Monahan, William Haade, Jack George, Paul Bryar, Ezelle Poule, Will Orleans, Richard Farmer, Jimmy Cross.

As You Were. R&L-Spartan/Lippert. Rl: 10/5/1951. D: Fred Guiol. Sc: Edward Seabrook. RT: 57 min. Cast: William Tracy, Joe Sawyer, Russell Hicks, John Ridgely, Sondra Rodgers, Joan Vohs, Edgar Dearing, Chris Drake, Ruth Lee, Margie Liszt, Roger McGee, John Parrish, Maris Wrixon.

Sky High. Spartan/Lippert. Rl: 10/29/1951. D: Sam Newfield. Sc: Orville H. Hampton. RT: 60 min. Cast: Sid Melton, Mara Lynn, Sam Flint, Douglas Evans, Fritz Feld, Marc Krah, Margia Dean, Paul Bryar, Thayer Roberts, Don Frost, John Pelletti, Ernie Venneri, John Phillips, Will Orleans, Peter Damon.

Sailor Beware. Paramount. 1/24/1952 (Los Angeles premiere); 1/31/1952 (New York City premiere) D: Hal Walker. Sc: James Allardice, Martin Rackin, Elwood Ullman. St: Kenyon Nicholson, Charles Robinson (play). Addl. Dlg.: John Grant. RT: 108 min. Cast: Dean Martin, Jerry Lewis, Corinne Calvet, Marion Marshall, Robert Strauss, Leif Erickson, Don Wilson, Vincent Edwards, Skip Homeier, Dan Barton, Mike Mahoney, Mary Treen.

A Girl in Every Port. RKO Radio. Rl: 2/13/1952. D/Sc: Chester Erskine. St: Frederick Hazlitt Brennan. RT: 86 min. Cast: Groucho Marx, Marie Wilson, William Bendix, Don DeFore, Gene Lockhart, Dee Hartford, Hanley Stafford, Teddy Hart, Percy Helton, George E. Stone.

About Face. Warner Bros. Rl: 2/28/1952(Nashville) 5/23/1952(NYC). D: Roy Del Ruth. Sc: Peter Milne. St: John Monks Jr., Fred F. Finklehoffe (play). RT: 94 min. Cast: Gordon MacRae, Eddie Bracken, Dick Wesson, Virginia Gibson, Phyllis Kirk, Aileen Stanley Jr., Joel Grey, Larry Keating, Cliff Ferre, John Baer. Technicolor.

Sound Off. Columbia. Rl: 4/11/1952. D: Richard Quine. Sc: Richard Quine, Blake Edwards. RT: 83 min. Cast: Mickey Rooney, Anne James, Sammy White, John Archer, Gordon Jones, Wally Cassell. SuperCinecolor.

Gobs and Gals. Republic. Rl: 5/1/1952. D: R.G. Springsteen. Sc: Arthur T. Horman. RT: 86 min. Cast: George and Bert Bernard, Robert Hutton, Cathy Downs, Gordon Jones, Florence Marly, Leon Belasco, Emory Parnell, Leonid Kinskey, Tommy Rettig, Minera Urecal, Olin Howlin, Donald MacBride, Henry Kulky, Marie Blake.

Jumping Jacks. Paramount. Rl: 6/11/1952. D: Norman Taurog. Sc: Robert Lees, Fred Rinaldo, Herbert Baker. St: Brian Marlow. Adl. Dlg: James Allardice, Richard Weil. RT: 96 min. Cast: Dean Martin, Jerry Lewis, Mona Freeman, Don DeFore, Robert Strauss, Richard Erdman, Ray Teal, Marcy McGuire, Danny Arnold.

Francis Goes to West Point. Universal-International. Rl: 6/23/1952. D: Arthur Lubin. Sc: Oscar Brodney, David Stern. RT: 81 min. Cast: Donald O'Connor, Lori Nelson, Alice Kelley, Palmer Lee [Gregg Palmer], William Reynolds, Les Tremayne, Otto Hulett, Dave Janssen, James Best.

Here Come the Marines. Monogram. Rl: 6/29/1952. D: William Beaudine. Sc: Tim Ryan, Charles R. Marion, Jack Crutcher. RT: 66 min. Cast: Leo Gorcey, Huntz Hall, Hanley Stafford, Myrna Dell, Murray Alper, Arthur Space, Tim Ryan, Bernard Gorcey, Gil Stratton Jr., David Condon [Gorcey], Bennie Bartlett, Paul Maxey, William Newell, Lisa Wilson, Riley Hill, Robert Coogan, Leo "Ukie" Sherin, Bob Peoples.

What Price Glory. 20th Century–Fox. Rl: 7/25/1952(Atlantic City premiere) 8/15/1952 (Los Angeles premiere) 8/22/1952 (New York City premiere). D: John Ford. Sc: Phoebe and Henry Ephron. St: Maxwell Anderson, Laurence Stallings (play). RT: 111 min. Cast: James Cagney, Corinne Calvet, Dan Dailey, William Demarest, Craig Hill, Robert Wagner, Marisa Pavan, Casey Adams [Max Showalter], James Gleason, Wally Vernon, Henri Letondal. Technicolor.

Fearless Fagan. MGM. Rl: 8/15/1952. D: Stanley Donen. Sc: Charles Lederer. St: Sidney A. Franklin Jr., Frederick Hazlitt Brennan. RT: 79 min. Cast: Janet Leigh, Carleton Carpenter, Keenan Wynn, Richard Anderson, Ellen Corby, Barbara Ruick, John Call, Robert Burton, Wilton Graff, Parley Baer, Jonathan Cott.

Back at the Front. Universal-International. Rl: 10/2/1952. D: George Sherman. Sc/St: Lou Breslow, Don McGuire. Sc: Oscar Brodney. St: Bill Mauldin (book). RT: 87 min. Tom Ewell, Harvey Lembeck, Mari Blanchard, Richard Long, Palmer Lee [Gregg Palmer], Barry Kelley, Russell Johnson, Vaughn Taylor, Aram Katcher, Aen-Ling Chow, Benson Fong. Reissued as **Willie and Joe Back at the Front.**

The WAC from Walla Walla. Republic. Rl: 10/10/1952. D: William Witney. Sc: Arthur T. Horman. RT: 83 min. Cast: Judy Canova, Stephen Dunne, George Cleveland, June Vincent, Irene Ryan, Roy Barcroft, Allen Jenkins, George Chandler, Elizabeth Slifer, Thurston Hall, Ellanor Needles, Dick Wessel, Pattie Chapman.

Mr. Walkie Talkie. Rockingham/Lippert. Rl: 11/28/1952. D: Fred Guiol. Sc: George Carleton Brown, Edward E. Seabrook. RT: 65 min. Cast: William Tracy, Joe Sawyer, Margia Dean, Robert Shayne, Alan Hale Jr., Russell Hicks, Frank Jenks, Wong Artane, Hanna Landy, Dorothy Neumann, Tom Hubbard, Kay Medford.

Never Wave at a WAC. Independent Artists/RKO Radio. Rl: 1/28/1953 (Washington DC premiere). D: Norman Z. McLeod. Sc: Ken Englund. St: Frederick Kohner, Fred Brady. RT: 87 min. Cast: Rosalind Russell, Paul Douglas, Marie Wilson, William Ching, Arleen Whelan, Leif Erickson, Hillary Brooke, Charles Dingle, Lurene Tuttle, Regis Toomey, Frieda Inescort, Louise Beavers, Vince Townsend Jr., Gen. Omar N. Bradley.

All Ashore. Columbia. Rl: 3/3/1953. D: Richard Quine. Sc: Richard Quine, Blake Edwards. RT: 80 min. Cast: Mickey Rooney, Dick Haymes, Peggy Ryan, Ray McDonald, Barbara Bates, Jody Lawrence, Fay Roope, Jean Willes, Rica Owen, Patricia Walker, Edwin Parker, Dick Crockett, Frank Kreig, Ben Welden, Gloria Pall. Joan Shawlee. Technicolor.

The Girls of Pleasure Island. Paramount. Rl: 4/1/1953. D: Alvin Ganzer, F. Hugh Herbert. Sc: F. Hugh Herbert. St: William Maier (novel). RT: 95 min. Cast: Leo Genn, Don Taylor, Gene Barry, Elsa Lanchester, Dorothy Bromiley, Audrey Dalton, Joan Elan, Peter Baldwin, Philip Ober, Barry Bernard, Arthur Gould-Porter. Technicolor.

Off Limits. Paramount. Rl: 7/8/1953. D: George Marshall. Sc/St: Hal Kanter, Jack Sher. RT: 89 min. Cast: Bob Hope, Mickey Rooney, Marilyn Maxwell, Eddie Mayehoff, Stanley Clements, Jack Dempsey, Marvin Miller, John Ridgely, Tom Harmon, Norman Leavitt, Art Aragon, Kim Spalding, Jerry Hausner, Mike Mahoney, Joan Taylor, Carolyn Jones, Mary Murphy.

Clipped Wings. Allied Artists. Rl: 8/14/1953. D: Edward Bernds. Sc: Charles R. Marion, Ellwood Ullman. St: Charles R. Marion. RT: 65 min. Cast: Leo Gorcey, Huntz Hall, Bernard Gorcey, Renie Riano, Todd Karns, June Vincent, Fay Roope, Mary Treen, Anne Kimbell, David Condon [Gorcey], Bennie Bartlett, Elaine Riley, Lou Nova, Philip Van Zandt, Lyle Talbot, Ray Walker.

Francis Joins the WACs. Universal-International. Rl: 7/30/1954. D: Arthur Lubin. Sc: Devery Freeman. St: Herbert Baker. RT: 95 min. Cast: Donald O'Connor, Julia [Julie] Adams, Chill Wills, Mamie Van Doren, Lynn Bari, ZaSu Pitts, Joan Shawlee, Allison Hayes, Mara Corday, Karen Kadler, Elsie Holmes, Patti McKay, Anthony Radecki, Olan Soule, Richard Deems.

Hit the Deck. MGM. Rl: 3/4/1955. D: Roy Rowland. Sc: Sonya Levien, William Ludwig. St: Hubert Osborne (play); Herbert Fields (musical adaptation). RT: 112 min. Cast: Jane Powell, Tony Martin, Debbie Reynolds, Walter Pidgeon, Vic Damone, Gene Raymond, Ann Miller, Russ Tamblyn, J. Carrol Naish, Kay Armen, Richard Anderson, Jane Darwell, Alan King, Henry Slate, The Jubilaires. Metrocolor; Cinemascope.

Mister Roberts. Warner Bros. Rl: 7/10/1955 (Los Angeles premiere) 7/14/1955 (New York premiere). D: John Ford, Mervyn LeRoy. Sc: Frank Nugent, Joshua Logan. St: Thomas Heggen (novel and play); Joshua Logan (play). RT: 123 min. Cast: Henry Fonda, James Cagney, William Powell, Jack Lemmon, Betsy Palmer, Ward Bond, Phil Carey, Nick Adams, Perry Lopez, Ken Curtis, Robert Roark, Harry Carey Jr., Pat Wayne, Frank Aletter, Tiger Andrews, Fritz Ford, Jim Moloney, Buck Kartalian, Denny Niles, William Henry, Francis Connor, William Hudson, Shug Fisher, Stubby Kruger, Danny Borzage, Harry Tenbrook Jim Murphy, Kathleen O'Malley, Maura Murphy, Mimi Doyle, Jeanne Murray, Lonnie Pierce, Martin Milner, Gregory Walcott, James Flavin, Jack Pennick, Duke Kahanamoku. WarnerColor; Cinemascope.

The Private War of Major Benson. Universal-International. Rl: 8/2/1955. D: Jerry Hopper. Sc: Richard Alan Simmons, William Roberts. St: Joe Connelly, Bob Mosher. RT: 105 min. Cast: Charlton Heston, Julie Adams, William Demarest, Tim Hovey, Nana Bryant, Tim Considine, Sal Mineo, Milburn Stone, Mary Field, Donald Keeler, Gary Pagett, Mickey Little, Don Haggerty, David Janssen, Richard H. Cutting, Mary Alan Hokanson, Butch Jones, Yvonne Peattie, Kay Stewart. Technicolor.

Francis in the Navy. Universal-International. Rl: 8/24/1955. D: Arthur Lubin. Sc/St: Devery Freeman. RT: 80 min. Cast: Donald O'Connor, Martha Hyer, Richard Erdman, Jim Backus, David Janssen, Clint Eastwood, Martin Milner, Paul Burke, Phil Garris, Myrna Hansen, Betty Jane Howard, Virginia O'Brien, William Forrest, James Pryor.

The Lieutenant Wore Skirts. 20th Century–Fox. Rl: 1/11/1956. D/Sc: Frank Tashlin. Sc/St: Albert Beich. RT: 99 min. Cast: Tom Ewell, Sheree North, Rita Moreno Rick Jason, Les Tremayne, Alice Reinheart, Gregory Walcott, Jean Willes. Deluxe Color; Cinemascope.

The Iron Petticoat. London-Romulus-Remus/MGM

(United States release only). Rl: 6/30/1956 (West Berlin premiere); 1/7/1957 (United States release). D: Ralph Thomas. Sc: Ben Hecht [not credited in some prints]. RT: 87 min. Cast: Bob Hope, Katharine Hepburn, Noelle Middleton, James Robertson Justice, Robert Helpmann, David Kossoff, Alan Gifford, Nicholas Phipps, Paul Carpenter, Sid James, Alexander Gauge, Sandra Dorne, Richard Wattis, Tutte Lemkow, Olaf Pooley, Martin Boddey, Richard Leech, Eugene Deckers, Stanley Zevic, Alexis Chesnakov, Andre Mikhelson. Technicolor; VistaVision.

The Teahouse of the August Moon. MGM. Rl: 10/17/1956 (Los Angeles Premiere); 12/1/56 (general release). D: Delbert Mann. Sc: John Patrick. St: John Patrick (play); Vern J. Sneider (novel). RT: 123 min. Cast: Marlon Brando, Glenn Ford, Machiko Kyô, Eddie Albert, Paul Ford, Eddie Albert, Henry (Harry) Morgan, Jun Negami, Nijiko Kiyokawa, Mitsuko Sawamura. Metrocolor; Cinemascope.

Top Secret Affair. Carrollton/Warner Bros. Rl: 1/30/1957. D: H.C. Potter. Sc: Roland Kibbee, Allan Scott. St: John P. Marquand (characters from novel). RT: 100 min. Cast: Kirk Douglas, Susan Hayward, Paul Stewart, Jim Backus, John Cromwell, Roland Winters, Arthur Gould-Porter, Michael Fox, Frank Gerstle, Charles Lane. WarnerScope.

Joe Butterfly. Universal-International. Rl: 7/17/1957. D: Jesse Hibbs. Sc: Marion Hargrove, Sy Gomberg, Jack Sher. St: Evan Wylie, Jack Ruge (story). RT: 90 min. Cast: Burgess Meredith, Audie Murphy, George Nader, Keenan Wynn, Kieko Shima, Fred Clark, John Agar, Charles McGraw, Shinpei Simazaki, Reiko Higa, Tatsuo Saitô, Chizu Shimazu, Herbert Anderson, Eddie Firestone, Frank Chase, Harold Goodwin, Willard Willingham. Technicolor; Cinemascope.

Operation Mad Ball. Columbia. Rl: 8/17/1957. D: Richard Quine. Sc: Jed Harris, Arthur Carter, Blake Edwards. St: Arthur Carter (play). RT: 105 min. Cast: Jack Lemmon, Ernie Kovacs, Katherine Grant, Arthur O'Connell, Mickey Rooney, Dick York, James Darren, Roger Smith, William Leslie, Sheridan Comerate, L.Q. Jones, Jeanne Manet.

Looking for Danger. Allied Artists. Rl: 10/6/1957. D: Austin Jewell. Sc: Ellwood Ullman, Edward Bernds. RT: 62 min. Cast: Huntz Hall, Stanley Clements, Lili Kardell, David Gorcey, Jimmy Murphy, Richard Avonde, Eddie LeRoy, Otto Reichow, Michael Granger, Peter Mamakos.

Kiss Them for Me. 20th Century–Fox. Rl: 11/6/1957. D: Stanley Donen. Sc: Julius J. Epstein. St: Luther Davis (play); Frederic Wakeman (novel). RT: 105 min. Cast: Cary Grant, Jayne Mansfield, Leif Erickson, Suzy Parker, Ray Walston, Larry Blyden, Nathaniel Frey, Werner Klemperer, Jack Mullaney. Deluxe Color; Cinemascope. Reissued as **Shore Leave.**

Don't Go Near the Water. MGM. Rl: 11/13/1957. D: Charles Walters. Sc: Dorothy Kingsley, George Wells. St: William Brinkley (novel). RT: 107 min. Cast: Glenn Ford, Gia Scala, Earl Holliman, Anne Francis, Keenan Wynn, Fred Clark, Eva Gabor, Russ Tamblyn, Jeff Richards, Mickey Shaughnessy, Howard Smith, Romney Brent, Mary Wickes, Jack Straw, Robert Nichols, John Alderson, Jack Albertson, Charles Wattis. Metrocolor; Cinemascope.

The Sad Sack. Paramount. Rl: 11/27/1957. D: George Marshall. Sc: Edmund Beloin, Nate Monaster. St: George Baker (comic strip). RT: 98 min. Cast: Jerry Lewis, David Wayne, Phyllis Kirk, Peter Lorre, Joe Mantell, Gene Evans, George Dolenz, Lilliane Montevecchi, Shepperd Strudwick, Abraham Sofaer, Mary Treen, Ken Becker. VistaVision.

No Time for Sergeants. Warner Bros. Rl: 6/27/1958. D: Mervyn LeRoy. Sc: John Lee Mahin. St: Ira Levin (play); Mac Hyman (novel). RT: 119 min. Cast: Andy Griffith, Myron McCormick, Nick Adams, Murray Hamilton, Howard Smith, Will Hutchins, Sydney Smith, James Milhollin, Don Knotts, Jean Willes, Bartlett Robinson, Henry McCann, Dub Taylor, William Fawcett, Raymond Bailey.

Imitation General. MGM. Rl: 8/29/1958. D: George Marshall. Sc: William Bowers. St: William Chamberlain. RT: 88 min. Cast: Glenn Ford, Red Buttons, Taina Elg, Dean Jones, Kent Smith, Tige Andrews, John Wilder, Ralph Votrian. Cinemascope.

The Perfect Furlough. Universal-International. Rl: 10/8/1958. D: Blake Edwards. Sc: Stanley Shapiro. RT: 93 min. Cast: Tony Curtis, Janet Leigh, Keenan Wynn, Linda Cristal, Elaine Stritch, Marcel Dalio, Les Tremayne, Jay Novello, King Donovan, Gordon Jones, Alvy Moore, Lilyan Chauvin, Troy Donahue, Dick Crockett, Eugene Borden, James Lanphier. Eastmancolor; Cinemascope.

Onionhead. Warner Bros. Rl: 10/25/1958. D: Norman Taurog. Sc: Nelson Gidding. St: Weldon Hill (novel). RT: 111 min. Cast: Andy Griffith, Felicia Farr, Walter Matthau, Erin O'Brien, Joe Mantell, Ray Danton, James Gregory, Joey Bishop, Roscoe Karns, Claude Akins, Ainslee Pryor, Sean Garrison, Dan Barton, Mark Roberts, Peter Brown, Tiger Andrews, Karl Lukas.

Rally 'Round the Flag, Boys! 20th Century–Fox. Rl: 12/23/1958. D: Leo McCarey. Sc: Leo McCarey, Claude Binyon. St: Max Shulman (novel). RT: 106 min. Cast: Paul Newman, Joanne Woodward, Joan Collins, Jack Carson, Dwayne Hickman, Tuesday Weld, Gale Gordon, Tom Gilson, O.Z. Whitehead. Deluxe Color; Cinemascope.

Don't Give Up the Ship. Paramount. Rl: 7/3/1959. D: Norman Taurog. Sc: Herbert Baker, Edmund Beloin, Henry Garson. St: Ellis Kadison (TV play). RT: 89 min. Cast: Jerry Lewis, Dina Merrill, Diana Spencer, Mickey Shaughnessy, Robert Middleton, Gale Gordon, Mabel Albertson, Claude

Akins, Hugh Sanders, Richard Shannon, Chuck Wassil.

A Private's Affair. 20th Century–Fox. Rl: 8/14/1959. D: Raoul Walsh. Sc: Winston Miller. St: Ray Livingston Murphy. RT: 93 min. Cast: Sal Mineo, Christine Carère, Barry Coe, Barbara Eden, Gary Crosby, Terry Moore, Jim Backus, Jessie Royce Landis, Robert Burton, Alan Hewitt, Bob Denver, Tige Andrews. Deluxe Color; Cinemascope.

It Started with a Kiss. MGM. Rl: 9/4/1959. D: George Marshall. Sc: Charles Lederer. St: Valentine Davies. RT: 104 min. Cast: Glenn Ford, Debbie Reynolds, Eva Gabor, Gustavo Rojo, Fred Clark, Edgar Buchanan, Henry (Harry) Morgan, Robert Warwick, Frances Bavier, Netta Packer, Robert Cunningham, Alice Backes, Carmen Phillips. Metrocolor; Cinemascope.

Operation Petticoat. Granart/Universal-International. Rl: 12/5/1959. D: Blake Edwards. Sc: Stanley Shapiro, Maurice Richlin. St: Paul King, Joseph Stone. RT: 124 min. Cast: Cary Grant, Tony Curtis, Joan O'Brien, Dina Merrill, Arthur O'Connell, Gene Evans, Dick Sargent, Virginia Gregg, Robert F. Simon, Robert Gist, Gavin MacLeod, George Dunn, Dick Crockett, Madlyn Rhue, Marion Ross, Clarence E. Lung, Frankie Darro, Tony Pastor Jr., Robert Hoy, Nicky Blair, John W. Morley. Eastmancolor.

The Rookie. 20th Century–Fox. Rl: 12/18/1959. D: George O'Hanlon. Sc: Tommy Noonan, George O'Hanlon. RT: 84 min. Cast: Tommy Noonan, Pete Marshall, Julie Newmar, Jerry Lester, Claude Stroud, Norman Leavitt, Joe Besser, Vince Barnett, Herb Armstrong, Richard Reeves, Don Corey, Rodney Bell, George Eldredge, Peter Leeds, Patrick O'Moore. Cinemascope.

Wake Me When It's Over. 20th Century–Fox. Rl: 4/8/1960. D: Mervyn LeRoy. Sc: Richard L. Breen. St: Howard Singer (novel). RT: 126 min. Cast: Ernie Kovacs, Dick Shawn, Margo Moore, Jack Warden, Nobu Atsumi McCarthy, Don Knotts, Robert Strauss, Noreen Nash, Parley Baer, Robert Emhardt, Marvin Kaplan, Tommy Nishimura, Raymond Bailey, Robert Burton, Frank Behrens. Deluxe Color; Cinemascope.

The Wackiest Ship in the Army? Columbia. Rl: 12/29/1960. D/Sc: Richard Murphy. St: Herbert Carlson (short story); Herbert H. Margolis, William Raynor (screen story). RT: 99 min. Cast: Jack Lemmon, Ricky Nelson, John Lund, Chips Rafferty, Tom Tully, Joby Baker, Warren Berlinger, Patricia Driscoll, Mike Kellin, Richard Anderson, Alvy Moore, Joseph Gallison, Teru Shimada, George Shibata. Eastmancolor; Cinemascope.

Cry for Happy. Wm. Goetz Prod./Columbia*. Rl: 1/11/1961. D: George Marshall. Sc: Irving Brecher. St: George Campbell (novel). RT: 110 min. Cast; Glenn Ford, Donald O'Connor, Miiko Taka, James Shigeta, Miyoshi Umeki, Michi Kobi, Howard St. John, Joe Flynn, Chet Douglas, Tsuruko Kobayashi, Harriet E. MacGibbon, Robert Kino, Bob Okazaki, Harlan Warde, Nancy Kovack, Ted Knight, Bill Quinn, Ciyo Nakasone. Eastmancolor; Cinemascope. *According to screenwriter Irving Brecher, executive producer William Goetz originally intended this film for a Universal-International release.*

All Hands on Deck. 20th Century–Fox. Rl: 3/30/1961. D: Norman Taurog. Sc: Jay Sommers. St: Donald R. Morris (novel). RT: 100 min. Cast: Pat Boone, Buddy Hackett, Dennis O'Keefe, Barbara Eden, Warren Berlinger, Gale Gordon, David Brandon, Joe E. Ross, Bartlett Robinson, Paul von Schreiber, Ann B. Davis, Jody McGrea, Owasso the Turkey. Deluxe Color; Cinemascope.

On the Double. Dena Prod./Paramount. Rl: 5/19/1961. D: Melville Shavelson. Sc: Melville Shavelson, Jack Rose. RT: 92 min. Cast: Danny Kaye, Dana Wynter, Wilfrid Hyde-White, Margaret Rutherford, Diana Dors, Alan Cuthbertson, Jesse White, Gregory Walcott, Terence de Marney, Rex Evans, Rudolph Anders, Edgar Barrier, Pamela Light, Ben Astar. Technicolor; Panavision.

The Last Time I Saw Archie. Mark VII-Manzanita-Talbot/United Artists. Rl: 5/27/1961. D: Jack Webb. Sc: William Bowers. RT: 98 min. Cast: Robert Mitchum, Jack Webb, Martha Hyer, France Nuyen, Louis Nye, Don Knotts, Del Moore, Joe Flynn, Richard Arlen, James Lydon, Robert Strauss, Harvey Lembeck, Claudia Barrett, Theona Bryant, Elaine Davis [Devry], Marilyn Burtis, Howard McNear, Gene McCarthy, Bill Idleson, James Mitchum, John Nolan, Lillian Powell, Nancy Kulp, Don Drysdale, Bill Kilmer.

The Honeymoon Machine. Avon-Euterpe/MGM. Rl: 8/16/1961. D: Richard Thorpe: Sc/St: Lorenzo Semple Jr., George Wells. RT: 87 min. Cast: Steve McQueen, Brigid Bazlen, Jim Hutton, Paula Prentiss, Dean Jagger, Jack Weston, Jack Mullaney, Marcel Hillaire, Ben Astar, William Lanteau, Ken Lynch, Simon Scott. Metrocolor; Cinemascope.

The Sergeant Was a Lady. Twincraft/Universal-International. Rl: 9/12/1961. D/Sc: Bernard Glasser. RT: 72 min. Cast: Martin West, Venetia Stevenson, Bill Williams, Catherine McLeod, Roy Engel, Gregg Martell, Chicke Lind, Jomarie Pettit, Mari Lynn, Joan Barry, Francine York, Rhoda Williams, Doris Fessette, Lonnie Blackman, Richard Emory, James Dale, Dan White, Hal Torey, John Mitchum, Mike Masters.

Everything's Ducky. Barbroo/Columbia. Rl: 11/6/1961 (national); 12/20/1961 (NY) P: Red Doff. D: Don Taylor. Sc: John Fenton Murray, Benedict Freeman. RT: 80 min. Cast: Mickey Rooney, Buddy Hackett, Joanie Sommers, Jackie Cooper, Roland Winters, Elizabeth MacRae, Gene Blakely, Gordon Jones, Richard Deacon, James Milhollin, Jimmy Cross, Robert Williams, King Calder, Walker Edmiston.

The Horizontal Lieutenant. Euterpe/MGM. Rl: 4/18/1962. D: Richard Thorpe. Sc: George Wells.

St: Gordon Cotler (novel). RT: 90 min. Cast: Jim Hutton, Paula Prentiss, Jack Carter, Jim Backus, Charles McGraw, Miyoshi Umeki, Marty Ingels, Lloyd Kino, Linda Wong, Yoshio Yoda, Yuki Shimoda. Metrocolor; Cinemascope.

The Pigeon That Took Rome. Llenoc/Paramount. Rl: 6/20/1962. D/Sc: Melville Shavelson. St: Donald Downes (novel). RT: 103 min. Cast: Charlton Heston, Elsa Martinelli, Harry Guardino, Salvatore Baccaloni, Marietto, Gabriella Pallotta, Brian Donlevy, Arthur Shields, Rudolph Anders, Vadim Wolkowsky. Panavision.

A Ticklish Affair. Euterpe/MGM. Rl: 8/18/1963. D: George Sidney. Sc: Ruth Brooks Flippen. St: Barbara Luther (short story). RT: 88 min. Cast: Shirley Jones, Gig Young, Red Buttons, Carolyn Jones, Edgar Buchanan, Eddie Applegate, Edward Platt, Billy Mumy, Bryan Russell, Peter Robbins, Robert Foulk, Milton Frome. Metrocolor; Cinemascope.

Soldier in the Rain. Solar/Allied Artists. Rl: 11/27/1963. D: Ralph Nelson. Sc: Blake Edwards, Maurice Richlin. St: William Goldman (novel). RT: 88 min. Jackie Gleason, Steve McQueen, Tuesday Weld, Tony Bill, Tom Poston, Ed Nelson, Lew Gallo, Rockne Tarkington, Paul Hartman, John Hubbard, Chris Noel, Sam Flint, Lewis Charles, Adam West.

The Incredible Mr. Limpet. Warner Bros. Rl: 1/28/1964 (Florida premiere) 3/28/1964 (general release). D: Arthur Lubin. Sc: John C. Rose, Jameson Brewer, Joe DiMona. St: Theodore Pratt (novel). RT: 99 min. Cast: Don Knotts, Carole Cook, Jack Weston, Andrew Duggan, Larry Keating, Oscar Beregi, Charles Meredith, Elizabeth MacRae, Paul Frees. Technicolor.

Dr. Strangelove Or: How I Learned to Stop Worrying and Love the Bomb. Hawk/Columbia. Rl: 1/29/1964. D: Stanley Kubrick. Sc: Stanley Kubrick, Terry Southern, Peter George. St: Peter George (novel). RT: 95 min. Cast: Peter Sellers, George C. Scott, Sterling Hayden, Keenan Wynn, Slim Pickens, Peter Bull, James Earl Jones, Tracy Reed, James Creley, Frank Berry, Robert O'Neil, Glen Beck, Roy Stephens, Shane Rimmer, Hal Galili, Paul Tamarin, Laurence Herder, Gordon Tanner, John McCarthy.

McHale's Navy. Universal. Rl: 6/4/1964. D: Edward Montagne. Sc: Frank Gill Jr., George Carleton Brown. St: Si Rose. RT: 93 min. Cast: Ernest Borgnine, Tim Conway, Joe Flynn, Bob Hastings, Gary Vinson, John Wright, Carl Ballantine, Billy Sands, Edson Stroll, Gavin MacLeod, Yoshio Yoda, Jean Willes, Claudine Longet, George Kennedy, Marcel Hillaire, Dale Ishimoto, John Mamo [Fujioka]. Eastmancolor.

Advance to the Rear. MGM Rl: 6/10/1964. D: George Marshall. Sc: William Bowers, Samuel A. Peeples, Robert Carson. St: Jack Schaefer, William Chamberlain (novel). RT: 100 min. Cast: Glenn Ford, Stella Stevens, Melvyn Douglas, Jim Backus, Joan Blondell, Andrew Prine, Jesse Pearson, Alan Hale Jr., James Griffith, Whit Bissell, Michael Pate. Panavision.

Ensign Pulver. Warner Bros. Rl: 6/31/1964. D: Joshua Logan. Sc: Joshua Logan, Peter S. Feibelman. St: Thomas Heggen, Joshua Logan (characters and incidents from play and novel). RT: 104 min. Cast: Robert Walker Jr., Burl Ives, Walter Matthau, Tommy Sands, Millie Perkins, Kay Medford, Larry Hagman, Pete Marshall, Joseph Marr, Gerald S. O'Loughlin, Diana Sands, Robert Matek, Jack Nicholson, Al Freeman Jr., Richard Gautier, George Lindsey, Sal Papa, James Farentino, James Coco, Don Dorrell. Technicolor; Panavision.

The Americanization of Emily. Filmways/MGM. Rl: 10/27/1964. D: Arthur Hiller. Sc: Paddy Chayefsky. St: William Bradford Huie (novel). RT: 115 min. Cast: James Garner, Julie Andrews, Melvyn Douglas, James Coburn, Joyce Grenfell, Edward Binns, Liz Fraser, Keenan Wynn, William Windom, John Crawford, Douglas Henderson, Edmon Ryan, Steve Franken, Paul Newlan, Gary Cockrell, Alan Sues, Bill Fraser, Lou Byrne, Alan Howard, Linda Marlowe, Janine Gray, Judy Carne, Kathy Kersh. Reissued as **Emily**.

McHale's Navy Joins the Air Force. Universal. Rl: 7/9/1965. D: Edward Montagne. Sc: John Fenton Murray. St: William J. Lederer (novel). RT: 90 min. Cast: Tim Conway, Joe Flynn, Bob Hastings, Gary Vinson, Billy Sands, Edson Stroll, John Wright, Yoshio Yoda, Gavin MacLeod, Tom Tully, Susan Silo, Henry Beckman, Ted Bessell, Jean Hale, Cliff Norton, Willis Bouchey, Berkeley Harris, Jacques Aubuchon, Len Lesser, Henry Corden, Jack Bernardi, Norman Leavitt, Joe Ploski, Andy Albin, Clay Tanner, Tony Franke. Technicolor.

Sergeant DeadHead. American-International. Rl: 8/18/1965. D: Norman Taurog. Sc: Louis M. Heyard. RT: 89 min. Cast: Frankie Avalon, Deborah Walley, Cesar Romero, Fred Clark, Gale Gordon, Harvey Lembeck, John Ashley, Buster Keaton, Reginald Gardiner, Pat Buttram, Eve Arden, Romo Vincent, Donna Loren, Mike Nader, Ed Faulkner, Norman Grabowski, Tod Windsor, Patti Chandler, Luree Holmes, Mary Hughes, Salli Sachse, Bobbie Shaw, Sue Hamilton, Ed Reimers, John Hiestand, Bob Harvey, Andy Romano, Dwayne Hickman (credited cameo). Pathécolor; Panavision.

Not with My Wife, You Don't! Feywood-Reynard; Norman Panama Prod./Warner Bros. Rl: 11/2/1966. D: Norman Panama. Sc: Norman Panama, Larry Gelbart, Peter Barnes. St: Norman Panama, Melvin Frank. RT: 118 min. Cast: Tony Curtis, Virna Lisi, George C. Scott, Carroll O'Connor, Richard Eastham, Eddie Ryder, George Tyne, Ann Doran, Donna Danton, Natalie Core, Buck Young, Robert Cleaves, Karla Most, Betty Bresler, Alfred Shelly. Technicolor.

What Did You Do in the War, Daddy? Mirisch-Geoffrey Productions/United Artists. Rl: 8/31/1966. D: Blake Edwards. Sc: William Peter Blatty. St: Blake Edwards, Maurice Richlin. RT: 116 min. Cast: James Coburn, Dick Shawn, Sergio Fantoni, Giovanna Ralli, Aldo Ray, Harry Morgan, Carroll O'Connor, Leon Askin, Rico Cattani, Jay Novello, Vito Scotti, Johnny Seven, Art Lewis, William Bryant, Kurt Krueger, Robert Carricart, Ralph Manza, Danny Francis, Herb Ellis, Ken Wales, Eric Anderson, Ken Del Conte, Thomas Hunter, Kelly Johnson, Jerry Martin. Deluxe Color; Panavision.

The Secret War of Harry Frigg. Albion/Universal. Rl: 2/29/1968. D: Jack Smight. Sc: Peter Stone, Frank Tarloff. St: Frank Tarloff. RT: 110 min. Cast: Paul Newman, Sylva Koscina, Andrew Duggan, Tom Bosley, John Williams, Charles Gray, Vito Scotti, Jacques Roux, Werner Peters, James Gregory, Fabrizio Mioni, Johnny Haymer, Norman Fell, Buck Henry, Horst Ebersberg, Richard X. Slattery, George Ives. Technicolor; Techniscope.

The Private Navy of Sgt. O'Farrell. Beck-Naho/United Artists. Rl: 5/8/1968. D/Sc: Frank Tashlin. St: Robert M. Fresco, John L. Greene. RT: 92 min. Cast: Bob Hope, Phyllis Diller, Jeffrey Hunter, Mylène Demongeot, Gina Lollobrigida, John Myhers, Mako, Henry Wilcoxon, Dick Sargent, Christopher Dark, Michael Burns, William Wellman Jr., Robert Donner, Jack Grinnage, William Christopher. Technicolor. Rated G.

The Extraordinary Seaman. MGM. Rl: 9/?/1969. D: John Frankenheimer. Sc: Phillip Rock, Hal Dresner. St: Phillip Rock (novel). RT: 79 min. David Niven, Faye Dunaway, Alan Alda, Mickey Rooney, Jack Carter, Juano Hernandez, Manu Tupou, Barry Kelley, Leonard O. Smith, Richard Guizon, John Cochran, Jerry Fujikawa. Metrocolor; Panavision. Rated G.

MASH. Aspen-Ingo Preminger Prod./20th Century–Fox. Rl: 1/25/1970 (NYC); 3/?/1970 (general release). D: Robert Altman. Sc: Ring Lardner Jr. St: Richard Hooker (novel). RT: 116 min (R-rated version); 112 min. (PG-Rated Version). Donald Sutherland, Elliott Gould, Tom Skerritt, Sally Kellerman, Robert Duvall, Roger Bowen, Rene Auberjonois, David Arkin, Jo Ann Pflug, Gary Burghoff, Fred Williamson, Michael Murphy, Indus Arthur, Ken Prymus, Bobby Troup, Kim Atwood, Tim Brown, John Schuck, Dawne Damon, Carl Gottlieb, G. Wood, Bud Cort, Danny Goldman, Corey Fischer. Deluxe Color; Panavison. Rated R (later modified to PG).

Kelly's Heroes. Avaka/Katzka-Loeb/MGM. Rl: 6/23/1970. D: Brian G. Hutton. Sc/St: Troy Kennedy Martin. RT: 145 min. Cast: Clint Eastwood, Telly Savalas, Don Rickles, Carroll O'Connor, Donald Sutherland, Gavin McLeod, Hal Buckley, Stuart Margolin, Jeff Morris, Richard Davalos, Perry Lopez, Tom Troupe, [Harry] Dean Stanton, Dick Balduzzi, Gene Collins, Len Lesser, David Hurst, Fred Pearlman, Michael Clark, George Fargo, Dee Pollock, George Savalas, John Heller, Stephen Sanders, Karl Otto Alberty, Ross Elliott, Phil Adams, Hugo De Vernier, Frank J. Garlotta, Harry Goines, David Gross, Robert McNamara, Read Morgan, Tom Signorelli, Donald Waugh, Vincent Marcacecchi. Metrocolor; Panavision. Rated PG.

Catch-22. Filmways/Paramount. Rl: 6/24/1970. D: Mike Nichols. Sc: Buck Henry. St: Joseph Heller (novel). RT: 121 min. Cast: Alan Arkin, Martin Balsam, Richard Benjamin, Art Garfunkel, Jack Gilford, Buck Henry, Bob Newhart, Anthony Perkins, Paula Prentiss, Martin Sheen, Jon Voight, Orson Welles, Seth Allen, Bob Balaban, Susanne Benton, Norman Fell, Charles Grodin, Austin Pendleton, Peter Bonerz, Jon Korkes, John Brent, Collin Wilcox-Horne, Phil Roth, Bruce Kirby, Jack Riley, Felice Orlandi, Marcel Dalio, Evi Maltagliati, Elizabeth Wilson, Richard Libertini, Liam Dunn, Olimpia Carlisi, Wendy D'Olive, Gina Rovere, Fernanda Vitobello. Technicolor; Panavision. Rated R.

Suppose They Gave a War And Nobody Came? ABC/Cinerama. Rl: 9/11/1970 (NY). D: Hy Averback. Sc: Don McGuire, Hal Captain. RT: 113 min. Cast: Brian Keith, Tony Curtis, Ernest Borgnine, Ivan Dixon, Suzanne Pleshette, Tom Ewell, Bradford Dillman, Arthur O'Connell, John Fiedler, Don Ameche, Robert Emhardt, Cliff Norton, Grady Sutton, Jeanne Bates, Pamela Britton, Dorothy Green, Maxine Stewart, Paula Stewart, Carolyn Williamson, Monty Margetts, Christopher Mitchum, John Lasell, Buck Young, Eddie Firestone, William Bramley, Sam Edwards, David S. Cass Sr., Paul Sorenson, John James Bannon, Vince Howard, Stan Barrett, Jean Argyle, Pamela Branch, Janet E. Clark, Lee Stanley. Technicolor. Rated M/PG.

Welcome to the Club. Welcome Prod./Columbia. Rl: 9/1/1971. D: Walter Shenson. Sc/St: Clement Biddle Wood. RT: 88 min. Cast: Brian Foley, Jack Warden, Andy Jarrell, Kevin O'Connor, Francesca Tu, David Toguri, Al Mancini, Art Wallace, Marsha A. Hunt, Joyce Wilford, Lon Satton, Christopher Malcolm, John Dunn-Hill, Lee Meredith, Louis Quinn, Lionel Murton, Jeanne Darville, Anisha, Claus Ersbak, Ueda, Oliver Norman, Eve Marie Petryshyn. Eastmancolor. Rated R.

The Last Detail. Acrobat/Bright-Persky/Columbia. Rl: 12/12/1973 (LA) 2/11/1974 (NYC). D: Hal Ashby. Sc: Robert Towne. St: Darryl Ponicsan (novel). RT: 105 min. Cast: Jack Nicholson, Otis Young, Randy Quaid, Clifton James, Carol Kane, Michael Moriarty, Luana Anders, Kathleen Miler, Nancy Allen, Gerry Salsberg, Donna McGovern, Pat Hamilton, Michael Chapman, Jim Henshaw, Derek McGrath, Gilda Radner, John Castellano. Metrocolor. Rated R.

Chesty Anderson, U.S.N. Atlas/Cinefilm. Rl: 11/?/1976. D: Ed Forsyth. Sc/St: H.F. Green, Paul

Pompian. RT: 88 min. Cast: Shari Eubank, Dorrie Thorson, Rosanne Katon, Constance Marie, Fred Willard, George Lane Cooper, Frank Campanella, Timothy Carey, Phil Hoover, Tim Wade, Scatman Crothers, Mel Carter, Lynne Guthrie, Brenda Fogarty, Joyce Mandel, Roy Applegate, Stanley Brock, Dyanne Thorne, Uschi Digard, Pat Parker, Mark Lawhead, Jim Cranna, Mark Forsyth, Matthew Forsyth, Richard Rifkin, Murphy Dunne, Pax Quigly, Betty Thomas, Deborah Harmon, Ira Miller, Bill Walker, Adair Jameson, Pam Rice, Nancy Noble, Marilyn Brown, Elizabeth Johnson, Kim Kahana, Gerald Okamura, Paul Pompian. Eastmancolor. Rated R. TV and Video Title: **Anderson's Angels.**

MAD Magazine Presents Up the Academy. Warner Bros. Rl: 6/6/1980. D: Robert Downey Sr. Sc/St: Tom Patchett, Jay Tarses. RT: 87 min. Cast: Ron Leibman (uncredited), Wendell Brown, Tommy Citera, J. Hutchison [Hutch Parker], Ralph Macchio, Herry Teinowitz, Tom Poster, Ian Wolfe, Antonio Fargas, Stacey Nelkin, Barbara Bach, Leonard Frey, Luka Andreas, Candy Ann Brown, King Coleman, Rosalie Citera, Yvonne Francis, James G. Robertson, Rosemary Eliot, Louis Zorich, Robert Lynn Mock, Tyrees Allen, Eric Hanson, Ken White, William J. L. Bunting, Sheri Ann Hoffhines, Allyson Downs, Brenda A. Rohr, Tanya Boyd, Ernest Vishneske, Myra Benson. Technicolor; Panavision. Rated R. TV and Video Title: **Up the Academy.**

Private Benjamin. Warner Bros. Rl: 10/10/1980. D: Howard Zieff. Sc: Nancy Meyers, Charles Shyer, Harvey Miller. RT: 110 min. Cast: Goldie Hawn, Eileen Brennan, Armand Assante, Robert Webber, Sam Wanamaker, Barbara Barrie, Mary Kay Place, Harry Dean Stanton, Albert Brooks, Alan Oppenheimer, Robert Hanley, Lee Wallace, Gretchen Wyler, Maxine Stuart, Lillian Adams, Sandy Weintraub, Tim Haldeman, Stu Nahan, J.P. Bumstead, Hal Williams, Toni Kalem, Damia Jo Freeman, Alston Ahern, P.J. Soles, Craig T. Nelson, James R. Barnett, Clayton D. Wright, Keone Young, George Roberts, Helen Baron, Paul Marin, Mimi Maynard, Alice Hirson, Wil Albert, Richard Herd, Sally Kirkland, Denise Halma, Lilyan Chauvin, David Olivier, Elie Liardet. Technicolor. Rated R.

Getting Wasted. Photon Films/Diversfied. Rl: ?/?/1980. D: Paul Frizler. Sc: Paul Frizler, John Flaherty. RT: 98 min. Cast: Brian Kerwin, Cooper Huckabee, George O'Hanlon [Jr.], Ken Michaelman, Stephen Furst, Dennis Howard, Stefan Arngrim, Wendy Rastatter, Ronnie Claire Edwards, Jeanne Lange, Tracey Walter, Haskell Gordon, Fredric Cook, Herb Voland, Ivan Bonar, Peter Alsop, Shell Kepler, Mary-Margaret, Robyn Pohle, Eric Greene, Rolly Fanton, Kristine Greco, Gina Gallego, Mike Gomez, Lois Foraker, Jo Jo Malone, Thomas Rosales, Vernon Weddle, John Kerry, David Buanno, Lee Lomask, Paul Cardin, Ward Rudick, David Caruso, Dick Haynes, Cory Yothers, Bud Cook, Pat Flahive, Jean Le Bouvir, Timothy Jerome, Shirley O'Hara, Herb Vigran, Barbara Mulch, Richard Doetkott, Jim Borress. Color. Rated R.

Stripes. Columbia. Rl: 6/26/1981. D: Ivan Reitman. Sc/St: Len Blum, Daniel Golberg, Harold Ramis. RT: 105 min.* Cast: Bill Murray, Harold Ramis, John Candy, Warren Oates, P. J. Soles, Sean Young, John Candy, John Larroquette, John Vodstad, John Diehl, Lance LeGault, Robert Leighton, Conrad Dunn, Judge Reinhold, Antone Pagan, Glenn-Michael Jones, Bill Lucking, Fran Ryan, Joe Flaherty, Nick Toth, Dave Thomas, Robin Klein, Robert J. Wilke, Lois Hamilton, Samuel Briggs, Hershel B. Harlson, Timothy Busfield, Solomon Schmidt, Gino Gottarelli, Gene Scherer, Craig Schaefer, Arkady Rakhman, Pamela Bowman, Bill Paxton. Metrocolor. Rated R. *This film is also available in an "extended cut" DVD version running 122 minutes. Included is an 18-minute sequence excised from the theatrical release print, in which the characters played by Bill Murray and Harold Ramis stow away on a commando mission to South America.

Weekend Pass. Marimark/Crown International. Rl: 2/3/1984 (Bismarck ND premiere). D/Sc: Lawrence Bassoff. RT: 88 min. Cast: D.W. Brown, Peter Ellenstein, Patrick Houser, Chip McAllister, Pamela G. Kay, Hilary Shapiro [Shepard], Graem McGavin, Daureen Collodel, Grand L. Bush, Sara Costa, Valerie McIntosh, Cheryl Song, Peter Bailey-Britton, Theodore Wilson, Bunny Summers, Phil Hartman, Tony DeLia, Lynn [Marie] Stewart, John Graves, Mona Charles, Debbie Christofferson, Joan Dykman, Kirk Calloway, Henry G. Sanders, Anthony Penya, Jacqueline Jacobs, Ashley St. Jon. Color. Rated R.

Tank. Lorimar-Universal. Rl: 3/16/1984. D: Marvin J. Chomsky. Sc: Dan Gordon. RT: 113 min. Cast: James Garner, Shirley Jones, C. Thomas Howell, Mark Herrier, Sandy War, Jenilee Harrison, James Cromwell, Dorian Harewood, G.D. Spradlin, John Hancock, Guy Boyd, Daniel Albright, Ron Baskin, Keith Jerome Brown, Robert Henry Bryant, CWO Frederick W. Clark, Alan G. Cornett, Bill Crabb, T. Renee Crutcher, SSG David J. Dominick, Raymond D. Eckel, J. Don Ferguson, Bill Fleet, Jeff Folger, Doneal G. Gersh, Jim Jackson, Bob Hannah, Mark McGee, Wallace Merck, Bob Neal, Russ Spooner, Danny Nelson, James T. Newton, Kathy Payne, Don Young, Joan Riordan, Beth Smallwood, Andy Still, Roy Tatum, Ben Walburn, Alan Walker, Thomas P. Ryan, Wallace Wilkinson, Laura Whyte. Metrocolor. Rated PG.

Best Defense. Cinema Group Ventures/Paramount. Rl: 7/20/1984. D: Willard Huyck. Sc: Willard Huyck, Gloria Katz. St: Robert Grossbach (novel). RT: 94 min. Dudley Moore, Eddie Murphy, Kate Capshaw, George Dzundza, Helen Shaver, Mark

Arnott, Peter Michael Goetz, Tom Noonan, David Rasche, Paul Comi, Darryl Henriques, John Polis, John A. Zee, Matthew Laurance, Christopher Maher, Lorry Goldman, Stoney Richards, Tyler Tyhurst, Eduardo Ricard, William Marquez, Deborah Fallender, Raye Birk, Ellen Crawford, Gene Dynarski, John Hostetter, David Paymer, Dennis Redfield, Jerry Hyamn, Hugo Stranger, Tracey Ross, Michael Scalera, Rob Wininger, Gary Bayer, Ronald Salley, Paul Eiding, Stephen Bradley, Ziporah Tzaban, Gabi Amrani, Itzhak Bbi Neeman, Patricia Pivar, Rick Dees, Chuck Street. Movielab Color. Rated R.

Basic Training. Entertainment Events/Playboy/Moviestone. Rl: 11/?/1985. D: Andrew Sugerman. Sc/St: Bernard M. Kahn. RT: 88 min. Ann Dusenberry, Rhonda Shear, Angela Aames, Will Nye, Walter Gotell, Marty Brill, William A. Forester, Christopher Pennock, Mark Withers, Gerard Prendergast, Marty Cohen, Orly Oh, Linda Hoy, Kenny Ellis, Gerald Berns, Michael Greene, Mark Lowenthal, Sam Scarber, Ari Barak, Fred Saxon. Color. Rated R. Video Title: **Up the Military.**

Weekend Warriors. Convy-Fimberg Prod./Moviestore. Rl: 8/29/1986 (San Antonio premiere) 10/?/1986 (general release). D: Bert Convy. Ph: Charles Minsky. Sc: Roy M. Rogosin, Bruce Belland. St: Bruce Belland. RT: 85 min. Cast: Chris Lemmon, Lloyd Bridges, Vic Tayback, Graham Jarvis, Brian Bradley, Alan Campbell, Marty Cohen, Daniel Greene, Art Kimbro, Matt McCoy, Jeff Meyer, Frank Mugavero, Juney Smith, Tom Villard, Camille Saviola, Brenda Strong, Bruce Belland, Jeff Allin, Monique Gabrielle, Gretchen Gray, Bob Libman, Randal Patrick, Stephen F. Schmidt, Wanda H. Tilson, Gene Wood, Greg Aikens, Stephen M. Bottroff, Mark L. Taylor, Gail Barle, LaGena Hart, Jennifer Convy. Color. Rated R. Video Title: **Hollywood Air Force.**

Good Morning, Vietnam. Silver Screen Partners III/Touchstone. Rl: 12/23/1987 (limited release) 1/15/1988 (general release). D: Barry Levinson. Sc: Mitch Markowitz. RT: 120 min. Cast: Robin Williams, Forest Whitaker, Tung Thanh Tran, Chintara Sukapatana, Bruno Kirby, Robert Wuhl, J.T. Walsh, Noble Willingham, Richard Edson, Juney Smith, Richard Portnow, Floyd Vivino, Cu Ba Nguyen, Dan Stanton, Don Stanton, Danny Aiello III, James McIntire, Peter Mackenzie, Ralph Tabakin, Sangad Sangkao, Vanlap Sangko. Deluxe Color. Rated R.

Biloxi Blues. Rastar/Universal. Rl: 3/25/1988. D: Mike Nichols. Sc/St: Neil Simon. RT: 106 min. Cast: Matthew Broderick, Christopher Walken, Matt Mulhern, Corey Parker, Markus Flanagan, Casey Siemaszko, Michael Dolan, Penelope Ann Miller, Park Overall, Alan Pottinger, Mark Evan Jacobs, Dave Kienzle, Mitthew Kimbrough, Jeff Bailey, Bill Russell, Natalie Canerday, A. Collin Roddey, Christopher Ginnaven, Morris Mead, Norman Rose, Ben Hynum, Andy Wigington, Scott Sudbury, Michael R. Haley. Color; Super 35. Rated PG-13.

A Man Called Sarge. Cannon. Rl: 2/2/1990. D/Sc: Stuart Gillard. RT: 88 min. Cast: Gary Kroeger, Gretchen German, Marc Singer, Jennifer Runyon, Andy Greenhalgh, Michael Mears, Bobby Di Cicco, Howard Busgang, Travis McKenna, Andrew Burnatari, Chris England, Jeffrey Wickham, Peter Dennis, Bruce Jenner, Yehuda Efroni, Aviva Marks, Lior Hashin, Zafrir Kohanovsky, Josef Bee, Natasha Leon, Tomer Yoseph, Alexander Peleg, Amikam Levi, Yuval Vill, Gabi Shoshan, Don LaFontaine. Color. Rated PG-13.

Hot Shots! 20th Century–Fox. Rl 7/31/1991. D: Jim Abrahams. Sc: Jim Abrahams, Pat Proft. RT: 85 min. Cast: Charlie Sheen, Cary Elwes, Valeria Golino, Lloyd Bridges, Kevin Dunn, Jon Cryer, William O'Leary, Kristy Swanson, Efrem Zimbalist Jr., Bill Irwin, Heidi Swedberg, Bruce A. Young, Ryan Stiles, Rino Thunders, Mark Arnott, Ryan Cutrona, Don Lake, Kelly Connell, Judith Kahan, Jeff Bright, Jimmy Lennon Jr., Marie Thomas, Ryan Fitzgerald, Al Clegg, Pat Proft, Marc Sahiman, Charles Barkley, Bill Laimbeer, Gene Greytak, Tony Lorea, Jerry Haleva, Bob Lenz, Willie Collins, Nancy Abrahams, Joseph Abrahams, Jamie Abrahams. Deluxe Color. Rated PG-13.

Going Under. Warner Bros. Rl 8/?/1991. D: Mark W. Travis. Sc: Darryl Zarubica, Randolph Davis. RT: 80 min. Cast: Bill Pullman, Wendy Schaal, Ned Beatty, Robert Vaughn, Roddy McDowell, Chris Demetral, Tyrone Granderson Jones, Dennis Redfield, Lou Richards, Ernie Sabella, Elmarie Wendel, Richard Masur, John Moschitta, Joe Namath, Rif Hutton, Michael Winslow, Dianne Turley Travis, Shawne Zarubica, Frank Bonner, Andrea Stein, Artur Cybulski, Ivan G'Vera, Darryl Zarubica, Tad Horino, Dean Cain, Robert Clotworthy. Technicolor. Rated PG.

Chasers. Morgan Creek/Warner Bros. Rl: 4/22/1994. D: Dennis Hoper. Sc: Joe Batteer, John Rice, Dan Gilroy. St: Joe Batteer, John Rice. RT: 102 min. Cast: Tom Berenger, Erika Eliniak. Cast: Tom Berenger, William McNamara, Erika Eliniak, Crispin Glover, Matthew Glover, Grand L. Bush, Dean Stockwell, Bitty Schram, Gary Busey, Seymour Cassel, Frederic Forrest, Marilu Henner, Dennis Hopper, Scott Marlowe, Jim Grimshaw, Mick McGovern, Charles Page, Richard Pelzman, Laura Cathey, Jim Bath, Michael Flippo, Rick Warner, Gene Dann, Michael O'Brien, Tony Donno, Wallace Wilkinson, Toni Prima. Technicolor. Rated R.

Renaissance Man. Cinergi-Parkway/Touchstone. Rl: 6/3/1994. D: Penny Marshall. Sc: Jim Burnstein. RT: 129 min. Cast: Danny DeVito, Gregory Hines, James Remar, Ed Begley Jr., Lillo Brancato Jr. Stacey Dash, Kadeem Hardison. Richard T. Jones, Khalil Kain, Peter Simmons, Greg Sporleder, Mark

Wahlberg, Cliff Robertson, Ben Wright, Ann Cusack, Jennifer Lewis, Alanna Ubach, Isabella Hofmann, Samaria Graham, Don Reilly. Technicolor. Rated PG-13. Reissued as **By the Book**.

In the Army Now. Hollywood/Buena Vista. Rl: 8/12/1994. D: Daniel Petrie Jr. Sc: Ken Kaufman, Stu Krieger, Daniel Petrie Jr., Fax Bahr, Adam Small. St: Steve Zacharias, Jeff Buhai, Robbie Fox. RT: 91 min. Cast: Pauly Shore, Andy Dick, Lori Petty, David Alan Grier, Esai Morales, Lynn Whitfield, Art LaFleur, Fabiana Udenio, Glenn Morshower, Beau Billingslea, Peter Spellos, Barry Nolan, Coleen Christie, Ryan Cutrona, Paul Mooney, Richard Assad, Maurice Sherbanee, Tom Villard, Howard J. Von Kaenel, Daniel Petrie Jr. Color. Rated PG.

Major Payne. Wife 'n' Kids/Universal. Rl: 3/24/1995. D: Nick Castle. Sc: Dean Lorey, Damon Wayans, Gary Rosen, William Roberts (earlier SC); Richard Alan Simmons (earlier SC). St: Joe Connelly, Bob Mosher (earlier film). RT: 95 min. Cast: Damon Wayans, Karyn Parsons, William Hickey, Michael Ironside, Albert Hall, Steven Martini, Orlando Brown, Andrew Harrison Leeds, Damien Wayans, Chris Owen, R. Stephen Wiles, Carolyn Walker, Mark W. Madison, Ross Bickell, Dean Lorey, R.J. Knoll, Stephen Coleman, Peyton Chesson-Fohl, David DeHart, Scott "Bam Bam" Bigelow, Michael Gabel. Color. Rated PG-13.

Operation Dumbo Drop. Walt Disney-Polygram-Interscope/Buena Vista. Rl: 7/28/1995. D: Simon Wincer. Sc: Jim Kouf, Gene Quintano. St: Jim Morris. RT: 107 min. Cast: Danny Glover, Ray Liotta, Denis Leary, Doug E. Doug, Corin Nemec, Dinh Thien Le, Tchéky Karyo, Hoang Ly, Vo Trung Anh, Marshall Bell, James Hong, Long Nguyen, Tim Kelleher, Scott N. Stevens, Kevin Larosa, Christopher Ward, Michael Lee, Le Minh Tien, Mac Van Nam, Chern Dao Van, Nick Satriano. Eastmancolor; Panavision. Rated PG.

Down Periscope. 20th Century–Fox. Rl: 3/1/1996. D: David S. Ward. Sc: Hugh Wilson, Andrew Kurtzman, Eliot Wald. St: Hugh Wilson. RT: 92 min. Kelsey Grammer, Lauren Holly, Rob Schneider, Harry Dean Stanton, Bruce Dern, William H. Macy, Ken Hudson Campbell, Toby Huss, Duane Martin, Jonathan Penner, Bradford Tatum, Harland Williams, Rip Torn, Patton Oswalt, Dennis Fimple. Deluxe Color. Rated PG-13.

Sergeant Bilko. Imagine/Universal. Rl: 3/29/1996. D: Jonathan Lynn. Sc: Andy Breckman. St: Nat Hiken (original TV series). RT: 93 min. Cast: Steve Martin, Dan Aykroyd, Phil Hartman, Glenne Headley, Daryl Mitchell, Max Casella, Eric Edwards, Dan Ferro, John Marshall Jones, Brian Leckner, John Ortiz, Pamela Segall [Adlon], Mitchell Whitfield, Austin Pendleton, Chris Rock, Cathy Silvers, Steve Park, Debra Jo Rupp, Richard Herd, Steve Kehela, Rance Howard, Travis Tritt. Color; Super 35. Rated PG.

Mchale's Navy. Bubble Factory-Sheinberg Prod./Universal. Rl: 4/18/1997. D: Bryan Spicer. Sc: Peter Crabbe. St: Peter Crabbe, Andy Rose. RT: 109 min. Cast: Tom Arnold, Dean Stockwell, Debra Messing, David Alan Grier, Tim Curry, Ernest Borgnine, Bruce Campbell, French Stewart, Danton Stone, Brian Haley, Henry Cho, Anthony Jesse Cruz, Tommy Chong, Scott Cleverdon, Honorato Magaloni, Eduardo Lopez Rojas, Tom Ayers, Paco Mauri, Jean Rebolledo, Diego Vazquez Lozano, Lucy Moreno, Mineko Mori, Alejandro Reyes, Eric Champnella, Bryan Spicer. Deluxe Color. Rated PG.

Buffalo Soldiers. FilmFour-Good Machine-Gorilla Entertainment-Grosvenor Park-Odeon/Miramax. Rl: 9/8/2001 (Toronto Intl. Film Festival) 1/21/2003 (Sundance Film Festival) 7/25/2003 (limited United States theatrical release). D: Gregor Jordan. Sc: Gregor Jordan, Eric Axel Weiss, Nora Maccoby. St: Robert O'Connor (novel). RT: 98 min. Cast: Joaquin Phoenix, Ed Harris, Scott Glenn, Anna Paquin, Elizabeth McGovern, Michael Peña, Leon Robinson, Gabriel Mann, Dean Stockwell, Brian Delate, Sheik Mahmud-Bey, Kirschfield, Noah, Tom Ellis, Kick Gurry, Haluk Bilginer, Idris Elba, Glenn Fitzgerald, Kirmo Wills, Enoch Frost, Jimmy Ray Weeks, Roger Griffiths, Alexis Rodney, Joel Ostendorf, Paul Conway, Ilhani Terzi. Technicolor; Super 35. Rated R.

All the Queen's Men. Atlantic Steamline-B.A. Filmproduktion-Dor Film Prod.-Phoenix/Strand Releasing. Rl: 10/14/2001 (Mill Valley Film Festival); 10/25/2002 (limited United States theatrical release). D: Stefan Ruzowitzky. Sc: David Schneider. St: Digby Wolfe, June Roberts, Joseph Manduke. RT: 99 min. Cast: Matt LeBlanc, Eddie Izzard, James Cosmo, Nicolette Krebitz, David Birkin, Edward Fox, Udo Kier, Oliver Korittke, Karl Markovics, Sissi Perlinger, Pip Torrens, Maria Petz, Paul Williamson, Gillian Hanna. Color; Super 35. Rated PG-13.

Military Intelligence and You! Pax Americana/Anywhere Road Entertainment. Rl: 10/21/2006 (Austin Film Festival); 2/10/2008 (first United States theatrical showing). D/Sc: Dale Kutzera. RT: 78 min. Cast: Patrick Muldoon, Elizabeth Ann Bennett, Mackenzie Astin, John Rixey Moore, Eric Jungman, Clive Van Owen. Not Rated.

Delta Farce. Lions Gate. Rl: 5/11/2007. D: C.B. Harding. Sc: Bear Adelman, Tom Sullivan. RT: 90 min. Cast: Larry the Cable Guy, Bill Engvall, DJ Qualls, Keith David, Danny Trejo, Marisol Nichols, Christina Moore, Lisa Lampanelli, Lane Smith, Glenn Morshower, Parker Goris, Ed O'Ross, Bill Doyle, Alejandro Patino, Luis Chávez, Nicholas Guilak, Albert Santos, Emilio Rivera, Tony Perez, Danielle Hartnett, Carlos Moreno Jr., Jeff Dunham, Joseph Nunez, Esteban Cueto, Craig Susser, Matt Riedy, Amy Powell. Color. Rated PG-13.

Major Movie Star. BenderSpink-DiNovi-Emmett/

Furla-Family Room-Gerber-Grand Army Entertainment-Major Prod.-Millenium-Papa Joe Films (no American theatrical distributor has picked up this film as of 2012; released in Russia by Top Film). Rl: 10/8/2008 (Russian theatrical premiere). D: Steve Miner. Sc: April Blair, Kelly Bowe. St: April Blair. RT: 98 min. Jessica Simpson, Vivica A. Fox, Steve Guttenberg, Aimee Garcia, Olesya Rulin, Keiko Agena, Jill Marie Jones, Ryan Sypek, Cheri Oteri, Gary Grubbs, Bryce Johns, Floriana Tullio, Katie Chonacas, Andy Milonakis, Jennifer Paige Finley, Harley Pasternak, Lara Grice, Trevor Schuldt, Marco St. John, Drew Waters, Kurt Fuller. Color; Super 35. Rated PG-13.

The Men Who Stare at Goats. BBC/Smokehouse/Westgate/Winchester Capital Partners/Overture. Rl: 9/25/2009 (Austin Film Festival); 11/6/2009 (theatrical release). D: Grant Heslov. Sc: Peter Straughan. St: Jon Ronson (book). RT: 94 min. Cast: George Clooney, Ewan McGregor, Jeff Bridges, Kevin Spacey, Stephen Lang, Robert Patrick, Waleed Zuaiter, Stephen Root, Glenn Morshower, Nick Offerman, Tim Griffin, Rebecca Mader, Jacob Browne, Todd Latourrette, Brad Grunberg, Matt Newton, Robert Curtis Brown, Hirach Titizian, Shafik N. Bahou, Sean Curley, Morse Bicknell, Kevin Wiggis, JJ Raschel, Arron Shiver, Jaime Margarida, William Sterchi. Color; Panavision. Rated R.

Bibliography

Books

Abbott, George. *"Mister Abbott."* New York: Random House, 1963.
Agee, James. *Agee on Film: Volume One.* New York: Putnam, 1958.
Allardice, James Burns. *At War with the Army: A Farce-Comedy in Three Acts.* New York: Samuel French, 1948.
Allon, Yoram, Del Cullen and Hannah Patterson, editors. *Contemporary North American Film Directors: A Wallflower Critical Guide, 2d ed.* London, New York: Wallflower, 2002.
Anderson, Hesper. *South Mountain Road: A Daughter's Journey of Discovery.* New York: Simon & Schuster, 2000.
Armstrong, Richard. *Billy Wilder, American Film Realist.* Jefferson, NC: McFarland, 2004.
Bakish, David. *Jimmy Durante: His Show Business Career, with an Annotated Filmography and Discography.* Jefferson, NC: McFarland, 2007.
Basinger, Jeanine. *The Star Machine.* New York: Knopf, 2007.
Beck, Jerry, and Will Friedwald. *Looney Tunes and Merrie Melodies: A Complete Guide to the Warner Bros. Cartoons.* New York: Henry Holt, 1989.
Berg, A. Scott. *Goldwyn: A Biography.* New York: Knopf, 1989.
Blesh, Rudy. *Keaton.* New York: Macmillan, 1966.
Borgnine, Ernest. *Ernie: The Autobiography.* New York: Citadel, 2008.
Brando, Anna Kashfi, and E.P. Stein. *Brando for Breakfast.* New York: Crown, 1979.
Brando, Marlon. *Brando: Songs My Mother Taught Me.* New York: Random House, 1996.
Brinkley, William. *Don't Go Near the Water.* New York: Random House, 1956.
Brownlow, Kevin. *The Parade's Gone By.* New York: Knopf, 1968.
_____. *The War, the West and the Wilderness.* New York: Knopf, 1979.
Bruskin, David N. *Behind the Three Stooges: The White Brothers.* Los Angeles: Directors Guild of America, 1993.
Bryant, Roger. *William Powell: The Life and Films.* Jefferson, NC: McFarland, 2006.
Budahn, P.J. *What to Expect in the Military: A Practical Guide for Young People, Parents, and Counselors.* Westport, CT: Greenwood Press, 2000.
Cagney, James. *Cagney by Cagney.* New York: Doubleday, 1976.
Campbell, Bruce. *If Chins Could Kill: Confessions of a B-Movie Actor.* New York: Thomas Dunne-St. Martin's Press, 2001.
Cannon, Lou. *President Reagan: The Role of a Lifetime.* New York: Simon & Schuster, 1991.
Carey, Harry, Jr. *Company of Heroes: My Life as an Actor in the John Ford Stock Company.* Metuchen, NJ: Scarecrow Press, 1994.
Chandler, Charlotte. *Nobody's Perfect: Billy Wilder, a Personal Biography.* New York: Simon & Schuster, 2002.
Coghlan, Frank Jr. *They Still Call Me Junior: Autobiography of a Child Star; with a Filmography.* Jefferson, NC: McFarland, 1993.
Cullen, Frank, Florence Hackman and Donald McNeilly. *Vaudeville, Old and New: An Encyclopedia of Variety Performers in America.* New York: Routledge, 2007
Curtis, Tony. *American Prince: A Memoir.* New York: Harmony Books, 2008.
Davis, Ronald L. *Words Into Images: Screenwriters on the Hollywood System.* Jackson: University of Mississippi Press, 2007.
DeBauche, Leslie Midkiff. *Reel Patriotism: The Movies and World War I.* Madison: University of Wisconsin Press, 1997.
DePastro, Todd. *Bill Mauldin: A Life Up Front.* New York: W.W. Norton, 2008.
Deschner, Donald. *The Films of Spencer Tracy.* New York: Citadel, 1968.
Dick, Bernard F. *Forever Mame: The Life of Rosalind Russell.* Jackson: University of Mississippi Press, 2006.
_____. *The Star-Spangled Screen: The American World War II Film.* Lexington: University Press of Kentucky, 1985.
Dickens, Homer. *The Films of Gary Cooper.* Secaucus, NJ: Citadel, 1970.
_____. *The Films of James Cagney.* Secaucus, NJ: Citadel, 1972.
Doherty, Thomas. *Pre-Code Hollywood: Sex, Immorality, and Insurrection in the American Cinema, 1930–1934.* New York: Columbia University Press, 1999.

Dooley, Roger. *From Scarface to Scarlet: American Films in the 1930s*. New York: Harcourt, Brace Jovanovich, 1981.

Duchovnay, Gerald, ed. *Film Voices: Interviews from Post Script*. Albany: State University of New York Press, 2004.

Dunaway, Faye, with Betsy Sharkey. *Looking for Gatsby: My Life*. New York: Simon & Schuster, 1995.

Dunigan, James F., and Albert A. Nofi. *Dirty Little Secrets of the Vietnam War*. New York: Thomas Dunne, 1999.

Dixon, Wheeler Winston. *The Early Film Criticism of François Truffaut*, with translations by Ruth Cassel Hoffman, Sonja Kropp, and Brigitte Formentin-Humbert. Bloomington: Indiana University Press, 1993.

Ebert, Roger, ed. *Roger Ebert's Book on Film*. New York: W.W. Norton, 1997.

Emery, Robert J. *The Directors, Take One*. New York: Allworth Press, 2002.

Ephron, Nora. *Wallflower at the Orgy*. New York: Viking Press, 1970.

Everson, William K. *The Bad Guys*. New York: Citadel, 1964.

Ewen, David. *Complete Book of the American Musical Theater*. New York: Henry Holt, 1959.

Eyman, Scott. *The Speed of Sound: Hollywood and the Talkie Revolution*. New York: Simon & Schuster, 1997.

Fantle, David, and Tom Johnson. *Reel to Reel: 25 Years of Celebrity Interviews from Vaudeville to Movies to TV*. Oregon, WI: Badger Books, 2004.

Fonda, Henry, and Howard Teichmann. *Fonda: My Life*. New York: New American Library, 1981.

Franklin, Joe, and William K. Everson, research assistant. *Classics of the Silent Screen*. New York: Citadel, 1959.

Furmanek, Bob, and Ron Palumbo. *Abbott and Costello in the Movies*. New York: Perigee Books, 1991.

Fyne, Robert. *Hollywood Propaganda of World War 2*. Metuchen, NJ: Scarecrow Press, 1994.

Gallagher, Tag. *John Ford: The Man and His Films*. Berkeley: University of California Press, 1986.

Gehring, Wes D. *Joe E. Brown: Film Comedian and Baseball Buffoon*. Jefferson, NC: McFarland, 2006.

Gemünden, Gerd. *A Foreign Affair: Billy Wilder's American Films*. New York: Berghan Books, 2008.

Gilmour, David. *The Film Club*. New York: Twelve, 2008.

Ginibre, Jean-Louis. *Ladies or Gentlemen; A Pictorial History of Male Cross-Dressing in the Movies*. New York: Filipachi, 2005.

Giroux, Henry A. *Disturbing Pleasures: Learning Popular Culture*. New York: Routledge, 1994.

Godard, Jean-Luc. *Godard on Godard: Critical Writings*. Edited by Jean Narboni and Tom Milnes. New York: Viking, 1972.

Goldberg, Lee. *Unsold Television Pilots: 1955 through 1989*. Jefferson, NC: McFarland, 1990.

Goldstein, Malcolm. *George S. Kaufman: His Life, His Theater*. New York: Oxford University Press, 1979.

Gordon, Ruth. *My Side*. New York: Harper & Row, 1976.

Goulart, Ron, ed. *The Encyclopedia of American Comics: From 1897 to the Present*. New York: Facts on File, 1990.

Hagman, Larry, with Todd Gold. *Hello Darlin': Tall (and Absolutely True) Tales About My Life*. New York: Simon & Schuster, 2001.

Hargrove, Marion. *See Here Private Hargrove*. Foreword by Maxwell Anderson. New York: Henry Holt, 1942.

Harris, Mark. *Pictures at a Revolution: Five Movies and the Birth of the New Hollywood*. New York: Penguin Books, 2008.

Hayde, Michael. *My Name's Friday: The Unauthorized But True Story of Jack Webb*. Foreword by Harry Morgan. Nashville: Cumberland House, 2001.

Hayes, David, and Brent Walker. *The Films of the Bowery Boys*. Secaucus, NJ: Citadel, 1984.

Heggen, Thomas. *Mister Roberts*. Illustrated by Samuel Hanks Bryant. Boston: Houghton Mifflin, 1946.

_____, and Joshua Logan. *Mister Roberts: A Play in Two Acts*. New York: Dramatists Play Service, 1948.

Heil, Douglas. *Prime-Time Authorship: Works About and by Three TV Dramatists (The Television Series)*. New York: Syracuse University Press, 2002.

Helfer, Ralph. *The Beauty of the Beasts: Tales of Hollywood's Wild Animal Stars*. New York: St. Martin's, 1990.

Heller, Joseph. *Catch as Catch Can: The Collected Stories and Other Writings*. Edited by Matthew J. Bruccoli and Park Buckner. New York: Simon & Schuster, 2003.

_____. *Catch-22*. New York: Simon & Schuster, 1961.

_____, and Adam J. Sorkin. *Conversations with Joseph Heller*. Jackson: University Press of Mississippi, 1993.

Henry, Ken, and Don Keith. *Gallant Lady: A Biography of the USS Archerfish*. New York: Forge, 2004.

Heston, Charlton. *The Actor's Life: Journals, 1956–1976*. Edited by Hollis Alpert. New York: Dutton, 1978.

Higham, Charles, and Joel Greenberg. *The Celluloid Muse: Hollywood Directors Speak*. London: Angus & Robertson, 1969.

Hill, Lee. *A Grand Guy: The Art and Life of Terry Southern*. New York: HarperCollins, 2001.

Hirschhorn, Clive. *The Columbia Story*. New York: Crown, 1990.

Hooker, Richard [H. Richard Hornberger]. *MASH: A Novel About Three Army Doctors*. New York: William Morrow, 1968.

Hopp, Glenn, and Paul Duncan. *Billy Wilder*. New York: Taschen, 2001.

Horn, Maurice, ed. *100 Years of American Newspaper Comics: An Illustrated Encyclopedia*. New York: Gramercy Books, 1996.

Horton, Andrew. *Ernie Kovacs and Early TV Comedy: Nothing in Moderation*. Austin: University of Texas Press, 2010.

Huie, William Bradford. *The Americanization of Emily*. New York: Dutton, 1959.

Hyman, Mac. *No Time for Sergeants*. New York: Random House, 1954.

Jackson, Carlton. *Picking Up the Tab: The Life and Movies of Martin Ritt*. Bowling Green, OH: Bowling Green State University Popular Press, 1994.

Jessel, George. *So Help Me: The Autobiography of George Jessel*. Foreword by William Saroyan. New York: Random House, 1953.

Jewell, Richard B., with Vernon Harbin. *The RKO Story*. New York: Arlington House, 1982.

Kael, Pauline. *The Citizen Kane Book*. With the shooting script by Herman J. Mankiewicz and Orson Wells. Boston: Little, Brown, 1971.

_____. *Kiss Kiss Bang Bang*. Boston: Little, Brown, 1968.

Kanfer, Stefan. *Somebody: The Reckless Life and Remarkable Career of Marlon Brando*. New York: Knopf, 2008.

Kapsis, Robert E., and Kathie Coblentz, eds. *Clint Eastwood: Interviews*. Jackson: University Press of Mississippi, 1999.

Kaufman, Stanley, and Bruce Hensell, eds. *American Film Criticism: From the Beginnings to Citizen Kane*. New York: Livewright, 1972.

Kerr, Walter. *The Silent Clowns*. New York: Knopf, 1975.

Knotts, Don, and Robert Metz. *Barney Fife and Other Characters I Have Known*. Foreword by Andy Griffith. New York: Berkeley Boulevard, 1999.

Kostilibas-Davis, James, and Myrna Loy. *Myrna Loy: Being and Becoming*. New York: Knopf, 1987.

Lahue, Kalton C., and Terry Brewer. *Kops and Custards: The Legend of the Keystone Films*. Norman: University of Oklahoma Press, 1968.

Lederer, William J. *All the Ships at Sea*. New York: William Sloane, 1950.

Lehman, Courtney, and Lisa S. Starke, eds. *Spectacular Shakespeare: Critical History and Popular Cinema*. Fairleigh Dickinson University Press, 2002.

Levin, Ira. *No Time for Sergeants: A Comedy in Two Acts*. Adapted from the novel by Mac Hyman. Included in *Best American Plays: Fourth Series, 1951–1957*; edited and with an introduction by John Gassner. New York: Crown, 1958.

Lewis, Jerry, and James Kaplan. *Dean & Me (A Love Story)*. New York: Doubleday, 2005.

Lewis, Robert. *Slings and Arrows: Theater in My Life*. New York: Applause Books, 1997.

LoBrutto, Vincent. *Stanley Kubrick: A Biography*. New York: Donald I. Fine, 1997.

Louvish, Simon. *The Man on the Flying Trapeze: The Life and Times of W.C. Fields*. New York: W.W. Norton, 1997.

Lynn, Kenneth Schuyler. *Charlie Chaplin and His Times*. New York: Simon & Schuster, 1997.

Lyons, Jeffrey. *Jeffrey Lyons' 100 Great Movies for Kids*. New York: Fireside Books, 1996.

Lupack, Barbara Tepa. *Take Two: Adapting the Contemporary American Novel to Film*. New York: Popular Press, 1994.

MacGillivray, Scott. *Laurel & Hardy: From the Forties Forward*. Foreword by Steve Allen. Lanham, MD: Vestige Press, 1998.

Maltin, Leonard. *The Great Movie Shorts*. Foreword by Pete Smith. New York: Crown, 1972.

_____. *The Disney Films*. New York: Crown, 1973.

_____. *Movie Comedy Teams*, rev. ed. Foreword by Billy Gilbert. New York: New American Library, 1985.

_____. *Of Mice and Magic: A History of American Animation*, rev. ed. New York: New American Library, 1987.

_____. *Hollywood: The Movie Factory*. New York: Popular Library, 1976.

_____, and Richard W. Bann. *The Little Rascals: The Life and Times of Our Gang*. New York: Crown, 1992.

Marquand, John P. *Melville Goodwin, U.S.A.* New York: Little, Brown, 1952.

Martin, Len D. *The Republic Pictures Checklist: Features, Serials, Cartoons, Short Subjects and Training Films of Republic Pictures Corporation, 1935–1959*. Jefferson NC: McFarland, 1998.

Mauldin, Bill. *The Brass Ring*. New York: W.W. Norton, 1971.

McBride, Joseph. *Whatever Happened to Orson Welles? A Portrait of an Independent Career*. Lexington: University Press of Kentucky, 2006.

McCall, Douglas L. *Film Cartoons: A Guide to 20th Century American Animated Features and Shorts*. Jefferson, NC: McFarland, 1998.

McCarthy, Todd. *Howard Hawks: The Grey Fox of Hollywood*. New York: Grove Press, 1997.

McDougal, Dennis. *Five Easy Decades: How Jack Nicholson Became the Biggest Movie Star in Modern Times*. Hoboken, NJ: John Wiley & Sons, 2008.

McGilligan, Patrick. *Robert Altman: Jumping Off the Cliff: A Biography of the Great American Director*. New York: St. Martin's, 1989.

_____, ed. *Backstory 3: Interviews with Screenwriters of the 1960s*. Berkeley: University of California Press, 1997.

McGowan, Kenneth, and Harold Clurman, eds. *Famous American Plays of the 1920s and 1930s*. Garden City, NY: Fireside Theater. 1988.

McKay, James. *Dana Andrews: The Face of Noir*. Jefferson, NC: McFarland, 2010.

Meade, Marion. *Buster Keaton: Cut to the Chase*. New York: HarperCollins, 1995.

Michaud, Michael Gregg. *Sal Mineo: A Biography*. New York: Crown, 2010.

Miller, Don. *B Movies*. New York: Curtis Books, 1973.

Mitchell, Glenn. *A-Z of Silent Film Comedy: An Illustrated Companion*. London: B.T. Batsford, 1998.

_____. *The Chaplin Encyclopedia*. London: B.T. Batsford, 1997.

Mitgang, Herbert. *Newsmen in Khaki: Tales of a World War II Soldier Correspondent.* Lanham, MD: Taylor Trade. 2004.

Morris, Donald R. *Warm Bodies.* Illustrated by Frederick E. Banbery. New York: Simon & Schuster, 1957.

Mulholland, Jim. *The Abbott and Costello Book.* New York: Popular Library, 1975.

Munden, Kenneth W., exec. ed. *The American Film Institute Catalog of Motion Pictures Produced in the United States.* Three volumes. BerkeleyUniversity of California Press, 1971–1999.

Neibaur, James L. *The Fall of Buster Keaton: His Films for M-G-M, Educational Pictures, and Columbia.* Lanham, MD: Scarecrow Press, 2010.

Nickels, Cameron C. *Civil War Humor.* Jackson: University Press of Mississippi, 2010.

Nollen, Scott Allen. *Abbott and Costello on the Home Front: A Critical Study of the Wartime Films.* Foreword by Chris Costello. Jefferson, NC: McFarland, 2009.

O'Connor, Robert. *Buffalo Soldiers.* New York: Knopf, 1993.

Okuda, Ted. *Grand National, Producers Releasing Corporation, and Screen Guild/Lippert: Complete Filmographies with Studio Histories.* Jefferson, NC: McFarland, 1989

_____. *The Monogram Checklist: The Films of Monogram Pictures Corporation, 1931–1952.* Jefferson, NC: McFarland, 1987.

Osborne, Hubert. *Shore Leave: A Sea-goin' Comedy in Three Acts.* New York: Samuel French, 1933.

Parish, James Robert. *Fiasco: A History of Hollywood's Iconic Flops.* New York: John Wiley and Sons, 2006.

_____. *The Great Movie Series.* New York: A. S. Barnes, 1971.

_____, William T. Leonard, Gregory W. Mank, and Charles Hoyt. *The Funsters.* New York: Arlington House, 1979.

Patrick, John. *Teahouse of the August Moon: A Comedy in Three Acts.* Adapted from the novel by Vern J. Sneider. Included in *Best Plays of 1953–54*; edited by Louis Kronenberger. New York: Dodd, 1954.

Phillips, Gene D. *Some Like It Wilder: The Life and Controversial Films of Billy Wilder.* Lexington: University Press of Kentucky, 2010.

Pomerance, Murray, ed. *Enfant Terrible! Jerry Lewis in American Film.* New York University Press, 2002.

Portnoy, Kenneth. *Screen Adaptations: A Scriptwriting Handbook.* Boston: Focal Press, 1998.

Potts, Stephen W. *From Here to Absurdity: The Moral Battlefields of Joseph Heller.* San Bernardino, CA: Borgo Press, 1982.

Pratt, Theodore. *Mr. Limpet.* Illustrated by Garrett Price. New York: Knopf, 1942.

Quinlan, David. *The Illustrated Guide to Film Directors.* New York: Rowman & Littlefield, 1983.

Quirk, Lawrence J. *Bob Hope: The Road Well-Travelled.* New York: Applause Books, 1998.

_____. *The Films of Paul Newman.* Secaucus, NJ: Citadel, 1971.

Reid, John. *Cinemascope Two: Twentieth Century–Fox.* Lulu.com (self-published), 2010.

_____. *Movie Mystery and Suspense.* Lulu.com (self-published), 2006.

Reilly, Adam. *Harold Lloyd: The King of Daredevil Comedy.* New York: Collier, 1977.

Rinehart, Mary Roberts. *23½ Hours' Leave.* New York: George H. Doran, 1918.

Robertson, James C. *The Casablanca Man: The Cinema of Michael Curtiz.* New York: Routledge, 1993.

Robb, David L. *Operation Hollywood: How the Pentagon Shapes and Censors the Movies.* Amherst, NY: Prometheus, 2004.

Ronson, Jon. *The Men Who Stare at Goats.* New York: Simon & Schuster, 2004.

Rosenberg, Bernard, and Harry Silverstein. *The Real Tinsel.* New York: Macmillan, 1970.

Sandford, Christopher. *McQueen: The Biography.* New York: Taylor Trade, 2003.

Sarris, Andrew. *American Cinema: Directors and Directions, 1929–1968.* New York: Dutton, 1968.

Schaefer, Jack. *Company of Cowards.* Boston: Houghton Mifflin, 1957.

Schelly, William. *Harry Langdon: His Life and Films.* Metuchen, NJ: Scarecrow, 1982.

Shales, Tom, et al. *The American Film Heritage.* Washington, D.C.: Acropolis Books, 1972.

Sheward, David. *It's a Hit! The Back Stage Book of Longest-Running Broadway Shows: 1884 to the Present.* New York: Back Stage Books, 1994.

Shulman, Max. *Rally Round the Flag, Boys!* Garden City, NY: Doubleday, 1957.

Sikov, Ed. *Mr. Strangelove: A Biography of Peter Sellers.* New York: Hyperion, 2002.

Silverman, Stephen M. *Dancing on the Ceiling: Stanley Donen and His Movies.* New York: Knopf, 1996.

Silvers, Phil, with Robert Saffron. *The Laugh Is on Me: The Phil Silvers Story.* Englewood Cliffs, NJ: Prentice-Hall, 1973.

Simon, Neil. *Biloxi Blues.* New York: Random House, 1985.

Skretvedt, Randy. *Laurel and Hardy: The Magic Behind the Movies.* Foreword by Steve Allen. Beverly Hills: Moonstone Press, 1987.

Slide, Anthony. *Eccentrics of Comedy.* Lanham, MD: Scarecrow, 1998.

Slifkin, Irv. *Videohound's Groovy Movies: Far-Out Films of the Psychedelic Era.* Canton, MI: Visible Ink Press, 2004.

Sneider, Vern. *The Teahouse of the August Moon.* New York: Putnam, 1951.

Stern, David. *Francis.* Illustrated by Garrett Price. New York: Farrar, Strauss, 1946.

Suid, Lawrence H. *Guts and Glory: The Making of the American Military Image in Film.* Lexington: University Press of Kentucky, 2002.

Sylbert, Richard, and Townsend. *Designing Movies: Portrait of a Hollywood Artist.* New York: Praeger, 2006.

Thomey, Ted. *The Glorious Decade.* New York: Ace Books, 1971.

Thompson, Frank. *Lost Films: Important Movies That Disappeared.* Secaucus, NJ: Citadel, 1996.

Toohey, John L. *A History of the Pulitzer Prize Plays.* New York: Citadel, 1967.

Turse, Nick. *The Complex: How the Military Invades Our Everyday Lives.* New York: Metropolitan Books, 2008.

Van Gelder, Peter. *That's Hollywood: A Behind-the-Scenes Look at 60 of the Greatest Films of All Time.* New York: HarperPerennial, 1990.

Ward, Richard Lewis. *A History of the Hal Roach Studios.* Carbondale: Southern Illinois University Press, 2006.

Wasson, Sam. *A Splurch in the Kisser: The Movies of Blake Edwards.* Middletown, CT: Wesleyan University Press, 2009.

Watz, Edward. *Wheeler & Woolsey: The Vaudeville Comic Duo and Their Films, 1929-1937.* Foreword by Dorothy Lee. Jefferson, NC: McFarland, 1996.

Weaver, Tom. *Double Creature Feature Attack: A Monster Merger of Two More Volumes of Classic Interviews.* Jefferson, NC: McFarland, 2003.

Widener, Don. *Lemmon: A Biography.* New York: Macmillan, 1975.

Wilk, Max. *The Wit and Wisdom of Hollywood: From the Squaw Man to the Hatchet Man.* New York: Atheneum, 1971.

Williams, Gurney. *I Meet Such People!* New York: Farrar, Strauss, 1946.

Wilson, Staci Layne. *Animal Movies Guide.* Rancho Palos Verdes, CA: Running Free Press, 2007.

Wissolik, Richard Davis, and Katie Killen, *They Say There Was a War.* Latrobe, PA: Saint Vincent College Center for North Appalachian Studies, 2005.

Witt, Linda. *A Defense Weapon Known to Be of Value: Servicewomen of the Korean War Era.* Hanover, NH: University Press of New England, 2005.

Zadja, Joseph I. *Education and Society.* Albert Park, Australia: James Nicholas, 2001.

Zuckoff, Mitchell. *Robert Altman: The Oral Biography.* New York: Borzoi Books, 2009.

Magazine and Newspaper Articles

Frequently Reference Sources

Animato
Billboard
Boys' Life
Chicago Sun-Times
Chicago Tribune
Deseret News
Entertainment Weekly
Film Bulletin
Film Daily
Films in Review
Filmfax
Jet
Life
Los Angeles Times
Milwaukee Journal-Sentinel (two separate newspapers prior to 1995)
Motion Picture Magazine
New York
New York Herald-Tribune
New York Times
People
Pittsburgh Post-Gazette
Pittsburgh Press
The Onion
San Francisco Chronicle
Time
TV Guide
USA Today
Variety
Village Voice
Washington Post

Print Articles, Interviews and Short Stories

Bennett, Ray. "*The Extraordinary Seaman*: Chopping Spoils Satirical Film." *Windsor* [Ont.] *Star,* April 10, 1970.

Bentley, Rick. Article on *Stripes. Kentucky New Era,* December 27, 1980.

Boyle, Hal. Interview with Bob Hope. Associated Press, May 9, 1968

Bryer, Jackson. "Interview with Neil Simon." *Studies in America 1945-Present,* Vol 6. No. 2, 1991.

Burns, Diana Hubbard. Interview with Joshua Logan. *Palm Beach* [FL] *Post,* February 10, 1980.

Carlson, Herbert. "Big Fella Wash-Wash." *Argosy,* July 1956.

Coons, Robbin. Interview with Wally Brown and Alan Carney. "Hollywood Sights and Sounds," nationally syndicated newspaper column, June 30, 1943.

Eaton, Marcia. "A Strange Kind of Sadness," *Journal of Aesthetics and Art Criticism* #41,1982.

Everly, Steve. "Era of *Dr. Strangelove* Produced a Recently Uneartherd Air Force Film." McClatchy Newspapers, January 25, 2010.

Franklin, Richard. Article on *The Extraordinary Seaman. The Age* (Sydney, Australia), March 11, 1969.

Hazard, John W. "The Flying Teakettle." *The New Yorker,* January 21, 1950.

Heffernan, Harold. Article on "Soldier in the Rain." *Virgin Island Daily News,* Sept. 24,1963.

Interview with Ivan Reitman. Associated Press, July 19, 1981.

Johnson, Erskine. Interview with Jack Lemmon. "Hollywood Today," nationally syndicated column, May 9, 1960.

Kleiner, Dick. Interview with Hy Averback. "Hollywood Correspondent," nationally syndicated column, May 28, 1969.

Kulp, Michael. Review of *Mad Magazine Presents Up*

the Academy. Penn State University *Daily Collegian*, June 20, 1980.
Lederer, William J. "We Kept Our Home the Navy Way." *This Week*, Sept. 12, 1948.
McGrear, Chris. "How the US Took On *Dr. Strangelove* and Tried to Make Americans Love the Bomb." *The Manchester Guardian*, February 11, 2010.
"Motion Picture News and Views." Articles on *Behind the Front*. Norwalk [CT] *Hour*, Sept. 12, 1925.
"Obituary: David Stern III." Lafayette [LA] *Daily Advertiser*, November 26, 2003.
Parsons, Louella. Item about *A Southern Yankee*. Hearst Newspapers, Dec. 24 1947.
Sheffield, Skip. Interview with Goldie Hawn. *Boca Raton* [FL] *Daily News*, Oct. 23,1980.

Internet Sources

Frequently Referenced Websites

Allmovie (previously All Movie Guide) http://www.allrovi.com/movies
The A.V. Club http://www.avclub.com
Bruce Bairnsfather and Old Bill http://www.olebill.zoomshare.com
City of Monroe [Michigan] Website http://www.ci.monroe.mi.us
Civil War Humor http://home.valstar.net/~jcraig/humor.htm
A Collection of Civil War Humor http://wesclark.com/jw/cw_humor.html
DVD Savant http://www.dvdtalk.com/dvdsavant/
The Drudge Report http://drudgereport.com
Film in America http://www.filminamerica.com
The General http://www.angelfire.com/indie/busterkeaton/BKGeneral.html
Google News Archive Search http://news.google.com/archivesearch
Greenbriar Picture Show http://greenbriarpictureshows.blogspot.com
Hollywood Heyday http://hollywoodheyday.blogspot.com
Huffington Post http://hollywoodheyday.blogspot.com
Internet Archive http://www.archive.org
Internet Broadway Database http://www.ibdb.com/index.php
Internet Movie Database http://www.imdb.com
ISSUU http://issuu.com
Key West History http://www.keywesttravelguide.com/key-west-history.html
The Kubrick Site http://www.visual-memory.co.uk/amk/
Maritime Database http://www.maritime-database.com
moviediva.com http://www.moviediva.com
NavSource Photo Archives http://www.navsource.org/archives/12/15idx.htm
Out of Step: Military Jokes and Military Humor Blog http://www.miljokes.com
RvB's AfterImages cinematical.com
Silents are Golden http://www.silentsaregolden.com
Snopes.com http://www.snopes.com
Steve McQueen Online http://www.mcqueenonline.com
Third Banana http://thirdbanana.blogspot.com
Wikipedia. http://www.wikipedia.org
William K. Everson Collection http://www.nyu.edu/projects/wke/notes.htm

Internet Articles and Interviews

Barthold, Jim. "The Real Life of Adrian Cronauer." *Urgent Communications*, March 1, 2005. http://urgentcomm.com/mag/radio_real_life_adrian/
Cookson, Christopher. "Echo." *Marlborough Online*, August 17, 2003. http://www.marlboroughonline.co.nz/index.mvc?ArticleID=51
Cunningham, Doug. "An Interview with Dale Kutzera." *Cineaste*, Vol. 33, no. 4, Fall 2008. http://www.cineaste.com/an-interview-with-dale-kutzera.htm
Heckman, Hugh M. "USS Virgo (AKA-20): The Wacky Ship of Mr. Roberts." *Sea Classics*, January 1979. http://www.uss-virgo.com/wacky.htm
Holman, Curt. "Wasted Warriors: *Buffalo Soldiers* Director Marches into Controversy." *Creative Loafing* [Atlanta] May 12, 2004. http://clatl.com/atlanta/wasted-warriors/Content?oid=1243044
Interview with William Peter Blatty. *Screenwriters on Film*, Jan. 10, 1994. http://www.youtube.com/watch?v=EvKJCj6DM7g
Interview with Larry the Cable Guy. *On the Record*, Fox News Channel, May 10, 2007. http://www.foxnews.com/story/0,2933,271292,00.html
"Jon Ronson Interview: Questions & Answers Session." Rinf.com, January 14, 2007. http://www.rinf.com/articles/jon-ronson-q-a.html
Laurier, Joanne. "*The Men Who Stare at Goats*: US Military Goes for the Paranormal." World Socialist website, Nov. 26, 2009. http://www.wsws.org/articles/2009/nov2009/goat-n26.shtml
Lindley, Dan. "Study Guide to Kubrick's *Dr. Strangelove*." http://www.nd.edu/~dlindley/handouts/strangelovenotes.html
Newley, Patrick. "Obituary: Bert Bernard." *The Stage*, May 10, 2004. http://www.thestage.co.uk/features/obituaries/feature.php/2064/bert-bernard
Twatio, Bill. "Bootlickers and Bureaucrats: Hollywood and Wartime Censors During the War Years." *Esprit de Corps*, December 1, 2004; reprinted at the Free Library website. http://www.thefreelibrary.com/Bootlickers+%26+bureaucrats%3A+Hollywood's+wartime+censors%3A+during+the...-a0126387424

Index

Numbers in ***bold italics*** indicate pages with photographs.

Abbott, Bud 12, 31, 48, 56, 59, 67, 68, 69, 70, 71, 78, 90–91, ***91***, 92–94, ***94***, 95–96, 97, 98, 99, 100, 102, 104–105, 120, 153
Abbott, George 254, 255, 304, 305
Abbott and Costello in the Foreign Legion 105, 384
Abbott and Costello Meet Frankenstein 102, 120
ABC *see* American Broadcasting Company
About Face (Hal Roach, 1942) 109–110, 382
About Face (Warner Bros., 1952) 256, 385; *see also* *Brother Rat*
Abraham Lincoln 322
Abrahams, Jim 359, 360, 361, 362, 363; *see also* Z-A-Z
Abroad with Two Yanks 155–156, 383
Abu Ghraib 210
Ace in the Hole 371
Ackroyd, Jack 28
Adam, Ken 339
Adams, Jimmie 46, 85; *see also* Ranch Boys
Adams, Julie 122, 258, ***258***
Adams, Nick 164, 185, ***186***
Adamson, Harold 283
Adler, Buddy 309
Adlon, Pamela (aka Pamela Segall) 231
Adoree, Renee 46
Advance to the Rear (*Company of Cowards*) 328–330, ***330***, 331, 389
Adventures of a Rookie 13, 102–103, ***103***, 383
The Age 345
Agee, James 192, 300, 303
Agena, Keiko 273
Aim, Fire, Scoot 88
Air Raid Wardens 299, 383
Airplane! 359–360, 361, 362–363
Aitken, Spottiswoode 24
Aladdin's Lamp 371
Albee, Edward 347
Albert, Eddie 137, 174, 200, 254, 255, ***255***, 256
Albertson, Frank 254
Alberty, Karl-Otto 228
Alcoa Theater 73
Alda, Alan 344, 345
Aldridge, Kay 137
Aletter, Frank 164
Alexander, Frank *see* Ton of Fun

Alexander, Jason 234
Alexander, John 209
Alexander, Katherine 300
Aley, Albert 232
All Ashore 140–141, ***141***, 142, 216, 241, 386
All at Sea 38, 379
All Hands on Deck 15, 257, 296–297, 388
All Night Long 27
All Quiet on the Western Front 11, 358
All-Star Bond Rally 285
All the Queen's Men 283–284, 393
All the Ships at Sea 242; *see also* *McHale's Navy Joins the Air Force*
Allardice, James B. 67, 69
Allen, Barbara Jo (Vera Vague) 305
Allen, Fred 214
Allen, Gracie 191
Allen, Seth 348
Allen, Steve 185
Allen, Woody 197, 366
Allied Artists Corporation 113, 117, 118, 223, 224; *see also* Monogram Pictures
Allyson, June 215
Altman, Robert 352–355, 356, 367
Alvin Theater (New York City) 163, 185
Ameche, Don 312
American Broadcasting Company (ABC) 167, 182, 187, 188, 232
American Carol 367
American Forces Vietnam Network (AFVN) 331–332, 333
American-International Pictures 244
The Americanization of Emily: 1959 novel 341; 1964 film 341–342, ***343***, 389
Ames, Elsie 51
Anchor Films 31
Anchors Aweigh 139, 280
Anderson, Herbert 137
Anderson, John 84
Anderson, Maxwell 10, 146, 149, 189–190
Anderson, Richard 207
Andre, Nicolle 128
Andrews, Dana 64, 66, 139, 301
Andrews, James J. 318
Andrews, Julie 75, 342, ***343***
Andrews, Tige 163, 164, 218
Andrews Air Force Base 83

Andrews Sisters (Patty, Maxine and Laverne) 12, 90–91, ***91***, 92–93, 95, 102
The Andy Griffith Show 185, 187, 188, 280
Angelletti, Carlo 277
Angrim, Stefan 263
Anhalt, Edward 73
Animal House (*National Lampoon's Animal House*) 246, 261, 262
Annapolis Academy 253
Anybody's War 78, 379
The Apartment 3–4
"Apple Blossom Time" 92
Appleby, Dorothy 51
Arabian Tights 86
Aragon, Art 62
Arbuckle, Roscoe "Fatty" 25, 26, 79
Archer, John 240
USS *Archerfish* 203
Arden, Eve 60, 61, 244
Argosy magazine 204–205, 207, 208
Aristophanes 7
Arkin, Alan 347, ***347***
Arkin, David 353
Arlen, Richard 35, 155, 219–220
Arms, Russell 366
Armstrong, Robert 34
Army Daze 88
The Army-Navy Screen Magazine 373, 375
Arnold, Edward 299, 301
Arnold, Jack 357
Arnold, Tom 234, 236
Around the World in Eighty Days 153
Arthur, George K. 11, 37–38, 39, 53
Arthur, Jean 286, 301
As You Were 112, 385
Ashley, John 244
Askin, Leon 225, 227
Assante, Armand 272
Astaire, Fred 135
Astin, John 204
Astin, Mackenzie 366
Astor, Gertrude 136
Astor, Mary 42, ***43***, 305
At Ease 46
At War with the Army: 1949 play 67–68, 254; 1950 film 67–69, 70, 254, 384
Atkinson, Brooks 173
Atkinson, Michael 284
Atlantic Monthly 160
Atwood, Kim 353

Auberjonois, Rene 353, **354**
Aubrey, James 229
Aubrey, Jimmy 46
Avalon, Frankie 244–245, 352
Averback, Hy 312
Avery, Tex 369, 371
A.W.O.L. 369
Axelrod, George 309–310
Aykroyd, Dan 231
Ayres, Lew 33, 69, 136

Babbitt, Art 282
"Baby Burlesks" 89
Baby Wants a Bottleship 372–373
Bacall, Lauren 290, 291
Baccaloni, Salvatore 277
Bach, Barbara 262
Bacharach, Burt 73
Back at the Front (*Willie and Joe Back at the Front*) 131, 386
Back from the Front 87, 89
Backus, Jim 241, 291, 295, 329, 330
Bacon, Kevin 167
Bad Girl 52, 137
The Bad Guys 368
Badger, Clarence 316
Baer, Parley 124
Bailey, Raymond 185
Bailey, Richard 193
Bairnsfather, Bruce 28, 129
Baker, Art 326
Baker, Eddie 46
Baker, George 13, 71–72, 73
Baker, Henry 73
Balaban, Bob 349
USS *Balao* 203
Baldwin, Alan 128
Ballantine, Carl 233, 242
Balsam, Martin 348
Baltimore Sun 273
Banks, Monty 17
Baptism of Fire 366, 368
Barclay, Joan 104
Bari, Lynn 81, 122
Barkley, Charles 363
Barnes, Binnie 153
Barnett, Vince 76, 77
Barney and Friends 210, 212
Barney Google and Snuffy Smith 126–128
Barrat, Robert 58
Barré, Raoul 369
Barry, Gene 157
Barry, Phyllis 87
Barry, Wesley 31, 100
Barthelmess, Richard 134
Bartlett, Bennie 114, 116, 117
Barton, Charles 102
Bary, Jean 149
USS *Bashaw* 69
Basic Training 272–273, 392
Basinger, Jeanine 204
Bates, Barbara 141, **141**, 142
Batman (TV series) 302, 359
The Battle of Gettysburg 315
The Battle of Who Run 17, 314–315
Battleground 240
Battling Sisters 46
Bazlen, Brigid 222
Bean, Orson 163
Beatty, Ned 364, **365**

Beau Hunks 55
Beaudine, William 114, 115, 116
Beavers, Louise 322, 324, 327
Beck, Jerry 369
Beckley, Paul V. 218
Beery, Noah 107
Beery, Noah, Jr. 107, 108, 109
Beery, Wallace 11, 35–36, **36**, 37, 40, 53, 107
Beetle Bailey 376
Behind the Front 11, 35–36, **36**, 37, 40, 41, 378
Behrman, S.N. 180
Beich, Albert 269
Belasco, David 133, 134
Bell, Rodney 76
A Bell for Adano 169
Bellamy, Ralph 157
Beloin, Edmund 72, 73
Benaderat, Bea 375
Bendix, William 44, 80–81, 130, 155, 156
Benedict, Billy 113, 114, **115**, 116
Benitez, Angelica 86
Benjamin, Dick 348
Bennett, Alma 32
Bennett, Bruce 101
Bennett, Elizabeth Ann 366
Bennett, Ray 344, 345, 346
Bentham, Josephine 299
Berenger, Tom 143
Bergen, Polly 68
Berkes, Johnny 59
Berle, Milton 214
Berlin, Irving 135
Berlinger, Warren 297
Bernard, Felix 100
Bernard Brothers (George and Bert) 74–76
Bernds, Edward 117, 118
Bernstein, Leonard 140
Berry, Chuck 231
Berti, Marina 131
Bessell, Ted 242
Besser, Joe 77, 86, 88; *see also* Three Stooges
Best, Willie 98
Best Defense 245, 391–392
The Best Years of Our Lives 301, 304
The Better 'Ole (1926 film) 11, 28–29, **29**, 30, 31, 52, 58, 378
The Better 'Ole: The Romance of Old Bill (play) 28
Bevan, Billy 32, 45, 265
Bevan, Donald 183
Biddle, Clement 356
"Big Fella Wash-Wash" 204–205; see also *The Wackiest Ship in the Army?* (film)
The Big Parade 3, 10–11, 21, 42, 46, 98, 146, 358
The Big Pie-Raid 47
Bill, Tony 223
Billboard 68, 117, 131, 184, 185
Billings, George 316
Biloxi Blues: 1985 play 14, 189, 194–196; 1988 film 194, 195, **195**, 196–198, 392
Biltmore Theater (New York City) 254

Binder, Henry 369
Binyon, Claude 310
Bioscope 321
Birkin, David 283
Bishop, Joey 187
Bissell, Whit 330
Black-Foxe Academy 257
Blackburn, William 180, 188
Blake, Robert (aka Mickey Gubitosi) 88
Blanc, Mel 373
Blanchard, Mari 131
Blatty, William Peter 225–226
Bleifer, John 114
The Blitz Wolf 371
The Blitzkiss 89
Block-Heads 54
Blocker, Dan 338
Blonde Ambition 273
Blondell, Joan **57**, 58, 137, 329, 330
"Blondie" film series 106, 126, 139
Blondie's Hero 106
Blore, Eric 5
Blue, Monte 298
Blum, Len 246
Blunder Below 372
Blunder Boys 88
Blyden, Larry 292
Blystone, John G. 153
Blystone, Stanley 46, 87
Boardman, True 18
Boasberg, Al 49
Bogart, Humphrey 60, 151, 155, 290, 291, 366
Boland, Mary 59
Bolger, Ray 135, 242
The Bond 18
Bond, Ward 25, 164
Bonnie Scotland 55–56, 380
Boobs in Arms **86**, 87, 88
Booby Traps 374
"Boogie Woogie Bugle Boy" 92
Boom Boom 369
Boone, Pat 256, 294, 296, 297
Booth Theater (New York City) 67
Borg, Veda Ann 110, 266
Borgnine, Ernest 232, 233, 234, 235, **235**, 236, 242, 288, 312
Borzage, Danny 164
Bosko the Doughboy 369, **370**
Bosley, Tom 277, **278**
Boston Globe 245
Boteler, Wade 31
The Bottletop Affair 241; see also *The Horizontal Lieutenant*
Bow, Clara 33
Bowen, Roger 353
Bowers, Charles 369
Bowers, William 14, 103, 217–219, 221, 328
Bowery Batallion 114, 115, 116, 384–385
Bowery Boys 105, 113–119, 183
U.S.S. *Bowfin* Submarine Museum and Park 201
Bowman, Lee 92, 93, 301
Box Office magazine 367
Boyd, William 42, 43, **43**, 44
Boyd, William "Stage" 44, 148
Boyer, Charles 277
Boylan, Malcolm Stuart 148

Boyle, Hal 63
Boys' Life 126
Bracken, Eddie 96, **97**, 98, 256, 300
Brackett, Charles 285
Bradley, Gen. Omar 268
Brancato, Lillo, Jr. 249, **250**
Brando, Jocelyn 163
Brando, Marlon 164, 173–174, **174**, 175–176, 288, 310
Bray Studios 47
Breen, Richard 177, 285
Brendel, El 89, 150, 151, 153
Brennan, Eileen 271, 272
Brennan, Wallis 9
Brennan, Walter 136, 187
Brezner, Larry 332
Brian, Mary 35, 138, 139
Brice, Monte 40, 316
Bridgeport [CT] *Sunday Herald* 80
Bridges, Jeff 210
Bridges, Lloyd 229, 360, 361
Bright Honor 253, 254
Brighton Beach Memoirs 195
Brill, Patti 102
Brinkley, William 14, 287
A Briny Boob 46
Brisson, Frederick 266
British Film Institute 339
Britton, Pamela 140
Broadway Bound 195
Broderick, Matthew 195, **195**, 196
Bromiley, Dorothy 156
Bronson, Charles 200
Brooks, Albert 271
Brooks, Leslie 137
Brooks, Louise 33, 34, 36
Brooks, Mel 81, 227, 359
Brooks, Phyllis 139
Brophy, Ed 48, 49
Brother Rat: 1936 play 67, 254–255; 1938 film 107, 255, **255**, 256–257, 263, 381
Brother Rat and a Baby 256
Brown, Joe E. 11, 49, 56–57, **57**, 58–59, 94, 99
Brown, Johnny Mack 56
Brown, Orlando 260
Brown, Phyllis George 247
Brown, Scott 84
Brown, Wally 13, 102–103, **103**, 104
Brown, Wendell 261, **262**
Browne, Bothwell 22, 23
Brownlee, Frank 85
Brownlow, Kevin 9, 18, 28, 319
Bruce, Carol 95
Bruckman, Clyde 318
Bruskin, David N. 358
Brusso, Pete 209, 210
Bryan, Jane 255
Bryant, Nana 259
The Bubble Factory 234
Buchman, Harold 304
Buchman, Sidney 303
Buck Privates (1928 silent film) 31, 91, 379
Buck Privates (1941 Abbott & Costello film) 12, 16, 31, 37, 56, 59, 75, 91, **91**, 92–94, 95, 96, 97, 98, 99, 100, 102, 104, 107, 120, 121, 153, 241, 381–382

Buck Privates Come Home 104–105, 384
Buckley, Floyd 184
Buckley, Hal 227
Budahn, P.J. 83
Bud's Recruit 9, 11
Buena Vista 82
Buffalo Soldiers: film 4, 236–239, 393; novel 236, 237–238
Bugs Bunny Nips the Nips 370
Bull, Peter 339
Bulletin of Atomic Scientists 338
Bullock, Dale Allen 161
Burdick, Eugene 340
Bureau of Censorship 299
Bureau of Motion Pictures 14, 153; *see also* Office of War Information
Burghoff, Gary 352
Burke, Paul 122
Burns, David 179
Burns, George 179, 187, 188, 191
Burnstein, Jim 247
Burr, William 341
Burrows, Abe 222
Burt Reynolds Theater (Florida) 163
Burton, George 46
Bush, George W. 210, 367, 368
Bussey, Sgt. Norma 267
Butterworth, William E. 352
Buttons, Red 218, 219, 307
By the Book see *Renaissance Man*
Byington, Spring **305**

Cactus Flower 271
Cagney, James 113, 139, 158, 164, 165, 166, 167, 366
Cahiers du Cinéma 270
Cahn, Sammy 61
Cal-Aero Air Academy 95
Calbes, Eleanor 179
Calhern, Louis 174, 175, 176
Call, John 124
Call Out the Marines 14, 153, 382
Calling All Tars 59
Calvet, Corinne 69, **157**, 158, 308
The Cameraman 49
Cameron, Gene 39, **39**
Cameron, James 364
Camp Minden (Louisiana) 273
Campbell, Alan 136
Campbell, Bruce 234, 236
Candy, John 246
Cannon, Lou 256
Canova, Judy 269
Cantor, Eddie 64
Capitol Theater (New York City) 321
Capra, Frank 27, 53, 373
Capshaw, Kate 245
Captain, Hal 312
Card, Kathryn **305**
Carère, Christine 294
Carey, Harry, Jr. 164, 165, 166
Carleton, Claire 104
Carlisle, Mary 136
Carlson, Herbert 205
Carne, Judy 342
Carney, Alan 13, 102–103, **103**, 104
Carol, Sue 60
Carpenter, Carleton 124

Carré, Ben 28
Carroll, Georgia 137
Carroll, John 301
Carson, Jack 130, 310
Carter, Arthur 215
Carter, Jack 242, 345
Caruso, David 264
Casella, Max 231
Cassel, Seymour 144
Castle, Nick 92
Castle, William 73
Catch-22: 1961 novel 346, 347, 348–349, 350, 352; 1970 film 4, 6, 15, 196, 311, 337, 346–347, **347**, 348, 349–350, 353, 355, 356, 357, 390
Caught in the Draft 12, 13, 58, 59, 90, 91, 93, 96–97, **97**, 98, 99, 382
Caulfield, Joan 301
CBS *see* Columbia Broadcasting System
Cerf, Bennett 180, 287, 288
Chamberlain, William 327
Chandler, Chick 139
Chandler, George 56
Chaney, Stewart 64
Changing Times 199
Channel 4 (Great Britain) 208
Channing, Carol 60
Channon, Jim 209, 212
Chaplin, Charlie 10, 17–19, **20**, 21, 25, 28, 29, 40, 99
Chaplin, Syd 9, 28–29, **29**, 52, 58
Chapman, Marguerite 137
Charlier, Dr. Roger H. (aka Henri Rochard) 273–274, 275
Charlita **115**
Charlotte News 189
"Charmaine" 148, 158
Chase, Charley 85–86, 88, 108, 110, 322
The Chaser 27
Chasers 143–144, 392
Chayefsky, Paddy 341
Cheech & Chong 234, 245, 246
Chesty Anderson, U.S.N. 270, 272, 390–391
Chevalier, Maurice 277
Chicago Daily News 321
Chicago Sun-Times 249
Ching, William 267
Chiniquy, Gerry 282
Chong, Tommy 234, 235; *see also* Cheech & Chong
The Chow Hound 373
Christie Studios 40, 46, 133
A Chump at Oxford 106
Churchill, Winston 345
Cinefilm 270
Cinema Group 245
Cinemascope Two 294
Cinerama Corporation 310
Citera, Tom 261, **262**
Civil War Humor 8
Clampett, Bob 371, 373, 375
Clark, Fred 52, 163, 176, 244, 288, 302
Clark, Harry 183
Classics of the Silent Screen 19, 148
Clayton, John 218
Clements, Stanley 62, 118
Cleveland, George 153

Cleverdon, Scott 236
Clifton-James, M.E. 66
Cline, Eddie 127, 154
Clipped Wings 117–118, 386
Clooney, George 210, *211*, 212
Clute, Chester 139
Clyde, Andy 32, 187
Coal Black and de Sebben Dwarfs 371
Coburn, Charles 28, 303, **304**
Coburn, James 225, 227, 342, ***343***
The Cock-Eyed World 11, *12*, 149, *149*, 150, 151, 379
Coco, James 169
Coe, Barry 294, 295, ***295***
Coe, J.W. 201
Coghlan, Frank, Jr. 306
Cohen, Harold W. (aka Harold V. Cohen) 78, 81, 287
Cohen, Nat 117
Cohen, Sammy 11, 38–39, ***39***, 40, 98, 149, 150
Cohen Saves the Flag 17, 315
The Cohens and the Kellys 41
Cohn, Harry 35, 304, 305
Collier's magazine 189, 307
Collins, Gary 208
Collins, Joan 310, ***311***
Collins, Monty *51*, 315, ***316***
Collins, Ray 120, 191, 200
Collyer, June 118
Columbia Broadcasting System (CBS) 188, 213, 214, 272
Columbia Pictures 27, 35, 49, 51, 53, 86, 88, 89, 100, 106, 117, 118, 125, 126, 139, 140, 142, 178, 204, 205, 214, 215, 216, 240, 245, 246, 280, 288, 300, 301, 302, 303, 304, 305, 306, 315, 328, 340, 346, 347, 356, 369
Columbia Records 78
Columbia University 180, 205
Combs, Richard 345
Comden, Betty 140
Come On Marines 11, 155, 380
Commando Duck 372
Company of Cowards (book) 327–328; see also *Advance to the Rear*
Compson, Betty 316
Conat Sales 117–118
Conklin, Chester 22–23, 40, 45
Conklin, Heinie 23, 44
Conklin, William 24
Connelly, Joe 257, 259
Conrad, Eugene 111
Convy, Bert 229
Conway, Tim 233–234, 236, 242, ***243***, 244
Cook, Carole 281
Cook, Clyde 32, 46
Cook, Elisha, Jr. 65, 366, 368
Cooke, Alistair 18
Cookson, Peter 301
Coons, Robbin 103, 104
Cooper, Gary 11, 58, 199–200, ***200***, 205, 328
Cooper, George *41*, 42, 44, 136
Cooper, Jackie 125
Coots, J. Fred 57
Corbin, Virginia Lee 317
Corby, Ellen 124

Corday, Mara 122
Corday, Rita 103
Corman, Gene 362
Corrigan, Lloyd 316
Cort, Bud 353
Cosmo, James 283
Costello, Lou 12, 31, 46, 48, 56, 59, 67, 69, 70, 71, 78, 90–91, ***91***, 92–94, ***94***, 95–96, 97, 98, 99, 100, 102, 104–105, 120, 153, 266
Cotler, Gordon 241
Coulouris, George 326
The Court Jester 327
Crabbe, Larry "Buster" 69, 136
Crabbe, Peter 234
The Cradle Snatchers: 1926 play 59–60, 147 (see also *Let's Face It* [play and film]); 1928 film 60
Crain, Jeanne 302
Cramer, Richard 324
Crane, Stephen 328
Crazy Rulers of the World 208, 209, 210, 212
Cristal, Linda 293
Crockett, Dick 142
Cronauer, Adrian 331–334, 336
Cronyn, Hume 301
Crosby, Bing 62, 68, 98, 269, 294
Crosby, Bob 192
Crosby, Gary 294, ***295***
The Cross-Red Nurse 265
Crown International 142
Crowther, Bosley 131, 175, 176, 200
Crutcher, Tim 116
Cruze, James 137
Cry for Happy 178–179, ***179***, 388
Cryer, Jon 361
Crystal, Billy 231
Cue magazine 357
Curry, Tim 234, 236
Curtis, Alan 92, 93
Curtis, Dick 87
Curtis, Jamie Leigh 204
Curtis, Ken 164
Curtis, Tony 122, 202, ***203***, 204, 208, 293, 294, 302, 312
Curtiz, Michael 53
The Cute Recruit 369

Da Costa, Morton 180, 184, 186
Daffy—The Commando 370
Dahl, Arlene 325, 327
Daiei Studios 175
Dailey, Dan ***157***, 158, 292, 307, ***308***
Dalio, Marcel 294, 350
Dalton, Audrey 156
Daly, Maggie 222
Dames Ahoy 136, 379
Damita, Lily *12*, 58, ***149***
Damone, Vic 135
Dane, Karl 11, 37–38, *39*, 42, 53
Daniels, Mickey 47
Danton, Ray 187
Dare, Danny 64
Darin, Bobby 179
Darnell, Linda 44
Darrin, James 216
Dash, Stacey 249, ***250***
Daumery, Claire 88
David, Keith 84
David, Mack 68, 70

Davidson, Max 108
Davis, Ann B. 297
Davis, Benny 57
Davis, Jack 47
Davis, Joan 95
Davis, Luther 292
Davis, Mildred 26
Davis, Ossie 184
Davis, Owen, Sr. 64
Davis, Randolph 364
Davis, Richard 292
Davis, Ronald L. 120, 307
Davis, Sammy, Jr. 215
Dawber, Pam 306
Dawson, Doris 27
Dawson, Richard 66
Day, Laraine 266
Day, Marceline 37
Deacon, Richard 125
Dead End (play and film) 113
Dead End Kids 113; see also Bowery Boys
Dean, James 69
Dean, Margia 113
Dear Ruth 301, 384
DeBeck, Billy 126, 127, 128
Defore, Don 81
Deigh, Khigh 179
Deitch, Gene 375, 376
Deitch, Seth 375
Dell, Gabriel 113, 114
Dell, Myrna 116
Delmar, Viña 52
Del Rio, Dolores ***147***, 148
Del Ruth, Roy 44
Delta Farce 16, 83–85, 393
Demarest, William 32, ***258***, 259, 300, 309
DeMille, Cecil B. 9, 19, 257
Demongeot, Mylène 63
Denby, David 196, 249
Dennis, Sandy 169
Dent, Vernon 27, 50–51, 87
Denver, Bob 294
de Putti, Lya 31–32
"Dere Mable" 9
Dern, Bruce 250
DeRose, Peter 256
Deseret News 236, 252
Desperate Journey 368
Destination Tokyo 202, 204
A Devil with Women 155, 380
Devine, Andy 121, 136
DeVito, Danny 247, 249, ***250***
Devorska, Jesse 151
Diary of a Sergeant 285
Dick, Andy 82, 83
Diehl, John 246
Dietrich, Marlene 286–287
Diggins, Peggy 137
Diller, Phyllis 63, 64
Dillman, Bradford 312
Dime a Dance 64
Dingle, Charles 266, 267, ***326***
Diplomaniacs 80
Dirty Dozen Brass Band 232
Disney, Walt 280, 318–319, 371–372, 373
Disney Studios 65, 104, 282, 334–336
Disturbing Pleasures 332

Ditch and Live 366
Dive! see *Going Under*
Diversified Film Distribution 263
Dixon, Ivan 312
The Dizzy Diver 46
Dizzy Yardbird 88
Dmytrk, Edward 110
Dr. Strangelove Or: How I Learned to Stop Worrying and Love the Bomb 15, 337, 338–339, **339**, 340, 341, 342, 350, 365, 389
Dodd, Claire 93
Dodd, Jimmie 127, 128
A Dog's Life 18
Dogs of War 47, 88, 323
"Dogville" comedies 358–359
Donald Duck 371–372
Donald Gets Drafed 371, 372
Donen, Stanley 124, 140, 292
Donlevy, Brian 277, 300, 327
Donohue, Jack 57, 58
Donovan, "Wild Bill" 30
Don't Give Up the Ship 73–74, **75**, 387–388
Don't Go Near the Water: 1956 novel 287–288; 1957 film 287, 288, **289**, 387
Don't Kill Your Friends 118–119
Dooley, Billy 46, 133
Dors, Diana 66
D'Orsay, Fifi 151, **152**
Doug, Doug E. 335, **335**, 336
The Doughboy 45–46
Doughboys **5**, 48–49, **50**, 51, 55, 99, 244, 265, 379–380
Douglas, Chet 178
Douglas, Kirk 291
Douglas, Melvyn 328, 330, 342
Douglas, Paul 267
Dowling, Constance 64, 66
Down Periscope 250–251, **251**, 252, 329, 393
Downes, Donald 276
Downey, Robert 261, 262
Downey, Robert, Jr. 261
Downs, Cathy 75
Dozier, William 266
Dragnet 219, 221
Dresner, Hal 344
Dressler, Marie 40, 265
Dreyfuss, Richard 356
Driscoll, Patricia **206**, 207, 208
Dru, Joanne 76, 200
Drucker, Mort 263, 360
Drysdale, Don 220
Dubin, Al 58
Duchovnay, Gerald 261
Duck Soup 80
Duckworth, Willie 240
Dugan, Tom 33
Duggan, Andrew 277, 282
Dumke, Ralph 178
Dumont, Margaret 110
Dunaway, Faye 344
Duncan, Bud 126–127, 128
Duning, George 141, 205, 240, 241
Dunn, Conrad 246
Dunn, James 137
Dunne, Irene 154, **154**, 155, 303, **304**
Durant, Jack 13, 33, 100, 101, **101**

Durante, Jimmy 12, 99–100, 138, 371
Durbin, Deanna 259
Durning, Charles 167
Dusenberry, Ann 272
Duvall, Robert 335–336, 352
Dvorak, Ann 44
Dwan, Allan 139, 155, 156
Dwan, Dorothy 31

Earle, Dorothy 17
East Side Kids 113; see also Bowery Boys
The Easter Dinner 276; see also *The Pigeon That Took Rome*
Eastman, Phil 373
Eastwood, Clint 123, 227, 228, **228**, 229
Easy and Hard Ways 245; see also *Best Defense*
Easy Rider 143
Eaton, Marcia 223
Eben, Al 114
Ebert, Roger 143, 245, 249, 333, 344
Echanis, Michael 209, 212
USS *Echo* 204, 207
Eden, Barbara 295, 296, 297
Educational Pictures 46, 49, 51, 64, 89
Edwards, Blake 141, 202, 204, 215, 216, 223, 225–226, 227, 241, 294
Edwards, Cliff 48, 49
Edwards, Eric 231
Edwards, Ronnie Clare 263
Egan, Richard 341
The Egg and I 120, 121
Eilers, Sally 32, 49, **50**, 136, 137, 265
Eisenhower, Dwight D. 290
Elan, Joan 156
Eleniak, Erika 143, 144
Elg, Taina 218
Elliot, Arthur 28
Elliott, Dick 118
Elliott, Scott 300
Ellison, James 11, 25, 156
USS *Elmyra* 222
Emhardt, Robert 183, 312
Emily see *The Americanization of Emily*
Englund, Ken 267
Engvoll, Bill 83, 84
Ensign O'Toole and Me 303
Ensign Pulver 167–168, **168**, 169, 389
Entertainment Weekly 84, 252
Ephron, Henry 158
Ephron, Nora 349
Ephron, Phoebe 158
Erdman, Richard 70
Erickson, Leif 292
Ernest in the Army 6
Esmond, Carl 366
Estrada, Juan José 145
Eubank, Shari 270
Evans, Charles **304**
Evans, Gene 73
Evans, Maurice 172–173, 180, 183
Evans, Muriel 86
Evans, Ray 127, 158, 294
Everson, William K. 40, 53, 97, 150, 368
Everything's Ducky 6, 125–126, 388

Ewell, Tom 130, **130**, 131–132, 269, 270, 312
Exhibitor's Forum 152
The Extraordinary Seaman 342, 344–346, 348, 390

Fabray, Nanette 60
A Face in the Crowd 185
Fail-Safe 340
Fain, Sammy 283
Fairbanks, Douglas, Sr. 19
Fall In 110–111, **111**, 113, 383
Fall Out — Fall In 371–372
Famous Studios 373; see also Paramount Pictures
Fantasy II 364
Fantle, David 236
Fantoni, Sergio 225, **226**
Farentino, James 169
Farr, Felicia 187
Farr, Jamie (Jameel Farah) 186
Farrar & Strauss 119
Farrell, Glenda 137
Fawcett, William 185
Faye, Alice 33
Faye, Herbie 231
Faylen, Frank 13, 100, 113
Fazenda, Louise 32, 40, 44, 60, 99
Fearless Fagan 123–124, 385
Feiffer, Jules 338, 375
Fenneman, George 175
Ferre, Cliff 256
Ferrer, José 254
Ferris, Audrey 30
A Few Quick Facts About Fear 374
Fiedler, John 312
Fielding, Edward 192
Fields, Dorothy 60
Fields, Herbert 60, 134
Fields, Stanley 81
Fields, W.C. 40, 127
Fifi Blows Her Top 88
Fightin' Fools 88–89
The Fighting 69½ 369, 374
Fillmore, Clyde 110
Film Bulletin 263
Film Daily 45
Film Voices 261
The Films of Paul Newman 310
Fine, Larry 86, **86**; see also Three Stooges
Fine, Sylvia (Mrs. Danny Kaye) 60, 64, 66
Finklehoffe, Fred 67, 253–254
Finlayson, James 53, 55, 56, 112, 324
First Earth Batallion 209, 210
The First Earth Manual 209
First Motion Picture Unit 366, 373
First National Pictures (aka First National Exchange) 17, 18, 21, 27, 32, 41, 52, 56, 134
Fisher, Fred 158
Fiske, Richard 87
Fitzgerald, Barry 68
Fitzgerald, F. Scott 237
Fitzpatrick, Daniel 132
Flaherty, Joe 247
Flaherty, John 263
Flannery, William 269
Flavin, James 155, 166

Fleischer, Max 280, 369, 371, 372
The Fleet's In (1928) 33, 136, 379
The Fleet's In (1942) 33, 69, 136, 382; see also *Sailor Beware*
Fleets of Stren'th 372
Fleming, Victor 35
Flight Command 92
Flippen, Jay C. 213
Flippen, Ruth Brooks 306
The Flying Deuces 55–56, 381
"The Flying Teakettle" see *You're in the Navy Now*
Flynn, Errol 257
Flynn, Joe *179*, 219, 220, 221, 233, 242, *243*, 244
Foley, Brian 356
Follow the Fleet 135, 381; see also *Shore Leave* (1922 Osborne play)
Fonda, Henry 162, 163–164, 165, *165*, 166, 184
Foran, Dick 95
Ford, Glenn 174, 175, 176, 178–179, *179*, 216, 217, 218, 219, 288, 302, 328, 329, *330*, 331
Ford, John 34, 40, 107, 148, 157, 158, 164, 165–166, 169, 176, 186, 307, 309
Ford, Paul 173, 175, 176, 179, 231
Ford, Wallace 138
A Foreign Affair 285–287, 384
Foreman, Carl 340
Forsythe, John 163, 173, 179
Fort Benning (Georgia) 70, 313
Fort Bragg (North Carolina) 189, 209
Fort Huachuca (Arizona) 311
Fort Jackson (South Carolina) 248
Fort Knox (Kentucky) 247
Fort Lee (Virginia) 266, 269
Fort Ord (California) 91, 123
Fort Roach (California) 73, 366; see also Roach, Hal
Fort Sill (Oklahoma) 82
45th Division News 128
Forward March 46
Foster, Ron 232
Fox, Virginia 23
Fox, Vivica A. 273
Fox, William 146–147
Fox Film Corporation 33, 34, 35, 38–39, 45, 60, 89, 98, 137, 145, 147, 148, 149, 150, 153, 155, 157, 280; see also 20th Century–Fox
Fox News Channel (FNC) 83
Foxe, Earle 257
Foxworthy, Jeff 83
Fowley, Douglas 107
Foy, Eddie, Jr. 154, *154*
Francis: 1946 novel 14, 119–120, 121; 1949 film 120–121, *121*, 122, 123–124, 125, 384
Francis, Anne 288
Francis, Bob 184, 185
Francis, Noel 56
Francis Goes to the Races 122
Francis Goes to Washington 119
Francis Goes to West Point 122, 385
Francis in the Haunted House 123
Francis in the Navy 122–123, 386
Francis Joins the WACs 122, 269, 386

"Francis the Talking Mule" series 119–125, 282
Francisco, Betty 39
Frank, Melvin 327
Frankenheimer, John 340, 342, 344–346
Franklin, Joe 19, 148
Franklin, Sidney, Jr. 123
Fraser, Hugh 282
Frawley, William 57, 58
Frazee, Jane 92
Freed, Arthur 140
Freeman, Al, Jr. 169
Freeman, Benedict 125
Freeman, Howard 184
Freeman, Mickey 231
Freeman, Mona 70, 301
Freeman, Stan 179
Frees, Paul 123, 281
Freleng, Friz 373
French, Charles K. 317
Friedwald, Will 369
Frizler, Paul 263
Fuller, Samuel 73
Fuller, Willam Allen 318, 319, 321
The Fuller Brush Man 325
Funicello, Annette 244
"Funny Torture" 209; see also *Crazy Rulers of the World*
Furmanek, Bob 92
Furst, Steven 263

Gabor, Eva 288, *289*
Gage, Erford 103, 104
Gage, Frank 85; see also Ranch Boys
Gallo, Lew 223
Gandy Goose 371
Gannett, Lewis 190
Garbo, Greta 330
Gardiner, Reginald 55, 244
Gardner, Ava 325
Garfunkel, Art 348
Gargan, William 96
Garick, Lt. Robert M. 115
Garner, James 312, 342, *343*, 352
Garner, Paul "Mousie" 77
Garnett, Tay 47, 192, 193
Garrett, Betty 140, 141
Garson, Henry 73
Gassner, John 173
Gates, Larry 173, 185
Gaver, Jack 185
The Gay Retreat 39, *39*, 98, 149, 378
The Geezer of Berlin 17, 358
Gehrig, Wes D. 58
Geisel, Theodore ("Dr. Seuss") 373
Geller, Uri 208, 209, 211
The General 8, 16, 26, 48, 318, 319, *320*, 321–322, 325, 327, 331, 378
General Nuisance 49, 51, *51*
General Spanky 322–323, *323*, 324, 331, 381
Genn, Leo 156
George, Peter 337, 338, 340
Geray, Steven 366
German, Gretchen 363
Gerrard, Charles K. 29
Getting Wasted 263–264, 391
GI Dood It 88
G.I. Honeymoon 301, 383
Gibson, Mel 236

Gifford, Alan 62
Gilbert, John 11, 42, 46
Gilford, Jack 348
Gill, David 18
Gillett, John 319
Gilliard, Stewart 362
Gillis, Anne 266
Gillmore, Margalo 290
Gilmore, Virginia 256
Gilroy, Bert 102, 103
Gilson, Tom 311
Girard, Bernard 232
The Girl He Left Behind 194
A Girl in Every Port (Fox, 1928) 8, 33, *33*, 34, 379
A Girl in Every Port (RKO, 1952) 80–81, 385
The Girls of Pleasure Island 156–157, 386
Giroux, Henry A. 332
Give Me a Sailor 59, 381
Glass, Ned 315
Gleason, Jackie 13, 76, 101, *101*, 102, 137, 223, 224, *224*
Gleason, James 107, 108
Gleason, Lucille 139
Glenn, Scott 237
Glover, Danny 335, *335*, 336
"The Gob" (stage sketch) 56; see also *Son of a Sailor*
The Gob (film) 56; see also *Son of a Sailor*
Gobs and Gals 75–76, 385
Godard, Jean-Luc 270, 294
Godfrey, Arthur 283
Goetz, William 129
Going Under 6, 364–365, *365*, 366, 392
The Gold Rush 21, 99
Goldberg, Daniel 246
The Golden Fleecing 221–222; see also *The Honeymoon Machine*
The Golden Turkey Awards 126, 175
Goldie 34–35, 380
Golding, Dave 129
Goldman, William 223, 224
Goldstein, Leonard 129, 130
Goldstein, Murray 117
Goldwyn, Samuel 64–65, 113, 301
Goldwyn, Samuel, Jr. 257
Gomberg, Sy 14, 176, 307
Gomer Pylce USMC 188
Gone with the Wind 324
The Good-Bye Kiss 32, 379
Good Morning, Vietnam 332, *332*, 333–334, 336, 392
Goodman, Dody 169
Goodwin, Harold 107
Goodwins, Leslie 102
A Goofy Gob 46
Goodwin, Harold 28
Gorcey, Bernard 114, 118
Gorcey, David (aka David Condon) 105, 113, 114, *115*, 117, 118
Gorcey, Leo 113, 114, 115, *115*, 116, 117, 118
Gordon, Gale 73, 244, 297
Gordon, Max 303
Gordon, Robert 9
Gordon, Ruth 302–303
Gorman, Buddy 114, *115*, 116

Gosfield, Maurice 231
Gottlieb, Alex 90, 95
Gottlieb, Carl 353
Gould, Elliott 352, 353–354, **354**
Goulding, Alf 45
Grable, Betty 59, 269
The Graduate 197, 347
Graham, Sheila 219
Grainger, Edmund A. 328
Grammer, Kelsey 250, **251**
Grand National Pictures 25, 48, 138
Grand Slam Opera 51
Le Grande Illusion 99, 294
Grandma's Boy 26, 315–316, 377–378
Granger, Michael 118
Grant, Cary 185, 202, **203**, 204, 208, 221, 274, **274**, 275, 292, 293, **293**
Grant, John 69, 92, 93, 95
Grant, Katherine 215
Graves, Peter 360
Gray, Charles 277
Grayson, Kathryn 140
The Great Dictator 21
Great Guns 12, 39, 56, 98, 382
The Great Locomotive Chase (book and film) 318–319
Green, Adolph 140
Green, Paul 181
Greenberg, Joel 42
Greene, Danford B. 353
The Greenwich Village Follies of 1923 56
Greer, Jane 200, **200**
Gregg, Virginia 202
Gregory, James 277
Grey, Clifford 134
Grey, Joel 256
Gribbon, Eddie 31, 136
Grier, David Alan 82, 83, 234, 236
Griffin, Carleton 85
Griffith, Andy 180, 181, 183, 184, 185, 186, **186**, 187
Griffith, D.W. 314, 322
Griffith, James 329
Griffith, Raymond 26, 316–317, **317**, 318, 322, 327
Grippo, Jan 113, 114, 116
Groody, Louise 134
Grossbach, Robert 245
Guardino, Harry 277
Guernsey, Otis L., Jr. 200
Guest, Christopher 366
Guinness, Alec 338
Guiol, Fred 107–108, 112, 155
Guthman, Edward 284
Guttenberg, Steve 273

Haas, Hugo 193
Haber, Joyce 267
Hackett, Buddy 125, 126, 296, 297
Hagman, Larry 169
Hail the Conquering Hero 309
Haines, William 38, 136, 137, 145, 155
Hal Roach Laff-Time see *Here Comes Trouble*
Hale, Alan 136
Hale, Alan, Jr. 113, 330
Hale, Creighton 45
Haley, Jack 88, 101, 137, **138**

Half Shot at Sunrise 78–79, **79**, 80, 85, 380
Half Shot Shooters 86–87, 88
Hall, Alexander 131
Hall, Arch, Jr. 220
Hall, Archie 217–218, 219, 220
Hall, Charlie 13, 100
Hall, Huntz 113, 114, **115**, 116, 117, 118
Hall, James 33
Hall, Juanita 136
Hall, Mordaunt 151, 155
Hall, Thurston 94
Halliwell, Leslie 107
The Halls of Montezuma 145
Halop, Billy 113
Ham and Bud 126
Ham and Eggs at the Front 44, 379
Hamilton, Frank 153
Hamilton, Lloyd 46, 126
Hamilton, Murray 163, 185
Hamilton, Neil 78
Hamlet 249
Hamlin, Tom 24
Hammett, Dashiel 227
Hands Up! 26, 316–318, 322, 327, 331, 378
Hanna-Barbera 371
The Happiest Days of Your Life 261
Happy Birthdaze 373
Hardison, Kadeem 249, **250**
Hardy, Oliver 11, 12, 17, 31, 39, 47, 53–54, **54**, 55–56, 98, 100, 105, 106, 107, 108, 109, 112, 155, 158, 217, 299, 322, 361
Hargrove, Dean 194
Hargrove, Marion 13, 176, 189–193, 194, 205, 208
Harlan, Kenneth 57
Harlan, Otis 136
Harlem Players 136
Harlow, Jean 35
Harman-Ising Productions 375
Harmon, John 118
Harmon, Mark 107
Harmon, Steve 167
Harmon, Tom 107
Harrigan, William 163
Harris, Ed 237, 238
Harris, Jack H. 338
Harris, Jed 215
Harris, Mildred 35
Harrison, Rex 274
Hart, Teddy 81
Hart, William S. 321
Hartford, Dee 81
Hartman, Don 65
Hartman, Phil 142, 231
Harvey, Paul 25
Harvey Publications 72
Hastings, Bob 183, 233, 242, **243**
Hathaway, Henry 155, 199
Hatley, Marvin 85; see also Ranch Boys
Hatton, Raymond 11, 35–36, **36**, 37, 40, 53
Haver, Phyllis 148
Havoc 145, 147
Hawks, Howard 8, 34, 110, 274, 275
Hawmps 7
Hawn, Goldie 15, 270–271, **271**, 272, 273

Hawthorne, Jim 88
Hay Foot 108–109, **109**, 382
Hay Foot, Straw Foot 24, 377
Hayden, Russ 156
Hayden, Sterling 339
Hayes, Allison 122
Haymes, Dick 141, **141**
Hays, Robert 167
Hayward, Leland 161, 163
Hayward, Susan 291
Haywood, Drexie 327
Hayworth, Rita 288, 300
Hazard, John W. 199
Headly, Glenn 231, 232
Hearn, Edward 31
Heart Trouble 27–28, 32, 52, 379
The Heavy Parade 46, 358
Hecht, Ben 63
Hecht, Ted 104
Heckman, Hugh M. 160
Heermance, Richard 118
Heflin, Van 130, 303
Heggen, Thomas 14, 159–162, 163, 165, 166, 167
Heil, Douglas 190
Held, John, Jr. 42
Helfer, Ralph 126
Heller, Joseph 346–349, 350
Hell's Angels 44, 52
Helton, Percy 118
Hemingway, Ernest 34
Hendra, Tony 260
Henner, Marilu 167
Henreid, Paul 61, 306
Henry, Buck 347–348, 349
Henry, Buzz 331
Henry Holt & Company 190
Hepburn, Katharine 62–63
Her First Mate 137, 380
Her Private Husband 45
Her Torpedoed Love 17
Herbert, F. Hugh 156, 300
Herbert, Hugh 137
Here Come the Marines 116, 117, 385
Here Come the Waves 5, 95
Here Comes Trouble 112
Herman, Lt. Col. Ruby E. 269
Hernandez, Juano 136
Hersey, John 169
Hersholt, Jean 53
Heslov, Grant 210, 212
Hesseman, Howard 167
Heston, Charlton 163, 257, **258**, 259, 260, 276–277
Hewitt, Alan 295
Hewitt, Virginia 114
Hey Rookie 5, 88
Heydt, Louis-Jean 192
Hiatt, Ruth 45
Hibbs, Jesse 176
Hickey, William 260
Hickman, Dwayne 310
Hickox, Harry 187
Hicks, Chris 236, 252
Hicks, Russell 112
High Button Shoes 213–214
High-Cs 85, 88
Higham, Charles 42
Higher Than a Kite 87
Hiken, Nat 214
Hill, Doris 30

Hill, George Roy 352
Hill, Steven 163
Hill, Thelma 127
Hill, Weldon (William R. Scott) 187
Hillbilly Blitzkrieg 127–128, 382–383
Hiller, Arthur 270, 342
Hilliard, Harriet 135
Hilton, Les 120
Hinds, Samuel S. 56
Hines, Gregory 249
Hinson, Hal 249
Hirschhorn, Clive 356, 357
A History of the 69th 8
Hit the Deck: 1927 play 134; 1930 film 11, 134–135, **135**, 379; 1955 film 135, 386; see also *Shore Leave* (1922 Osborne play)
Hitchcock, Alfred 67, 270
Hi'ya Sailor 139, 383
Hoffman, Jordan 212
Hogan, Bill 129
Hold That Ghost 93, 95, 96
Holden, William **4**, 136, 164, 301, 342, 366
USS *Holland* 201
Holland, John 266
Holliday, Judy 215, 292
Holliman, Earl 288
Holloway, Sterling 100
Holly, Lauren 251, **251**
Hollywood Air Force see *Weekend Warriors*
Hollywood Pictures 82
Hollywood Reporter 108, 124, 158
Holmes, Phillips 322, 324
Holmes, Stuart 88
Holt, Tim 102
The Honeymoon Machine 15, 221, 222, 224, 242, 388
Hooker, Richard see Hornberger, H. Richard
Hope, Bob 12, 58, 59, **60**, 61–64, 70, 71, 90, 96, **97**, 98, 327
Hopper, Dennis 143, 144
Hopper, Jerry 257
Horizon magazine 346
The Horizontal Lieutenant 241–242, 388–389
Horman, Arthur T. 75, 91
Hornbeck, William 32
Hornberger, H. Richard (Richard Hooker) 351
Horne, James W. 85
Horvath, Charles 331
Hoskins, Allen "Farina" 47
Hot Pepper 153
Hot Shots! 16, 360–362, **362**, 363, 392
Houghton Mifflin 160, 161
House, Don 161
Hovey, Tim 258, 259, 260
Howard, Curly 86, **86**; see also Three Stooges
Howard, Leslie 324
Howard, Moe 86, **86**; see also Three Stooges
Howard, Shemp 86, 87–88, 95; see also Three Stooges
Howard, William K. 157

Howell, C. Thomas 312
Hughes, Carol 100
Hughes, Howard 42, 44, 52, 148, 283
Hui, William Bradford 341
Hull, Warren 137
Humeston, Earl 123, 124
Humeston, Floyd C. 123, 124
The Hungry Goat 373
Hunnicutt, Arthur 110
Huns and Hyphens 17
Hunt, Marsha 301
Hunt, Marsha A. 356
The Hunt for Red October 364
Hunter, Jeffrey 64, 318
Hunter, Tab 194
Hurlock, Madeleine 45, 265
Hurst, David 227
Husmann, Ron 179
Huss, Tony 252
Huston, John 285
Hutchins, Will 187
Hutchinson, J. 261, **262**
Hutton, Betty **60**, 61, 69, 95, 136, 300
Hutton, Brian 228
Hutton, Jim 222, 241, 242
Hutton, Robert 75, 299
Hyams, Joe 283
Hyde-White, Wilfred **65**, 66
Hyden, Steven 84
Hyer, Martha 52, 220
Hyman, Earle 184
Hyman, Mac 14, 180, 181, 183, 184, 186, 188
Hyman, Ray 208
Hymer, Warren 34, 35, 138
Hyuck, Willard 245

"I Love the Men" 113
I Spied for You 89
"I Was a Male War Bride" (newspaper article) 274, 275
I Was a Male War Bride (1949 film) 274, **274**, 275, 384
I Was Monty's Double 66
Identification of a Japanese Zero 366, 368
If I Had a Million 11
"I'm Glad My Number Was Called" 100
I'm in the Army Now 372
"I'm Nobody" 256
"I'm Proud I'm a Navy Man" 139
"I'm So Unlucky" 141
Imagine Entertainment 230
Imhof, Roger 138
Imitation General 4, 14, 103, 217–218, 225, 328, 387
The Impatient Years 301, 383
Imperial Theater (New York City) 57, 60
"In My Arms" 192
In the Army Now 82, **82**, 83, 84, 393
In the Meantime, Darling 302
In the Navy 12, 46, 93–94, **94**, 95, 96, 100, 382
Ince, Thomas H. 24, 25, 314, 315
The Incredible Mr. Limpet 279, 280–281, **281**, 282–283, 389
Independent Artists 266

Ingels, Marty 242
International Pictures 120, 129; see also Universal-International
Ireland, John 76, 327
The Iron Petticoat 62–63, 386–387
Irving, William 46
It Started with a Kiss 301–302, 388
It's a Mad Mad Mad Mad World 104, 126
It's Murder She Says 374
Ives, Burl 169
Ives, George 167
Izzard, Eddie 283, 284

Jackson, Harry 173
Jackson, Mary Ann 45
Jackson, Sammy 187
Jackson, Selmer 114
Jagger, Dean 222
James, Anne 241
James, Claire 137, 138
Janie 299, 300, 305, 383
Janis, Conrad 305–306
Janssen, David 122, 131
Jarrell, Andy 356
Jarvis, Graham 229
Jason, Rick 269
The Jazz Singer 30, 47
Jefferson Productions 137
Jenkins, Allen 115, 137
Jenkins, Gordon 76
Jenks, Frank 116
Jenner, Bruce 363
Jerry the Giant see Madden, Jerry
Jessel, George 30
Jester Comedies 17
Jet magazine 245, 260
Jewell, Austin 118
Jewell, Isabel 138
Joe Butterfly 176–177, 178, 387
Johanna Enlists 298, 313, 377
Johnson, Arte 184
Johnson, Emory 298
Johnson, Noble 318
Johnson, Russell 131
Johnson, Tom 236
A Jolly Good Furlough 373
Jolly Tars 46
Jolson, Al 30, 47
Jones, Chuck 373
Jones, Dean 218, 303
Jones, F. Richard 22
Jones, Gordon 125, 240
Jones, James Earl 339
Jones, Jennifer 168
Jones, John Marshall 231
Jones, Shirley 306
Jordan, Bobby 113, 114
Jordan, Gregor 237–238
Jory, Victor 137
Joyce, Natalie 34
Judels, Charles 88
Jumping Jacks 15, 70–71, **71**, 73, 385

Kadison, Ellis 73
Kael, Pauline 3, 81, 235, 279
Kain, Kahlil 249, **250**
The Kaiser—Beast of Berlin 9, 17, 358
Kaiser Wilhelm 9, 17, 19, 22–23
Kalem Films 318

Kane, Carol 142
Kanin, Garson 18, 302
Kardell, Lili 118
Karloff, Boris 169
Karlweiss, Oskar 173
Karnelly, Leila 149
Karns, Roscoe 11
Karns, Todd 117
Karr, Hillard *see* Ton of Fun
Kashfi, Anna 288
Katz, Gloria 245
Katzenberg, Jeffrey 332
Katzman, Sam 113
Kaufman, George S. 303
Kaye, Danny 60, 61, 64–65, **65**, 66, 70, 71, 74, 277, 327
Kazan, Elia 185
Keating, Larry 282
Keaton, Buster **5**, 8, 25, 26, 30, 46, 48–50, **50**, 51, **51**, 52, 55, 99, 139, 244, 265, 315, **316**, 318–319, **320**, 321–322, 325–326, 327
Keaton, Michael 231
Keavy, Hubbar 92
Keep 'Em Flying 12, 95–96, 382
Keep Your Powder Dry 266
Keighley, William 256, 366
Keith, Brian 163, 311
Keith, Ian 43
Keith, Robert 163
Kellerman, Sally 352, 353, 354, 356
Kellin, Mike 68, 207, 208
Kelly, Gene 139, 140, **140**
Kelly, Patsy 322
Kelly, Paul 153, 290
Kelly, Sean 260
Kelly's Heroes 227–228, **228**, 229, 348, 390
Kemp, Matty 32
Kemper, Charles 88
Kennedy, Arthur 366
Kennedy, Edgar 28, 127, 128
Kennedy, George 234
Kennedy, John F. 224
Kennedy, Merna 56
Kennedy, Tom 44, 89
Kennedy-Martin, Troy 227
Kenny, Doug 260, 261
Kent, Dorothea 51
Kentucky Film Commission 247
Kentucky Fried Movie 359, 364
Kerr, Deborah 124, 292, 310
Kerr, Walter 19, 28, 37, 316, 319
Kerwin, Brian 263
Ketcham, Hank 375
Keys, Katherine 89
Keystone Studio 9, 154, 314
Kibbee, Roland 290
Kickin' the Conga Around 372
Kilmer, Bill 220
King, Charles 134
King, Dennis, Jr. 292
King, Henry 24
King, Joseph 58
King, Judy 39
King, Paul 201
King, Walter Woolf 111
King Features 376
King Henry IV 7
King Henry V 249
The King's Men 153

Kingsley, Sidney 113
Kingston, Natalie 27, 34
Kirby, Bruno 332
Kirk, Phyllis 72, 73, 256
Kiss and Tell 300, **300**, 301, 304, 305, 384
Kiss Them for Me: 1945 play 292; 1957 film 291, 292–293, **293**, 387; see also *Shore Leave* (Wakeman novel)
Kissinger, Henry 338
Klages, Raymond 100
Klemperer, Werner 293
Knotts, Don 177, 185, 219, 221, 280–281, **281**
Knox, Alexander 303, **304**
Knox, Elyse 107, 108, 139, 266
Kobayashi, Tsuruko 178
Kobi, Michi 178
Kolb, Clarence 96
Korff, Arnold 49
Korittke, Oliver 283
Korkes, Jon 349
Kornman, Mary 47
Koscina, Sylva **278**, 279
Kouf, Jim 335
Kovacs, Ernie 177, 178, 205, 216–217, **217**
Kramer, Stanley 126
Krasna, Norman 301
Krebitz, Nicolette 283
Kroeger, Gary 362
Krueger, Kurt 225
Kruger, Stubby 164
Kubrick, Stanley 338–339, 340, 350, 352
Kulky, Henry 88
Kulp, Michael 263
Kurnitz, Harry 190, 192, 193
Kutzera, Dale 366, 367, 368
Kyô, Machiko 174, 175, 176

Ladd, Alan 366
Ladies' Home Journal 306
Lady Be Careful 33, 68, 136, 381; see also *Sailor Beware*
LaFontaine, Don 362
Laimbeer, Bill 363
Lake, Arthur 25, 60, 139, 375
Lamb, John 264
Lamont, Charles 123
Lamour, Dorothy 33, 96, **97**, 136
Lancaster, Burt 340
Lanchester, Elsa 157
Landis, Jessie Royce 295
Landis, John 359
Landry, Margaret 102
Lane, Charles 110
Lane, Lola 44, 255
Lane, Lupino 46
Lane, Priscilla 255, 256
Lane, Richard 118
Lane, Rosemary 255
Lang, Jennings 232–233
Lang, Stephen 210
Langdon, Harry **26**, 27–28, 30, 32, 45, 52–53, 240
Lanteau, William 67, 222
Lantz, Walter 280, 371, 375
Lanza, Mario 124
Lardner, John 129

Lardner, Ring, Jr. 129, 352, 353, 355
Larkin, Peter 180, 184
Larroquette, John 246
Larry the Cable Guy (Dan Whitney) 81, 83–84
The Last Detail 8, 142–143, **143**, 144, 390
The Last Round-Up 371
The Last Time I Saw Archie 14, 103, 219, **219**, 220–221, 280, 328, 388
Laughlin, "Froggy" 88
Laurel, Stan 11, 12, 39, 47, 53–54, **54**, 55–56, 98, 100, 105, 106, 107, 108, 109, 112, 155, 217, 299, 322, 361
Laurie, Piper 122
Lawrance, Jody 141
Lawrence, Rosina 322
Lazarus, Sidney 49
Le, Dinh Thien 335, **335**
Lear, Norman 227
Leary, Denis 335, **335**, 336
The Leathernecker 27, 53
Leathernecking 11, 154, **154**, 155, 380
Leave It to the Marines 156, 385
LeBlanc, Matt 283, 284
Leckman, Brian 231
Lederer, William J. 14, 242, 303
Lee, Canada 136
Lee, Doris *see* May, Doris
Lee, Dorothy 78, 79
Lee, Lila 31
Lee, Gen. Robert E. 8
Lee, Rowland V. 147
Lees, Robert 70, 71
Leguizamo, John 234
Lehrman, Henry "Pathe" 30, 40
Leibman, Ron 262, **262**
Leigh, Janet 124, 293, 294
LeMassena, William 179
Lembeck, Harvey 131, 163, 200, 219, 220, 221, 231, 244
Lemmon, Chris 229
Lemmon, Jack 73, 164, 165, 166, 168, 205, **206**, 208, 214–216, 217, 229, 239, 288, 352
le Picard, Marcel 116
LeRoy, Eddie 118, 183
LeRoy, Mervyn 165, 178, 180, 185, 186
Leslie, Joan 303
Lesser, Sol 23
Lester, Jerry 76, 77
Lester, Richard 345, 347, 357
Let It Rain 154, 378
Let There Be Light 285
Let's Face It: 1941 play 60–61; 1943 film 59, 60, **60**, 61, 64, 383; see also *The Cradle Snatchers*
Let's Go Navy 15, 114–115, **115**, 116, 385
"Let's Not Talk About Love" 61
A Letter for Evie 301, 384
Levin, Ira 180, 181, 182–183, 184, 186, 187
Levinson, Barry 332
Levy, Mike 120
Lewis, Jerry 66–71, **71**, 72–75, **75**, 76, 77, 105, 136, 254, 256, 277
Lewis, Robert 173

Index

Lewis, Sheldon 31
Lewis, Sylvia 269
Lieber, Fritz 81
Liebman, Max 60
The Lieutenant Wore Skirts 269–270, 386
Life magazine 66, 68, 92, 120, 123, 175, 184, 190, 217, 267, 287, 292, 321
Life with the Flying Cadets 95
Lights Out 371
Linden, Doris 127, 128
Linden, Eric 138
Lindsey, George 169
Lionsgate Films 83
Liotta, Ray 335, **335**, 336
Lippert Pictures 72, 112–113, 156
Lisi, Virna 302
Little Tough Guys 113; *see also* Bowery Boys
Littlefield, Lucien 128
Litto, George 352
Livingston, Jay 68, 70, 127, 158, 294
Lloyd, Art 324
Lloyd, George 153
Lloyd, Harold 25, **25**, 26, 111, 315–316
"The Lobby Number" 65
Lockhart, Gene 81
Loder, John 156
Loder, Lotti 52
Loeb, Leo 21
Loesser, Frank 139, 192
Loew's State Theater (New York City) 102
Logan, Joshua 161, 162–167, 169, 171, 181, 184
Lollobrigida, Gina 63, 64
Lombard, Carole 191
The Long Gray Line 164
Longet, Claudine 234
Looking for Danger 118, 387
Loos, Mary Ann 307
Lorch, Theodore 29
Lord, Del 315
Lord, Marjorie 109
Loren, Sophia 277
Lorey, Dean 259
Lorimar Productions 312
Lorraine, Louise 37
Lorre, Peter 73
Los Angeles Times 367
Lost at the Front 41, 378
Louise, Tina 204
Louvish, Simon 40
Love, Montague 316
Love and Duty 17
Love at First Bite 87–88
The Lovely Ladies, Kind Gentlemen 179; *see also Teahouse of the August Moon*
Lovett, Dorothy 153
Lowe, Edmund 52, **147**, 148, 149, **149**, **152**, 153, 154, 157
Loy, Myrna 32, 34, 44
Lubin, Arthur 91, 95, 96, 120, 121, 122, 123, 124, 125, 282
Lubitsch, Ernst 107
Luce, Claire Boothe 290
Luce, Henry 290
Lugosi, Bela 151

Lumet, Sidney 340, 352
Lund, John 205, 286
Lundigan, William 139, 199
Lundin, Walter 324
Lupino, Ida 155
Lupino, Wallace 46
Lupton, John 318
Lusitania 9
Luther, Barbara 306
Lyceum Theater (New York City) 134, 135
Lydon, James 220
Lynch, Edward A. 57
Lynn, Betty 266
Lynn, Jeffrey 131
Lynn, Mara 156
Lynn, Vera 339
Lyon, Ben 52
Lyon-Lamb Animation 263

Ma and Pa Kettle 120
MacArthur, Douglas 205, 290
MacBride, Donald 69, 99, 100, 114
Macchio, Ralph 261, **262**
MacDonald, Edmund 98
MacDonald, J. Farrell 60, 127
Mace, Fred 315
MacFarlane, George 78, 79
MacGibbon, Harriet **179**
MacGillivray, Scott 98
Mack, Charlie (The Two Black Crows) 78, 81; *see also* Moran, George
Mack, Marion 321
Mack, Roy 127
Mackaill, Dorothy 134
MacLean, Douglas 24–25, 154, 298
MacLeod, Gavin 204, 228, 233, 242
MacMahon, Horace 138
MacRae, Elizabeth 125, 281
MAD magazine 260–261, 263, 360
MAD Magazine Presents Up the Academy 260–262, **262**, 263, 264, 391
Madden, Jerry (Jerry the Giant) 39
Magnus, Annabel 47
Mahin, John Lee 186, 187
Mahoney, Jock 87
Majestic Theater (New York City) 179
The Major and the Minor 257
Major League 250, 360
Major Movie Star 273, 393–394
The Major Payne 259–260, 263, 393; see also *Private War of Major Benson*
Mako 63
Maley, Peggy 163
Maltin, Leonard 59, 65, 77, 150, 177, 372
A Man Called Sarge 362–364, 392
Mandel, Johnny 342
Mandy, Jerry 85
Mankiewicz, Don 266
Mann, Delbert 174, 175
Manning, Knox 65, 107
Mansfield, Jayne 77, 270, 292, **293**
Mantell, Joe 72
Many Tanks 372
Marcus, James 31

Mardi Gras 5, 256–257, 294, 296
Marietto *see* Angelleti, Carlo
Marimark Productions 142
The Marines Are Coming 155, 380
Marion, Charles R. 116, 117
Maris, Mona 155
Markey, Enid 306
Marlow, Brian 70
Marquand, John P. 289, 290, 291
The Marquis Chimps 296
Marriage Is a Private Affair 301
The Marry-Go-Round 373
Marsh, Mae 309
Marshall, George 55, 72, 217, 328
Marshall, Joan 73
Marshall, Marion 69
Marshall, Penny 247, 249, 250
Marshall, Peter 76–77, **77**, 169
Martell, George 156
Martin, Dean 66–71, **71**, 72, 73, 74, 75, 76, 105, 136, 254
Martin, Jill **316**
Martin, Richard 102–103, **103**, 104
Martin, Steve **230**, 231–232, 234, 366
Martin, Tony 135
Martin Beck Theater (New York City) 173, 174
Martinelli, Elsa 277
Marton, Andrew 348
Marvin, Lee 200
Marx, Groucho 80–81, 110, 301; *see also* Marx Brothers
Marx Brothers 37, 80, 81, 110
Mascot Pictures 155
MASH: 1968 novel 352–353; 1970 film 15, 16, 85, 145, 229, 230, 238, 297, 311, 312, 334, 337, 351, 353–354, **354**, 355–356, 357, 368, 390
*M*A*S*H* (TV series) 15, 129, 167, 332, 355, 356
Maslin, Janet 144
Mason, Shirley 154
Masquers Club 158
Matthau, Walter **168**, 169, 187, 291, 352
Mauldin, Bill 13, 28, 128–129, 130, 131–132
Maxey, Paul 116
Maxwell, Bert *see* Bernard Brothers
Maxwell, Marilyn 62
May, Doris [Doris Lee] 24
Mayehoff, Eddie 62
Mayer, Louis B. 325
Mayer, Ray 138
Mayo, Virginia 301
Mazurki, Mike 110
MCA 202, 204
McBride, Joseph 34
McCabe, John 21, 361
McCarey, Leo 53, 309–311
McCarthy, Frank 254
McCarthy, Nobu 177
McCormick, Myron 184, 185
McCourt, Malachi 353
McCoy, Adrian 364
McCrary, Todd 239
McDaniel, Hattie 324
McDonald, Ray 141, **141**
McDougal Alley Kids 47
McDowell, Charles 256

McDowell, Roddy 184, 364
McFarland, George "Spanky" 88, 322, *323*
McGavin, Darren 71
McGilligan, Patrick 309
McGovern, Elizabeth 238
McGraw, Charles 242
McGregor, Ewan 211
McGregor, Malcolm 31, 91
McGuire, Don 311, 312
McHale's Navy: 1962 TV series 204, 232, 236, 242, 347; 1964 film 233–234, *235*, 242, 389; 1997 film 6, 232, 234–236, 393
McHale's Navy Joins the Air Force 116, 234, 242–243, *243*, 389
McHugh, Frank 57
McIntire, John 120, 200
McKay, Scott 301
McKee, Raymond 45
McKimson, Robert 282
McLaglen, Victor *12*, *33*, 34, 52, *147*, 148, 149, *149*, *152*, 153, 154, 155, 157
McLeod, Norman Z. 267, 270
McNamara, Ted 11, 38–39, *39*, 40, 98, 134, 149, 150
McNamara, William 143
McQueen, Steve 222–223, 224–225
Meadows, Jayne 290
Meatballs 246, 261
Medcraft, Russell 59
Medford, Kay 169
Medina, Patricia 120
Medved, Harry and Michael 126, 175
Meeker, Ralph 163
Meet John Doughboy 369
"Melody in 4F" 60, 64
Melton, Sid 156
Melville Goodwin, U.S.A. 289–290; see also *Top Secret Affair*
Melvin, Allan 231
Men O'War 54
"Men Who Stare at Goats" (TV episode) 208–209; see also *Crazy Rulers of the World*
The Men Who Stare at Goats: 2005 book 210, 212; 2009 film 8, 16, 210–211, *211*, 212, 394
Menander 7
Mercer, Johnny 342
Mercouri, Melina 277
Meredith, Burgess 176, 177
Merkel, Una 173
Merrill, Dina 73, *75*, 202
Merrill, Gary 67
Messing, Debra 234, 236
Metro-Goldwyn-Mayer (MGM) 5, 10, 13, 35, 37–38, 41–42, 48–49, 53, 54, 55, 62, 73, 88, 106, 123–124, 129, 135, 136, 140, 146, 174, 175, 190, 191, 192, 193, 217, 218, 221, 222, 227, 229, 240, 241, 242, 266, 280, 288, 299, 301, 303, 306, 322, 324, 325, 328, 329, 330, 331, 341, 342, 344, 345, 346, 358, 371
Meyer, Russ 270
Meyers, Nancy 270
MGM *see* Metro-Goldwyn-Mayer
Michael, Gertrude 137

Middleton, Noelle 62
Middleton, Robert 73
Midler, Bette 92
A Midsummer Night's Dream 249
The Mighty Navy 372
Miles Gloriosus 7
Milestone, Lewis 42, 44
Milhollin, James 125, 184, 185
Military Intelligence and You! 6, 366–368, 393
"Military Policemen" 62
Miljan, John 30, 32
Miller, Ann 88, 135, 141
Miller, Barry 196
Miller, Don 301
Miller, F.E. 102
Miller, Harvey 270
Miller, Marvin 62
Miller, Patsy Ruth 30
Miller, Penelope Ann 196
Miller School of Albermarle (Virginia) 259
Milner, Martin 166
Minciotti, Silvio 131
Mineo, Sal 258, 294, 295, *295*
Miner, Steve 273
Minnelli, Vincente 303
Minnevitch, Borrah and His Harmonice Rascals 102
The Miracle of Morgan's Creek 299–300, 301, 383
Miracle Pictures 264
Miramax Films 236, 239
Mirisch Brothers 225
The Misfit 46
Misrock, Henry 253
Miss Pacific Fleet 137, 380–381
Mr. Limpet 279–280; see also *The Incredible Mr. Limpet*
Mister Roberts: 1946 novel 14, 159, 160–161, 168; 1948 play 161–163, 171, 173, 181; 1955 film 4, 16, 163–165, *165*, 166–167, 168, 169, 185, 186, 188, 214, 223, 386; 1965 TV series 167; 1984 TV special 167
Mr. Walkie-Talkie 113, 386
Mr. Winkle Goes to War (novel and film) 279
Mitchell, Darryl 231
Mitchell, David 195
Mitchell, Duke 74
Mitchell, Frank 33, 58, 77, 100, 331
Mitchell, Glenn 318
Mitchell, Margaret 324
Mitchell, Millard 199, 200, 286
Mitchell, Norman 59
Mitchum, Robert 219, *219*, 221
Mitgang, Herbert 129
Mizoguchi, Kenji 176
Monahan, Kasper 324
Monaster, Nate 72
Monks, John C. 253–254
Monogram Pictures 31, 100, 113, 126–128, 266, 301
Monroe, Marilyn 270
Monsieur Verdoux 21
Montagne, Edward J. 233
Montevecchi, Liliane 73
Montgomery, Gen. Bernard Law 66
Monthly Film Bulletin 345
Mooching Through Georgia 315, *316*

"Moon Walk" 306; see also *A Ticklish Affair*
Mooney, Russ 264
Moore, Alvy 125, 205
Moore, Del 219, 220
Moore, Dudley 245
Moore, Michael 367
Moore, Margo 177
Moore, Terry 295
Morales, Esai 82, 84
Moran, Frank 137
Moran, George (The Two Black Crows) 78, 81; see also Mack, Charlie
Moran, Lois 33
Moreland, Mantan 100, 102
Moreno, Rita 269, 270
Morgan, Harry 174, 225, 227
Morgan, Kewpie 31
Morgan, Ralph 322
Morgan Creek Productions 143
Morris, Donald R. 14, 296
Morris, Howard 375
Morris, Jim 334
Morris, Wayne 255, *255*, 256
Morros, Boris 55
Mosel, Tad 68
Mosher, Bob 257, 259
Moss, Jack 305
Motion Picture 21, 321
Motion Picture Herald 37, 116
Motion Picture News 18, 24
Motion Picture World 154
Movie Mystery and Entertainment 345
Moviestone Films 272
Moviestore Entertainment 229
Moving Aweigh 373
MTV 82
Muir, Esther 137
Muir, Jean 56
Muldoon, Patrick 366
Mullaney, Jack 222
Munro 375–376
Munshin, Jules 140, *140*
Mura, Corinna 153
Murphy, Audie 176, 177
Murphy, Eddie 245
Murphy, Jimmy 118
Murphy, Michael 353
Murphy, Richard 199, 200, 205
Murray, Bill 15, 238, 246–247, *248*
Murray, Charlie 11, 23, 41
Murray, Forbes *326*
Murray, John Fenton 125, 244
Murray, Ken 154, *154*
Murrow, Edward R. 14
"My Love, My Life" 158
My Wonderful World of Slapstick 325
Myers, Zion 358
Myhers, John 63

Nader, George 176
Nagel, Conrad *41*, 42, 155
Naho 63
Namath, Joe 364
Nathan, George Jean 134
National Broadcasting Company (NBC) 63, 73, 167, 179, 208, 280
National Lampoon 260–261

Navy Blue Days 47
Navy Blues (MGM, 1929) 38, 136
Navy Blues (Republic, 1937) 138–139, 381
Navy Blues (Warner Bros., 1941) 101, 137–138, **138**, 382
Navy Blues Sextette 137–138
Nazarro, Cliff 128, 139
Neal, Tom 100, 115
Needham, Hal 331
Neidler, Werther **154**
Neilan, Marshall 88
Nelson, Barry 185
Nelson, Dick 98
Nelson, Ed 223
Nelson, Kenneth 179
Nelson, Ralph 224
Nelson, Ricky **206**, 207–208
Nemec, Corin 335, **335**, 336
Nerves 145
The Nervous Wreck (play and film) 64; see also *Up in Arms*
Never Wave at a WAC (film) 266–268, **268**, 269, 270, 271, 386
"Never Wave at a WAC" (*Schlitz Playhouse of Stars* TV play) 266–267
New Christy Minstrels 329, 331
New England Film News 55
New Orleans Item 120
New School for Social Research 53, 97
New York Civic Center 163
New York Herald Tribune 67, 200, 218
New York Magazine 196, 245, 249
New York Post 119, 185
New York Times 21, 66, 131, 144, 151, 154, 155, 175, 190, 200, 262, 263, 296
The New Yorker 199
Newfield, Sam 156
Newhart, Bob 331, 348, 350
Newman, Paul 181, 277–278, **278**, 279, 310
Newmar, Julie 76, 77
Newsweek 129
The Nicholas Brothers 74
Nichols, Mike 196, 346, 347, 348, 349, 350, 353
Nicholson, Jack 142, 143, **143**, 169
Nicholson, Kenyon 69, 135
Nickels, Cameron C. 8
Nielsen, Leslie 360
"Night Watch" 160; see also *Mister Roberts*
Nikki, Mariko 173
Nimbus Libéré 370
Nimoy, Leonard 122
1941 6
Nishimura, Tommy 178
Nissen, Greta 150, **152**
Nixon, Marion 317
Nixon, Richard 333
Niven, David 344, 345
No Time for Sergeants: 1954 novel 14, 159, 180–183, 188; 1955 play 183–185; 1955 TV production 181–183; 1958 film 16, 185–186, **186**, 187, 188, 280, 288, 387; 1964 TV series 187–188

Noble, Maurice 282
Nolan, Lloyd 366
Noonan, Tommy 76–77, **77**
Normand, Mabel 32, 40, 45, 315
North, Sheree 269–270, 295
Norton, Barry 158
Not with My Wife, You Don't 302, 389
Novak, Kim 288
Novello, Jay 225, 227
Now We're in the Air 36, 148, 379
Nugent, Elliott 64, 65, 303
Nugent, Frank 165, 166, 169
Nuyen, France 220, 221
Nye, Louis 219, 220, 221

Oakie, Jack 11, 33, 101, 134–135, **135**, 136–137, 138
Oates, Warren 246, 247
O'Brien, Conan 273
O'Brien, George 33, 158
O'Brien, Joan 202
O'Brien, Tom 11, 42
O'Connell, Arthur 202, 216
O'Connor, Carroll 225, 227
O'Connor, Donald 120, **121**, 122–123, 124, 125, 130, 178–179, **179**
O'Connor, Kevin 356
O'Connor, Robert 236–237
O'Donoghue, Michael 260, 261
O'Donohue, James T. 148
Of Fox and Hounds 369
Off Limits 15, 62, 386
"Off the Record" 74
Offerman, George, Jr. 191
Office of Censorship 13
Office of Information (U.S. Navy) 164
Office of War Information (OWI) 13, 14, 104, 139, 190, 265, 266, 299
O'Flaherty, Patrick 8
Oh, Charlie see *Hold That Ghost*
Oh, How I Hate to Get Up in the Morning 369
O'Hanlon, George 76
O'Hara, Maureen 158
Okazaki, Bob 174
O'Keefe, Dennis 156, 297
Oland, Warner 30
O'Laughlin, Gerald S. 168
The Old Army Game 372
Old Bill 28–30, 31, 129; see also Bairnsfather, Bill
O'Leary, William 361
Olive Oyl and Water Don't Mix 372
Oliver, Edna May 59, 79
Oliver, Gordon 256
Olsen & Johnson 91, 127
Olson, Frank 210
"On a Buck and a Quarter a Day" 58
On Dress Parade 113, 257
On the Double 65, **65**, 66, 388
On the Town 140, **140**, 141, 142, 384
One Hour Married 45
One Little Indian 7
One Night in the Tropics 90, 92
O'Neill, Charles 318
Onera, Sho 173
The Onion 84, 245, 284
Onionhead 187, 387

Operation Dumbo Drop 334–335, **335**, 336, 393
Operation Mad Ball 214, 215–217, **217**, 225, 387
Operation Petticoat: 1959 film 16, 201–203, **203**, 204, 208, 212, 225, 233, 293, 388; 1977 TV series 204
Operation Teahouse 175
O'Rourke, P.J. 260
Osborne, Hubert 133
Osborne, Vivienne 137
Oteri, Cheri 273
Our Gang 47, 88–89, 111, 112, 322, 323, 324
Our Relations 54
Over Thereabouts 45, 265
Over 21: 1944 play 302–303; 1945 film 302, 303, **304**, 383–384
Overall, Park 197
Overman, Lynne 96, **97**, 98
Overture Films 210
Owen, Gary 56

Pack Up Your Troubles (1932 Laurel & Hardy film) 54, **54**, 55–56, 105, 380
Pack Up Your Troubles (1939 Ritz Brothers film) 81, 381
Padden, Sarah 127
Padila, Marguerita 134
Palmer, Betsy 164
Paloma, Gabriella 277
Palumbo, Ron 92
USS *Pampanito* 252
Panama, Norman 327
Pangborn, Franklin 6, 60, 153
Pantoliano, Joseph 167
Papp, Joseph 339
Paquin, Anna 236, 237
Paramount Pictures 3, 11, 24, 33, 35–37, 40, 53, 59–62, 65, 67, 69, 70, 71, 72, 78, 90, 93, 96, 98, 136, 155, 156, 223, 245, 246, 257, 276–277, 285, 299, 301, 316, 318, 346, 347, 348, 350, 359, 361, 371, 372, 373, 375, 376
Paramount Theater (New York City) 102
Parker, Cecilia 138
Parker, Corey 196
Parker, Dorothy 136, 230, 302
Parker, Fess 318, 319
Parker, Jean 55
Parker, Suzy 292, **293**
Parker, Trey 374
Parnell, Emory 75
Parrish, James Robert 113
Parry, Mark 366
Parsons, Karyn 260
Pasha, Kalla 23
Pasternak, Joe 306, 307
Patchett, Tom 261
Pate, Michael 329, 330
Pathé Pictures (aka Pathé Exchange) 21, 25, 30, 47, 127, 136, 315
Patrick, John 165, 171–172, 173, 174, 175, 179, 181
Patrick, Lee **304**
Patrick, Robert 211
Patterson, Lorna 272
Patton, Gen. George C. 129, 290

Pavan, Marisa 158
Pax-Americana Pictures 366
Payne, John 44
Pearson, Jesse 329
Peary, Harold 373
Peeples, Samuel A. 328
Pendleton, Austin 232, 348, 352
Pendleton, Nat 92, 100, 104, 151
Penn State University Collegian 263
Pennick, Jack 40, 56, 164, 309
People magazine 261
Perez, Marcel 17
The Perfect Furlough 14, 225, 293–294, 387
Perkins, Anthony 348
Perkins, Gil 325
Perkins, Millie 169
Perlinger, Sissi 283
Perrin, Nat 327
Peters, Don 282
Peters, Susan 266
Petrie, Daniel 292
Petrillo, Sammy 74
Petty, Lori 82, 83
Pflug, Jo Ann 352
The Phil Silvers Show see *You'll Never Get Rich*
Phillips, William "Bill" 191, 193
Phoenix, Joaquin 237, 238, 239
Photo Analysis for Aerial Bombardment 366
Photoplay 28, 29
Pichel, Irving 322, 324
Pickens, Slim 338
Pickford, Mary 298, 313
Picture Play 30, 321
Picturegoer 321
The Pigeon That Took Rome 259, 277, 279, 389
Pimpernell, John 8
Pittenger, William 318–319
Pitts, ZaSu 31, 61, 88, 120, 122, 137, 265
Pittsburgh Post-Gazette 78, 81, 287
Pittsburgh Press 245, 262, 324, 364
Place, Mary Kay 272
Plane Daffy 371
Platt, Edward C. 269
Plautus 7
Playboy Films 272
Pleshette, Suzanne 222, 312
Plymouth Theater (New York City) 146
Police Academy 230, 250, 335, 364
Pollard, Snub 45–46
Ponicsan, Darryl 142
Popeye the Sailor 371, 372–373
Porter, Cole 60, 183, 374
Porter, Jean 110, 193, 194
Poston, Tom 222, 223, 262
Povah, Phyllis 61
Poynter, Nelson 13
Powell, Dick 93, 123, 288
Powell, Eleanor 325
Powell, Jane 135
Powell, William 164, 166, 167, 169
Pratt, Hawley 282
Pratt, Theodore 279, 280, 283
Preminger, Ingo 352, 355
Preminger, Otto 156, 157, 302

Prentiss, Paula 222, 241, 242, 348, 350
Present Arms 154, 155; see also *Leathernecking*
Presle, Micheline 158
Presley, Elvis 294
Preston, Robert 185
Prevost, Marie 23
Price, Garrett 280, 281
Prince, Hughie 93
Princeton University Players 184
Private Benjamin: 1980 film 15, 16, 230, 270–271, *271*, 272, 273, 391; 1981 TV series 272
Private Buckaroo 95
Private Izzy Murphy 11, 30, 378
Private Jones 48
The Private Navy of Sergeant O'Farrell 63–64, 390
Private Pluto 371
"Private Snafu" cartoon series 373–374, *374*, 375
Private Snafu Presents Seaman Tarfu In the Navy 375
Private Snafu vs. Malaria Mike 374
Private Snuffy Smith 127–128, 382
Private Valentine: Blonde and Dangerous see *Major Movie Star*
The Private War of Major Benson 257–258, **258**, 259, 260, 386
A Private's Affair 15, 257, 294–295, **295**, 296, 388
Proft, Pat 360, 361, 362, 363
Project Jedi 209, 210
"Psychic Footsoldiers" 210; see also *Crazy Rulers of the World*
PTA Magazine 126
Pulitzer Prize Playhouse 290
Pullman, Bill 364
Pulver, Richard 161
Punchy Cowpunchers 87
Punsly, Bernard 113
Purcell, Dick 138
Purviance, Edna 18, 19
Pyle, Ernie 59

Quaid, Randy 142
Qualls, DJ 84
USS *Queenfish* 203
Quillan, Eddie 139
Quine, Richard 140–141, 215–216, 217, 241
Quintano, Gene 335
Quirk, Lawrence J. 310

Rabin, Nathan 245
Rackin, Martin 69
Rafferty, Chips 207, 208
Raguse, Elmer A. 324
Ralli, Giovanna 225
Rally 'Round the Flag, Boys!: 1957 novel 309–311; 1958 film 6, 309–311, *311*, 387
Rambeau, Marjorie 373
Ramis, Harold 246, 247
Ranch Boys 85–86
Rand, Sally 34
Randall, Lt. Col. Herbert 160
Randall, Rebel 110
Randall, William 324
Random House 180, 287

Ransohoff, Martin 342
Rapée, Ernö 148
Rapf, Harry 37
Rasche, David 245
Rastar Productions 194
Rastatter, Wendy 263
Rath, E.J. 64
Ration fer the Duration 373
Ray, Aldo 225
Ray, Charles 24, 26
Raye, Don 93
Raye, Martha 59, 61, 95, 137, 214
Raymond, Gene 59
Readers' Digest 160, 274
Reading (PA) *Eagle* 148
Reagan, Ronald 123, 255, **255**, 256, 366, 368
Recon Pilot 366
The Recruit 17
Red Alert 337–338, 340; see also *Dr. Strangelove*
The Red Badge of Courage 129, 328
Reed, Donna *191*, 192, 193
Reed, Marshall 240
Reed, Tracy 340
Reid, John 294, 345
Reiner, Carl 366
Reinhold, Judge 246
Reis & Dunn 369
Reisner, Charles F. 29
Reitman, Ivan 246
Remar, James 249
Renaissance Man 247–250, **250**, 392–393
Rennie, James 134
Renoir, Jean 71, 99, 294
Republic Pictures 75–76, 138–139, 220, 269
Resisting Enemy Interrogation 366, 368
Reville with Beverly 5–6
Revue Productions 232; see also Universal Pictures
Reynolds, Burt 352
Reynolds, Debbie 76, 135, 301–302
Reynolds, Joyce 299
Reynolds, Marjorie 100
Rhue, Madlyn 202
Rialto Theater (New York City) 136
Riano, Renie 117
Rice, Adnia 187
Rice, Florence 101, **101**
Richards, Cully 61
Richards, Frank 117
Richards, Jeff 288
Richardson, Thomas 252
Richlin, Maurice 201, 223, 225
Richmond, Ted 328
Richter, Mischa 189
Rickles, Don 228
Riddle, Meredith "Rip" 204
Ride 'Em Cowboy 94–95
Rinaldo, Fred 70, 71
Rinehart, Mary Roberts 24
Ritt, Martin 342
Ritz Brothers (Al, Harry, Jimmy) 81, 90
RKO-Pathé 155
RKO Radio Pictures 14, 55, 78, 80, 81, 102–104, 108, 134, 135, 137, 153, 154, 266

Roach, Bert 22, *41*, 42
Roach, Hal 25–26, 45, 46, 47, 53, 54, 55, 72, 85, 86, 88, 106–108, 109, 110, 111, 112, 113, 155–156, 255, 322, 323, 324
Roach, Hal, Jr. 112, 315
Robbins, Peter 307
Roberson, Chuck 331
Roberti, Lyda 322
Roberts, Beverly 58
Roberts, Joe 46
Roberts, Stanley 129
Roberts, William 259
Robertson, John S. 134
Robins, Leo 134
Robinson, Charles 69, 135
Robinson, Hubbell 214
Rock, Chris 231
Rock, Joe 46–47
Rock, Philip 344
Rodgers and Hammerstein 374
Rodgers and Hart 154, 155
Rogers, Charles 155
Rogers, Emmett 180, 183
Rogers, Ginger 135, 257
Rogers, Jimmy 109
Rogers, Will 109
Roman, Phil 282
Romero, Cesar 244
Ronson, Jon 208–210, 212
The Rookie 76–77, *77*, 388
Rookie Revue 369
Rookies 37–38, 45, 148, 378
Rookies in Burma 13, 104, 383
Rooney, Mickey 62, 72, 73, 123, 125–126, 140–141, *141*, 142, 216, 240–241, 345
Roosevelt, Franklin D. 90, 244
Roosevelt, Theodore 9
Root, Stephen 210
Rose, John C. 280
Rose, Si 233
Rosen, Gary 259
Ross, Joe E. 297
Ross, Kewpie *see* Ton of Fun
Ross, Marion 202
Ross, Michael 117
Ross, Shirley 139
USS *Rotanin* 159, 161
Roth, Joe 360
Roth, Lillian 136
Rough Seas 85–86
Roux, Jacques 277, *278*
Rowan and Martin's Laugh-In 271, 283
Roxy Theater (New York City) 148, 150
Rubin, Benny *154*
Ruck, Alan 196
Ruge, Billy 17
Ruge, Jack 176
Ruggles, Charlie 190
Ruggles, Wesley 190–191, 192, 193
Rulin, Olesya 273
Rumsfeld, Donald 209
Russell, Harold 285
Russell, Jane 283, 341
Russell, Rosalind 216, 266–267, *268*, 269
The Russians Are Coming, the Russians Are Coming 6

Rutherford, Margaret 66
Ryan, Irene 6
Ryan, Peggy 141
Ryan, Sheila 98
Ryan, Tim 6, 116
Ryan, William 153

SAC Command Post 340–341
The Sad Sack: comic strip 13, 71–73; 1957 film 71–73, 74, 387
Sahl, Mort 229
Saiko, Tatsuo 176
Sailor Be Good 11, 137, 380
Sailor Beware: 1933 play 33, 69, 135–136, 137, 138–139; 1952 film 69–70, 71, 136, 385
Sailor Izzy Murphy 30, 378–379
A Sailor-Made Man 10, 25, *25*, 26, 377
Sailor's Holiday (Columbia, 1944) 139, 383
Sailor's Holiday (Pathé, 1929) 136, 379
Sailor's Lady 139, 381
Sailor's Luck 8, 137, 380
Sailors on Leave 139, 382
"The Sailor's Polka" 70
A Sailor's Sweetheart 32, 378
Saint, Eva Marie 163
St. Catherine's School (California) 257
St. Clair, Mal 22, *23*
St. Louis Post-Dispatch 132
St. Marie, Nick 77
Saks, Gene 195
Sale, Richard 307
Salt Water Daffy 88
A Salty Sap 46
"Same Old Army" 294, 295
Sandburg, Carl 321
Sands, Billy 231, 233, 242
Sands, Diana 169
Sands, Tommy 169, 294
San Francisco Chronicle 284
San Francisco Maritime Museum 252
USS *Saratoga* 56
Sargent, Dick 64
Sarris, Andrew 21, 227, 309, 340
Saturday Evening Post 35, 327, 340
Saturday Night Live 245, 362
Savalas, George 228
Savalas, Telly 227
Savelli, Guy 209, 210
Sawyer, Joe 56, 61, 107, 108, 109, 111, *111*, 112, 138
Scala, Gia 288
Schaefer, George 179
Schaefer, Jack 327
Schary, Dore 174
Schelling, Thomas 338
Schelly, William 28
Schenck, Joseph 318, 321
Schildkraut, Joseph 81
Schildkraut, Rudolph 81
Schilling, Gus 118
Schindler's List 234
Schlesinger, Leon 373, 374, 375
Schneider, Rob 251
Schuck, John 353, *354*
Schulberg, Budd 185

Schwalb, Ben 117, 118
Scott, Allan 290
Scott, George C. 302, 339, 348, 361
Scott, Randolph 135
Scott, Raymond 373
Scotti, Vito 225, 227, 278
Scrap the Japs 373
Screenland 38
SCTV 246, 247
Sea Legs 11, 136, 380
Seabrook, Edward E. 107, 111
USS *Seadragon* 201
"Seaman Hook" cartoons 375
The Secret War of Harry Frigg 277–278, *278*, 279, 310, 390
Sedgwick, Edward 44, 325
Sedgwick, Eileen 42
See Here, Private Hargrove: 1942 novel 189, 190, 195, 205; 1944 film 13, 168, 176, 190–191, *191*, 192–193, 194, 197–198, 383
Seein' Red White and Blue 373
Segal, Alex 183
Seiter, William A. 17
Selby, John 180
Sellers, Peter 338, 339, *339*
Semels, Harry 87
Semon, Larry 17, 30–31
Semple, Lorenzo, Jr. 221–222
Sennett, Mack 9, 17, 22, 27, 32, 40, 45, 53, 314–315
Sergeant, John 209, 212
Sergeant Bilko *230*, 231–232, 234, 393
Sergeant DeadHead 6, 244–245, 252, 389
"Sgt. Doubleday" series 72, 106–113
The Sergeant Was a Lady 122, 269–270, 388
Service with a Guile 373
Seven, Johnny 225
"Seven Against the Sea" (*Alcoa Premiere* TV episode) 232–233; see also *McHale's Navy*
Seven Days Ashore 104
The Seven Year Itch 270
Shakespeare, William 7, 249
Sham Battle Shenanigans 371
Shapiro, Joseph M. Viertel 253
Shapiro, Stanley 201, 294
Sharp Shooters 33, 379
Shaughnessy, Mickey 73, 288
Shavelson, Mel 66, 276, 277
Shaver, Helen 245
Shaw, David 285
Shaw, Irwin 285
Shaw, Wini *57*, 58
Shawn, Dick 177, 225, *226*, 227
She Learned About Sailors 33, 380
Shear, Rhonda 272
Sheekman, Arthur 301
Sheen, Charlie 360, *362*
Sheen, Martin 163
Sheffield, Skip 271
Sheinberg, Bill 234
Sheinberg, John 234
Sheinberg, Sid 234
Shell Socked 46
Shenson, Walter 357
Sher, Maury 191
Sheridan, Ann 137, 155, 274

Sherman, George 131
Sherman Said It 86
Sherwood, Robert E. 321–322
She's in the Army 266, 267
Sheward, David 161, 195
Shibata, George 207
Shield, LeRoy 86
Shields, Arthur 277
Shigeta, James 178, 179
Shima, Kieko 177
Shimoda, Yuki 241
Shore, Dinah 64
Shore, Mitzi 82
Shore, Pauly 81–82, **82**, 83
Shore Leave (1922 Osborne play) 32, 133–134, 137, 138
Shore Leave (1925 film) 10, 38, 134–135, 378
Shore Leave (1944 Wakeman novel) 291–292; see also *Kiss Them for Me*
Shoulder Arms 10, 16, 17–19, **20**, 21, 22, 85, 377
Shulman, Max 161, 162, 309, 310
Shumate, Harold 90–91
Shyer, Charles 270
Sibbald, Laurie 187
Sidney, George (actor) 11, 41
Sidney, George (director) 316
Siemaszko, Casey 196
The Silent Clowns 319
Silo, Susan 243
Silverman, Fred 194
Silvers, Cathy 231
Silvers, Phil 49, 99–100, 138, 175, 213–214, 230–232, 239
Simmons, Beverly 105
Simmons, Peter 249
Simmons, Richard Allan 259
Simon, John 195
Simon, Neil 14, 189, 194–196, 197, 359
Simon, Robert F. 202
Simon, S. Sylvan 325
Simon & Schuster 210, 296
Simpson, Jessica 273
Sinatra, Frank 310, 312
Singer, Howard 177
Singin' in the Rain 122, 124
Six Hits and a Miss 153
Skelly, Hal 56
Skelton, Red 100, 325–326, **326**, 327
Skerritt, Tom 353
USS *Skipjack* 201
The Skipper Surprised His Wife 303, **305**, 384
Skirts Ahoy 140
Skretvedt, Randy 98
Sky Devils 44, 380
Sky High 156, 385
Sky Trooper 371, 372
Slattery, Richard X. 167
Sleeman, Philip 86
Sloane, Bill 190
Sloane, Paul 79
Small, Edward 155
Smight, Jack 279
Smith, Alexis 137
Smith, Howard 185, 288
Smith, Kent 218, 366

Smith, Paul Girard 56, 107
Smith, Robert 153
Smith, Roger 167, 216
Smith, Sydney 185
Smith, Wonderful 100
Smith's Army Life 45
Snafu: 1945 play 304–305; 1946 film 304–306, 384
Sneider, Vern J. 14, 165, 169–171, 172, 173
Snopes.com 201
"Snuffy Smith" film series 126–128
Snyder, William L. 375, 376
So Proudly We Hail 253, 254
So Quiet on the Canine Front 358–359
Soldier in the Rain 4, 223–224, **224**, 225, 389
Soldier Man 27, 45
A Soldier's Plaything 30, 52–53, 380
Soles, P.J. 246, 272
Solomon, Louis 304
Sommers, Jay 296
Sommers, Joanie 125
Son of a Sailor 56–57, 58, 94, 380
Sons o' Guns: 1929 play 57, 58, 381; 1936 film 49, 57, **57**, 58, 99
Sothern, Ann 325
"Sound Off" (marching song) 240
Sound Off 15, 140–141, 216, 240–241, 385
South Pacific 136, 207
Southern, Terry 338, 339
A Southern Yankee 325–326, **326**, 327, 384
"Souvenir" 73; see also *Don't Give Up the Ship*
Spacey, Kevin 211
Special News Service 92
Spence, Hartzell 189
Spence, Ralph 35–36, 42
Spencer, Diana 73, **75**
Spicer, Bryan 234
Spielberg, Steven 234
Spies and Guys 88
Spinach fer Britain 373
Spinach-Packin' Popeye 373
"Spoils of War" 35; see also *Behind the Front*
Sporleder, Gregory 249
Spradlin, G.D. 312
Spuds 30–31, 378
Stabile, Dick 68, 70
Stack, Robert 360
Stafford, Hanley 116
Stalag 17 3–4, **4**, 183, 217, 219
Stalling, Carl 373
Stallings, Laurence 10, 146, 149, 150
Stander, Lionel 88
Stang, Arnold 373
Stanley, Aileen, Jr. 256
Stanton, Harry Dean 271
Stanwyck, Barbara 306
Star Wars (film series) 209, 211
Starlift 5, 76, 77
Starr, Frances 134
Stars and Stripes 13, 119, 128, 129, 131
Stebbins, Bill 205
Stedman, Vera 46
Stengel, Leni 79

Sterling, Ford 22, **23**, 315
Sterling, Jan **305**
Stern, David, III 14, 119–120
The Steve Allen Show 219, 280
Stevens, Angela 88
Stevens, Craig 202
Stevens, George 108
Stevens, Stella 329, **330**, 331
Stevenson, Adlai 338
Stevenson, Venetia 122
Stewart, French 234
Stewart, James 257
Stewart, Paul 291
Stine, Harold C. 282
Stockwell, Dean 144, 234, 236, 238
Stoloff, Benjamin 34
Stone, Ezra 67, 254
Stone, Joseph 201
Stone, Matt 374
Stone, Milburn 258, 259
Stone, Peter 279
Die Störenfried 370
Storm, Gale 301
The Story of G.I. Joe 3, 129
Strand Releasing 283
Stratton, Gil, Jr. 116, 117
Straughan, Peter 210
Strauss, Richard 350
Strauss, Robert 69, 70, 219, 220, 221
Streeter, Edward 9–10
Stripes 15, 82, 230, 238, 245–247, **248**, 252, 272, 391
Stritch, Elaine 293, 352
Stroll, Edson 233, 242
The Strong Man **26**, 27, 52, 378
Stuart, Nick 40, 60
Stubblebine, Maj. Gen. Albert 208–209, 210
Sturges, Preston 59, 299, 309
Styne, Jule 61, 139
A Submarine Pirate 9
Suid, Lawrence H. 332
Sukapatana, Chintara 333
Summersby, Kay 290
Summerville, Slim 137
Sundance Film Festival 239
Suppose They Gave a War and Nobody Came? 311–313, 390
Sutherland, Dick 26
Sutherland, Donald 227, 228, **228**, 229, 352, 353, 354, **354**
Sutherland, Edward 35, 40, 44
Sutton, Grady 312
Sutton, Lon 356
Swain, Mack 316, 317
Swanstrom, Arthur 57
Swat the Spy 17
Sweetheart of the Navy 138, 381
Swing It Sailor 138, 381
Switzer, Carl "Alfalfa" 322, **323**
Swope, Herbert Bayard 302
Swor, Bert 78
Swor, John 78
Sylbert, Richard 348, 350

Taka, Miiko 178
Take Heed, Mr. Tojo 375
Talbot, Lyle 65, 266
Tallman, Frank 348
Talton, Alix 138
Tamblyn, Russ 288

Tank 312–313, 391
Tanks a Million 107–108, 110, 112, 382
Tapps, Jonie 140, 241
Target for Today 366
Tars and Stripes 50–51
Tarses, Jay 261
Tashlin, Frank 64, 269–270, 373
Tashman, Lilyan **154**
Tatum, Bradford 252
Taurog, Norman 70, 74, 244, 297
Tayback, Vic 229
Taylor, Don 126
Taylor, Gilbert 339
The Teahouse of the August Moon: 1951 novel 14, 159, 165, 170–172, 173; 1953 play 165, 171–174, 175, 176, 179, 181, 183, 185; 1956 film 174, **174**, 175–176, 177, 178, 179, 186, 188, 288, 328, 387; 1962 Hallmark Hall of Fame TV special 179
U.S.S. *Teakettle* 199, 200; see also *You're in the Navy Now*
Teal, Ray 70
Teller, Edward 338
Temple, Shirley 89, 300, 323
Terry, Sheila 56
Terrytoons 371
Thalasso, Arthur 27
Thalberg, Irving 49
Thatcher, Eva 23
Theater Guild 181
Theodore Huff Society 40, 150
There's Something About a Soldier 369
They Came to Cordura 328
Third Banana website 77
Thomas, Billie "Buckwheat" 88, 322, **323**, 324
Thomas, Bob 244
Thomas, Dave 246
Thomas, Jerry 116
Thomey, Ted 214
Thompson, Frank 315
Thompson, Howard 64
Thompson, Keene 40
Thorpe, Richard 193, 222, 242
¡*Three Amigos!* 84
Three Little Sew-and-Sews 87
Three Sailors and a Girl 140
Three Sons o' Guns 48
Three Stooges 50, 86, **86**, 87, 89, 315
Three's a Crowd 27
A Ticklish Affair 306–307, 389
Tiffany-Stahl 48
Tillie's Punctured Romance (Christie/Paramount, 1928) 40, 41, 39
Tillie's Punctured Romance (Sennett, 1914) 18, 40
Time magazine 33, 67, 78, 183, 221–222, 290, 334
Tin Hats 11, 41, **41**, 42, 193, 378
Tire au Flanc 71
Tobias, Charles 256
Tobias, Scott 284
"Today" 331
Todd, Thelma 56, 85, 86, 88, 265
Tokio Jokio 370
Tokyo Woes 375
Toler, Sidney 44

Tombes, Andrew 6
Tommy Atkins in Berlin see *Yankee Doodle in Berlin*
Ton of Fun 46–47
Toomey, Regis 99, 100
Top Gun 360, 361
Top Secret Affair 289, 290–291, 387
Top Sergeant Mulligan (Anchor, 1928) 31, 100, 379
Top Sergeant Mulligan (Monogram, 1941) 13, 31, 100, 382
Torn, Rip 251
Toronto Film Festival 238
Totheroh, Rollie 18
Touchstone Films 247, 249, 332
Towne, Robert 142
Townsend, Colleen 307
Tracy, Spencer 34, 35, 44, 104, 157, 164, 288
Tracy, William 107, 108, 109, 111, **111**, 112, 255
Tramp Tramp Tramp 13, 100–101, **101**, 102, 223, 382
Tranh, Tung Than 333
Travis, Mark W. 364
Trejo, Danny 84
Tremayne, Les 269
Troopers Three 48
Tropic Thunder 6
The Tropical Twins see *Cock-Eyed World*
Troup, Bobby 353
True to the Army 269
True to the Navy 136
Truffaut, François 70
Truman, Bess 345
Truscott, Harold 28
Tryon, Glenn 136
Trzcinski, Edmund 183
Tu, Francesca 356
Tucker, Forrest 101
Tugend, Harry 325, 327
Tully, Tom 207, 242–243
Turan, Kenneth 367
Turner, Lana 266, 301
Turner Classic Movies (TCM) 28
Turpin, Ben 23
TV Guide 214
Twain, Mark 180
20th Century–Fox 60, 76, 77, 81, 98, 99, 139, 157, 158, 177, 199–201, 250, 256, 257, 269, 270, 274, 275, 288, 291, 292, 294, 295, 302, 307, 309, 350, 352, 353, 354, 355, 360, 361; see also Fox Film Corporation
"21 Dollars a Day — Once a Month" 100
23 1/2 Hours' Leave: 1918 novel 24; 1919 film 10, 24–25, 31, 154, 377; 1937 film 11, 25, 381
Two Arabian Knights 42–43, **43**, 44, 148, 378
Two Black Crows see Moran, George; and Mack, Charlie
The Two Black Crows in the A.E.F. 78; see also *Anybody's War*
Two Hours to Doom see *Red Alert*
Two Marines and a General (*War Italian Style*) 52
Two Tars 54, 109, 110
Tytla, Vladimir "Bill" 282

UGO website 212
Ullman, Elwood 69, 117, 118
Umeki, Miyoshi 178, 179, 242
Uncivil Warbirds 315
Uncivil Warriors 86, 315
Underwood, Franklin 179
United Artists 42, 44, 63, 106–107, 112, 219, 221, 225, 318, 321
United Features Syndicate 129
United Press International 185
Universal-International 104, 120, 121–123, 124, 128, 129, 131, 176, 177, 201, 202, 204, 232, 257, 293
Universal Pictures 12, 17, 31, 37, 48, 90–91, 92, 93, 94, 95, 96, 107, 113, 120, 129, 136, 137, 139, 154, 194, 230, 233, 234, 242, 259, 277, 312; see also Universal-International
University of Nevada-Las Vegas 42
Up Front: comic panel 129, 131; 1951 film 129–130, **130**, 131, 132, 385
Up in Arms 64–65, 66, 383
Up the Academy see *MAD Magazine Presents Up the Academy*
Up the Military see *Basic Training*
UPA (United Productions of America) 280, 373, 374
The U.S. Steel Hour 181
USA Network 272

Vance, Vivian 60
Van Doren, Mamie 77, 122
Van Eyck, Peter 366
The Vanishing Private 371, 372
USS *Vanmen* 74
Van Owen, Clive 367
Van Susteren, Greta 83
Van Zandt, Phil 117
Variety 22, 28, 84, 239, 252, 367
Vaughn, Robert 364, 365
Vavitch, Michael 155
Vélez, Lupe 153
Vera-Ellen 141
Vera Vague see Allen, Barbara Jo
Vernon, Bobby 46
Vernon, Wally 6
The Victors 340
Videohound's Groovy Movies 346
Vidor, King 9, 11, 21, 97–98
The Village Voice 21, 284
Vim Comedies 17
Vincent, June 117
Vinson, Gary 233, 242
Virginia Military Institute 253–254, 255–256, 257
USS *Virgo* 159–160
Vitagraph Pictures 46
Vitaphone Studio 59, 88, 127
Vitascope 52
Vivyan, John 202
Vohs, Joan 112
Voight, Jon **347**, 348
von Brincken, Wilhelm **154**
Von Zell, Harry 200

A WAC from Walla Walla 269, 386
Wackiest Ship in the Army (TV series) 208
The Wackiest Ship in the Army? (film) 4, 204–205, **206**, 207–208, 388

Wagner, Robert 158
Wahlberg, Mark 249, **250**
Wake Me When It's Over 177–178, 280, 388
Wakeman, Frederick 291, 292
Walcott, Gregory **65**
Walken, Christopher 197
Walker, Edwin D. 340
Walker, Hal 70
Walker, Helen 156
Walker, Polly 134, **135**
Walker, Robert 168, 191, **191**, 193, 194, 213, 303, **305**
Walker, Robert, Jr. 168, **168**, 169
Walker, Terry 25
The Walking Dead 169
Wallace, Richard 305
Wallach, Eli 173
Walley, Deborah 244
Wallis, Hal 67, 69, 70, 71, 72, 73, 99
Walsh, J.T. 332
Walsh, Raoul 8, 137, 147–148, 149, 150, 151, 153, 157, 294
Walston, Ray 292
Walters, Charles 288
War Babies 89, 358
War Dogs 371
War Italian Style see *Two Marines and a General*
War Mamas 88, 265
Ward, David 250
Ward, Edward 108
Warden, Jack 177, 200, 208, 356
Warm Bodies 296; see also *All Hands on Deck*
Warner, Jack L. 185, 186, 281, 282
Warner Bros. Pictures 28, 30, 44, 48, 52–53, 56, 58, 88, 90, 93, 94, 99, 101, 102, 113, 137–138, 143, 163–164, 165, 166, 167, 185, 187, 214, 220, 255, 256, 260, 270, 280, 282–283, 289, 290, 299, 301, 364, 368, 369, 370, 371, 373, 374, 375
Warren, Harry 58
Washington Post 249
Wasserman, Lew 202
Watkin, Pierre 303
Watson, Bobby 66
Watz, Ed 80
A WAVE, a WAC and a Marine 266
Waxman, Franz 166
Way Way Out 6, 66
Wayans, Damon 259–260
Wayne, David 71, 72, 73, 130, **130**, 131, 162–163, 173, 176, 179
Wayne, John 158, 213
Wayne, Patrick 164, 166
Weaver, Doodles 6, 77
Weaver, Tom 126
Webb, Jack 200, 219, **219**, 220, 221
Webber, Robert 184, 272
Webster, Steve 321
Wee Wee Monsieur 87
"Weegie" (Arthur Feelig) 338
Weekend Pass 142, 391
Weekend Warriors 229–230, 392
Weeki Wachee Springs 283
Weil, Richard 62
Weiss-Artclass Pictures 45, 46
Welcome to the Club 356–357, 390
Weld, Tuesday 223, 224, **224**, 310

Welles, Orson 277, 305, 347, 348
Welles, Virginia 300
Wellman, William 129
Wells, Billy K. 150
Wells, George 222, 242
We're in the Legion Now 48
We're in the Navy Now 36, 378
Wessel, Dick 73, 88
Wesson, Dick 256
West, Mae 191
West, Martin 122
West Point Academy 253
Weston, Jack 222, 281, 282
What Did You Do in the War, Daddy? 225–226, **226**, 227, 389–390
What Next, Corporal Hargrove? 42, 192–194, 384
What Price Glory: 1926 film 11, 38–39, 40, 52, 89, 145, 147, **147**, 148–150, 151, 157, 158, 358, 359, 378; 1952 film 157, **157**, 158, 385
What Price Glory? (play) 10, 42, 145–147, 148, 149, 158, 189
What Price Porky? 369
What to Expect in the Military: A Practical Guide for Young People, Parents and Counselors 83
Wheaton, Glenn 209, 210, 212
Wheeler, Bert 11, 78–79, **79**, 80, 81, 85, 108
Wheeler, Harvey 340
Whelan, Arleen 267
When Willie Comes Marching Home 158, 176, 307–308, **308**, 309, 384
Which Way to the Front? 66
Whitaker, Forrest 333
White, Jules 51, 358, 359
White, Marjorie 151
White, Ron 83
White, Sammy 241
Whitfield, Lynn 82
Whitfield, Mitchell 231
Whiting, Jack 59
Whitney, Dan see Larry the Cable Guy
"Who Did It? I Did! Yes I Did!" 61
Who Killed Doc Robbin? 112
Whoopie! 64; see also *Up in Arms*
Why Bring That Up? 78
Why Leave Home? 60; see also *The Cradle Snatchers*
Why Sailors Go Wrong 39, 149, 379
Widmark, Richard 292
Wife 'n' Kids Productions 259
Wilcoxon, Henry 64
Wild Train 318
Wilder, Billy 3–4, 216, 217, 257, 285–287, 292
Wilder, Gene 348
Wilder, Thornton 302
Wiley, Hugh 35
Wilke, Robert J. 247
Willes, Jean 187, 234
Williams, Albert 186
Williams, Andy 234
Williams, Esther 124, 325
Williams, Hal 271, 272
Williams, Hank 229
Williams, Herschel 299
Williams, John 277

Williams, Robin 231, 247, 332, **332**, 333–334
Williamson, Fred 353, **354**
Willie and Joe 13, 28, 128–131; see also Mauldin, Bill
Willie and Joe Back at the Front see *Back at the Front*
Willingham, Noble 332
Willis, Matt 110
Willock, Dave 61
Wills, Chill 120–121, 122, 123, 192, 193, 194
Wilson 303
Wilson, Don 121
Wilson, Hugh 250
Wilson, Janis 306
Wilson, Lewis 139
Wilson, Marie 80–81, 267, **268**, 271
Wilson, Tom 44
Wilson, Warren 107
Wilson, Woodrow 9, 303
Wincer, Simon 335
Winchell, Walter 200
Windsor, Claire 42
Windsor [Ontario] Star 344, 345
Winslow, Michael 364, **365**
Winters, Roland 125
Winters, Shelley 139
With Love and Hisses 53, 55, 56, 108
Withers, Jane 81
Witherspoon, Cora **304**
Wolf, William 357
Wolfe, Digby 283
Wolfe, Ian 262
Wolheim, Louis 42, **43**, 148
Women of All Nations 11, 150–152, **152**, 153, 155, 380
Wood, Ernest 45
Wood, G. 353
Wood, Sam 37
Woods, Donald 139
Woods, Edward 139
Woodward, Joanne 310
Woodworth, Marjorie 112
Woolsey, Robert 11, 78–79, **79**, 80, 81, 85, 108
The World of Abbott and Costello 244
Wright, Helen 136
Wright, John 233, 242
Wuhl, Robert 333
Wyler, William 137, 342
Wylie, Evan 176
Wyman, Jane 99–100, 255, **255**
Wynn, Ed 371
Wynn, Keenan 124, 176, 191, 192, 193, 194, 213, 288, 291, 293, 339, 342
Wynter, Dana 66

Yank 13, 71, 189
Yankee Doodle in Berlin 10, 22–23, **23**, 32, 377
Yanks Ahoy 111–112, 113, 383
Yates, Herbert 75
Yes Yes Babette 46
Yoda, Yoshio 233, 242
York, (Sgt.) Alvin 58
York, Dick 216
York, Francine 122
York Productions 67

Yorkin, Bud 352
You Bet Your Life 80
You'll Never Get Rich (The Phil Silvers Show) 14, 175, 213, 214, 231, 232, 233; see also *Sergeant Bilko*
Youmans, Vincent 134
Young, Alan 62, 72, 73
Young, Gig 306
Young, Noah 26, 33, 44
Young, Otis 142, **143**
Young, Sean 246, 247
Youngman, Henny 266

"You're a Lucky Fellow, Mr. Smith" 92
You're a Sap, Mr. Jap 373
You're in the Army Now 12, 49, 98–99, 138, 382
You're in the Navy Now (U.S.S. Teakettle) 200, **200**, 201, 205, 208, 385

Zanuck, Daryl F. 23, 29, 44, 274, 307
Zarubica, Darryl 364

Z-A-Z 360–361, 362, 363, 364, 367; *see also* Abrahams, Jim; Zucker, David; Zucker, Jerry
Zelaya, José Santos 145
Zero Hour! 359–360, 361
Zieff, Howard 270
Zimbalist, Efrem, Jr. 361
Zinsser, William K. 346
Zuaiter, Walee 211
Zucker, David 359, 367; *see also* Z-A-Z
Zucker, Jerry 359; *see also* Z-A-Z

www.ingramcontent.com/pod-product-compliance
Lightning Source LLC
Chambersburg PA
CBHW081533300426
44116CB00015B/2608